DATE DUE	
AUG 10 1999	
OCT 21 1999	
DEC 16 1999	—
MAY 17 2010	
MAY -4 2	
27	

Terrorism in the 20th Century

BOOKS BY JAY ROBERT NASH

FICTION
On All Fronts
A Crime Story
The Dark Fountain
The Mafia Diaries

NONFICTION
Dillinger: Dead or Alive?
Citizen Hoover
Bloodletters and Badmen
Hustlers and Con Men
Darkest Hours
Among the Missing
Murder, America
Almanac of World Crime
Look for the Woman
People to See
The True Crime Quiz Book
The Innovators
Zanies: The World's Greatest Eccentrics
The Crime Movie Quiz Book
Murder Among the Mighty
Open Files: The World's Greatest Unsolved Crimes
The Toughest Movie Quiz Book Ever
The Dillinger Dossier
Jay Robert Nash's Crime Chronology
Encyclopedia of Organized Crime
Encyclopedia of 20th Century Murder
Encyclopedia of Western Lawmen and Outlaws
Crime Dictionary
Spies

POETRY
Lost Natives & Expatriates

THEATER
The Way Out
Outside the Gates
1947 (Last Rites for the Boys)

MULTI-VOLUME REFERENCE WORKS
The Motion Picture Guide (15 volumes)
The Encyclopedia of World Crime (6 volumes)

TERRORISM IN THE 20TH CENTURY

A Narrative Encyclopedia from the Anarchists, through the
Weathermen, to the Unabomber

JAY ROBERT NASH

NASH

M. Evans and Company, Inc.
New York

M. Evans and Company, Inc.
216 East 49th Street
New York, New York 10017

**Library of Congress
Cataloging-in-Publication Data**

Nash, Jay Robert
    Terrorism in the 20th century : a narrative encyclopedia from the anarchists, through the weathermen, to the unabomber / Jay Robert Nash
        p.   cm.
    Includes bibliographical references and index.
    ISBN 0-87131-855-5 (paper)
    1. Terrorism—History—20th century I. Title.
HV6431.N366   1998
303.6'25—dc21   98-22532

All photos are from the author's collection, unless otherwise indicated.

DESIGNED AND TYPESET BY RIK LAIN SCHELL

Printed in the United States of America

9   8   7   6   5   4   3   2   1

·CONTENTS·

·Introduction·

Terrorists come in all forms. They are not simply violent political fanatics out to further their cause by any means, although this is a popularly held misconception. The Federal Bureau of Investigation defines domestic terrorism as the "unlawful use of force or violence, committed by a group(s) of two or more individuals, against persons or property to intimidate or coerce a government, the civilian population, or any segment thereof, in furtherance of political or social objectives." Under this restrictive definition, the notorious Unabomber and scores like him in the past cannot be labeled terrorists, which Theodore Kaczynski certainly was. Moreover, the motivations of the terrorist cannot be limited strictly to a political or social cause.

It is obvious that the FBI does not wish to include lone terrorists as such in their limited lexicon—and for good reason. To do so is to then greatly enlarge the Bureau's responsibility for identification and apprehension, forcing it to make tremendous expansions and expenditures in personnel and operations, a task perhaps too daunting for this budget-conscious agency. Moreover, by extending its definition to include single persons, the Bureau's success rate in apprehending such elusive individuals would certainly spell a decline in its overall percentage of yearly arrests.

It is the lone terrorist that all fear most. He operates erratically, as would a serial killer, often committing terrorist acts over long periods of time, going for years without striking, then re-emerging to perform a bombing or killing. Terrorist groups select their targets and victims with some measurement of reason, their actions governed by the political results that might be brought about. On the other hand, the lone terrorist is not governed by any such logic. He often acts on impulse and his victims are varied according to class and profession. When the victims of the lone terrorist are consistently selected by race or nationality, law enforcement agencies may have some means of identifying the perpetrator, but such avenues of pursuit present slim leads and often demand years of dogged research and investigation.

Many lone terrorists operate for the simple thrill of terrifying others, such as the many serial killers who have plagued the U.S. and other countries over the decades, a social phenomenon peculiarly rampant in the twentieth century. These maniacal murderers in the U.S., such as the Ax Man of New Orleans; the 3-X slayer of New York; the Mad Butcher of Cleveland; the Bludgeon Killer of Tulsa, Oklahoma; and Son of Sam (David Berkowitz); along with their equally hideous counterparts in Europe—the Ogre of Hanover (Fritz Haarmann), the Monster of Dusseldorf (Peter Kürten), the Monster of Florence—terrorize and kill for the perverse love of terror and killing.

Whether or not they terrorize a small community (the child killer of Detroit's suburbs in the late 1970s), a large city (New York's Mad Bomber, George Peter Metesky), or even a country (the coast-to-coast strangler Earle Leonard Nelson of the late 1920s), these terrorists are as dangerous and lethal as their politically-motivated counterparts. Further, such lone-wolf terrorists are much more difficult to track down.

These shadowy creatures have no confederates or associates to provide information to anti-terrorist authorities on their operations and whereabouts. Their movements and actions are less predictable than the terrorist belonging to an organized group whose base of operations is generally rooted to a single country (the Baader-Meinhof Gang of Germany) or geographical area (the PFLP of the Middle East). They often move from state to state in the U.S., or from city to city in a given country.

Almost always, the lone terrorist either reveals his own identify through error or is identified to authorities by friends or relatives, as was the case with Theodore Kaczynski, whose own brother recognized his writings as that of the Unabomber and put federal agents on his trail. With the case of the periodic terrorist-killer Peter Kürten of Germany, authorities were led to his doorstep by his own wife after he casually informed her that he was the Monster of Düsseldorf, the brutal serial killer sought for two decades. (Kürten suggested to his wife that she collect the substantial reward posted for his capture; she did.) With Sylvestre Matuschka, the Hungarian train bomber of the early 1930s, his own greed for money stemming from fantastic insurance schemes led to his identification and capture.

Snaring Timothy McVeigh, the vicious bomber of the federal building in Oklahoma City in 1995, was a matter of hindsight and luck when a police officer recalled arresting McVeigh for weapons violations just after the explosion and believed he might fit the description of the bomber. The identification and apprehension of groups of terrorists, on the other hand, present different problems for law enforcement officials.

Investigators must operate in this domain chiefly through informants and what little forensic evidence they might be able to piece together following a terrorist bombing, kidnapping or killing. When dealing with groups, the investigator's opportunity for capitalizing on mistakes is greater. Had it not been for the niggardly greed of Palestinian terrorist Mohammed Salameh in collecting a $200 deposit on the Ryder truck used to bomb the World Trade Center, that case might never have been solved and the terrorists never brought to justice.

Islamic terrorists, in fact, present the most challenging confrontations to anti-terrorist forces today through their tactics of total sacrifice. They have proven again and again their willingness to suicidally attack those they deem their enemies. Like the kamikaze pilots of World War II, many Arab terrorists believe that by sacrificing themselves while killing as many of the "enemy" as possible, they enhance their spiritual after-life by furthering the political cause of their religion, as preached in Iran and Iraq as "holy wars." This is an ancient belief that dates back to the twelfth century and the mythical Old Man of the Mountain and his Order of the Assassins, one of the first known terrorist groups that was dedicated to the murder and elimination of European leaders of the crusades, those "infidels" who had dared to invade the sacred soil of Islam.

In the twentieth century, Islamic terrorism expanded as one Arab country after another emerged from beneath the yoke of European colonialism. Islamic terrorists in the Middle East attacked European authority, as well as other Arab nations slow to embrace Islam as the ruling political force of any land. Dictatorial leaders like Egypt's Nasser and the Shah of Iran held Islamic terrorism in check for decades but when Iran came under the total control of Ayatollah Khomeini, terrorism in the Middle East secured a national base of operations.

Added to Iranian terrorist groups were those who operated under the direction and sponsorship of Libya, ruled by Western foe Muammar Qaddafi, and in Iraq, where military dictator Saddam Hussein plotted conquest not only against Israel and the West but against his own Arab neighbors. Further, Yasir Arafat, head of the PLO, was for years the inspiration of many Palestinian terrorist groups and their bloody actions, until assuming the role of a peace-seeking political leader.

Another consistently terrorist-plagued area throughout the twentieth century is Northern Ireland, which had been separated from the Free State (later the Republic) of Ireland in a controversial agreement between Great Britain and IRA leader Michael Collins in 1922. From that time to the present, the clandestine Irish Republican Army (IRA) has waged an almost non-stop guerrilla war with British forces in an effort to reunite the six northern Irish counties to the Republic. It has been a slaughterhouse campaign of relentless bombings and shootings, the British-backed Northern Irish forces committing as many heinous terrorist acts as their IRA counterparts. Both have been widely discredited for their senseless waste of human life and their inability to reach a peaceful settlement.

In the United States, at the turn of the century, terrorism reared its hydra-headed presence in the form of ruthless anarchists, who were looked upon by the general population as strange creatures from another world. Small in numbers, the anarchists made their presence known through bloody public demonstrations and confrontations with police. One of them, Leon Czolgosz, reached out in 1901 and fatally shot President William McKinley. Anarchism also seeped into the most radical labor movements, particularly the IWW (Wobblies), producing such terrorists as Harry Orchard who blew up mines, trains, and government officials in the western states, and the McNamara brothers who destroyed the Los Angeles Times Building in 1910.

Also at the turn of the century, following the large Italian immigration to the United States, the Black Hand, an extortion racket first begun by the Sicilian Mafia, terrorized Italian enclaves in New York, Chicago, New Orleans, and other metropolitan areas. Scores of Italian and Sicilian immigrants were compelled to regularly pay extortion or suffer the kidnapping of their children, the destruction of their businesses, or death. Thousands of businesses were set afire or bombed and hundreds were killed in a terror campaign that did not end until the beginning of Prohibition and the appearance of the Jazz Age gangster.

Five years before this time, in 1915, the Ku Klux Klan was reborn, carrying its nineteenth-century racism into the modern era, and all the ancient trappings that symbolized the "Invisible Empire"—the white hoods and robes, the flaming crosses, the grandiose titles bestowed upon the foremost bigots in its ranks—became the hallmarks of race hatred. And with the rebirth of this ancient evil came increased beatings, burnings, lynchings, chiefly focused upon black victims, but Catholics, Jews, and foreigners also felt the wrath and fury of the Klan.

After spreading like wildfire throughout the South, Klan membership mushroomed into Northern industrial states like Illinois and Michigan. Blue collar workers, told by Klan leaders that blacks and foreigners would take their jobs unless they took action, swelled the KKK ranks to millions. State governments were taken over by Klan leaders. Almost all of the government offices in Indiana were controlled by Klan leaders during the 1920s. The Klan brazenly marched down America's main streets waving the flag of the United States. A half million Klan members marched down Pennsylvania Avenue in Washington while dread-filled spectators stood silent, much as crowds watched in fear as Benito Mussolini's Black Shirts, his private army of terrorists, marched along the streets of Italy at the beginning of the 1920s.

A decade later, Adolf Hitler's Brown Shirts (SA) in Germany began a terror campaign that would not only sweep over his own country but engulf most of Europe and bring about the mass murder of more than twelve million human beings. At this time, in the United States, gripped by Depression, labor and strike-breaking gangs clashed in northern industrial cities, bringing back the labor terrorism of old.

During World War II, terrorism in Europe was kept up at a furious pace by Hitler's SS and Gestapo thugs, who had replaced the Brown Shirts, and their power and influence even reached into the U.S. to murder any German prisoner-of-war displaying pro-Western sympathies. Following World War II, terrorism in Palestine increased as right-wing Israeli groups, such as the Stern Gang and their Palestinian counterparts, slaughtered each other. The IRA stepped up its terror campaign in Northern Ireland and in England. In the U.S., Puerto Rican nationalists attempted to assassinate President Truman and they sprayed the House of Representatives with bullets. In Kenya, the Mau Mau, a secret black terrorist sect, launched a campaign of widespread murder and destruction.

In the 1960s, the controversial Vietnam War encouraged widespread dissension in the U.S. and abroad. Students became increasingly militant and formed numerous underground anti-government groups, many of these adopting the tactics of terrorism during the 1968 Democratic Convention in Chicago, seeing a police riot in response. Blacks formed several paramilitary underground groups—the Black Panthers, the Symbionese Liberation Army (SLA), the Death Angels—and fought police in the streets of America. The KKK resurfaced in force to spread their old terrors through the South, attacking and killing freedom riders and civil rights workers, both white and black.

Europe in the 1970s was suddenly bathed in blood with the emergence of ultra-violent terrorist groups—the Baader-Meinhof Gang of Germany, the Red Brigades and Red Guards of Italy, Algerian nationalists in France and in the Middle East the equally ruthless PFLP, Black September, and the Hanafi Moslem extremists. Most of these killer organizations were from the radical left, launching an all-out attack on democracies. Their kidnappings, bombings, and murders were committed on crowded streets, restaurants, bars, buses, trains, planes, inside government buildings. Nothing, not the fear of imprisonment nor death itself seemed to daunt these fanatics.

By the 1980s, international terrorism was a chilling reality that threatened every country and every citizen. Arab terrorists led the way, skyjacking airplanes and even cruise ships such as the *Achille Lauro*, kidnapping and killing at will. Such demoniac persons as Carlos, known as the Jackal (Ilyich Ramirez Sanchez), kidnapped government and business leaders and collected millions in ransom as the democracies made one concession after another, wrongly believing that these terrorists could be appeased, mollified, bought off.

When political kidnappings and abductions resulted in concessions from officials and governments, particularly the release of imprisoned terrorists, worldwide terrorist organizations accelerated these crimes, realizing that they were effective. After repeated failures in negotiating with terrorists, governments began to take a harder line with these uncompromising fanatics. In some cases, kidnap victims were killed, but, often as not, the terrorists came to realize that by murdering their hostages they would only assure the full wrath of governmental purging of their ranks.

Some governments adopted the "no payment of any kind" posture, making political kidnappings futile gestures. Those who murdered their hostages in the face of stubborn governmental refusal to negotiate, did so simply out of brutality or frustration, further condemning themselves in the eyes of the world community. This has been the lot of the myriad terrorist organizations in Europe, the Middle East, Asia, and South America.

By the 1990s, the democracies began to fight back, unwilling to compromise, knowing now that concession was a futile diplomacy with uncompromising terrorists. It became all-out war, kill or be killed, so that most terrorist groups now realize that they will be relentlessly pursued, hunted down, and tracked to imprisonment or death for their heinous crimes. The police of all democracies set up anti-terrorist divisions headed by specialists and manned by dedicated anti-terrorist teams and organizations. Military units such as the U.S. Delta Force, trained to especially combat and destroy terrorists, can now fly to all points of the globe to confront and overwhelm this persistent enemy.

The isolated terrorist remains a constant problem; these lone killers still strike from anonymity and obscurity, such as the demented Unabomber, Theodore Kaczynski, and they are capable of mass destruction and murder, such as the bombing of the federal building in Oklahoma City by Timothy McVeigh. The only defense against such killers is vigilant security systems and the help of those who can bring information to authorities in advance of a kidnapping or bombing. Had Timothy McVeigh confidante Michael Fortier, who knew in advance that the federal building in Oklahoma City was targeted for bombing, taken his information to authorities, he might have prevented the enormous loss of life. As it was, Fortier, a spineless, drug-taking hanger-on, turned state's evidence to save his own hide and could, after being given a prison term as an accessory in 1998, only murmur meaningless apologies to the survivors of the blast.

McVeigh, condemned to death and universally viewed as one of America's worst mass murderers, symbolizes the new and dangerous terrorist threat today in America, one stemming from the extreme right, a killer without conscience or remorse. He is championed only by small self-styled paramilitary groups obsessed with the notion that the government is the enemy. Such groups in Michigan, Montana, and in the Deep South are heavily armed with automatic weapons and train for confrontation against constitutional authorities. The image of these groups, however, has been considerably sullied by the actions of McVeigh and others like him, branding them advocates of terrorism instead of patriotism.

As we fast approach the twenty-first century, international terrorism, instead of diminishing, has increased, finding safe havens in third-world countries, particularly those that have emerged from the shattered Soviet Union and throughout the Middle East. As India and Pakistan misguidedly sought to enhance their international standings by detonating nuclear bombs in 1998, terrorists in Europe and elsewhere have stepped up their efforts to steal from heavily guarded sources of precious uranium, plutonium, and lithium, the very substances vital to the creation of nuclear bombs.

Their objective is clear—to use nuclear weapons as a way of dictating terms to a world society that no longer tolerates their crimes against humanity. Their conspiracy is obvious—to overcome all resistance by confronting the world with Armageddon, the final anarchism of total destruction. To that the nations of the earth can only answer with indefatigable pursuit and apprehension of these terrorists, hopefully preventing the unthinkable from happening, and avoiding the worst of all man-made disasters.

Jay Robert Nash
Chicago, 1998

·ONE·
TERRORISM COMES TO AMERICA

1900

The Killing of a Kind Man

The twenty-fifth president of the United States typified a comfortable America. William McKinley was a friendly, outgoing man who loved to greet his fellow citizens, wading into crowds to clasp all the hands he could reach before Secret Service agents edged him away. Elected to the presidency in 1896, McKinley's first administration had presided over a land of booming industries and ever-expanding business.

McKinley had also fought and won in record time a "little war" with Spain, mostly at the insistence of his sabre-rattling Assistant Secretary of the Navy, the fiery Theodore Roosevelt. The Spanish-American War of 1898 saw U.S. fleets steam into Cuban and Filipino waters to destroy Spanish warships. Roosevelt quit his Washington post, formed a group of shock troops he named the Rough Riders and stormed San Juan Hill. America's swift

triumph brought about the annexing of vast, exotic lands—Hawaii, Wake Island, Samoa, and the outright acquisition of the Philippines, Cuba, Puerto Rico and Guam.

By McKinley's second term in 1901, with Roosevelt as his vice president, America was suddenly a world power. This posture warmly nurtured the ambitions of an elitist group of industrial tycoons headed by J. P. Morgan. A thriving middle class also gloried in the new broad-shouldered American image, even though other major nations dismissively viewed the U.S. as a farm boy flexing over-developed muscles.

The lowest strata of American society was, for the most part, oblivious of such concepts. The laboring immigrant class concerned itself with day-to-day survival under near slave wages and health-wracking work conditions. Its members worked ten-hour days and its male population had an

Anarchist Leon Czolgosz, a revolver hidden beneath a handkerchief, is shown shooting and mortally wounding President William McKinley at the Pan-American Exposition in Buffalo on September 6, 1901.

average life expectancy of forty-eight years. Within this grimy, uneducated class was a laborer named Leon F. Czolgosz (pronouned Cholgosh), the least likely person to introduce terrorism to a tranquil America in the first year of a bright new century.

Unlike his overworked peers, Czolgosz did not eat a plain meal in the evening before collapsing from exhaustion. His unschooled mind burned with curiosity. He stayed up late, devouring pamphlets and books about anarchy—the violent overthrow of governments, the destruction of monarchs, theories reveling in bloody revolution and assassination. Born in Detroit in 1873 to Polish immigrants, Czolgosz was the fourth of eight children. His father was a common laborer and his mother died giving birth to her last child when he was twelve. Without formal education, Czolgosz went to work in a Cleveland wire mill.

At night, in the small room of a cheap boarding house, Czolgosz read anything he could find about anarchy—books, magazines, newspapers. He embraced this philosophy as he would his own mother and seethed with hatred for an American government branded as an enemy of the people by anarchist leaders Emma Goldman and Alexander Berkman. He visited Goldman at her Chicago headquarters but, she later claimed, he made such a pest of himself that he was ordered to go away and never return.

Czolgosz nevertheless remained an avid anarchist. He was electrified by the exploits of another anarchist, Gaetano Bresci. This immigrant Italian laborer working in New Jersey, had

Assassin Leon Czolgosz stated that he shot President McKinley "because I thought it was my duty."

sailed to Italy where he shot and killed King Humbert I on July 29, 1900. So excited did Czolgosz become over this assassination that he could not sleep. When he did try to sleep he dozed off clasping the thumb-worn stories of the Humbert murder. Then he read that President McKinley would be visiting the Pan-American Exposition in Buffalo, N.Y. This was his opportunity, he told himself, to duplicate the act of Gaetano Bresci. He would kill William McKinley.

The Pan-American Exposition was a marvel to behold. Its many exhibits included new mechanical devices, including automobiles, a host of ethnic restaurants, parades, bands, a giant, wonderful picnic to which flocked parasol-twirling women in long-flowing dresses and men wearing winged collars, frock coats, and high-buttoned shoes—tens of thousands of them.

Into this sea of humanity plunged McKinley. Ever the politician, he intended to shake the hands of thousands—he was adept at it, able to clasp the hands of hundreds within an hour. To that end, the president, on September 6, 1901, went to the large auditorium called the Temple of Music. Outside, thousands patiently lined up to enter single file to shake his hand.

Earlier McKinley had stood on the speaker's platform at the Esplanade and addressed more than 50,000 respectful visitors (there were 116,000 at the Exposition that day), telling them that with America's new expansionism (imperialism, some said), the days of isolation were over and that the United States, with its "almost appalling" prosperity, must establish fair trade agreements with nations. "God and man have linked the nations together," he emphasized. "The period of exclusiveness is past."

The Secret Service was on hand to protect the president. When President James A. Garfield had been mortally wounded in a Washington, D.C., railway station on July 1, 1881, by political malcontent and assassin Charles Julius Guiteau, he had had no protection at all. Neither had Abraham Lincoln two decades earlier. Since that time, precautions had been taken. McKinley was guarded by three Secret Service agents—George Foster being the commander. When McKinley positioned himself in front of a dais in the Temple of Music, a guard flanked him on either side; Foster on one side,

agent Samuel R. Ireland on the other. Another agent stood only a few steps distant. "Let them come," the smiling president said and the doors were opened to a public that streamed inside to greet him.

Foster scrutinized each person as they stepped up to McKinley to shake his hand. Shuffling forth in the long line was a pale-faced youth who caught the eye of the Secret Service chief. His face was expressionless, his eyes a dull glaze. Wrapped about his right hand was a white handkerchief, which the young man raised to his forehead to wipe away sweat. Foster took no warning from this. It was a hot day. (The president himself carried three handkerchiefs that day to wipe away the perspiration.) Further, Foster surmised that the youth had somehow injured his hand and was using the handkerchief as a bandage. Oddly, Ireland later remembered, before Czolgosz approached McKinley, another man with three fingers of his right hand bandaged "had shaken hands with his left."

At 4:07 P.M., Czolgosz finally reached the president. An organist was playing a Bach sonata as McKinley, believing that the slightly built young man in the black suit before him had injured his hand, reached out for Czolgosz's left hand. The anarchist slapped it away and stretched out his handkerchief-cloaked right hand under which he clutched a short-barreled .32-caliber Iver-Johnson revolver. He lurched toward the president and, standing stone-faced before him by only a few inches, fired twice.

Smoke steamed from two holes in Czolgosz's handkerchief and billowed upward so that the two men were almost enveloped in the small cloud. McKinley's face froze in a look of astonishment. He clutched his abdomen into which one bullet had tunneled. Foster and Ireland leaped forward, as did a half dozen city detectives, pouncing on the assassin, dragging him to the center of the stage, punching and kicking him.

McKinley was helped to a nearby chair, aides fanning him, his secretary, George B. Courtelyou, fumbling at his breast and belly. McKinley saw Czolgosz being pummeled and said: "Don't let them hurt him. Be easy with him, boys." He raised his hand to drop it weakly on Courtelyou's shoulder and could see that it was coated with blood. "My wife," he said in a whisper, "be careful, Courtelyou, how you tell her—oh, be careful."

By then pandemonium had seized the crowd inside the building. Hundreds of terrified men and women stampeded toward the doors, fighting to get outside, roaring with panic, screaming with hysteria. A motorized ambulance arrived with a half dozen men in white jackets rushing to the platform, and the half-conscious McKinley was carried outside through a stunned, moaning and keening crowd. The beloved president appeared lifeless.

The nation was shocked into disbelief. The hand of terrorism had reached out of a murky past to bring violent death to America's leader, a kind and gentle man who, the electorate knew full well, had always attempted to avoid violence and had even tried to evade the confrontation with Spain, a war he knew America could easily win. The bloody spectors of John Wilkes Booth and Charles Guiteau suddenly rose smirking from their graves, and the memory of the Haymarket Riot in Chicago in 1886, when anarchist bomb-throwers murdered eight policemen and wounded sixty-seven other officers, became white hot.

Here was another ancient bloodletter of the same stripe. Czolgosz, once in custody, proudly admitted that he was an anarchist, a follower of Emma Goldman. He admitted that after hearing Goldman give one of her rousing lectures, he was determined to "do something heroic for the cause." He was quick, however, to state that he acted alone, that Goldman and other leading anarchists had not sent him on his terrible mission to Buffalo. Police learned that Czolgosz had been using the alias of Fred Nieman. The last name translated into "Nobody," Fred Nobody.

"I shot President McKinley," Czolgosz said in a monotone to reporters, "because I thought it was my duty . . . I didn't believe that one man should have so much service and another man should have none."

Not for a moment did anyone believe that the terrorist had acted alone. He was part of a widespread anarchist conspiracy harped the newspapers, and all believed that an evil cabal with equally evil ideas imported from a morally corrupt Europe was behind the attack. Anyone who criticized McKinley as he lay dying for eight days, from ministers to policemen, were fired from their jobs, beaten, some even tarred and feathered.

It was first reported that McKinley would recover. Immediately after the shooting, he had been rushed to a small hospital on the Exposition grounds where Dr. Matthew D. Mann, a skilled Buffalo surgeon, discovered that Czolgosz's first bullet had struck the president's chest but had only grazed his ribs. The unimpassioned assassin, however, was conscious of his aim and, to make sure he struck a vital spot, lowered his revolver before firing his second shot.

The second bullet pierced the stomach, lacerating both front and back walls. Dr. Mann and other physicians decided to operate immediately before the light failed in the small hospital. Since the building had no electricity, one of the doctors used a mirror to reflect the sun's dying rays through a window onto the area where Mann and others were operating. Toward the end of the operation, a small light bulb was rigged up to be hand-held over the doctors as they worked. Dr. Mann located and removed the bullet, cleaned the peritoneal cavity and sutured the holes in the stomach left by the bullet. He then closed the wound and covered it with an antiseptic bandage. McKinley was then removed to the Buffalo home of a friend, John G. Milburn.

McKinley appeared to recover, his physicians reportedly feeding him a liquid diet of raw eggs and whiskey. They neglected the development of gangrene, however, and when it came time to act, the apprehensive doctors decided that another operation might be too risky. On September 13, 1901, the president lapsed into a coma. He revived briefly to recognize his wife, aides, and doctors, saying to them softly: "It's useless, gentlemen. I think we ought to have a prayer." He moved his lips silently as the tearful group recited the words of the Lord's Prayer.

"Goodbye, goodbye all," McKinley then said. "It is God's way. His will, not ours, be done." He drew his wife close to him, whispering the words of his favorite hymn, "Nearer, my God to Thee, Nearer to Thee." He held onto his wife's hand for some time before she was led away weeping. McKinley's eyesight failed but he reached out for her as if he were a groping child. A physician took his hand and held it until he died at 2:15 A.M., September 14, 1901.

National mourning was quickly replaced by universal anger and vindictiveness. A wave of reprisals against all anarchists was demanded. Emma Goldman, authorities were sure, had orchestrated the assassination. When first told that McKinley was dead, she snapped with typical anarchist fervor: "Suppose the president is dead. Thousands die daily and are unwept. Why should any fuss be made about this man?" She was arrested on September 10, 1901, as were hundreds of other anarchists. From her prison cell Goldman issued a statement that disavowed her having any association with Czolgosz: "Anarchism did not teach men to do the act for which Czolgosz is under arrest. We work against the system and education is our watchword."

Led by guards from his death row prison cell in New York's Auburn Prison, Czolgosz (center) begins his walk toward the electric chair on October 29, 1901; once strapped into chair, the terrorist said: "I am not sorry for my crime."

After Chicago mayor Carter Harrison expressed the opinion that Goldman was not personally involved with McKinley's assassination, she was released on September 24. The incident so irked the fiery Goldman, however, that she threw her support to Czolgosz, even though she had privately described him as "a dim-witted terrorist." She attempted to stir up support for the assassin, but even those in her inner circle refused to work for Czolgosz's release. Visibly angry, Goldman perceived this reaction to be a sell-out of Czolgosz and she soon quit Chicago, going to New York where she temporarily withdrew from the anarchist movement, working as a nurse in tenement hospitals under the alias of Miss E. G. Smith.

Meanwhile, no time was lost in putting Czolgosz on trial. Within two weeks of the shooting, he appeared on the witness stand. He offered no defense, freely, almost proudly admitting his guilt. He was careful, however, to again state that "there was no one else but me. No one told me to do it. No one paid me to do it." This latter statement had been blurted with such enthusiasm that it was later claimed that one of Goldman's followers had visited the assassin in prison and had urged him to say that he had acted alone, that Emma Goldman had not sent him to kill McKinley.

Condemned, the terrorist's execution was prompt. At 7 A.M., on October 29, 1901, he was taken from his cell in New York's Auburn Prison and led to the electric chair. He wore a winged collar, black tie, and a neatly pressed suit. His shoes had a high gloss as Czolgosz had spent his last early-morning hours mindlessly buffing them.

Out of more than a thousand applicants, twenty-six spectators had been allowed into the death room. As the head, arm, and leg straps of the electric chair were adjusted about the assassin's body, spectators heard an official ask Czolgosz if he had any last words to say. "I am not sorry for my crime," came his dull response. He then added: "I am awfully sorry that I could not see my father."

The current was thrown and the terrorist was pronounced dead at 7:17 A.M. The deaths of McKinley and Czolgosz marked a dividing line in history; one side representing a genteel lifestyle of security that would be no more, the other, for dark, unclear purposes, an instrument of unpredictable and horrendous violence. At first, Czolgosz's deed was thought to be a random and rare act of madness. It would be repeated, however, with alarming regularity as the century deepened, until it was chillingly clear that his breed had proliferated beyond imagination, that terrorism could claim the twentieth century as its own.

"Something Ought to be Blown Up!"

By the time Leon Czolgosz stoically pulled the trigger in Buffalo, a small American labor organization had surfaced, calling itself the Industrial Workers of the World, its members labeled "Wobblies" (or "I Wont Works") by their opponents. Led by William Dudley "Big Bill" Hayward, the IWW recruited to its narrow ranks poorly paid miners of several western states. Hayward was an ex-cowboy and miner who approached unionizing with an iron fist and the motto of "Good Pay or Bum Work." Anarchists to the core, he and his lieutenants had, like Czolgosz, embraced revolutionary ideas that had nothing to do with peaceful negotiations. Unless his terms were met by management, Hayward threatened mine owners with strikes, mayhem and violence.

Frightened mine owners immediately hired the Pinkerton Detective Agency to protect their properties and to root out the IWW radicals among their workforces. The IWW responded by calling strikes and attacking those miners who refused to join the radical labor organization. Those who would not strike were beaten or run out of town.

Colorado became the hub of IWW activity at the turn of the century. The mine owners of this state had grown enormously rich from the near slave labor of their miners, who worked ten-hour shifts and faced health and safety conditions that were no less than horrific. There were few or no safety measures provided. The miners constantly breathed in lung-crippling coal fumes, and flickering kerosene lamps affixed to the tops of their helmets could, at any moment, in a pocket of heavy coal dust, set off violent explosions.

The Western Federation of Miners, an arm of the IWW, finally called a general strike, demanding better wages and improved safety and health conditions. The mine owners refused to budge. They would not meet the relatively minor expense of providing air fans to blow the mine shafts clean of coal fumes and dust. They would not raise wages or cut down the ten-hour shifts. They brought in a small army of Pinkerton guards to protect their property. Their workers, the mine owners reasoned, would soon reach starvation and be forced to return to work without any concessions granted.

Adding to Hayward's problems were the workers themselves. Many miners shunned the radical laborites, fearful of the violence they advocated.

IWW leaders (left to right) Charles Moyer, William "Big Bill" Hayward, and George Pettibone, charged in 1907 with attempting to terrorize mine owners into Union contracts through bombings and murder.

Further, Hayward viewed Idaho governor Frank R. Steunenberg, who had taken the side of management in the strike, as his main opponent. Steunenberg, a good-natured journalist at the beginning of his career, had been the editor of the pro-labor *Caldwell Record*. He had been Idaho's governor in 1896 and again in 1898. It was by then apparent to labor that Steunenberg, who inherited the widespread mining strike, would do nothing for the miners.

A state of open warfare erupted in the Coeur d'Alene district, with strikers and strikebreakers battling each other. Mobs attacked the Pinkerton guards at mining sites. Steunenberg did nothing. Hayward took the road to revolution. He called to his office a clever, ruthless labor thug, Albert E.

Horsley, who went under the name of Harry Orchard. "Something ought to be blown up!" he emphasized to Orchard, jabbing his finger onto a map pinpointing the mines.

Orchard, an explosives expert, quickly went about the business of acquiring dynamite. A short time later the Sullivan and Bunker Hill mines blew up. Two men were killed and the mines were completely incapacitated. Steunenberg called in federal troops (there being no state militia) and hundreds of striking miners were arrested and placed inside barbed wire enclosures. Hundreds of miners fled the state. Denounced by every union organization, Steunenberg was branded an enemy of labor.

Meanwhile, Orchard went on blowing up mines and killing people

Top: Eugene V. Debs, who headed the rail-road firemen's union and who was tried and convicted of attempting to undermine the U.S. Government after his strike turned into widespread violence.

throughout the West. When the Wobblies were locked out of the Vindicator Mine in Cripple Creek, Colorado, Orchard blew up the mine works and more men were killed. At the orders of Hayward, he later insist-ed, he went to Independence, Colorado, where strikebreaking miners had rejected a union takeover by the Wobblies. This time, the miners them-selves became the victims. Orchard planted a hundred pounds of dynamite he had stolen from the Cripple Creek mine under the railroad platform at Independence. He rigged a triggering device with a bottle of acid to set off the charge when he turned a windlass.

Orchard lurked in the shadows, tim-ing his detonation for a change of shift when tired workers would be waiting on the railroad platform. When the platform became crowded, he set off the charge. More than one hundred miners were sent skyward. Twenty-six were killed and another fifty seriously injured. The mass murder was routine for the vicious, unconscionable Orchard, who later stated: "Through the dark I could hear the strikebreaking miners—quite a crowd of them—com-ing out of the mine and going to the depot. The train was on time. I heard her whistle for the station at 2:35, and a moment later she drove in. Just then I pulled on the wire. A second later the charge went off with a tremendous roar." When Orchard reported the results of his carnage to Hayward, the IWW leader reportedly slapped his hands in jubilation, shouting: "Good

Right: Clarence Darrow, the brilliant criminal attorney who failed to win an acquittal for Debs, argued so eloquently on behalf of "Big Bill" Hawyard that the IWW leader walked free.

work, Harry! That will force the bas-tards to come in with us!"

There was no stopping Hayward now. He would terrorize miners into joining the IWW and murder any mine-owner or official who blocked his way to power. He would use explosives to rid himself of his enemies, a method of destruction and murder that he knew would be indentified with his labor movement. Hayward immediatley dispatched Orchard to San Francisco where he was to blow up Fred Bradley, a staunch and intractable member of the Mine Owners Association.

The charge Orchard set in the front double doors of Bradley's home went off when Bradley opened them, ripping the facade of the house to pieces and blowing Bradley across the street. Orchard, who activated the explosion from hiding, was sure that Bradley was dead but was later surprised to learn that his victim had survived, although he was crippled for life. The labor terrorist went to his boss Hayward, asking if he should return to finish off Bradley. "Don't bother," Hayward reportedly told him, "he and his friends got our message." He then ordered Orchard to murder Judge Luther M. Goddard of the Colorado Supreme Court because this judge had ruled against the Wobblies in a recent case.

Orchard spent considerable time constructing a bomb inside of a purse, then placed this item on a snow-swept path the judge regularly took to his Denver office. The terrorist hid behind a building, watching Goddard approach. Before he reached the spot where the purse had been dropped, Goddard was hailed by a friend and stopped to chat. Merritt W. Walley, a Denver citizen, suddenly appeared on the path, picked up the purse and was instantly blown to pieces, his body parts spread over a radius of half a block. Again, Hayward was pleased, telling Orchard that Goddard's witnessing the awful death of an innocent bystander was "a better lesson than his own death might have been."

One man, however, was not to be overlooked. His death had to be a certainty, Hayward told Orchard. Former Idaho governor Frank Steunenberg was to be killed and no mistakes made. By that time, Steunenberg was out of office and had become the president of the Caldwell Bank. To Hayward, however, he was still the symbol of resistance to organized labor and, in particular, the radical, bomb-wielding Wobblies.

Using the same method employed in his attempt upon Bradley, Orchard affixed a bomb to the front gate at Steunenberg's home. When the banker returned home on the evening of December 30, 1905, he opened the gate and was instantly shredded to death by a violent explosion. Police immediately identified the terrorist killing as the work of the IWW but, as had been the case for many years, they could prove nothing.

Then Harvey K. Brown, a visiting sheriff from Baker City, Idaho, went to the Caldwell police, telling them that he had recognized a man whom he believed was an IWW terrorist and bomber, one who might have been involved in Steunenberg's death. He was staying at a Caldwell hotel under the name of Tom Hogan, Brown said, "pretending to be a sheep buyer." The next day, January 1, 1906, police were led to Hogan's room by Brown, catching Hogan as he was about to leave, suitcases in hand. Hogan was arrested and taken to police headquarters where he was identified as Harry Orchard.

Orchard denied any guilt in the Steunenberg killing. "I've been buying sheep for some ranchers in Montana," he insisted, but he could provide no receipts of purchase, no bills of sale, no evidence that a single lamb had been shipped to Montana or anywhere else. The labor terrorist then clenched his teeth and remained silent. He was put into solitary confinement for ten days but this failed to break his spirit or loosen his tongue. He was then removed to a regular jail cell, which he shared with another prisoner, an affable inmate who befriended him.

The other prisoner was the ablest Pinkerton detective in America, James McParland, head of the agency's Denver office. It was McParland who had, in 1875, successfully penetrated the secret society called the Molly McGuires and exposed their terrorist acts and leaders in the mining districts of Pennsylvania. He was an expert at disguises and even more expert in getting felons to confide in him. So trusting of McParland did Orchard become that he detailed his many terrorist bombings and murders to him, taking smug pride in his ability to kill anyone marked for death by the illustrious Big Bill Hayward.

At the end of thirty days, McParland was ostensibly released. He then had Orchard brought to his office and confronted him with his own statements. Orchard broke down and made a full confession, which he signed. The lengthy confession detailed dozens of terrorist bombings and killings Orchard had committed over a decade, all at the behest of the IWW, specifically Big Bill Hayward. (This chilling memoir was published a year later under the title *Confessions and Autobiography of Harry Orchard*, which proved to be a minor best-seller.)

Orchard stated that Charles H. Moyer, president of the Western Federation of Miners, and Hayward, its treasurer, had hired him to perform each and every act of terrorism. Union executives Jack Simpkins and George Pettibone had aided and financed him, Orchard said, and Steve Adams, another IWW terrorist, had assisted him in killing Steunenberg, the blowing up of the railroad depot in Independence and many of his other crimes.

Adams was arrested and thrown into a prison cell. He was promised immunity if he would confess, and he quickly added his admissions to those of Harry Orchard. Idaho officials promply asked the governor of Colorado to extradite Hayward, Moyer, and Pettibone. All three were arrested on February 17, 1906, at their union headquarters in Colorado and taken to Idaho under heavy guard. Though many questioned the legality of the extradition, state and federal courts upheld the action.

The prosecution was confident that it would, with the testimony of Orchard and Adams, quickly get a conviction against Hayward and the others, hoping to end forever the wave of terror spread by the violent IWW leaders. Prosecutors had not reckoned, however, on the most brilliant lawyer of the land—Clarence Darrow —coming to the defense of the Wobbly leaders. The Chicago lawyer was the champion of American labor who, in 1894, had abandoned a comfortable law practice (with the Chicago and Northwestern Railroad as his main client) to take up the cause of decidedly underdog unions and their

IWW terrorist and bomber Harry Orchard (Albert E. Horsely), who murdered dozens of people in the labor wars of the far West in 1903-1905.

leaders, first defending Eugene V. Debs, secretary-treasurer of the Brotherhood of Locomotive Firemen.

Debs had called his union out on strike to support striking Pullman workers resisting a 25 percent pay cut. The nationwide strike crippled all railroads west of Chicago, and federal troops were called out to protect strikebreakers, as well as force union members back to work. When mob violence broke out and more than thirty persons were killed, Debs was placed on trial, charged with conspiracy to undermine the government.

Darrow's defense of Debs was vigorous and inspired. Unlike other labor lawyers of the past, Darrow's defense was built upon an aggressive attack. He went to the heart of the problem—unfair wages paid to union workers and miserable working conditions. He was really defending the right of unions to exist. His stirring summation to the jury in the Debs case caused jury members to weep. Though Debs was jailed for violating an injunction, Darrow emerged as the most eloquent spokesman of American labor—he was a white knight who rode to the rescue of the common man.

The lawyer again made headlines when he brilliantly defended anthracite miners on trial in Scranton, Pennsylvania, in 1902–1903. When Hayward and the IWW called him to their defense, Darrow did not hesitate, although he was unnerved in defending an element of labor that intrinsically believed in violence and terrorism as a means of solving labor disputes.

When Darrow arrived in Idaho in December 1906, he was joined by defense attorneys Edmund Richardson, John Nugent, Edgar Wilson, and Fred Miller. He immediately put together a plan to save Hayward and his lieutenants, a legal thrust aimed at Steve Adams, Orchard's co-terrorist who had in his confession supported all of Orchard's indictments of Hayward and the IWW. Darrow knew that if the case against Adams was shattered, Adams would not testify against Hayward. Adams was tried in February 1907, his defense arguing mightily for his innocence, saying that his confession had been forced from him, that while in prison Adams had been alternately promised immunity or death by hanging.

When Adams openly renounced his confession, enough doubt was planted in the minds of the jury to render it indecisive. When it could not agree on Adams' guilt or innocence, the defendant was returned to prison. Darrow had won the first round; Adams would not be a state witness in the case against Big Bill Hayward.

That trial began on May 9, 1907. The prosecution team represented some of the most influential men in the West, William E. Borah, James H. Hawley, Charles Koelsche and Owen M. Van Duyn. For the first time Orchard's confession was made public by the prosecution and each word describing his terrorist career was published by a national press greedy for sensationalism. To give credence to Orchard's character, the prosecution postured him as a reformed man who had gotten religion and had renounced his criminal past. Hawley, who presented the opening argument for the state, pointed out that Orchard would testify as a penitent man. He then launched into a withering denunciation of Hayward and his "terrorist" union organization.

On the stand, Orchard recounted his crimes over the many years, stating that he had been in the pay of Hayward, Moyer, and Pettibone and that they had instructed him who to kill and when. Not including the twenty-six miners he murdered in the Independence bomb explosion, he admitted to eighteen terrorist killings done at the behest of the IWW leaders. He said that Pettibone was an amateur chemist and had instructed him in the arts of explosives and poisons. Orchard also said that Pettibone had

given him strychnine, which he originally thought to use in murdering Bradley. He said he put this into a bottle of milk delivered to the Bradley home but the cook took a sip of it, thought it bitter, and threw it out. Then he resorted to the bomb that tore away the front of Bradley's three-story house and blew his victim across the street.

Darrow centered his remarks on Hayward, profiling him as a self-made man who had come from humble beginnings, going to work in the mines at the age of nine, forced to go without education or a future, a man who had struggled to free himself from poverty and the merciless rule of oppressive mine owners. Though in ill health and without notes, Darrow spoke for an astonishing eleven hours, discrediting Orchard's testimony, labeling him a habitual liar and a ruthless terrorist who had acted on his own, or, he inferred, had done his awful deeds on behalf of the mine owners to discredit the unions. "He never did a courageous thing in his life, not one," Darrow said in describing Orchard to the jury.

The thundering Darrow leaned close to the jurors and told them that, yes, they could hang Bill Hayward but that the American labor union would continue with others "who will risk their lives in that great cause which has demanded martyrs in every age of the world." Near collapse, his voice reduced to a whisper at the end of his summation, Darrow defied anyone to convict a man solely on the basis of Harry Orchard's testimony. This, of course, was his trump card. Without Adams, Orchard's statements were without corroboration.

On July 29, 1907, the jury retired for seven hours, returning to pronounce Hayward not guilty. The courtroom sat in stunned silence. Big Bill walked from the court a free man, but Darrow's job was not finished. He handled the defense in Adams' second trial. Again, a jury disagreed about the defendant's guilt or innocence. Then Pettibone was brought to trial and Darrow continued the defense. He appeared in court in a wheelchair, apologizing to the court and saying that he could no longer proceed. He was taken to a hospital where he wavered between life and death, according to one report. Pettibone was nevertheless acquitted and the state dropped its case against Moyer.

Darrow had won a staggering victory, but one that was bittersweet. When he recovered from his illness, he confided to a friend that he suspected Hayward was guilty, that the boisterous, volatile union leader was "capable of awful violence." He told friends that he intended to quit the defense of labor. This would not be the case, however. Four years later, he would take on the defense of two brothers who, like Big Bill Hayward, preferred to settle union issues with explosives. Two months after Hayward's acquittal, on September 30, 1907, Sheriff Harvey K. Brown was blown to pieces by a bomb reportedly planted in his home by an IWW terrorist, in retaliation for Brown's identification of Orchard.

Harry Orchard, who had been condemned for his many murders, had saved his neck by becoming a state's witness. His sentence was commuted to life imprisonment. Hayward continued to vex and intimidate mine owners until 1917 when he and other IWW leaders were indicted for sabotaging vital war industries. He was convicted and given a twenty-year prison term but was released on bail pending an appeal. Hayward fled the country, going to Russia where the Bolsheviks welcomed him with open arms. Upon his death he was given a state funeral and buried on May 18, 1928, at the Kremlin, close to the bodies of Lenin and John Reed, the American who had lionized the Russian Revolution in his book, *Ten Days That Shook the World*.

One of the millions of readers avidly consuming every detail of the Hayward trial was Michael Silverstein, a Russian immigrant and a devout anarchist. In the year following Hayward's release, Silverstein went to work making bombs. He threw one of these infernal machines into a crowd of policemen milling about in New York City's Union Square. The officers spotted the bomb, its long fuse blazing, and dashed to safety, but one bystander was killed when it went off with a mighty roar.

Silverstein was caught on the spot as he attempted to flee. He was sent to prison for life. It was later reported that he had thrown the bomb at police whom he said had been extorting too much money from prostitutes, one of them being his own sister. The anarchist had thought to organize the prostitutes into a union like Hayward's IWW, but when none responded to his call, he decided to act on his own. Silverstein wrote letters from his cell to Hayward for years. All were returned unopened.

Enter La Mano Negra

As the anarchists preyed upon union members and company owners in the first decade of the twentieth century, an even more sinister terrorism haunted the burgeoning Italian-Sicilian immigrant population pouring into New York, Boston, Philadelphia, Detroit, Chicago, New Orleans, St. Louis, Kansas City, and San Francisco. This was the ubiquitous *La Mano Negra,* or the Black Hand. Unlike the anarchists in the American labor movement who sought power through violence, the Black Hand practiced terrorism for profit.

Never an organized criminal society as was the Italian Camorra or the Sicilian Mafia, the Black Hand was made up of independent terrorists. These killers invariably came from the ranks of the Italian and Sicilian criminal families that sanctioned Black Hand operations in given areas, demanding and receiving a percentage of whatever extortion monies were obtained. In Italy, Black Hand terrorists had been operating since 1750, but this extortion racket became widespread in the U.S. only after 1900, chiefly because there were hundreds of thousands of new, ignorant and superstitious Italian immigrants who served as easily terrified victims.

The Black Hander's technique was prosaic—and deadly. He would threaten various types of violence to extort money from a well-to-do victim, usually an Italian or Sicilian shopowner or businessman. Sometimes the Black Hander would simply kidnap the victim's child and hold him for ransom. At other times he would threaten to blow up an office or shop or to attack, injure or kill a family member of the recipient of the Black Hand note.

In the U.S., the Black Hand note was invariably written in broken English, blatantly demanding a specific amount of money and giving instructions on how the cash was to be delivered. Sinister symbols and images always adorned the Black Hand note—daggers dripping blood, a bomb exploding, a skull and crossbones, a gun smoking at the barrel, a body dangling on a rope by the neck. Invariably, the signature was unmistakable—a hand imprinted in heavy black ink, thus the sobriquet, *La Mano Negra* (the Black Hand).

In New York, at the turn of the century, the sprawling Italian community was terrorized by a hulking Black Hand thug known as Lupo the Wolf, real name Ignazio Saietta (he was later profiled in Mario Puzo's *Godfather* as Don Fanucci and brilliantly essayed in the film *The Godfather, Part II* by Gaston Moschin). Each month, Saietta regularly sent out his Black Hand notes and extorted tens of thousands of dollars from terrified victims, most of whom knew that he was the extortionist but, to protect their lives and property, said nothing.

There was good reason to maintain the code of silence known as *omerta*. Saietta routinely murdered people as an example to those who disbelieved his willingness to kill. More than thirty persons were known to have been murdered by Saietta when they refused to pay up. He simply entered their homes, and, often in front of wives and children, strangled the male member of the household to death, dragged the body outside to his horse-drawn carriage—he later used an automobile—and drove to a livery stable he owned in Harlem. There he hacked up the bodies, burned parts of them and buried what would not burn in his backyard.

An enterprising terrorist, Saietta also loaned himself out to other Black Handers as an enforcer. For a substantial fee he shot, stabbed, strangled, and beat victims into submission. There was an element of hazard for Black Handers hiring Saietta to commit his gruesome chores. He enjoyed his work so much that he often went too far, killing the Black Hand victim

Police photos of Ignazio Saietta, the Black Hander who terrorized New York's Little Italy and who was known as Lupo the Wolf.

before he had a chance to pay his extortionist.

Criminally bent Italian and Sicilian young men grew to admire Saietta and his success. He wore expensive clothes and sported diamond rings on his fingers. He lived in a large house and employed several servants who were also Black Hand accomplices. He was driven throughout New York's Little Italy in a fine carriage and dined in the district's best restaurants. All paid him homage as he strolled through the neighborhoods, boldly reaching into the tills and money drawers of shopkeepers to take a percentage of the day's profits.

Young gangsters came under Saietta's evil spell. They acted as his agents in Manhattan and Brooklyn, delivering Black Hand notes and collecting extortion payments for him until, with his approval, they branched out as independent Black Handers paying him a percentage of their weekly take. So powerful did Saietta become that no criminal activities could be conducted in his districts without his approval and his receiving kick-backs from cash or loot taken. Saietta's graduates of his Black Hand terrorist racket included Ciro Terranova, who rose to gangland prominence as the "Artichoke King," Frankie Yale (Uale), who later became one of the crime bosses in New York during the 1920s, and Johnny Torrio, who became head of the dreaded Five Points Gang before moving to Chicago where he was, in the early 1920s, the crime overlord of half the city, until being shot by rival gangsters and turning over his multimillion-dollar oper-

ation to his enforcer, Al Capone.

On rare occasions, Saietta's Black Hand victims thought to fight back. One victim whose daughter had been brutally beaten and raped by Saietta went to the Black Hander's home with the intent to kill Lupo the Wolf. Saietta, however, was a man always prepared for death. In the evening, his heavily armed servants boarded up the windows of his house and bolted all doors. One guard always sat in a chair at the head of the stairs leading to Saietta's bedroom with a shotgun cradled in his lap.

Upstairs, Saietta slumbered in a huge four-poster bed, razor sharp knives and loaded revolvers close at hand. A shotgun on a pedestal had been rigged in such a way that it would blast anyone entering his bedroom unannounced. This is exactly what happened when the enraged father somehow got into Saietta's house and found an unguarded back stairway leading to his bedroom. As he burst through the door, both barrels of the shotgun roared, tearing away the man's head. The terrorist jumped from his bed, dragging the bloody body into the hall. As his guard came running to blubber excuses, Saietta stabbed him to death for failing in his duty. He then dragged both corpses downstairs, loaded them into his cart, and drove to Harlem where he disposed of the bodies. His guard thereafter sat outside his bedroom door, wide awake.

Authorities were almost helpless in stopping Saietta. Few persons would even acknowledge knowing the Black Hand terrorist, let alone be willing to

The heroic NYPD Lt. Joseph Petrosino who was murdered by the Mafia in Palermo, Sicily in 1909 while tracking down Black Handers.

His name still sent fear shuddering down the spines of Italian immigrants.

One New York police officer, however, had no fear of Lupo the Wolf. He was Lieutenant Joseph Petrosino, a big-fisted, 200-pound officer who hated the Black Hand and the terror it brought to his community. Petrosino had several times confronted the terrifying Saietta, and he had helped Agent Richey to build the case against him. It was Petrosino who, in 1901, discovered a Manhattan gravesite where more than sixty Black Hand victims had been anonymously buried by their killers. Many of these victims were those of Saietta and his henchmen, but since the property was not in Saietta's name, no case could be proved against him.

Petrosino was truly a remarkable man. Born in Italy in 1860, he immigrated with his family to the U.S. when he was a child. Joining the police department in 1883, he soon proved incorruptible, refusing to take payoffs from gambling house and brothel owners. In 1895 he was promoted to detective and posted to the Lower East Side, which housed the greatest share of Italian and Sicilian immigrants. It was here that he began his lifelong battle with the Black Hand.

For ten years, Petrosino battled Black Handers, tracking down and jailing dozens of them. His methods were uncompromising. To demean the omnipotent image of the Black Hand, Petrosino would catch and parade the terrorists he caught down the streets of Little Italy, cuffing and

testify against him. On the few occasions when he was arrested and charged with Black Hand activities, a battery of expensive lawyers appeared to quickly have the charges dropped. Saietta's success at avoiding conviction led him to believe that he was immune from prosecution, so much so that he boldly branched out into other criminal pursuits, including counterfeiting. This was his undoing. Bills printed by a press he controlled were traced back to him by an intrepid undercover Secret Service agent, Larry Richey. This time Lupo the Wolf was convicted and given a thirty-year prison term. He would die behind bars. During his first few years in prison, Saietta continued to oversee Black Hand operations in Little Italy.

kicking these Black Handers in front of shopkeepers and immigrant Italian workers. On occasions he would shout to the crowded tenement dwellers: "Is this what you fear—cowards like this!" With that he would affix his heavy foot to the backside of a Black Hander and send him sprawling into the gutter.

This kind of naked humiliation was not endured lightly by the Black Handers, who vowed to murder their antagonist. Petrosino received dozens of Black Hand notes each year. Each promised to bring about his death by terrible torture. The police officer simply filed the notes in a box he kept at home. Black Handers shot at him from ambush, tried to knife him in crowds, and even tried to run him over with horse-drawn carts. Poison was slipped into his food in restaurants. He not only survived but his reputation became so widespread that he was repeatedly decorated by the city of New York. The Italian government honored him by bestowing upon him a gold watch. At one point, the great Italian tenor Enrico Caruso, through one of his aides, asked Petrosino to pay him a visit while he was performing at the Metropolitan Opera House.

The great Italian tenor Enrico Caruso (shown in the role of Pagliacci), a Black Hand victim many times over.

Caruso surprised Petrosino by telling him that he, too, had received dozens of Black Hand notes regularly and showed him a recent death threat affixed with the traditional Black Hand. The singer admitted that he had been paying off the Black Hand for years, and, at one point, estimated that $1,000 of every $10,000 he earned went to these terrorists. Then Caruso showed Petrosino the most recent Black Hand demand, one that ordered the singer to pay $20,000 in cash or die. The note stated that lye or other corrosive agents would be slipped into Caruso's wine or tea. It also promised that the singer's wife and children would be kidnapped, tortured, and then killed.

Petrosino studied the note carefully and identified one of the symbols on it, a maltese cross. He had earlier arrested a Black Hander who had used just such a symbol. Tracking down his prey, Petrosino beat a confession out of the Black Hander. Then, ignoring deportation laws, he dragged the man to a ship sailing for Italy and put him on board. When the two were inside a small stateroom, Petrosino withdrew his revolver and jammed the barrel of the weapon into the terrorist's mouth, reportedly saying: "If you return to this country, I will blow your brains out! If you ever bother Mr. Caruso anywhere on earth, I will find you and blow your brains out!"

The Caruso incident was reported to Police Commissioner William McAdoo who commended Petrosino for his prompt action. He then ordered the officer to establish an all-Italian squad of hand-picked men that was to dedicate itself to the total destruction of the Black Hand in New York. "Tear it out," McAdoo said, "branch and root!"

Again, Petrosino went to work with Larry Richey of the Secret Service. Through this undercover agent, Petrosino identified and arrested dozens of Black Handers, including the man who had taken Saietta's position of boss, a ruthless killer named Enrico Alfano. Petrosino learned that Alfano, as a member of the Camorra in his native Naples, had murdered a couple who had balked at paying him Black Hand extortion. He had been identified by Italian police and fled to New York where he organized widespread Black Hand operations.

After Richey located Alfano, Petrosino, alone, marched up the stairs of an old brownstone in Manhattan and ordered the Black Hander to surrender. Alfano and one of his henchmen stood behind the apartment door with drawn guns and defied the tough policeman to arrest them. The powerful Petrosino promptly kicked down the door, jumped on top of it and pinioned Alfano and his aide beneath. Because he knew that Alfano was wanted in Italy for murder, he was able to arrange for the Black Hander's deportation to Naples where he was imprisoned.

It was the Alfano case that gave Petrosino the idea of traveling to Palermo, Sicily, where he thought to search the files of the local police and thus identify many Black Handers who had committed serious crimes in Sicily before fleeing to New York. In this way, he thought he would be able to deport legions of criminals from American shores. He went to then Police Commissioner Theodore Bingham and requested that he be sent to Sicily to search the police files.

Bingham had serious reservations. He pointed out to Petrosino that by traveling to a foreign country, especially to Sicily where the Mafia dominated politics and the government itself, he would be placing himself in grave danger. The Mafia, Bingham said, had spies inside the New York Police Department, and, if that most secret criminal organization learned of his mission, he might be murdered. Petrosino was persuasive, however, and finally got Bingham's reluctant permission to go to Sicily.

Petrosino sailed to Sicily in February 1909. Diligently, he searched the police files in Palermo, pulling criminal background cards on dozens of Black Handers he identified as being in New York and wanted in Italy and Sicily for serious crimes. Petrosino sent this information to Bingham who, in turn, ordered the twenty-seven-man Italian squad to round up these wanted felons and hold them for deportation back to Sicily.

Mafia bosses in New York learned that many of their men were being picked up and held for extradition. They then learned that all of this was the work of Petrosino, who was in Sicily. A courier was sent to report this to the Mafia bosses in Palermo, Don Vito Cascioferro (or Cascio Ferro), and Don Paulo Marchese, both of whom sat on the Mafia's Grand Council. Cascioferro, who had been run out of New York by Petrosino many years earlier, took great delight in planning the detective's murder. He later claimed that he witnessed the killing of Petrosino and he often stated that he himself had fired the fatal bullet into his old nemesis.

Actually, it was Cascioferro who had really imported the Black Hand to America. Born in Sicily in 1862, Cascioferro's first criminal charge was for assault in 1884. He climbed the Mafia ladder quickly and soon supervised widespread kidnapping, extortion and other rackets until, following a murder, he fled to the U.S. In New York, he established the Black Hand, tutoring such willing recruits as Ignazio Saietta in the dark art of extortion. He also invented the protection racket where he and his minions took weekly payments from intimidated Italian businessmen. He was careful to point out to his henchmen that they should never demand payments so large as to force the victim into bankruptcy. "When the man makes money, we make money," Cascioferro instructed.

Ernest Borgnine, left, enacted the role of the brave New York Police Detective, Joseph Petrosino in the 1960 film, Pay or Die.

Cascioferro became known as "Don Vito" in his Lower East Side neighborhood, a man to whom everyone paid Black Hand money. Though an outright extortionist, he was thought to be fair, as well as generous in his contributions to charities. He was also cruel toward anyone he thought to be a weakling. (All of these personality traits were fused into the character of "Don Vito" Corleone in Mario Puzo's novel, *The Godfather*, as well as the careers of American gangsters Charles Lucky Luciano and, chiefly, Carlo Gambino, long-time head of one of New York's ruling Mafia families.)

That lethal streak of cruelty undid Cascioferro when he murdered a man named Benedetto Madonia, a Black Hand victim who had resisted paying extortion money. Cascioferro dismembered his victim's body and hid it in a barrel, one found by an inquisitive policeman, Joseph Petrosino. A few days after the discovery of the body, Petrosino tracked Cascioferro to a restaurant. He sat down at the Black Hander's table, reportedly saying: "I know you killed and chopped up that guy Madonia. You were seen. No one will say so in court but I know you did this."

Cascioferro withdrew a large wad of bills from his pocket and shoved it across the table to Petrosino. The officer stared at the money for a moment, then picked it up, and, with one large hand forced open the Black Hander's mouth and jammed the money into it with the other. The startled, enraged Cascioferro gripped his knife and fork until his knuckles showed white but he did not react. "You see this?"

Petrosino said, pulling a police mugshot of Cascioferro from his pocket, then withdrawing his revolver and placing it atop the photo. "The next time we meet," Petrosino said as he got up and started to leave, "go for your gun because I will shoot you down like the murdering beast you are!" Cascioferro realized he had met a man as tough and uncompromising as himself. He left New York and returned to Sicily where he joined the Inglese family, rising to the rank of a Mafia boss within a few years.

Then Petrosino arrived in Sicily in 1909 and Cascioferro worked up a scheme to murder him. Petrosino, however, was unaware that Cascioferro had become a Mafia don in Palermo and that he had been marked for murder by the very man he had earlier vowed to shoot on sight in the streets of New York. On the night of March 12, 1909, Petrosino met with an informer in a Palermo restaurant. The informer had promised to turn over a list to Petrosino that would contain the names of the top Mafia bosses in Sicily and Italy, as well as details on Black Hand operations throughout the United States. The informer was Marchese who, indeed, did turn over this information to Petrosino. He then chillingly, according to one report, while sliding a forkful of spaghetti into his mouth, casually admitted that he himself was on the list, bragging that he was one of the top Mafia dons in Sicily and that Don Vito Cascioferro was also on the list as a ruling Mafia boss. He pointed to a nearby table where Cascioferro sat eating with a distinguished-looking gentleman. Cascioferro slowly turned in Petrosino's direction, smiled and nodded.

Petrosino, shaken, got up from the table, pocketing the sheaves of paper Marchese had given him, and fled the restaurant, going to a postal station near the huge statue of Garibaldi that towered in the Piazza Marina. The detective managed to slip the information into a postal slot (it was later retrieved by Mafia members) before dozens of Black Handers closed in on him from all points of the square. Drawing his revolver, Petrosino began firing at his pursuers, who fired back. More than one hundred shots were reportedly fired before Petrosino fell mortally wounded. It was at this point that Casioferro sauntered up to the prone detective and fired a bullet into his brain, the coup de grace.

The detective's body, pockets emptied, was found the following morning and immediately shipped back to New York. Tens of thousands of mourners lined the streets of Little Italy to glimpse Petrosino's funeral cortege. The city honored Petrosino as a martyr in the cause of law enforcement, a knight battling the forces of evil. His widow, Angelina Salino Petrosino, was awarded a pension from the city, along with $10,000 in cash that had been donated by the people of Little Italy, the poor immigrants Joseph Petrosino had spent a lifetime protecting and in the end for whom he sacrificed his life.

The Petrosino killing caused an international incident, with U.S. authorities exchanging harsh notes with Italian government officials. One American federal official went so far as to blame Italy and Sicily for being "lawless countries where no one is safe from the Black Hand and the Mafia." An Italian official reminded the American of the horrendous mass lynchings of reported Mafia members in New Orleans in 1890 after that city's police chief, David Peter Hennessey had been shot to death by Mafia killers after he had attempted to crack down on the Black Hand.

The Italian government, however, promised that its police would not rest until Petrosino's killers were found, arrested and punished. No one was ever apprehended for the murder, although Cascioferro was brought in for questioning. A high-ranking Sicilian police official, Cavaliere Ponzi, arrested Cascioferro and brought him to his office on April 3, 1909. Cascioferro had the perfect alibi—at the moment Joseph Petrosino was being shot to death, he was dining with a member of the Italian parliament. Cascioferro was released with apologies. He would dominate the Sicilian Mafia until 1926 when Italian dictator Benito Mussolini, determined to wipe out the criminal brotherhood, personally ordered Cascioferro's arrest. He was sent to prison for life, following his conviction of murdering two wealthy men who had refused to pay his Black Hand demands. He died behind bars in 1945.

Paulo Marchese was not as fortunate as Cascioferro. Witnesses did tell police that they had seen him with Petrosino only a short time before the detective was killed. An arrest war-

Chicago crime boss James "Big Jim" Colosimo (left), Colosimo's father, and Johnny Torrio in 1911; Colosimo brought Torrio from New York to rid himself of Black Handers.

rant was issued for the Mafia don but he fled Sicily, going to New York where he changed his name to Paul di Cristina. The Italian Squad, however, got on his trail and he went to New Orleans. Here Di Cristina again plied his trade as a Black Hander, terrifying the large Italian community. He soon became head of the Mafia in New Orleans.

So successful did Di Cristina become that he took to signing his Black Hand notes with his own name and delivering these in person to Italian and Sicilian businessmen. No one resisted him, except a stubborn grocer named Pietro Pepitone

who had already thrown several of Di Cristina's men from his store. Di Cristina decided to settle matters himself. He drove a wagon to the front of Pepitone's shop and tethered the horses to a hitching post. He solemnly walked up the stairs to the store's porch but before he could enter, Pepitone suddenly appeared, a shotgun in his hands.

The grocer uttered not a single word as he pulled both barrels. The blast tore the Black Hand terrorist in half. Convicted of manslaughter, Pepitone was sent to prison for twenty years and was released after six years in 1915. (Pepitone's son,

Michele, would be murdered ten years after Di Cristina's deserved demise, in October 1919, ostensibly in belated reprisal for the Black Hander's death.)

Though its exponents were jailed and killed, the Black Hand continued to flourish in the Italian communities of New York, New Orleans, and elsewhere. In Chicago, such fearsome Black Hand terrorists as James "Sunny Jim" Cosmano grew rich from their murderous extortion racket. One of Cosmano's consistent victims was crime boss James "Big Jim" Colosimo who operated scores of brothels and gambling dens. Cosmano regularly sent Black Hand notes to Big Jim, demanding large cash payments. Unless these were made, Cosmano promised, his Black Handers would torch the Colosimo operations. Big Jim paid and paid until little Johnny Torrio arrived from New York in 1909.

Torrio, once boss of the Five Points Gang, had fled New York rather than face a murder charge. He was to aide Colosimo in managing a vast criminal empire, but one of his first assignments was to rid Big Jim of the Black Hand terrorists. Torrio, who had been a Black Hander himself in New York, set up a meeting with Cosmano's men, ostensibly to make a huge and final cash payment. When three Black Handers appeared, Torrio and his men shot and killed the extortionists. Later, Big Jim asked his enterprising aide what had happened to Cosmano's men. Torrio shrugged and said: "I looked back and they didn't wave goodbye." Cosmano never bothered Colosimo or Torrio again.

The Black Hand nevertheless remained in Chicago, terrorizing the sprawling Italian community. Statistics show that between 1900 and 1918, more than eight hundred bombs were set off in the city by Black Hand terrorists. Between January 1, 1910, and March 26, 1911, no less than thirty-eight Black Hand victims were killed on one Chicago streetcorner, at Oak and Milton streets in Little Italy. Most of the victims were openly murdered on the street and in broad daylight by a hulking thug who was called Shotgun Man since he cradled a shotgun in his long, heavy arms as he hunted for those who had refused to pay off.

The Black Hand theories carefully advanced by Cascioferro in New York, were completely abandoned in Chicago. A Black Hand victim was given only one opportunity to pay an extortion note before being killed by the terrorists. Squandering uncooperative victims through murder was acceptable to Chicago Black Handers since, in their cold-blooded viewpoint, other extortion victims were plentiful. The police appeared powerless to stop the Black Handers. In 1910, a police sweep of Little Italy ensnared more than 200 Italian and Sicilian gangsters practicing Black Hand extortion, but since no witnesses came forward to testify against them, they were released to carry on their terroristic trade.

Leaders in the Italian community tried to fight back by establishing the White Hand Society, which encouraged Black Hand victims to identify their tormentors, urged the police to vigorously pursue and arrest the terrorists and exhorted the press to conduct a vigorous campaign against the Black Hand. The Society saw little success. Most Italian immigrants were indifferent to this crusade and feared reprisal. Police were slack in their detection of the terrorists, believing this to be "an ethnic matter best settled by community leaders." Also, offices of the Society were bombed by Black Handers like Sam Cardinelli and his henchmen, a retarded giant named Frank Campione and an eighteen-year-old psychopathic killer, Nicholas "The Choir Boy" Viana.

Not until 1918 were these three notorious Black Hand terrorists caught in the act of murder and finally convicted and later hanged. Their deaths coincided with the demise of the Black Hand terror. About the same time, Prohibition went into effect, offering a much more lucrative racket—peddling bootleg beer and liquor, a racket that would mushroom into a multimillion-dollar criminal industry, enrich the lives of once unknown thugs like Al Capone and make them undisputed crime bosses, as well as go far in establishing the national crime syndicate in the U.S.

The Black Hand did not die an easy death. Terrorists using Black Hand techniques continued operations into the 1920s, although Prohibition gangsters thought them old-fashioned. The last Black Hand gang in Chicago was headed by Andrew Kerr, a non-Italian racketeer who specialized in bombing offices of unions who resisted mob control. Kerr openly admitted that he had "the best bombers in Chicago" and even named his men—Con Shea, Jim Sweeney, and "Soup" Bartlett. When Kerr and his men were sent to prison, he was replaced by Joseph Sangerman, who became the chief bombing terrorist for the mobs.

Sangerman's berserk lieutenant, George Matrisciano, alias Martini, had been a Black Hander since 1905. As Sangerman's chief union terrorist, Matrisciano reveled in his status of "top bomber." He brazenly paraded about Little Italy with two sticks of dynamite jutting from his coat pocket, and he would stop total strangers to show them with idiot pride a fading newspaper clipping that described him as a "terrorist." Such blatant public displays convinced Sangerman that Matrisciano was a risk to his organization. He ordered his lieutenant murdered. By then, the Black Hand was, throughout the land, like Matrisciano's newspaper clipping, a mercifully fast-fading nightmare.

·TWO·
RETURN OF OLD
EVILS

1910

The Siege of Sidney Street

By 1910, England was faced with a great flood of immigrants from Eastern Europe. The conservatives in Parliament attempted to block this immigration, especially opposing those with known anarchist backgrounds. Those anarchists who had legally migrated to England and those who had smuggled themselves into the country met in secret meetings, vowing to take vengeance in the form of violence and robbery against a government hostile to their politics.

On December 10, 1910, several of these anarchists attempted to rob a jewelry store in the Exchange Buildings in Houndsditch, a section of London's East End. Police were summoned to the area by a resident complaining of loud noises. Officers soon discovered that the anarchists were trying to bore a hole through a wall to reach a jeweler's safe in an adjacent office. (They had hoped to rob the safe and fund a widespread terrorist campaign throughout London.)

Inside the building and working by dim lights were six or more Eastern European anarchists who had been driven out of their countries for subversive activities and were associated with the Italian anarchist Malatesta. These included, Peter Piatkow, alias Peter Schtern or Peter the Painter, the nominal leader; George Gardstein, alias Mouremtzov, a Latvian; Max Smoller, a wanted fugitive in the Crimea; Jacob Peters, who had been tortured by the Okhrana, the czar's secret police; Joseph Levi; Yourka Dubof, a locksmith who was to open the jeweler's safe; and Nina Vassileva, Gardstein's mistress, who stood watch outside the store.

When Vassileva saw police arrive, she alerted the gang, who stopped their

London police massing for the attack during the Siege of Sidney Street in 1911.

drilling. Sergeant Bentley positioned his four men around the building and then went to the front door of the shop, politely knocking. Gardstein opened the door a crack to stare at Bentley.

"Have you been working or knocking about inside?" Bentley asked.

Gardstein shrugged, pretending he did not understand English. He then slammed the door and retreated into the rear of the building. Bentley and other officers entered the building but could see nothing. As they groped about in the dark, a rear door swung open and a man with a gun began to fire at them. Then a hail of bullets seem to come from everywhere in a terrific cross fire. Bentley was instantly hit in the neck and shoulder and collapsed. Constable Woodhams leaped forward to help his sergeant and was also shot. Constable Tucker then stepped forward and was shot square in the chest. He died instantly.

Gardstein then attempted to flee, knocking down Constable Choate who stood in his path. Dubof and Peters, both armed, then shot Choate as they fled past him—he was later found dead with twelve bullets in his body. The last constable, Sergeant Bryant, tried to club the killers with his nightstick and was also shot down. The fleeing terrorists fired wildly and a bullet struck one of their own men, Gardstein, but the entire gang still managed to escape. The policemen were, except for their nightsticks, unarmed. Three officers were dead and two seriously wounded from the savage attack, an unprecedented massacre in the history of the British police. London was suddenly seized by anarchist terror.

Criminals and political zealots in the past had used force and created violence in England but no one had ever ruthlessly shot down unarmed

British bobbies. The crime was unthinkable except when attributed to anarchists, who had long been profiled as bestial and inhuman. An enraged Winston Churchill, then Home Secretary, demanded that police hunt down the terrorists and kill them if need be in their apprehension. This did not take long. Police simply followed the trail of blood left by the wounded Gardstein to the apartment of Fritz Svaars, Peters' cousin and an instigator of the abortive robbery.

The anarchists quickly concluded that the seriously wounded Gardstein was a liability. They placed him on a bed and left him to bleed to death. He was later found dead, a loaded pistol tucked beneath his pillow. As they fled, Dubof, Peters, and Svaars' mistress, Luba Milstein, were caught by policemen. Smoller vanished and Svaars himself escaped. Though he had taken no direct part in the robbery-murder, Svaars was branded a fugitive. Fearing that he faced deportation back to Russia where a death sentence awaited, Svaars vowed that he would not be taken alive and took great pains to avoid a police entrapment, moving from one anarchist hideout to another.

Police conducted a thorough city-wide search for the fugitive, unraveling in the process a conspiracy that horrified the public and sent shock waves through the hierarchy of government. Dozens of anarchists had banded together to form a deadly conspiracy that was aimed at assassinating government leaders and even setting London ablaze, according to information pieced together by police from their informants and from the sketchy remarks made by those in custody. At the head of this conspiracy was the mysterious anarchist known as Peter the Painter. It was he who had devised a series of robberies to finance the reign of terror.

Detective Superintendent John Ottaway and Inspector Frederick Wensley ordered their men to penetrate every known anarchist haunt in their desperate search for Svaars. Hundreds of anarchists and those suspected of harboring such political beliefs were rousted as officers disrupted the meetings of social and political clubs, barged into pubs and invaded coffee houses. A £500 reward was posted for information leading to the arrest of Svaars.

Meanwhile, those in custody from the Houndsditch shootings said nothing. Only young and frightened Nina Vassileva finally talked, but she knew very little. It was from her that police learned about the ubiquitous Peter the Painter. She portrayed him as the anarchist mastermind who intended to "kill all the politicians and generals and set fire to London." Through her, a photo of Peter the Painter was obtained, a man shown in profile wearing a business suit, a winged collar, a narrow black tie, and with a decided German bearing. His hair was cropped, and he wore a thick, upturned waxed mustache in the manner of Kaiser Wilhelm.

On January 1, 1911, police received a tip that the much-wanted Svaars, along with a jeweler known only as "Joseph," and a woman, Betsy

Gershon, were hiding in an apartment at 100 Sidney Street. The jeweler was later identified as Joseph Marx, alias Jacob Vogel. Ottaway and Wensley went to the address with several officers but proceeded with caution, knowing that they were dealing with armed men who would not hesitate to shoot anyone who might attempt to apprehend them. Complicating their task was the building itself in which the fugitives hid. It was one of ten four-story apartment buildings packed with people, each building separated from the next by fireproof walls.

More than 200 policemen, all given weapons, were brought to 100 Sidney Street. They hid behind fences, walls, buildings, and in shops. They blocked all avenues of escape and then Ottaway sent his men quietly into the buildings to safely remove the other residents. This took more than a day to accomplish as constables softly knocked on doors and whispered their orders to the startled tenement dwellers. By 4 A.M., January 3, 1911, the buildings were empty except for the second-floor apartment where Svaars and Vogel were hiding. (Betty Gershon had been apprehended as she was returning to the apartment with groceries on January 2.)

At 7:30 A.M., Sergeant Leeson hurled pebbles at the windows of the second-floor apartment, attempting to draw Svaars and Vogel forward so that they could be told they were surrounded and to give themselves up. A second officer pounded on the front door, which had been bolted by the men inside. The response was a hail of gunfire steaming from one of the upper windows. Bullets spattered the cobblestones of the street and sharded shop windows as officers dashed frantically for cover. Sergeant Leeson lay wounded in the street. For two hours police traded shots with the anarchists.

About this time Winston Churchill was taking his morning bath. His valet informed him of events and Churchill hurriedly dressed. When informed of the ensuing battle, which was later to be called the Siege of Sidney Street, Churchill ordered police to "use whatever force necessary" to bring the situation under control. A detachment of heavily armed Scots Guards arrived at the scene from the Tower of London at 10:15 A.M. Police and military officers immediately fell into furious debates as to how they should proceed. Ottaway still wanted to attempt to negotiate with the anarchists but a military officer shouted that "these damned terrorists must be blasted out of there!"

Though it was a serious breach of protocol that would bring widespread criticism in days to come, Churchill suddenly arrived at Sidney Street to personally take charge of the siege. With him were Superintendent Quinn of the Special Branch and Melville Macnaghten, head of the Central Intelligence Division. The Home Secretary's visit to the site of the battle would later be considered a major public relations *faux pas*. Still, Churchill, who had reveled in his harrowing experiences during the Boer War, could never resist the lure of adventure.

Standing inside a shop and peering from its window to see a steady stream of gunfire pouring from the upstairs window of the anarchists' apartment, Churchill grimaced, then barked an order to bring in field artillery and reduce the apartment building to rubble if necessary. A battery of horse artillery rumbled into the area from the St. John's Woods Barracks. Churchill was persuaded not to use the big guns and it was soon decided that the building would be stormed before the artillery went into action. By then six more policemen had been wounded by the withering marksmanship of the anarchists.

The Scots Guards, holding rifles, took their position in the middle of the street, phalanxes of police officers behind them. Before the attack took place, however, an officer pointed to the roof of 100 Sidney Street where a thin wisp of smoke was curling upward. The building was on fire, a blaze that had apparently started in the upper floors and was quickly working its way downward. Suddenly, one of the gunmen poked his head from a window gushing smoke. Dozens of rifles and pistols cracked and the gunman was struck in the head, falling back inside the apartment.

The fire soon raged through the bullet-ridden building. When the fire brigade arrived, Churchill ordered the firemen to hold back. Not until the upper floors of the building collapsed from the blaze did the firemen open their hoses. The small army of guardsmen, police officers and firemen watched as 100 Sidney Street collapsed in smoldering rubble. Five firemen were injured when a wall of the building collapsed on them. Police then cautiously moved through the still-smoking debris to find the

Peter Piatkov, alias Peter the Painter, one of leaders of the anarchists who created murder and mayhem in London in 1911.

charred bodies of Marx and Svaars, both of whom had been the top lieutenants of Peter the Painter.

Marx had been the man shot in the window. Svaars was also shot through the head but not by a police or guardsman's bullet. Officials concluded that the terrorist had shot himself as the flames enveloped him. Looking at the bodies, Churchill grimly nodded and walked away. The remaining members of the anarchist gang were brought to trial for the Houndsditch shootings but, ironically, were released for lack of evidence.

Churchill was later lambasted in the press for overplaying his hand—never had it taken so many to bring down so few. The Siege of Sidney Street drew criticism from politicians and the press the world over who claimed that officials, chiefly Churchill, had overreacted and that if they had developed a clear and proper plan of seizure, the anarchists might have been taken alive. "The police can hardly be congratulated upon their success in dealing with this formidable conspiracy," sneered the *London Daily Mail*. To a friend the tenacious Churchill reportedly confided: "What were we to do—wait until the bastards shot us in our beds?"

Peter the Painter, so-called because he painted scenery for anarchist dramas, remained at large. He was never found or convicted but he was well remembered, especially after police reproduced his photo on wanted posters that were plastered on walls all over London. Some of these posters, especially in Whitechapel and other gathering areas for anarchists were preserved with pride for years. When Alfred Hitchcock filmed his first version of *The Man Who Knew Too Much* (1935), he reenacted the Siege of Sidney Street, switching the anarchists to spies led by an insidious kidnapper, Peter Lorre. A British police officer who had been at the actual siege saw the Hitchcock film and said: "It was nothing like the real thing. The real thing was a nightmare with brave officers shot down. Film actors get off the floor after a scene and go to a party."

Jules Bonnot, who led an anarchist terror gang through France from 1911 to 1913, robbing banks and killing at will and whim.

Bonnot's Reign of Terror

In the same year that the London anarchists went to ashes, an adventurous young racetrack driver named Jules Joseph Bonnot struck terror in France. Bonnot had made a name for himself as one of the most daring race car drivers in the early era of the auto. He took to drinking in Paris clubs frequented by anarchists who persuaded him through flattery to lend his name to their cause. Within months, he announced that he, too, was an anarchist and was opposed to the government of France, to any government for that matter.

Some time later in 1911, Bonnot agreed to supply his anarchist mentors with cash to fund their underground operations. To accomplish this end the race driver would use his own skills. He would rob French banks and escape in an auto, a robbery technique never before employed anywhere. (Henry Starr, nephew of American bandit Belle Starr, would be the first U.S. bank robber to use a car in a getaway in 1914, fully three years after Bonnot's inventive ploy.)

Forming a gang of young race car drivers and friends, all of whom had embraced anarchism, Bonnot committed his first terrorist robbery on December 21, 1911. He and others waylaid a bank messenger named Gaby of the Societé Générale in Paris' Rue Ordener, shooting him and taking a pouch stuffed with a half million francs, then the equivalent of £25,000 or $200,000, an enormous haul that stunned the French police. They drove off in a Delaunay-Belleville car. Before authorities had the chance to respond, the gang invaded an army arsenal on the Grand Boulevard in Paris and removed scores of rifles, revolvers, and many boxes of ammunition. Again, the terrorists escaped in a car. At the wheel was Bonnot, waving wildly to the helpless, weaponless gendarmes chasing on foot. Much of the arms and ammunition Bonnot distributed to anarchist groups, but he kept the more modern weapons for his own gang.

After another half dozen sensational robberies, Bonnot and his men, who acted openly, were identified and more than 10,000 wanted posters advertising rewards for their capture were distributed throughout Paris and neighboring cities. An alarmed Prime Minister Poincaré announced that "Bonnot must be brought to justice by whatever means and whatever cost." Poincaré authorized the creation of the French Garde Mobile, or Flying

Squad, which also employed cars and whose single assignment was to track down and capture the terrorists.

Bonnot meanwhile robbed a factory and shot down several supervisors and managers as an anarchistic act against authority. He and his gang then motored to Belgium to visit other anarchist groups and encourage them to raid Belgian banks and arsenals. Bonnot then boldly returned to Paris. As he drove past a policeman, the gendarme recognized him and leaped upon the running board of the car. Bonnot and others inside the car drew revolvers and shot the officer three times in the chest. He fell dead from the speeding car.

Police seeking photographs of the elusive terrorist-bandits were aided by a flamboyant and successful author, H. Ashton-Wolfe, who made a living by writing fanciful tales about supposedly real-life criminals. Ironically, he pointed out to police, he had at one time employed Bonnot as his chauffeur. He then offered the officers a photo showing himself in his car and his chauffeur, Bonnot, at the wheel. The police reprinted the photo on new wanted photos; it was the first to be used in identifying the terrorist.

Once he learned that his car, then a Dion-Bouton, had been identified, Bonnot looked about for another fast auto. These were rare in that the auto had still not become the conveyance of the land; most still traveled by horse-drawn carriage and cart. Bonnot learned that the Marquis de Rougé, a well-known sporting figure, had just purchased a speedy touring car. In March 1912, Bonnot and other gang members drove their car onto a path taken by the Marquis's car, blocking the route.

The terrorists shot both the Marquis and his chauffeur, throwing their bodies into a ditch before abandoning the Dion-Bouton and stealing the touring car. Bonnot, Francois Callemin, his top lieutenant, and others then drove to Chantilly where they parked the touring car and sauntered into the local bank. They all carried rifles and revolvers and, without warning, fired their weapons as they entered the bank, immediately killing one clerk and wounding two others. Then the terrorists leaped over the tellers' cages and scooped up the money in the drawers (a technique that would later be employed by bank robber John Dillinger in the early 1930s).

Outside the bank, Callemin and others fired their rifles to ward off citizens who had come running at the sound of the first gunfire. The scene was something out of the American West a half century earlier. With Bonnot rushing from the bank holding a sack of money, the bandits leaped into the car and, firing their weapons into the air, drove quickly out of town. A policeman fired at the speedily retreating car and managed to wound Callemin. This so enraged the terrorist that he fired at an innocent motorist traveling in the opposite direction.

The Chantilly raid spurred the Sûreté Nationale to make an all-out effort to capture the terrorists, assigning hundreds of its best men to track down Bonnot and his gang. Poincaré reflected the astonishment of the country at Bonnot's crimes and his ability to elude capture, saying that he was "the most

Police closing in on Bonnot's hideout.

dangerous criminal of this century or the last." As if to prove that claim, Bonnot and his men next attacked the ancient fortress of Vincennes in what was close to a military operation. The terrorists overpowered guards, shooting one to death in the process. Then, while looting the great arsenal of weapons and ammunition, they shot down several more guards.

The gang was now hunted everywhere in France, police and military units on the trail of its members. Bonnot acted out the part of the dedicated anarchist, publicly stating that he would kill anyone who dared to come near him or his men. Pierre Garnier, one of Bonnot's men, wrote taunting letters to the Sûreté. One

missive admitted: "I know that you will get the better of me in the long run. All the strength is on your side. But I will make you pay for it dearly."

One by one, Bonnot's gang members were cornered and caught. Callemin, his top aide, was trapped by police in Paris in March 1913 as he peddled down a narrow street on a bicycle. As he was dragged away, the anarchist screamed: "I was ready for you! But you had all the luck! You will find that my three revolvers are all loaded!"

Bonnot had also made enemies within his own ranks. One of his anarchist followers, a few days after Callemin was captured, sent a letter to the police, telling them that Bonnot

Above: Using moving barricades, French police inch closer to the Bonnot gang, holed up and firing from the farm building beyond. *Below:* Civilian volunteers firing on Bonnot's hideout.

could be found at his rural hideout at Choisy-le-Roi. "I hope you get the skunk!" the informer added. "He killed one of my best friends."

As had been the case at Sidney Street in London, a small army of French police and soldiers swarmed into the countryside around a farmhouse in Choisy-le-Roi. Hundreds of men threw up barricades around the building, others dug trenches and set up machine guns. It was as if the French had gone to war.

Using carts and mattresses filled with hay as shields, more than two hundred heavily armed men moved slowly toward the house. Suddenly, Bonnot began firing at them, dozens of rounds that instantly killed one officer and wounded several more. He ran from window to window, firing and screaming oaths, a lethal maniac.

TERRORISM IN THE 20TH CENTURY

Bonnot's letter, found after he had been killed in his last battle.

The police and troopers fired back in a gun battle that lasted six hours. When there was no more gunfire from the house, the attackers crept cautiously forward, entered the house and climbed the stairs.

They found Bonnot on the floor, bleeding to death, struck by four bullets. He was in a half coma and with his dying breath he cursed the officers staring down at him. Nailed to a wall was a letter he had written during the gun battle. It read: "I am famous. My name is trumpeted to the four corners of the globe and the publicity given to my humble person must make all those people jealous who try in vain to get into the papers. As far as I am concerned, I could have well done without it." He added that certain persons who had harbored him were not anarchists and were innocent of his crimes.

Bonnot died in front of the officers who then carefully inspected his corpse, determining that the fatal bullet to the head had been inflicted by Bonnot himself. He had opted to commit suicide rather than be taken into custody. Several other gang members chose the same inglorious exit, including a gang member named Corouy who gulped down a glass of prussic acid when gendarmes burst into his room. Callemin and two other gang members, Soudy and Monier, were tried, found guilty of murder and terrorist activities, and were sentenced to the guillotine. They were all beheaded on April 21, 1913.

Garnier and another gang member found themselves trapped in a hideout on May 14, 1913. They shot it out with police and were both killed. The remaining members of the terrorist gang were rounded up and given long prison terms. In the following year, the last violent words of Pierre Callemin were recalled. Before the guillotine severed his head, he had shouted: "Within a year, you will all die at the hand of anarchy!" Many of those soldiers present at his execution were dead a little more than a year later, but not at the hand of anarchy. It would be the guns of the Kaiser that would take their lives in the opening bloody battles of World War I.

A Bomb for a
Publishing Magnate

At the time British authorities were contending with the flow of anarchists into England, Harrison Gray Otis, the most influential publisher in California, was waging his own war against entities he thought more dangerous than anarchists—unions. Otis headed the all-powerful Merchants and Manufacturers Association and was the publisher of the equally omnipotent *Los Angeles Times*. For twenty years, Otis had used the association and the editorial pages of the *Times* to combat unionism. "We employ no union men!" was his staunch motto. During those twenty years open shops prevailed in Los Angeles.

In 1907, the American Federation of Labor called Otis "the most unfair, unscrupulous and malignant enemy of organized labor in America." The publisher did little to change this perception. He was frequently observed driving about Los Angeles with a small cannon mounted on the running board of his car, fully prepared to blow anarchist laborites into oblivion.

In 1910, the AFL tried hard to once again bring unions into Los Angeles. Otis countered by having the Merchants and Manufacturers Association

pressure the city into outlawing picketing. The unions then placed their considerable political support behind the Socialist candidate for mayor, Joe Harriman, who won a dramatic upset over the incumbent in the primary.

Then, on October 1, 1910, a tremendous explosion decimated the *Los Angeles Times* Building. The blast blew out an entire wall, creating an inferno in which scores of screaming, running workers were horribly burned. Twenty workers were dead and dozens more injured. An enraged Otis announced that the explosion was no accident but a bomb planted by organized labor. He added that he had been getting bomb threats for years and that these threats were known to his workers, who had to labor under the strain and apprehension of being murdered by anarchist labor leaders. Now, it had happened.

The incumbent mayor, at Otis' urging, immediately hired William J. Burns to find the bombers. Burns was at the time considered to be the greatest detective in America, and he went about his diligent business with great skill. Inspecting the ruins and finding bomb fragments, Burns and his aides soon saw a pattern that linked the

The smoking ruins of the Los Angeles Times *Building, blown up by labor terrorists on October 21, 1910*

Times bombing to a series of bombings attributed to the leaders of the Bridge and Structural Iron Workers Union. Digging further, Burns produced evidence against the union's secretary-treasurer, twenty-eight-year-old John J. McNamara, and his twenty-seven-year-old brother, James McNamara. The evidence was in the form of a confession supplied by Ortie McManigal who was

Return of Old Evils

Above: William J. Burns (left) with Times owner Harrison Gray Otis; operatives from Burns' famous detective agency tracked down the terrorists who planted the bomb. Left: Clarence Darrow, the greatest criminal lawyer of his day, at the time of the McNamara trial.

to you—well, I believe you will have to stand alone." McManigal buckled, writing out a full confession, saying that he had hired two anarchist bomb experts, David Caplan and Matthew Schmidt, on behalf of the McNamaras, and that they had all smuggled the bomb into the *Times* Building and set it off with a timing device.

The extraordinary Burns then went to Indianapolis, Indiana, where on April 26, he marched into the Iron Workers headquarters and, with state police backing him, personally arrested the McNamara brothers. By decidedly extralegal means, Burns managed to send the brothers to Los Angeles for trial. The hue and cry from labor over this questionable extradition was universal. Public sentiment was highly in favor of the McNamaras. Most felt that they were being railroaded by ruthless businessmen and a huge fund was raised to defend them.

The McNamaras and their supporters then turned toward Chicago to summon the champion of labor, Clarence Darrow. The great defense attorney, however, at first did not respond. He had grown weary of labor murders and had resolved never again to enter that arena after his exhausting defense of Big Bill Hayward and his Wobblies in 1907. Union representatives pleaded, pointing out that there was no one more able to protect the rights of the defendants. Moreover, they promised that there would be a $200,000 defense fund and that the McNamaras would personally pay him a fee of $50,000. Darrow accepted and went to Los Angeles, a journey he would later bitterly regret.

tracked down in Detroit, Michigan, by Burns' operatives in April 1911.

McManigal was visited by Burns, who warned him that under existing conspiracy laws, he would be held equally guilty with the McNamaras for the *Times* bombing. "The McNamaras will undoubtedly have all the financial resources of organized labor behind them at the trial," Burns told McManigal. "But when it comes

Unlike the maverick IWW union headed by Big Bill Hayward in Colorado during the mine bombings of the early 1900s, the union represented by the McNamaras was supported universally by American labor. Venerable labor leader Samuel Gompers branded the case against the brothers a "capitalist conspiracy," a sentiment echoed across the land in every union hall and on the pages of pro-labor newspapers. Unions and the general public rallied around the brothers, who were portrayed as scapegoats in a vicious frame-up. Radical labor leader Eugene V. Debs insisted that the "rigged trial" called for a nationwide work stoppage, thundering: "Let the striking toilers of the Pacific Coast raise the red standard of revolt, and the workers of other states fall in line and swell the hosts of American freeman in their fight to rescue their kidnapped brothers from the clutches of a murderous plutocracy!"

In Los Angeles, Darrow was faced by a quagmire of corruption involving the trial. As he gathered evidence for the defense, he slowly came to realize that his clients were guilty. Worse, minions from the District Attorney's office and operatives working for Burns (who worked for Otis) practiced widespread bribery. Darrow's people bribed back. The great labor lawyer was in a quandary. He wanted to quit the case, but to abandon his clients would also mean personal fraud and deceit. As a moral man he could not do it. His dilemma was solved, in part, by labor writer and Darrow's close friend, Lincoln Steffens, who was covering the trial. After Darrow confided in him,

Steffens suggested that he plead his clients guilty as the only method of saving them from the death penalty.

Through his intermediary, publisher E. W. Scripps of San Diego, Darrow proposed to Otis that he would have his clients plead guilty if the publisher would drop his demands for the death penalty. Otis reluctantly agreed. Then James McNamara got up in open court and admitted setting the bomb "for moral purposes." He was sent to San Quentin Prison for life. His brother John received a fifteen-year term, serving ten years before being released. Caplan and Schmidt were sent to prison for life.

Socialist mayoral candidate Harriman lost the election and was ruined politically. The conviction of the McNamaras also set back the cause of unions in Los Angeles for years. Labor then turned its wrath on Darrow, saying that he had sold out the cause that he had championed for decades and abandoned American workers to the despotic rule of capitalists.

Darrow's enemies were on all sides, with Otis being the most vengeful. The publisher caused the District Attorney to charge Darrow with bribery. He was arrested and held for trial while Otis and his forces put together evidence that claimed one of Darrow's assistants had offered bribe money to two prospective jurors through a private detective.

Darrow, meanwhile, went broke paying for his own defense. He never received his fee from the McNamaras nor a cent of the labor defense fund in that case. When he called upon labor leaders like Gompers to help him defray his enormous legal costs, his appeals were answered with refusals. Piqued with Darrow, Gompers wrote to him at this time, saying: "I am free to say to you that in my judgment any general appeal for funds to defend you or the men under indictment would fall upon deaf ears and elicit little if any response at this time."

Now he was alone, vowing to never again take up the cause of Labor, one that showed so little gratitude for his lifetime of service. To Darrow's rescue came the flamboyant, unpredictable and heavy-drinking criminal attorney Earl Rogers. Throughout the long, dreary and exhausting trial, with Otis vindictively urging Darrow's conviction and imprisonment, Rogers remained sober and effectively argued his client's case.

Darrow himself provided some of his own defense, but it was the flashy, eloquent Rogers who carried the load and made the final, brilliant summation, moving confidently along the jury box, peering into the eyes of each juror as his resonant voice intoned: "Will you tell me how any sane, sensible man who knows anything about the law business—and this defendant has been at it for thirty-five years—could make himself go to a detective and say to him: 'Just buy all the jurors you want. I put my whole life, my reputation, I put everything I have into your hands. I trust you absolutely. I never knew you until two or three months ago and I don't know much about you now. But there you are. Go to it!'"

Two jurors refused to convict Darrow and the trial ended in a hung jury. Following a second trial, the case

Labor terrorists Jim and John McNamara at trial, after admitting their guilt in planting a bomb in the Los Angeles Times *Building.*

ended in an acquittal and Darrow, penniless, went back to Chicago. He vowed to earn money the way his esteemed friend Rogers did, by defending wealthy men accused of criminal acts. To that end, Darrow enriched his coffers during the 1920s by defending millionaire Chicago gambler Mont Tennes and others. But he won a startling victory in the 1924 murder case of Richard Loeb and Nathan Leopold, managing to preserve the lives of these horrific thrill killers. He successfully battled narrow-minded fundamentalism in Tennessee in the Scopes Trial and won an impressive victory in the Massie murder case in Hawaii but he seldom took labor cases. That was a cause, he reasoned, that had abandoned *him*.

TERRORISM IN THE 20TH CENTURY

Joe Hill, IWW Terrorist and Manipulated Martyr

Where radical labor leaders discarded its legal champion Clarence Darrow, they shamelessly used the life and death of their handpicked terrorist, Joe Hill, to further their cause. Best known today for his songs and poems created in the infant days of the American labor movement, Hill was executed for murdering a one-time Salt Lake City police officer and his son. He became a martyr to the radical union movement, but he was unmistakably a brutal killer who deserved his grim fate.

Born October 7, 1879, in Gävle, Sweden, as Joel Emmanuel Hägglund, he was one of nine children. When his father, Olaf, a railroad conductor, was killed in an accident, the eight-year-old Hill went to work to help support his starving family. A short time later he went to sea, sending his earnings to his mother. When she died in 1902 and his brothers and sisters were grown, he immigrated to America, changed his name to Joe Hillstrom and tried unsuccessfully to organize laborers in Chicago. He would be known far and wide simply as Joe Hill, the name under which he wrote a number of stirring union songs.

Though unschooled, Hill had a deep talent for songwriting, his most memorable union tunes being "Casey Jones, the Union Scab," and "The Preacher and the Slave," which contained a line that later became a permanent part of American idiom: "You'll get pie in the sky when you die." He advocated primitive Marxism or early-day communism, ranting that workers would never enjoy the good things of life until capitalism was completely eradicated.

In 1910, Hill joined the IWW and volunteered to work as a Wobbly terrorist. He went to Los Angeles where he reportedly helped to plant the bomb that blew up the Los Angeles *Times* Building, a crime for which the McNamara brothers and other IWW terrorists went to prison. In 1913, Hill went to work in a Utah mine, attempting to organize miners into IWW ranks. He was, like Harry Orchard a decade earlier, handpicked by IWW

The legendary Joe Hill, labor terrorist and murderer, who was executed for his crimes on November 19, 1915.

leader Big Bill Hayward to spread terrorism and murder staunch anti-laborites.

In Salt Lake City, the Eselius brothers acted as Hayward's top lieutenants, issuing guns and bombs to IWW terrorists, along with lists of those to be executed. On the list was John Morrison, a wealthy Salt Lake City storeowner. As a former Salt Lake City police officer, Morrison had helped to break many strikes and had uncovered several IWW plots to bomb mines. He had made countless arrests and survived shoot-outs with union terrorists, killing and wounding a number of Wobblies.

After leaving the police force, Morrison opened a store in Salt Lake City, one he successfully operated with his two grown sons, Arling and Merlin. The Morrisons were under no delusions concerning their own safety. John Morrison had many times received terrorist threats that his store would be bombed and his family members killed. He had survived two vicious attempts on his life, and he and his sons kept loaded revolvers behind the counters of their store and never went anywhere without their weapons.

On the night of January 10, 1914, Hill and another Wobbly terrorist, Otto Applequist, left the town of Murray, Utah, which was just outside Salt Lake City. Two hours later, at about 10 P.M., two men wearing masks and brandishing guns burst through the doors of the Morrison grocery store just as Morrison and his sons were about to close the place.

"We've got you now!" one of the intruders shouted. He and his partner opened fire on the Morrisons, who dove for their revolvers. A wild gun battle occured within several seconds, smoke filling the store. When it cleared, the two terrorists had fled and John and Arling Morrison lay dead on the floor. Merlin stood up and retrieved his brother's gun, discovering that a single bullet had been fired from its magazine.

Joe Hill suddenly appeared at 11:30 P.M. at the home of Dr. Frank F. McHugh, displaying a gunshot wound that had passed through his body,

TERRORISM IN THE 20TH CENTURY

grazing his left lung. Hill said: "Doctor, I've been shot. I got into a stew with a friend of mine who thought I had insulted his wife." Then and thereafter Hill would not reveal the name of the "friend" who had shot him.

Dr. McHugh dressed and bandaged the wound, telling Hill that it was not serious and that he would recover quickly. Hill went to the home of the Eselius brothers to recuperate. When McHugh heard about the Morrison shootings, however, he informed police of Hill's wound. Officers raced to the Eselius home and, barging through the door, found Hill sitting at a table. He suddenly reached for something and an officer fired off a shot that shattered Hill's hand. The object Hill had been reaching for was a handkerchief.

By the time Hill was brought to Salt Lake City headquarters, four other suspects in the Morrison murders were already behind bars. They were released when Hill was jailed and officially charged with the killings. Applequist, the man who had accompanied Hill on the night of the terrorist attack, was never again seen.

The case against Hill was thought to be "airtight." He was a known IWW terrorist. He could not or would not explain his whereabouts on the night of the Morrison killings, or identify the person who had inflicted his mysterious bullet wound. Moreover, he had been heard repeatedly to state that he would be "getting even" with Morrison for past union offenses by the ex-policeman.

Hill's lawyers found him to be a troublesome client. He argued with them constantly and refused to supply information that might clear him of the murder charge. He fired his attorneys and when the court appointed new lawyers to defend him, Hill refused to cooperate with them. In court, Hill refused to reveal how he had been wounded. The circumstantial evidence was persuasive enough to bring about his conviction. Hill was sentenced to die on July 18, 1914.

At this time Big Bill Hayward and the IWW, which had been strangely inactive during Hill's trial, suddenly launched a massive campaign to save their terrorist's life. Hayward profiled Hill as a sacrificial lamb to be slaughtered on the altar of capitalism. The campaign caused several appeals and stays of execution but Hayward privately admitted that Hill would be executed and before that time the terrorist was to be used to gain sympathy and funding for his IWW. Utah authorities received many pleas for clemency from distinguished American citizens, including President Woodrow Wilson, Helen Keller, and Swedish Foreign Minister W. A. F. Ekengren.

In the end, Hill had no delusions, wiring Hayward: "Don't waste any time mourning—organize!" As it still does today, the State of Utah offered Hill the options of being executed by hanging or being shot by a firing squad. "I'll take shooting," Hill replied. "I'm used to that. I have been shot a few times in the past and I guess I can stand it again."

On the morning of November 19, 1915, guards came to take Hill from his cell and before a firing squad. They found his cell door tied to bars with strips of blanket Hill had torn apart. He then used his bunk and mattress to barricade himself against the guards who took almost a half hour to break into the cell. Hill fought violently with his guards, struggling and kicking as he was dragged into a courtyard and strapped into a wooden chair.

"Well," Hill sighed. "I'm through. You can't blame a man for fighting for his life." As he stared at a large canvas twenty feet away, a paper target was pinned to his shirt over his heart. Behind the canvas were five sharpshooters, the barrels of their rifles poking through five holes in the canvas. As is still the custom, one of the marksmen in the five-man squad had a blank cartridge in his rifle. None in the squad knew who had the blank so that all would aim to kill and no one would know who had actually executed the condemned man.

A guard then shouted: "Ready . . . aim . . ."

Hill interrupted him, shouting for his own execution: "Fire! Go on and fire!"

The rifles barked. Three bullets smacked dead center into the heart of Joe Hill, killing him instantly. From that moment on, he became a martyr to the cause of unionism and, as late as the radical 1960s, a coffeehouse hero where his songs were wailed by folksingers who had, for the most part, never heard of the IWW, Wobblies, Big Bill Hayward or, specifically, John and Arling Morrison, who were murdered in cold blood and for whom no poignant, rousing tunes had ever been written.

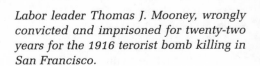

Labor leader Thomas J. Mooney, wrongly convicted and imprisoned for twenty-two years for the 1916 terorist bomb killing in San Francisco.

TERRORISM IN THE 20TH CENTURY

Railroading a Rebel

In the annals of terrorism, American labor leader Tom Mooney is the most shocking example of the wrongly convicted. For twenty-two years Mooney chose prison over freedom, a choice based upon moral principles. To accept anything else than an outright pardon from the governor of California was, in his determined view, an admission that he was responsible for bombing the San Francisco Preparedness Day Parade on July 22, 1916, a horrendous terrorist explosion that left ten persons dead and another fifty seriously injured.

Mooney and his young protégé, Warren Knox Billings, were arrested, charged and convicted of murder based on the perjured evidence of two wholly unreliable witnesses. Even the presiding judge in the case, Frank Griffin, expressed his doubts. Griffin called the Mooney conviction "one of the dirtiest jobs ever put over."

Thomas Jeremiah Mooney, born in 1882 to Irish immigrants Bernard and Mary Mooney, was exposed to labor struggles at early age. His father was active in the Knights of Labor movement in Iowa. Upon his father's death, Mooney and his siblings moved with their mother to Holyoke, Massachusetts. It was here that Mooney first displayed his penchant for being a rebel. He was loudly scolded by a priest at the Catholic school he attended for his habitual truancy, particularly for sneaking away to a Protestant church to sample some free candy.

Bristling at the priest's reprimand, Mooney quit the parochial institution and enrolled himself in a nearby public school. By 1907, Mooney was deeply involved in labor union politics, running as a nominee for delegate to the International Molder's Union convention in Philadelphia. He lost by seven votes. Later that year, Mooney used his life savings to sail to Europe where he thought to fulfill his ambition to become an artist. The trip would change his life and his political views forever.

While strolling through a Rotterdam art museum, Mooney met Nicholas Klein, an American delegate to the International Socialist Convention. Klein had been drawn to Mooney when he spotted the membership pin of the Molder's Union Mooney proudly wore on his lapel. For two days, Klein and Mooney discussed the class struggle between workers and management and the objectives of the American labor movement. Mooney then abandoned his ambition to become an artist. Instead of studying great paintings, Mooney spent the rest of his time in Europe observing laborers and the socioeconomic problems they confronted, all under Klein's guidance.

When he returned to the U.S., Mooney found the country in a panic. The news from the West, where Big Bill Hayward and the IWW were accused of murdering mine officials and strikebreaking miners, caused a wave of terror to ensue. Anarchists were behind every laborer wielding a pick and shovel roared the press. By then, however, Mooney had fully embraced the cause of labor and socialism. He joined the Socialist Party and began subscribing to its organ, *Appeal to Reason*. In 1908, Mooney traveled with radical labor leader Eugene Victor Debs on the "Red Special," a train traversing the country as Debs, the Socialist candidate for president, barnstormed the nation.

Following the acquittal of Hayward, Mooney came to believe in the cause of Hayward's union, the International Workers of the World. In March 1910, Mooney joined the IWW. Later that year he went to San Francisco to run as the Socialist candidate for judge of the Superior Court. He lost but stayed on in California where, in May 1911, he, along with Austin Lewis and Cloudsley Johns, founded the publication *Revolt: The Voice of the Militant Worker*. Immersing himself in radical causes on the West Coast, Mooney supported James and John McNamara, who, in 1910, were accused of employing anarchist bombers to destroy the *Los Angeles Times* Building, owned by anti-labor publisher Harrison Gray Otis. When the McNamaras confessed to the bombing, Mooney and all other IWW leaders were branded subversives and dangerous terrorists. They were singled out for surveillance.

Mooney; his wife, Rena; and Warren Billings were caught up in one of San Francisco's bitterest labor disputes in May 1913. At that time, outside linemen belonging to the Electrical Worker's Union walked off the job in a wage dispute with the Pacific Gas and Electric Company of California. The use of explosives by labor radicals to destroy property and intimidate strikebreakers during the dispute typified the kind of "class warfare" advocated by labor anarchists Emma Goldman, Alexander Berkman and Joe Hill

Because Mooney and his aides backed the strikers, they were immediately branded terrorists. Warren Billings, returning from New York to San Francisco, was arrested and charged with possession of dynamite. In November 1913, he was convicted and sent to Folsom Prison to serve a two-year sentence. A month later Mooney was arrested and charged with plotting to blow up the PG&E Towers that spanned the Carquinez Straits. Prosecutors failed to provide evidence for the charge, unable to show a single stick of dynamite in Mooney's possession. He and a codefendant were released.

Mooney was nevertheless a marked man. John J. Barrett, the leading attorney for Pacific Gas, walked up to Mooney's defense attorney, Maxwell McNutt, a few minutes after Mooney

Some of the dead from the Preparedness Day Parade bomb that exploded in San Francisco on July 22, 1916, killing ten and seriously injuring forty more.

was acquitted. A day of reckoning was coming, he said, adding: "Well, Mac, you got Mooney out of this but we put a red shirt on him and we'll get something on him some day."

The day came three years later in 1916. In July of that year, Tom and Rena Mooney, along with Billings, who had been released from prison, attempted to organize the railway car motormen. Try as they might, the Mooneys could not convince the motormen to walk off the job; most expressed fear of reprisals from management. Exhausted, the union orga-

nizers decided to take a vacation along the picturesque Russian River.

At the same time, San Francisco businesses heavily advertised the Preparedness Day Parade, which was scheduled for July 22. The day was fast approaching when the U.S. would enter the war in Europe. The parade was a show of patriotic support for the allied cause, which many citizens had tacitly endorsed by 1916, despite President Wilson's reelection credo of "Too Proud to Fight." The IWW and radical trade unionists, including Mooney, had openly condemned

Return of Old Evils

entering the war. Mooney and Billings had made their feelings well known in the radical press and were therefore likely suspects when a powerful dynamite bomb exploded during the parade near the intersection of Market and Steuart streets, a searing blast that instantly killed ten people, wounded fifty, others and could be heard blocks away.

Men, women, and children had been killed and maimed in this brutal terrorist attack. The huge fireball from the explosion shot upward, and a sickening cloud of black smoke towered above the tallest buildings, so that it could be seen from any place in San Francisco. Hundreds of thousands of people shuddered in fear as they were herded to their homes and police fanned out in search of the bombers. Police Chief David Augustus White had dozens of suspects on his list. Agents of the Kaiser may have set off the bomb; or Mexican insurgents resentful of General John J. Pershing's incursion into their country in a quest for bandit Pancho Villa; or even members of the Black Hand. Little, however, could be learned from the actual site of the bombing, so thorough was the devastation in the area.

The *San Francisco Chronicle* posted a reward of $14,100 for the capture of the "bomb fiends" and this amount was supplemented by the San Francisco Chamber of Commerce, which offered an additional $5,000 reward. On July 26, Billings was taken into custody and the police announced that those responsible for the terrible bombing would all be under arrest within forty-eight hours. Several more persons were then arrested, including Dr. Edward D. Nolan, Israel Weinberg, and Belle Lavin, who were only slightly connected to radical groups. The only reason why Lavin was picked up was because she ran a boarding house where union members sometimes met. All were arrested without warrants.

Only hours after the bombing, District Attorney Charles Fickert arrived at police headquarters. Fickert was the political tool of United Railroads, with whom Mooney had frequently bumped heads in his effort to unionize railroad workers. Accompanying Fickert was Martin Swanson, a brawny detective employed by the railroads. They immediately told Chief White that one man had masterminded the bombing—Tom Mooney.

On July 26, when Billings and others were being arrested, however, Tom Mooney was unaware that police were searching for him. He and his wife had gone on a picnic at Montesano. When they saw a newspaper reporting Billings' arrest, Mooney wired Chief White to advise him that he was returning to San Francisco on July 27, 1916, to tell his side of the story.

Other stories, however, were told on August 1, before a grand jury when Fickert brought forth a prostitute and accused murderer, Estelle Smith, and an unemployed waiter, John McDonald. Both supplied damaging statements against Mooney and Billings. McDonald insisted that he had seen Tom Mooney standing at the corner of Market and Steuart streets carrying the suitcase that police believed contained the bomb. Smith echoed McDonald's statements and an eight-count murder indictment was brought against Mooney, Billings, Nolan and Weinberg.

Fickert's evidence against Dr. Nolan and Weinberg was based on their friendships with Mooney, though no one placed either man at the scene of the explosion. (Charges against Nolan, Weinberg and Lavin were later dropped.) The district attorney also supplied the motive. Mooney set off the bomb to destroy the offices of United Railroads, which were nearby. He later switched the motive, saying that the real object of Mooney's bomb was the nearby headquarters of the Preparedness Day Parade.

The celebrated Mooney trial began before Judge Frank Griffin on January 3, 1917. The labor leader was unruffled when he testified, saying that when the bomb went off he and his wife, Rena, were a distance of more than a mile from the devastation, watching the parade on a roof of an office building where Mooney rented space. "Mrs. Mooney and I were in her studio on the fifth floor of the Eilers Building," he said. "A large flag covered the window. We could not see the parade so we went up on the roof. On the roof was Wade Hamilton, an Eilers employee with a small camera making pictures. In the sweep of his camera, he caught us as well as the parade. A clock down the street also was in the picture. In three of his pictures the clock showed the time to be 1:58 P.M., 2:01 P.M., and 2:04 P.M. The time of the explosion was 2:06 P.M."

Prosecutors insisted that Mooney had had the photos retouched, but it was later proven that District Attor-ney Charles Fickert had actually tried to have photo developers alter the hands on the clock. Fickert, however, had no need of doctored photos to convict Mooney and Billings. He had the sworn statement of McDonald and that of a surprise witness, Frank C. Oxman, a traveling salesman from Durkee, Oregon.

Oxman took the stand to state that he had arrived in San Francisco on July 22 and watched the parade. He said he saw Mooney and Billings appear in front of a saloon and place the black suitcase against the wall of a saloon and that the explosion went off at that very spot some minutes after they left the area. Mooney could offer no rebuttal against the statements of this eyewitness.

On February 9, 1917, a jury returned a verdict of guilty on all counts. Jury members had taken ten ballots before voting to convict. Their conviction was solely based on the testimony of McDonald and Oxman. Judge Griffin then sentenced Mooney to death by hanging, but before the execution could be carried out, President Woodrow Wilson intervened with California Governor William Dennison Stephens. Mooney's sentence was commuted to life imprisonment. He was sent to San Quentin. Billings was given a life term and sent to Folsom Prison.

Following the conviction of Mooney and Billings, it was learned that Oxman had lied on the witness stand. He had been nowhere near the Preparedness Day Parade on July 22 but more than 100 miles away, on business in Woodland, California. It was also proved that he had been induced to commit perjury. He was tried for perjury in September 1917, but to no one's surprise, he was acquitted. In 1921, McDonald recanted his testimony, signing an affidavit that he, like Oxman, had lied. In fact, he said he had been ordered to commit perjury by the police. In both instances, the large reward money paid to Oxman and McDonald was an important factor in their decision to perjure themselves. None of this did Mooney or Billings any good. An archaic California law prevented the perjury cases of McDonald and Oxman from being reintroduced into the Mooney case. According to the ancient law, no such evidence could be presented after a conviction.

The union men fell out when Billings stated that he would accept a state parole. Mooney responded that to do so would be tantamount to an admission of guilt. He insisted that he be given a full and unconditional pardon. Unless he got it, he vowed to rot in prison. Mooney petitioned the governor of California for that pardon in 1930 and again in 1935. On both occasions, his petition was denied.

The case would not die. The National Commission on Law Observance and Enforcement expressed serious doubts about Mooney's 1917 conviction. A Gallup poll conducted in January 1938 revealed that most Americans believed that Mooney and Billings had been the victims of a serious miscarriage of justice and that they had been convicted for their political beliefs, not for the specific crime for which they had been charged.

In the fall elections of 1938, the California governorship went to a Democrat for the first time in forty-four years. The new governor, sixty-two-year-old Culbert Levy Olson, almost immediately reviewed the Mooney case and concluded that the Preparedness Day bombing was not his work nor that of Billings. In January 1939, Olson ordered Mooney taken from his cell in San Quentin and transported to the state capitol in Sacramento. There, in front of a surging press corps, Governor Olson announced that he was granting Tom Mooney a full and unconditional pardon. Throngs of well-wishers who had worked hard for that day pressed close to the uncompromising union organizer, who choked out the words: "Governor Olson, I shall dedicate the rest of my life to work for the common good." Billings was released on October 15, 1939. He was asked what he wanted most now that he was a free man. Billings did not hesitate, blurting: "A ripe persimmon! Boy, do I want a ripe persimmon!" The actual terrorist who set off the murderous Preparedness Day bomb was never apprehended.

"$250 a Head for Policemen!"

Akron, Ohio, was a peaceful enough town in the fall of 1918. It had its share of crime but it also had a diligent, honest police force to combat that crime. For one person it was too much diligence. He was Rosario Borgio, Akron's Mafia boss who controlled all the rackets in town, from bordellos to gambling dens. He also operated a widespread protection racket, an offshoot from his days as a Black Hand chieftan. He was a *padrone* and his word was law in Akron's underworld.

His headquarters was a sprawling resort offering gambling and women. He had made the place, according to his own term, "cop-proof." He had installed alarms on the doors leading to the front and back stairs. Several steps on the stairways were fixed so that they would, at an operator's manipulation, open backward to drop intruders into pits filled with razor-sharp foot-long spikes upon which they would be impaled and killed. If an invader managed to get by the stairs, he would be faced with solid steel doors impossible to batter down. Behind the doors was an arsenal of shotguns, rifles, pistols, submachine guns and grenades.

Borgio had many local officials on his payroll, but he was unable to penetrate the Akron police force, its officers refusing bribes and payoffs from Borgio's bagmen. Borgio was just another thug to the Akron police force. Raids on his gambling joints and bordellos increased in the fall of 1918. At such times the operators and the patrons were locked up. By jailing Borgio's patrons, the Mafia don knew, the police were intent on putting him permanently out of business.

The raids enraged the swarthy, volcanic Borgio, who swore vendetta, the ancient Italian credo of killing off all enemies. He called together every thug, goon and Black Hander in the Akron area, more than two dozen professional criminals who stood quietly in the back room of Borgio's gambling casino.

The boss moved catlike before them, growling: "These cops raiding my places . . . this is gonna stop right now." He turned to stare from face to grim face. Borgio then announced the most incredible decision ever made by a U.S. crime boss. If the police declared war on him, he would do the same. If the police would frighten his customers, he would terrorize the police. He would do even more than that. He

The terrorist mob which systematically began exterminating the Akron, Ohio police force in 1918: 1) Gunman Pasquale Biondo; 2) Crime Boss Rosario Borgio, who paid $250 for every dead cop; 3) Gunman Paul Chiavaro; 4) Gunman Guiseppe Mazzano; 5) Gunman Lorenzo Biondo; and 6) Gunman Tony Manfredi, thought to be an informer and who was marked for death by the mob.

took a wad of bills from his pocket and waved this in the air, saying in an even voice: "Two hundred and fifty dollars a head for policemen!"

Paul Chiavaro, one of Borgio's top enforcers, was puzzled. "You mean you're putting a price tag on cops?"

"On all cops," Borgio said. "I want them all killed, every one of them."

"The whole force?" asked Lorenzo Biondo.

"That's right, I want the whole goddamned police force wiped out! You get paid right away, right after you kill one of those bastards, on the spot, two hundred and fifty dollars for every dead cop! Just make sure you kill him, not just hurt him. He never gets up again. Dead, all of them, dead!"

The gangsters stared in disbelief but the gang boss repeated his order and his price for the life of each Akron police officer. Nodding, the gangsters filed out. Borgio had not long to wait before making his first payment.

On the night of December 26, 1918, Patrolman Robert Norris was walking down a dark residential Akron street, making his appointed rounds. Someone shot him from ambush. Norris' body was found a few hours later when a passerby stumbled over it; he had been shot in the back several times.

A few days later officers Edward Costigan and Joe Hunt, on patrol, were both shot dead. Patrolman Gethin Richards was killed a few days after the double slaying. Akron police detectives were baffled at the killings. There existed no apparent motive for the murders, which were committed in different parts of the city, ruling out local gangs. None of the officers was robbed after being killed. Detectives concluded that they were dealing with a lone murderer, a cop-hating maniac. In the latter assumption they were correct.

The killings caused a wave of terror to ensue among Akron's police force.

Patrolmen were backed up by other cops who followed them. Their street beats were changed and they never walked their beats by the same routes. Then Chief of Detectives Harry Welch received a phone call from an anonymous woman who told him that "a gang of killers was going to murder every policeman in Akron." She went on to nervously tell Welch that one of the men involved in the killings had gone to New York. She gave no names, only a bizarre description of the man, then hung up.

Welch, desperate, immediately called one of the finest detectives in New York, Michael Fiaschetti, who had taken over the Department's Italian Squad after its erstwhile leader, Lieutenant Joseph Petrosino, had been murdered ten years earlier in Palermo, Sicily, while tracking down Black Handers. Welch told Fiaschetti the incredible story about how someone had given orders to indescriminately murder every police officer on the Akron force. One of those involved, Welch said, according to his tipster, was an Italian and then passed on this description: "All we have is this: Look for the man with the hole in his hand."

With only this thin clue, Fiaschetti alerted the members of his squad who knew the Italian community well, having plumbed its depths for more than a decade. They contacted all their informants and regularly checked hoodlum hangouts. Not until late January 1919 did Fiaschetti make headway. At that time he received a call from a poolroom operator, one of his best informants. "He was in my place last night," the tipster said. "Looks like he has been shot through the hand."

That night Fiaschetti went to the poolhall and found two men playing pool. He watched until one of them placed his hand on the pool table to show a livid scar in the middle of his hand. He then arrested both men, Tony Manfredi, the man with the hole in his hand and his companion, Pasquale Biondo. He quickly secured an extradition order, then boarded an Akron-bound train with his prisoners. He studied both men who sat silently handcuffed across from him in a locked stateroom. Biondo was a snarling, savage gunman full of guile and hatred for the law.

Manfredi, however, was an outgoing type who liked to sing, and Fiaschetti encouraged him to render some songs with his tenor voice. He decided that Manfredi was the man most likely to provide him with information. Locking Biondo to a handrail in the stateroom, Fiaschetti took Manfredi to the lounge car and bought him several drinks. The handsome, egotistical gangster then began to talk about himself, admitting that a few weeks earlier he was walking along a dark Akron road with three friends, heading toward a roadhouse, when his friends began shooting at him. A bullet smashed through the palm of his right hand before he escaped into some woods.

"Why did they do that to you, your friends?" Fiaschetti asked.

"I don't know," Manfredi shrugged. "Some grudge maybe."

"Was Biondo with them?"

"Biondo? No, he's my friend. Had he been there he would never have let them do such a thing to me." Manfredi then went on to explain that after he escaped into the woods, he had returned to Akron where he met with Biondo. "He told me how dirty they were," Manfredi said, proud of his association with Biondo, saying that his friend had suggested that they both leave Akron for a short time and go to New York "until this police thing dies down."

It was at this point that Fiaschetti, a shrewd, tough cop who had been handling gangsters for years, decided to confront the vain Manfredi with what he knew and bluff his way along with his own suspicions (which later proved correct). "Listen, Manfredi," he said in a confidential tone, "I know all about those policemen killed in Akron. You were in on it and so was Biondo. The gang that tried to knock you off had planned to take you for a ride because you knew too much and they were afraid you would talk. When they made a mess of the job, what else could they do? Biondo wasn't in on the shooting so the gang knew you would trust him. He wanted you to go to New York where he planned to kill you. It is his job to get it done right this time."

Manfredi stared at the detective with a gaping mouth. Fiaschetti smoothly went on with his lie: "That's the tip that's come from Akron. When the word came, it was up to me to keep Biondo from sending you to the morgue. I jumped in just in time to save your life. If you had left that poolroom with him, you would have been dead a few minutes later. The gun I took from him would have been used on you."

The gangster sat in stony silence. His face was white with fear. The gangster plot outlined by Fiaschetti was perfectly logical to Manfredi. Then the detective played his trump card: "Come clean, Manfredi, and you won't burn. Do the right thing and you'll get away with a prison sentence instead of the electric chair. Remember, that man in the compartment has only one thing on his mind. To kill you and to do it even though you're in custody, if he can get away with it."

Manfredi cursed, then broke. "And I thought he was my friend!" With that Manfredi outlined the entire terror campaign ordered by Rosario Borgio and how he had paid off on the dead bodies of the Akron policemen. He named all the members of the gang and who pulled the triggers. When Fiaschetti arrived in Akron with his prisoners, he detailed the entire murder conspiracy to Akron detectives. Borgio and his gang members were quickly arrested.

Rosario Borgio was convicted and sent to the electric chair. So, too, were Paul Chiavaro, Vito Mezzano and Lorenzo Biondo (Pasquale's brother). Manfredi was given a twenty-year prison term as was Biondo, the man assigned to kill him. (Manfredi survived, was later paroled and disappeared.) When the extraordinary detective Fiaschetti returned to New York, he received a commendation from his own Department. He was later awarded a gold medal for valor from the governor of Ohio for smashing the Akron terror gang.

Combating the "Red Menace"

After World War I, and before the decade of the 1910s closed, anarchists and Communists in the U.S. stepped up terror campaigns in an all-out effort to provoke a widespread revolution. Through bombings and attempted assassinations, the anarchists only provoked heavy-handed repression from governmental agencies, which would later become known as the notorious Red Raids. So reactionary was the government that it moved to purge America of every suspected terrorist, as if to say to its citizens and the world "enough is enough."

The anarchists opened with their first salvo in Washington, D.C., on June 2, 1919, placing a bomb on the front doorstep of the home of A. Mitchell Palmer, U.S. attorney general. The bomb exploded with a terrific blast at 11:15 P.M., tearing away the facade of Palmer's house and killing the anarchist who placed it there. He had literally been blown into tiny pieces. The largest fragment remaining was his bloody foot, still encased in a shoe, blown across the street to land at the front door of the assistant secretary of the Navy, Franklin Delano Roosevelt.

The same anarchist group planted eight other bombs that night all about Washington. The facades of several government buildings were blown away. At the sites of these explosions police found the same strange message scribbled on scraps of paper. It read: "The powers that be make no secret of their wills to stop the world-wide spread of revolution. The powers that be must reckon that they will have to accept the fight they have provoked. A time has come when the social question's solution can be delayed no longer; class war is on and cannot cease but with a complete victory for the international proletariat."

Thirty-eight other bombs were sent to members of the federal government throughout the country. These intended victims were those known to be outspoken opponents to anarchists, Communists and radicals on the far left. None were killed. Pressured to react quickly, Palmer turned to the Department of Justice, which offered a so-called "Red Menace" expert, a young attorney named J. Edgar Hoover. In quickly prepared briefs, Hoover showed Palmer a short history of the Bolshevik-Communist movement in Russia and the terrorist measures these fanatics took to achieve political power.

Hoover went further, providing Palmer with a long list of anarchist and Communist associations, brotherhoods and organizations known to be dangerous as revolutionary groups bent on toppling the government through violent means. Armed with Hoover's briefs, hundreds of federal agents from the Department of Justice's Bureau of Investigation swarmed throughout the land. Their numbers were swelled by hundreds of local law enforcement members, as well as those who were hastily deputized as U.S. federal deputy marshals, the latter having no law enforcement training whatsoever.

The first raids were led against members of the Federation of the Union of Russian Workers. Leading Socialists and anarchists like Emma Goldman and Alexander Berkman were arrested and jailed. Hoover personally prosecuted Goldman and Berkman, pointing out their long careers as anarchist leaders who had incited to riot and encouraged terrorism. He outlined how, in 1892, Berkman had attempted to murder industrialist Henry Clay Frick and had been sent to prison. He inferred that Leon Czolgosz, who had assassinated President McKinley in 1901, had been a star anarchist pupil of the unfeeling Emma Goldman.

Berkman, Hoover illustrated, was released from prison in 1906 and immediately went back to his elderly lover and mentor, Goldman, and from that point onward they had encouraged the terrorism spread by anarchists, particularly in the radical IWW union movement, along with the criminal bombings by union terrorists

*Left: Anarchist Alexander Berkman who is about to shoot and wound industrialist Henry Clay Frick in his office in 1892; Berkman later became one of J. Edgar Hoover's targets in the notorious Red Raids of 1919-1921. **Right:** J. Edgar Hoover saved his most wrathful indictments for anarchist-socialist leader Emma Goldman (shown in 1919), the leader of the radical left in the U.S. at the time of the Red Raids.*

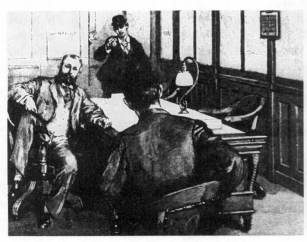 

TERRORISM IN THE 20TH CENTURY

Top: J. Edgar Hoover (shown in 1970 when he was the all-powerful chief of the FBI), after a crash course in leftist politics, prepared the legal briefs which brought about the Red Raids and the subsequent mass deportations of anarchists from the U.S. in 1919-1921.

in the pay of left-wing leaders Big Bill Hayward and the McNamara brothers. Hoover pointed out how Goldman and Berkman had published an anarchist magazine, *Mother Earth*, which encouraged violence and terrorism, and how they had vociferously denounced America's entry into World War I and had demonstrated before draft boards to the point where they were arrested and convicted of obstructing conscription in 1917, how they were jailed, then released in 1919 just in time to be rearrested following the anarchist bombings. They and hundreds of others were ordered deported to Russia.

On December 21, 1919, Goldman, Berkman and 245 other anarchists, Communists and political radicals were marched up the gangplank of the ancient liner *Buford*, which the press had labeled the "Red Ark." William J. Flynn, then head of the Bureau of Investigation, personally escorted the prisoners to the dock. He thought it a cheery outing and was seen to laugh and joke with his agents, especially the youthful J. Edgar Hoover, who had recently joined the Bureau (and would later, as a result of his instigation of the Red Raids, become the totalitarian head of the Bureau, which would be renamed the FBI).

Right: William J. Flynn, chief of the Bureau of Investigation (precursor to the FBI, later headed by Hoover), personally escorted Alexander Berkman onto a deportation ship, then jammed a cigar into the mouth of the startled anarchist.

Flynn walked Berkman up the gangplank of the ship, standing with him on deck and wagging a finger in Berkman's face, telling him that if he ever again stepped foot in America he would be thrown into a cell. Berkman only glared at Flynn, who suddenly laughed and pulled out a cigar, jamming this into the startled Berkman's mouth. "Aww, don't be so glum," Flynn laughed. "You're alive, aren't you?" He added: "You better enjoy that cigar, because you won't be getting any more where you're going!"

A crowd of Washington dignitaries appeared at dockside just as the *Buford* began to pull away. The politicians gloated and waved to Berkman and Goldman. One congressman shouted: "Merry Christmas, Emma!" Goldman thumbed her nose at him, and Berkman, incensed at their humiliating treatment, shouted from the rail: "We'll come back, and when we do, we'll get you bastards!"

Goldman had been resigned to her deportation. She had earlier quit her appeals and stated: "Rather than give our enemies a chance to defeat me, I have decided to tell them to go to hell." Goldman would remain in exile, becoming disillusioned with Russian communism and writing a book about its failures. She would die in 1940, little remembered. Her lover and most devoted follower, Berkman, would also become disillusioned with Soviet oppression. He quit Russia and went to Paris, where he haunted bistros and cafes trying without success to interest others in his faded anarchist cause. He committed suicide in France on June 28, 1936.

The deportation of Goldman and Berkman did not cease Palmer's Red Raids. Government agents resumed raiding the homes of suspects on January 20, 1920. They barged into homes without search warrants. They beat suspects unmercifully without ever having to answer for these brutal attacks. Thousands of suspects were dragged to jail cells without ever being charged and without the benefit of any legal counsel.

William J. Flynn's Bureau of Investigation supervised these continuing illegal raids. Flynn himself was unconcerned about how his agents acted, turning over the campaign to rid America of radicals to his chief assistant, Frank Burke, telling him: "I leave it entirely to your discretion as to the methods by which you should gain access to such places [the sites to be raided]."

Anarchists fought back by planting more bombs, the worst of these explosions occurring at the corner of Broad and Wall Streets on September 16, 1920. A lone terrorist drove a horse-drawn wagon to this spot and alighted from it. Minutes later, at 11:59 A.M.— undoubtedly timed to kill the many people crowding the area during lunch time—the entire wagon, which was packed with explosives, blew up with a terrific roar. Thirty-eight innocent persons were found dead in the smoking debris. Hundreds more had been injured, scores crippled for life. The offices of J. P. Morgan, thought to be the terrorist's target, were thoroughly damaged. The terrorist was never caught.

This and other bombings spurred the government agents to step up their raids, which continued through the beginning of 1921, reaching into thirty-three major U.S. cities. Thousands of suspects were rounded up, herded like cattle into cells while their identities were sorted out and charges filed against them. Out of more than 10,000 persons arrested, only 446 were eventually deported on June 30, 1921. The backlash from the press and especially from labor leaders had already begun. Published reports detailed how federal agents acted

Top: *The carnage of the bomb that exploded at Broad and Wall streets in NYC at 11:59 a.m., on September 16, 1920; the terrorist, never caught, had hacked 500 pounds of iron sash weights into tiny slivers and packed these into a horse-drawn cart, then set off the tremendous explosion, the flying metal killing thirty-eight and wounding hundreds more.*

Above right: *The wrecked offices of J. P. Morgan Company, which was across the street from the horrific blast on Wall Street and thought to be the true target of the terrorist; Morgan's chief clerk, Thomas Joyce, was blown to pieces as he stood next to the window at right.*

without warrants, made wholesale assaults, forged documents, and perjured themselves on the witness stand to get convictions.

Assistant Secretary of Labor Louis F. Post accused the press of producing a "great terroristic scare in the country" by profiling federal agents in a bad light. Lawyers for the Department of Labor, however, disagreed, stating that Attorney General Palmer had acted in "absolute ignorance of American principles." As criticism against him mounted, Palmer grew angry and bitter. When he appeared before the House Rules Committee to answer official complaints, Palmer shouted that he had been pressured into acting prematurely and that his untrained men were sent out to conduct the raids with little or no evidence because of the lack of time involved.

"I say that I was shouted at from every editorial sanctum in America from sea to sea!" Palmer thundered. "I was preached upon from every pulpit! I was urged—I could feel it dinned into my ears—throughout the country to do something and do it now, and do it quick, and do it in a way that would bring results to stop this sort of thing [bombings] in the United States! I accept responsibility for everything they [his agents] did. If one or two of them, overzealous or perhaps outraged as patriotic American citizens—and all of them were—by the conduct of these aliens, stepped over the bounds and treated them a little roughly, I forgive them. I do not defend it, but I am not going to make any row about it."

Palmer's blatant endorsement of his agent's illegal activities spelled his end in government. By the end of 1921, Palmer left office. The anarchist terror subsided as the 1920s began to roar, vanishing like a bad dream. The Jazz Age, however, brought with it a new kind of terror, one that would spread for a decade through half the nation as an invisible empire of ruthless terrorists rose up beneath white hoods and sheets, whipping, shooting and killing thousands of random victims beneath the glare of fiery crosses.

·THREE·
GHOST GOVERNMENTS

Beneath the White Hood

Following the Civil War, the rigors of Reconstruction imposed upon a devastated South gave birth to a secret society called the Ku Klux Klan, the KKK. Organized in 1865 by fiery ex-Confederate cavalry General Nathan Bedford Forrest (although he never admitted being present at the society's birth), the strange name of the society was derived from the combination of the Greek word *kuklos* (circle) and the Scottish word "clan."

Actually, six ex-Confederate soldiers in Pulaski, Tennessee, who had ridden with Forrest, and with his approval, established the Klan to combat the evils imposed upon whites by the corrupt Freedman's Bureau. Created by Northern abolitionists, this organization placed uneducated blacks in positions of total authority over whites, giving blacks the opportunity to take vengeance upon former slave owners or whites in general without fear of prosecution since the Union Army still occupied the defeated Confederacy.

Widespread crimes were committed by black members of the Freedman's Bureau—whites were ruthlessly attacked and beaten, some were whipped, some murdered in the streets of Southern towns. Most of the offenses committed by blacks at this time were aimed at white women. White females were openly insulted, degraded and even raped by blacks at the vengeful urging of Northern white officials called carpetbaggers since they traveled about the South seizing property and valuables, carrying large satchels made of cloth.

The KKK sought to terrorize and suppress blacks they suspected of oppressing and harrassing whites. Playing upon the childish fears of

Left: *Ex-Confederate general Nathan Bedford Forrest, who is credited with organizing the first Ku Klux Klan following the Civil War to reportedly combat outrages by blacks and carpetbaggers in the war-shattered South.*

Right: *Klan members in costume during the Reconstruction era.*

Below: *Phillis, a young freedwoman in North Carolina is whipped by Klan members for striking a white girl; Union occupation forces caught six of the KKK members and jailed them.*

most uneducated blacks at the time, the Klan adopted white hoods and robes, and even the horses its members rode were covered in white shrouds. The reason for the hoods and robes was obviously to hide the identities of these night riders, but it was also to convince gullible blacks that the frightening KKK members who confronted them were the ghosts of dead Confederate soldiers. To enforce this eerie perception, Klan riders wore false heads and handed these to terrified blacks, or they would clutch the hand of a black with a skeleton's hand.

The dispossessed and disenfranchised whites of the South flocked to the Klan's banner in record numbers. The society adopted formal rules for members and created a secret oath that, when recruits were sworn in, demanded that the identities, rituals and practices of the Klan never be revealed under pain of death. Dozens, then hundreds of similar groups sprang up throughout the South until more than a half million Klan members went about righting wrongs to whites. They initially believed themselves to be champions of the oppressed, riding to the rescue of all that was sacred to the white culture of the antebellum South.

Some wrongs were righted by Klan members, chiefly against white land-grabbing carpetbaggers, but it was quickly realized that the KKK inflicted more wrongs upon superstitious and naive blacks. They beat and whipped black men and women who stood accused of insulting whites. Those accused of more serious crimes—rape or murder—were summarily swooped up by the night riders in white hoods and taken to a secluded area where they were, without trial, executed by lynching.

By 1868, the whites began to wrest back control of Southern state legislatures, creating "Black Codes," which established a segregation policy that would last into the mid-twentieth century. Blacks were thus kept out of the election process and the educational system. They were, under the Black Codes, arrested wholesale for vagrancy, drunkenness, and disorderly conduct, some guilty, most not. Enforcing the white edicts was the Klan, which had become the most powerful force in the South, with more than a half million white members.

In the mid-1870s, however, the Klan, led by ex-Confederate officers, was out of control. Instead of defending hearth and home, the Klan was made up of gangs of terrorists bent on burning, looting, and robbing. They operated simply as bandit-terrorists and murdered blacks in large numbers under the cover of what Forrest had called "an

A carpetbagger about to be lynched by Klan members in Georgia.

invisible empire." Forrest quit the Klan in 1872, stating that it had become a lawless organization lost in Halloween gibberish and vicious outlawry.

In 1877, when the Democrats won back total control in the South and were able to subject the black population to their will, there was no more need of the Klan. Its local and state units were disbanded, its hoods and robes stored away as mementoes of a bygone, bloody era. It took the murder of a thirteen-year-old girl in Atlanta in 1913 to summon into the twentieth century the awful spector of the Klan and give rebirth to its rotting carcass.

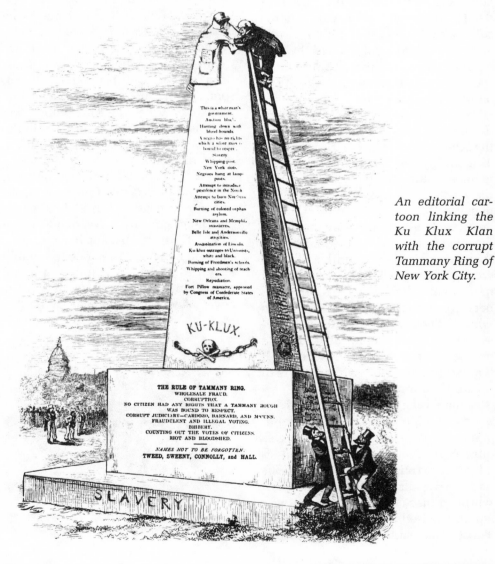

An editorial cartoon linking the Ku Klux Klan with the corrupt Tammany Ring of New York City.

TERRORISM IN THE 20TH CENTURY

"A Little Girl is Dead"

Mary Phagan, thirteen years old, was found murdered and sexually molested in an Atlanta pencil factory on April 26, 1913; her death would give rebirth to the long dead Ku Klux Klan.

Mary Phagan was one of nine teenage girls who worked on the assembly line at the National Pencil Company in Atlanta, Georgia. She lived in Marietta, fourteen miles from Atlanta, and on April 26, 1913, a Saturday, she arrived to collect some back pay, $1.20 for a single day's work. Leo Max Frank, the office manager, gave Mary her money and she left his office. A short time later she was dead, murdered. She was only a week from turning fourteen.

The girl's body was found by the black night watchman, Newt Lee, in the factory basement beneath a pile of rags the following morning at 3:30 A.M. She had been strangled to death by a cord. Her clothes had been torn and it was later determined that she had been sexually molested. The near-hysterical Lee called Frank at home, and not getting an answer, phoned police.

Three Atlanta detectives arrived. When J. S. Starnes glimpsed the body for the first time, he exclaimed: "Great Jesus in the morning! It's a white woman!" One of the girl's eyes had been blackened as if she had been struck by a heavy blow. A tiny gold bracelet she wore had been twisted so

hard that it was embedded in the flesh. Part of the victim's head and face was covered by a makeshift bandage, a strip of cloth torn from her petticoat.

Britt Craig, a reporter from the *Atlanta Constitution* who had accompanied the detectives, knelt in the dust to retrieve two small notes written in a scribble and employing awful grammar. The first read: "he said he wood love me and land me down like night witch did it but that long tall black negro did by his slef." The second note read: "mam, that negro hire down here did this i went to make water and he push me down that hole a long tall negro black that who it was long sleam tall negro i wright while play with me."

Craig immediately looked at Lee, a tall, slim black man. He then said: "Symbolic retribution. Girl murdered in pencil factory, identifies her killer." The detectives fixed the beams of light from their flashlights onto Lee's face. The night watchman screamed: "It looks like he's [the killer] trying to put it off on me!" He was handcuffed and jailed under suspicion of murder.

At 7 A.M., Starnes and other detectives went to Frank's home and asked him to accompany them to headquarters, telling them that Mary Phagan, one of his employees, had been found dead in the factory he managed. His wife, Lucille Frank, called to him from another room, asking what the callers wanted. "A little girl is dead," Frank replied.

Frank was taken to a mortuary where he identified the girl. "Do you have any idea who did it?" he asked. Detectives informed him that his night watchman Lee had been arrested on suspicion. A short time later, Frank was brought to headquarters for questioning. A meek, nervous young man, Frank answered all questions until Luther Z. Rosser, one of the best criminal attorneys in Atlanta, arrived at police headquarters and told Frank not to answer questions. He then lambasted Police Chief John Beavers and, especially, Chief of Detectives Newport Lanford for abusing Frank's rights by insisting he identify the body and report to police headquarters without serving an arrest warrant.

Frank, at his lawyer's insistence, stripped to show that he had no scratches or blood on him, marks and stains that certainly would be evident in the struggle with the victim had he been the killer. Moreover, police checked every item of clothing in the Frank home and found no bloodstains. Frank was nevertheless arrested and charged with killing Mary Phagan. By that time most of the authorities in Atlanta knew the identity of the murderer, the factory's drunken, brutish black janitor, Jim Conley, who had been seen in the basement a short time after Mary Phagan left Frank's office with her pay voucher.

Conley, too, was jailed. He was asked to write out copies of the notes found next to the victim. He said he could not write. He later admitted that he could write, and he scribbled out what was dictated to him. His writings and the original notes were almost identical in handwriting and down to the spelling errors and bad grammar. A shrewd and devious man, Conley then admitted to police that he, indeed, did write the notes, but he had done so on Frank's order, that Frank had raped the girl and killed her in the process, then ordered Conley to hide the body in the basement and write the notes so that it would appear that the night watchman, Newt Lee, had committed the crime.

All of this was presented at Frank's prolonged trial, although it was apparent that the soft-spoken, well-educated Frank, a devoted family man, would not have attacked one of his own employees, or be so stupid as to have another employee hide the body on the premises of his own factory and then blithely proceed about his business, oblivious to the bold fact that the corpse would easily be found. During Frank's trial, Conley's own court-appointed lawyer, William Smith, went to the trial judge, Leonard Strickland Roan, and told

Leonard Strickland Roan, and told him that his client had told him not once but many times that he, not Frank, had raped and murdered the girl. Judge Roan reminded the attorney that he was violating confidential attorney-client information and refused to allow the information into the record.

Much more than legal protocol was behind the railroading of Leo Max Frank. He was a Northerner and he was also a Jew and, as such, the object of hatred by many serving on Atlanta's police force and in the district attorney's office. Moreover, the most important and influential man in Georgia, the great populist leader Tom Watson, wanted Frank convicted. Watson was a racist and bigot through and through; his hatred for blacks was only exceeded by his loathing for Jews. When he was informed that Jim Conley was undoubtedly the killer of Mary Phagan, Watson turned to his political stooge, Huge Mason Dorsey, the slippery, underhanded solicitor general for Fulton County, and sneered: "Hell, we can lynch a nigger any time in Georgia, but when do we get the chance to hang a Yankee Jew?"

It was Watson who personally saw to it that Frank was persecuted relentlessly in his own racist newspaper, the *Jeffersonian*, in which the accused man was described as a "lascivious sodomite," a pervert, and a child-killer throughout Frank's lengthy trial. Through pressure from Watson, police forced a local whorehouse operator, Nina Formby, to sign an affidavit stating that Frank was one of her most regular customers,

Tom Watson, the Populist leader of Georgia; expressed his rabid racism in his newspaper, the Jeffersonian, *blatantly stating that Frank ought to be lynched, inciting the so-called "Knights of Mary Phagan"—a precursor to the revived Ku Klux Klan— to do exactly that.*

that he craved sex all the time, and that, on the day of Mary Phagan's murder, Frank had come to her and asked if he could bring the girl, whom he thought was only unconscious, to one of her rooms until she revived. Even the press, biased as it was against Frank, challenged this incredible claim.

The Frank family cook, Minola McKnight, was forced by detectives to sign a statement that Frank was adulterous and regularly cheated on his wife. McKnight bravely redeemed herself, however, by repudiating her statement when she took the witness stand, saying she had been coerced into signing the statement and that Frank was a decent, upstanding family man.

The trial itself was a farce. Judge Roan tolerated every kind of legal abuse from Dorsey, who brushed aside

Leo Frank was reserved and unemotional at his murder trial; his wife is shown seated behind him.

ings, and terrorized witnesses into depicting Frank as a sex fiend. Throughout this farce, Tom Watson's supporters packed the spectator gallery, hooting for conviction. One of those who shouted loudest for Frank's head was the bespectacled "Colonel" William Joseph Simmons, a traveling salesman and part-time fundamentalist preacher, a religious circuit-rider who peddled soap and sermons to the backwoods folk of Georgia and points south.

Simmons sneered and booed as Frank took the stand in his own defense to softly but bravely deny his guilt, calling the statements of Conley and others outright lies. It was difficult to hear Frank speak above the catcalls and jeers from Watson's goons in the courtroom and the hundreds who stood outside the court building, roaring for Frank's conviction and execution.

As was expected, Frank was convicted and Judge Roan sentenced him to be executed. Frank's attorneys filed an appeal with the U.S. Supreme Court, which was denied, with Justices Charles Evans Hughes and Oliver Wendell Holmes writing strong dissenting opinions. Said Holmes: "Mob law does not become due process of law by securing the assent of a terrorized jury. We are not speaking of mere disorder or mere irregularities in procedure, but of a case where the processes of justice are actually subverted . . ."

Reading this, elderly Judge Roan reexamined his own conduct at the trial, and, conscience-stricken over not revealing what Conley's lawyer had told him, wrote a letter to Georgia Governor John M. Slaton, expressing his doubts about Frank's adjudged guilt. Roan died a short time later.

Slaton, however, had already suspected that Frank had been railroaded, and he conducted his own thorough investigation, concluding that Conley was the true killer and Frank was completely innocent.

Though he knew he was placing himself in political jeopardy and even physical danger, the courageous Slaton commuted Frank's death sentence to life imprisonment, believing that the true facts of the case would later emerge in a calmer atmosphere, and that Frank would eventually be released and Conley, the real killer, brought to trial. None of this came to be.

Watson and his myriad racist minions exploded, as police in Atlanta had anticipated. Police Chief Beavers had warned Slaton that he would not be responsible for what might happen if the governor signed the commutation. Slaton signed it anyway, only twenty days before he was to leave office in 1915. The day before this was done, Beavers sent his men to contact all the Jews living in Atlanta to leave town, warning them that because of the impending clemency shown to their fellow Jew, a man most believed guilty of child-murder, they would soon be in physical danger.

Jews by the thousands departed Atlanta by carriage, car and train. The scene at the train depot that day was one that brought disgrace to the decent citizens of Atlanta. As hundreds of defenseless Jewish children were herded onto trains leaving the city, scores of Watson's anti-Semitic thugs stood nearby cursing them and their terrified parents, theatening to hang and shoot them all. Uniformed Atlanta police-

men stood in the crowds of Watson men and did nothing. Some even joined in the racist chorus. An elderly Jewish businessman who had just put his grandchildren aboard the train turned to the crowd and shouted: "What is the matter with you men— have you no shame or decency? These are children!"

"No they h'aint!" came one response, "they's Jews!"

The businessman then confronted a young police officer he knew personally. "I see some of your men in this crowd of heroes who want to hurt innocent children."

"It's because of Leo Frank," the embarrassed policeman said. "I can do nothing about them."

"And what can you do for yourself?"

The young officer stared at the Jewish elder for a moment, then slowly nodded and, with a swipe of his hand, tore his badge from his uniform and threw it beneath the wheels of the train. He walked away, quitting the force on the spot. He, like John Slaton, was a rare exception in a state that had had its deep-seated racial hatreds upturned by Tom Watson's plough.

Slaton himself was not safe. He personally came under violent attack by an throng of heavily armed, enraged racists, who invaded the governor's grounds on the day Slaton signed the commutation. Thousands of Watson's followers stormed into the area, scores breaking into the governor's mansion where one shotgun-toting intruder screamed: "Where is that Jew-loving son-of-a-bitch!"

A regiment of horse-mounted national guardsmen wielding swords

Left: Georgia's Governor John Slayton, who conducted his own investigation and determined that black janitor Jim Conley had murdered Mary Phagan; he courageously quashed Frank's death sentence and it cost him his political career and almost his life. Above: The dangling body of Leo Frank, victim of a Klan lynch mob, on the night of August 16-17, 1915.

arrived at the governor's mansion. For two days the troopers battled the howling, blood-thirsty mobs bent on killing Slaton or any Jews they could find in Atlanta. The rioters even cried out for Mrs. Slaton's blood, calling her "a rotten liberal." Slaton and his family escaped, leaving the state and remaining in exile for years. Over many years to come he was repeatedly warned by Watson's stooges, state officials, that if he returned to Georgia, he would be murdered.

Watson then began to lobby for the lynching of Leo Frank, who had been removed to the Milledgeville Prison Farm immediately after Slaton's reprieve. There, a berserk inmate, William Green, crept up on Frank as he slept on his bunk in an open barracks and slit his throat. Frank survived, thanks to the quick action of another prisoner, a doctor, who was able to close the wound with twenty-five stitches and stop the bleeding.

When hearing of this Watson commended Green but expressed his disappointment over Frank's survival. The arch racist confided his fears to friends that the longer Frank survived the better chance he might have of proving his innocence. Watson then conferred with none other than William J. Simmons, the backcountry preacher who had led the riotous spectators at Frank's trial.

Simmons had by then organized a large group of racists under the banner of the Knights of Mary Phagan. He had been one of the first to pay $2 to see the D. W. Griffith film, *The Birth of a Nation*, in Atlanta and had excitedly gripped the arms of his theater seat as the KKK riders of the Reconstruction era were shown galloping to the rescue on screen. He later insisted that this film inspired his reestablishment of the old Klan, causing him to gather a few followers to climb to the top of Stone Mountain, set fire to a large wooden cross, and dedicate his Knights of Mary Phagan to seeking revenge for the child's murder.

Watson enthusiastically supported Simmons' hood- and robe-wearing group, stating in his newspaper that he saw "the invisible power" of these "knights" bringing justice in the Frank case, where the state had failed in its duty to render that justice. Watson thus provided Simmons with another title, which he would quickly reshape into "The Invisible Empire of the Ku Klux Klan." Watson then published an article that, in any state other than Georgia, would have brought about his arrest for inciting to riot and murder. He declared in print: "The next Jew who does what Frank did is going to get exactly what we give to Negro rapists!" He had pronounced Leo Frank's death sentence.

Simmons and his Knights of Mary Phagan responded quickly to this order, spreading their "Invisible Empire" over Georgia on the night of August 16, 1915. They first cut the telephone wires to Milledgeville Prison Farm, then, in Marietta, packed eight cars full of "knights," and drove to the prison farm. The first to see the headlights of the cars approaching the prison was trustee J. W. Turner. He rushed up to a guard on duty and shouted: "They are coming for Frank! Get him out the back way!" The guard turned away, saying nothing.

Turner and another trustee named Bruce then rushed to the warden's office, but guards there ignored their warnings about invaders coming for Frank and ordered the trustees to return to their barracks. A few minutes later, the lynch mob of about twenty-five heavily armed men broke through the front gates of the prison farm without opposition from armed guards standing nearby. Only three of the men were masked, one of them being an older man who was later thought to be Simmons himself. The mob split into four parties, as if following a military drill, and began their systematic search for Frank.

One group burst into the home of Warden Smith and snapped handcuffs on him. A man poked a rifle at Smith's head and said: "We have come for Leo Frank. You will find him tomorrow on Mary Phagan's grave. You can come with us, if you want."

"Damned if I go any place with you," replied Smith.

Smith was held prisoner and watched glumly as all of his guards were rounded up and handcuffed. None resisted and some appeared as if they had known in advance that the raid would take place. Another group, its leaders knowing exactly where to locate Frank, ran to a barracks and raced to a second floor. They searched the bunks of sleeping men and found Frank, a large bandage still on his neck, covering Green's vicious knife wound. The invaders had been informed of this bandage and used it to identify the man they were seeking. Frank was grabbed by his hair, arms, and legs and yanked from his bed. As he moaned in pain, the intruders handcuffed him, then half carried him out of the barracks to a waiting car.

Warden Smith was freed of his handcuffs the minute the mob drove off. He had difficulty in reaching city police because the lines had been cut but he finally managed to call offficers in Augusta. It took him more than half an hour to convince state officials that Frank had not been released by his Jewish friends, as they had been informed, but that a very real lynch mob from Marietta had kidnapped the prisoner.

It was several hours after Frank had been taken before state police mobilized a widespread search for him and the mob. Sheriffs in a fifty-mile radius put together car posses, the first time autos were used for such a purpose in Georgia, and began a desperate search. William Frey was the only man to spot the mob. An ex-sheriff, he was not part of the search effort, although he had been informed of the police dragnet.

Frey was driving down the Roswell Road near Marietta at 7 A.M. when eight cars packed with gun-clutching men drove past him. The thirty-one-year-old Frank was in the back seat of the third car, sitting between two men who held revolvers to his head. Frey stopped his car for a moment. He was unarmed and no longer a sheriff. There were more than two dozen men in those cars, all heavily armed. "I didn't stand any more of a chance than Frank did," Frey later admitted. He kept driving in the opposite direction.

A short time later the grim caravan came to a stop on the Roswell Road next to a giant oak tree outside of Marietta. About thirty men jumped from the cars. A few were masked, most were not. A group of surveyors working along a railroad track that dawn began to walk toward the group of men but the lynch mob waved them off with their weapons. Across the road, a farmer named Chandler was driving his team in a nearby field and he witnessed Frank dragged from one of the cars.

Frank was placed beneath the oak tree and a heavy rope was put about his neck. He wore only a nightshirt. His hands were handcuffed and someone knelt to place handcuffs about his small feet. Chandler crept up on the group to stand behind some bushes, quaking in terror. He overheard the following conversation: "Mr. Frank, we are going to do what the law said to do—hang you by the neck until you are dead. Do you want to say anything before you die?" (This was said by the ringleader, who was later identified as a former Marietta police officer.)

Frank stood cooly staring back at his self-appointed executioners. He said nothing for some moments and then he replied: "No."

Then the ringleader asked a question that belied the very existence and purpose of the lynch mob: "We want to know if you are guilty or innocent of the murder of Mary Phagan."

The heroic Frank refused to dignify the question of a lynch mob leader by responding. Instead, he calmly held up his handcuffed hands, elevating a finger bearing his wedding ring. He said in a firm voice: "I think more of my wife and my mother than I do of my own life. Would you return my wedding ring?"

The ringleader glanced over his shoulder at a older masked man standing behind him. The man gave a slow nod. (This was thought to be William J. Simmons.) A member of the lynch mob slipped the ring from Frank's finger. (The ring was later returned to Mrs. Frank by a reporter who said he was handed the ring by a man on an Atlanta street before running off into a crowd.)

Frank was then hoisted to the top of a small, battered table. The rope was tied tautly to a branch of the oak tree. The ringleader then kicked the table from beneath Frank, who jerked downward, his body convulsing as he strangled to death. The lynch mob stood silent, patiently watching him die. When his body was at last lifelessly, gruesomely swaying slowly from the end of the rope, the lynch mob members walked casually back to their cars and drove away.

Farmer Chandler ran to Marietta where a large ceremony was in progress at the town square, honoring the slain Mary Phagan. "They got him!" shouted Chandler to the crowd, "they got him!" Hundreds, then thousands quickly followed the farmer on foot, and in carriages and cars to the site of the lynching. There the throngs stood to view Frank's pathetic, swaying body. Though there were Marietta police officers present, none of them made an effort to take down the corpse. An amateur photographer took two photos showing scores of gaping men, women, and children standing beneath the hanging body. These photos would be displayed for fifteen years in the windows of small Georgia shops and on postcards sold for a nickel in rural drugstores. Every member of Simmons' "knights" carried a copy in his wallet.

The rage felt by U.S. citizens across the land over the lynching was universally expressed by the press, even in Georgia, but it solved nothing. The members of the lynch mob were never arrested, although most of their identities were well known. When hearing the news, Governor Slaton wept openly. Thomas E. Watson, who had released the forces of human malice, ignorance and prejudice, was jubilant, gloating in a press conference he gave on the front porch of his mansion at

Hickory Hill, one in which he commended Frank's killers for meting out "justice in Georgia."

In appreciation for his service of railroading Frank, the power-brokering Watson sent his venal henchman Dorsey to the U.S. Congress for two terms. When Dorsey told Watson he wanted to run for the U.S. Senate, Watson turned him down. He wanted that post for himself and, in 1920, the worst racist in America became a U.S. senator from Georgia. He did not live long enough to enjoy his exalted political post, dying of bronchial asthma on September 26, 1922. Not one of his peers in the Senate sent condolences.

Mary Phagan's real killer, Jim Conley, was convicted of being an accessory after the fact (in supposedly aiding Frank to hide the body) and was sent to a chain gang to serve a year and a day. In 1919, he was convicted of instigating a riot that brought about the death of one man, and he was sent to prison for fourteen years. Upon his release he continued living in Atlanta where he died in 1962 at the age of seventy-six. He never publicly admitted his guilt.

In 1982, Alonzo Mann, who had been a fourteen-year-old black office boy working in the pencil factory, came forth to state that he saw Jim Conley carrying the unconscious body of Mary Phagan from the second floor of the factory on the day of the murder. The girl was alive at the time, he said. He saw her breathing and her hands twitching. He went on to say that Frank was not even in the building at the time he saw Conley, who said to him: "If you ever mention this to anyone I will kill you!"

The boy ran home and told his mother everything. She told him to keep quiet, that she feared for his life. He said nothing until 1953, when, stricken with conscience and while Conley was still alive, he said he went to several reporters with the story but the newsmen dismissed his tale. In 1983, Mann took a lie detector test and passed it before he signed affidavits naming Conley as the killer of Mary Phagan. "I know deep down in my heart what I say," said Mann at the time, "and that Frank did not do this."

It was not until 1986 that Georgia's State Board of Pardons and Paroles granted a posthumous pardon to Leo Frank, but even then, the pardon was couched with reservations, saying that the pardon was based on the state's "failure to protect the person of Leo Frank and thereby perserve his opportunity for continued legal appeal on his conviction, and as an effort to heal old wounds."

Invisible Empire

Imperial Wizard Hiram Wesley Evans, in a fearsome KKK costume, 1929; calling himself "the most 100 percent American," Evans wrested control of the Klan from Simmons, who had become an alcoholic.

Those "old wounds" had been inflicted for seventy years by the hooded thugs who murdered Frank under the direction of William J. Simmons. He later stated that he had created his Knights of Mary Phagan some time in 1913 as an enforcement arm of the will of the people. Later still, when he changed the name of his terrorist group to the Knights of the Ku Klux Klan, Simmons claimed that he had envisioned reestablishing the old hooded vigilantes as early as 1900 after reading a book of anecdotes about the Klan.

Simmons fell asleep one night, he said, with this book in his hands and had deep dreams about the old, galloping night riders. "On horseback in their white robes," he excitedly recounted to one newsman, "they rode across the wall in front of me and as the picture faded out I got down on my knees and swore that I would found a fraternal organization which would be a memorial to the Ku Klux Klan."

The self-righteous Simmons took his time to fulfill his oath. He encouraged the idea of the Klan wherever he traveled, but he concentrated upon saving souls at this time. Simmons traveled throughout the South as a Methodist preacher, using his fists to bully unruly flocks to church on Sunday. The strong-armed tactics of preacher Simmons were condemned by Methodist Bishop Wilson, who eventually suspended him from all religious activities for "inefficiency." The circuit-rider defied this edict and continued delivering his fiery sermons. Bishop Wilson, so enraged over this defiance, tracked Simmons down to a backwoods church and, using a switch, whipped him from the pulpit and out of the building.

Undaunted, Simmons established his own brand of religion, gathering about him malcontented Methodists who served as his disciples. To supplement the meager income that stemmed from church donations, Simmons sold women's garters and undergarments to small-town general stores. He and his backwater preachers continued sermonizing to their

Above: William J. Simmons, who created the "Knights of Mary Phagan" in 1913, gave rebirth to the Ku Klux Klan in 1915, becoming its Imperial Wizard and promoting widespread race hatred and clandestine violence.
Below: The frontpiece of Thomas Dixon's novel, The Clansman.

scanty congregations until 1913 when the Frank case erupted in Georgia, which allowed Simmons to gather a new flock to the banner of racism and hatred mounted by Tom Watson.

By 1915, Simmons' "knights" numbered in the hundreds, with thousands in support of their cause, which was to terrorize Jews and blacks. Simmons received regular dues from members and additional funding from Watson. His organization then received an incredible boost in the form of one of the greatest motion pictures ever made, *The Birth of a Nation*, directed by David Wark Griffith. Based on the inflammatory novel, *The Clansman*, by Rev. Thomas Dixon, the film glorified the old Klan, portraying the nineteenth-century night riders as champions of female honor and the defenders of the weak and the helpless during the Reconstruction Era. The film, which created riots in Northern cities, also depicted blacks as shiftless drunks and lascivious rapists.

In Atlanta, however, no blacks dared oppose the film. While thousands of white Atlantans queued up for the premier showing of the film, Simmons and his knights circulated in the crowds. Wearing a cutaway frock coat and striped trousers—the traditional garb of the Southern preacher—Simmons addressed the throngs: "I am he who from the realms of the unknown wrested the solemn secret from the grasp of the night and became the sovereign Imperial Master of the Great Lost Mystery." It was all gobbledygook, of course, but citizens eagerly responded to the racism and bigotry put forth by Simmons and his followers.

TERRORISM IN THE 20TH CENTURY

Simmons continued to use the publicity surrounding the epic film to promote the rebirth of his own self-styled Klan, although Griffith, when hearing of this, disavowed any association with Simmons and his knights. His film, however, helped to create an aura of respectability for the KKK, which, in its heyday of the 1920s, swelled to a membership of more than seven million.

Incorporating the Klan in Atlanta, Simmons placed advertisements in newspapers and on billboards throughout Georgia. "A Classy Order for Men of Character," one ad was headlined. It went on to state: "No Roughnecks, Rowdies, nor Yellow Streaks Admitted. It is of and for men who are in all things 100 percent American and no other." Simmons did not advertise the real reason for the Klan's existence—race and religious hatred and bigotry.

When new recruits arrived, they quickly learned that the Klan opposed the immigration of all foreigners to American shores. It condemned Catholics, Jews and, especially, blacks. The hatred for blacks was rampant among its members, and Simmons made no excuses for the rabid racism he and his followers embraced. Simmons would open his meetings by placing a brace of pistols and a horsewhip on a table and then shout to his hooting supporters: "All right, now bring on your niggers!"

The old night riders on horseback were replaced by hooded thugs in autos who raced about the Georgia countryside, dragging blacks and Jews from their beds in the middle of the night and administering whippings or

Above: The Klan rides in a scene from D. W. Griffith's masterful The Birth of a Nation, *the 1915 film which reportedly inspired Simmons to reorganize the KKK.* **Right:** *Director David Wark Griffith openly denounced the Klan and resented the fact that it had used his film as a promotion piece to recruit new members to its hooded ranks.*

worse to these hapless victims. The Klan spread like wildfire through the Carolinas, Alabama, Virginia, Arkansas, Mississippi, Louisiana, Florida, Texas and Tennessee—the solid South of the old Confederacy. It then crept into Northern states with large rural populations and finally into the industrial cities of the Midwest where blacks and other minorities had made headway into the assembly lines of previously all-white workforces.

Hundreds of thousands of bigots flocked to the Klan banner in Maryland, Ohio, Michigan, Indiana,

Illinois, Kentucky, and Missouri. Detroit was widely infected by the secret society, and in Chicago, in the early 1920s, the Klan boasted of more than 50,000 dues-paying members. Everywhere Klan members appeared in their long-flowing white robes and pointed hoods to hold mass meetings before blazing crosses and then embark on their night missions to terrorize blacks, Jews, Catholics, and foreigners.

The Klan adopted brutal, medieval methods to quash opposition to its whippings and lynchings. Its members took to branding unruly blacks and whites who opposed them. The Reverend Orrin Van Loon, pastor of a community church outside of Detroit, openly criticized the Klan in 1924 from his pulpit. The next night a gang of hooded men forced their way into his home and dragged him to a waiting car that sped off to a lonely spot where Van Loon was branded on the back with three large letters: KKK. The shootings, mutilations, burnings, and lynchings spread unchecked. The terrorists were abetted by many lawmen who were themselves Klan members, as were the political bosses of local and state governments.

For the Klansmen of the early 1920s, life was, in the words of one of its hooded leaders, "roaming through the clover." Simmons and the top leaders of the Klan grew enormously rich by charging their members a $10 initiation fee, $1-a-month dues, and $6.50 for a simple white robe and hood with peaked cap. (Later, from the 1950s on, the Klan would not sell these costumes but rented them for each meeting to get maximum cash flow from Klan trappings.)

Simmons also made considerable money by selling titles to the richest of his bigoted followers. It was the secret society's best fund-raising device, and through the Klan's haphazard rites, a member with enough money could quickly become a Nighthawk, Klokann, Klexter, Klagaro, Kladd, Klabee, Kilgrapp, Kludd, Klokard, or Klaliff. Seniority brought august titles such as Exalted Cyclops, Kleagle, King Kleagle, and Grand Goblin. There was, of course, only one Imperial Wizard. That was Simmons.

Banking tens of thousands of dollars each month, Simmons lived in an Atlanta mansion and was waited upon by servants (white). He and his minions spewed forth a nonstop stream of KKK propaganda in the form of pamphlets, booklets, and their own newspaper, all of which were sold to eagerly buying members who reveled in their bigoted statements. Said one 1924 KKK broadside: "The Klan is for a Christian country, free, clean and Democratic. We want clean politics. We want the elimination of the bootlegger. [This was a joke in that many Klan leaders were becoming rich through their bootlegging activities during Prohibition.] We want the elimination of the prostitute, gambler, niggers, Mexicans, Irish, Jews, Germans, Huns, and, in fact, all foreigners, so that they will not be able to appropriate to themselves the policies and destinies of the Great and Glorious American Republic." It was the Know-Nothing Party all over again, but this time it hid beneath a sheet and clutched a shotgun and a whip.

The power of the KKK during the 1920s—500,000 Klansmen march down Pennsylvania Avenue in Washington, D.C.

Klan leaders placed blacks at the top of their hate list, urging that all be either killed or "shipped back to Africa." When black leader Marcus Garvey developed a confidence swindle in the mid-1920s to transport all American blacks to Africa, the Klan actually offered Garvey money for this purpose. Next on the KKK hit list were the Jews. "Jesus Christ is the leader of the Ku Klux Klan," droned Simmons, "and we are for Him. The Jew is not for Him, and therefore the Jew has shut himself out of the Klan." Next came the Catholics: "The Pope will sit in the White House when hell freezes over!"

In 1922, Klan leaders tried to pressure Atlanta's Board of Education into firing all of the city's Catholic teachers. Those on the Board who resisted this move were threatened with death. In September 1922, the city council, which was infected with Klan members, denounced in a formal resolution the Catholic fraternal order, the Knights of Columbus, as an un-American organization. Its passage was blocked at the last minute by Mayor James Key, who angrily vetoed the measure.

One of the more virulent Klan leaders was Imperial Kludd Caleb A. Ridley, a pastor of the Central Baptist Church and the national chaplain for the Klan. Though he openly expressed his hatred for Jews and Catholics, Ridley reserved his special venom for the Pope, saying: "I can't help being what I am racially. I am not a Jew, nor a Negro, nor a foreigner. I am an Anglo-Saxon white man, so ordained by the hand and will of God, and so constituted and trained that I cannot conscientiously take either my politics or my religion from some secluded ass on the other side of the world."

Ghost Governments

White Southern ministers who opposed the Klan's witch-hunting philosophy, such as Dr. Plato Durham and Reverend M. Ashby-Jones—they dared to address blacks as "mister" and treated them as equal to whites—were branded "Negrophiles." Their churches were picketed, vandalized, and burned by Klansmen, their congregations threatened with torture and death.

During the mid-1920s, Klan rallies and marches were regular occurrences, not only throughout the South but in the Northern cities. In Detroit, the Klan marched under white hoods down the main thoroughfares, 20,000 strong, with tens of thousands cheering them and applauding their racist banners. In Chicago, 50,000 Klansmen marched down Michigan Avenue to the same accolades. In Washington, as was the case with every Klan parade, a massive march was preceded by many Klan leaders holding large American flags—there were 500,000 white-robed bigots in that procession alone.

The Klan was patriotic, it claimed, and it proudly reported how, in Hammond, Indiana, a Klansman murdered an immigrant for saying "to hell with the United States," and how he was acquitted by an all-white jury of Klansman. Hooded thugs did as they pleased, patrolling the streets of Southern towns, punishing people suspected of breaking racial rules established by the Klan. A white woman and her black lover were whipped for "immoral behavior." Two white men were beaten senseless and thrown into a garbage dump for patronizing black prostitutes. An Atlanta barber was charged with "cut-

ting the hair of an inferior race," and using the same scissors on white men. He was taken to a remote spot, stretched between two trees, and beaten so severely with a cleated belt that he died of his wounds.

When Congress edged toward investigating the Klan, Simmons pressured U.S. congressman W. D. Upshaw from Atlanta to threaten a congressional investigation of the Knights of Columbus. The Washington investigations collapsed. Throughout the 1920s, the Klan was all-powerful in more than twenty states. It was responsible for the lynchings and murders of at least five thousand men and women (mostly blacks but whites, too, were lynched). Most of these victims were those accused or convicted of serious crimes, from rape to murder, but those suspected of lesser offenses were also executed by the rope. Typical was Fred Sullivan, a black man, who was taken from a jail in Byhalia, Mississippi, as well as his wife. They were awaiting trial for burning down a plantation barn. When a deputy sheriff and his posse attempted to interfere, Klansmen held off the lawmen with guns, forcing them to watch as the man and woman were hanged.

The smallest Klan infraction might bring death. Henry Scott, a black railroad porter, was accused of insulting a white female passenger. The train was stopped near Tampa, Florida. Scott was dragged from a Pullman car and promptly hanged from a tree next to the railroad siding while many white men witnessing the execution cheered from the open windows of the train. In Duluth, Minnesota, three black circus workers accused of attacking a seventeen-year-old white girl, were lynched from the poles holding up the main tent. More than 3,000 Klansmen stormed the jail in Paris, Texas, to drag twenty-eight-year-old Herman Arthur and his nineteen-year-old brother, Irving, from their cells. The sharecropping brothers stood accused of murdering their landlord, a high-ranking Klansman. Both were burned to death at the stake. Photos were taken of the charred bodies and copies were sent to every black family in the county.

The brutality of the Klan was boundless. In Datura, Texas, Alexander Winn was lynched for reportedly attacking a white girl. When the local Klan leader learned that the black man had been hanged, he exploded, shouting: "I told you to burn that bastard!" The white-robed lynch mob went to the funeral home where Winn's body lay, dragged it to a street, soaked it with kerosene, and then dutifully burned the corpse. In Perry, Florida, a white teacher, Ruby Hendry, was murdered by Charles Wright, a black man and a confessed killer. Wright was lynched, and the next day, Arthur Young was also lynched because he had been Wright's best friend.

No one was safe, especially behind bars. Klansman stormed into jails, even prisons, to drag their prey to death. More than 1,500 Klans-

Above: Klan atrocity, 1919: Omaha, Neb., a Negro accused of raping a white woman was burned to death while KKK supporters gather about the grisly remains of the victim.
Below: Klan atrocity, 1933: Alabama, a Negro charged with rape and murder was lynched while KKK supporters celebrate.

men stormed into the Texas state prison in Huntsville on December 14, 1922, to drag George Gay outside the prison walls where he was shot to death with more than 1,000 bullets. The twenty-five-year-old black man had been accused of sexually attacking a white woman. In Columbia, Missouri, on April 29, 1923, James T. Scott, a black janitor at the University of Missouri, was taken from a strong jail by more than 500 Klansmen and women. He was taken to a bridge and hanged from one of the steel arches. Scott had been accused of attempting to assault the fourteen-year-old daughter of a faculty member of the university.

Black workers were especially singled out for punishment. Jake Brooks, an employee of a packing house, joined some other workers on a picket line and was immediately seized and lynched. Near Guernsey, Arkansas, John West, a black laborer working at a paving site, accidentally used a drinking cup reserved for whites to slake his thirst. He was lynched that night by Klansman, "for polluting white water." Dallas Sewell was dragged from his home in Eufala, Oklahoma, to a remote area by hundreds of hooded Klansman. The light-skinned Sewell had been recently hired by an employer who thought he was white. A Klan leader read his death sentence for committing the offense of "passing for white and for associating with white people." He was then hanged.

When anyone protested the widespread terrorism practiced by the Klan, they were themselves targeted for injury or worse. Clarence Darrow appeared in Mobile, Alabama, on March 11, 1927, at a large civic gathering. He condemned the Klan lynchings and mob actions, urging "mutual respect and cooperation through toler-

Left to right, Imperial Kleagle Edward Young Clarke, Simmons' right-hand man, who was arrested for drunkenness and indecent exposure. Mrs. Elizabeth Tyler, Klan publicist, who was arrested for disorderly behavior with Clarke. David Stephenson, Grand Dragon of the KKK and political boss of Indiana during the early 1920s; his hand-picked Klansmen occupied almost all high offices in the State. Stephenson was later convicted of raping and murdering a State employee and sent to prison for life.

TERRORISM IN THE 20TH CENTURY

ance." Before he finished talking, scores of Klansmen appeared carrying weapons, and Darrow had to flee the city while protected by dozens of policemen.

By then, however, Klan power had begun to wane, mostly due to the scandals and crimes committed by Klan leaders themselves. The *New York World* made the Klan its special target, assigning reporters to follow Klan leaders about and report their nefarious doings. Edward Young Clarke, Imperial Kleagle, and Simmons' right-hand man, had been arrested for drunkenness and indecent behavior, the paper reported, but not a word of this appeared in the *Atlanta Constitution* where Clarke's brother, Francis Clarke, was the managing editor.

The story involved Clarke and Mrs. Elizabeth Tyler, Klan publicist and vice chairman of the Georgia Committee of the Republican Party, who had been arrested with Clark on the disorderly charge. No one in Atlanta read the tale since Klan members seized the thousands of copies of the *World* to be distributed in the city and burned them.

Simmons himself had become an incurable alcoholic and was so consistently drunk that, by 1922, he was not permitted to appear in public by other Klan leaders. His place was taken by an overweight dentist, Hiram Wesley Evans, who called himself "the most 100 percent American." Evans, who had been the Klan's secretary for a number of years, coveted Simmons' power and encouraged the leader's excessive drinking habits until he could no longer function. When Simmons realized that Evans was taking

over, he threatened to create a schism in the Klan. Evans paid him off by giving him a Klan severance of $146,000.

In Indiana, a mainly farming state, the Klan ruled supreme during the early 1920s under the iron-fisted leadership of Grand Dragon David Curtis Stephenson. He literally controlled the entire state, having engineered Klan members into the state house and the assembly. Almost every mayor of every city was a Klan member, as were most of Indiana's ranking police officers. Stephenson did what he pleased, ordering whippings and lynchings at will.

Stephenson also traveled throughout the South, preempting the authority of other Klan leaders by taking over meetings and selecting from the crowds the most attractive women present, ordering these confused, semi-literate females to his bed. They complied but complaints from their sweethearts and husbands soon brought Klan censure. Stephenson, on January 1, 1924, was tried by Klan officials who threw him out of the Klan "for committing indecencies in several states."

Stephenson returned to Indiana where his Klan authority went unchallenged. In January 1925, he met Madge Oberholtzer, a voluptuous young woman who worked for the Indiana State Department of Public Instruction. The Klan leader first appeared to be a gentlemen, taking the woman to dinner several times without ever making an advance. Then, on the night of March 15, 1925, Stephenson called Oberholtzer to his home. When she arrived, she found him drunk, telling her: "I love you more than any woman I have ever known." He gave her something to drink and she quickly became drowsy.

With two Klan members, Earl Klinck and Earl Gentry, Stephenson half carried the semi-conscious woman to a car, then to a train depot where the four boarded a train. Oberholtzer revived as she was being placed into a stateroom and saw that all three men were carrying guns. As Klinck and Gentry stood guard outside the stateroom, Stephenson undressed the helpless Oberholtzer, causing open wounds by viciously biting her. He then repeatedly raped her.

The group disembarked at Hamilton, Indiana, and checked into a hotel. There, Gentry dressed the wounds Stephenson had inflicted on the half-delirious woman. He then dressed her and, at her request, took her to an all-night drugstore where she purchased bichloride of mercury pills. She later ingested six pills in an attempt to commit suicide. On March 17, Stephenson and his men drove Oberholtzer to her parents' home, informing them that their daughter had been in a car accident. On April 14, 1925, Madge Oberholtzer died from internal poisoning.

Stephenson, Klinck, and Gentry were charged with murder by a prosecution team that had nothing to do with the Klan, except to brand it a lunatic organization that spread terror throughout Indiana and elsewhere and to announce that the leading terrorist was Grand Dragon Stephenson. Though threatened by KKK members, the district attorney would not dismiss his case. To obtain immunity, Klinck and Gentry turned on their Klan boss and testified against him. He was convicted of rape and murder and sent to prison for life. The shock wave through the Invisible Empire was tremendous. Thousands quit the Klan, some even burned their robes.

Others, however, tens of thousands, clung to the Klan for the next decade until the Depression of the 1930s saw a drastic decline of Klan membership. By 1939, Evans realized that the Klan was no longer a going concern and he quit the organization, selling its charter, property, and trappings to Samuel Green and Dr. James H. Colescott, a veterinarian from Terre Haute, Indiana.

The Klan was so desperate for funds in 1940 that it joined with the Nazi American Bund to survive. When the Bund was branded un-American, the Klan was all but dissolved. It lingered until Pearl Harbor united all America in a common cause that obliterated the racist purposes of the Klan. In 1944, the Klan received a death blow from the Internal Revenue Service, which charged the KKK with owing more than $600,000 in back taxes. Green and Colescott held a final meeting of the Klan in Atlanta on April 23, 1944, officially dissolving this most sinister of terrorist organizations.

The Klan would return, however, gradually in the 1950s and with great strength in the 1960s in fierce and deadly opposition to freedom riders traveling the Deep South. The Klan would once again unleash the forces of murder and terrorism in a final effort to maintain segregation and recapture its ancient, evil powers.

"Pineapples" and Primaries

As David Stephenson ruled Indiana during the early 1920s, the city of Chicago was similarly dominated by crime czar Al Capone, whose enormous criminal empire of bootlegging, bordellos, and gambling brought him an estimated $50 million each year in illegal, tax-free profits. As the Klan was the ghost government in many Southern states, Capone was the ghost mayor of Chicago. As Stephenson's Klan was protected by Indiana officials, Capone's crime cartel was shielded by Chicago politicians, not the least of whom was William Hale "Big Bill" Thompson, the bragging, boozing, elected mayor of Chicago. Thompson's administration was not only wholly venal, but its minions reveled in their corruptibility.

By 1927, Capone had all but eliminated competition from rival gangsters and his rule was absolute in Chicago. In April of that year, however, a reform candidate, Senator Charles S. Deneen, promised to change all that. He vowed that he would wrest the Republican primary from Thompson and, once in office, would sweep out the gangsters, chiefly the infamous Mr. Capone.

The mob boss, however, had Thompson in his pocket, along with State's Attorney Robert E. Crowe and even Illinois governor Len Small, who immediately paroled any Capone mobster who was unlucky enough to be sent to prison. Crowe was utterly corrupt and a blatant cog of the Capone organization. In 1923, there were 23,862 Prohibition violations and felony cases charged against

Al Capone, crime boss of Chicago during the 1920s; he ran a bootleg empire worth $50 million each year and he ruled through terrorism.

Chicago bootleggers, chiefly those commanded by Johnny Torrio and Al Capone. In every instance, Crowe's representatives had the charges dismissed or reduced to petty fines. Small was no better. He would later be sent to prison for embezzling public funds.

Deneen's coattails were not clean either. He received the financial and strong-arm backing of another Chicago gangster, Joseph "Diamond Joe" Esposito, who thought to oust Capone through a political power play. The stage was set for one of the most bloody political primaries in U.S. history, the architect of its carnage being Capone's chief terrorist, James "King of the Bombers" Belcastro.

Belcastro was an expert at making all sorts of bombs, especially those with long delay mechanisms that allowed him to set these explosives off at great distances. The terrorist had long employed bombs to further his criminal activities, beginning with his days as a Black Hander in Chicago's Little Italy, where he grew rich extorting money from his fellow Italians.

Knowing his reputation as a bomb terrorist, Scarface summoned Belcastro in the early years of Prohibition, employing him as his top terrorist-enforcer in the distribution of Capone beer and liquor. If a saloonkeeper or bartender proved reluctant to buy Capone beer, and continued to purchase beer from a rival gangster-owned brewing firm, Belcastro was ordered to blow up the saloon. This he did with deadly precision and alacrity, with more than 100 deaths

Left: William Hale "Big Bill Thompson," the boozy, loud-mouthed Mayor of Chicago whose 1927 election was financed by crime boss Al Capone.
Top: Johnny Torrio, Capone's mentor, shown in 1925, a scarf hiding a bullet wound in the neck from rival gunmen, turned over his crime empire to Scarface and retired a multimillionaire.
Above: Terrorist James "King of the Bombers" Belcastro was employed by Capone to blow up the homes of political opponents and polling sites before and during Chicago's 1927 primary elections.

TERRORISM IN THE 20TH CENTURY

Left: *Judge John A. Swanson, a Thompson-Capone adversary, was marked for extermination in Capone's 1927 "Pineapple Primary."* **Right:** *The Chicago home of Judge John A. Swanson, demolished by a bomb planted by terrorist Belcastro during the 1927 primary.*

attributed to his "infernal machines" during the mid to late 1920s.

In retaliation, one rival gang built its own bomb factory in an attempt to blow up Capone-controlled saloons, but Belcastro located the explosives plant and blew it up, along with a half dozen bomb-making thugs. In 1927, fearful that reform candidate Deneen might oust his political shield, Mayor Thompson, Capone told Belcastro to "use your pineapples" on the opposition. A series of bloody explosions took place in early 1927. The first bombs went off at the homes of City Controller Charles C. Fitzmorris and Public Service Commissioner Dr. William H. Reid. Next came the residence of Judge John A. Swanson, Deneen's candidate for state's attorney, and then Deneen's own home.

None of the politicians were killed, but Diamond Joe Esposito, who ignored the many Capone threats against his life, was finally assassinated as he walked down his neighbor-hood street between two bodyguards, shot to death from a moving car in which Belcastro was seen riding. (This was a rare instance wherein the terrorist used a gun to dispose of a victim.)

Attacking politicians was not enough for Scarface. He intended to terrorize all those citizens who might think to vote Deneen into office. He unleashed Belcastro and his henchmen against the public. The terrorists planted bombs in several polling places known to be hostile to Thompson's reelection. When more than a half dozen of these bombs were personally exploded by Belcastro, fifteen voters were killed and scores more were horribly injured. The Chicago press dubbed the slaughter-house election "The Pineapple Primary," and began its first serious campaign to rid the city of Capone.

Supporting the press campaign was one of Thompson's most outspoken political opponents, Octavius Granady, a prominent black attorney. He

Ghost Governments

called the mayor a stooge for Capone and so vilified Thompson and the mob boss that Scarface erupted and told Belcastro to "kill this bird—use a bomb on him—blow him to hell—or anything else, but get rid of him!" The terrorist concluded that it would take too long to construct and plant a bomb, so he and three henchmen got into a car on the night of April 10, 1927, the very eve of the primary election, and went in search of Granady.

They spotted the lawyer talking to some friends on the street and opened fire from their fast-moving auto. Their aim was poor and Granady survived the fusillade, dashing to his car and driving off at breakneck speed. Belcastro and his men pursued. At one intersection, Granady attempted to turn a corner, but lost control of his car and smashed into a tree.

Staggering from the steaming wreck, Granady was caught in the glare of the lights from the gangsters' car as it roared toward him. Belcastro was seen to lean from the window of the car with a submachine gun in his hands. He fired almost point blank into Granady, cutting him in half. The "King of the Bombers" was arrested the next day and tried for this murder, but witnesses suddenly lost their memories or disappeared. Belcastro was acquitted.

When prosecutors described Belcastro as a notorious terrorist and bomber, attorneys for Capone's enforcer pointed out that there had been sixty-two bombings over the last six months, and that "this included some of the homes of Thompson-Crowe allies," as if to say that if one side was bombing, it was all right for the other to retaliate in the same fashion.

A few days before the primary was held and following Belcastro's bombing of the Swanson and Deneen homes, State's Attorney Crowe gave a press conference in which he deplored the terrorism. He put up $10,000 of his own money for information leading to the conviction of the bomber. He then boldly put the bombings on the victims themselves, saying: "I am satisfied that these two bombings are the result of a conspiracy upon the part of a few Deneen leaders to win the primary. . . ." The primary went as Capone planned, with Thompson and his cronies winning the Republican nominations.

The general election was a different matter. The Chicago public had had enough of bombs and terrorists and soundly defeated the Thompson-Crowe machine. This was the turning point for Scarface Al Capone. He had terrorized a public that had formerly thought him to be no more than a colorful bootlegger supplying cheap beer. Now, he was thought of as a terrorist who ruthlessly murdered his way to power. Public pressure to get rid of Capone increased, until, four years later, he was convicted of income tax evasion and sent away to prison. James Belcastro, his personal bomber, escaped retribution. He rose inside the ranks of the old Capone mob and quietly died in bed three decades later.

Black Shirts and Skulls

Italian dictator Benito Mussolini; he rose to power through the terrorist tactics of his Black Shirts.

At about the same time Capone rose to power in Chicago, another Italian seized an entire country, employing the same terror tactics. Benito Mussolini, a farm boy and failed journalist, turned to politics, first as a Socialist at the turn of the century, then swinging to the extreme right as the founder of fascism just after World War I. In his first office he mounted a black flag upon which was a leering white skull and crossbones, signifying death rather than defeat.

Mussolini favored black, wearing black shirts and black ties and black pants—he thought it gave him individuality. He would later insist that his fascist followers don black as a symbol of their loyalty to his political cause. The Black Shirt in Italy would come to symbolize repression, racial bigotry, military aggression, terror, and murder.

Tens of thousands of soldiers could find no employment in Italy following the War. Mussolini sold them fascism and a hunger for power. In 1919, he went to Milan, industrial center of the country, where unemployment was widespread. He seized upon this economic disaster by organizing thousands of disgruntled soldiers into his new fascist party, Fasci di Combattimento. This was the beginning of the fascist state in Italy.

There was little philosophical substance to Mussolini's new political party but trappings galore. For two years he drew a vast army of ex-soldiers to his banner—a black flag bearing a skull and crossbones, symbolizing Mussolini's "Victory or Death" motto—and he costumed his hoardes of thieves and cutthroats in a simple uniform: black shirts and ties, riding pants, black boots, and a small fez-like cap with a jaunty tassel.

Secretly funded by Italian industrialists to rid the country of Communists and Socialists, Mussolini's Black Shirts invaded the streets, savagely beating political opponents. They stormed into the offices of political adversaries and wrecked everything in sight. Mussolini's thugs even destroyed the offices of *Avanti*, the Socialist newspaper that "Il Duce" had once edited.

In November 1921, Mussolini organized the Partito Nazionale Fascista, the official fascist party in Italy. By

Mussolini in 1912, arrested for labor terrorism.

then his Black Shirts ran wild throughout the land, bullying everyone to vote fascist. Those who refused were beaten senseless. Those who persisted in refusing were kidnapped, tortured, even murdered.

With the reassurance that King Victor Emmanuel III and the army would not oppose him, Mussolini led his Black Shirts, an estimated 100,000 men, on an "historic" march on Rome in 1922 to seize the government.

During the march, Black Shirts seized all anti-fascist newspapers and radio stations, prefectures, police stations, and trade associations. In Parma, there was stiff resistance against the fascists by the People's Arditi under Guido Picelli, but 20,000 Black Shirts swarmed into the city and killed all of the officials, losing 139 men in the process. Picelli fled to Spain, where he was later tracked down and murdered by Black Shirts.

Once the Black Shirts reached Rome, only a few working-class quarters showed resistance. Socialists from one section attacked the Black Shirts, who killed seven of them, wounding seventeen more. Black

Shirt thugs found a young Communist leader and painted his face green, white, and red, Italy's national colors, then forced him to swallow several quarts of castor oil and run through the streets shouting "Viva il Fascio!"

By the end of his short march, Mussolini controlled almost all communication in Italy, which was destined to hear but one voice, one thought, that of fascism. On October 30, 1922, Mussolini came to power, appointed the new head of state and allowed to pick his own ministers to all important cabinet posts. He gradually placed his fascist stooges in these positions while his Black Shirts cuffed and cowed the citizenry into voting fascist representatives into Italy's stooge parliament.

One lone voice cried out against him and his terrorist legions, that of the brilliant, courageous Giacomo Matteotti, the Socialist leader in the Italian parliament. On May 30, 1924, Matteotti arose in the Chamber of Deputies to accuse Mussolini and the fascist majority of rigging the recent elections and having conducted for two years a terror campaign that had stilled the voice of democracy. His two-hour speech was frequently interrupted by angry taunts and threats from most of the 357 fascist deputies present.

At the end of his attack on Mussolini and his Black Shirts, Matteotti prophetically announced to his supporters in parliament: "Now you can prepare orations for my funeral." Mussolini, livid with rage, retorted through the pages of his party newspaper, *Popolo d'Italia*, signing

his arch foe's death warrant: "Matteotti, that infamous swindler, that well-known coward and most despicable liar, would do well to be careful, if, one day, his brains should happen to be beaten out, he would have no right to complain in view of the things he has said and written."

Six weeks later, on June 10, 1924, Matteotti left his home in Rome at 4:30 P.M. to attend a meeting at the parliament building. At that time, a janitor working in the building across the street observed a suspicious-looking car containing six men parked on the street. Thinking that these men might be planning a burglary, he jotted down the license plate number: 55 1216. A few minutes later, he watched these same men, all Black Shirts, seize a pedestrian who looked like Matteotti and drag him into their car,

Top: Mussolini's early day newspaper office (Il Popolo d'Italia) where he proudly displayed his black flag with skull, the fascist symbol of terrorism adopted by his Black Shirt followers.

Right: The infamous Black Shirt march on Rome, 1922; left to right, Emilio de Bono, Attilio Terruzi, Italo Balbo, Mussolini, Cesare de Vecchi, Francesco Giunta.

Ghost Governments

not an uncommon sight in Italy during those fascist years. Since Mussolini came to power in 1922 there had been more than 2,000 abductions carried out in the name of the fascist party.

The outcry from the liberal members of the parliament in response to the abduction was deafening. Mussolini then addressed parliament, saying: "As soon as the police were advised of Matteotti's absence, I myself gave strict orders that investigations be made diligently in Rome and at the border stations. The police are already on the track of suspects and everything will be done to clear up this affair, to arrest the guilty and bring them to justice."

Mussolini knew exactly who the suspects were, of course, since he had personally handpicked Matteotti's kidnappers and killers, a group of diehard Black Shirts who were none too careful in their work. Il Duce learned with purple rage that the police had traced the license plate of the abduction car to one of Mussolini's most ardent supporters, Filippo Filippelli, editor of the fascist newspaper, *Corriere Italiano*. Filippelli suggested in the editorial pages of his newspaper that Matteotti had probably gone on an extended vacation, which he was known to have done in the past.

Two months later, on August 16, 1924, Matteotti's decaying remains were discovered in the woods of Quarterella, outside of Rome. He had been repeatedly stabbed to death and his body hidden in a shallow grave. A hunter's dogs dug up the corpse.

Giacomo Matteotti, the lone voice raised against Mussolini in Italy's Chamber of Deputies; he was kidnapped and murdered by some of Mussolini's Black Shirt thugs on June 10, 1924.

"What are we to do?" a high-ranking police official asked Mussolini. He rubbed his shaved head and barked: "Arrest the bastards and tell them to keep their mouths shut. We will take care of them."

Filippelli was arrested, along with an Italian-American gangster, Amerigo Dumini. Then members of Il Duce's inner circle, assistant secretaries of state in the Interior Ministry, were charged with the conspiracy to kill Matteotti—Francesco Giunta and Aldo Finzi. Also arrested were Giovanni Marinelli, who was treasurer of the fascist party, and press chief Cesare Rossi.

The suspects were told by their police interrogators to deny every-

The secret burial of the assassinated Matteotti.

thing and remain quiet. Filippelli, however, had prepared a detailed memorandum, no doubt as a method of self-preservation, which directly implicated Mussolini and his top aides in the murder and cover-up. Il Duce exploded: "Those rascals! They want to blackmail me!" He brought the Black Shirts to a secret meeting where he attempted to convince them to put the interests of the state ahead of their own. Rossi pretended to agree, then fled, leaving behind a document that accused Mussolini of planning Matteotti's murder.

A new Minister of the Interior, Luigi Federzoni, a non-fascist, was appointed by Mussolini in the hopes that this appointment would appease his enemies. Federzoni promptly ordered the rearrest of all the conspirators who had been released pending further investigation. Albino Volpi, who had actually commanded those involved in the kidnapping, was arrested, as were Rossi, Filippelli, and Marinelli. Rossi's document clearly showed Mussolini to be behind the murder, but when this was brought before King Victor Emmanuel III, the monarch refused to act. He realized that if he dismissed his prime minister, Mussolini's Black Shirts would quickly topple his throne.

On January 3, 1925, Mussolini boldly went before parliament and claimed full responsibility for the actions of his associates. He challenged his opposition to take action but he knew none would be forthcoming. Il Duce ruled Italy through his Black Shirt legions, and if the state endorsed murder, there was nothing anyone could do about it. On December 21, 1925, fascist judges in a Rome court dismissed all charges against Filippelli, Rossi, and Marinelli. In 1926, four other conspirators were arrested and tried with Dumini in the tiny village of Chieti in rural Italy, far from the site of the murder.

Dumini was absolved of all guilt by the court because, as one prosecutor politely pointed out, he had been sitting in the front seat of the kidnap car and could not have participated in the actual murder of Matteotti, who was stabbed to death in the back seat. The other four killers were convicted on the charge of manslaughter without premeditation. (They claimed that they only wanted to talk to Matteotti but he struggled so violently that they had to stab him to death in defending themselves.) All four men served less than two months in prison. When released, Dumini and the others were given large sums of money.

Only one man, Amerigo Dumini, ever paid a proper penalty in the murder of Matteotti. Following World War II, on January 21, 1947, he was tried and convicted of Mussolini's state-endorsed murder of Giacomo Matteotti. Dumini, then paralytic and near death, was found guilty and sent to prison for thirty years, dying behind bars a short time later.

The Black Shirts continued to do Mussolini's wholesale kidnappings and murders. They formed part of the Italian SS, modeled after Hitler's terror legions, who tracked down helpless Jews and others branded as enemies of the state, sending these victims to starve in concentration camps. Black Shirts made up Il Duce's private guard, which had the honor of murdering anyone he called enemy. Michele Shirru, an American anarchist, arrived from New York and admitted before he ever got near the dictator that he had come to kill Mussolini. Black Shirts shot him in the back, killing him on May 29, 1931.

On the following June 17, Angelo Sbardellotto admitted that he had been *thinking about* assassinating Il Duce. He, too, was executed by Black Shirts, who shot him in the back. On the following day, Domenico Bovone was also executed for throwing bombs at Black Shirts in Turin, Genoa, and Bologna. More than 1,000 Black Shirts vied for the honor of killing Bovone.

Mussolini distrusted his Black Shirt followers, knowing they were the worst sort of human derelicts, criminals, and perverts. When mounting his invasion of helpless Ethiopa, he sent his Black Shirt legions to fight and hopefully to die in Africa. He also sent most of his diehard fascists to Spain to fight against the Republic in the Civil War, also hoping that the Black Shirts would be slaughtered.

Typical of Mussolini's fanatical terrorists was Arconovaldo Bonaccorsi, who led the first Black Shirt contingents to Spain. He commanded a fighter squadron know as "The

The ignoble end of the Black Shirt leader, April 29, 1945, Benito Mussolini and his mistress Clara Petacci, dead and mutilated, hanging from the girders of a gas station in Milan, Italy.

Ghost Governments

Dragons of Death." He wore the traditional black shirt on which was emblazoned a huge white skull and crossbones. He and his men soon bombed the Republican defenders on Mallorca into submission. Bonaccorsi had all the captured and wounded Republicans brought to a town square where he personally supervised their massacre. He then posed with his foot on the neck of one of the murdered men while photographers took his picture as he joyously shouted: "Il bel tempo è tornato"—"Happy days are here again!"

As Hitler dragged Mussolini into their doomed partnership in a war of aggression, there would be too few more happy days for the Italian Black Shirts. Their ranks were decimated in Africa and Spain, and those who were sent to fight in Russia alongside German divisions were annihilated. As this core of terrorists dwindled, so, too, did Mussolini's power. He was deposed, then restored by the Germans and finally captured by Italian partisans who shot him, his mistress Claretta Petacci, and a few of his loyal Black Shirt followers. The bodies were taken to Milan and, on April 29, 1945, were mutilated, desecrated, and then strung upside down by the heels from the girders of a gas station in the Piazzale Loreto where SS guards had earlier executed a number of Italian partisans.

When General Dwight D. Eisenhower was told of the grisly execution, he replied: "God, what an ignoble end! You give people a little power and it seems like they can never be decent human beings again." He was referring to the partisans but his comment could have been made of the Black Shirts themselves, who had abused their power for two decades and made Italy a country of terror and sudden death.

In the end, the Black Shirts who survived burned their uniforms or tore them to shreds before stepping into streets, waving tiny Allied flags and cheering victorious American and British troops rumbling past them. In Germany, at the same time, while Allied armies closed in from all sides, men who had belonged to similar but even more sinister organizations, were also burning uniforms. Some were black, some were the color of brown.

·FOUR·
FEARMAKERS OF THE 1930s

Brown Shirts and Swastikas

The terror brought to Italy by Mussolini's Black Shirts paled before the Brown Shirts of Germany. Here, Adolf Hitler, a failed Austrian artist, malcontent, and hater of anything other than things German, sought to emulate Mussolini's rise to power. In 1923, attempting to duplicate Il Duce's successful political coup of marching on Rome, Hitler and WW I leader General Erich Ludendorft led a group of right-wing fanatics through the streets of Munich in an attempt to take over the government.

Unlike Mussolini's Black Shirts, Hitler's legions—he had dressed them in brown shirts, riding pants and boots—met with disaster. Local police and military units fired on the marchers and Hitler's putsch failed. Tried and sent to prison, Hitler became a martyr to the right wing cause of his lunatic fringe party, the

National Socialists, or Nazis. He wrote a book in jail, *Mein Kampf* (My Struggle), in which he advocated the German takeover of the world and the suppression and annihilation of all races he considered inferior, chiefly Jews and the Slavic nationalities.

Once released, he began to systematically build up his Brown Shirt forces, called the SA or Storm Troopers (*Sturmabteilung*). They marched through German streets carrying banners emblazoned with the emblem of the swastika, ironically an obscure American Indian symbol. Although the Communists in Germany were the avowed enemies of Hitler and his Brown Shirts, the Nazis, like the KKK in the U.S., equally aimed hatred toward Jews, Catholics and foreigners. They went further, attacking teachers, trade unionists, writers, democrats, and fraternal

Above: German dictator Adolf Hitler, shown in the early days of the Nazi movement (1925), wearing the symbols of his terrorist stormtrooper army, the Brown Shirt and the Swastika.
Below: Hitler, standing, giving the Nazi salute at a Brown Shirt meeting in 1932.

organizations not approved by the Nazis.

Like the Black Shirts in Italy, the Brown Shirts took to their ranks soldiers embittered over the loss of World War I, spreading the myth that Germany had been "stabbed in the back" by the harsh conditions of the Versailles Peace Treaty. Further, the most sadistic criminals and perverts were welcomed by the Nazis. The Brown Shirts were originally headed by Hermann Goering, Hitler's right arm. When Goering was promoted to Reichsmarshal and made head of the Gestapo, Germany's secret police, Ernst Roehm, who had helped to organize the Brown Shirts in the beginning, became the SA chief. Roehm had broken with Hitler in 1925 and had gone to Bolivia to serve as a military adviser. He returned to Germany in 1930 at Hitler's request, to reorganize and stablize the SA which, Hitler complained, was becoming unruly. Roehm did reform the SA, but he maintained his own perversions; he was a notorious homosexual whose top cadres were also homosexual, as well as brutal sadists who delighted in inflicting pain upon helpless citizens.

Meanwhile, Hitler advanced another paramilitary organization headed by Heinrich Himmler, the SS, whose members wore black shirts and served as Hitler's personal bodyguard. As both the SA and the SS grew in number and power, Hitler pitted these organizations against each other, while using them both, more than one million strong, to intimidate the regular German army (Wehrmacht), before and just after he came to power as chancellor of Germany in 1933.

TERRORISM IN THE 20TH CENTURY

Adolf Hitler with Ernst Roehm at a massive Brown Shirt rally in 1933.

Fearmakers of the 1930s

German schoolboys in class wearing Brown Shirts and giving the Nazi salute to their teacher.

Throughout the 1920s, the SA was the dominant Nazi force in Germany, and by 1930, it had swelled to more than 500,000 men. Brown Shirts marched about without weapons, waving large black flags adorned with white skull and crossbones (just as Mussolini's Black Shirts had done). They nevertheless had at their disposal all the arms they needed when making their night raids into homes, beerhalls and political meetings. At first, the SA struck at the Communists, waging street battles with the Reds. These streetfights occured in every major German city and were bloodbaths where the SA, through sheer dint of numbers, invariably emerged victorious.

One of the early Brown Shirt martyrs of this period, or so he was later touted by propaganda minister Paul Josef Goebbels, was Horst Wessel. The son of a Protestant minister, Wessel joined the Brown Shirts in 1926, abandoning his music studies and family in Berlin. He moved into an apartment with a prostitute, Erna Jaenecke, whom he had taken away from another Nazi thug, Ali Hoehler.

Wessel spent much of his time beating up Jews and religious leaders. The terrorist was fond of clubbing ministers over the head as the emerged from

Above: Hermann Goering, the first chief of the SA, better known as the Brown Shirts; when Goering became Reichsmarshal under Hitler, Ernst Roehm took over the SA. Below: Nazi propaganda poster of two stormtroopers preparing to do street battle against Communists in the early 1930s.

churches, an expression of hatred for his father, no doubt, who had disowned him. Since the SA paid very little—its coffers were kept purposely low by Nazi leaders "to keep the wolves hungry"—Wessel earned most of his money by pimping for the voluptuous, bosomy Jaenecke. On the strength of his mistress' sexual favors to Nazi superiors, Wessel was promoted to the rank of Group Leader of the SA in Berlin.

Hoehler, who, like Wessel, was a pimp, seethed over losing Jaenecke who had also been his meal ticket. He went to Jaenecke's former landlady, Frau Salm, and got from her the new address where the prostitute and Wessel were living. On January 14, 1930, he broke into their Berlin apartment and shot Wessel in the mouth, grabbing Jaenecke and fleeing.

When Goebbels learned of the scandal, he promptly turned the shooting into a Brown Shirt myth. Covering up the real facts, Goebbels told the German public that Wessel had courageously battled a gang of bloodthirsty Communists and, outnumbered, had been fatally wounded. To make sure that his story was not contradicted, Goebbels had Ernst Roehm, head of the SA, send Brown Shirt thugs to track down Jaenecke, Hoehler, and Salm. They were all murdered, their bodies secretly buried.

Wessel lived long enough to see himself transformed from obscure thug to national hero and martyr, reading on his deathbed about his own legendary feats as envisioned by the imaginative Goebbels in the pages

Fearmakers of the 1930s

of *Der Angriff.* After Wessel died on February 23, 1930, Goebbels, rummaging through his personal effects, found several amateur songs Wessel had written, choosing one of these to promote.

The maudlin "Horst Wessel Song," which plaintively cried out the glories of the Nazi struggle and promised eventual political victory ("For the last time the rifle is loaded . . . Soon Hitler banners will wave over the barricades"), was just the thing to inspire Hitler youth, Goebbels concluded. Hitler himself decreed that the song was to be sung by National Socialist members at the close of all meetings, and it soon became the Nazi anthem, adding to the mythical rituals of the Nazis and Adolf Hitler.

Hitler made much of the SA during the early 1930s. He asked that Brown Shirts who had been injured in street battles with the hated Communists be brought to him for personal congratulations and decorations. He visited

Above: *Horst Wessel, who was murdered by a fellow Brown Shirt in 1930, became a martyr to the Nazi cause.*
Below: *Brown Shirts are shown burning books in Luchino Visconti's film profile of the early Nazi years,* The Damned *(1970).*

Brown Shirts who were hospitalized, extolling their heroics in battling the enemy. He bestowed titles and commendations upon SA groups, holding their battle standards at massive rallies, blessing them as blood banners as a priest might bless a rosary.

This all the more encouraged the Brown Shirts to commit more savage acts. They terrorized and beat anyone who disagreed with their right-wing beliefs, reserving their most vicious behavior for the hapless Jews of Germany. Brown Shirts painted the Star of David on the windows of shops owned by Jews and stood outside of these stores screaming foul oaths at the owners and threats to anyone who dared to enter. These Nazi thugs stopped Jews in the street and made them kneel to wash the cobblestones and shine their boots. If Brown Shirts caught any German women fraternizing with Jewish men, they hung signs about their necks that read: "I am a swine," or "I have tainted my German blood by sleeping with Jewish pigs."

In Hamburg, a group of Brown Shirts dragged a young blonde woman and a small Jewish man from an apartment. They forced them to pose with them for photographs. About the woman's neck they placed a sign that read: "I am the biggest swine in the place and cohabit only with Jews." The Jewish man was forced to wear a sign that read: "Being a Jewish lout, I take only German girls to my room." After the photos were taken, the man and woman were taken into an alley and their heads were crushed with steel bars.

Brown Shirts also singled out Catholics and other religious organizations for special persecution. They burned churches and attacked priests, beating them senseless in front of their parishioners.

Prior to the 1932 general election, Brown Shirt thugs made sure that Nazi deputies were elected to the Reichstag by beating 99 persons to death in a single month and seriously injuring another 1,125 when breaking up political meetings held by opposition parties. In 1933, the year in which Hitler seized power, Goering proclaimed the SA a legitimate auxiliary police force. He launched the Brown Shirts, the Gestapo, and the regular police in a massive, nationwide terror campaign against the last islands of democratic resistance. Goering told the SA leaders that they were to employ "the severest methods to drive out anti-State organizations, including, if necessary, ruthless use of armed force . . . in this case, I have no obligation to abide by the law; my job is simply to annihilate and exterminate. . . ."

Goering gave free rein to tens of thousands of sadistic killers, who vented their rage on countless victims. In the words of one historian, "Prussia was turned into a terrorist's witches' cauldron. Mobile squads of the SA swept through the streets of the towns, the worst thugs being in Berlin." Thousands were dragged from huts, cellars and other hiding places and were tortured and beaten in fifty impromptu concentration camps, which were really underground bunkers where the Brown Shirts took their victims to commit their atrocities.

The Brown Shirts ran amuck, so much so that Goering could not control them and it took Rudolph Diels (who was not a Nazi but a toady to Goering), head of Goering's Gestapo, to actually raid Brown Shirt torture chambers and stop the wholesale slaughter. One of these sites was located at 10 Hedemannstrasse in Berlin. On the fourth floor, Diels and his men found Brown Shirt "victims . . . half dead from starvation. In order to exort confessions from them, they had been kept standing for days in narrow cupboards. 'Interrogation' consisted simply of beating up, a dozen or so thugs being employed in fifteen-minute shifts to belabour their victims with iron bars, rubber truncheons and whips. When we entered, these living skeletons were lying in rows on filthy straw with festering wounds."

Goering was forever intriguing with SA leaders, attempting to undermine Roehm's control. In 1931, he plotted to regain control of the Berlin SA, working with Captain Walther Stennes, head of the Brown Shirts in the city. The coup failed and Stennes was later seized by the SS and held incommunicado. In 1933, however, Goering ordered Diels to rescue Stennes from a death sentence edicted by his rival Heinrich Himmler. Diels led Gestapo agents into SS headquarters and boldly demanded that Stennes be released to his custody. Stennes, accompanied by his wife and a German training officer attached to the Chinese Army, then slipped across the Dutch frontier. Stennes later became the commander of Chiang Kai-shek's bodyguard.

Stennes was replaced by Edmund Heines as SA commander of Berlin with his chief of staff being Karl Ernst. Both were notorious homosexuals who had earlier been Roehm's lovers. Roehm's homosexuality led to child molestation. One of his ex-lovers, Peter Granninger, served as Roehm's pimp. He abducted young boys for Roehm from the Gisela High School in Munich, eleven in all, according to his later count, after molesting the helpless youths himself.

Though Hitler had heard of Roehm's sexual abnormality, he refused to believe such reports, insisting that "hard evidence" be placed before him. Goering, on the other hand, knew full well that the SA leadership was rife with homosexuals, but it mattered not to him as long as those Brown Shirts did his dirty work. One of Goering's "dirty jobs" fell to Karl Ernst.

On the night of February 27, 1934, Goering, at Hitler's bidding, concocted a plan to rid Germany of the few remaining Social Democrats and other opposition party deputies in the Reichstag. He would simply burn down the building and blame the old enemy, the Communists. An underground passageway that connected the central heating system of the Reichstag and the President's Palace offered a secret entry to the building. Karl Ernst led a small group of Brown Shirts through this tunnel to the Reichstag where they set fire to the building by soaking the place with gasoline and self-igniting chemicals. They then ran back to the palace and safety.

Minutes later a raging fire lit up the sky over Berlin as the Reichstag

Above: Germany's parliament building, the Reichstag, burning on the night of February 27, 1934.

Far left inset: S.A. leader Karl Ernst, the Brown Shirt leader who, at
Goering's orders, set fire to the Reichstag in 1934.

Above inset: Marinus van der Lubbe, a Dutch halfwit, was blamed for
the Reichstag fire and was promptly beheaded by the Nazis.

Fearmakers of the 1930s · 109

burned to ashes. Oddly, the fire attracted a half-witted Dutch Communist, Marinus van der Lubbe, who entered the building and set a few small fires of his own. He was arrested almost immediately. Actually, SA men had heard the mentally defective arsonist boasting in a beerhall days earlier how he would set the Reichstag and other buildings on fire. He was steered to the building by Brown Shirts and shoved inside just after Ernst and his men left.

The gutted Reichstag Building was all Hitler needed to launch a full-scale purge of all those suspected of being Communists or Communist conspirators. The so-called Communist threat also permitted Hitler to take complete power as dictator until the Red Menace was eliminated. That day would never come. Hitler remained in permanent power. Van der Lubbe was quickly convicted of setting the fire and was decapitated by an axe, a brand of execution reserved for Communists. For the leaders of his own Brown Shirts, Hitler reserved rifles and pistols.

By June 1934, the SA under the command of Roehm had become first an embarrassment to Hitler, then an outright threat. When the Fuhrer learned that Roehm envisioned the regular German Army being fused to his SA, with himself as military chief, he quickly gave the order to stamp out the Brown Shirts. The leaders were to be executed. Heinrich Himmler relished the assignment. His 50,000 handpicked SS men despised the dissolute SA, and he quickly established murder squads to eradicate Roehm and his top aides, who were conve-

niently off guard on the night of June 30, 1934, frolicking at a retreat in Wiesee, a lakeside resort near Munich.

Hitler personally went to Munich where he tore the insignias from two top-ranking SA leaders and ordered them shot immediately for treason. He then went to the Wiesee resort accompanied by Himmler and a heavily armed SS guard. He marched into the Hanselbauer Inn at 6:30 A.M. Roehm and top SA leaders were still sleeping. Hitler stood at Roehm's door, clutching a revolver. When an aide banged on the door, Roehm threw it open. Half naked, he gaped at his Fuhrer who accused him of treason and ordered him imprisoned. Roehm was taken to the cellar and locked up. He was later removed to Stadelheim Prison in Munich.

Edmund Heines, another SA leader, answered Hitler's loud banging. Behind him could be seen a male sleeping partner. Hitler exploded at the scene, which Goebbels later described as "revolting, almost nauseating." Hitler hissed to one of his SS guards: "Repugnant beasts," and ordered Heines and other Brown Shirt leaders taken to Stadelheim with Roehm. At the prison in Munich later that morning, Hitler went into a tirade against Roehm and the SA such as none of his closest SS aides had ever before witnessed. "A gob of foam shot out of his mouth," one SS man later recalled as Hitler raved about Roehm's treason. He ordered the SA leaders shot at once.

Sepp Dietrich, who was later to command SS panzer divisions in WW II, arrived to carry out his Fuhrer's orders. In short order, Heines, August Schneidhuber, Wilhelm Schmid, Hans Peter von Heydebreck, Hans Hayn, and Count Hans Joachim Graf von Spreti-Weilbach were all taken outside, placed against a wall, and shot by firing squad. The startled SA leaders simply gave the Nazi stiff-armed salute, shouted "Heil Hitler," and died. Roehm, because of his long association with Hitler, was given a pistol and ordered to kill himself. Roehm insisted that Hitler shoot him personally. When the SA leader delayed committing suicide, two SS killers, Theodor Eicke and Michael Lippert, entered his cell and shot him to death. Karl Ernst, en route to a vacation spot, was pulled from a boat and shot to death in Berlin. (Goering had Ernst on his list so that no one would ever be able to trace the Reichstag fire to him.)

Now it was the turn of the SS to terrorize the land in what later became known as the "Night of the Long Knives." SS thugs barged into homes throughout Germany, summarily executing anyone who had been put on the list of Roehm's so-called co-conspirators. This list had been drawn up by Hitler, Goering, Goebbels and Himmler. On it were the names of every enemy or near-enemy the four top Nazis could remember. Eighty-three men were murdered without trial or a chance to defend themselves, at least that was the official count

later reported. The actual number of victims will never be known, but the bloodbath certainly encompassed more than 1,000 victims.

The victims included General Kurt von Schleicher, Germany's last chancellor before Hitler, who had strenuously opposed Hitler's cabinet. When he opened the door of his villa outside of Berlin, he was immediately shot to death by SS men. His wife of only eighteen months ran forward and she, too, was shot to death. Gregor Strasser, who had been one of the founding fathers of the Nazi party and had fallen out with Hitler, was also murdered that night. Catholic Action leader Erich Klausner was shot to death in his office and his office staff shipped to a concentration camp. Gustav von Kahr, who had betrayed Hitler in the 1923 Munich Putsch, was taken to a forest near Dachau by SS thugs and hacked to death with pickaxes.

SA terrorism in Germany was thereafter replaced by SS terrorism. Himmler's SS continued to randomly seek out countless victims over the next decade. The SS would also establish a horrendous concentration camp system in which more than twelve million would be exterminated before Germany collapsed, following Hitler's welcomed suicide in a Berlin bunker in 1945, ending one of the worst terror-plagued eras in the history of mankind.

Depression-Era Terrorists

The doings of the Brown Shirts in Germany held little interest for Sylvestre Matuschka of Hungary. He had served in the Hungarian Army during WW I and felt fortunate enough to escape the horrendous battles that destroyed the legions of Austro-Hungary. He was glad to see the collapse of the old, autocratic Hapsburg dynasty, for it allowed enterprising men like himself to develop new business opportunities.

During the 1920s, he began several businesses, seeing considerable success. He lived well in Budapest, affording a large house, servants, and mistresses he culled from the chorus lines of music halls. A large man with a heavy black beard and eyesight so poor that he was compelled to wear thick-lensed glasses, Matuschka did not attract attention from females. He bought their favors with money and jewelry. When his businesses began to fail, he began new enterprises, selling stock. Toward the end of the 1920s, these firms also failed and Matuschka was accused of fraud.

Though acquitted, the Hungarian entrepreneur had spent almost all of his fortune. He was forced to sell his property in Budapest before moving to Vienna. Here, Matuschka developed a brand new scheme to enrich himself. He would blow up trains, pretend to be among the passengers, and, as a seriously injured survivor, claim and collect large insurance payments.

After studying the use of explosives, Matuschka planted dynamite along the rail line near Ansbach, in an attempt to derail the Vienna-Passau Express on New Year's Day, 1931. The bomber exploded the dynamite too late, waiting until the engine and most of the cars had passed over the spot where the explosives were planted between the rails. The train was only partially wrecked, with a few cars sliding off the tracks. When Matuschka scrambled up the embankment to mingle with passengers, he was shocked to see that all of those on the cars were soldiers. He had wrecked a troop train and there was no way in which he could have passed himself off as a passenger.

When it was determined that the train had been purposely blown off its tracks, officials began a search for the "insane fiend," but their investigations led nowhere. Matuschka next struck on

August 8, 1931, blowing a train off its track near Juelerboy, Hungary. Several coaches rolled down an embankment, injuring twenty-five people. Again, Matuschka was foiled in his scheme by not being able to go down the steep embankment to join the passengers. "I thought about it going down there," he said later, "but the cliff was too dangerous. After all, the idea was to kill others and make myself appear to be injured, not to kill myself."

Again, authorities discovered the bomber's apparatus near the site and this time widespread panic set in. Someone, a madman, said the press, was blowing up trains at random. Detectives and military police combed the countryside near the sites of the two train wrecks but unearthed no clues to the bomber's identity. One Austrian official predicted that more train bombings would be forthcoming. When asked how he knew this, the official smiled and said: "We are dealing with a demented person who *likes* to blow up trains."

Train passengers became wary and many postponed business trips and vacations, waiting until the fiend was caught. Others boarded trains with apprehension as police searched luggage and cargo shipments. Suspects were yanked from seats or compartments and thoroughly grilled. Extra guards carrying guns rode the passenger trains, and special headlights were installed on engines so that the tracks ahead were illuminated for great distances in hopes that an alert engineer might spot explosives or the dynamiter himself.

Knowing that he was being sought

Hungarian terrorist Sylvestre Matuschka planted bombs on trains in a wild insurance scheme whereby he would collect damages by being an injured passenger.

in several countries, Matuschka waited for more than a year before making his next move. Not until September 12, 1932, did the terrorist strike again, this time blowing a Hungarian Railways express off a steel viaduct at Bia-Torbagy. Cars fell off the elevated track and were bent like pretzels as they struck rocks. Some telescoped into one another. Twenty-two persons were killed and scores more were injured.

This time, Matuschka was ready, hiding in the gorge. After blowing the train off its tracks, he left his hiding place between some large rocks and went to a railway car which was on its side. He spotted several dead persons, and from their open wounds he gathered some blood and smeared this on his face and arms. Then he lay down among the screaming victims and waited to be found.

Matuschka was removed from the train wreck along with the others and taken to a shelter where he somehow managed to bandage his own imaginary wounds. He then gave his name and address in Vienna. Once he returned home, Matuschka promptly filed suit against the railroad. Police inspectors, however, could not find a record of his fare—by then all passengers were being registered when they purchased tickets—and, moreover, no one on the train remembered seeing him as a passenger.

Several detectives then went to Matuschka's home. When he gave evasive answers, he was arrested. Police then searched his home and found explosives and detonators. They also found Matuschka's detailed plans to blow up trains in France, Italy, and the Netherlands. He had marked railway maps throughout these countries, which, for a year, he had explored, locating what he thought to be the best places to blow up trains. Confronted with this evidence, Matuschka confessed to wrecking the three trains.

The first of two trials began on June 15, 1933. Matuschka insisted that his bombings were not designed as insurance swindles but that he was afflicted with a strange mental illness that compelled him to wreck trains, that he took sexual gratification from blowing up trains. "It's the only way in which I can satisfy myself," he insisted. "I cannot find sexual pleasure in any other manner. I must blow up trains! It's only when the cars roar off the track that I can find release—it's maddening, don't you see?"

When asked by the prosecution how this odd mental malady began,

Matuschka blamed an evil hypnotist he had met at a county fair. "This Satanic creature implanted in my brain a lust to wreck trains." He was a gypsy, Matuschka said, adding: "I think he suffered from the same strange passion. I think he had blown up trains in the war and afterward. It had warped his mind and he was able to warp mine when he put me under his spell." The terrorist could not remember the name of the gypsy hypnotist.

When the prosecution ridiculed this story, Matuschka changed his tale, saying that he now remembered the strange force that had directed him to destroy trains. It was a spirit named Leo who came to him at night. The jury was dumbfounded and could not reach a verdict. Matuschka was tried again and this time he was convicted and sentenced to be hanged for mass murder. At the last minute, Matuschka was saved from the gallows. Officials were not quite sure of his sanity and his sentence was commuted to life in prison. When the Soviets liberated Budapest from the Nazis in 1944, Matuschka was released from his cell. He reportedly went to work for the Russians as an explosives expert.

Though Matuschka's publicly stated motives to murder were strange, the killings by the New York terrorist of the same era who was known as the 3-X slayer were even more bizarre. The killer claimed to belong to a secret international society whose mission was to procure a set of papers, and, if he failed, fourteen persons and possibly more would meet an untimely end. A series of cryptic letters written to the *New York Evening-Journal* identified the writer as "3-X," who, in the summer of 1930, terrorized the borough of Queens and precipitated a panic, as police commenced the wildest manhunt in city history up to that time.

The first victim of the 3-X killer was Joseph Moyzynsky, a College Point grocer, who was shot and killed in the presence of his nineteen-year-old girlfriend, Catherine May, on June 11, 1930. The killer employed a modus operandi that would be duplicated almost to the letter by New York's terrorist-murderer David Berkowitz (the Son of Sam) in the 1970s. Moyzynsky was parked in an auto with May in Whitestone, Queens, when the killer advanced from behind. He fired a revolver through the open window of the vehicle, killing Moyzynsky immediately.

May was dragged from the car and taken to the main road where the killer put her on the first bus. When later questioned by police, May identified Albert Lombardo as the assailant. Lombardo was a gangster from the Lower East Side of Manhattan, who provided police with an unshakable alibi. He was released and May was held as a material witness.

Six days later, on June 17, twenty-six-year-old Noel Sowley was murdered in a similar fashion as he sat in his car in a secluded spot in Creedmore, Queens, a short distance from the state hospital. Sowley, who worked as a mechanic for the Cable Radio Tube Corp in Brooklyn, was in the company of twenty-year-old Elizabeth Ring when the lone gunman crept up next to the car, snarling: "You're going to get what Joe got!" He then fired two shots into his victim's head.

The killer then rifled through Sowley's pockets while the girl sat petrified next to the corpse of her dead lover. The man mumbled something under his breath about killing thirteen men and one woman. Ring, who was released by the killer to catch a bus on Rocky Hill Road, later described the killer as a foreigner, about five feet six inches in height. Police inspecting the murder victim found in Sowley's pockets a number of newspaper clippings about the Moyzynsky murder with a pencil-scrawled note reading "here's how."

The letter the killer left at the murder scene was addressed to the police. "I am the agent of a secret international order," it read, "and when I met Moyzynsky that night it was to get from him certain documents, but, unfortunately, they were not in his possession at the time. We always get them through their women." The killer then threatened the life of a third, unnamed person. When this note was published, the citizens of Queens realized that they were dealing with a berserk killer who, despite his claims to the contrary, murdered victims at random. The terrorist caused a widespread panic.

Police Commissioner Edward Mulrooney ordered more than 2,000 uniformed policemen to sweep across the less-traveled roads of Queens. Several suspects were picked up and taken before Ring but she could identify none of them as the killer of Sowley.

The next day, police inspector John Gallagher received two more threatening notes from 3-X. The missives were penned on cheap notepaper and written in blue ink. One read: "Thirteen more men and one woman will go if they do not make peace with us and stop bleeding us to death." The residents of Queens and the other New York boroughs became terror-stricken.

Husbands and fathers began carrying weapons, escorting their wives and children to school and on the smallest of errands. Men were routinely seized by police and questioned. Reports concerning 3-X streamed in from everywhere, causing detectives to chase down thousands of blind alleys. The killer's next correspondence originated in Philadelphia on June 20, a letter sent to Joseph Moyzynsky's brother John, who worked as a plumber. The note read: "You must have those papers, they're mine. Give them to me by putting them in a newspaper and leaving it back door entrance to men's room, Broad Street Station, Sat. af. If you don't have them, leave word who has. No foolin and keep the gumshoe squad off."

Moyzynsky told Philadelphia police that he had no idea what the note-writer was talking about, nor what he wanted. The next and ninth letter in the 3-X series was sent to a Brooklyn man, Meyer Newmark, who was threatened with death unless he handed over document "U.J. 4-3-44." Meanwhile, detectives in Coatesville, Pennsylvania, questioned a former soldier, Dewey Ede, who said he had spoken with a man who told him of being selected for a secret mission by

the "Red Diamond of Russia" and "now that the papers have been returned, I can return to my country."

The case went from bizarre to macabre when, on June 25, Rebecca Hirsch, a 35-year-old Brooklyn woman, stumbled into a precinct station with most of her clothes charred and bearing severe burns. The hysterical woman choked out a frightening story, saying that a man had entered her room and tied her to a bedpost. Before fleeing out the window, he set fire to her clothing. Police inspected the woman's room and found a note signed "Maniac," which also bore a drawing of the moon accompanied by two large X's.

Letters and even phone calls came from the reported terrorist and still the New York City police were no closer to establishing the identity of 3-X. On June 28, the private secretary to George U. Harvey, president of the borough of Queens, received a threatening phone call. "This is 3-X," the caller intoned. "You put the cops after me and I'm going to get you next!" The secretary had received an earlier call from the same man and police were ready to trace the second call. The secretary kept the man on the line long enough for police to trace the second call to a pay phone in a cigar store at Lexington and 12th Street, but by the time officers arrived at the location, the caller had disappeared.

Inspector Thomas Mullarkey of the Fifteenth Inspection District met with reporters and summed up the frustration of police in apprehending 3-X. "The man responsible for these murders," said Mullarkey, "was a man with a delusion that certain conditions needed reforming. He has either come to the conclusion that he has succeeded in doing what he set out to do or he has been scared away by the vigilance of the hunt we are making for him."

Hampering police was a series of anonymous phone calls made to investigators by a private detective who said that he could furnish clues leading to the arrest and conviction of 3-X in return for a cash reward. The caller was identified as Aaron Blattman, a thirty-three-year-old fingerprint expert working for the Bronx Magistrates Court. During the inconclusive and sensational Hall-Mills murder trial of the 1920s, Blattman had been scheduled to appear as a defense witness but was never summoned. He later unsuccessfully sued Mrs. Edward Hall for $56,000 in lost wages from a series of articles he was supposedly hired to write for a newspaper syndicate. Blattman was branded a crackpot and was found guilty of misconduct unbecoming a court officer when making his assertive phone calls to police.

In early August 1930, a third man, Prudential Insurance agent Hector Avalone, was found murdered. Police concluded that Avalone had been killed by a 3-X copycat. The bullets removed from the body did not match those taken from the corpses of Moyzynsky and Sowley. Convinced that 3-X had left the area, Police Commissioner Mulrooney quietly removed the police guards assigned to the back roads of Queens. Almost a year later, Chief Inspector John

O'Brien received a letter, postmarked from Pittsburgh and threatening a renewed round of violence.

"Ha! Ha!" gloated the note sender to O'Brien. "In my own little efficient way I have removed another undesirable from this world. A Pittsburgh girl between eighteen and twenty-five is next. Tell Pittsburgh police to watch out for me and try to catch me." O'Brien did contact Pittsburgh police, notifying Inspector Frank R. Boyd of the latest communication from 3-X.

Not until June 1, 1936, however, did authorities get a break in the case. On that day, a suspect was arrested in Elizabethtown, New York, and identified as the likely 3-X killer. State troopers Walter Rockburn and Elmer Salisbury picked up twenty-nine-year-old Frank Engel in a public garage after the officers had noted his "queer actions."

Engel, a member of the College Point Volunteer Life Saving Corps, freely confessed to the 1930 3-X murders after the troopers arrested him on a disorderly conduct charge. Eye witnesses to the 3-X murders Catherine May and Elizabeth Ring were both taken to the district attorney's office and asked to provide a positive identification. "No, he is not the man," Ring told District Attorney Charles Sullivan. "The man you want was older in 1930 than this man is today." May agreed with Ring.

On June 11, 1936, State Supreme Court Justice George E. Brower declared Engel mentally incompetent and committed him to the state hospital for the insane. The mysterious and deadly killer known as 3-X was not

Inset: Florence Polillo, a 36-year-old prostitute, one of the victims of the Mad Butcher of Cleveland, a berserk killer who terrorized the city for more than four years.

Above: *January 26, 1936: Cleveland Police officers carrying the dismembered remains of Florence Polillo.*

Left: *August 18, 1938: Police detectives raiding Cleveland's shantytown; Asst. Safety Director Robert Chamberlain (cigarette in mouth), is shown making an arrest of a vagrant suspected of being the Mad Butcher, who by then, had slain twelve persons, random killings all. The suspect was released.*

heard from again. His brand of lone-wolf terrorism was well-known to another city that had been fear-gripped by a murderous maniac throughout the 1930s. He was called the Mad Butcher of Cleveland.

For four years, headless corpses turned up in remote locations in and around Cleveland, Ohio, the first murder occurring in September 1934 when the remains of an unknown woman were found in the Kingsbury Run section. The second victim, a small-time hoodlum named Edward Andrassy, was found on September 23, 1935, also in Kingsbury Run. Andrassy's body had been dismembered with surgical precision, suggesting to police that the killer might have medical experience.

By the time that the grisly remains of thirty-six-year-old prostitute Florence Polillo were found in a bushel basket on January 26, 1936, the city was in a frenzy. Victims seemed to be selected at random and the police were powerless to track down the maniac killer. As had been the case with the 3-X murderer in New York, citizens responded to the Cleveland terrorist by arming themselves. Vigilante groups patrolled neighborhoods carrying shotguns and police had difficulty in disarming apprehensive residents. On one occasion a man who lived near Kingsbury Run pulled a gun on a city detective and fired off a couple of shots, thinking the plainclothesman was the Mad Butcher.

More mutilated victims turned up. In June 1936, the headless remains of another young man were found in Kingsbury Run. Fingerprints were

July 6, 1937: Cleveland police detectives meet with National Guardsmen, who found the mutilated remains of the tenth victim of the Mad Butcher floating in the Cuyahoga River.

taken but failed to identify the victim. The body, however, bore six unmistakable tattoos. The head was later found and, in an effort to identify the victim, a death mask of the victim was displayed at the Cleveland Exposition of 1936–1937. Though tens of thousands of spectators stared at this death mask, no one came forward to make an indentification.

One strong suspect was former meat butcher Frank Dolezal who had been "fingered" by private detective Lawrence "Pat" Lyons. The private investigator found blood traces in Dolezal's room, and police grilled the tough, hard-drinking Dolezal for forty hours, after which he confessed to killing Polillo and disposing of her head, but he changed his story several times. Police concluded that they had a lunatic on their hands but not a murderer. Before questions could be answered, Dolezal committed suicide by hanging himself in his jail cell in September 1939.

Though the Cleveland murders appeared to cease, three similar murders were reported in Pittsburgh in May 1940, where someone had severed the heads of three persons in a railroad car. A year earlier a headless

Fearmakers of the 1930s

body had been found in Newcastle, Pennsylvania. The last such murder occurred in Pittsburgh in 1942, which convinced the Cleveland police that the killer had moved on. Frank Dolezal's guilt or innocence remains in doubt.

Left: July 7, 1939: Frank Dolezal, a Cleveland vagrant and alcoholic, shown after being grilled non-stop for forty hours, his shirt streaked with sweat, confessed to murdering and decapitating Florence Polillo. Police thought they had finally apprehended the Mad Butcher but Dolezal changed his story many times, was thought to be insane, and, before his trial, committed suicide in his cell.

Below: May 3, 1940: Pittsburgh, Pa. police detectives remove the body of one of three men, all decapitated, from a freight car, the bloody hand of this headless victim raised in the wicker casket. The word "Nazi" was crudely carved across the chest of one body. The car had been sitting idle for about a year at a Youngstown, Ohio siding before being moved to a junk yard. It was thought that this was the work of the elusive Mad Butcher of Cleveland, credited with twelve killings in that town before moving on to Pennsylvania to continue his random mutilations and murders.

The Black Legion

Where New York, Cleveland and Pittsburgh were plagued by maniac terrorists who murdered at will and seemingly without motive, there was a purpose to the terror spread by the Black Legion in Detroit during the 1930s. The Black Legion had been created solely to keep assembly-line jobs at auto works in the hands of native-born American whites at any price, including kidnapping, torture, and murder.

Organized in 1933 by Harvey Davis, an employee of Detroit's Public Lighting Commission, the Black Legion was a variation of the Ku Klux Klan. Its credo, as were its costumes and paraphernalia, was modeled after the Klan. The Legion operated secretly behind its pseudonym, the Wolverine Republican League, and recruited only those who were white, native-born and Protestant. Davis established the criteria of the secret organization, which was, ostensibly, to defend decency and womanhood in the U.S., creating a vigilante group that would actively eradicate Jews, blacks, Catholics, Communists, and anarchists. The costume of this organization was almost identical to that worn by KKK members, except that the robes and hoods were black.

Initiation rites were founded on an image of terror. Members in good standing stood in a circle wearing their robes while initiates kneeled before them. Members held guns to the heads of the initiates who were then ordered to chant a long, rambling oath which, in part, read: "In the name of God and the Devil, one to reward, the other to punish, here, under the black arch of God's avenging symbol . . . I will exert every possible means in my power for the extermination of the anarchist, the Communist, the Roman hierarchy and their abbettors . . . I will show no mercy but strike with an avenging arm as long as my breath remains . . . I pledge . . . never to betray a comrade, and that I will submit to all the tortures mankind can inflict, rather than reveal a single word of this, my oath."

An exact number of Black Legion members was never determined, but most reliable reports show the figure at about 20,000 dues-paying members. Davis and his lieutenants actually made considerable profit from the sale of robes, whips, symbolic rings, women's jewelry, along with weapons consisting of knives and revolvers.

They charged exorbitant prices for bullets.

Members knew full well what the Legion's purposes were—to make the automotive workforce in Detroit all-white and Protestant, along with electing local officials who would enforce the edicts of the Black Legion. The long-standing criminal organization of Detroit, the Purple Gang, a mixture of Jewish and Italian gangsters, came under the Legion's scrutiny and many of the gang members were attacked and hospitalized during the Legion's heyday, although the Purples had largely been rendered ineffective by that time through an aggressive political and law enforcement campaign.

The bigoted Davis reserved the organization's deepest hatred and wrath for political and racial foes, selecting his first victims in 1935. In that year, police began to turn up bodies of those who had obviously been murdered, but baffled investigators could not provide a single reason for the strange homicides. Early that year, the body of Silas Coleman, a black man, was discovered in a swamp about forty miles from Detroit. He had been shot several times. Union organizer John Bielak was found dead outside of Monroe, Michigan, a short time later. His killers had tortured him, literally slicing his flesh before hacking him to pieces with what seemed to be swords or machetes.

A short time later, another union organizer, Edward Armour, was riddled with gunfire from a passing truck as he walked down a Detroit street. Armour survived to tell police that he had no idea why a truckload of gunmen would want to murder him. The killings continued, inexplicably, murders that remained unsolved but struck terror into racial minorities and Catholics who had been anonymously contacted by Legion members and told to leave town.

Then, in May 1936, a body was found behind the wheel of a car on Gulley Road on Detroit's far West Side. The victim, shot five times, was taken to the morgue where fingerprints identified him as Charles Poole, whose only criminal record was an ancient vagrancy charge in Kansas City. While puzzled detectives stared down at Poole's riddled remains, believing they had another of the many unsolved murders on their hands, a couple entered the morgue. The man and wife had been summoned to the morgue to identify an accident victim. As they were passing the slab holding Poole's exposed body, the couple stopped dead still and gasped.

"I know that man," said the wife. "He's a friend of my brother's."

"Who is he to you?" one of the detectives asked the woman.

"We called him Chap," she replied. "But none of us have seen him in a good, long while." Then the woman added as an afterthought: "People say that he has been running around with a man named Tennessee Slim."

The detectives then learned that the dead man's wife was in the hospital and about to have a baby. Before her delivery, Mrs. Poole told detectives that Tennessee Slim was none other than Harvey Davis. Police quickly took Davis into custody, jailing him. He smugly told officers from his jail cell that his lawyers would soon have him on the street again.

Meanwhile, Detective Jim Havrill located Owen and Marsha Rushing who had known the dead Poole very well. Mrs. Rushing was visibly upset when Havrill questioned her and her husband.

"What's your wife hiding, Owen?" Havrill asked Rushing. "See—she's eating her heart out. Don't let her go on like that."

Before Rushing could respond, Marcia Rushing, shaking with fear, blurted: "We can't tell you! You don't know those people!"

"What people?"

"That—that organization! They kill people who talk! They carry guns and there are thousands and thousands of them. They are like the Ku Klux Klan, only bigger and more awful!"

The Rushings began to talk, as did others and soon Detroit Police had uncovered the story of the Black Legion. They began to make more arrests, capturing Erwin Lee who was carrying a .38-caliber revolver and a blackjack in his pockets, en route to "an assignment," he admitted.

Next, police rushed into the home of John Bannerman where they found thousands of black robes and hoods decorated with skull and crossbones. Bannerman had tried to burn the robes but there were too many to destroy before police arrived.

Then, Dayton Dean, one of Davis' cowed followers, was picked up. Dean began to talk, unraveling all the secrets of the Legion. He admitted that

Humphrey Bogart in the 1937 film, Black Legion *(shown in a publicity still from the movie with Erin O'Brien-Moore, left, and Ann Sheridan, right), portrayed the role of Dayton Dean, the real-life informant who exposed Detroit's terror gang.*

he had joined the Ku Klux Klan in 1922 but had moved his allegiance to the Legion, when Davis, also a one-time member of the KKK, organized the Legion in 1933. Dean said that Davis had ordered the murders in 1935 either for political or racial reasons, adding that Davis was angry that blacks and other minorities were obtaining jobs in the automotive industry.

What about Poole, detectives asked. Dean replied that Poole was a Legion member and a friend of Davis but that the leader had decreed Poole unfit for membership when learning that he had beaten his pregnant wife. Dean was chosen to lure Poole to his death because he was Poole's best friend and would be trusted by the victim. He said that once Poole joined him, Davis and six others took him to a secluded spot outside the city. There the terrorists donned their black robes and Davis pronounced a death sentence on Poole for "defaming womanhood by beating a pregnant woman." All of the members then each fired a single bullet into the victim.

Davis was also personally responsible for the death of Silas Coleman, said Dean, "because he wanted a nigger to shoot." He went on to describe how Davis and others drove Coleman to a swamp outside of Detroit and then ordered him to "run for his life." As the terrified black man raced into the darkness, the Legion members all pulled out revolvers and used the fleeing Coleman for target practice.

"Don't miss!" screamed Davis, according to Dean. "Or you may get an extra bullet sent your way!" This last quoted remark was typical of Davis, who kept his members together through death threats and constant fear that they, too, might be marked for execution if they were thought to be disloyal to the Legion, or, more specifically, to Davis.

Dean, who learned that he had been put on Davis' "hit list" for informing, went on cooperating with authorities, bravely repeating his testimony in court where Davis and his lieutenants were tried *en masse*. All were convicted and given life sentences. Dean, for turning state's evidence, was given a short prison term. He would later be profiled by actor Humphrey Bogart in Warner Brothers' straight-from-the-headlines film production, *The Black Legion*.

With Davis and his top aides in prison, the Legion quickly disintegrated. In the late months of 1936, police counted more than 15,000 black robes once worn by the dedicated terrorists of the Legion. The robes had been dumped into garbage cans throughout the Detroit area. "The ones that worry me," said one detective at the time, "are the robes that were not thrown away, the ones that went into trunks, chests, closets and attics, the ones that might be worn again." His fears were, thankfully, unfounded. The Black Legion never again surfaced.

·FIVE·
TERROR, U.S.A.

Fiends on the Loose

While the U.S. was at war and millions of men fearfully faced death on foreign battlefields, the peaceful town of Tulsa, Oklahoma, was terrorized by a murderous, unknown fiend who horrified residents and baffled police and the FBI. Five grisly murders were committed over a six-year period during the 1940s, all on the North Side of the city. To this day, no one has ever solved the Tulsa bludgeoning murders.

The terror began on the sultry day of July 10, 1942. On that morning, Helen Brown, a twenty-year-old expectant mother, said goodbye to her husband, Bill, as he went off to work. A few minutes later, an intruder entered the Brown home on Main Street through an open window. The intruder caught Mrs. Brown by surprise, striking her across the face repeatedly, and then strangled her into unconsciousness. She was found some time later that morning by neighbors and rushed to

St. John's Hospital, but efforts to save her life and that of her unborn child were futile.

Police were shocked to learn from the examining physicians that the bruises on Mrs. Brown's stomach indicated that, in addition to the bludgeoning, she had been trampled to death. Tulsa detectives took her husband, William C. Brown, into custody, grilling him for five straight hours before he was released as a suspect. Brown, a fruit-truck driver who was seen at work at the time of his wife's murder, told police that his wife did not have an enemy in the world.

County Attorney Dixie Gilmer met with members of the press, saying that robbery was not a factor in the case as nothing had been taken from the Brown home. He admitted that he could establish no motive for the senseless killing nor did some scant clues shed any light on the murderer's identity. Tulsa newspapers reported the grim facts of the terrorist killing that kept the city on edge for months to come.

Then, with the Brown killing still fresh in memory, the fiend struck again. On January 14, 1943, J. B. Underwood, an attorney, called police to tell them that one of his employees, thirty-one-year-old Georgia Green, a stenographer, had been slaughtered in a similar fashion. When Green failed to report for work that day, Underwood called her residence several times but received no answer. Following dinner that night, Underwood decided to visit Green's apartment but, failing to get a response to his doorbell ringing, he summoned a tenant who let him inside.

Underwood walked into a bedroom to recoil in shock. There, on the bed was Green, along with her mother, Mrs. Clara Luzila Stewart. Both were dead, soaked in blood. Police examiners quickly determined that the two women had been hacked to pieces with an ax. Police Chief George Blaine immediately took charge of the case before county authorities could intervene (and save him considerable loss of face). Blaine expressed the opinion that neither woman had been criminally assaulted.

Not so, contradicted Dr. J. Jeff Billington, who reported that both women had been raped *after* they had been bludgeoned to death. Police went on to report that seven eggshells had been found in the kitchen sink and the residue of scrambled eggs was found in a frying pan, all pointing to the fact that the killer had made himself a hearty breakfast after assaulting the women with an ax and had

leisurely eaten it while his victims lay dead in the bedroom. Though the ax was found by school children a few blocks from the murder scene, it offered no clues, except for the fact that it had been stolen from the garage of a local man who said he used it for carpentry.

When police openly concluded that the double murder had been committed by the same lunatic who had killed Mrs. Brown six months earlier, the citizens on the North Side of Tulsa panicked. Women were guarded night and day by husbands, fathers and brothers. Police added special patrols in their search for the madman. Since he had struck during the daytime, protection was even more difficult, particularly when men were obligated to go to their jobs.

Two years passed before the killer struck again. On May 15, 1945, Panta Lou "Pat" Liles, a twenty-year-old factory worker at the Douglas Aircraft company, was found sprawled on her blood-soaked bed. Her murderer had administered repeated blows to her head, using a heavy, blunt instrument, before raping her. The murder was almost identical to the Brown-Green-Stewart killings. There was an additional, tantalizing fact—the killer actually spoke on the phone with Liles' roommate, Irma Seburn, either before or after he killed Liles.

Seburn, who worked as a night nurse for a Tulsa manufacturing company, was Liles' roommate, and called at 5 A.M. to awaken her. She let the phone ring for almost five minutes before someone picked up the receiver. A voice that sounded "gruff," answered, according to Seburn's recollection. "Pat?" she questioned. The masculine voice at the other end of the line mumbled an almost inaudible response that sounded like "yes." The conversation broke off a few seconds later with Seburn unsure of whether she had spoken with her roommate or not. She called back at 5:10 A.M., to ask Liles if she was going to work with "Edith" or not. The voice answered in the affirmative, only no "Edith" existed. Seburn, who had used the imaginary name "Edith" as a test, then called police.

To everyone's surprise, police arrested thirty-three-year-old Leroy Benton on June 7, 1945, after he surrendered voluntarily once he had heard that a warrent for his arrest had been issued. Benton, a black man who had been convicted of rape in 1927, worked as a porter in several Tulsa cafes and department stores following his release from prison in 1929. When queried by the press, officials brought forth Captain Phil Hoyt of the Kansas City, Missouri, Police Department.

"The only thing I can say is that Benton has a guilty knowledge of the crime," reported Hoyt. "He either saw it committed or committed the crime himself."

Benton was grilled around the clock and, after being given a lie detector test, admitted the murder of Liles. He later told reporters: "I confessed because I thought I might get a life sentence and because I thought while I was serving my time the real murderer might be found and I would be released."

Still later, Benton insisted that he had never entered Liles' apartment and offered to undergo more lie detector tests to prove his claim. After a five-day trial, however, Benton was convicted, mostly on the strength of an FBI lab report linking him to the crime. He was sent to the state penitentiary at McAlester to begin serving a life term on November 24, 1945. Tulsa residents breathed a collective sigh of relief, believing that the terrorist-killer had finally been captured.

Benton had nevertheless appealed his conviction, which the state criminal court overturned on the grounds that his confession had been coerced by "third degree" methods and that the Tulsa police had denied him the right to legal counsel. On March 3, 1948, the wrongly convicted Benton was released to the sheriff of Tulsa County. He immediately moved to Hammond, Indiana.

The unknown bludgeoning killer did not vanish with Benton. Four months later, on July 2, 1948, the sex fiend attacked four females. The first victim was forty-five-year-old Ruth Norton, a building service employee who lived on North Cheyenne Avenue. The killer entered her apartment and raped Norton before beating her to death. Police found no signs of struggle in the apartment and, after discovering a billfold containing thirty-three dollars in cash on the woman's bedstand, ruled out robbery.

Boldly, later that night, and in the same apartment building, the murderer launched another attack, this time raping and bludgeoning into unconsciousness thirty-eight-year-old Mrs.

J.B. (Alsey) Cole, her daughter Doris, thirteen, and a neighbor girl, LeVon Gabbard, fourteen. All three had been assaulted in their beds as they slept. Rushed to a hospital in critical condition, Mrs. Cole and her daughter died. Gabbard could not identify the killer.

Police made desperate appeals to Tulsa residents to disclose any information they might have, "no matter how ridiculous it may sound," but the killer remained unidentified. Suspects by the dozens were dragged to police headquarters for questioning, including Gabbard's twenty-five-year-old brother-in-law, Sam McCutcheon, but all were released and cleared. Benton, of course, was immediately suspected but he was able to prove that he was in Hammond with friends at the time of the killings. The bludgeoning murders then inexplicably ceased. Despite an intense investigation that went on into the 1950s, the killer who had terrorized Tulsa was never apprehended.

A few hundred miles to the west, the good citizens of Texarkana, Texas, squatting on the Texas-Arkansas border, suffered a similar reign of terror, except that the madman who plagued that town vented his murderous spleen not over several years but within three bloody weeks. The unknown killer committed five heinous murders in "lover's lane," beggining in late February 1946.

Parked on Morris Lane, a mile west of Texarkana, Lou Denton and his girlfriend, Irma Black, were listening to the radio and necking when suddenly a masked assailant crept up from behind the car, viciously striking

Denton over the head with the butt of a revolver, knocking him unconscious. He then dragged Black from the car, beating and raping her. After rifling Denton's wallet and Black's purse, the attacker fled.

The victims were discovered by Sheriff W. H. Presley and Deputy Zeke Hensley, telling the officers that the attacker had been at least six feet tall and weighed about 185 pounds. A check on nearby tire tracks failed to identify the car driven by the assailant. Though Denton and Black had undergone a terrible ordeal, they later considered themselves fortunate, compared with the fate of other victims of the terrorist killer who came to be known as the Lover's Lane Murderer of Texarkana.

On the night of March 24, 1946, twenty-four-year-old Richard Griffin and his nineteen-year-old girlfriend, Polly Ann Moore, parked their car on North Park Road, less than a mile from where Denton and Black had been assaulted. Lurking in the shadows fifty feet away was the Lover's Lane Murderer. As police later reconstructed his movements, the killer advanced on Griffin and Moore carrying a small caliber handgun.

The next morning a cafe worker named Charles Walters noticed a car parked in a patch of woods. He approached and then stood dead still, recoiling in horror at what he saw. Lying 200 yards away was Moore's body. She had been raped and shot to death. Griffin was only a few yards away. He, too, was dead, murdered. "I'd say this man was killed at least two hours before the young woman was," concluded an examining physician brought to the murder site by police. "The murderer held his gun very close to the victims. Powder burns are evident around the wounds in both bodies."

Found nearby were tire tracks that matched those in the Denton and Black assault. Police realized that they had a homicidal maniac on their hands. Texas Rangers were called and dozens of officers conducted a house-to-house search for the car in an attempt to identify the tires. Sheriff Presley was convinced that the killer of Griffin and Moore was the same person who had raped Black. "It's not possible that two criminals are driving cars with identical tires," he said.

The police search netted nothing. Jittery residents of Texarkana began to carry weapons. They flooded the police department with reports of strangers prowling about neighborhoods, especially in popular lover's lanes. Six suspects were questioned but were released. Though police warned everyone to stay away from spooning spots in the evening, young lovers continued to visit the areas at night.

Less than a month after the Moore-Griffin killings, on the night of April 14, 1946, seventeen-year-old Paul Martin and his fifteen-year-old girlfriend, Betty Jo Booker, left a VFW dance and drove along the North Park Road, parking close to where the recent murders had occurred. The next morning, insurance salesman G. W. Weaver slowed his car, saying to his wife: "Look, there's a man lying on the ground over there! He's a mess of blood!" Weaver called Sheriff Presley.

Martin had been shot three times in the back. Booker was found a few yards away. Her stomach and abdomen had been savagely slashed open. Clues were almost nonexistent. A friend of the couple told police that Booker had left the dance carrying a saxophone, and state police conducting a dragnet examined every car on the road for just such an instrument. By this time the police of Texas, Arkansas, Oklahoma, and Louisiana were on the lookout for the terrorist killer, but he apparently had not left the Texarkana area, striking again on May 3, 1946, ten miles outside the city limits.

Virgil Starks had just sat down to read his evening paper when a bullet crashed through the front window of his home, striking him in the head and neck. He crashed to the floor, dying. His wife, who was upstairs doing chores, ran down the stairs and, as she rushed to her husband's side, two more bullets smashed through the window, striking her in the face.

Despite her severe wounds, Mrs. Starks did not lose consciousness. Staggering out of her house, she made her way to the home of a neighbor, A. V. Prater. After seeing to Mrs. Stark's wounds and calling police, Prater grabbed his hunting rifle and went out looking for the gunman. Arkansas Sheriff W. E. Davis arrived at the Starks home a short time later to find several spent .22-caliber cartridges. He also found that the lock on the back door of the house had been broken and that bloody footprints were left inside.

"The slayer must have broken in before he knew that Starks' wife had escaped," Davis later reported. "It is only by the grace of God that Mrs. Starks got away. Otherwise there's no doubt that she would have received the same treatment as those other women got at the hands of the sex fiend."

The investigation was intensified and continued for months as a feeling of dread permeated Texarkana and surrounding towns. The terror murders were reported by the nation's press, which caused no less than six persons to come forth to confess to the killings. They were all dismissed as crackpots and lunatics. Police even questioned every person stationed at Barksdale Field in Shreveport, Louisiana, but nothing came of the interrogations.

As weeks, then months dragged on and no new killings occurred, police were at a loss to explain why the killer had ceased his activities. Then authorities looked back to May 7, 1946. On that date, four days after the Starks' home had been shot up, a drifter matching the description of the rapist in the Denton-Black case wordlessly stepped in front of a fast-moving train outside of Texarkana, Arkansas.

The dead man had no identification, but he was not a homeless vagabond in that he wore good clothes and shoes and carried cash in his pocket. Not far away, on that day, police found a car parked in a heavily wooded area. It was on fire, burned beyond recognition. All of its tires had been removed, making it impossible to match tread marks with those left at the murder scenes. Police could not determine whether or not the car had belonged to the suicide-bent stranger.

One detective surmised that the dead man and the killer were one and the same: "It was only four days after the Starks shooting. He knew we had more than a thousand heavily armed men in the area looking for him—day and night. The papers had reported it. He had scared the wits out of everyone but we were getting closer and he knew it and he also knew he could not get out of the area. So he took the tires from the car, burned the vehicle, and then waited for the express train to arrive. The son-of-a-bitch probably grinned when he faced the engine. We still don't know who he was. We will probably never know."

The American Internment
Camp Murders

About the time the Tulsa terrorist began indiscriminately bludgeoning victims to death, an otherwise tranquil America saw the rise of dozens of internment camps designed to house Axis prisoners of war. In May 1942, at the time of the first Tulsa killings, there were only thirty-two Axis prisoners of war locked up in America, one Japanese and thirty-one Germans. By May 1945, hundreds of internment camps throughout America contained more than 425,000 Axis prisoners, mostly captured German troops. Of that number, fewer than 3,000 escaped American internment camps throughout the war and all but one lone German were recaptured.

The camps were clean, well-guarded, and, when it came to the German camps, operated with great efficiency. That efficiency was due to the German prisoners themselves. The first to arrive in large numbers were members of Irwin Rommel's elite Afrika Korps, made up of veteran Wehrmacht soldiers and diehard Nazis. American military commanders in charge of the camps marveled at the self-discipline practiced by these men. So well organized were they that U.S. Army commanders more or less allowed the prisoners to run the camps themselves, assigning living quarters inside wooden barracks and tents and even designating work details.

As the war progressed and the number of prisoners began to swell, the type of German prisoner changed dramatically. Those who had been conscripted into the German Army were not the fanatical followers of Adolf Hitler. These drafted soldiers were nationalists, to be sure, but they were far from enthusiastic supporters of the Third Reich. Statistics later show that 40 percent of all prisoners in the U.S. during the war were sympathetic toward the Nazi ideology, and of these, 10 percent were ardent party members and fanatical Nazis. These consisted, for the most part, of thugs and killers whose racist mentality permitted no deviation from Hitler's ambition to conquer the world and destroy those nationalities as he deemed "unfit" for life.

Although U.S. officials attempted to reeducate the German prisoners by printing and distributing through the camps a number of pamphlets exposing Hitler's lies and propaganda, no headway was made with the diehard

German prisoners-of-war in a U.S. POW camp raise the Nazi salute during the funeral of one of their comrades as American army guards stand by. Any prisoner who showed the slightest sympathy for the Allies or cooperated with U.S. guards met with beatings and death.

Nazis. Several hundred thousand other prisoners, however, were receptive to this information. When they showed signs of accepting American ideas and rejecting the race hatred preached by Hitler, they were often ostracized by other prisoners. Some were punished. Some were even murdered.

The slightest show of empathy toward the Allied cause on the part of prisoners could bring criticism and threats from the Nazis. At Camp McCain, near Jackson, Mississippi, Sergeant Werner Baecher was assigned by ranking German prisoners to go through American newspapers and assemble a news bulletin on events in Europe, presenting this to the prisoners in the mess hall, following the evening meal. One night he announced that American troops had landed in Sicily. His report was met with stony

silence. Then a young officer cadet approached him, saying with a sneer: "You know, certainly, that you are a traitor!" When Baecher asked why, the young cadet snapped: "Because you are repeating enemy propaganda—giving news items that are not true!" Baecher stopped giving reports, which were taken up by Nazis. Subsequent news bulletins fabricated German victories—that Leningrad had been captured and England invaded.

Hitler had long been feeding his troops fantastic lies to bolster morale. Paul Josef Goebbels, his propaganda minister, had widely distributed reports as early as 1941, for instance, that German bombers had flown to America and reduced New York's skyscrapers to rubble. This blatant lie was easily exposed to German prisoners arriving in New York when they saw the buildings still standing. Yet, Nazi enforcers maintained camp authority.

When American officials opened a church inside the internment camp at Fort DuPont, Delaware, for those wishing to attend Sunday Mass, an ardent Nazi posted himself outside the church and warned other prisoners that if they entered, he would write down their names "and they would discover the consequences when they got back to Germany." On another occasion, a German chaplain conducting Easter Mass closed his sermon with the words: "Let us pray for our poor, suffering Fatherland. May peace come quickly." The prisoners booed and hissed him. As he walked from the dais, several Nazis struck him in the face. The chaplain asked that he be moved to another camp for his own protection and was sent to an internment center in Alva, Oklahoma.

New prisoners arrived at the camps with edicts from Heinrich Himmler, dreaded leader of the Gestapo and the SS. He warned those "succumbing to Jewish-Bolshevik" influences that they would be identified in prisoner exchanges (which did not exist) or following the war, when they would be repatriated. Their families would be punished and so would they, promised Himmler. Reported the *Boston Globe*: "Fifty percent of the German noncoms definitely support Hitler and his government. They are, in reality, a police force in the camp . . . The effect of their rule is a little Germany, where persecution of the anti-Nazis is thorough and violent."

Gestapo units were organized inside the camps to enforce Nazi edicts. The *New York Times* criticized those in charge of the camps for failing to realize "that they were capturing Nazi gangsters as well as run-of-the-mill soldiers." The Nazis soon made the camps into houses of terror where any German soldier who appeared to fraternize with guards, ask about life in America or repeat the real facts of Germany's setbacks was tried in a kangaroo court and invariably punished in the form of a beating. Some Germans were murdered outright and their deaths passed off as suicides.

American camp commanders were lax during the early years of the war in protecting prisoners against the camp Gestapos, preferring to let the Nazi fanatics run well-disciplined camps. One camp commander so admired this discipline that he insisted that Germans reporting to him give him the stiff arm "Sieg Heil" salute. Another proudly marched his prisoners to church in a small town on Sunday, reveling in the fact that the Germans were lustily singing en route. Not knowing their language, he was later upbraided and embarrassed when told that the Nazis were singing the "Horst Wessel Song," one praising Hitler and packed with race hatred.

When Provost Marshal General Archer L. Lerch discovered that Germans were being tried by their fellow inmates for showing empathy toward the Allies, he immediately ordered bulletins posted throughout the camps stating that "any prisoner who fears for his own safety need only report that fear to the nearest American officer or enlisted man, and he will be given protection."

This did little good for many prisoners. One new group of captured Germans arrived at Camp Ellis, Illinois. Within its ranks was a young aviator named Pips, who made the mistake of saying to veteran prisoners that the war was lost. Hans Werner Richter later recalled how he, Pips, and others in his group were given the silent treatment by other prisoners when they entered the compound for the first time.

Suddenly, other grizzled veterans hissed: "Traitors! Deserters! Bandits!"

"They're nuts!" one of Pips' friends said.

"All from the *Afrika Korps*," Pips said.

"Where are you from?" a prisoner asked with a snarl.

"Italy."

"Deserters, in other words. You'll pay for it!"

"Shut your trap!" Pips shouted back.

Richter remembered how that "same evening we met up with what was called the 'Lagergestapo,' the camp gestapo . . . Pips was seized in the barracks and badly beaten, then dragged by the legs out of the barracks and badly beaten, his poor bloody head bouncing over the ground." He was later taken to the hospital where he survived. Pips was transferred to another camp.

The diehard Nazis routinely beat those of other nationalities who had been conscripted into the German Army later in the war when Germany's own supply of men dwindled. Lieutenant-Colonel C. P. Evers, commander at Camp Ellis, offhanded-ly reported that "on one occasion fifteen Nazis so unmercifully assaulted a Polish prisoner that he required hospital treatment for several days."

The slightest infraction of Nazi rules could bring painful reprisal. One prisoner insisted upon writing a letter to his father, who was a U.S. citizen, despite warnings not to communicate with a German who was "not a good Nazi." He was beaten senseless. American guards did little to protect prisoners marked for punishment. When one badly frightened prisoner went to guards at Camp Breckinridge, Kentucky, to say that he feared for his life, he was given a bottle of gentian scent, "which he was to hurl at his assailant so that the latter might be identified by the scent in the morning."

Beatings and torture were followed by outright murders, particularly between September 1943 and April 1944. One of the first homicides was that of Captain Felix Tropschuh at Camp Concordia, Kansas, who had criticized Hitler's philosophy in his diary which was read by Nazi thugs. On October 18, 1943, he was brought before a Nazi kangaroo court and condemned. Tropschuh was taken to a room where he was left with a rope and a chair, guards posted outside the door. The implication was clear. He was found hanging from a rafter the next morning, and his death was ruled a "suicide" by camp authorities.

On the night of November 4, 1943, Corporal Johann Kunze was summoned to a secret meeting in the mess hall at Camp Tonkawa, Oklahoma, where more than 200 prisoners were present. Kunze watched as the doors

Heinrich Himmler, ruthless director of the SS, dictated the fate of any defecting German prisoners-of-war—death.

10, 1945, the first foreign prisoners of war ever so punished in the U.S. The killers of twenty-four-year-old Corporal Hugo Krauss, however, escaped American justice altogether.

Krauss was born in Germany but lived with his migrated parents in New York from 1928 to 1939. He spoke English fluently and acted as an interpreter for the American commander at Camp Hearne, Texas. This fact alone condemned him in the eyes of veteran Nazis, who considered him a turncoat. The fact that his parents were naturalized American citizens and that Krauss openly expressed admiration for the American way of life, sealed his fate.

Nazi vengeance came on the night of December 17, 1943. According to one report "from six to ten men entered the compound [where Krauss and other 'protected' prisoners slept] through a hole they had cut in a wire fence . . . and invaded Krauss' barracks. He screamed for help but no one came to his aid. His barracks mates looked on while his skull was fractured, both arms were broken and his body was battered from head to foot." Five days later, Krauss died in the hospital. No one could identify the killers, who were never brought to trial.

In early January 1944, a similar fate befell Franz Kettner, a thirty-nine-year-old German private, who was hated by most of his fellow inmates simply because he was an Austrian. Moreover, when he refused to steal items from the camp storeroom, he was openly booed in the mess hall, then tried by a kangaroo court and condemned. Kettner was found dead

were barred and several Nazis rose to denounce him as a traitor. Gestapo agents impersonating soldiers who had been captured with Kunze stated that upon his capture he had given information to American G-2 inquisitors regarding secret installations in Hamburg that would have been useful in later Allied bombings of that city. Found guilty by a Gestapo tribunal, Kunze was grabbed by other prisoners and then beaten to death with clubs and broken milk bottles.

This blatant murder did not go unpunished. The five men responsible for Kunze's death, all hardened sergeants of the Afrika Korps, were identified and later tried for murder at Camp Gruber, Oklahoma. Found guilty, they were all executed on July in his bunk, his wrists slashed, on the night of January 11, 1944, his death ruled "a suicide."

So, too was that of Werner Dreschler, a young sailor in the German Navy who had arrived at Papago Park Camp, outside of Phoenix, Arizona. Within six hours of Dreschler's arrival at the camp on March 13, 1944, his body was found hanging from a rafter in a barracks latrine. Colonel A. H. Means thought the death suspicious and immediately launched a full-scale investigation. Dreschler had served aboard a U-boat and he and his fellow submariners had been captured. It was learned that the other submariners had tried Dreschler and condemned him because he had supplied American interrogators with information about his U-boat.

Dreschler was labeled by fellow crewmen "a dog who has broken his oath," and he was then beaten and strangled to death in his barracks by his fellow shipmates, who then strung him up in the washroom in an attempt to fob off his death as a suicide. When Means learned the identities of the seven U-boat men who had killed Dreschler, he ordered their court-martial. Dreschler's shipmates were not repentant. In fact, they bragged about how they had proudly meted out Nazi justice. All seven were condemned and were hanged by the U.S. Army on August 25, 1945, at the Disciplinary Barracks at Fort Leavenworth, Kansas.

A prisoner's military record stood for nothing, if he was thought to be an American sympathizer. Hans Geller, twenty-one, had an excellent war record as a German paratrooper. He had been wounded twice and decorated several times for battlefield heroism. His three older brothers, all German soldiers, had all been killed in action. Geller was a methodical, well-disciplined prisoner, but the fact that he fluently spoke and read English made him suspect among his fellow prisoners at Camp Chaffee, Arkansas. He also appeared to be too cooperative with American officers, and when he had two new German prisoners removed from a work detail because their Nazi politicking interfered with their duties, he was condemned to death by a kangaroo court.

On the night of March 25, 1944, a German officer, who was apparently friendly toward Geller, went to the door of his fellow inmate and told Geller that a new prisoner had arrived, one who was a native of Geller's home town of Sudern, Germany. Geller, thinking the man might have news of his parents, sought out this man in a dark barracks. He was met by a towering, murderous Nazi thug, Sergeant Edgar Menschner, who strangled Geller to death in a matter of seconds. Menschner was later identified, tried and condemned to hang. His death sentence was commuted by President Harry Truman on July 6, 1945, to twenty years imprisonment at the Disciplinary Barracks of Fort Leavenworth, Kansas.

The last known murder committed by Nazis against their fellow prisoners was that of twenty-four-year-old Corporal Horst Gunther who was found hanging from a lamppost near Camp

Gordon, Georgia, on April 6, 1944. Gunther was suspected of informing American officers of an impending work stoppage at his internment camp. Moreover, he was a lover of American jazz, which, in and of itself, was enough to condemn him in the eyes of diehard Nazis, who thought such music "degenerate" since it originated with the black race.

Gunther was tried and condemned by a kangaroo court, and two brutal German sergeants, Rudolf Straub and Erick Gauss, were assigned to execute Gunther. They wordlessly strangled him to death while five other prisoners looked on in horror. Two of these prisoners talked and both Straub and Gauss were arrested. Tried under courts-martial at Fort McPherson, Georgia, Straub, and Gauss were found guilty and condemned to hang. They were executed at Forth Leavenworth, Kansas, on July 14, 1945.

Though the official count of prisoners murdered by their fellow inmates during the war was seven, at least another hundred met a similar fate. (One report had 176 such victims during the war.) Evidence in these cases, however, was not substantial enough to prove homicide. Several prisoners were shot to death by guards as escapees after rushing the barbed wire fences of their compounds. These men did so in fear for their lives or after being ordered to do so by Nazi thugs. Though several prisoners saw another prisoner being thrown under the wheels of a moving passenger train near Camp Hearne, Texas, no one could be induced to testify against the perpetrators. The same held true at Camp Grant, Illinois, where a group of fanatical Nazis locked forty-two suspected anti-Nazis in their barracks and attempted to burn them to death by setting fire to the building.

Because of these murders and forced suicides, as well as the thousands of beatings and persecution of anti-Nazi German prisoners, camp officials began a slow process of separating the Nazi fanatics from those who appeared to seek "re-education." Any German prisoner asking for asylum from his fellow prisoners was eventually sent to a "safe camp." Three of these camps were Fort Devens, Massachusetts; Camp McCain, Mississippi; and Camp Campbell, Kentucky.

Many requesting safe camps were intellectuals who had been imprisoned in Germany before being conscripted into the German Army and were easily identified by U.S. intelligence. Those who volunteered themselves for transfer to the safe camps were ostensibly anti-Nazis, but they were thoroughly screened in the event that the self-styled camp Gestapo agents attempted to infiltrate these camps. The problem remained difficult. In the waggish words of one American camp officer: "About the only way to distinguish a Nazi from an anti-Nazi is when you see a man being pursued by a crowd of fifty others who are howling for murder, you can be sure that the man who is running is an anti-Nazi."

Gestapo agents did manage to penetrate Fort Devens, four of them, who arrogantly presented themselves to the camp commander, announcing that they had obtained all the information they needed in order to report hundreds of "disloyal" Germans to Nazi officials in other camps for later reprisal. These four agents then asked to be reassigned to "Nazi" camps. The camp commander was too shrewd to release these terrorists, ordering them to remain at Devens where they were "well-subdued by the anti-Nazis."

Oddly, some American officers commanding internment camps felt that the anti-Nazis were a constant source of annoyance, that they were opposed to everything and, especially, that they maintained very little discipline and that discipline in the camps controlled by the Nazis was far superior. Those in the anti-Nazi camps were faced with the dim prospect of retribution following the war. Their names had been recorded and, following repatriation after hostilities, they would return to a Germany hostile to them, or so they all envisioned.

This was really not the case. The Germany to which they returned was in ruins and almost all anti-Nazis were given jobs of authority by the occupying Allied forces. It was this segment of the German POWs that fared well, not the fanatical followers of Adolf Hitler, who found themselves to be social paraiahs in a new Germany that wanted nothing more to do with Nazis and world conquest. The terror they had inflicted on their fellow prisoners-of-war came to haunt them as they were thought to be war criminals. At best, they were given menial jobs, poor housing and limited opportunity to advance in civilian careers. The conscience of the new Germany dictated that these monsters be scrubbed clean from the national fabric. They were socially "deloused," then sent into oblivion.

Target Truman

President Harry Truman was an affable politician but a no-nonsense chief executive. Inheriting the presidency upon the death of Franklin D. Roosevelt in 1944, Truman aggressively pursued an end to World War II, ordering the two atomic bombs dropped on Hiroshima and Nagasaki, which collapsed Japan's once-fanatical will to win. Truman, however, was also the consummate Democrat, and his desire to see democracy spread throughout the world was unwavering. To that end he was a staunch friend of the new Jewish state of Israel; the U.S., under Truman's administration, being the first to recognize Israel as an independent and sovereign nation. It is therefore puzzling to realize that Jewish elements in Palestine, before that recognition came, targeted Harry S. Truman for assassination.

The threat came from the Stern Gang, an ultra-right wing splinter group of the Jewish underground force known as the Irgun Zwei Leumi. The terrorist Stern Gang was originally led by Abraham Stern, a Zionist zealot who had been born in Poland in 1907. After traveling through several wars and revolutions, the fifteen-year-old Stern reached Palestine in

1922. He enrolled in the Hebrew University and joined the underground organization called Haganah. A secret home guard designed to protect Israeli settlers against oppressive Arabs when the British could not or would not (Palestine then being a British protectorate), the illegally armed members of the Haganah fought off Arab raids and established an intelligence system within Arab territories that warned against future attacks.

This was insufficient for the aggressive Stern. He had won a scholarship to Florence, Italy, where, at the age of twenty-one, he grew to admire the tactics of dictator Benito Mussolini. Upon his return to Israel, Stern bristled at the Haganah's refusal to enact reprisals against Arab attacks. He formed a group of tough, uncompromising commandos known as the Revisionists, which eventually evolved into the Stern Gang, which was loosely connected with the more militant Jewish underground group, the Irgun.

Shortly before World War II, in 1939, Stern went to Poland where he procured arms and ammunition for his group. When he returned to the Palestine, he launched an all-out attack against Arab and British factions. The attacks involved lightning raids into Arab strongholds and British camps where adversaries were mowed down by Stern Gang machine gunners.

Stern and his men became bomb experts and planted and detonated explosives in the camps of the enemy. Though the Irgun tacitly endorsed the activities of the Stern Gang, the more conciliatory Haganah disavowed them. The attacks continued long after Stern himself was shot and killed by a British police officer in February 1942.

Following WW II, the Stern Gang increased its terrorist campaign in an effort to force British authorities and their allies into recognizing Jewish independence. In June 1947, Stern Gang members constructed sophisticated mail bombs and sent eight of these to British officials, including Foreign Secretary Ernest Bevin and former Foreign Secretary Anthony Eden. Suspicious British police carefully opened one of the small packages, a cream-colored envelope eight by six inches. Inside of this was a smaller envelope marked "Private & Confidential."

Inspecting this envelope, bomb experts found powdered gelignite, a pencil battery, and a small detonator rigged to explode the gelignite when the envelope was opened. Although British politicians escaped injury from the Stern Gang mail bombs, one British citizen did not. On May 3, 1948, a package was received at a home in Wolverhampton, addressed to Captain Roy Alexander Farran. The home was that of Farran's parents.

His brother, twenty-five-year-old Rex Francis Farran, opened the package to find a deluxe edition of Shakespeare's plays. When he lifted the cover, the book, packed with explosives, blew up, devastating the Farran cottage and mortally wounding Rex Farran, who died of his wounds two days later.

Captain Farran, who was then vacationing in Scotland, knew that Jewish terrorists intended to murder him ever since he left Palestine, where he had served with the British police. He had been removed from his duties after being charged with murdering a Jewish youth named Alexander Rubowitz. Court-martialed, but acquitted, Farran was relieved and sent back to England. Before departing Palestine, he was repeatedly warned by members of the Stern Gang that he would pay for the killing of Rubowitz. One note he received read: "We will follow you to the end of the world."

Bomb experts carefully examined the debris in the shattered cottage and determined that explosives had been placed in the hollowed-out pages of the book, attached to a trigger mechanism that set off the explosives once the front cover of the book was lifted. Rex Farran's death was attributed to Jewish terrorists and at the top of the suspected groups was the Stern Gang, although the actual killers were never identified.

British experts concluded that each bomb was powerful enough to kill or, at least, maim anyone opening one of the envelopes. When, a few weeks later, a number of these same type of envelopes arrived at the White House,

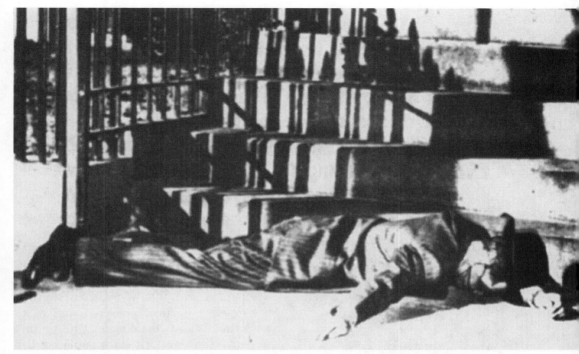

Oscar Collazo, Puerto Rican nationalist and would-be assassin of President Harry Truman, lies wounded and bleeding at the steps of Blair House in Washington, D.C., November 1, 1950.

one addressed to Truman, officials in the White House mail room, previously alerted by British officials, turned the small packages over to U.S. Army bomb experts who defused all of the bombs.

This had not been the first time Harry Truman had been marked for assassination by terrorists. A year earlier, Secret Service agents learned that the president would be shot by a sharpshooter armed with a high-powered rifle as he crossed the field at the Army-Navy football game. It is customary for the president to sit on one side, with Army, in the first half of the game and then ceremoniously cross the field to sit with the Navy in the second half of the game.

Told of this threat, Truman said he would attend the game and cross the field at half-time, come what may. Frustrated, the Secret Service pressed every man into duty, stationing agents at every conceivable vantage point in the stadium where a rifleman might take up a hidden position. When Truman crossed that field, he was flanked by Secret Service agents filled with anxiety, especially when Truman leisurely strolled to the other side and boldly took off his hat and waved it at the cheering crowds as he smilingly walked through the turf, almost as a signal to any hidden marksman that he was daring him to fire that fatal shot. It never came. As one retired Secret Service agent of Irish descent later told the author: "That boyo had guts!"

Actor Sal Mineo portrays a terrorist in the 1960 film Exodus, *a member of a right-wing group that is based upon the notorious Stern Gang, which sent bombs to British officials and to the White House in hopes of killing President Truman.*

Truman's fortitude was as much in evidence on November 1, 1950, the day he was scheduled to be assassinated by the Independence Party of Puerto Rico, a small faction of fanatics who thought to kill American officials in an effort to intimidate the U.S. into granting the commonwealth full independence. Oddly, Truman had, for years, urged Congress to do exactly that.

As early as October 16, 1945, Truman had told Congress: "It is now time, in my opinion, to ascertain from the people of Puerto Rico their wishes as to the ultimate status which they prefer and within such limits as may be determined by Congress to grant to them the kind of government they desire." Truman did not exclude the possibility of complete independence.

The president went further on February 20, 1948, when, during a visit to San Juan, he stated: "The Puerto Rican people should have the right to determine for themselves Puerto Rico's political relationship to the United States." Because of Truman's strong urging, Congress passed laws that allowed Puerto Rico to elect its own governor and other officials and create a constitution that gave the Puerto Rican people control over local affairs.

As a result, the Popular Democratic Party led by Munoz Marin, which favored commonwealth status, and the Statehood Party, which wanted Puerto Rico to become the forty-ninth state, overwhelmed the Independence Party at the polls. The *Independistas*, who made up a tiny fraction of Puerto Rico's population, nevertheless went on a terrorist rampage, shooting and kidnapping local officials and setting off bombs through the island.

Two fanatical *Independistas* living in New York, Griselio Torresola and Oscar Collazo, decided that they would kill President Truman and that this assassination would somehow compel the U.S. into overturning the will of the Puerto Rican electorate and bringing about total independence. Born in Puerto Rico in 1914, Collazo automatically became a U.S. citizen when he was three under the Jones Act. At the age of seventeen, he went to New York, where he worked at a number of unskilled jobs.

Collazo met and married Rosa Mercado who had two daughters from a previous marriage. The family moved to the Bronx where Collazo continued to work at menial jobs. Embittered by his inability to make more money and encouraged by his politically active wife, he joined the *Independistas*. After obtaining a job as a metal polisher, Collazo became a union leader in the factory where he worked. He also became one of the leaders of the *Independistas* in the U.S.

In 1948, Griselio Torresola arrived in the U.S., moving to the Bronx so he could be close to Collazo. Little is known about Torresola, except that he was born in Puerto Rico in 1925, and that he was a fanatical *Independista* who had participated in many terrorist activities in Puerto Rico. Authorities later learned that Torresola was an *Independista* assassin whose job it was to organize the assassination of President Truman. To that end, he directly involved Collazo, who enthusiastically embraced the plan such as it was. The pair did not move, however, until late October 1950, when they traveled to Washington, D.C. Both took hotel rooms, checking in with guns and ammunition hidden in their suitcases.

The assassins had not been thorough in their research of Truman's schedules. They had originally thought to somehow invade the White House and shoot the president in his office or in his bed, indescriminately killing any Secret Service man, presidential guard, white house staffer, or even family members, if need be. They were surprised to learn upon their arrival that Truman and his family were not staying at the White House, which was then under renovation.

The president was living at Blair House, which fronted on Pennsylvania Avenue, separated from the street by only a thin strip of grass. The house itself fronted directly onto the sidewalk and it was a Secret Service man's nightmare. The Service did its best to provide maximum security, stationing guards in booths at the west and east ends of the house. Secret Service agents were inside the house and a White House policeman guarded the front steps.

Torresola and Collazo decided to simply blast their way into Blair House, seek out the president and shoot him dead. It was a suicide mission, both agreed, but their fanatical beliefs overrode any consideration of survival. About 2 P.M., on November 1, 1950, both men approached the front entrance of Blair House from opposite directions. White House policeman Donald T. Birdzell was guarding the entrance to the front door. When he heard a faint click, he turned to see a man standing only eight feet away. It was Collazo, aiming a Walther P-38 automatic pistol at him.

The gun first misfired, but when Collazo pulled the trigger a second time, a bullet ploughed into Birdzell's right leg. The guard made a grab for his own pistol as he staggered out into Pennsylvania Avenue. Collazo bolted up the steps. The front door was wide open and only a screen door with a light latch on it was between him and the interior of Blair House. "The guards in the east booth were, thank God, on the alert," Margaret Truman later recalled. These were Joe Davidson and Floyd Boring, who began shooting at Collazo, as did the wounded Birdzell.

Collazo reached the second step before bullets cut him down. He fell to the bottom of the stairs, still clutching his weapon. He tried to rise, and Private Leslie Coffelt, a guard in the west booth, shot him in the chest. Meanwhile, Torresola, who had hidden behind a hedge in front of the building, began firing rapidly at Birdzell, hitting him in the left knee and toppling him to the pavement.

Coffelt returned Torresola's fire, as did the other guards. Torresola turned to Coffelt and fired twice at him. The bullets struck the guard in the chest and abdomen. Though dying, the heroic Coffelt managed to get off one more shot, a bullet that struck Torresola square in the forehead and killed him instantly. Coffelt collapsed and would die three and a half hours later in the hospital. Twenty-seven bullets had been fired during the hectic three-minute gun battle.

At the moment the gun battle began, Truman and his wife, Bess, were dressing to attend the dedication of a statue of British Field Marshal Sir John Dill, who had been a member of the World War II Combined Chiefs of Staff. Bess Truman, hearing the shots, went to a window facing Pennsylvania Avenue and saw Birdzell lying in the street, blood streaming from his leg wounds. She gasped and said to her husband: "Harry—someone's shooting our policemen!"

While gunfire was still being exchanged with Torresola, President Truman ran to the window, pushing his wife away. He stuck his head out the window. At that moment, several Secret Service agents had rushed from Blair House into the street, guns drawn. Torresola was at that second a dead man, collapsing into the hedge.

One of the Secret Service men looked up to see Truman and shouted to him: "Get back! Get back!"

Truman obeyed quickly. He finished dressing, then hurried downstairs to confer with aides who told him that there had been only two assailants, one dead, the other wounded and on his way to the hospital. Truman decided he would attend the ceremonies for Dill. Within minutes, panicky rumors spread throughout Washington that the president and seven Secret Service agents had been killed. A short time later, a very much alive Harry and Bess Truman arrived at Arlington Cemetery for the statue ceremonies. When an official next to Truman learned of the attempted assassination, he immediately suggested that the president go to a safe house. Truman waved away the idea, saying quietly: "A President has to expect these things."

A search of Torresola's clothing produced a letter to him from Pedro Albizu Campos, leader of the Puerto Rican Nationalist Party (the *Independista* party). The letter spoke of the possibility of Torresola assuming the leadership of the party in the U.S., with the clear implication that this might occur if his mission was successfully accomplished.

Collazo, meanwhile, removed to a hospital with the other injured men, talked freely with investigators, confessing his plot to murder the president as a way of drawing attention to his cause for Puerto Rican independence. He admitted that he and Torresola had poorly planned their raid and did not even know if Truman was inside Blair House when they made their attack. They had not even consulted a newspaper to track Truman's movements. Had they done so, they would have learned of the president's trip to Arlington that day. It was shudderingly realized by the Secret Service that if the two assassins had learned of that trip, they could have easily shot Truman as he left Blair House or at Arlington and killed the president at the cemetery where he would have been out in the open for a prolonged period.

Promptly arrested, Collazo was indicted on three charges: the murder of Coffelt, assault with intent to kill two guards, and intent to kill the president. Rosa Collazo was also arrested and charged with complicity but was later released. In March 1951, Collazo was found guilty of Coffelt's murder, and he was sentenced to die in the electric chair on August 1, 1952. Though he declined his right to plead for clemency, on July 24, 1952, President Truman commuted Collazo's sentence to life imprisonment. Truman's announcement came just one day before Puerto Rico became a "free commonwealth." In September 1979, President Jimmy Carter granted clemency to Collazo and three other Puerto Ricans convicted on an armed attack on the House of Representatives in 1954. Carter gave "humanitarian reasons," as the motivation for his act.

New York's Mad Bomber

On March 29, 1950, seven months before the abortive attack on Blair House and President Truman's life, New York City's Grand Central Station was suddenly swarming with police as explosives experts, tipped by a threatening note, frantically searched for a hidden bomb. The bomb squad detonated the bomb before it could do any damage. A month later, another bomb was found in a phone booth near the New York Public Library and still another at the Grand Hotel. Three more duds were found in short order but the bomb experts admitted that each deadly device was more powerful than the last. The creator of these bombs was well known to authorities. He had been terrorizing New York for a decade and was known as the "Mad Bomber."

Authorities searched frantically for the faceless terrorist who monitored their movements through fear-peddling newspaper reports. This was George Peter Metesky, a short, fat man with thin hair. He wore gold-rimmed glasses that gave him a harmless, myopic appearance. Metesky seethed with hatred for a corporate enemy, his one-time employer, Consolidated Edison. Working as a wiper at Con

Ed's Hell Gate plant, he was stunned on September 5, 1931, when a blast of hot, noxious gasses threw him to the ground.

Examing doctors found nothing wrong with Metesky, although he continued to complain that serious and constant headaches prevented him from working regularly. He hotly pursued disability payments, but the company turned him down flat. For nine years, Metesky raged at Consolidated Edison but got nowhere. Then, on November 16, 1940, he decided to strike back by terrorizing the city of New York, which he had somehow come to view as the symbol of the utility firm that had ruined his life.

On that day the police bomb squad found a pipe bomb Metesky had made and planted in the Edison Building on West Sixty-Fourth Street in Manhattan. The crude device had been placed inside a tool box, along with a note reading: "Con Edison crooks, this is for you." This was the first of thirty-seven bombs Metesky was to plant over the next sixteen years at scattered sites throughout Manhattan. The second bomb was recovered at a location on Nineteenth Street, Manhattan, in September 1941. Though more powerful than the first, this bomb proved to be a dud.

Police expected a series of planted bombs in the near future but were surprised to receive in December 1941 a note from the "Mad Bomber," as the terrorist was described by the press, one which exemplified his strange patriotism. "I will make no more bomb units for the duration of the war," wrote Metesky. "My patriotic feelings have made me decide this—later I will bring the Con Edison to justice—they will pay for their dastardly deeds." It was signed "F.P.," which investigators later discovered stood for "Fair Play."

George Peter Metesky, right, under arrest and en route to court to face charges of planting dozens of bombs in New York City for more than a decade. He went to an asylum.

Throughout the war, however, Metesky did not remain inactive. He sent a series of letters to theaters, restaurants and newspapers, promising to make the City of New York suffer. Not until 1950, however, did he again act, placing the bombs at the Grand Central Station and in other locations. Four years passed before Metesky placed a bomb beneath Radio City Music Hall in 1954. This device exploded, seriously injuring two persons and causing extensive damage.

In 1955, Metesky planted six bombs throughout New York, four of these exploding. A bomb planted in Grand Central Station seriously injured a redcap. Other targets the terrorist chose were all high-visibility locations—Macy's Department Store, the Radio Company of America, and the Paramount Theatre in Brooklyn. Police conducted a widespread manhunt for Metesky, even establishing a special squad to track him down, but they came up empty.

At one point, police asked James A. Brussel, assistant commissioner of mental health for the state of New York, to provide a pyschological profile of the suspect. Brussel studied the string of bombings and the notes from the terrorist calling himself "F.P." He then reported that the suspect was a paranoid and that he was of Slavic origin, explaining that these people had had a long history of such terrorist bombings. Brussel then added: "When you find this man, he will be wearing a double-breasted suit."

What bothered police most was the fact that the terrorist was improving his techniques. Each one of his newly planted bombs proved to be more powerful and more sophisticated than the last, as was the device Metesky planted on the Staten Island Ferry which injured several persons and demolished the interior of the boat. The special investigative unit searching for Metesky ran down hundreds of leads and took countless suspects into custody. It all came to nothing.

It remained for a Consolidated Edison team headed by Alice Kelly to finally pinpoint Metesky as the "Mad Bomber." Examining thousands of employee files, Kelly and others determined that the most serious malcontent among ex-employees was George Peter Metesky. Police found the meek-looking Metesky in Water-bury, Connecticut, at the home of his spinster sisters, where he had been living.

When he answered the door, Metesky glared at officers for a moment, then gave them a sheepish smile and said: "I think I know why you fellows are here." Inviting them inside, he said without a quaver in his voice: "You think I'm the Mad Bomber." He then dressed in a pinstripe, double-breasted suit and accompanied detectives to headquarters. In April 1957, the fifty-four-year-old Metesky was found of unsound mind by Judge Samuel Leibowitz, who ordered him confined in a mental institution.

Metesky spent the next sixteen years in various mental facilities before earning a final release from custody on December 13, 1973. At the time, the man who had terrorized New York for almost two decades met briefly with newspapermen and gave them a wide smile. "I don't look like a Mad Bomber, do I?" he asked before stepping into a car that took him home to his elderly sisters. "That guy's right out of *Arsenic and Old Lace*," quipped one newsman. "The character Jonathan, the monster brother, fooling around in the basement and making plans you don't want to hear about."

·SIX·
OTHER WORLD TERRORISTS

The Mau Mau of Kenya

1950

One of the most feared secret criminal societies in Africa was Mau Mau, a blood-thirsty terrorist organization that sought to oust European settlers from the native lands of British-controlled Kenya at any price, including torture, beating and mass murder. In the 1950s, Mau Mau terrorists oppressed both white settlers and blacks who refused to join the secret society.

The land the Mau Mau sought was the vast and fertile Highland region bounded by Mount Kenya, Nairobi (the nation's capital), the Aberdare Mountains, and Nyeri, where the huge Kikuyu tribe had dwelled since the sixteenth century. The Highland region itself had been the traditional and ancestral home of the smaller Wanderobo tribe of hunter-gatherers and some of its members owned as much as forty square miles of land.

Though the Kikuyu tribe had the numbers and strength to take the region by force, their religious beliefs and legal customs prevented such land-grabbing. Consequently, Kikuyus who wanted land negotiated for it by bartering animals or other goods. The Kikuyu would also propose a ceremony of "mutual adoption," which, by making the Wanderobo an adopted Kikuyu, validated the transaction.

Most of the Highland region was inhabited by Kikuyu farm families, and the tribe proliferated in blossoming settlements at Nyeri, Muranga, and the Kiambu district by the late nineteenth century. In the 1890s, however, the area was beset by a number of calamities, including a smallpox epidemic, an outbreak of rinderpest, a locust plague, and then several years of drought that brought famine and widespread death. Between 20 and 50 percent of the Kikuyu population died. Survivors abandoned their farms and moved to Nyeri and Fort Hall.

Though most of their farms had reverted to the bush, former displaced owners still considered themselves the rightful owners of the land and that their displacement was only a temporary condition. The Kenya-Uganda Railroad disputed such claims. Begun in 1896, the railroad reached the Highland region in 1902, bringing with it trains packed with European settlers.

Viewing the region as virgin land, the European colonists began dividing the area into farms. Where Kikuyus were still present on farms, the Europeans simply purchased the land. Kikuyus selling the land, however, believed they were renting it and that they still retained ownership. This misunderstanding was greatly compounded by the ignorance of both Kikuyus and British settlers for each other's laws and customs.

British settlers assumed that, since no other African tribes with whom they had had experience ever owned any lands, the Kikuyus had no actual legal claim to the fertile fields of the Highland region. All uncultivated land was set aside by the British as "Crown Land," with the exception of areas called "Reserves" that were set aside for the native population.

The Kenya Civil Service agency had been set up to protect the interest of native Kenyans, but this agency better served white interests. Moreover, the British-controlled legislative council that ruled Kenya had ten representa-tives for the 10,000 white settlers of 1923 while having only one representative for the blacks, who numbered in the millions, and even that representative was not a black until 1944.

Following World War II, black ex-serviceman and mission-trained African nationalists attempted to reclaim tribal lands in the Highland region but were rebuffed. They revived the Kikuyu Central Association, the KCA, an organization begun in 1922, using this to lobby for the return of tribal lands. The KCA had been outlawed in 1940 and was revamped by Eliud Mathu as the Kenyan African Union, the KAU. The leader of this new movement was later to make his mark as one of Africa's most celebrated leaders, Jomo Kenyatta (Johnstone Kamau).

In 1946, Kenyatta returned from England after a sixteen-year exile (having been the secretary of the outlawed KCA in 1928). He was appointed principal of the Kenya Teacher's College in Githunguri. At the time, he offered his services to the legislative council, but Governor Sir Philip Mitchell refused, suggesting that Kenyatta study politics on the local level before seeking national recognition.

Instead, Kenyatta saw this as an opportunity to gain power through the KAU. He moved from village to village, recruiting members to the association and, in 1947, became its president. This position, however, gave Kenyatta no more power than that which was willed by the association's leaders. Kenyatta's will, however, dominated another group he formed during this period, a secret

Rock Hudson, with Dana Wynter at left, discover the hacked-up remains of a white planter in Kenya, the victim of Mau Mau terrorists, in the 1957 film, Something of Value.

organization called Mau Mau, a corruption of the phrase "*Uma Uma*," meaning "Out! Out!"

Mau Mau members were recruited ostensibly to the KAU but were in reality given the secret organization's oath, called the Oath of Unity, *Ndemwa Ithatu*, administered in a ceremony incorporating many tribal rites. The first oath a Mau Mau inductee took was a pledge of his loyalty to the cause of restoring the Kikuyu's lands. The only specific requirement of this level of membership was a small donation to the organization's coffers (sixty-two shillings and fifty cents and a ram). Successive levels of membership were accompanied by different oaths requiring greater commitment. The most extreme level of membership demanded the *Batuni* Oath or Platoon Oath, which required the initiate to kill all enemies of Mau Mau, white or black.

This oath was the most solemn of Mau Mau vows. It was held while the initiate squatted naked in front of the

oath-giver. The initiate then had to thrust his penis into a hole made in the skinned thorax of a slain goat. While holding this bloody meat, the initiate vowed:

If I am called on to kill for our soil, if I am called on to shed my blood for it, I shall obey and I shall never surrender. I shall never betray our country or anybody of this movement to the enemy, whether the enemy be European or African. If I am called during the night or the day to burn the store of a European who is our enemy, I shall go forth without fear and I shall never surrender. If I am called to go to fight the enemy or to kill the enemy—I shall go even if the enemy be my father or mother, my brother or sister. If the people of the movement come to me by day or by night and if they ask me to hide them, I shall do so and I shall help them. I shall never take away the woman of another man, never walk with prostitutes, never steal anything belonging to another person in the movement, nor shall I hate any other member for his action. I shall never sell my country for money or for any other thing. I shall abide until my death by all the promises that I have made this day. I shall never disclose our secrets to our enemy or to anybody who does not belong to the movement and if I transgress against any of the vows that I have thus consciously made, I shall agree to any punishment that the movement shall decide to give me and if I fail to do these things, may this oath kill me.

By 1952, KAU was nothing but a shell used by Mau Mau, which had recruited thousands to its secret cause. Whites who learned of Mau Mau believed its aims to be the elimination of the white race in Kenya, the expulsion of all foreigners, the restoration of tribal customs and land ownership, the wiping out of Christianity, the ending of soil terracing, and the institution of secular education that would preach race hatred and other forms of xenophobic beliefs. The whites were not far from wrong.

As Mau Mau spread throughout Kenya, its oath-givers became more and more aggressive, forcing reluctant Kikuyu tribal members to swear secret allegiance to the organization. Some who refused were chopped to death with *pangas* (double-edged blades). In several instances, whole villages that showed reluctance to join Mau Mau were attacked by Mau Maus using arson as their terrorist weapon. The villages were burned to the ground by ruthless Mau Mau killers who waited until families had bedded down inside thatched huts before setting the inflammable buildings afire. When

the screaming inhabitants attempted to flee, including women and children, they were speared to death or slashed by Mau Mau thugs standing at the doorways.

Until 1948, British authorities were unaware of Mau Mau, and when they did learn of its existence, they learned little about the organization because of its highly secret nature. As the violence increased in Mau Mau recruitment, the government soon realized the danger involved in this new movement. An informer described to authorities the various oaths administered by Mau Mau and, to counteract and nullify the oaths among superstitious tribes, the government sent medicine men or witch doctors to the villages to remove the oath through witchcraft ceremonies.

This so enraged Mau Mau leaders that, on May 15, 1952, two Kikuyu who had cooperated with British authorities were seized, tortured, and then horribly murdered. Their mutilated bodies were found in the Kirichwa River near Nairobi. A black informer who found the bodies was himself murdered. Although six suspected Mau Mau members were arrested and brought to trial, the case collapsed for lack of evidence against them. Witnesses refused to testify after they had been told they would be killed should they defy Mau Mau.

This is what happened to scores of villagers who resisted Mau Mau on September 25, 1952. Three gangs of Mau Maus, numbering about fifteen terrorists in each gang, set fire to five farms in Timau, between Meru and Nanyuki. More than 120 cattle were killed or maimed and other herds wounded. Hundreds of sheep were slaughtered, the animals disemboweled.

Shortly before the government declared a State of Emergency on October 21, 1952, Mau Mau launched a massive recruitment campaign, sending its top-ranking members from Nairobi in cars and jeeps into the Reserves. These motorized "oathing" teams could perform sweeping Mau Mau initiation rites before government officials persuaded the naive tribes to reject the murderous society. Thus, Mau Mau was able to intimidate new members into supporting the organization's bloody ends. Some of the traveling "oathing" teams were able to recruit as many as 800 to 1,000 persons at a time.

Again, however, Kikuyus refused to join Mau Mau and a wholesale slaughter ensued. Hundreds were killed. Villages were burned and property was devastated by marauding Mau Maus. All of this greeted Sir Evelyn Baring, the new governor, upon his arrival in Nairobi. In fact, during his first inspection, he was horrified to hear that one of his own government officials had been assassinated by Mau Mau thugs in broad daylight. This was Senior Chief Waruhiu who was hacked to pieces on an open road.

Baring called in British troops, which arrived on October 20, 1952, on twelve RAF troop carriers. Reinforcements poured in to supplement the Lancaster Fusilers and other units that began sweeping the countryside in search of Mau Maus. Eighty-three

Kenyan leaders suspected of being Mau Mau organizers, including Jomo Kenyatta, were arrested and held for trial. The Mau Maus struck back in bloody reprisal, attacking government officials and white settlers. The Mau Maus were so bold as to conduct oathing sessions in front of Kenyan officers. Senior Chief Nderi, along with two police officers, approached a crowd that was taking the Mau Mau oath, and the mob turned on them, hacking Nderi to pieces with long blades.

White farmers barricaded themselves inside their large country houses and fought off Mau Mau attacks. Often, they ran out of ammunition and were overwhelmed before British troops could come to their aid. White men captured alive were savagely mutilated before being killed. Women were gang-raped and children were horribly butchered. (The killing of a white child, six-year-old Michael Ruck, caused widespread and passionate hatred for Mau Mau not only among the white settlers but among the majority of loyal blacks.) Eric Bowyer, an elderly European farmer, was slaughtered along with his two houseboys. So, too, was Commander Meiklejohn, a retired naval officer living at Thomson's Falls.

Blacks were also killed indescriminately. Nairobi City Councillor Tom Mbotela, a Luo tribesman and former vice president of KAU, was murdered on November 26, 1952. Mbotela had openly denounced Mau Mau, and he had given evidence against its leaders, including Jomo Kenyatta.

In some cases, Mau Mau members were servants inside white house-

While tribesmen look on, a Kenyan witch doctor delivers incantations intended to break the spell and secret oath of Mau Mau. Government officials used many such tribal witch doctors in combating Mau Mau terrorism in the early 1950s.

holds who betrayed their employers to the invading terrorists. One houseboy who had taken the Mau Mau oath only a few hours before his employer's rural home was attacked, slipped up behind his white employer and drove a blade into his back, then hacked off his head and, holding this gory trophy, ran screaming in murderous triumph to his fellow Mau Maus lurking in the dark beyond the house.

The white settlers and the loyal Kikuyu fought back, organizing the Kikuyu Home Guard, which worked with the African tribal police. By mid-January 1953, the Home Guard numbered more than 10,000. A few Mau Mau in their midst were quickly purged when they refused to denounce Mau Mau, a requirement for Home Guard membership.

Mau Mau fought back furiously, first attacking and capturing the police station at Naivashi on March 26, 1953, where all of the officers and their families were slaughtered. The Mau Maus looted the place of considerable arms and ammunition, and then mounted a huge attack against the village of Lari, which had remained loyal to the government and had provided a large number of Home Guard members.

The entire town was massacred by Mau Maus. When Home Guard troops arrived, they counted eighty-four bodies of men, women, and children, but many more residents were missing and it was thought that the Mau Maus had taken them hostage. (These victims were later found, several hundred, their bodies strewn over a distance of several miles.) Chief Luka, who had opposed Mau Mau, had been chopped to pieces, along with his eight wives. An escaping woman who had had her arm cut off at the joint, told how she had witnessed a drunken Mau Mau decapitate her baby and then watched in horror as the little corpse was passed from hand to hand by the terrorists who drank its blood. This woman survived to identify fifty Mau Maus, all neighbors she recognized. These men were taken into custody and later executed.

In April 1953, Kenyatta and five of his aides were found guilty of "managing Mau Mau." Kenyatta was sentenced to seven years in prison at hard labor. Other important Mau Mau leaders, however, remained at large, and the government went through the tedious task of identifying these men and tracking them down. The first of these fugitives to be captured was Waruhiu Itote. Born in 1922, Itote had

been a corporal in the King's African Rifles and later a fireman on the East African railway. He claimed that he had been forced to take the Mau Mau oath in 1951 but that he voluntarily served as a spokesman for KAU at public meetings and as an executioner at secret Mau Mau sessions. He had assumed command of Mau Maus on Mount Kenya and had promoted himself to the rank of "General China."

Helping to snare Itote was a clever Kenyan-born Englishman, Ian Henderson, who knew well the culture, history and traditions of the Kikuyus. The twenty-seven-year-old Henderson was assistant superintendent of police. He talked with Itote for three days and finally persuaded "General China" to return to Mount Kenya and arrange the surrender of more than 5,000 Mau Maus camped on the slopes. Henderson, through his Kikuyu contacts, was able to provide British authorities with intelligence about Mau Mau activities. Through this intelligence, Henderson and others were able to identify and convert group after group of Mau Maus, using them to convert or capture their fellow Mau Maus.

In May 1955, Kikuyu police teams, each accompanied by ex–Mau Maus, flushed out and killed twenty-four of the fifty-one top Mau Mau leaders. Finally, on October 26, 1956, the last important Mau Mau leader, Dedan Kimathi, was captured. Kimathi had been the most ruthless of Mau Mau leaders, having ordered almost all of the most brutal attacks and massacres. Kimathi, born in 1920, had been blessed by his dying grandmother on her deathbed, a sign, he later insisted, that meant he was to rule all of the Kikuyus. He was clever, and, as a child, he stole from the old man who had sponsored him and sent him to school. He was driven from the village and later repaid his benefactor by sending Mau Mau thugs to kill him.

Kimathi began as an enforcer at KAU meetings and was later promoted to secretary. He took the Mau Mau oath in 1952 and became the chief oath-giver. It was Kimathi who was giving the oath to the group of Kikuyus when Officer Nderi approached him, and it was Kimathi who had hacked this official to death. Though captured after this murder, Kimathi escaped, bribing a jail guard with a stolen bicycle.

Fleeing to the Aberdare forests, he organized Mau Mau actions and, holding up the Bible he had stolen from his benefactor years earlier, announced that the good book had revealed him to be the reincarnation of Abraham, Moses, and the Messiah. Those who appeared to challenge his authority were sent on impossible suicide missions. If they returned, they were killed and their bodies "left to the hyenas." It was Henderson who tracked Kimathi through the Aberdare forests and finally captured him on October 26, 1956. He was quickly tried and convicted of mass murder. Upon his execution, the spirit of the militant Mau Mau was broken.

A total of 10,527 Mau Maus had been killed by official count. An equal number of innocent and loyal Kikuyus had been murdered, and thirty-two white settlers had been killed

by Mau Mau members. Sir Patrick Renison, another new governor, officially proclaimed the end of the Emergency in January 1960. Between 1952 and 1956, the Mau Mau movement cost the British and Kenyan governments more than $154 million. The terrorists tied down eleven infantry battalions and more than 21,000 police officers before the State of Emergency was recalled.

This was not the end to Mau Mau, however. The organization continued to survive and administer oaths into the 1960s. In hopes of driving out white settlers once and for all, Mau Mau activity increased dramatically in 1963, just before Kenya's independence was announced. To no one's surprise, Kenyatta, released by the British in 1961, became the country's first prime minister (1963–1964). It had been Kenyatta who had negotiated the terms of Kenya's independence at the London Conference in 1962. (He would go on to become the country's long-lasting president from 1964 until his death in 1978.)

Many former Mau Mau members were elected to seats in the National Assembly. Two separate periods of amnesty were declared in order to reclaim Mau Mau members. Those who did come forward to take advantage of this amnesty, as well as one offered in 1964, proved to be a great disappointment to their leaders. Instead of occupying the farms assigned to them, they returned to the forests and jungles. The failure of Kenyatta to reintegrate his former Mau Mau members into mainstream Kenyan society emphasized the death of the criminal secret society. Mau Mau in Kenya was no more.

A strange and bloody footnote to Mau Mau was written in Chicago almost two decades later when a black gang of terrorists calling itself De Mau Mau ran amuck, slaying two white families and others in 1972. The gang was made up of embittered Vietnam War veterans whom Cook County Sheriff Richard J. Elrod referred to as "gang leaders and triggermen."

This group of young black men attended Malcolm X University on Chicago's West Side. There they terrorized students and faculty alike. They challenged and threatened teachers, white and black, who disagreed with their views. They beat up dozens of students who refused to either join their group or pay them homage. The gang members said their group was called De Mau Mau, a black activist group that had taken its name from the secret terrorist society in Kenya of the 1950s, but they never specified their political beliefs or aims. All were expelled in spring of 1972. School president Charles G. Hurst, Jr., described the gang members as "desperate men venting their frustration." He added: "There never seemed to be a motivation to their violence."

The terror gang exploded on the night of August 4, 1972, driving through the western suburbs of Chicago and committing random murders. The De Mau Maus invaded the Barrington Hills home of insurance executive Paul Corbett, shooting and stabbing everyone in the house— Corbett, his wife, stepdaughter, and sister-in-law. They drove on to Monee,

Illinois, where they murdered Stephen Hawtree and two members of his family. Next, in Highland Park, the group slew William Richter, an army specialist. Driving to West Frankfort, the gang murdered Michael Gerchenson.

Police had little difficulty in tracking down the terrorists. Witnesses gave authorities the license number of their car. Once in custody, six gang members—Reuben Taylor, 22; his brother Donald Taylor, 21; Michael Clark, 21; Nathaniel Burse, 23; Edward Moran, Jr., 23; and Robert Wilson, 18—were charged with murder.

Tried in the courtroom of Associate Judge Paul D. Caesar, four of the gang members—Clark, the two Taylor brothers, and Burse—entered the circuit court building, swearing at reporters and TV camera crews. A report had it that fellow terrorists would attempt to shoot up the courtroom in an effort to free the De Mau Maus, which prompted a search for concealed weapons of everyone entering the courtroom. Angry at delays and at cameramen taking his picture, Clark shouted to a deputy sheriff: "What the hell's going on? Richard Speck [a notorious mass murderer] didn't get as much publicity as this."

Arrogant and smug, Donald Taylor suggested that the gang "sing a song for the pigs," and all four rendered a screaming, bone-chilling chorus of "God Bless America." Reuben Taylor then asked a deputy for marijuana in payment for the song. On November 10, 1972, all four pleaded not guilty to charges of murdering the Corbett family when arraigned before Judge

Richard J. Fitzgerald.

Moran and Burse never went to trial. They were found dead in their cells in the Lake County, Illinois, jail; they had been strangled to death, but their killers were never identified. It was reported that other De Mau Mau gang members killed them when learning that they might testify against them.

On October 10, 1974, Clark and the Taylor brothers were found guilty of murdering the Corbetts. Waiting in a holding cell before being sentenced, one of the Taylor brothers grew nervous, believing that he was about to be sentenced to death. "What are you worrying about," chanted the cold-blooded Clark. "You know what's going to happen to us—the same thing that happened to Speck, nothing!" (Speck, killer of eight Chicago nurses in 1966, had received life imprisonment after the U.S. Supreme Court abolished capital punishment.) Donald Taylor and Michael Clark were given 150 to 200 years in prison; Reuben Taylor and Robert Wilson were given 100 to 150 years. The De Mau Mau terror gang, like its more potent predecessor, ceased to exist as the killers went behind bars for life.

Triad Terrorism

Where Mau Mau was a fleeting and bloody moment in the long, dark history of Africa, the Triad Society was an ancient secret organization, which, like the Mafia, was corrupted from a once patriotic movement to a criminal organization whose chief weapon was terror. The Triads were actually made up of many Chinese sects, also known as the Dagger Society, Heaven & Earth Society, Hung Society, and Red Society. They came into existence during the late seventeenth century as organizations designed to overthrow the oppressive yoke of the Ch'ing emperors.

Triad leaders backed many coups and rebellions against the corrupt Chinese dynasties but always fell short of gaining total power. The Society's members infested the Boxers, who ostensibly rebelled against the last Chinese dynasty but were really under the direction of the empress, who attempted to oust the European communities that had seized power in China in 1900. The Boxers and the dynasty all but collapsed when a powerful multinational European army came to the relief of Boxer-besieged foreign legations in Peking on August 14, 1900.

Sun Yat-sen, himself a Triad member, came to power in China in 1911, dissolving the dynasties. He recognized the Triads at the time, which caused a wave of bureaucrats and politicians to join the Society to enhance their prestige and reputation in the new Republican government. Soon the Triads had spread their influence and control of opium, their chief source of income, to Malaya, Singapore, and Hong Kong. Triad chiefs directed all criminal pursuits in China and throughout Southeast Asia, organizing widespread prostitution, gambling, drug taking and any other vices and illegal operations from which lucrative profits could be drawn.

Triad influence became so powerful that people were forced to take the oath to the Society in order to keep their jobs, down to the most menial laborer or rickshaw runner who paid 17¢ a month in Triad dues. In Hong Kong, criminal pursuits of the Triads increased dramatically after the Japanese invasion of 1941. Prior to that time, only about 8 percent of the population belonged to the Society. Within fifteen years, that percentage doubled.

The occupying Japanese did much to encourage the Triads, secretly working with them in an effort to prevent sabotage and subversion. In return, the Triads were given free hand in controlling all criminal pursuits, paying large monthly tributes to their Japanese commanders. It was the same in Singapore and those areas of mainland China occupied by Japanese troops.

When Japan was defeated in World War II, China underwent civil war, with the Communists driving Chiang Kai-shek's Nationalist forces to the sea and onto the island of Taiwan. Tens of thousands of mainland refugees streamed into Hong Kong, and awaiting them were members of the Triad known as the Green Pang, who enlisted these naive Chinese with the promise of work, housing, and education for their children. Instead, these hapless refugees were forced into criminal pursuits, their daughters dragged into white slavery, their sons driven into drug peddling.

The Green Pang Triad, which had fought with the Nationalists, soon dominated the labor forces in Hong Kong, as well as the distribution of all narcotics and the supervision of gambling and prostitution. It also operated a protection racket in which shopkeepers were extorted of a deep percentage of their weekly profits under the threat of being burned out of business, an extortion racket that is widely practiced by the Triads today throughout East Asia. The Green Pang, however, concentrated its efforts more with the rich than with the poor. More than 600,000 refugees squatting in Hong Kong's shanty towns had brought from mainland China their own Triad, which was known as the 14K Association.

Posing as anti-Communist organizations, the Triads in Hong Kong energetically recruited new members so as to meet the challenge of power each Triad posed to another. To be admitted into a Triad carried with it a heavy obligation, the penalty of death imposed upon members who violated the tenets of the secret, oath-bound brotherhood. (Today, there are thirty-six oaths a new member must swear.) Those who refused to join the Triads were branded as pro-Communist, a tactic encouraged by government leaders.

By the mid-1950s, the Triads in southwestern Asia were all-powerful, their influence and operations unchallenged by local governments. At his citadel in Taiwan, Generalissimo Chiang Kai-shek thought to use the Triads to expand his power and, hopefully, gain enough support to reinvade and recapture mainland China for the cause of nationalism. He was, no doubt, the inspiration for the raising of Nationalist Chinese flags over the huge refugee center in Hong Kong on October 10, 1956.

This act violated a police mandate in Hong Kong that proscribed either Chinese government from raising its flag in the neutral British colony. When the police tore down the flags, thousands of Triad members rioted, taking to the streets and challenging the police. The bloody riots went on for two days, turning the district of Kowloon into a battle zone.

British citizens and other Europeans were warned to steer clear of the area, but Swiss chancellor Fritz Ernst and his wife, Ursula Marguerita Ernst, ignored the order, driving into the middle of the mob. Thinking that his diplomatic immunity would somehow protect him, Ernst had a quick lesson in mob violence. His car was turned over by Triad thugs who set it afire. Ernst escaped with severe burns, but his wife was not so fortunate; she was killed.

The rampaging Triad members pillaged more than $25 million in goods during the riots and committed many murders. The mass arrests that followed revealed to authorities just how deeply Triad influence and power ran and shocked public opinion into pressuring authorities to put the Triads in check. Yet, only four Triad members were actually convicted and executed for the Kowloon Riots of 1956. Moreover, Hong Kong, with its three million residents in 1958, continued to pay tribute to the Triads, about $40 million a year. Everyone paid, from shoe-shine boys to rickshaw coolies, from dancehall girls to prostitutes, from restaurant owners to hotel keepers. The Triads made money from black market goods of all kinds, including theater and sports tickets.

As authorities brought increasing pressure to root out Triad members in Hong Kong, the secret sect increased its terrorist activities. In 1958 alone, Triad thugs murdered more than 800 persons, many of these being government officials and policemen. In September 1958 alone, police record-ed 350 killings that they attributed to the Triads. A typical victim was a prosperous merchant named Ko Sun Wei, who lived in the Kowloon district. He had resisted paying tribute to the Triads, who sent squads of killers to invade his premises. Wei, two daughters, one son and his wife were found dead in their home. The women had been raped repeatedly and then tortured to death with knives.

Despite a constant battle to identify Triad leaders and disrupt the Society by British authorities, the sects not only survived but flourished. In Singapore alone, there were thousands of active Triad members belonging to nine different sects, all cooperating to run that city's criminal activities, and collecting millions in tribute. In recent years, the Triads moved into Hawaii and recruited Chinese-Americans into the Society by the thousands. By the late 1980s, Triad activity spread throughout the West Coast of the U.S. and Canada. In southern California, Triad members concentrated on the stealing of expensive foreign-made cars—Mercedes-Benz, BMW, Rolls Royce—boldly taking these autos from restaurant parking lots or even stopping motorists on streets and freeways, randomly shooting them, and fleeing with the cars. These autos were then driven to Long Beach and other California ports where they were quickly loaded onto ships sailing for China and other East Asian ports, where they were instantly sold for five and six times their original cost.

Voodoo and the Ton Ton Macoutes

At the time the Triads of Hong Kong discarded their secret ways to wage open warfare, a smooth-talking, clever little man named Francois Duvalier came to power in poverty-stricken Haiti. Elected president in 1957, Duvalier was a trained doctor who had worked in a U.S. medical aid program before turning to politics. He was known to his followers as "Papa Doc" Duvalier.

Duvalier's naive followers were thrilled to have a leader who described himself as a medicine man and a skilled witch doctor with roots that ran deep into the black magic of voodoo. Duvalier promised to share his wonderful powers with his followers, claiming to summon the devil to his bidding through witchcraft and black magic.

Duvalier had vowed to his supporters that he would use the millions of dollars of American aid, Haiti's main income, to raise the living standards of a country with 90 percent illiteracy, an average life span of thirty-five years and an average personal income of £1 per week. A short time after his election, it was obvious to all that Duvalier had no intention of sharing his power or the national treasury with anyone.

Diverting most of the American aid

to his own personal bank accounts, Papa Doc retreated to a lavish mansion surrounded by heavily armed guards to enjoy the good life, gulping imported foods and wines and entertaining a bevy of expensive call girls. In 1964, Duvalier declared himself president for life, and then ordered the army to kill all of his political opponents—or anyone who spoke out against him for that matter—and specified that their mutilated corpses be hung from the lampposts in Port-au-Prince with voodoo symbols engraved in their flesh.

To the stunned and frightened populace of Haiti, Duvalier announced that the dissenters had been destroyed by the forces of "Baron Semedi," the avenging spirit of witchcraft, a voodoo demon whose soul had been raised from the dead to do the bidding of the devil. This his gullible supporters actually believed, as they had for decades believed in the existence of zombies, dead persons who, through the cabalistic rites of voodoo, had been raised from their graves to do the bidding of all-powerful witch doctors such as Papa Doc.

Terrifying the populace even more was the existence of a special secret police force Duvalier established early in his evil reign, the brutal Ton Ton Macoutes, a 10,000-member secret police force that, over the years, murdered thousands of citizens and army officers suspected of plotting Duvalier's overthrow. Uniformed in blue denim and red neckerchiefs, the Macoutes protected the political, social, and religious interests of dictator Duvalier. For more than thirty years, this above-the-law force used random violence and voodoo fear tactics to enforce Duvalier's wishes and whims.

The Macoutes were largely illiterate and mostly sadistic in nature. They had been recruited from Haiti's slums and small villages, and they unsentimentally exercised their uncontrolled power, often against their own class. They were present on every level of government and business, in government offices and local service industries. Carrying guns at all times, as well as bolos and machetes, the Macoutes lounged inside buildings, inspecting natives and foreigners alike. They abused foreign visitors, extorted money from shopkeepers, and raped and pillaged at will.

Haitian dictator Francois "Papa Doc" Duvalier, who controlled his corrupt regime through his small army of terrorists, the Ton Ton Macoutes.

The Macoutes—a Creole name meaning "Bogeyman"—were patterned after Hitler's SS troops. They killed with impunity on election days, often leaving corpses on display to ensure victories for Duvalier's candidates. The Macoutes were deeply influenced by voodoo as exercised by the crafty Papa Doc, and frequently his decisions and penalties were determined by ancient voodoo rites.

When a traitorous Macoute was alleged to have turned himself into a dog to escape punishment, Duvalier ordered the mass execution of dogs throughout Haiti. The poor animals were hunted in the streets of Port-au-Prince and in the homes of the poor and middle class. Despite the pleas of their owners, mongrels and poodles alike were shot, stabbed and hacked to pieces.

Living above the law, the Macoutes commandeered autos without paying, rode free in taxis and buses, took food when hungry, took money from all as they pleased. The reign of the Macoutes perpetuated the despotism of the Duvaliers over one of the poorest countries in the world for three decades.

President John F. Kennedy, shown with wife Jackie and children Caroline and John on April 15, 1963, condemned Duvalier's dictatorship and cut off all aid to Haiti as long as Duvalier remained in power. Papa Doc put a curse on the American leader and when Kennedy was later assassinated, Duvalier claimed that his hex had destroyed the U.S. President.

President John F. Kennedy was given a detailed report of Duvalier's repressive regime in 1963, and he announced that U.S. aid would be discontinued to Haiti as long as Duvalier was in control. Papa Doc responded by telling his people that he had put a curse on Kennedy. When the president was assassinated six weeks later, the Haitians were convinced that Papa Doc's voodoo hex was the cause.

Duvalier was soon literally bleeding his people dry, rounding up thousands of Haitians daily and giving them a week's wages for a liter of blood, which he then sold to America for transfusions at £12 a liter. Dying of heart disease and diabetes in 1971, Duvalier altered the nation's constitution to allow his nineteen-year-old

son, playboy Jean-Claude Duvalier, known as "Baby Doc," to become president for life.

"Baby Doc" Duvalier continued in power, enriching himself and his extravagant wife, Michele, while Haiti's decline continued until it was by far the poorest nation in the Western Hemisphere. Unrest and open rebellion finally drove Jean-Claude Duvalier from power, and he and his family fled the country on February 14, 1986. They landed in the ski resort of Grenoble, France, where they began to lavishly live on the estimated $400 million they had stolen from their country. Meanwhile, the Ton Ton Macoutes were hunted down and killed in Haiti, as they had earlier hunted down their helpless victims.

·SEVEN·
MALCONTENTS, MISFITS, AND THE AMERICAN LEFT

Terror in the Skies

The international crime of skyjacking was rare before World War II, and even in the postwar years the act of hijacking an airplane was confined mostly to those attempting to escape Communist-controlled nations. Nothing like it had occured in the U.S. until August 3, 1961, when Leon Bearden, a politically disgruntled car salesman, decided that he would opt for Cuban citizenship. His decision unfortunately involved his naive seventeen-year-old son, Cody. The skyjacking haphazardly conducted by the Beardens set the precedent for the many dangerous terrorist acts to come, skyjackings that became, to the horror of passengers, airlines and the public, all too commonplace.

Boarding a Continental B-707 jetliner in Phoenix, Arizona, the thirty-eight-year-old Bearden and his son took their seats and waited for the plane to become airborne. Bearden had nur-

tured the idea of skyjacking a U.S. commercial plane for months. Unemployed and brooding about his dire economic plight, this was not to be Bearden's first criminal act. He had a twenty-year criminal record that included prison terms for forgery, robbery, and grand theft. His son, Cody, however, was an innocent youth who idolized his father and followed him blindly.

When the plane was airborne for some time, the Beardens left their seats and walked to the cockpit of the plane. Drawing guns, they both entered the cockpit, where Leon Bearden put a .38-caliber pistol to the head of Captain Byron D. Rickards, saying: "We are going to take this plane to Cuba. Alter your course forty-five degrees to the south."

It was grimly ironic that Captain Rickards knew more about skyjacking at that time than perhaps any other pilot in the world. He had been the first pilot to be hijacked on record in 1931. At that time, Rickards had been a young pilot for a domestic Peruvian airline, which had been boarded by revolutionaries who demanded that he use his plane to drop propaganda leaflets over Peruvian cities, as well as transport rebels to safe areas. Though he had been under the threat of death, Rickards had refused and managed to talk the skyjackers into surrendering to authorities.

Certainly, when the gun-brandishing Beardens entered his cockpit, Rickards must have thought back to the skyjacking he had endured thirty years earlier. He stalled for time, telling Bearden that he did not have enough fuel to make the flight to Cuba and would have to stop off at El Paso to refuel. Bearden agreed and Rickards radioed a message in which he described his predicament. When he landed the plane in Texas, El Paso police, border patrolmen, and FBI agents were waiting at International Airport.

The small army of lawmen waited in hiding while a ground crew busied itself with refueling the plane. Since it was assumed that the skyjackers were henchmen of Cuban dictator Fidel Castro, President Kennedy was kept informed of events by phone. A pregnant woman passenger then became hysterical. Bearden decided to allow sixty-one of the passengers to disembark, keeping four passengers and the crew as hostages.

When the ground crew appeared to be stalling, Bearden grew impatient and fired a bullet between the legs of a terrified passenger, demanding that the plane take off. Fuel tanks were hurriedly filled and Rickards taxied the plane onto a runway. As he did so, a motorcade packed with heavily armed lawmen rushed from hiding places and poured machine-gun fire into the undercarriage of the moving plane, flattening its tires and knocking out an engine.

As the plane came to a halt, FBI agent Francis Crosby boarded the jetliner to negotiate with Bearden. Realizing that his foolhardy plan had backfired, Bearden himself became hysterical, shouting that he would shoot one of the passengers and then kill himself if the plane did not take off. At that moment, one of the male hostages blind-sided Bearden with a sucker punch and knocked him senseless to the floor of the plane. Crosby grabbed his gun and Cody Bearden meekly surrendered.

The Beardens were quickly taken into custody and the hostages were released, having undergone a ten-hour ordeal. The Beardens were charged with kidnapping, illegally transporting a plane (the word skyjacking had yet to be introduced), and obstructing commerce by robbery. Cody Bearden had pleaded guilty to his part in the skyjacking and was sent to a correctional institution for juveniles until he was twenty-one. His hardened father admitted to nothing. On October 18, 1961, he was found guilty in a U.S. District Court of violating three federal laws. On October 31, Leon Bearden was sentenced to life imprisonment.

The Bearden skyjacking of 1961 did not inspire an immediate surge in air kidnapping, but American citizens turned terrorists did begin to escalate such activities. David Healy and Leonard Oeth skyjacked a chartered plane over Miami to Cuba on August 13, 1962. Both men were returned to the U.S. and imprisoned. On November 17, 1965, Thomas H. Robinson, brandishing two pistols, took over a National DC-8 flight carrying ninety-one people from Houston to New Orleans, ordering the pilot to fly to Cuba. Robinson was caught and imprisoned.

It was not until 1968, however, when skyjackings to Cuba proliferated at an alarming pace. On February 18 of that year, James Boynton of Kalamazoo, Michigan, skyjacked a one-passenger, one-crew-member Miami-bound Piper Apache to Cuba. He was returned to the U.S. and was sent to prison for kidnapping. Three days later, on February 21, 1968, Lawrence M. Rhodes skyjacked a DC-8 flying from Tampa, Florida, to West Palm Beach, ordering the pilot to fly to Cuba. Rhodes, who had a history of mental illness, was later confined in an asylum. On June 29, 1968, E. H. Carter, armed with a revolver, ordered the pilot of a Southeast DC-3 to fly to Cuba where he successfully escaped.

Cuba-bound skyjackers suddenly began appearing on U.S. planes in droves. On July 1, 1968, Mario Velasquez Fonseca skyjacked an eighty-five passenger Northwest B-727 en route from Chicago to Miami. After forcing the pilot to land in Cuba, he escaped. John H. Morris attempted to skyjack a TWA B-727 flying from Kansas City, Kansas, to Las Vegas, Nevada, on July 4, 1968. Morris claimed he had a gun and some dynamite, but he had neither. Over-

Two of America's first skyjackers (left to right), Cody and Leon Bearden, who skyjacked a jet in 1961.

powered, he was later imprisoned. Eight days later, on July 12, 1968, Leonard S. Bendicks skyjacked a private Cessna-210, with two persons on board, flying from Miami to Key West. Bendicks ordered the pilot to fly to Cuba, which he did, but Bendicks was returned to the U.S. and was imprisoned. On the same day, Oran D. Richards skyjacked a forty-eight passenger Delta CV-880 en route from Baltimore to Houston, ordering the pilot to land in Cuba. Richards was later sent to a mental institution.

On July 27, 1968, a National DC-8, en route from Los Angeles to New Orleans with fifty-seven passengers on board, was skyjacked by Rogelio Hernandez Leyva. Armed with a pistol, Leyva ordered the pilot to fly to Cuba and, after landing, he successfully escaped. Willis Jessie took his three-year-old daughter along when, on August 4, 1968, he skyjacked a chartered Cessna 182 in Naples, Florida, flying to Cuba. Jessie was later sent to prison for kidnapping. On August 22, 1968, Bill McBride, wielding a revolver, skyjacked a chartered Cessna 336, flying en route from Nassau, Bahama Islands, to Georgetown. McBride diverted the plane to Cuba and escaped.

Dozens of skyjackings occured throughout 1968 and 1969 and would continue with deadening regularity long into the troubled 1970s. One of the most unusual skyjackings involved Anthony Raymond, a fifty-six-year-old alcoholic and one-time used-car salesman (he oddly shared the same trade as the trend-setting Bearden). A native of Baltimore, Raymond boarded an Eastern Airlines Boeing 727 en route to Miami on June 26, 1969.

When boarding the plane, Raymond was wearing a T-shirt, shorts, and sandals. He was in a state of drunkenness at the time, according to one report. Once the plane was aloft, the myopic Raymond held on to his loose-fitting horn-rimmed glasses with one hand and pulled out a pocketknife with the other. Waving the knife in front of a terrified stewardess, Raymond forced her to open the cockpit door. Standing wobbly-legged in the cockpit, Raymond babbled almost incoherent threats while ordering the pilot to fly to Cuba, which he did.

Castro's government officials welcomed the boozy skyjacker with open arms. Eastern's crew of seven and the ninety-six passengers on board were safely returned to the U.S. When Raymond sobered up some weeks later, he began to lobby Cuban authorities for permission to return to the U.S. He wrote his sister in Baltimore that he wanted to return home, that it had all been a mistake. By then, a half dozen other American skyjackers were sitting about Havana, also wanting to go home. These included Thomas George Washington, who, after reading about Willis Jessie's skyjacking in 1968, also took his small daughter along when he skyjacked an Eastern Airline plane on December 19, 1968, in Philadelphia.

Also waiting to return to the U.S. was Ronald T. Bohle, who had skyjacked an Eastern flight on January 9, 1969; Robert L. Sandlin, who had skyjacked a Delta Airlines plane in Dallas on March 17, 1969; and Joseph Calvin Crawford, who had diverted a Continental Airlines flight from El Paso, Texas, to Cuba on July 26, 1969. Most of these skyjackers were unemployed and mentally unstable. Anthony joined them after Fidel Castro, becoming fed up with the skyjackings, ordered all of the American skyjackers sent home. All were prosecuted and sent to prison.

Raymond's defense attorney claimed that his client was almost unconscious with drink when he boarded the plane he skyjacked and that the airline was responsible in that it had not ejected him. Moreover, the attorney emphasized, Raymond would never have committed the crime had it not been for a credit card firm sending him an unsolicited credit card. Immediately after receiving the card, the lawyer pointed out, Raymond used it to get drunk, charge his air ticket and then stagger on board the Miami-bound Eastern flight that he skyjacked in a comatose state.

It was a whim, the attorney said, conjured from Raymond's dim recall of the many planes skyjacked to Cuba. The defendant was nevertheless sentenced to fifteen years in prison by Baltimore Judge Alexander Harvey II, who summed up Raymond's plight as being "the tragic case of an alcoholic whose life is a failure at the age of fifty-six." Harvey then took to task the flight crew of the skyjacked Eastern plane, stating that he could not understand why the crew had meekly obeyed "the drunken orders of a little man holding a penknife." By then, however, as Harvey may have known, skyjacking occured with such regularity that few questions, if any, were asked of the terrorists. All they had to do was point toward Cuba.

The Klan Rides Again

When John Fitzgerald Kennedy assumed the office of the presidency, he immediately launched an active campaign to desegregate southern schools and public places. The federal move was met with fierce resistance in the Deep South, and at the core of local defiance was a new generation of Ku Klux Klan members hiding beneath old robes and hoods. Blacks who attempted to enter white schools, eat in restaurants, or shop at stores patronized by whites were attacked and beaten.

Reacting to this new wave of terrorism, a New York City activist group calling itself the Congress of Racial Equality (CORE) organized several interracial bus trips to the heart of the South in the early 1960s as a protest against the region's racially motivated violence. Many of these Freedom Riding trips ended in disaster.

The first group of Freedom Riders boarded two buses in Washington, D.C., in May 1961. They passed through several southern towns with only slight interference, but all that changed when the buses crossed into Alabama. "I could tell the difference when we crossed the state line," said eighteen-year-old Charles Person, one of the Freedom Riders. "The atmosphere was tense."

A line of cars was waiting for the buses when they crossed into Alabama. When the first bus stopped in Anniston, the cars overtook it and a passenger from one of the cars tossed a homemade bomb into the bus through an open window. It exploded inside, shooting fire the length of the bus and burning several passengers. The bus began to move, but the fire inside caused the desperate Freedom Riders to smash the windows.

With black smoke billowing from the windows, the bus was forced to the side of the road. As the young Freedom Riders leaped screaming from the bus, some with clothes burning, a mob of white men from the car caravan was waiting for them. KKK thugs beat them as they fled. As the first bus caught fire and began to burn to a cinder, the second bus arrived in Anniston. Eight men, identified later as members of the KKK, boarded the bus and began striking the young passengers with clubs and bats as they sat helpless in their seats.

News of the vicious attacks spread to nearby Birmingham, where supporters rode to the rescue of their fellow Freedom Riders, gathering the two busloads of CORE workers and putting them onto other buses, which then drove to Birmingham. Another mob, dominated by KKK leaders, was waiting for the Freedom Riders, and when they alighted at the city bus terminal, the youths were attacked by men wielding pipes and blackjacks. Dozens of the youths suffered concussions, broken ribs and arms.

Throughout the attack, white Birmingham police officers stood by and did nothing. Later that day, an arrogant Eugene "Bull" Connor, Birmingham's Police Commissioner, told the press: "Our people of Birmingham are a peaceful people, and we never have any trouble here unless some people come into our city looking for trouble."

In Montgomery, Alabama, the Freedom Riders met the same fate. Whites attempted to shoot protestors and ignited the clothing of one black man and watched him burn. Alabama Governor John Patterson lamely reported that: "I cannot guarantee the protection for this bunch of rabble-rousers."

Freedom Riders entering Jackson, Mississippi, a short time later, were given the same brand of southern hospitality. Authorities there rounded up 164 Freedom Riders and jailed them for "breach of the peace." Many paid fines and were released, while others were held in the maximum security cells at Parchman State Penitentiary.

President John Kennedy and his brother Robert Kennedy, then U.S. Attorney General, were enraged by what they clearly saw as a new rising of the Ku Klux Klan. Robert Kennedy ordered 400 U.S. deputy marshals and Treasury agents to patrol the streets of Alabama, chiefly to escort the northern protestors. President Kennedy

went further, declaring war on the KKK-backed southern rioters and their stooge politicians. "I hope that state and local officials in Alabama will meet their responsibilities," he said. Kennedy added ruefully: "The U.S. Government intends to meet its."

Despite the threats and violence, Freedom Riders increased in number. By 1964, they went into southern states by the thousands and worked tirelessly to register black voters. One of their main targets was the backwater state of Mississippi, where only 5 percent of the state's 500,000 black population was registered. The most active CORE member in the state was twenty-four-year-old Michael Schwerner, who moved to Meridian, Mississippi, and worked for six months to register black voters. Aiding him were twenty-year-old Andrew Goodman and James Chaney, twenty-one, a Negro who was their link to the black community.

Klan residents of Meridian hated Schwerner and Goodman not only for their efforts to "line up the niggers," as one KKK leader intoned, but because they were Jewish northerners, a sentiment that had run so deep in Georgia fifty years earlier that a Jewish businessman, Leo Max Frank, had been railroaded and later lynched for a crime he did not commit. So incensed did Sam H. Bowers, Jr., become over Schwerner's activities that he marked him for execution. The forty-three-year-old Bowers was the Imperial Wizard of the Ku Klux Klan in Neshoba County, Mississippi.

On the night of June 21, 1964, Schwerner, Goodman, and Chaney were driving back from Philadelphia, Mississippi, where they had visited congregation members of a burned-out black church that had been recently torched by KKK members. The CORE activists encouraged the blacks to fight back with their vote. As the trio approached Meridian on a deserted road, the glaring lights of a squad car flooded their car, a siren went on and they were pulled to the side of the road by Neshoba County Deputy Sheriff Cecil R. Price, who was a secret KKK member.

Price arrested the trio on trumped-up charges of speeding, releasing them about 10 P.M. that night. As the three drove off, Price followed. Schwerner, at the wheel, sped up, and soon a high-speed chase developed, with Price once again pulling the CORE workers to the side of the road. Price had planned his moves well, engineering the car driven by Schwerner to a remote spot where a KKK lynch mob waited.

Dragged from their car, the three young men were shoved into the arms of the grinning Bowers and his KKK terrorists. The terrified youths were led to a small cove of trees where Schwerner tried to reason with the Imperial Wizard, telling Bowers: "Sir, I know just how you feel."

"You do, huh?" came the grunted reply. With that, Bowers and others cold-bloodedly shot each young man in the head and then dragged their lifeless bodies to shallow graves that had already been prepared. About a week later, the Klansmen returned to the murder site and created an earthen dam over the graves. When news of the disappearance of the CORE work-

ers broke, the nation's press focused its attention on Mississippi.

Thousands of altruistic young persons had joined the Freedom Riders early in 1964. The summer of that year was a time of optimism and hope for civil rights workers, with more than 1,000 college students working in Mississippi to register black voters, hoping that their labor would focus national attention on the evils of segregation, which it did. Mississippi, however, was one of the most effectively segregrated, states in America. The powerful Ku Klux Klan, with its law enforcement and political connections, intimidated the black community through terror tactics. Fear of Klan bombings of homes and churches, cross-burnings, and beatings had kept blacks from seeking basic voting rights. Those courageous blacks who did attempt to register, simply vanished.

When state authorities appeared lethargic in searching for the missing Freedom Riders, the FBI stepped in, code-naming its investigation "Miburn" because the case began with the burning of the black church. For five months, 150 FBI agents worked on the case, piecing together evidence of the KKK plans to execute the three CORE workers. Enormous pressure against the FBI to produce results came from civil rights workers around the country, as well as members of the grieving families of the missing youths.

Forty-four days after the executions, and after weeks of wading through vast, swampy land areas, volunteer searchers unearthed the badly decomposed bodies of the slain civil rights workers. Bureau agents learned through a single informant and a lone confession that the Ku Klux Klan had ordered and carried out the three murders.

Twenty-one men were initially charged with murder and conspiracy to murder, but their prosecution was thwarted when the state court refused to allow the Department of Justice to introduce the testimony of Horace D. Barnette, one of the accused who had confessed to his part in the crime. The case was dismissed and the Department was forced to seek a grand jury indictment. Aided by the testimony of Barnette, the FBI's star witness, James E. Jordan, and Philadelphia resident Florence Mars, the grand jury indicted eighteen men on an old federal law prohibiting conspiracy against the rights of another citizen. Convictions could bring each defendant a ten-year prison sentence and a $5,000 fine.

The two-week trial generated national press coverage, focusing upon the defiant, surly defendants and an aloof jurist, U.S. District Court Judge W. Harold Cox. The judge, decidedly unsympathetic to civil rights, was once heard publicly to state that several blacks registering to vote reminded him of a "bunch of chimpanzees." An all-white jury deadlocked when it could not convict all of the defendants.

Judge Cox further instructed the jury that it could find individual defendants guilty. A verdict was reached on October 20 and seven men were found guilty of conspiracy to murder: Sam H. Bowers, Jr.; Cecil R. Price; Horace Barnette; thirty-year-old truck driver Jimmy Arledge; thirty-year-old gas station operator Billy Wayne Posey; thirty-

four-year-old laundry truck driver Jimmy Snowden; and Alton W. Roberts, a twenty-nine-year-old salesman. The jury, however, acquitted eight men, including Neshoba County Sheriff Lawrence Rainey, and came to no judgment on three other defendants.

After the verdict was read, Judge Cox surprised many by stating: "I very heartily enter into this jury's verdict." He then castigated Roberts and Price and ordered their immediate imprisonment because of the threats they had made before the jury returned its verdict. On December 29, 1964, Cox sentenced Bowers and Roberts to ten years imprisonment; Price and Posey to six years; and Barnette, Snowden and Arledge to three years. None of those convicted received fines. Federal witness Jordan, after a separate trial on January 13, 1965, received a four-year prison sentence.

The KKK executions and trial made a tremendous impact on Mississippi and on the civil rights movement. Blacks came to dominate the movement and abandoned nonviolence for militant action. Yet the voter registration campaigns that summer brought into the political process tens of thousands of blacks who had never before registered as voters. The town of Philadelphia, Mississippi, showed the most drastic change. The public schools were desegregated and job opportunities for blacks were broadened. Despite the tragic killings, Freedom Rider Haywood Burns echoed the sentiment of civil rights workers when he stated: "It was our finest hour."

The hours of the KKK were dismal. The Mississippi trial had exposed the organization for the brutal terrorist fraternity it truly was, but the Klan's long tentacles continued to grotesquely twitch throughout Mississippi and the Deep South. Vernon Dahmer, a black activist, was killed on January 10, 1966, by a Ku Klux Klan bomb in Hattisburg, Mississippi. On June 30, 1968, Thomas Albert Tarrant and Kathy Ainsworth, two KKK supporters who had made threats to several Jewish leaders in Meridian, Mississippi, were stopped by police as they were planting dynamite outside the home of a Jewish businessman. Ainsworth fled and was shot and killed by police.

In the backwoods of Alabama, the Klan still clung to its lynch-mob authority as late as the 1980s. In 1981, a black man was charged with the murder of a Birmingham police officer. KKK members were much in attendance and were incensed when the accused was sent to Mobile under a change of venue to be tried in that city. When the jurors in Mobile were unable to come to a decision and a mistrial was declared on March 30, 1981, Klan members vowed revenge.

In retaliation, Klan members, twenty-nine-year-old Henry Francis Hays and seventeen-year-old James Llewellyn Knowles, went out one night, searching for a black man to murder. Any black man would do. The pair saw nineteen-year-old Michael Donald and drove their car next to him, catching him off guard by politely asking for directions. When Donald leaned close to the car, they grabbed him and tossed him in, holding him hostage at gunpoint as they drove to the next county.

When the car stopped, Donald broke free and fled into the dark wilderness but the Klansmen tracked him down, beating him into unconsciousness with tree branches before killing him by slitting his throat. Next, Hays and Knowles dumped the body into their car and drove to a Klan party at the home of Bennie Jack Hays. There the celebrants hung Donald's body from a tree while they drank heavily and danced "victory jigs" beneath the swaying corpse.

Someone at the party turned informant, and Hays and Knowles were arrested and tried before one black and eleven whites. On December 10, 1983, the Klan was stunned when the jury returned a verdict of guilty, recommending life imprisonment for both men. On February 2, 1984, Circuit Judge Braxton Kittrell, Jr., ignored the jury's recommendation and sentenced Hays to death in the electric chair. Knowles, who had pleaded guilty to a federal civil rights charge, was given life imprisonment.

Some time later, Donald's mother, Beulah Mae Donald, and the National Association of Colored People (NAACP) sued the Ku Klux Klan, and on February 12, 1987, an all-white jury further shocked the KKK by awarding the plaintiffs $7 million in damages. This broke the back of the organized Klan and demoralized Klansmen throughout the South. Not only had their racial peers wholeheartedly condemned the Klan but imposed a fine impossible to pay, a moral and financial judgment from which the Klan could never recover.

Havoc in Chicago

The bustling, hustling city of Chicago had played host to several presidential conventions. It was in a Chicago "smoke-filled" hotel room where cigar-chomping Republican bosses selected Warren G. Harding as the party's candidate for president in 1920, ushering in one of the most corrupt administrations in American history. In the years following World War II, Chicago was dominated by the Democratic Party, with the heavy-handed Richard J. Daley at its helm.

It was Daley who insisted that the Democratic National Convention be held in Chicago in 1968, despite all warnings that the atmosphere was volatile and that massive demonstrations promised to disrupt the convention. Democrats in power in Washington, especially under the unsteady hand of President Lyndon Baines Johnson, had aggresssively pursued the unpopular war in Vietnam and, to many, Democrats meeting in Chicago represented "the war party."

Deep divisions in American society had been created by the war. Many draft-age college students, including future president William Clinton, simply refused to serve in the military. A strong, nationwide anti-war movement encouraged campus protest and confrontational politics as a means of signaling disapproval of the U.S. involvement in Southeast Asia.

The "professional protestors," as they were later termed by Daley minions, who met in Chicago to disrupt the convention were, indeed, orchestrated by three militant protest organizations that had been established by vocal minorities: the Youth International Party (Yippies), Students for a Democratic Society (SDS), and the National Mobilization to End the War (MOBE). Through the highly organized underground press, the call went out to members to meet in Chicago for a week of public protests and demonstrations during the Democratic convention.

In April of that year, Chicago had undergone terrible riots on the West Side, following the assassination of Dr. Martin Luther King. Police used extreme restraint during these riots, which resulted in widespread and costly damage. Mayor Daley openly criticized the force for being too lenient. A hard line politician and a man who ruled Chicago with an iron fist, Daley resolved that demonstrators would not disrupt *his* conven-

Mayor Richard J. Daley, the autocratic political boss of Chicago during the disastrous 1968 Democratic convention. He ordered his police en masse into the streets and called up the National Guard to combat the thousands of rock-throwing protestors.

tion, and to that end, he mobilized the city into an armed camp, calling up some 6,000 Illinois National Guardsmen and 6,000 regular army troops to support the city's more than 15,000 policemen.

No question that the hippies, Yippies, and other out-of-town protestors were spoiling for physical confrontation. The author was present in Grant and Lincoln parks when leaders Jerry Rubin and Abbie Hoffman met with their hard-core followers and ordered them to recruit Chicago youths into the ranks of protestors. Thousands of naive teenagers, more eager to see some excitement than to alter the political process, joined the demonstration organizers who numbered in the hundreds and who had poured into the city by car, bus, train, and plane.

When the protest leaders asked for a permit to sleep outside in Lincoln Park on Chicago's north side, it was refused by City Hall. On August 25, 1968, protestors camped out in the area in brazen defiance of the 11 P.M. curfew. Police were ordered to clear the area and did so with few problems. It was a different story the next night. Hippie leaders Hoffman and Rubin urged scores of followers to resist the police and, as the author witnessed firsthand, showed teenagers how to hurl rocks and bottles at police and guardsmen.

Rubin spent a great deal of time displaying razor blades affixed with tape to the tips of his shoes and demonstrating how to kick police and guardsmen "in the chins until the bastards bleed." He and others handed out razor blades and tape to scores of demonstrators and this riot device and other ploys were later widely used by protestors to provoke officers into bloody retaliation. On the night of August 26, 1969, the protestors were ready when the police again attempted to sweep the park after curfew.

"The parks belong to the people!" Rubin, Hoffman, and other leaders began to chant, and this was taken up by hooting masses of rebellious teenagers. Police had to use force to drive the protestors out of the park. Protestors were anything but non-violent. They taunted police and hurled rocks and bottles at advancing officers. (Some of these were Molotov cocktails that failed to explode.)

Some injuries from this police sweep were counted on both sides, but the worst was yet to come. The three-day riot culminated on the night of August 29, 1968, when masses of protestors, led by Rubin, Hoffman, and others, set out on a march toward the International Amphitheater, where the convention was being held under tight security. The path of the marchers was blocked by guardsmen armed with rifles fixed with bayonets.

Protestors responded by hurling bottles, rocks, and other objects at the guardsmen. Many ran into the startled guardsmen, kicking their legs with razors affixed to their shoetips. They mercilessly taunted the youthful guards with foul language and endless oaths. The guardsmen held rifles empty of bullets. When police closed in, officers received the same physical and verbal abuse. They responded by advancing on the huge throng, tossing tear gas bombs into their midst and beating many protestors who refused to give way. Some reporters and photographers in the crowd were also beaten and thrown to the ground.

The author, present at this time, noted that most of these reporters and/or photographers were from the underground press and were highly partisan in favor of the protestors; these "news people" also called police vile names and many, more or less, taunted officers or defied them to strike out at them. Most of the reporters from established newspapers and local and network TV witnessed the confrontation from the safety of the guarded entrance of the Conrad Hilton Hotel on Michigan Avenue, their view of the demonstrators obstructed; these members of the press saw only the steady march of the guardsmen toward the crowds, which they construed as a brutal act, but they did not see the many provocational acts committed by the political terrorists jabbing at the guardsmen with pointed sticks, the razor-blade kicking, the bottle and rock throwing as did the author who was in the surging, defiant crowd itself.

It is true that many enraged police officers swung their nightsticks indiscriminately at those in the crowd. Hearing of this, many TV commentators inside the amphitheater, such as Walter Cronkite, condemned the police. On the floor of the convention, Senator Abraham Ribicoff protested the police behavior, calling for an end to the harsh law enforcement tactics. From his seat in the Chicago delegation, Mayor Daley, angrily red-faced at such criticism, shouted curses at the senator.

In many instances, the overreaction of the police was seen firsthand by the author. On one occasion, the author was in Lincoln Park after curfew, watching officers wildly chase teenagers through the park area. A young girl wearing a serape was dodging the nightsticks of three officers when I interrupted them. As the girl fled, they turned on me, then stopped. One officer, his nightstick raised a few feet from my head, paused to look at my press credentials. (I was then editor-in-chief of *ChicagoLand* magazine.) Moreover, my appearance was that of a businessman as I was attired in a three-piece suit and was carrying a briefcase. Appearances were everything to these policemen.

I asked the officers why they had gone after the girl.

"She's wearing a cape, like the rest of those goddamn anarchists!"

"She's wearing a serape."

"Whatever it is, who knows what she's got under it—a knife, a gun, a bomb!"

"She's a kid—can't be more than sixteen," I said.

"Yeah," said one of the other officers, "well, a fifteen-year-old put a buddy of mine in the hospital last night after hitting him on the head with a lead pipe!"

A group of youngsters standing at a clump of trees nearby began shouting curses at the officers who were certainly spooked by events. To them, Chicago had been invaded by a host of vicious terrorists wanting to destroy the city's well-organized system of law and order.

"There's some more of 'em," said one officer, "Let's go!"

They ran off, chasing hooting teenagers for whom the riots were nothing more than a wild and exciting game. There were others, however, with ideas of revolution and massive destruction in mind.

A short time later, I encountered a group of demonstrators who were older, unshaven, carrying rocks, bottles, and knives. One of them held a strange-looking package wrapped in black masking tape, an object that could have easily been construed to be a homemade bomb.

"What are you?" one of them challenged. "A goddamned detective?" I showed them my press credentials. They were still suspicious. Like the police, appearances counted for everything with the hard-core protestors. "Just don't ask us any questions," the ringleader said. "Wait and see what happens tomorrow night though!" Off they went, looking for policemen to challenge.

Daley later charged that the convention week riot had been carefully planned by the leaders of the Yippies, SDS, MOBE, and other organizations, citing Abbie Hoffman, Jerry Rubin, Rennie Davis, and Tom Hayden. These four were later among the seven indicted for conspiracy to foment a riot. Although an independent investigating committee headed by future Illinois governor Daniel Walker concluded that the Chicago police had rioted, it was clear to anyone witnessing events that, for the most part, authorities had been savagely provoked by well-organized demonstrators bent on violent confrontation.

These were, indeed, American terrorists who had formed a political coalition before the riots with certain 1930s leftists such as fifty-four-year-old David Dellinger, chairman of MOBE. Linking up with Dellinger were Hayden and Davis of SDS and Rubin and Hoffman of the Yippies. Chicago police intelligence had identified these ringleaders long before the riots began, and following the bloody confrontations in which scores of police and demonstrators were injured, a grand jury was empaneled to decide whether or not to bring the leaders of the demonstration to trial for inciting to riot.

On March 20, 1969, the jury returned indictments against eight of the anti-war activists: Jerry Rubin, Abbie Hoffman, Rennie Davis, David Dellinger, Thomas Hayden, John Froines, Lee Weiner, and Bobby Seale of the Black Panther Party. They were charged with forming a "combine" to "conspire, confederate, and agree together on or about April 12, 1968 . . . to travel in interstate commerce with the intent to incite, organize, promote, encourage, participate in and carry on a riot."

The celebrated "Conspiracy Trial" began on September 26, 1969, in the courtroom of seventy-four-year-old Judge Julius Hoffman. The case became the "Chicago Seven Trial" when Seale was later granted a separate trial. William Kunstler and Leonard Weinglass represented the defendants, and the prosecution was headed by U.S. Attorney Thomas Foran and Richard Schultz.

On the first day of the trial, the violent Seale accused Judge Hoffman of racism after he denied Seale's motion for a separate trial. Hoffman was deeply offended by Seale's volatile remarks, stating to the defendant: "Do you know you are addressing the judge who ordered the first desegregation of schools in the North?" Seale's repeated outbursts of vile oaths and threats caused Hoffman to order marshals to bind and gag Seale, a controversial decision that caused Hoffman to be severely criticized by the press. Seale nevertheless sat in court strapped to a chair with his mouth taped.

Abbie Hoffman, one of the most vocal and active protestors during the bloody riots in Chicago in 1968.

The five-month trial was needlessly prolonged by the publicity-seeking defense counsels and limelight-loving defendants, particularly Rubin and Hoffman who verbally sparred with Judge Hoffman at every opportunity. On one occasion, the author was present in a cloakroom adjoining the courtroom where the defendants were assembled, plotting with their lawyers their disruptive moves in court that day. "I'll read the newspaper," Rubin told Hoffman, "and you spit on the floor a lot." Hoffman wanted center stage: "No, I'll read the newspaper with my feet on the table and you spit on the floor!"

Such mindless, sophomoric anarchy was at the core of the so-called defense, tactics and conduct encouraged by the devisive Kunstler who, in reality, had no real defense for the terrorist tactics employed by most of his

Chicago police in riot gear, about to storm into a line of protestors during the Democratic Convention, 1968. It was later determined that the widespread violence was the result of a "police riot," but the author saw more than enough provocation coming from protestors who attached razor blades to their shoes in order to slice the legs of the officers.

clients during the staged riots. Kunstler, instead, attempted to try the Chicago Police Department, the judicial system and Hoffman himself.

On February 14, 1970, the jury retired to consider a verdict. While they were sequestered, Judge Hoffman handed down contempt of court sentences. Dellinger received twenty-nine months in jail; Davis, twenty-five; Hayden, fourteen; Rubin, twenty-five; Hoffman, eight; Froines, five; and Weiner, two months. For calling the court "a medieval torture chamber," Kunstler was ordered to serve four years and thirteen days in prison. Weinglass received twenty months and nine days.

The jury returned its verdict the following day, on February 15, 1970. The defendants were acquitted of the charge of conspiracy. However, Dellinger, Davis, Hayden, Hoffman and Rubin were found guilty of crossing state lines to incite a riot. For lack

of enough evidence, accused bomb makers Froines and Weiner were acquitted of conducting workshops on the construction and detonation of incendiary devices.

None of the notorious Chicago Seven served time. A federal district judge overturned the convictions on May 11, 1972, on the grounds that Hoffman had waited too long to impose sentencing. The defendants had escaped through a legal loophole, which enraged Chicago authorities. On November 21, 1972, the convictions were permanently voided, thus ending a sensational criminal trial that had, for the first time, introduced anarchist street theater to the courtroom. The actors smugly took their bows in the underground press and continued to encourage others to emulate their questionable actions. Many did, some to the point of enacting outright revolution and bloody anarchy.

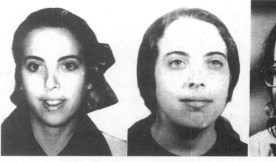

"... Which Way the Wind Blows"

Three different views of Brandeis honor student turned terrorist, Susan Edith Saxe, who made the FBI's Ten Most Wanted list in the 1970s after participating in a deadly Boston bank robbery. She remained at large for five years.

The Students for a Democratic Society, better known as SDS, which helped visit upon Chicago the convention riots of 1968, had among its ranks a radical element so violent that they soon broke away as a splinter group to form a small but effective terrorist organization. Calling itself the Weathermen, the group's name stemmed from a line in a Bob Dylan song: "You don't need a weatherman to know which way the wind blows."

Originally the group had called itself the Weathermen, but fifteen of the thirty-seven members were women, all fanatical feminists who insisted that the group drop its masculine gender identity. The terrorist band became the Weather Underground Organization. Its leaders stated that they had departed SDS to avoid police infiltration.

Made up mostly of college-educated white women and men, many members had parents who were wealthy or came from politically powerful families. In essence, they were the spoiled and pampered progeny of the upper class who disavowed laws and regulations and embraced anarchy and terrorism to destroy the American political process and capitalism. The spectors of Emma Goldman and Alexander Berkman rose mightily in their midst.

Weathermen led the forced occupation of five buildings at Columbia University in 1968 and, in response to the indictment of the Chicago Seven, led the maniacal 1969 four-day riots in Chicago ("Days of Rage"), in which hundreds of mostly out-of-city radicals, spearheaded by Weathermen, ran amuck down Loop streets, randomly bashing in windows of shops and businesses, destroying everything in their paths. Scores were arrested, charged, and convicted of wanton destruction of property.

The hallmark years for the Weathermen were 1969 and 1970. They set off more than 4,000 bombs in those two years, which, miraculously, killed no one other than some of the group's own members. The terrorist organization set the precisely timed bombs to detonate in the early morning hours, and then warned police so that no one would be killed in the explosions. The last Weatherman bombing was that of a New York bank in 1975. More lethal was the explosion that went off in the group's Greenwich Village bomb factory, killing three of the anarchists.

Leaders Mark Rudd, William Ayers, Jeff Jones, Jim Mellon, Terry Robbins, John Jacobs, and Bernadine Dohrn (the latter being the most radical of the lot) made sure that, over a seven-year period, more than twenty-five Weathermen bombs were planted at sites that they called "symbols of American imperialism," including the Pentagon and the Capitol Building in Washington. Continuously on the move to escape FBI and police drag-nets, Weathermen churned out a sophomoric magazine entitled *Prairie Fire*, promoting its crude ideology of anarchy and revolution.

During this time, the Weathermen promoted themselves in an under-gound film directed by Emile de Antonio. Appearing before the cam-eras and mumbling their revolution-ary slogans and credo were Dohrn, Ayers, Jones, Cathy Wilkerson, and Kathy Boudin. According to later reports, the group, much like the mur-derous Manson family of Los Angeles, used sex to fuse its membership. Monogamy among members was abol-ished and mass pot-smoking orgies were held. Members later restricted themselves to homosexual sex. Sex was coerced, "to level the bourgeois conceit surrounding pleasure and power," according to one report.

The most fanatical member of the Weathermen, Bernadine Dohrn, later claimed that she broke up the terrorist group by issuing a manifesto in January 1977, one in which she accused other leaders of "sins against ideological purity." This was, of course, nonsense; the Weathermen were simply tired of being hunted by

authorities. In New York in September 1977, Rudd, who had led the Columbia University sit-in in 1968, turned himself in. Rudd appeared in court in New York and Chicago, where he faced eight misdemeanor charges, including criminal trespass-ing, unlawful assembly, criminal solicitation, obstructing government administration, and jumping bail.

Rudd refused to talk to the press. He also refused to detail his activities, contacts, and hideouts during his flight to avoid prosecution. He later received an unconditional discharge. Rudd's actions caused other Weathermen ter-rorists to come forward, including twenty-seven-year-old Robert Roth and thirty-one-year-old Phoebe Hirsch, who received probation for their sav-age destruction of property in the "Days of Rage" rampage through Chicago in 1969.

Dohrn held out. A fanatical radical, Bernadine Rae Dohrn, raised in Wisconsin and a graduate of the University of Chicago Law School in 1967, was one of the founders of the Weathermen, and she, more than most, had organized the "Days of Rage" riots, as well as promoted the planting of bombs throughout the U.S., acts of terrorism that kept her on the run from police for eleven years.

Dohrn had the dubious distinction of being placed on the FBI's Ten Most Wanted list after involving herself in a bomb plot in Flint, Michigan. Federal charges against her involving the "Days of Rage" disorders were dropped when it was discovered that federal investigators had obtained evidence against Dohrn through illegal wiretaps,

Arrogant and defiant, Bernadine Dohrn, leader of the terrorist Weathermen group, holding a press conference, predicting an offensive that would spread from coast to coast. A short time later, Weathermen bombs exploded along the West Coast. Dohrn was a fugitive for more than a decade.

but she nevertheless still faced three state indictments, including mob action, flight to avoid prosecution, and assault (kicking a policeman in the groin and striking another with a club). The charges represented Class 3 felonies and carried with them a maximum five-year sentence.

When other Weathermen turned themselves in, Dohrn angrily denounced them. She lived with Ayers in New York under an assumed name and worked as a waitress in a restaurant. In 1980, tired of her drab, hum-drum life, Dohrn hired a lawyer, Michael Kennedy, and, after negotiations were held with Chicago's State's Attorney Bernard Carey (who was then about to leave office), she surrendered.

Appearing in Cook County's Criminal Court on December 3, 1980, Dohrn

pleaded not guilty to the charges against her. As expected, she used the occasion to launch into a diatribe of her radical political views, which no one cared to hear. Dohrn's case was transferred to the court of Judge Fred G. Suria, Jr., who had heard a number of other cases involving the terrorist disorders of the late 1960s.

Kennedy told Judge Suria that his client was financially destitute in his plea to have Dohrn's $300,000 bail reduced. Suria reduced it to $25,000. On January 13, 1981, Dohrn began her trial by changing her plea to guilty to all outstanding charges against her. Placed on probation for three years, she was fined $1,500. When released, the still arrogant terrorist told the press that she and Judge Suria had "different views of America," and that

Malcontents, Misfits, and the American Left

she was still "committed to the struggle ahead."

Dohrn later went to work in New York as a practicing attorney, but she is remembered chiefly as one of the architects of American terrorism in the 1960s and 1970s. "She was the worst of us," one reformed Weatherman later anonymously commented— "Some wanted to kill her but I guess they realized that she would have enjoyed that—making her a martyr and all . . . We were all jerks, mad at our parents for having money, mad at politicians and corporate leaders because they were running things and we weren't. Dohrn was the biggest jerk of them all."

There were other Bernadine Dohrns in that generation, lots of them. One was Susan Edith Saxe, who, like Dohrn, was a political terrorist of the 1970s and, like Dohrn, was placed on the FBI's Ten Most Wanted list. The twenty-one-year-old honor student from Brandeis University was a campus activist who coordinated the National Strike Center in the wake of the Kent State shootings in May 1970, when jittery National Guardsmen shot and killed four rioting university students.

To fund their terrorist activities, Saxe and four other Brandeis students masterminded the armed robbery of the State Street Bank and Trust Company in Boston in September 1970. During the daylight robbery, the terrorists shot and killed forty-one-year-old officer William Schroeder. The terrorist band netted $26,000 from the robbery, money it reportedly intended to use in constructing bombs

and leading murderous raids against government agencies.

A short time after the robbery, a communique was issued by "Commander-in-Chief" Stanley Bond of the "Revolutionary Action Force East," one that claimed responsibility for the holdup. Bond, William Gilday, 41, and Robert Valeri of Sommerville, Massachusetts, were arrested within a week of the robbery-murder, but Saxe and a second female, Katherine Power, eluded capture and were added to the FBI's list of important fugitives.

Saxe managed to stay at large for five years, mostly through her extensive contacts in the then widespread radical feminist movement. She worked at menial jobs under assumed names and always kept on the move, criss-crossing the country, reportedly enjoying her status as a much-wanted felon. On March 27, 1975, however, Saxe was recognized by a policeman in Philadelphia, who promptly arrested her. She was promptly arraigned on separate charges of robbery and manslaughter, stemming from the Boston bank robbery and an earlier attack on the Bell Federal Savings and Loan in Philadelphia. According to the FBI, Saxe and Power had also participated in the theft of government property at the National Guard Armory in Newburyport, Massachusetts on September 1, 1970, when terrorists looted arms and ammunition.

For Susan Saxe, there was no defense. She pleaded guilty in Suffolk Superior Court to manslaughter and two counts of armed robbery. On January 17, 1977, Saxe was sentenced to twelve years in prison by Judge Walter McLaughlin. On February 11, 1977, Federal District Judge Alfred Luongo in Philadelphia sentenced her to an additional ten years for the savings and loan robbery and the National Guard Armory break-in. The sentences were to be served concurrently.

The white radicals of the 1960s who steeped themselves in terrorism received an enormous amount of publicity. To black radicals, however, these coddled middle-class revolutionaries were only playing at revolution. They knew nothing of the generations of poverty, spiritual degradation, and economic oppression endured by American blacks. As the civil rights movement of the 1960s spawned the white terrorist organizations, it also gave birth to the militant Black Panther Party, a coalition of American blacks bent on changing the system through violent and radical means.

The Jim Crow laws and in-place segregationist policies of the Deep South caused black activist Stokely Carmichael to coin a phrase in 1965 that would be embraced by all black radicals: Black Power. Following the march on Selma, Alabama, Huey P. Newton and Bobby Seale founded the militant Black Panther Party. Headquarters was established in Oakland, California, and chapters were opened in most major cities throughout the U.S. Many of the chapters had been organized through the offices of the national Student Nonviolent Coordinating Committee (SNCC), but the Panthers soon abandoned the advocacy of nonviolence. Newton indicted the police as enemies of social change and swore to prevent police brutality in black communities by whatever means possible.

Newton's decree caused Panthers to illegally arm themselves and fight several pitched gun battles with police. In 1968, Newton was convicted of voluntary manslaughter after shooting two Oakland police officers. He served twenty-two months in prison before his court-ordered release in 1970. A year earlier, on December 14, 1969, fourteen Chicago police officers raided a West Side apartment where members of the Black Panthers had reportedly stockpiled a huge arsenal of guns and ammunition.

A wild gun battle ensued in which at least 100 bullets were fired. It ended with the deaths of Black Panther leaders Fred Hampton, 21, and Mark Clark, 22. Four of the surviving Panthers were seriously wounded, and two police officers received minor wounds. State's Attorney Edward V. Hanrahan, whose office was responsible for the raid, was accused of planning a deliberate assassination attack, charges that Hanrahan denied. He pointed to the abundance of weaponry recovered from the Panther apartment and commended the officers in the raid for their "bravery, their remarkable self-restraint and their discipline in the face of this vicious Panther attack."

The seven surviving Panthers were indicted for attempted murder after a special coroner's jury, on January 30, 1970, exonerated the police officers by ruling the deaths of Hampton and Clark as "justifiable homicides." Yet the Hanrahan-ordered raid was more closely scrutinized by members of the press who counted the bullet holes in the apartment and proved that all but one shot had been fired by the police. A special investigation was ordered, which resulted in Hanrahan and thirteen others being indicted for covering up police misconduct.

This case dragged on for years, with the seven surviving Panthers and the relatives of Hampton and Clark filing a civil rights violation suit in which they asked for more than $47 million from Hanrahan and twenty-seven others. All were acquitted, but the U.S. Court of Appeals reinstated the charges in 1979, and on February 28, 1983, Judge John F. Grady approved a $1.85 million settlement in favor of the plaintiffs.

By that time, the Black Panthers had literally gone out of business. Newton had, a decade earlier, in 1972, renounced "the rhetoric of the gun," and urged his followers to improve conditions for blacks by working within the system. This came in the same year that FBI Director J. Edgar Hoover died. At the height of activity, with more than 2,000 members having been recruited in thirty cities, Hoover stated that the Panthers were "the greatest threat to internal security in the country." In some respects, Hoover was correct, at least when it came to the Black Liberation Army (BLA), a splinter group of the Black Panthers.

The BLA never had a membership of more than 200, and most of its recruits were street thugs with long criminal records. It conducted a terrorist campaign in 1971–1972 of systematic murder of police officers. Its members first struck on May 21, 1971, in Harlem, where two police officers, one white and one black, were gunned down while answering a phony call for help. Three months later, three BLA members sauntered into the police station in Ingleside, California, and shotgunned the desk sergeant to death before fleeing. Thus the BLA announced its program of death and defiance. Anthony Bottom, Albert Washington, and Herman Bell were later arrested and convicted for both attacks.

In January 1972, two more New York police officers, Gregory Foster, black, and Rocco Laurie, white, answering a distress call near the corner of Avenue B and Eleventh Street, were gunned down from behind by three BLA members. One of the killers did a "death dance" over the bodies of the dead officers. The next day, a note was received by authorities that promised a "new Spring offensive." It was signed: "The George Jackson squad of the BLA." Though no one was apprehended for these savage murders, the BLA soon disintegrated. The police dragnet for the killers of Foster and Laurie was so intense that BLA members scattered, abandoning all operations.

The radicals of the late 1960s in America soon gave way to even more devastating terrorists in Europe and the Middle East. None, however, were as savage as the political terrorists known as the Baader-Meinhof Gang, a bevy of youthful bloodlusting fanatics who stopped at nothing to achieve their anarchistic goals.

·EIGHT·
UNDERGROUND
GUERRILLAS

1970

Dark Hearts in Germany

Beginning in 1967, Germany was to suffer for almost a decade through a seemingly endless series of terrorist bombings, robberies, kidnappings, and murders, all performed with devilish care by the Baader-Meinhof (B-M) Gang. Its members were without conscience, utterly ruthless and fanatically dedicated to the destruction of a capitalist system that had weaned them in comfort and security, much like the 1960s hippies, Yippies, Weathermen, and other violence-prone activists in the United States.

The leaders of this terrorist group, Andreas Baader and Ulrike Meinhof, did not spring from impoverished gutter-life but evolved from Germany's middle class during that country's greatest economic post–World War II boom. Inspired by left-wing educators, the gang members represented Hitler's early-day Nazi Party in reverse. Although its philosophy embraced the

radical left, the tactics of the B-M Gang were identical to that of the Nazi Brown Shirts of the 1920s and early 1930s. At all times, the gang employed terror to achieve its ends, and, for a time, was so effective that German political and business leaders were compelled to barricade themselves in their own homes, which had been turned into armed fortresses.

Just as the Nazis used as a rallying point the "martyrdom" of Horst Wessel (a vicious Nazi thug killed in 1930), the university students who later formed the B-M Gang were galvanized by the death of an obscure West German student, Benno Ohnesorg. On June 2, 1967, the Shah of Iran was welcomed in Berlin by the West German government, setting off protests from the student left. Among the jeering students throwing rotten eggs and overripe tomatoes at the Shah's passing motorcade was Ulrike

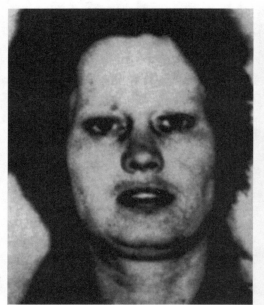

Left: *Ulrike Meinhof, the calculating leader of Germany's Baader-Meinhof Gang, one of the most ruthless terrorists of the twentieth century.*
Right: *Andreas Baader, wealthy playboy turned terrorist, the drug-taking pawn of Ulrike Meinhof and his demented lover, Gudrun Ensslin.*

Meinhof, self-appointed political journalist and devout Marxist. She would later become the guiding light of the terrorist gang bearing her name.

The demonstration against the Shah developed into one of the worst riots in Germany in decades. Police, alerted to possible violence on the part of demonstrators, overreacted to the students pelting the Shah's motorcade with rotten fruit and rocks. Officers employed the "liver-sausage" tactic of sealing both sides of the student group, which stretched for several blocks, forcing the students to flee at the ends and, as they burst forth, attacking them with rubber truncheons and nightsticks.

The main body of students fled down a narrow passageway, the Krumme Strasse. The police, hot on their heels, overtook many of them, beat them to the pavement and fell on top of them as more police in the rear rushed forward to run over those who had fallen. The students in the vanguard of this rushing mob suddenly saw masses of police in front of them and realized that they were trapped. They turned to desperately battle the police behind them.

In the free-for-all, Sergeant Heinz Kurras, a plainclothes officer, drew his revolver and fired a single shot. The crowd froze into silence, gathering mutely about the body of a young man with dark hair and a scraggly

TERRORISM IN THE 20TH CENTURY

mustache. The fallen student was twenty-six-year-old Benno Ohnesorg. He was married, his wife was pregnant and he had never before participated in a political demonstration. He had joined other students to jeer at the Shah simply because he thought "it would be fun."

Now he was dead, a martyr to a cause he knew nothing about. Ulrike Meinhof saw the corpse and immediately viewed it as a tool for her own political ends. She had railed in her column, published in the leftist *Konkret*, against the Shah's forthcoming visit to Berlin, and it was she, more than most, who had brought the students to the streets. Many in the crowd of students were, like Meinhof, diehard Marxists, but just as many others were apolitical, such as the dead Ohnesorg, who had, by his untimely death, become Meinhof's *cause celebre*.

Another event during that demonstration worked to create the future terrorist gang. Berndt Andreas Baader, a spoiled playboy-student who came from considerable wealth, met tall, blonde Gudrun Ensslin, a fanatical Communist. Both had been living with others and had produced children through these unions, but they immediately decided to abandon their mates and children for each other. Baader was easy pickings for Ensslin, a submissive sort who was dominated by his new lover. Ensslin was the epitome of the new, fanatical feminist; she had appeared in a pornographic movie and proudly took her friends and relatives to view it.

Moving to Frankfurt, Baader and

Ensslin frequented the cafes where students gathered. Almost every day Ensslin could be found shrieking her Communist philosophy into the ears of annoyed students. She would dramatically sweep glasses and dishes from tables to make her point, which was always urging a total revolution where all elected officials would be killed and ties with the "imperialistic" United States be severed. So vociferous was Ensslin that she caught the attention of spies working for Reinhard Gehlen's West German intelligence organization, and she was placed upon a suspect list of people to be watched.

The spy organization concluded that Ensslin was "a noisy crank and a drug-taking whore whose ravings

Terrorist Gudrun Ensslin, who appeared in pornographic films and gleefully planted bombs in department stores.

could easily be dismissed." Though most students with whom Baader and Ensslin lived soon grew bored with them and asked them to move on, the pair were welcomed by militant left students belonging to the SDS (*Sozialistischer Deutscher Studenbund*). Two of the more radical element of this group, Thorwald Proll and Horst Sohnlein, heavy drug takers like Baader and Ensslin, embraced the young woman's revolutionary plans. When Ensslin pointed out to these stooge-like followers that the Kaufhof and the Schneider, huge department stores that symbolized the core of capitalism, should be destroyed, her impulsive plan was embraced with enthusiasm. Obtaining some pamphlets that described how to build incendiary devices, Ensslin went about the business of making some crude bombs. Baader purchased hashish to keep the group in euphoric highs while they planned their revolution. Actually Proll, after obtaining the necessary chemicals, constructed the bombs.

The four revolutionaries began their so-called "People's War" on April 3, 1968, when they ostensibly sought revenge for the Berlin slaying of Ohnesorg, a young man they never knew. Wearing filthy clothes and so thoroughly drugged that they bumped into mannequins and furniture displays, the four entered the department stores and, in spite of drawing attention to themselves, managed to hide their firebombs. Then they went to a nearby outdoor cafe and ordered wine, waiting for the firebombs to explode.

Ensslin could not contain her excitement. She went to a phone and, with-out giving her name, called police, saying: "Soon there will be flames in the Schneider and the Kuafhof. It's a political act of revenge!" She hung up and rejoined her wine-gulping companions. They were drunk by the time customers began running from the Schneider store, where the terrorists had planted a firebomb in the toy department. The fire from this bomb was quickly extinguished. The other bomb failed to go off.

All four terrorists were quickly identified by store employees who particularly remembered the stoned Ensslin staggering about the toy departments. The foursome were brought to a police lineup and were pointed out by store clerks, one woman saying about Ensslin: "You could not forget her—she has the same rat's tails hairdo, the one with the sunken eyes and the flat chest—that's her standing up there."

By then, police had found the makings of bombs in Proll's car and had taken from the careless Ensslin's purse her own notes, copied from the pamphlet about incendiaries, of how to make a firebomb. Charged with arson, the four faced trial on October 13, 1968. As would be the case with the Chicago Seven trial, the apprentice terrorists made a mockery of the proceedings. Sohnlein tried to punch the bailiffs and had to be restrained. Both he and Proll shouted obscenities and Communist slogans throughout the trial. Baader made inane remarks having nothing to do with the case while his mistress, Ensslin, remained mute, slumped in her chair.

Toward the end of the trial, Ensslin and Baader jumped to their feet to insist that Proll and Sohnlein were innocent and that they alone were responsible for the bombs. It made no difference. The four were convicted and sent to prison for three years, in spite of the fact that the prosecution demanded twice that amount of prison time. The prosecutor had ruefully warned the court: "These people are not harmless—they are fanatics. They care nothing for life and they will do it again!"

Inside prison, Baader brooded for some time before he went about telling other inmates that he had fire-bombed two department stores to protest the Vietnam War. One prisoner looked at him, puzzled, then said: "That's the most idiotic thing I ever heard." Getting no response or respect from other prisoners, Baader began writing letters to Communist students, portraying himself as a martyr to the cause of the Left. Ensslin, also, played this role and was delighted to hear that she and her boyfriend had been elevated to the status of proletarian heroes by left-wing students.

A prison psychiatrist interviewed Ensslin at this time, asking her what she and the others hoped to achieve through terrorism. "We do not want to be merely a page in cultural history," she snapped at him. The examining physician concluded that Ensslin realized that she was emotionally dependent upon Baader and hated herself for this weakness, seeking revenge against her lover's strength by leading him into anarchy and personal disaster.

Expensive lawyers hired by the parents of Baader and Ensslin soon won for the terrorists an early release. All four were set free on June 13, 1969, to await an appeal hearing scheduled for the following November. They had served only fourteen months behind bars. Upon their release, the arsonists were hailed by SDS students as great heroes of the proletarian movement. They begged the four to lead them in an open revolution against the government. The self-serving foursome, however, had no intention of doing anything but furthering their own ends.

Baader, Ensslin, and Proll, funded by Proll's sister Astrid, fled to France where they remained in hiding. When the money ran out, Baader returned to Germany, moving from one city to another and reveling at the wanted posters showing his picture and describing him as "an escaped felon." In Berlin, he made contact with his most ardent supporter, Ulrike Meinhof, who had promoted his Frankfurt arson as a heroic achievement of the New Left. To her, the pensive playboy was another Lenin who would lead West Germany into the Communist camp.

The twenty-three-year-old Meinhof by then had abandoned her twin daughters, sending them to a boarding house, and divorced her husband, Klaus Roehl, publisher of *Konkret*, in which Meinhof's rabble-rousing column appeared. Baader and Meinhof sexually trysted but were not romantically involved with each other. Meinhof, like Ensslin, was the more dominant of the two. She made the plans and Baader took the orders. One of these was to retrieve some weapons hidden in a Berlin cemetery. When attempting to dig up the guns, Baader was recognized and arrested. He was sent back to prison.

Ensslin then arrived in Berlin to beg Meinhof to help her free her lover, saying: "I cannot live without 'Baby.'" Meinhof used her press connections to discover that Baader was taken out of Tegel Prison on certain days to do research at a small library in Dahlem operated by the German Institute for Social Questions. (The tolerance of Leftist fanatics by the government was later criticized by political analysts who found such accomodations mystifying.)

On May 14, 1970, Meinhof and others entered the library, brandishing submachine guns. They opened fire, shooting the place to pieces, riddling books and wounding two guards and injuring several library workers and patrons. Baader fled with the invaders. Once reunited, Baader, Ensslin, Meinhof, and others then embarked on a murderous terrorist spree unlike anything ever seen in Germany.

When the group made the decision to take their revolution to the streets, a decision was also made to learn how to become effective guerrillas. Help came from Horst Mahler, Baader's attorney during the arson trial. Mahler was the founder of the radical Red Army Faction, an underground organization dedicated to the overthrow of the West German government. He provided fake passports and funds for the group, which he accompanied to Beirut where contact was made with

the PFLP (Popular Front for the Liberation of Palestine).

The Arabs put the group through urban guerrilla training at a secret, rural camp, and the Germans proved to be adept with high-powered weapons, although the male members shunned the commando training. Baader complained about getting dirty, saying: "It is not necessary to crawl through the mud of an infiltration course to become an effective guerrilla." The keen-eyed marksmanship of Meinhof, Ensslin, and other females in the group astounded their Arab instructors.

The females, who dominated the German group, delighted in rolling their bodies out of moving vehicles and dashing through minefields. Baader and the other males, all of whom had been dominated as children by single-minded women, however, would escape to Beirut at every opportunity to sit captivated in movie theaters showing their favorite spy thrillers or westerns. Baader particularly enjoyed films starring Marlon Brando and was delighted when Meinhof and Ensslen called him by the movie star's name.

The group next moved to a tough training camp in Jordan. Here they underwent terrorist training, bomb making, and the many dark methods of kidnapping and murder. Peter Homann, one of Meinhof's many former lovers, was with the group at this time. He later told the German press that the Palestinian guerrillas had no use for Baader. Homann described Baader as "a coward performing the whole revolt to cover up his cowardice; they [the Palestinians] wouldn't even take him on patrol."

One course that captured the complete attention of the Germans was one dealing with bank robbery. The Germans were told that the easiest way to finance expensive terrorist activity was through bank robbery. They would soon put these techniques to use in their native land. Returning to Berlin with arms and the know-how to use them, the Germans began robbing banks with alacrity in fall 1970. Mahler became the nominal leader, and on some days, he supervised the robbery of as many as three banks in a single outing. Amassing tens of thousands of marks, Mahler warned members not to spend the money freely as it would draw attention to them.

The one-time lawyer now acted out the part of fantastic secret agent. During the robberies, Mahler wore grotesque disguises—donning false noses, phony beards and mustaches, and bright red toupees to hide his baldness. Police nevertheless were able to identify the terrorist from bank video camera pictures and, in October 1970, when he entered his apartment, twelve policemen were waiting for him inside, all pointing pistols at him.

"This must be some mistake," Mahler said, acting surprised. He produced forged papers that identified him as Gunter Uhlig.

An officer stepped close to him, smirking, and yanked the cheap red wig from the top of Mahler's head. "Do you still imagine that we can't recognize you, Herr Mahler?" he said.

Mahler was quickly tried and con-victed. He was sent to prison for fourteen years but none in the B-M gang mourned his loss. To the gang, Mahler was nothing more than an inept intellectual who talked and talked about revolution but never formed a plan to destroy the West German government. "He preferred to rob banks and hide the spoils for a rainy day," one of the gang later remarked.

From that point onward, Meinhof took over the gang, recruiting the most violent members of the radical SDS to her banner. The gang began to increase in number, so that by 1971, there were more than 150 members in branches located in Berlin, Frankfurt, and Munich. The bank robberies continued, each raid becoming more bloody. Meinhof encouraged her followers to "kill the pigs [policemen]," who offered the slightest resistance.

On January 15, 1971, the gang burst into two banks at the same time in Kassel. After looting two vaults, Meinhof realized that the stolen money was large enough for her to purchase a tremendous arsenal. From Al Fatah, an Arab terrorist organization, she bought boxes of automatic rifles, machine pistols and enormous amounts of ammunition. Meinhof then recruited to her ranks members of a bizarre radical group, SPK (Socialist Patients' Collection), all mental patients who had been organized by their equally unbalanced doctor, Wolfgang Huber, a physician at the Psychiatric-Neurological Clinic at the University of Heidelberg.

Huber had originally organized his patients as a political force against the university doctors controlling the clinic in order to force the faculty into giving them unlimited access to drugs. As a result, Huber and his patients were thrown out of the clinic, and the whole, crazy lot of them joined Meinhof. With the fusion of these lunatics to the gang, the killings began in earnest.

Meinhof instructed gang members to raid police arsenals to obtain weapons and ammunition, as well as to investigate banks and report back about which bank could be most easily robbed. The terrorists were also ordered to steal cars to be used in the robberies and, from 1971 onward, no road in Germany was safe from these terrorists. Typical was the conduct of two of Meinhof's robot-like followers, Petra Schelm and Werner Hoppe. The pair had stolen a BMW (the gang's favorite auto) and were speeding along when they ran into a police roadblock outside of Hamburg on July 15, 1971.

When police ordered the couple out of the car, Hoppe jumped to the roadway, firing a pistol at officers before running into some nearby woods. Schelm, one of Meinhof's closest associates, also leaped from the car, emptying a pistol at officers barricaded behind their vehicles. She then threw down the empty pistol and stood, glassy-eyed, staring at the officers who motioned her to advance and surrender.

From beneath a coat she was carrying, Schelm produced a Firebird Parabellum, a weapon carried by all members of the B-M gang. She sprayed the police with bullets, who returned fire with submachine guns.

Schelm fell to the pavement dead, almost cut in half. Hoppe was spotted an hour later running down a road. A police helicopter descended to allow officers to leap on top of the running fugitive. He was quickly convicted of theft and sent to prison.

Meinhof lost no time in elevating the dead Schelm to the status of hero to the movement. She ordered all members not known to the police to attend Schelm's funeral. More than fifty radical left students arrived to place a red flag on the casket of the dead girl, but this was quickly removed by officers who took photos of everyone attending the wake. Though this helped to identify B-M members, the ringleaders were next to impossible to run to earth as they hid in the homes of well-to-do radicals.

Those gang members found on the roads by police offered zealot-like resistance. On September 25, 1971, two officers saw a parked car on the Freiburg-Basel motorway. When they stepped close to investigate, two of the most vicious gang members, Holger Meins and Margrit Schiller, shot them down and escaped.

Police soon came to realize that in almost every encounter with gang members, they faced at least two or three terrorists, and, always, a woman was the driver of the car and apparently in command. It was always the woman who barked an order to the others to open fire on police. And in almost every instance, the terrorists appeared to be in a drugged state. Authorities later learned that Meinhof distributed generous doses of hashish each day to her followers.

On October 22, 1971, police recognized Schiller, but when an officer named Schmid approached her, she whipped out a pistol from her handbag and shot him dead at point-blank range. As other officers dashed forward, Schiller, a long-legged blonde, sprinted into a nearby park. Pursuing police were suddenly stopped by a fusillade of shots coming from the park, fired by three of Schiller's companions, all armed with automatic assault weapons. The gang members escaped, but the next morning, police spotted a tall, blonde-haired woman making a call in a phone booth.

As she stepped from the booth, officers demanded that she show them her identity papers. She gave them a crooked smile and produced an identity card that said she was Dorte Gerlach. As the police examined the card and other papers, the twenty-three-year-old blonde lasciviously stuck out her tongue and ran it slowly around her full lips, while fondling her own ample breasts. She leaned close to one of the officers and whispered her price in his ear, pretending to be a common prostitute.

One of the officers opened her bag and found a 9-mm-caliber pistol. Margrit Schiller was then promptly arrested and put into a police car where she shrieked foul oaths at the officers. She would later claim that others had killed officer Schmid. Sent to prison, Schiller was given a twenty-seven-month sentence, being released in 1973, only to be rearrested the following year for subversive activities. Schiller represented the most lethal element of the B-M gang as she was an original member of the offshoot SPK from the Heidelberg asylum.

In November 1971, Meinhoff ordered two new recruits, Wolfgang Grundmann and his blonde mistress, Ingeborg Barz, to case a bank in Kaiserslautern, thirty-five miles from Heidelberg. Grundmann was a dedicated Marxist, but Barz was merely a secretary who had worked for the Berlin Telephone Company. She joined the B-M gang simply because she was in love with Grundmann and, as she later lamely commented: "The organizations was made up of exciting people who knew how to have thrills."

Because Barz was the most presentable of the group, she was select-

Ingeborg Barz, a secretary in love with a Baader-Meinhof terrorist, tried to leave the group and was murdered by gang members. Andreas Baader crushed her skull with a rock, then threw her body into a river.

ed to go to a branch of the Bavarian Mortgage and Exchange Bank in Kaiserslautern to check on its security. On December 10, 1971, Barz entered the bank and loitered at a counter, pretending to fill out bank forms. Her overlong visit caused many to take notice of her.

Twelve days later, on December 22, 1971, a man entered the same bank and placed a tape recorder on a customer counter. He looked about, studying everyone in the bank. When he determined that there were no guards present, he turned on the tape recorder, which let loose a deafening blast of rock music, signaling to the terrorists outside the bank to enter. Three persons holding automatic weapons rushed into the bank. All wore anoraks and knitted balaclava helmets that covered their faces and left only sinister-looking slits for the eyes. One of them shouted: "Raid! Hands up! To the wall!"

Some of the customers began to nervously talk to each other, but the ringleader of the gang shouted: "Silence!" As three of the machine gun–waving terrorists leaped over counters and scooped up cash, the man who had turned on the tape recorder (and then hid his face beneath a mask) stood by the door, training a submachine gun on the customers and employees. One of the terrorists ordered an official to open the vault.

Outside the bank, Herbert Schoner, a thirty-two-year-old policeman, married with two small children, noticed a minibus illegally parked in front of the bank. He walked across the street and ordered the driver to move the vehicle. As Schoner stepped behind the bus, the driver threw the vehicle into reverse and almost crushed the officer into the car behind.

Schoner leaped out of the way and ran to the driver's side of the minibus, drawing his gun, shouting for the driver to get out. The driver fired several shots through the window, one of the bullets smacking into Schoner's neck. The officer's face was covered with blood from the cuts received from the flying glass. Falling to the pavement, Schoner fired three shots at the driver as he crawled toward what he thought was the safety of the bank doorway.

As Schoner pushed the bank door open, one of the gang members, sitting on the counter, covering the customers with his submachine gun, casually swung about, took deliberate aim, and fired a short burst into Schoner. The policeman fell backward through the door, into the street, dead. When Schoner collapsed, the gang members inside the bank abandoned the safe inside the vault, which was not yet opened by the fiddling bank officer, and ran from the bank with briefcases stuffed with money from the tellers' cages. They leaped into the minibus, which roared off down the street. Police alarms went off at two nearby stations, but when officers attempted to drive out, they found vehicles blocking their paths. The vehicles had been strategically parked by gang members for that purpose.

A witness at the bank later identified the man with the tape recorder. He was Klaus Junschke, one of the mental patients under Dr. Huber's care and one of the most ardent members of

Klaus Jünschke, a mental patient and member of SPK, a terrorist group working with Baader-Meinhof, helped rob a branch of the Bavarian Mortgage and Exchange Bank in Kaiserslautern in 1971; a policeman was shot dead during the robbery.

SPK. (Huber was no longer directing his patients in the ways of terrorism, having been arrested and jailed on July 7, 1971.) On December 28, 1971, police found the Kaiserslautern hideout used by the terrorists. It was littered with soiled mattresses, bomb-making and drug paraphernalia, revolutionary pamphlets and old clothes. Also found was a note written in Meinhof's handwriting that read: "Fat One 1330." This was a reference, police concluded, to the Volkswagen that had been used to block the exit of one of the police stations.

With Meinhof, Baader and others now identified and linked together in the bank raid, the press bannered their bloody exploit in Kaiserslautern with the headline: "Baader-Meinhof Murders On." Alarmed at the widespread killings committed by the terrorists, Chancellor Willy Brandt addressed the nation in a special television broadcast. He warned the terrorists that the government would do everything in its power to suppress their activities. "The free democracy which we have built from the ruins of dictatorship and war must not be understood as a weak state." Brandt then asked citizens to cooperate with police in identifying and tracking down the terrorists.

One of those watching the Brandt television broadcast was Ingeborg Barz. She had come from a well-to-do family and had never before been involved in illegal activities. She had been with Grundmann for about four months, the most frightening time of her life. The "thrills" she had sought had turned into horror after the murder of Schoner. All Barz thought about was escaping the B-M gang. She called her mother in Berlin and told her: "I have nothing to do with them here." Then she made the mistake of telling gang members she intended to leave.

Barz was reminded that she had taken an oath to the terror gang and that she could not desert their cause and to do so would mean death. She was ordered to call Meinhof who was in Berlin at the time. Meinhof told Barz to drive to a remote spot on the Rhine riverbed near Ludwigshafen. Meinhof would meet her there, she said, and work something out so that she could leave the gang without disgrace.

When Barz arrived at the rendezvous, she discovered Baader waiting for her, not Meinhof. The gang leader had sent Baader to murder the defecting young woman. According to gang member Gerhard Muller, who was later captured, Baader walked up to Barz and crushed her skull with a blunt instrument. He then affixed weights to her ankles and rolled the dead girl into the river before driving off in a stolen Alfa Romeo. The body surfaced in July 1973 and was identified. Meinhof's purpose in ordering Barz's death was simple; if she could not hold her gang members together through her political rhetoric, she would do so under threat of death. The Barz execution proved so effective that no other B-M gang member ever attempted to desert again.

Barz's boyfriend, Grundmann, did escape, right into the arms of the police. Grundmann had merely shrugged when he was told that his "chicken-hearted" girlfriend had to be killed. A short time later, Grundmann was living in Hamburg with Manfred Grashof, a demented anarchist. Both men had been planning, under Meinhof's directions, to blow up several government buildings. The gang was now entering its ultimate revolutionary stage, the mass bombings of buildings.

Acting on a tip, police learned of Grundmann's Hamburg hideout and, on March 2, 1972, they appeared before the apartment door. Grundmann answered a knock at the door; he shrank back in fear as he stared into the muzzles of five guns held in the hands of police officers. "Police!" one of them shouted. "Hands up!"

"Stop!" yelled the lip-quivering Grundmann. "Don't shoot—we're unarmed!"

Grashof, standing behind Grundmann and hidden from the sight of the officers, grabbed a machine pistol and, as Grundmann dove for the floor, opened fire, his bullets striking the officer in charge, who later died of his wounds. Grashof was himself shot and wounded in the withering return fire from the other officers. Both Grundmann and Grashof were jailed, with Grundmann being released in October 1976.

The arrests of these two terrorists spooked the B-M gang, which had moved into the Hamburg area. The terrorists split up into small groups and scattered throughout Germany. The hastily vacated hideouts were located by police and the fingerprints of Baader, Meinhof, Ensslin, Holger Meins, and Jan-Carl Raspe were found. Raspe was a particularly brutal radical who delighted in murder, having a gunsmith build a special stock on his gun so that he could have a better grip.

Incensed that they had been driven out of Hamburg, the gang decided that it would strike back by planting bombs in factories, government office buildings, and army posts. Under Raspe's direction, the gang operated a bomb factory where explosives expert Dierk Ferdinand Hoff constructed a number of powerful pipe bombs by hand. On May 11, 1972, Meinhof, Ensslin, Baader, and Raspe planted three of these bombs in the U.S. Army headquarters in Frankfurt.

The terrorists somehow managed to infiltrate the heavily guarded American post, placing the bombs, wrapped as gifts with flowers placed on top of them, in a large phone area used by unsuspecting GIs. As the grinning, joking group of terrorists left the post en route to a vacation in France, the bombs went off, one terrific explosion after another. Thirteen American soldiers near the phone area were flattened by the blasts. Lieutenant-Colonel Paul Abel Bloomquist, who was walking to his car, was hit by a bomb fragment. The thirty-nine-year-old Bloomquist collapsed and bled to death before help could reach him. A Vietnam hero, he left a widow and two small children. (When the terrorists later learned that they had murdered an American officer, they bought champagne and celebrated.)

The blast caused more than $1 million in damage and caused American commanders at all U.S. posts to put their men on alert. Orders were given that no one was to enter an American post without identification being checked and rechecked. Still, U.S. Army Supreme Headquarters in Heidelberg proved vulnerable. A woman drove into the parking lot of this post on May 24, 1972, parking her car. She had been admitted because her car bore USA-EUR green plates, those issued to American personnel; these plates had obviously been stolen from one of the many cars driven by Americans and parked throughout the city.

At 6 P.M., the lot began to fill up with army personnel en route to their homes. The car blew up with a tremendous roar, the blast tearing to pieces two American officers standing nearby, twenty-nine-year-old Captain Clyde Bonner, father of two, and Ronald Woodward, father of three. Several other servicemen were seriously injured. As had been the case following the Frankfurt blast, a female, most probably Meinhof, called the German Press Agency to proudly claim responsibility for the bombing on behalf of the Red Army Faction, saying that it had been planted in retaliation for the martyrdom of Schelm and as a protest against the Vietnam War.

In the name of the slain murderess, Schelm, Meinhof ordered bombs planted in the Augsberg police station. On May 12, 1972, two female

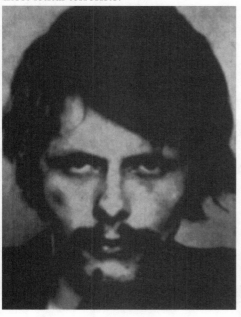

Jan-Carl Raspe, one of Baader-Meinhof's most lethal terrorists.

Damage is shown at the U.S. base in Heidleberg, Germany, following the explosion of a Baader-Meinhof bomb.

gang members, Irmgard Moller and Angela Luther, casually walked into the station to make an innocuous inquiry. They left two suitcases heavily packed with bombs that went off a few minutes later, causing the roof to collapse and five policemen to be seriously injured.

On the same day, Schelm was also "honored" by an explosion set off by the gang in the parking lot of the State Criminal Investigations Office in Munich. Sixty cars were blown up and the offices were badly damaged. Three days later, Baader, Meins, and Raspe located the Karlsruhe residence of federal judge Wolfgang Buddenburg and planted a bomb in his Volkswagen. Buddenburg had been the judge who had signed the arrest warrants for all of the known gang members. The judge, however, did not use his car on May 15, 1972. Instead, his

wife, Gerta Buddenburg, got into the car. When she turned on the ignition, the car blew up. She miraculously survived but was crippled for life.

The bombings went on and on as the authorities chased shadows, always barely missing the terrorists, who moved from hideout to hideout. Rewards in excess of hundreds of thousands of dollars were placed on the heads of the B-M leaders, but few dared to inform on these blood-lusting killers. When hearing of the dead or alive rewards, Meinhof got on the phone and called all over Germany to members, ordering the assassinations of businessmen, politicians and government leaders. When hearing of this, the West German government ordered the Ministry of Defense and the Federal Chancellory ringed with armed troops. Barricades were constructed around the homes of prominent businessmen and political leaders and armed guards patrolled the grounds around the clock.

VIP figures were told not to leave their homes until the leading terrorists were rounded up. This was impractical in that the B-M gang was widespread and highly financed through the millions it had gleaned from scores of bank robberies. They insulated themselves against identification by remaining mobile and anonymous. They could afford to pay for endless hideouts, fast cars, arms and ammunition.

On June 1, 1972, however, the authorities got their first big break. A tipster later identified only as "an old-age pensioner" called the Baader-Meinhof Commission to inform officials that a bomb factory in a garage on the North Side of Frankfurt was stored from floor to ceiling with "gas cylinders" that were being brought to the garage by "young people driving expensive cars." Heavily armed police squads rushed to the site and found the bomb factory. Inside they found hundreds of explosive devices. Bomb experts dismantled the bombs while the area was ringed with hundreds of officers wearing various disguises.

Officers closest to the garage pretended to be gardeners clipping hedges. Early the following morning, a lilac Porsche roared through the deserted streets of Frankfurt and came to a stop in front of the garage. Three men got out, one staying next to the car. The other two men entered the garage. Hundreds of officers crept forward from behind trees and bushes and on rooftops. The young man near the car spotted some of the officers, and he suddenly pulled a pistol and sprinted down the street, firing blindly behind him. When his pistol was empty, the officers closed in and tackled the man. He was Jan-Carl Raspe, one of the most important B-M leaders.

Inside the garage were even more important gang members, Andreas Baader and Holger Meins. Both men grew alarmed when they heard the shooting outside; this was Raspe, running from the scene and attempting to draw the police with him and away from his associates. Baader and Meins cracked the garage door to see police swarming past them down the alleyway in pursuit of Raspe. They quickly barricaded the door, and then attempted to employ the bombs against the police, but they found them rendered useless.

Soon, gas shells were smashing through the windows. An armored car rumbled down the alley. Gasping for air, Baader and Meins threw the gas cannisters back through the windows so that the alleyway was filled with smoke. Then they heard an officer talking to them through a bullhorn: "Come out one at a time. Nothing will happen to you. Think of your life. You are still young."

Baader opened the door a crack. He could be seen inserting bullets into the chamber of his revolver while smoking a cigarette clenched between his teeth. He spotted an officer on a rooftop and aimed, but the officer fired first, his bullet smashing into the terrorist's leg. Howling with pain, Baader dropped his revolver and

Baader-Meinhof terrorist Holger Meins, shirtless, is shown just after his capture in Frankfurt, Germany, June 1972.

retreated to the rear of the garage where he cowered.

Meins then went to the door. He stuck out his head, shouting to police that he wanted to surrender. The officers were taking no chances. They remembered the coat-over-the-arm trick practiced by the murderous Petra Schelm. Meins was ordered to strip. He obediently removed all his clothes, except his underpants, then hobbled outside; he had been grazed in the leg by a stray bullet. He screamed in fear, begging the officers not to hurt him.

"Who's still inside?" an officer asked.

"Andreas," replied Meins.

Television cameras had by then arrived at the scene, and Meins was photographed in his embarrassing state of undress. Police wasted no more time, a half dozen officers throwing open the garage doors. Baader lay in the back of the garage, holding on to his bleeding leg. He wore expensive tailor-made clothes and dark glasses. Next to him on the floor was his revolver. He made no move toward it as officers surrounded him. He was lifted up and placed on a stretcher as the cameras caught it all.

Seeing the cameras, Baader raised himself on one elbow; he could not resist grandstanding; he shouted: "You are all swine!" With that he fell back on the stretcher, and as he did so, a fully loaded pistol slipped from his pocket, falling off the edge of the stretcher. Baader was rushed to a hos-

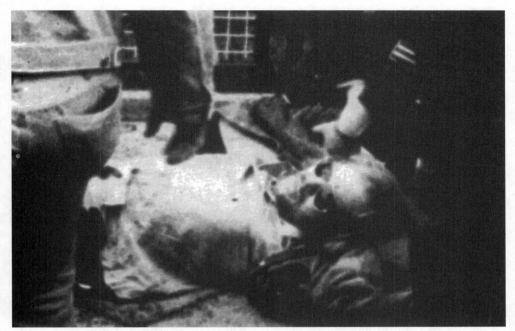

Andreas Baader lies wounded after a 1972 shootout with police in Frankfurt, Germany.

pital and given a transfusion. He was then returned to his long-vacated jail cell.

One by one, the top leaders of the terror gang fell into the hands of the authorities. Next came the vainglorious Gudrun Ensslin. She walked into a Hamburg boutique to try on a designer coat. She removed her jacket and placed this on a chair. When a salesgirl picked up the jacket, she noticed that it was extraordinarily heavy. Then she saw a machine pistol sticking out from the coat pocket and called police. Ensslin was taken without a battle and was soon whisked off to prison.

Only the mastermind, Ulrike Meinhof, remained at large. A week later, police received information that she might be in a Hanover apartment. Officers went to the address and knocked on the door. A dumpy woman with straggly dark hair and large dark circles under her eyes answered the door. She was immediately seized, her arms thrown behind her. She was handcuffed and dragged downstairs to a waiting police squad. The woman kicked and screamed: "You pigs! You pigs! You pigs!" They knew they had Ulrike Meinhof.

Found on Meinhof was a note from Ensslin that had been smuggled out of the prison where Ensslin had been taken. It read: "Mac is on holiday, four weeks, to be spent there." The "Mac" referred to in the note was Iain MacLeod, who had become the chief arms supplier to the terrorists.

MacLeod was a leading British terrorist with a quick trigger-finger. When police tracked him down to an apartment in Stuttgart, they took no chances. Officers stood before the door, holding submachine guns.

When MacLeod answered the door, he saw the officers and quickly slammed it in their faces. The police immediately opened fire, pouring dozens of rounds through the door. When they opened it, they found MacLeod dead on the floor. He was clutching a machine pistol. This death by no means ended the threat of the terrorist gang. Other deadly members remained at large who began to warn authorities that if their leaders were placed on trial, wholesale destruction of government buildings would commence. For two years, the government put off the trial, building a bomb-proof courtroom in Stammheim.

Meanwhile, gang members searched their own ranks for traitors, believing that insiders had tipped authorities as to the whereabouts of the captured leaders. Ulrich Schmucker, a twenty-year-old radical student, became the gang's chief suspect. He had been found sleeping inside of a car loaded with explosives by police on May 7, 1972, and was inexplicably released. A mock trial was held, and when Schmucker could give no reason for his release, he was condemned to death. His best friend, Gotz Tilgener, who had brought Schmucker into the organization, was ordered to shoot him. Tilgener refused, telling gang members: "You have gone too far."

The execution job went to another member, who casually shot the suspected traitor to death. His body was dumped in Grunwald Park in Berlin. (Another story has it that Schmucker was actually taken to the park, tied to a tree and shot by a firing squad of eight B-M members. Following the murder, a gang member called police to inform them that Schmucker had been "liquidated" because he had been "an instrument of the class enemy." Tilgener, the friend who had refused to execute Schmucker, was later found dead, his death attributed to drugs and alcohol, but murder was never ruled out since authorities found in his apartment many letters from gang members threatening his life.

Inside prison, the gang leaders went on defying the system, promising bloody reprisals for their incarceration. Holger Meins then went on a hunger strike, refusing food and water. After his death on November 9, 1974, Meinhof exploded and demanded that his suicide be revenged. She smuggled notes out of prison in which she demanded action by her followers, decreeing the death of Gunter von Drenckmann, president of the West German Supreme Court.

On November 14, 1974, when the jurist was celebrating his birthday at his Berlin home, the front doorbell rang. A servant told Drenckmann that "a group of nice young men" were at the doorstep with presents. The judge stood smiling in the doorway as several young men offered him small bouquets of flowers. As he reached out for a bouquet, the young men dropped the flowers to show guns that had been hidden beneath the bouquets. They emptied their weapons into Drenckmann. The old man fell dead in the doorway. Drenckmann, it was later pointed out, had been selected for death by Meinhof on whim; he had never been involved with any legal action against the gang.

B-M terrorists next kidnapped fifty-two-year-old Peter Lorenz, head of the Christian Democrat Party and the most popular candidate for the post of mayor of Berlin. Placed in a basement cell of a hideout, he was guarded night and day by six armed terrorists. In return for Lorenz's safe return, the gang demanded that the government release one of its most lethal leaders, Horst Mahler, along with five other B-M terrorists. The kidnappers did not ask for Meinhof, Baader, or Ensslin, believing they would better serve the cause by remaining "prison martyrs."

The kidnappers were led by Ralf Reinders, one of the young men who had murdered Judge Drenckmann. He, Fritz Teufel, and Angela Luther were now the leaders of the terrorists. Reinders had Lorenz photographed in his cell, and these photos were sent to officials with notes stating that unless the demands of the kidnappers were met, Lorenz would be executed.

Oddly, Mahler announced that he would not cooperate with the new B-M leaders. He refused to leave his cell. Secretly, Mahler feared that his fellow terrorists might want him free so that they could kill him for imagined traitorous acts. "Now they are all lunatics," he whispered to a guard.

The government then shocked the world by caving in, releasing the five

terrorists and giving them each 20,000 marks. Realizing that they had triumphed over the government, B-M leaders next schemed to have Meinhof, Baader, and Ensslin released. To that end, several terrorists broke into the West German Embassy in Stockholm on April 24, 1975. All of the gang members were later identified as part of Huber's "crazy brigade," the Communist mental patients. Ambassador Dietrich Stocker and several other diplomats were held hostage.

The terrorists inside the Embassy demanded that Meinhof, Baader, and Ensslin be released, given $500,000 and flown out of the country, along with twenty-three other B-M members held in prison. If the government refused, all of the diplomats would be killed, one by one. Silence was the only response from the Bonn government. Then Lieutenant-Colonel Andreas Baron von Mirbach was taken to the head of the stairs. (The terrorists were barricaded on the fourth floor of the building, negotiating with authorities on the third floor.)

Without a word, the military attache was shot several times and his body thrown down the stairs. One of the berserk terrorists laughed uproariously, shrieking that the Bonn authorities would certainly agree to terms now. The gang members fully believed that the government would submit as it had in the Lorenz case, but they were shocked to learn otherwise when Swedish police called up the stairs to them to say that the Bonn government had refused to negotiate. German Chancellor Helmut Schmidt and his ministers had had enough of the Baader-Meinhof gang.

In an effort to save the other hostages, Swedish authorities offered to let the terrorists leave the country if they would release the remaining diplomats. Gang members responded by shooting an enfeebled old man and dangling his body from a fourth-floor window. Still, Bonn would not yield. Swedish police then made plans to attack the terrorists with tear-gas shells, followed by a massive rush of heavily armed troops. It was not necessary. Shortly before 10 P.M., the terrorists gave up.

After releasing the hostages, the gang members decided on mass suicide. At midnight the Embassy building was rocked by a tremendous explosion that collapsed the floors of the building. Among the ruins was found the dead leader of the Embassy raid, Ulrich Wessel, a young man who had inherited millions but who had opted for Marxism and sudden death. Four other terrorists then stumbled from the smoking ruins—Hanna-Elise

Krabbe, Karl-Heinz Dellwo, Lutz Taufer, and Bernd Maria Rossner. The last to surrender was Siegfried Hauser, who died five days later from a crushed skull.

The trial of Meinhof, Baader, Ensslin, and Raspe finally took place on May 21, 1975. Either the terrorists would be convicted or the government would collapse, most reports concluded. Hundreds of pages listed the 600 capital offenses charged to the defendants. For a year the prosecution presented a litany of murders, bombings, torture, and robberies, and throughout the mostly uneventful trial, the defendants incessantly shouted obscenities and threats. On May 4, 1976, exhausted from the proceedings, Ensslin, attempting once again to take the limelight from her co-defendants, confessed to having caused three of the four murder-bombings with which the group was charged.

So despondent over this confession was Ulrike Meinhof that she resolved to end everything. She tore a towel

A defiant Ulrike Meinhof, imprisoned in 1975; she would hang herself in her cell.

into strips and tied the strips together to make a crude rope. She then fastened the rope to the window bars of her cell, stood on a chair and placed the noose around her neck. She then jumped from the chair. Hours later, guards found her dangling, quite dead, her tongue, black and drooling, sticking from between teeth that had almost cut it in two when her jaw had automatically clamped shut. She was given a huge funeral on May 15, 1976, in West Berlin. More than 4,000 radical students followed the funeral cortege. All wore masks so that police could not identify them.

The trial went on and so did the terrorist B-M killings. Siegfried Buback, chief federal prosecutor for West Germany, was shot to death by gang members while he drove down a street in Karlsruhe on April 7, 1977. This killing did not prevent the conviction of Baader, Ensslin, and Raspe on several murder counts on April 28, 1977. They were sent to prison with life terms. The killings nevertheless went on.

Terrorists attempted to kidnap Dr. Jurgen Ponto, head of the Dresden Bank, thinking to ransom him for the jailed terrorists. Ponto, however, opened the door of his Frankfurt home on July 30, 1977, and struggled with his abductors. They shot him dead. Ponto had been caught off guard since one of the callers at his door was his own goddaughter, Susanne Albrecht. She, along with several other B-M members, used the same trick employed in the Drenckmann shooting. Albrecht stood holding a bouquet of flowers with a gun hidden beneath the bouquet. Unknown to Ponto, his goddaughter had become the mistress of SPK killer Karl-Heinz Dellwo, who had been captured following the embassy attack in Sweden.

Dr. Hans Martin Schleyer, one of Germany's top industrialists, was next kidnapped by the terrorists, who swooped down upon his limousine, killing three of his bodyguards and his chauffeur before taking Schleyer captive. They again demanded the release of Baader, Ensslin, and Raspe. The Bonn government stalled as police conducted a desperate search for the kidnappers and their victim. Even after the terrorists released a photo of Schleyer, showing him in a state of complete collapse, the government did not act.

Desperate to make something happen, the terrorists asked the help of their Arab brothers in the PFLP. A splinter group of that organization promptly seized a Lufthansa airliner en route from Majorca to Frankfurt, holding its passengers captive, demanding that the Baader group be released, along with several Arab terrorists then in German prisons. They also demanded $15 million and an uninterrupted flight to a Middle Eastern destination.

The plane was shuttled about from airport to airport while Bonn refused to admit defeat. In Aden, the frustrated terrorists shot and killed the pilot, Jurgen Schumann, after forcing him to kneel in front of his passengers. They threw his body from the plane, threatening to kill more hostages if their demands went unanswered. After flying to Mogadishu, the terrorists made more demands, but this time they were met by a well-trained commando unit from the *Grenzschutz Gruppe 9*. The commandos stormed the plane and shot it out with the Arab killers. Three of the four terrorists were killed, the fourth wounded. All eighty-six passengers were released without serious injury, and none of the heroic German soldiers was wounded. It was a smashing triumph for governmental law and order.

Raspe, who operated a secret transmitter in his prison cell, learned of the terrorist defeat and somehow managed to have two guns smuggled into prison. Baader used one of them to blow out his brains, and Raspe used the other to kill himself. Ensslin, now all alone, followed Ulrike Meinhof's example and hanged herself in her cell.

In retaliation for these suicides, the B-M terrorists holding Schleyer murdered their hostage. His body was later found stuffed into the trunk of a car parked in Mulhouse, France. Some of his slayers were later apprehended and given long prison terms. The murder of Schleyer was the last significant criminal act by the Baader-Meinhof terrorist gang, which soon went out of existence as a viable force in world terrorism. The German nightmare, which had lasted a decade, was finally over.

Terror in Red and Black

Just as Germany suffered through the 1970s under the blood-soaked hands of the Baader-Meinhof gang, Italy underwent a similar and prolonged agony brought about by fanatical leftists of the self-styled Red Brigades. This ultra-leftist organization was founded in 1969 by Renato Curcio, a sociology student at the University of Trento. The original group confined its early criminal activities to vandalism, arson, and proselytizing about the need for "an armed proletariat vanguard to do battle against the imperialist state of the multinationals."

By the early 1970s, however, the Red Brigades became more dangerous as its members took to kidnapping mid-level corporate officials, who were released after admitting crimes at "people's trials." In 1970, the Brigades were content to distribute leaflets throughout Milan that listed "enemies of the people." In 1971, these Italian terrorists took to bomb making; they blew up three trucks on a test track at Pirelli.

The terrorists graduated to kidnapping the following year, seizing Idalgo Macchiarini, an executive for Sit-Siemens, on March 3, 1972. After being kept prisoner for only half an hour, Macchiarini was shoved from a car and was left standing in the middle of a roadway, wearing a sign stating that "nothing will remain unpunished. Hit one to educate 100. All power to the armed people." Bartolomeo di Mino, a member of an extreme right-wing political group, was seized next, released with the warning: "The fascist agitators must have no chance of political action in our districts, our factories, or anywhere else."

Fiat executive Ettore Amerio was kidnapped in 1973. Upon his release, Amerio nervously parroted Red Brigades' instructions, stating that his kidnapping had "served to mature me and make me reflect more deeply." One Italian police official snorted: "Sounds like he is reading from a script. They must have threatened to harm his family if he didn't spout their nonsense."

On April 18, 1974, the Red Brigades attacked the government directly by kidnapping deputy prosecutor Mario Sossi. He was photographed by the terrorists as he stood beneath a poster stating "carry the attack to the heart of the state." Unlike earlier hostages, Sossi was not released. The Red Brigades now demanded something in return for Sossi—eight imprisoned Red Brigade members were to be released and flown to Cuba, North Korea, or Algeria.

Genial and outgoing, Francesco Coco, a prosecutor in Genoa, smilingly agreed to the demands of the terrorists. When Sossi was released, however, Coco reneged on his promise. The terrorists bided their time, and two years later, Coco became the first political murder victim of the Red Brigades. By 1975, the Red Brigades thought of only one avenue by which to support their activities, ransom kidnapping. On June 4, 1975, factory director Dr. Vittorio Gancia was abducted and held for ransom.

Police discovered the hideout where Gancia was being held and mounted an assault. In the wild shootout, one policeman was killed and another wounded, as Gancia sprinted to freedom. Undaunted, the Red Brigades launched a series of kidnappings, twenty-six in all, that proved more successful. One abduction, that of shipping magnate Pietro Costa, netted Brigades terrorists $2.1 million. As the Red Brigades expanded its membership, it also aligned itself with other terrorist organizations such as Italy's other leftist revolutionary party, the Armed Proletarian Nucleus, or NAP, Germany's Red Army Faction and various Palestinian groups.

In 1975, forty-nine members of the Red Brigades were brought to trial in Turin. In retaliation, their comrades shot various government representatives in the kneecaps, or, as was the case with Coco, killed them. Next the terrorists murdered the head of an attorneys' association in Turin and then the chief of an anti-terrorist police squad.

In 1978, fourteen top members of the Red Brigades, including founder Renato Curcio, were arrested and placed on trial, charged with bombings and assassinations. The Brigadists responded almost immediately by kidnapping Aldo Moro, who had five times earlier served as Italy's prime minister. The Christian Democrat had brought socialists into mainstream Italian politics and government in 1963. In 1977, Moro was impressed when 40,000 young activists demonstrated on the part of the Communist Party, saying that communism had become a part of the political values of Italy's middle class. Moro sought to give the Communist Party an increased voice in the Italian government.

Though Communist in nature and philosophy, the Red Brigades sought to use the sympathetic Moro as their tool and to barter him for the release of the Brigadists in custody. On March 16, 1978, as Moro was being driven from church to a special session of parliament, his heavily guarded car was attacked by a party of Brigadists, including three women. Wielding automatic weapons, the terrorists shot down and killed five of Moro's bodyguards in their bloody ambush, and then hustled Moro into hiding.

Two days later, a photo of Moro posing before a Red Brigades flag arrived at a newspaper in Rome. With it was a note from the terrorists, who said they were going to try Moro for actions "against the interests of the people." On March 29, the Ministry of the Interior received a note from Moro himself, instructing the government to meet the demands of the terrorists because "there is the risk that I will be induced to talk in a manner that could be dangerous." An accompanying note stated that the "people's trial" of Moro was in progress.

On April 15, 1978, authorities received word from the Brigadists that Moro had been found guilty of "crimes against the people," and had been executed, that his body had been dumped into a lake. A desperate search failed to uncover the body. Two days later a newspaper received a photo of Moro in good health, along with another demand that Brigadist prisoners be released. Oddly, the Communists disavowed any association with the terrorists, saying that if the Christian Democrats caved in to Brigadists' demands, the Communist Party would refuse to enter into a political coalition. West Germany and the United States urged the Italian government to resist the demands of the terrorists.

Moro's family begged the unflinching government to negotiate with the terrorists. The Pope reportedly got down on his knees and prayed for the deliverance of the political leader. Seven more letters were received by government leaders from a pleading Moro. A terrorist note was then received that demanded the release of all Communist prisoners in Italy for Moro. The Communists openly rejected this offer and distanced themselves from the terrorists. On May 7, 1978,

Prospero Gallinari, terrorist leader of the Red Brigades in Italy, and killer of the kidnapped Prime Minister Aldo Moro in 1978.

Moro's wife received a final letter from her husband, one in which he stated: "Soon they will kill me. The friends could have saved me but did not. I kiss you for the last time. Kiss the children for me."

On May 9, 1978, police received an anonymous tip to search for a red car in the heart of Rome. They found such a car and, upon opening the trunk, they also found the bullet-riddled body of Aldo Moro. He had been shot eleven times in the heart. His hands and feet were chained. It had been fifty-five days since he had been kidnapped. In Turin, Brigades founder Renato Curcio hailed the assassination of Moro as a triumph of revolutionary justice, but Italy and the world were horrified by the brutality of Moro's slaying, and world leaders condemned the Brigadists and the sadistic manner in which they had tortured Moro's family with teasing promises of his release, announcements of his death, then more news that he was alive.

The terrorists continued to take more lives, killing seven more political victims within a week of Moro's murder. By early 1979, however, police were able to penetrate the hideouts of the Brigadists. They arrested twenty-two suspects, including Antonio Negri, a political science professor in Padua who, along with the others, was imprisoned in the maximum security prison at Trani, Italy. On December 28, 1980, the Brigadists led other prisoners in a mass breakout attempt. Two days later, commandos using helicopters swept into the prison yard and rescued eighteen hostages.

By 1983, sixty-three persons had been charged with the Moro kidnapping and murder. They were brought to trial before Judge Severino Santiapichi. Twenty-three of the terrorists were found guilty and were sentenced to life imprisonment, among them Prospero Gallinari, the man who had actually shot Moro to death. Nine other defendants received life sentences for other murders and kidnappings, the rest receiving sentences of between a few months to thirty years. Four were acquitted. (The matter did not end there; as late as 1988 warrants were still being issued for the arrest of terrorists involved in the Moro killing.)

By the 1980s, the Red Brigades had been decimated by massive arrests.

More than 450 Brigadists were in prison, yet the terrorist group lingered, mostly under the fanatical leadership of Antonio Savasta. The son of a Rome policeman, Savasta had abandoned his law studies to join the Red Brigades in the mid-1970s. It was he who actually masterminded the kidnapping of Aldo Moro. He had also engineered the kidnappings of Guiseppe Taliercio, a chemical company executive, and political leader Ciro Cirillo. In 1980, Savasta shot his way out of a police trap in the Sardinian city of Cagliari, a long-time stronghold of terrorist operations.

Savasta then pinpointed leaders of the North Atlantic Treaty Organization (NATO) as the next targets of the Red Brigades. He reasoned that NATO represented a common defense of western Europe against Communist aggression and, as such, was the mortal enemy of the Brigadists. Savasta targeted NATO chief and U.S. Brigadier General James Lee Dozier for kidnapping. On December 17, 1981, Dozier was seized by terrorists under Savasta's command from his apartment in northern Verona.

Dozier was taken to Padua and held captive in an apartment for forty-two days, as Savasta sent his demand to the Italian government, the release of Brigadists from prison. This time, the government met fire with fire. It turned the matter over to its crack anti-terrorist squad, the *Nucleo Operativo Centrale di Sicurezza* (NOCS), more commonly known as the "Leatherheads." The unit located the Padua apartment on January 28, 1982. As squad members prepared to storm the place, Savasta, realizing he had been located, approached Dozier, who was tied to a chair. He stood before the helpless American officer, raising a pistol to his victim's head. Before he could pull the trigger, the NOCS squad burst through the door and windows. One of the officers slammed a rifle butt onto Savasta's head, knocking him senseless before he could fire a single shot.

Retrieving Dozier safely marked the first time that a Red Brigades kidnap victim had been successfully rescued since 1975. In the wake of the rescue, more than 400 Brigadists were rounded up. The Italian government had finally broken the back of the worst terrorist gang in its history but not without the help of one of its worst terrorists. Savasta quickly lost his political fanaticism and readily agreed to cooperate with Italian police. He supplied the names of dozens of Red Brigades members to police and then wrote an open letter to Brigadists, imploring them to come out of hiding and surrender. Further, Savasta confirmed long-suspected ties between the Red Brigades and Yasir Arafat's PLO, and various Soviet block countries, chief suppliers of arms and ammunition to the terrorists.

On March 14, 1982, Savasta and sixteen others charged with the kidnapping of General Dozier went on trial in Rome. All seventeen terrorists were found guilty. Savasta was sent to prison for sixteen years and six months. His co-defendants received varying prison terms of two to twenty-seven years. With the imprisonment

of Savasta and his henchmen, the Red Brigades of Italy crumbled.

The destruction of the Red Brigades and, earlier, the Baader-Meinhof Gang disheartened its terrorist mentor, the Palestine Liberation Organization, which had, at its own expense, trained the Brigadists and B-M gang members, as well as funded some of their operations and equipped them with high-powered weapons. The same fate befell another, more distant PLO-backed terrorist organization, the Red Army of Japan.

Begun in 1969 by left-wing students in Japan, the Red Army sought to achieve its political goals through acts of terrorism. When the group made plans to assassinate Japan's leading politicians, twelve of its top members opposed the killings. All twelve were summarily executed on orders of Red Army leader Tsuneo Mori. To solidify its membership, as well as glean funding, the Red Army aligned itself with the PLO, functioning in many instances as an enforcement arm of the Arab terrorist organization. One of its "assignments" from the PLO, or, more specifically, from the Black September commando arm of the PLO's radical splinter group, Al-Fatah, was the Red Army attack on Lod Airport in Tel Aviv.

On May 13, 1972, three members of the Japanese Red Army, recruited by Black September, carried out a ruthless machine gun attack on innocent persons gathered at the Lod Airport terminal. Throwing hand grenades and firing bursts into crowds, the three terrorists slaughtered twenty-four persons, including thirteen

Puerto Ricans on a pilgrimage to the Holy Land, and wounded another twenty-six. Four of the wounded victims later died, and two of the three terrorists, Rakeshi Okudeira and Yoshuyiki Yasuda, were killed.

The surviving Red Army killer, Kozo Okamoto, was later tried and convicted, then sent to prison for life. (The prosecution did not seek the death penalty.) The Popular Front for the Liberation of Palestine (PFLP) later claimed responsibility for the Lod attack, saying that it had been a reprisal for an earlier Israeli attack against Palestinians.

Universally condemned, the Red Army was held up to the world as nothing more than a gang of murderous thugs who did the bidding of other terrorist organizations. Recruitment to the Red Army fell off drastically, and in 1973, Mori, the group's top commander, was imprisoned. He hanged himself in his cell that year. Remnants of the organization continued their terrorist attacks, hijacking a JAL plane in 1973.

In the following year, Red Army terrorists attempted to sabotage oil storage tanks in Singapore and, also in that year, the group took over the Japanese Embassy in Kuwait. This was the last significant terrorist act conducted by the group, which soon, for lack of funds and recruits, faded into oblivion.

The Palestinian terrorist group known as Black September died a harder death. Dedicated to the cause of Palestinian liberation through violent means, the organization took its name from the September 1970 war with Jordan in which Palestinian commandos were expelled from that country following a series of airline hijackings. The members of this radical splinter group of Al Fatah and the PLO carried out a series of terrorist attacks against Israel, its Western allies and anyone else opposed to the establishment of a Palestinian homeland.

Ironically, the first victim of Black September was an Arab, Jordanian prime minister Wasif Tell, who was shot and killed outside the Sheraton Hotel in Cairo in November 1971. Tell's assassin, Ezzat Rabbah, shot the prime minister as he stepped from his car without his usual complement of bodyguards, firing five rounds point-blank into Tell in the middle of a large crowd before the hotel entrance.

One of his henchmen, Monzer Khalifa, horrified the crowd of stunned European and American tourists by kneeling next to the mortally wounded Tell and, like a mad dog, lapping up his victim's blood from the floor. As one report had it, "his shocking action was a clear statement to the world that these were terrorists unlike any ever seen before." As Rabbah, Khalifa and two other confederates were seized and dragged away, they held up their fingers in a victory salute, screaming: "We are members of Black September!"

The group's second attack was performed by the Japanese Red Army Faction at Lod Airport. Unlike the Jihaz el-Rasd faction of Al Fatah, Black September did not confine its terrorist attacks to the Middle East. At the XX Olympiad in Munich, on July

18, 1972, eight Syrian-trained commandos scaled a six-foot fence surrounding the Olympic compound.

Their target was the dormitory housing the Israeli athletes, where they planned to hold the athletes hostage until 234 Arab terrorists were released from Israeli jails. They also insisted that German terrorists Andreas Baader and Ulrike Meinhof, then imprisoned in Germany, also be released. Upon their forced entrance into the Israeli quarters, the terrorists killed a coach and a weightlifter.

When officials stalled, the eight Black Septembrists announced that they would kill two Israeli athletes every half hour unless German authorities agreed to fly them to an Arab country of their choice. Failing to negotiate the release of the hostages, the German government agreed to provide a jet for the terrorists. The eight Black Septembrists and nine Israeli hostages were flown by helicopter from the Olympic compound to Fürstenfeldbruck air base and a waiting jet that was to take them to Cairo.

As the Black Septembrists appeared on the tarmac, holding the hostages at gunpoint, German sharpshooters opened fire. The terrorists, instead of returning fire against the Germans, immediately shot down their captives in cold blood, killing nine Israeli athletes. Five of the eight Arabs were then killed by withering fire from German commandos. Three of the Black Septembrists were taken into custody—Kadir el Dnawy, Mohammed Abdullah, and Ibrahim abd es. In retaliation for the Munich attack,

Israel launched a series of air attacks against several locations identified as Al Fatah training camps in Syria and Lebanon.

Although it was later stated that the PLO disavowed Black September, this horrific terrorist group was the official enforcement arm of Al Fatah, which was then under the direction of Yasir Arafat. This, Israeli intelligence always knew and knows to this day. The Munich massacre was directed by Black September leader Abu Iyad (Salah Khalaf), Arafat's closest collaborator and supporter. He was also responsible for the Black September attack on the Saudi Arabian Embassy in Khartoum on March 1, 1973, when U.S. ambassador Cleo A. Noel was wounded, and George Curtis Moore, American chargé d'affaires, was brutally murdered.

As Arafat began to embrace a softer approach to PLO activities, and the Arab League announced in 1974 that he was "the sole legitimate representative" of the Palestinian people, he ordered Black September to cease its brutal terrorist raids, absorbing most of its leaders into Al Fatah and PLO branches. Many of those killers are alive today, working with Arafat to secure Palestinian independence through peaceful negotiations with Israel.

Though Black September ceased operations under that name, its terrorist killers joined other Palestinian groups and continued to spread havoc in the Middle East and in Europe under the leadership of such murderous masterminds as Ilyich Ramirez Sanchez, who was also known as the

The most-feared international terrorist of the twentieth century, Ilyich Ramirez Sanchez, better known as Carlos, or the Jackal; he was sent to prison in France for life in 1997.

Jackal, or Carlos (who was devastatingly profiled in Frederick Forsyth's novel, *The Day of the Jackal*).

Born to a wealthy Venezuelan lawyer, a devout Communist, Sanchez was weaned on communism and trained as a terrorist while in his teens in Cuba. He aligned himself with the PFLP and soon became one of its independent terrorist leaders, masterminding the spectacular raid of an OPEC conference in Vienna, Austria, on December 21, 1975, leading eight others and taking eighty-one representatives of the oil-rich countries hostage.

Sanchez then negotiated a safe passage out of the country for this group and a number of African, South American, and Arab hostages, flying to Algiers and receiving a staggering $50 million ransom for his hostages from the Shah of Iran and King Khaled. He then disappeared inside Libya, a country ruled by one of his employers, dictator and fellow terrorist, Muammar Qaddafi. Sanchez vanished altogether in 1982 when he narrowly missed being killed in Beirut by Israeli commandos.

In 1992, Sanchez was tried *in absentia* in France and convicted of the murder of two police officers. He received a thirty-year prison sentence but remained at large, hiding somewhere in the Middle East, intelligence agents concluded.

Rumors of Sanchez's whereabouts abounded as agents from a half dozen countries tracked him. Finally, Sanchez was located in the Sudan where he was arrested by local police in 1994 and extradited to France, where he was held for trial. A considerable amount of money was paid to expensive lawyers working on Sanchez's defense before he was eventually brought to trial in Paris, these funds reportedly provided by Third World terrorist organizations.

For more than two years, Sanchez's attorneys argued that France had no right to try their client, let alone extradite him. Nevertheless, on December 24, 1997, the Jackal was convicted of the 1975 murders of two French intelligence agents and a Lebanese informant. He was sentenced to prison for life. The dreaded Carlos went behind bars still protesting the right of France to imprison him.

The Canadian Kidnappings

James Richard Cross, British trade commissioner for Canada, sits glumly while his FLQ terrorist kidnappers photograph him in 1970.

At the time the Baader-Meinhof gang, the Red Brigades, and Black September came into being, a fanatical French separatist group calling itself the *Front de Liberation du Quebec* (FLQ) launched a series of kidnappings and murders that terrorized Canadian citizens. The FLQ had long demanded that its separatist demands be met, but the Canadian government of Prime Minister Pierre Trudeau was unresponsive.

On October 5, 1970, Canada experienced its first political kidnapping when four armed FLQ gunmen seized forty-nine-year-old James Richard Cross, the British trade commissioner for Canada, from his Quebec home. In their ransom communique, the terrorists demanded that twenty-three of their compatriots be released from prison, that they receive $500,000 in gold, the reinstatement of several recently fired postal workers and safe passage for the kidnappers to either Cuba or Algeria. Unless these terms were met, the kidnappers promised, Cross would be killed. Enclosed with the note was a photo of a haggard-looking James Cross staring bleakly into the camera's eye.

Prime Minister Trudeau at first refused to deal with the terrorists, publicly stating: "You can't let a minority impose its views upon a majority by violence . . . It is a difficult decision when you have to weigh a man's life in the balance, but certainly our commitment to society is greater than anything else."

Refusing the FLQ demands, Trudeau offered to have the group's manifesto read over radio and television airwaves if Cross was released. This proposal was rejected by the FLQ, its leaders stating that unless its captive members were released by 6 P.M. on October 10, Cross would be killed. Ignoring the new terrorist demand, the government had parts of the FLQ manifesto read on television on October 8. Robert Lemiuex, an attorney acting on behalf of the terrorists, then accused the government of acting in bad faith.

The provisional government of Quebec countered with an offer of free passage for the kidnappers if Cross was released. Instead of negotiating further, the FLQ kidnapped Quebec's Minister of Labor, Pierre Laporte, two

Pierre Laporte, Canada's minister of labor, sits with his son; a short time later he was abducted by FLQ terrorists and later murdered.

masked men holding submachine guns and taking him from his Quebec home while he was playing football with his son and nephews. A short time later, the FLQ informed government officials that they would kill Laporte unless their demands were met. Officials stalled for time. Robert Lemiuex was arrested on October 11, 1970, charged with obstructing a police investigation.

Meanwhile, in captivity, Laporte wrote to Robert Bourassa, Quebec's premier, stating: "We are confronted by a well-organized escalation which will only end with the freeing of the political prisoners." He asked Bourassa to meet the demands of his kidnappers, ending with: "You have the power to decide on my life or death."

Bourassa appeared on TV to say that the government must have assurances that the men would be released unharmed before any demands were met. The govenment then added to the confusion by demanding that one man from each of the two known terrorist cells surrender. The FLQ would only give its "solemn pledge to the people of Quebec" that the hostages would be released if demands were met.

On October 15, the FLQ aroused the students at the University of Quebec, who took to the streets, demonstrating on behalf of the terrorists and insisting that their demands be met. This so alarmed Bourassa that, on October 16, he requested that federal troops be sent to guard public buildings and the homes of government officials, including his own.

One more offer was then made to the FLQ. If Cross and Laporte were released, five of the imprisoned FLQ members would be released and all concerned with the kidnappings could go free. For two days the terrorists remained silent. During this time the govenment issued the first peactime declaration of a state of "apprehended insurrection," which allowed the government to take any action required to ensure national security.

The FLQ was officially condemned and more than 250 persons suspected of FLQ connections were arrested. Then the government made another offer to the terrorists: The prisoners and kidnappers would receive safe escort to the Cuban consulate and all could depart for Cuba. Upon arrival in Cuba, Cross and Laporte would be set free by Cuban authorities. This latest offer enraged the frustrated terrorists, who murdered Laporte out of hand.

On October 18, 1970, police, following up on a tip, found Laporte's bullet-ridden and strangled corpse in the trunk of a car at St. Hubert's airport near Montreal. It was the first political slaying in Canada in more than 100 years. The police stepped up their search for the kidnappers. They located nineteen-year-old Bernard Lortie, an FLQ terrorist, on November 6, and, on December 2, police located a Montreal house where Cross was being held. (It was never publicly stated if Lortie gave investigators the location of the hideout.)

Rather than storm the house, the police negotiated with FLQ members who agreed to release Cross in exchange for safe passage to Cuba. Cross was then set free and three FLQ terrorists and four of their relatives were flown to Cuba, courtesy of the Royal Canadian Mounted Police. The matter did not end. Investigators grilled Lortie until he provided the names of three accomplices in the kidnappings and killing of Laporte— Paul Rose and brothers Jacques and Francis Simard.

Following a series of trials in 1971, Rose was found guilty of Laporte's kidnapping and murder, for which he received two concurrent life sentences. Francis Simard was given a life sentence for his involvement with the crimes, and Lortie was given twenty years. Jacques Simard was acquitted of all charges. The FLQ members who escaped to Cuba later went to France where the government "honored" the safe passage agreement made in Quebec. They were never prosecuted for their crimes.

Black Muslims, Death Angels, and Mass Murder

Although the Black Muslims of America had publicly preached nonviolence, its male membership, particularly in the mid-1960s, was mostly made up of young blacks across the country who had been imprisoned for strong-arm robbery, drugs, and murder. Such was the case with Malcolm Little, a small-time thief who reportedly underwent a religious transformation while serving time in prison in Charlestown, Massachusetts. He joined the Black Muslims under the leadership of Elijah Muhammed and soon became Malcolm X, one of the Muslims' most outspoken leaders, who was to be assassinated in 1965 by fellow Muslims.

The Muslims, since their inception in 1913 by Prophet Drew Ali, preached "Black Isolationism," which called for total segregation of the races and a separate black homeland to be established outside of the U.S. (a credo that black confidence man Marcus Aurelius Garvey expanded upon in the 1920s as he gathered a fortune from duped followers to ostensibly lease a huge flotilla of boats that would sail America's black population to Africa). Wallace D. Fard, who took over the Muslims in 1930, continued this doctrine until he mysteriously disappeared in 1934 and his place was taken by Muhammed.

Muhammed launched the widespread recruitment of militant blacks from American prisons and soon had a fierce following of uneducated and violent men, thousands of them, who hated a political and economic system that they claimed they would change through nonviolence. Those Muslims who actually believed in effecting change through nonviolent means, however, were either killed or driven out of the Muslim sect after being branded traitors and subjected to physical harrassment, even death, as was the case with Malcolm X.

In 1974, the so-called kidnapping of publishing heiress Patricia Campbell Hearst by the Symbionese Liberation Army (SLA), headed by the megalomaniacal Donald David DeFreeze, brought the Black Muslims into the camp of terrorism. On February 4, 1974, the nineteen-year-old Hearst was physically abducted from the Berkeley, California, apartment she shared with fiance Stephen Weed. After answering a knock on the door, Weed was beaten senseless by two men who swept Hearst from the apartment.

Above: Newspaper heiress Patricia Campbell Hearst, ostensibly abducted in 1974 by Symbionese Liberation Army terrorists.
Below: FBI wanted poster for SLA leader Donald David DeFreeze.

The kidnapping seemed faked, according to neighbors, who reported how Hearst's cries for help seemed feeble or feigned. A huge ransom was demanded of Hearst's father, publishing magnate William Randolph Hearst, Jr. The ransom was to be $70 million in foodstuffs to be delivered to California's poor. To convince Hearst that the kidnapping was real, SLA leader DeFreeze enclosed a tape recording of his captive; on it Patty Hearst, in a monotone, stated that "these people aren't just a bunch of nuts. They're perfectly willing to die for what they're doing."

Oakland, California, was designated as the distribution point for the food, and the Black Muslims, to the surprise of the press and public, were chosen by the terrorists as the "managers" of the food distribution. This was not so surprising after all, as it was later pointed out, in that many black SLA members were also Black Muslims. When the food was distributed, more than 13,000 persons jostling for position in food lines, suddenly rioted. (One report had it that Muslims instigated the riot by tossing food packages into the crowd in a disdainful manner.)

DeFreeze, a bomber and terrorist with a long criminal record, had apparently been recruiting members to the SLA from the ranks of the Black Muslims. He had formed the SLA in 1973, after escaping from prison, and one of his first edicts was to order the death of Marcus Foster, the black superintendent of schools in Oakland, who had been critical of the Black Muslims and who had proposed a

Black muslims, working with the SLA, distributed tons of foodstuffs in Oakland, California, to the black community as part of the ransom to be paid for the return of Patty Hearst in 1974. The SLA symbol is prominently displayed on a doorway.

plan wherein all Oakland students be photographed for identification purposes. DeFreeze and militant Black Muslim leaders believed that Foster was actually proposing a system whereby Muslims could be identified. Foster was shot to death with cyanide-tipped bullets on November 6, 1973.

On January 10, 1974, two of DeFreeze's men, Russell Little and Joseph Remiro were stopped by police in Concord, California. They jumped from their van, pulling guns and battling police until Little was wounded and captured. Remiro escaped but was

later captured. Both had been stopped only a few blocks from the SLA's bomb-making factory and headquarters, which police shortly discovered after it caught fire. In the debris, officials found revolutionary pamphlets and a note written in DeFreeze's handwriting: "Patricia Campbell Hearst on the night of the full moon of January 7."

Hearst's abduction followed on February 4. Following the ransom payment of food in Oakland, the SLA stepped up operations, its members, including an obviously very willing Patty Hearst who was recorded by

TERRORISM IN THE 20TH CENTURY

Patricia Hearst clutching an automatic weapon and posing next to the SLA logo; she would later be exposed as faking her own kidnapping and being a willing member of the terrorist organization. She would also go to prison for robbing a bank.

Underground Guerrillas

Firemen guarded by heavily armed police attempt to extinguish the flames consuming the SLA headquarters in Los Angeles, 1974. DeFreeze and five others perished in the blaze.

bank video cameras, robbing the Hibernia Bank in San Francisco's Sunset District. Prior to the robbery, Hearst had sent another tape to the press in which she stated that she had voluntarily joined the terrorists and should be henceforth addressed as "Tania." Although her family thought she was being coerced, it was later determined that Hearst had joined the SLA while a student at Berkeley and had play-acted her own abduction to milk food and money from her billionaire father.

Hearst later participated in the robbery of a sporting goods store in Inglewood, California, with white SLA members Emily and William Harris, spraying the facade with machine gun bullets. Three days later,

on May 17, 1974, police received a tip from a former SLA member that the main gang was holed up in a small stucco house at 1466 E. 54th Street, Los Angeles. More than 400 heavily armed officers, including FBI agents, attacked the place. Inside, DeFreeze, who now called himself "Field Marshal Cinque," directed return fire by his diehard followers.

More than 6,000 shots were fired before the building caught fire. Found in the smoldering ruins the next day were the bodies of DeFreeze; William Wolfe, reported to be Hearst's lover; Nancy Ling Perry; Camilla Hall; and Patricia Soltysik. SLA members still at large robbed a bank in Carmichael, California, in 1975, at which time Emily Harris reportedly shot and killed a woman. After attempting to bomb a police station on September 18, 1975, Hearst and Wendy Yoshimura were caught by police.

Hearst was convicted of armed robbery and sent to prison for seven years but, after she had served only two years, Hearst's sentence was commuted by President Jimmy Carter. Upon her release, Patricia Hearst insisted that she had really been kidnapped and held for fifty-some days in a closet and that she was repeatedly raped and then brainwashed into believing that the SLA members were the only people who cared about her.

William and Emily Harris were later caught and imprisoned for kidnapping; they were paroled in 1983. In June 1977, Joseph Remiro and Russell Little were sent to prison for life after being convicted of the murder of Marcus Foster. They were also each given six

TERRORISM IN THE 20TH CENTURY

Clockwise from above left: SLA member William Wolfe, reportedly Patty Hearst's lover and the real reason she joined DeFreeze's terrorist group; he died in the flames. SLA members Patricia Soltysik, Nancy Ling Perry, Angela Atwood, and Camilla Hall, all dead in the flames.

months to twenty years for the attempted murder of Robert Blackburn, Foster's deputy, who was wounded at the time of Foster's murder.

Despite the destruction of the SLA, the Black Muslims in California, however, did not remain inactive. They organized a murder cult known as the Death Angels, which was responsible for a series of racial and unprovoked murders of white San Francisco residents, a reign of terror lasting 179 days in 1973–1974. Five black men seeking membership in the Death Angels selected twenty-three white victims at random in the streets of San Francisco, shooting them down and killing fifteen of their number.

In desperate response, the city organized Operation Zebra (to indicate the black-on-white murders) and police began a widespread hunt for the terrorists, stopping more than 600 young black men on the streets, searching and questioning them. Civil rights advocates filed a complaint and the Operation was halted.

The interracial "Zebra killings" were solved when twenty-nine-year-old Anthony Harris, one of the five black killers, confessed and implicated four other blacks—Manuel Moore, 31; J. C. Simon, 29; Larry Craig Green, 24; and Jessie Lee Cook, 30. The slayers stated that the doctrine of the Death Angels compelled them to kill

Underground Guerrillas

LAPD Sgt. Charles Loust, before a chart detailing the SLA headquarters destroyed by the fire in the 1974 shootout. Before him is the terrorist arsenal recovered from the ruins.

whites at random, that all whites were evil and had to be destroyed. Their initiation into the murder cult required them to kill a number of whites. In March 1976, the second-longest trial in California history (a year and six days) took place when the five men went to court. After 181 witnesses testified, the five accused men were found guilty and sent to prison for life.

A spinter group of Black Muslims calling itself the Hanafi Moslems, launched a terror campaign in Washington, D.C., on March 9, 1977. Led by fifty-four-year-old Haamas Abdul Khaalis, a U.S. black citizen whose original name was Ernest

Timothy McGhee, small bands of Hanafi Moslems invaded three downtown buildings, killing one man, wounding eleven others and taking more than 100 hostages. Khaalis led a band of seven terrorists into the B'nai B'rith headquarters, the oldest and largest Jewish service organization in the U.S.

Entering the building at 11 A.M. Khaalis and his thugs moved upward floor by floor, seizing dozens of hostages, shooting at some of them, slapping and slashing others. At noon, three other Hanafi thugs entered the Islamic Center and took eleven hostages but without any display of violence. About two hours later, two more Hanafi terrorists entered the District Building only a few blocks from the White House, shooting at random and killing twenty-four-year-old Maurice Williams and wounding three other persons, including city councilman and later mayor, Marion Barry.

At first, authorities found it difficult to learn what the terrorists wanted. Finally, Khaalis stated that he would release all hostages after the government ordered a ban on the film, *Mohammad, Messenger of God*, a movie the Hanafi Moslems deemed sacrilegious. In addition, Khaalis demanded that five Black Muslims serving prison sentences for their part in the 1973 slayings of seven Khaalis family members be turned over to him for execution. If this particular demand was not met, Khaalis vowed that he would behead all of the more than 100 hostages held captive in the three buildings.

The FBI quickly provided a shocking profile of Khaalis to officials. He had been discharged from the army in World War II as mentally unstable. He had attempted to extort money from a bank in 1968, but charges were at that time dropped when it was learned that he was a mental patient. Volatile and emotionally unpredictable, Khaalis had joined the Black Muslims in 1958, but had broken with the group and had organized his own sect, the Hanafi Moslems. He had written a critical letter to the Muslims in 1972 that had apparently prompted the attack on his home/headquarters in Washington in 1973 where his six children and one grandchild were slain. Five black men

had been sent to prison for life for that crime.

Initially, authorities complied with Khaalis's first demand, officially banning the movie about Muhammad. They also reimbursed Khaalis $750 for legal fees caused by an earlier contempt of court citation. They refused, however, to deliver the five Black Muslims to Khaalis for execution. Instead, they persuaded three ambassadors of Islamic countries, those of Pakistan, Egypt, and Iran, to meet with the disturbed Khaalis in the lobby of the B'nai B'rith building. The ambassadors read excerpts from the Koran to him, passages forbidding the use of violence.

Khaalis finally agreed to release the hostages if he were allowed to go free. Officials agreed. Once the hostages were set free, Khaalis was taken to the courtroom of Harold Greene, chief judge of Washington's Superior Court, where he was released after promising the court to stay in Washington, give up all arms, surrender his passport, shun all pretrial publicity, and promise not to break the law again. The eleven Khaalis men were brought to court the next day. The three who had taken over the Islamic building where no violence occurred were released on their own recognizance. The remaining eight were held on high bail and trial for murder and kidnapping.

Khaalis and the eleven men went to trial in June and all were convicted of kidnapping and murder on July 23, 1977. Abdul Muzikir, the killer of Maurice Williams, was sent to prison for seventy-seven years to life. Khaalis was sentenced to serve from 41 to 123 years in prison. The rest of the prisoners received sentences of between twenty-two and seventy-two years.

By the end of the 1970s, the Black Muslims and their terrorist splinter groups had abandoned violence, or so their leaders emphatically claimed. In May 1985, Wallace D. Muhammad disbanded the American Muslim Mission in order to bring its members into the worldwide Islamic community. However, a militant faction that refused to accept Wallace Muhammad's new order was organized under the direction of Louis Farrakhan. Though the Muslims may have forsaken terrorism to honor Islamic beliefs, murder and mayhem were about to break loose in the heart of Islam itself.

·NINE·
DAY OF THE ARAB

A Murder in Egypt

To Western nations, Anwar Sadat, President of Egypt, was an enlightened leader who would take any legitimate action that might secure peace in the Middle East, a land that had known no peace for decades. To Israel, the sworn enemy of Egypt for untold generations, Sadat was a candid, forthright statesman determined to end forever the conflict between the two nations. To extreme fundamentalists, particularly the Egyptian terrorist organization called Takfir Wal-Hajira ("Repentence of the Holy Flight"), Sadat was a traitor to Islamic beliefs, one marked for the assassin's bullet. Sadat knew that was his eventual fate. Moments before he was fatally shot on October 6, 1981, he raised his arm and snapped a salute at the man about to send four bullets into his body.

The assassination of Sadat was not an impulsive act, but one that had been some time in the making. Many plots had been fermenting for several years, with some nearing completion almost two years earlier. The news that assassins were tracking him came as no surprise to Sadat. This was an accepted way of life for Arab leaders throughout the century. As one might expect regular elections in Western countries, one coup followed another in Egypt, as was the case in almost all other Arab countries. One despotic ruler replaced another in a weary system that saw the names of tyrants change but oppressive tyranny remain. Sadat would be one of the few Arab rulers to alter that system.

Born to middle class parents, Sadat became a cadet in the army in 1937, when he befriended another cadet, Gamal Abdel Nasser. Both teenagers believed that Egypt suffered under two corruptive influences, their own rulers and those who ruled their rulers, the British. Upon entering the Egyptian Officer Corps, Sadat organized a group he called the Free Officer Corps, a group dedicated to freeing Eygpt of foreign colonialism. Although he had never planned a violent overthrow of the government, Sadat was arrested and imprisoned for seditious activities in 1942. Released six years later, Sadat discovered that the Free Officer Corps

Anwar Sadat, the enlightened and coura-geous leader of Egypt, assassinated by Islamic terrorists in 1981. (Wide World)

had been nurtured into a potent force by his good friend Nasser.

With Nasser's help, Sadat was rein-stated in the army and served as Nasser's aide. Both worked diligently in planning a bloodless coup that would overthrow Egypt's venal King Farouk, which, they hoped, would terminate the overpowering influence of the British in Egypt. The British really controlled the country, as Sadat later pointed out, the British Secretary for Oriental Affairs in the British Embassy in Cairo actually dictating Egyptian policy and procedures.

On July 23, 1952, Nasser and Sadat would change all that. A full colonel in the Egyptian army, Sadat was delegated by Nasser to go to Alexandria and demand of King Farouk his abdication.

Sadat did exactly that, confronting the bloated monarch with the fact that Nasser and the army controlled Egypt and that his immediate abdication was mandatory. The corrupt sovereign had no choice. He packed his bags and went into lavish exile on the Riviera. "It was a boyhood dream come true," Sadat later commented, but it would be four more years before the British reluctant-ly evacuated the country, and even then democracy did not come to Egypt.

Sadat quickly realized that Nasser, despite his promises and well-inten-tioned plans, really had no intention of ever establishing a free electorate. He presided over a one-party system, a form of socialism that disguised a regime as totalitarian as that of the deposed Farouk. Sadat was kept on as Nasser's top aide and to him the Egyptian strongman confided his worst fears, for he was a man plagued by nightmares and the ghosts of assassins.

Nasser saw plotters and conspirators everywhere and distrusted all but Sadat, who served the paranoid Nasser loyally, if too silently. For eighteen years, Sadat dutifully served as Nasser's liege man but only toward the end of the dictator's life did Sadat real-ize that he was expected to replace Nasser. This Nasser confided to Sadat only a few months before he died of a heart attack in September 1970.

When Sadat was sworn in as presi-dent of Egypt, he inherited a nation in economic ruin. Worse, his predecessor had indentured Egypt to the U.S.S.R. The Soviets dictated policies and pro-cedures far in excess of what the British had mandated for decades. Without ever fulfilling their promises of economic support, the Soviets nevertheless made daily demands on Sadat, who could turn to no other major power for support. Nasser had alienated all the Western countries, especially the U.S., with his pro-Soviet policies.

This political stance had left Egypt on the brink of perpetual bankruptcy. As Sadat desperately tried to extricate his country from Soviet domination, Egypt's woes increased in 1967 when Israel soundly thrashed the country's army in a lightning war. Egypt's national image sank to an all-time low. Internally, the country was—thanks to Nasser's half-baked socialism—awash with scores of Marxist groups planning their own coups. In desperation, Sadat surprised the West by breaking with the U.S.S.R. in July 1972. He ordered more than 15,000 Soviet engineers and workers out of the country. To strengthen Egypt's economy, Sadat immediately opened friendly talks with the U.S.

In October 1973, Sadat again surprised the West by sending Egyptian forces in a swift tank attack that captured the Suez Canal and ripped through Israeli-occupied Sinai. This was later known as the Yom Kippur War, one that ended with Egypt with a slight military disadvantage but one that increased the country's prestige, as well as that of Sadat, who was then perceived to be a decisive, shrewd leader.

Sadat did not neglect internal affairs. He closed detention camps and prohibited arbitrary arrests. Becoming as popular as Nasser, Sadat was reelected to his post as president by the Egyptian parliament in 1976. As he became more aggressive in establishing friendly relations with the West, Sadat distanced

himself from the fanatical Islamic groups, giving only lip service to Yasir Arafat's PLO and its more dangerous arm, Al Fatah, behind which lurked a number of lethal terrorist organizations such as Black September.

In November 1977, Sadat shocked the West and bitterly angered his Middle East neighbors by boldly approaching Israel and proposing peace talks that would finally bring to an end the violence and wars between Egypt and Israel. Though Israel and its Western allies were pleased, radical Arab leaders and Islamic fundamentalists were incensed. Sadat nevertheless proceeded to cement relationships with Israel, going to that country to publicly embrace Prime Minister Menachem Begin. In September 1978, Sadat met with Begin and President Jimmy Carter at Camp David, Maryland, and signed peace accords that finally brought peace between Egypt and Israel, a truly historic agreement. For this far-sighted and heroic act, Sadat and Begin were awarded the Nobel Peace Prize.

This act also sealed Sadat's fate. Almost every Islamic radical and terrorist vowed to seek his death. He further infuriated his enemies by offering asylum to the dying Shah of Iran. The deposed dictator, suffering from an incurable illness, was allowed to die in Cairo, but Sadat's act of kindness was denounced in Teheran, particularly since Sadat had refused to return the dying man to Iran for trial and certain execution.

Another Arab leader who seethed with hatred for Sadat was Libyan dictator Muammar Qaddafi, financier of world terrorists who had long been lobbying for Sadat's assassination. Qaddafi announced that Sadat "is a traitor to Islam." That Qaddafi assigned killers to track down and murder Sadat was a grim fact to American intelligence leaders. In Spring 1980, Sadat flew to the U.S. to confer with President Carter. Sadat's plane was to stop over in the Azores, but CIA agents soon identified Libyan assassins arriving there before Sadat's plane was scheduled to land. Alerted to the assassination plot, Sadat's plane was rerouted. Qaddafi's killers had been outwitted.

Though condemned by many Arab leaders as a compromiser, Sadat continued his efforts to make peace on all fronts. In August 1981, he met with President Reagan, urging the American leader to meet with PLO chief Yasir Arafat in hopes that this would lead to peace negotiations between the Palestinian leader and representatives of Israel. Upon his return to Egypt, Sadat was faced with a concentrated effort on the part of radicals and terrorists to unseat him. Open resistence to his administration caused Sadat to jail more than 1,500 violent political dissidents. Among these was the brother of an Islamic fanatic, Khaled Ahmed Shawki el Islambouli, a lieutenant in the Egyptian Army and the leader of an extremist sect of terrorists, Takfir Wal-Hajira. The founder of this fanatical sect, Sayyed Kotob, had plotted the assassination of Nasser in 1966 and had been captured and executed before putting his plans into effect.

This thirty-year-old terrorist sect had but a few members in 1981. It was an offshoot of the long outlawed Muslim Brotherhood, which had been dedicated to the assassination of any Muslim who might be branded a heretic and traitor to Islamic fundamentalism. The Brotherhood proudly traced its origins back to the eleventh century, claiming to have historic links with the dreaded Order of the Assassins and its fierce, mystical leader, the Old Man of the Mountain. The Order had invented political assassination when sending trained killers to murder aristocratic leaders of the Third Crusade who had successfully recaptured parts of the Holy Lands. Ironically, this organization that had condemned Sadat had benefited most by him. Upon assuming power, Sadat had pardoned and released from prison most of the organization's members.

In 1981, however, Sadat had imprisoned many radicals opposed to his peace efforts with Israel, including the brother of Islambouli. The army officer used this as his excuse to plan the murder of Sadat. He chose October 6, 1981, for the day of the attack. On that day, Sadat would be reviewing troops in Cairo in celebration of the anniversary of the Yom Kippur War.

The terrorist's plan was a bold one. Sadat was to be exposed to public view, and the assassins would have instant access to him. Conversely, the Egyptian president would also be heavily guarded in the reviewing stand. In front of the stand and flanking it would be his special palace guard, commanded by General Mohammed Abdel-Halim Abu Ghazala, defense minister and the very man who had planned the 1973 sneak attack against Israel. Moreover, plain-clothes detectives would be planted throughout the reviewing stand.

In this startling photo, an assassin is shown firing directly into a reviewing stand; his bullets fatally wounded Egyptian President Anwar Sadat, October 6, 1981.

Sadat himself was aware that there was a serious plot against his life several weeks before the attack. He was, however, a charismatic, open man who refused to shelter himself behind phalanxes of guards and barred palace doors. That had been the way of Farouk, of Nasser, of scores of other despotic Egyptian rulers. Sadat felt that he had introduced a new and open society to his country and that the more visible he was, the more confidence his people would have in his administration. This Islambouli knew well, and he planned to take advantage of Sadat's willingness to expose himself.

Islambouli had studied his victim's habits and schedules and knew full well he could almost strike at will. Moreover, he chose the day of the big parade, which would be widely covered by the national and international press, and therefore, the killing and the cause of the assassins, he reasoned, would be widely publicized

and develop sympathy for the murderers and more quickly help to bring about the kind of government in Egypt as had been established by Ayatollah Ruhollah Khomeini in Iran.

The terrorist, who, ironically, was about the same age as Sadat when Sadat created *his* revolutionary cadre, felt he would need four others to accomplish the assassination. His top aide, Hussein Abbas Muhammad, was already in the army, a reservist who would have the right to appear in the parade. Three others, however, were civilians, and it would be difficult for Islambouli to smuggle these men onto the military parade grounds in Cairo. He solved this problem by ordering three soldiers to go on sick leave before the ceremonies and substituting the civilians in their place, having them don military fatigues as did he and Muhammad.

These five terrorists were to perform the actual murder, but at least seventeen others were involved in the plot one way or another. All of the plotters belonged to the terrorist group Takfir Wal-Hajira. Though small, this group had the endorsement of almost all the radical fundamentalists in the Middle East and, in particular, the sponsorship of Libyan strongman Muammar Qaddafi.

Normally no ammunition was issued at any military parade (in Egypt or anywhere else), but somehow Islambouli managed to obtain ammunition for his Kalashnikov submachine gun and the three AK47 assault rifles his men were to use. He also acquired two grenades and some stun bombs, and then loaded his men into the back of a Russian-built army truck that was to appear in that section of the parade displaying heavy artillery, a contingent that would arrive on the reviewing grounds at the end of the parade.

As had been the tradition with the Order of the Assassins nine centuries earlier when preparing to commit a political assassination, Islambouli distributed small doses of hashish to his men, ordering them to inhale and chew the drug to prepare their minds for what they were about to do. (Ulrike Meinhof of Germany's fierce Baader-Meinhof terrorist gang also made a practice of giving hashish to her followers before they committed bank robberies and murders.)

The parade began before noon. Islambouli and his men sat sweating in the rear of the truck for ninety minutes as the massive parade, with bugles blaring and drums beating, filed past the large reviewing stand where Sadat and other dignitaries sat casually chatting.

The president sat in the front row of the reviewing stand, flanked by his fifty-two-year-old vice president, Hosni Mubarak, and General Ghazala.

The sixty-two-year-old Sadat was unmistakable in the crowd. He wore a distinctive black army uniform and black boots and spurs. Around his neck gleamed his Star of Sinai medal. He appeared calm and happy in taking the salutes from his troops as they swung past him in tight formations. This was the kind of event Sadat relished. He enjoyed showing himself to his people, especially his troops, believing, and rightly so, that he had restored Egypt's self-pride and increased its status as an important power in the Middle East.

About 1 P.M., a roaring flight of F-4 Phantom jets, followed by Mirage trainer planes, began passing over the reviewing stand. Sadat and his retinue stood up, looking skyward, pointing at the air show. At that precise moment, the truck carrying Islambouli and his men stopped right before the reviewing stand. The lieutenant and his men jumped from the rear of the vehicle. To some in the reviewing stand who bothered to take their eyes from the air show, it appeared as if the truck had broken down and the men jumping from the rear were preparing to push it.

The men, however, unslung their weapons and began to run toward the reviewing stand, which was only twenty yards distant. Islambouli shouted to them as they ran: "Kill the traitor! Kill the traitor! Attack!" He threw a grenade that landed far short of the reviewing stand. It caused no injuries upon explosion. Another assassin threw a second grenade, which failed to explode. Islambouli and the others then charged the reviewing stand. At that precise moment, Sadat averted his eyes from the air show and stared at the onrushing soldiers. His thoughts at that moment may have been confused. He instinctively brought his hand to the bill of his cap in a short military salute. Perhaps he thought this might cause the attackers to pause and automatically revert to military protocol, ceasing their attack.

If so, Sadat had no way of knowing that three of his attackers were only civilians impersonating soldiers and that Lieutenant Islambouli was consumed with hatred for him and was bent on his death. The attackers responded to the salute by opening fire and riddling the crowd in the reviewing stand. Pandemonium seized the crowd in the reviewing stand. Most threw themselves to the ground. Sadat remained standing, a stoic figure, as his killers ran forward.

Fawzi Abdul Hefez, Sadat's personal secretary, grabbed a chair in desperation and tried to thrust this in front of Sadat to protect him from the onslaught. A hail of bullets struck the chair, one plowing into Hefez's leg and sending him crashing to the floor of the reviewing stand. Sadat was then struck by four bullets, two entering the left side of his chest, another striking the collarbone and lodging in his neck, and the fourth smashing into his right leg above the knee. (Doctors would later discover a huge gash in the right leg that they could not explain.)

For a second or two the president swayed, glassy-eyed, and then collapsed into his chair. At that moment, General Ghazala, receiving a slight head wound that caused his entire face to run blood, jumped for the microphone and began barking orders for his troopers to shoot down the assassins. The palace guard, however, was immobilized, shot to pieces, with several troopers already lying dead around the reviewing stand.

Ghazala kept shouting for his men to shoot down the assassins. At one point, Islambouli squarely faced the general but he did not fire his weapon. Either it was jammed, or he had hesitated for arcane reasons. (Some later claimed that Islambouli had no intentions of killing anyone other than Sadat.) In the confusion, troops and assassins mixed in front of the reviewing stand, the loyal soldiers unable to identify the killers since they wore the khaki uniforms of their own men. One guard reportedly picked up a pike and raced toward a man he thought to be one of the assassins, skewering the man on the spot.

Ghazala's troops began responding to his orders, waves of them dashing from the parade grounds and swarming over the assassins, disarming them and beating them to the ground. In the reviewing stand all was havoc and death. Eleven had been killed, including Omani prince Shabeb bin Teymour; Bishop Samuel of the Coptic Church; Major General Hassam Allam; and Mohammed Rashwan, Sadat's personal photographer, who had just finished snapping a photo of the skyward-looking and smiling Sadat before the fusillade killed him. Four Egyptian soldiers who had placed themselves before Sadat were also dead. Thirty people were wounded, and these included Said Marei, presidential adviser; Belgium ambassador Claude Ruelle; Australian first secretary John Woods; Irish defense minister Jim Tully; Abd Rabb Enabi Hafex, Sadat's military chief-of-staff; and Vice President Mubarak, who immediately went to the fallen Sadat and discovered that he was still alive.

As Islambouli and his men were led away, a helicopter landed at the parade grounds to remove Sadat to the Maadi Hospital, where Egypt's chief surgeon, Major General Karim, along with a dozen other top medical specialists, began a two-hour battle to save the president's life. Sadat, with blood gushing from his mouth, arrived at the hospital twenty minutes after he had been shot. Physicians immediately gave him blood transfusions and began massaging his heart. The president grew steadily weaker and died two hours later. The cause of death was listed as "violent nervous shock, internal bleeding in the chest cavity, with the left lung and major blood vessels at the bottom of the left lung torn."

Egypt had lost its most important leader of the century. Mubarak, a competent and loyal Sadat stalwart, took over the reins of government while more than 800 dissidents were arrested on suspicion of having been involved in the assassination. This number soon dwindled to twenty-four, who were indicted for premeditated murder and conspiracy. On November 21, 1981, this group was tried en masse in Cairo, placed in a large cage in open court. They clung to the bars and shouted revolutionary slogans, obscenities, and

threats at their accusers and prosecutors. The five assassins were identified as Muslim fundamentalist fanatics who had sought to overthrow the civilian government and replace it with a Khomeini-style religious regime.

Each of the assassins loudly proclaimed that it had been their ambition to end "permissive Western influence" in Egypt by killing Sadat. The arrogant Islambouli freely admitted to plotting the assassination and carrying it out with Muhammad and the others, but he emphatically denied that his acts had anything to do with eliminating the entire Egyptian administration. He demanded that Egypt's defense minister testify so that he could report Islambouli's conduct during the assassination. "Get Abu Ghazala here to testify," Islambouli shouted at one point. "Ask him. During the shooting I looked him in the eyes and said, 'I don't want you. I want your dog [Sadat]!'"

Five of the defendants, including Islambouli and Muhammad, were condemned to death, while seventeen others were given sentences ranging from small terms to life at hard labor in prison. Two of the defendants were acquitted. Islambouli and Muhammad, having been Egyptian soldiers, were afforded the military style of execution by firing squad, while the three civilians were ignominiously hanged, all of them dying on April 15, 1982. Islambouli, according to witnesses, went to his death calmly, stoically proclaiming the righteousness of his cause.

Many curious and unexplained facts were lightly touched upon at the mass trial of the assassins. Other puzzling facts were never mentioned. It was never explained how Islambouli knew exactly when Sadat's attention and that of most others in the reviewing stand would be riveted upon the skies to watch the air show. Even more puzzling was the fact that the bodies of two plainclothes detectives, part of a contingent of private guards who protected Sadat, had been found shot to death in the rear of the reviewing stand a few minutes *before* Islambouli and his men alighted from the truck to open fire on their presidential prey.

This, coupled to some of Sadat's strange wounds, tended to support the theory that there had been others in the reviewing stand who were part of the plot and opened fire from behind the dignitaries to coordinate an attack with Islambouli and his men who were charging from the front. President Mubarak later confirmed that the Sadat assassination had, indeed, been a concerted attack aimed at eradicating the entire administration. The question was also raised repeatedly by Western journalists how Muammar Qaddafi's government-controlled radio station in Libya had announced Sadat's assassination with exact details long before the Egyptian authorities had made those details public.

In the heart of Islam, for days following Sadat's ruthless assassination, there was jubilation in Beirut, Teheran and other Middle Eastern cities, with Islamic fanatics firing off endless rounds from automatic weapons, performing bizarre dances, and holding street fetes. Sadat was considered by these violent terrorists to be an arch foe of fundamentalism, the very reason why Sadat was heralded in the

Khaled Islambouli, terrorist and chief assassin of Anwar Sadat, is shown behind prison bars. He and four others were executed on April 15, 1982.

West as one of the most enlightened leaders of the Arab world.

Sadat was, in the world view, a paradoxical and unpredictable man who led his people with resolution, a man who put aside his own pride and national vanity for a greater good. To the fundamentalist Arab, Sadat's embrace of Israel was a sign of degenerate weakness. He was a defector from the ranks of Islam, one who had deserted the holy war to rid the Middle East of Israel and its Western allies. The fundamentalist terrorists, led by the Popular Front for the Liberation of Palestine (PFLP), would continue to seek out enemies and kill them. They would make strange alliances to achieve their ends, linking themselves to distant revolutionary causes such as that of the Irish Republican Army (IRA). Their victims would be the helpless and the innocent. The slaughter they inflicted would extend to almost every country, on the ground and in the air.

Day of the Arab

The Irish-Arab Connection

In 1974, Scotland Yard revealed that the lingering terrorist organization known as the Irish Republican Army (IRA) had signed a secret pact with the Popular Front for the Liberation of Palestine (PFLP). British informants had presented overwhelming evidence to Yard investigators that the PFLP had agreed to help fund and provide weapons to the IRA to continue its terrorization of Britain.

This news came only a few days after an assassination attempt on the life of J. Edward Sieff, owner of the Marks and Spencer store chain and a staunch supporter of the Zionist Federation of Great Britain and Ireland. Though wounded, Sieff quickly recovered and announced on television that his support for the Jewish cause would not be diminished. Sieff's resolve was no doubt bolstered by PFLP's claim that it had been behind the attempted assassination, alleging that Sieff had given millions of pounds to Israel to help finance the 1973 Middle Eastern war.

The IRA by this time had fallen into worldwide disrepute in that it had ruthlessly attacked and killed innocent British citizens in a seemingly endless series of bombings and other armed attacks in Northern Ireland and throughout England. Its fanatical crusade to pry loose the six most northern counties in Ireland from British rule was at the core of its existence and had been since the paramilitary terrorist organization began in 1922, when Michael Collins and other Irish Free Staters had negotiated a partitioned Ireland with the British.

This had spawned the present IRA, which combated the Free State and was driven underground during the 1922–1923 Irish Civil War. In 1939, the IRA saw a resurgence, with a series of bombings in England. At that time, as was the case with the PFLP forty years later, the IRA received considerable help from another mortal enemy of England, Nazi Germany. Agents from Germany brought guns, ammunition, and explosives to the IRA, which unleashed a new terror campaign in England. During World War II, five of the IRA's top leaders were captured and executed.

The terrorist organization went into sharp decline in 1948 when the Irish Free State withdrew from the British commonwealth and was reorganized as a republic. The IRA then concentrated on unifying Protestant Northern

Destruction of the police station in Belfast, North Ireland, October 16, 1975; the Belfast Brigade of the Provisional IRA claimed responsibility. (Wide World)

Ireland and the republic to the south. The Catholics in the north, however, were unwilling to endorse the aims of the radical IRA until the 1960s. At that time the Catholic minority rebelled at the discriminatory actions of the Protestants in Ulster who sought to exclude them from direct participation in the elective process.

The IRA actually split into two factions, the older members choosing to agitate for political freedom while younger Catholics in Ulster, called the Provos, branched off into a separate group that believed it could force British troops from Northern Ireland through terrorist tactics. In 1972, law and order in Northern Ireland all but collapsed after the largely Protestant

parliament at Stormont was abolished by order of the London government.

These actions further complicated a tense situation, resulting in the formation of Protestant secret societies, among them the Ulster Volunteer Force, the Red Hand Commandos, and the Ulster Defense Association, composed primarily of working-class men from the ghettos of Belfast. The once peaceful city became the battleground of an ugly, protracted guerrilla war.

On a single day in July 1972, twenty-two bombs were exploded in downtown Belfast, killing nine people and wounding 130. In the next few years, the IRA targeted British officials for assassination. Among the casualties were Ambassador Christopher Ewart-Biggs, killed in a bomb blast on July 21, 1976, as he drove from his residence outside Dublin to the embassy in Merrion Square. On August 27, 1979, British war hero and First Earl Louis Mountbatten was blown up on his boat as he fished off the coast of Donegal Bay.

By that time, the Provos of the IRA were umbilically linked to the PFLP. In 1973, in an effort to consolidate all terrorists around the globe in support of its cause, the PFLP sent emissaries to Japan to recruit the Red Army of Japan, to Germany to enlist the support of the Red Army Faction and Baader-Meinhof Gang, and to Turkey to seek out members of the Turkish People's Liberation Army and to especially establish an alliance with the IRA.

Representatives of all these groups were invited to Lebanon by PFLP leader George Habash to attend a "terrorist summit." Contact with the IRA was made by Habash's right-hand man, Mohammed Boudia, an actor and a member of Black September who was tracked down and killed by Mossad agents a short time later. The IRA Provos who attended the summit in Beirut were promised financial backing and military weapons if they worked in concert with the PFLP. Moreoever, the PFLP offered to train IRA recruits at their secret guerrilla training camps.

The IRA responded with alacrity, accepting money and arms from the PFLP and accommodating the Arab terrorist organization by executing attacks against British businesses and installations selected by PFLP for destruction. In accordance with the agreement reached at the Lebanon terrorist summit, the IRA would exchange intelligence with PFLP and would provide safe houses for Arab terrorists operating in England and Ireland. Moreover, IRA Provos would have the benefit of being trained at PFLP camps. IRA terrorists thus learned veteran Arab techniques and murder methods in Lebanese camps and, by the late 1980s, in guerrilla camps located in Libya. (The IRA terrorists were eventually given their own camp at Bir ad Dawim in Libya.)

IRA terrorism continued into the 1990s unabated, but much of the organization's support had dwindled in its homeland where the Provos were viewed as common criminals and fanatical killers who had long earlier abandoned the political process. British Prime Minister Margaret Thatcher, herself the target of a botched 1984 IRA assassination attempt, summed up the attitude of most Catholics and Protestants in present-day Ireland: "There can be no compromise with murder and terrorism." That is exactly what happened, however, when it came to the cold-blooded PFLP killers who took over the helpless Italian cruise ship *Achille Lauro*. In this instance it was not a case of compromise but outright capitulation to the terrorists.

A Mediterranean Murder

Abu Abbas (Mohammed Zaidan Abbas) has been for years one of the top advisers to Yasir Arafat, and according to most reliable reports, he is also the chief architect of PFLP terrorism from the 1970s. His record of planning effective strikes, however, is dismal. In 1980, Abbas sent an infiltrating terrorist into Israel via a hot-air balloon, but the saboteur was killed when the balloon blew up. Next, on March 7, 1981, Abbas ordered two suicide-bent terrorists to penetrate Israeli airspace by operating tricky hang gliders. The kamikaze-like terrorists were to glide over a refinery in Haifa and drop explosives on their target while in midair, a tactic that all but guaranteed their self-destruction.

The explosives strapped to one terrorist were released prematurely and exploded on Lebanese territory. The terrorist crashed on an Israeli kibbutz and was captured. The second terrorist so mismanaged his hang glider that it fell into a camp of the pro-Israeli Christian Militia, the South Lebanon Army (SLA), and he was turned over to the Israelis. On April 16, 1981, Abbas sent two more of his terrorists in a hot-air balloon to infiltrate Israel. The balloon was shot down by Israeli forces and the PFLP men were killed.

On June 5, 1984, Abbas ordered his four top terrorists to invade the Israeli kibbutz of Ein-Gev. All four were quickly captured. Abbas, who received direct support from Fatah and Arafat, as well as funds from Iraqi dictator Saddam Hussein, knew that his mounting failures made him appear ineffective, even clownish, to his masters. To polish his tarnished image, Abbas decided to perform a spectacular terrorist coup. He would seize the Italian cruise liner *Achille Lauro*, hold its passengers hostage and effect the release of scores of Arab terrorists from Israeli jails.

On October 7, 1985, four of Abbas' most fanatical followers boarded the 624-foot vessel in Alexandria, Egypt, carring on board several suitcases packed with guns and ammunition. (There was no security at all on board, as was the case with most tourist liners at that time.) The terrorists planned to seize the ship as it sailed to Port Said. Exactly what the terrorists hoped to achieve has never been determined. One theory had it that they would seize the ship and sail it to the Israeli port of Ashdod where they would threaten to blow it up unless their demands were

Leon Klinghoffer, shown with his wife Marilyn; the invalided American tourist was shot to death in his wheelchair by PFLP terrorists who hijacked the cruise ship Achille Lauro in 1985. (Wide World)

Asking for instructions, the terrorists waited until the PFLP contact in Genoa radioed PFLP chiefs in Tunis to receive a specific plan of action. It was during this transmission that the shipboard terrorists informed their chiefs that they and their weapons had been discovered by a curious ship's steward, causing them to advance their operations schedule. Apparently, Tunis had no specific instructions or any kind of plan in mind. A short time later, at 8:45 A.M., the four terrorists charged through the doors of the ship's dining room, firing off their weapons and wounding several passengers and crewmen.

Marching the captain to the control room, the terrorists ordered him to sail for Tartus, Syria. They then made radio contact with several port authorities, demanding that fifty imprisoned PFLP terrorists be released by Israel. Vernon Walters, U.S. Ambassador to the United Nations, was notified of the ship's seizure, and he immediately called Syrian President Hafez al-Assad. A short time later, the terrorists received a message from the Syrians. They would be refused entry to the port of Tartus.

Enraged, the terrorists herded the American passengers together, taking their passports. They shuffled the passports, playing a grim variation of Russian roulette, stating that the passport that wound up on top of the pile would represent the first U.S. victim. The passport of Leon Klinghoffer was taken from the top of the pile.

A terrorist studied the photo and then matched it to a sixty-nine-year-

met. Another version had the terrorists sailing into Syrian waters where they would murder all Jewish and American citizens on board.

Whatever the plan actually hatched in Abbas' head, the operation was haphazard at best, and his terrorists achieved nothing other than a senseless murder and international condemnation. Once on board, the terrorists bided their time, watching most of the passenger-tourists disembark at Alexandria, where they went on to see the Egyptian museums, the Sphinx, and the Pyramids. When the ship sailed for Port Said, the terrorists roused themselves, taking over the ship's radio room where they contacted a PFLP coordinator in Genoa, Italy.

old man in a wheelchair. Pointing to Klinghoffer, another terrorist fired into the helpless invalid's head, killing him instantly. Then, at gunpoint, the terrorists ordered several other American passengers to throw Klinghoffer's body into the sea. One of the terrorists then ran to the radio room and announced to listening Syrian authorities (a conversation monitored by Israelis and others): "We threw the first body into the water after shooting him in the head. Minutes from now we will follow up with the second one. Do not worry, Tartus, we have a lot of them here."

The blatant murder of the helpless Klinghoffer immediately exploded in the world's press. Arafat himself was shocked to see the operation so badly mismanaged. Knowing that the seizure of the ship could become a public relations nightmare, he ordered Abbas to publicly disassociate the PLO from the terrorists. Abbas, pretending to be a good Samaritan and a disinterested party acting for the benefit of all concerned, went to Port Said, saying that he had been "dispatched by Arafat to resolve the hijacking."

Abbas then contacted the ship, but he used a code name, Abu Khalid, one recognized by the terrorists on board the *Achille Lauro*. His ship-to-shore radio conversation was recorded by Israeli intelligence and later released. It was clear from the conversations between Abbas and the terrorists that he knew those on board, calling one by name, and that he was in charge of their operation in that he gave them orders, not advice, in an effort to resolve their dilemma and that of the PLO-PFLP. The following is from a transcript of the October 9, 1985 conversation:

PORT SAID [ABBAS]: Here is Abu Khalid, here is Abu Khalid, how do you hear me?

ACHILLE LAURO: Go ahead.

PORT SAID: This is Abu Khalid. Who is talking? Is this Magid?

ACHILLE LAURO: Correct.

PORT SAID: How are you feeling, Magid?

ACHILLE LAURO: Good, thank God.

PORT SAID: Listen to me carefully. First, you have to treat the passengers very well. You have to apologize to them and to the ship's crew and tell them it was not our goal to take control of the ship. Tell them your main goal and who—

ACHILLE LAURO: Right. We spoke to them and told them that our main goal was not to seize the ship.

The U.S. quickly exposed Arafat's ruse, stating through a Department of Justice official that "the evidence we have right now is that he [Abbas] participated in all of this, guiding them [the terrorists] throughout." Attorney General Edwin Meese then stated that the U.S. had "hard evidence" that Abbas was "a principal in the hijacking." The U.S. then ordered Seal Team Six at Charleston Air Force Base and the U.S. Army's Delta Force at Fort Bragg, North Carolina, to board planes that began flying toward a British base on Cyprus. The Americans intended to force a boarding of the ship, kill the terrorists and rescue the hostages.

The American Navy lost track of the Italian liner over the next day and a half, but Lieutenant-Colonel Oliver North of the National Security Council asked for help from Israeli military intelligence (AMAN) and was given the exact location of the ship. Before the American Seals and the Delta Force arrived to take action, the vessel sailed to Port Said where, on the evening of October 9, 1985, Abbas, still pretending to be a neutral arbitrator, "negotiated" the surrender of the terrorists to Egyptian authorities. Abbas promised the terrorists "safe conduct" out of Egypt.

The next day, Abbas and his four terrorists boarded an EgyptAir jetliner bound for Tunis. U.S. F-14 fighter jets, however, intercepted the Egyptian plane and forced it to land at Sigonella Air Base in Sicily. U.S. commandos from Seal Team Six surrounded the plane, but they, in turn, were surrounded by a large force of heavily armed *carabinieri*. For some time there was a tense standoff, before the U.S. forces reluctantly acknowledged the Italian sovereign rights and turned the five terrorists over to the Italians.

Rather than handing the terrorists over to the U.S., and to placate Arafat, the PLO, and its terrorist arm, PFLP, the Italian government of Prime Minister Bettino Craxi, cowardly betrayed its Western allies, allowing Abbas and a PLO official to board a Yugoslav Airlines plane and fly to Belgrade. Once in Belgrade, Abbas went to a PLO safe house and then disappeared.

The Italian government lamely stated that the U.S. had offered weak evidence of Abbas' "involvement in the hijacking." Said Prime Minister Craxi later: "We knew at the time only that Abbas had offered his good offices [to negotiate the return of the ship] as an intermediary." This, of course, was nonsense. Craxi and other Italian officials had been shown the ship-to-shore communique between Abbas and the terrorists, and they knew full well that Abbas was in league with the terrorists who were acting under his authority.

Though the Italian government refused to extradite the four terrorists in its custody, it eventually tried these men, as well as ten others, including Abbas *in absentia*. Italian prosecutors at that time identified Abbas as the mastermind of the *Achille Lauro* hijacking. Moreover, the prosecutors identified Abdel Rahim Khaled, Abbas' top aide, as having been aboard the ship until it reached Alexandria, and that he had given last minute instructions to the four terrorists before disembarking.

The four terrorists who committed the hijacking were all convicted in an Italian court. All received prison sentences, the stiffest being thirty years, which was meted out to Yussef Magid Molqi, the gunman who shot and killed Klinghoffer. Molqi had admitted this killing but later recanted his confession. Upon hearing his relatively light sentence (prosecutors had demanded a life term), Molqi began chanting in the courtroom: "Long live Italian justice, long live Palestine."

Ibrahim Abdelatif Fataier, Molqi's

right-hand man, was given a twenty-four-year term. Marouf Assadi was given fifteen years and Bassam al-Ashker, who had been a minor at the time of the crime, was turned over to juvenile authorities. Others received lighter sentences but Abbas, convicted *in absentia*, received a life term, a day of which he has yet to serve.

The U.S. later indicted Abbas, offering a $250,000 reward for information leading to his apprehension and effective prosecution and punishment. The Department of Justice later withdrew this offer on the grounds that Abbas had already been convicted in Italy, a move that enraged U.S. citizens and, in particular, the Klinghoffer family.

Yasir Arafat nevertheless was criticized in the world's top political circles as having tacitly endorsed the seizing of the *Achille Lauro*. He took extraordinary efforts to disassociate the PLO from the terrorist act. PLO foreign secretary to the United Nations Farouk Qadoumi announced that media reports of Klinghoffer's death were no more than a "big lie fabricated by the intelligence services of the United States." Denial and obfuscation was the order of the PLO position, a stance not dissimilar to that of former Nazis who insisted after World War II that reports of Himmler's death camps were nothing more than falsified Allied propaganda.

When Abbas again surfaced in Arab circles, he was acknowledged by Arafat as one of his most trusted aides. Abbas openly denied the fact that his armed terrorists had killed the helpless Klinghoffer in a May 1986 interview with NBC, one in which he labeled President Reagan "public enemy number one," and that he promised continued attacks on American citizens. The Big Lie was Abbas' defense: "What is the use of killing an old man anyway? Why? After all, he is old and would soon be dead anyway without killing. I do not believe our comrades on the boat carried out any killing."

PLO official Qadoumi, while addressing an Arab League luncheon, brutally joked about the Klinghoffer murder, suggesting that "perhaps it was his wife that pushed him over into the sea to have the insurance. Nobody even had the evidence that he was killed." In late 1988, Abbas attended a meeting of the Palestinian National Council in Algiers. Someone brought up Klinghoffer's death and the terrorist leader snickered: "Him? I hear he died when trying to swim for it!" The remark drew laughter. A few days later, according to best reports, PFLP terrorists managed to smuggle a bomb on board Pan Am Flight 103.

The PFLP Takes to the Air

By the late 1970s, the PFLP began sending its most ardent terrorists to board commercial airlines, to skyjack those planes, and hold them and their passengers for ransom. The ransom would invariably be the release of terrorists held in prisons around the world. The release of imprisoned terrorists did not always apply to Arab prisoners; the PFLP often demanded the release of those in terrorist organizations allied with the PFLP such as the IRA, the Red Army Faction, and the Baader-Meinhof Gang.

Typical of PFLP skyjackings was the seizure of a Lufthansa Boeing 737 jet on October 13, 1977. The plane was en route from Palma, Majorca, to Frankfurt, Germany, with eighty-two passengers and four crew members on board. Four Arab PFLP members hijacked the plane when it was passing over the French Riviera. Pulling guns and announcing that they were members of the Organization of Struggle Against World Imperialism, the terrorists ordered the plane to land in Rome where it was refueled. The plane then took off and flew over several Middle Eastern countries that refused it the right to land.

As this was happening, the PFLP terrorists informed a German rescue team that they wanted eleven political prisoners released, plus two Palestinians jailed in Turkey. They also demanded $15 million for expenses. When not getting a response, the terrorists, on October 16, shot the pilot of the plane and flew to Mogadishu, Somalia. By that time, German commandos, headed by Lieutenant-Colonel Ulrich Wegener, had flown after the skyjacked plane. In Mogadishu, the terrorists haggled with German negotiators before the commandos sucked the doors off the plane and lobbed grenades inside.

Three of the four PFLP terrorists were killed and the survivor wounded. Miraculously, all passengers and crew, with the exception of the slain pilot, survived the assault. Although the retaking of this plane was heralded as a victory, the Germans paid the price of another assassination, that of German industrialist Hans Martin Schleyer, who had been kidnapped by the Baader-Meinhof Gang in Germany. Schleyer, who had been kidnapped in Cologne and was being held by the B-M Gang for ransom, was to be exchanged for jailed gang members.

When this demand was not met, the B-M gang contacted the PFLP and asked for help. The Arabs responded by skyjacking the Lufthansa plane, a countermeasure that ended in disaster for the PFLP. The German terrorists, after three of their jailed comrades were found dead in their cells, killed Schleyer on October 19, 1977.

Despite this setback, the PFLP and other Fatah-backed terrorist groups continued to send terrorists on board airliners to capture crews and passengers and hold them hostage. Immad Mugniyeh, a Lebanese Shiite leader, head of the Musawi faction, and operational director of Hizbollah, engineered the hijacking of TWA Flight 847 in 1985, a seventeen-day terrorist action that saw one American passenger, a U.S. Navy diver, killed in cold blood.

The Arab terrorists dispensed with sending killers to board planes on April 3, 1986, and simply planted a powerful bomb on board TWA Flight 840, which was flying from Athens to Cairo. The bomb had been planted at the instructions of Abdullah abed al-Hamid Labib (AKA: Colonel Hawari), a Fatah-PFLP chief who had been trained as a terrorist in Algeria. The bomb blew a huge hole in the side of the TWA 727 jet, killing four Americans, one being an infant, when they were sucked out of the plane. Nine others, including five more Americans, were injured in the blast. It was later determined that the device contained about one pound of plastic explosive (Semtex, made in Czechoslovakia). One report had it that May Elias Mansur, a Lebanese working for Labib, had planted the bomb on the plane, an accusation she later emphatically denied.

In the case of Pan Am Flight 103, the PFLP again sent only a bomb to work its carnage, one that caused the 747 jumbo jet, bound for New York City with 259 people on board, to explode into a gigantic ball of flames over Scotland on December 21, 1988, raining debris onto the village of Lockerbie and destroying forty houses, several cars, and a gas station.

About one hour after taking off from London's Heathrow Airport, Pan Am Flight 103 exploded at an altitude of 31,000 feet. Burning wreckage was spread over a radius of ten miles in the worst disaster in British history. Mike Carnahan, a witness who was only a few hundred yards from the scene of the explosion, described how "the sky was actually raining fire. It was just like liquid." In addition to those killed in the plane, eleven persons on the ground were also killed. Occupants of the plane included Bernt Carlsson, Swedish ambassador to the United Nations Council for Namibia and thirty-eight students from Syracuse University.

Two weeks earlier, the U.S. Embassy in Finland had received an anonymous phone call in which an informant warned of a possible December bombing of a Pan Am flight bound for the U.S. from Frankfurt, Germany. The caller said that the Abu Nidal terrorist organization would be behind the bombing. The same caller had apparently called the Israeli Embassy in Helsinki with the same warning, as he did other embassies. On December 13, the Soviet Embassy issued a warning to its diplomats that a Pan Am flight might be bombed and suggested that they cancel any Pan Am flights and switch to another airline.

According to U.S. Federal Aviation Administration Director of Security

The shattered nose section of Pan Am Flight 103, guarded by a policeman at Lockerbie, Scotland, December 21, 1988; a PFLP bomb killed all 285 persons on board. (Wide World)

Ray Salazar, issuing security bulletins about the warning would not have been effective if they had been widely distributed because "then people would have circumvented the security measures." Jeffrey M. Kreindler, vice president in charge of security for Pan Am, explained that the airline policy for keeping security risks secret was the best way to enhance security and was not an action taken in commercial interests.

Scotland Yard and the FBI joined forces to probe for sabotage in the Pan Am disaster, both soon realized that explosives had blown up the jet. "Conclusive evidence of a detonating high explosive," was reported after a week of intensive investigation by the British Ministry of Defense's Royal Armament Research and Development Establishment in Kent, south of London. Evidence from two parts of the framework of a luggage pallet

revealed that a powerful plastic explosive must have been used to blow up the plane and that the device was so well timed and so devastating that its maker or makers must have had considerable technical skill and resources.

The identity of the bombing source, however, could not be determined. The U.S. government offered $500,000 for information. On February 7, 1989, sources in the international terrorist movement reported that Ahmed Jibril, head of the PFLP, was responsible for exploding the Pan Am plane in midair. Omar Shehabi, a spokesman for the group, denied that the PFLP had anything to do with the bombing. According to anonymous sources, however, Jibril, identified as a former Syrian military intelligence officer, was working for Libyan strongman Muammar Qaddafi who was seeking revenge for American air raids in his country in April 1986.

On the same day that the PFLP connection was announced, relatives of crash victims accused the U.S. government of neglecting to warn passengers and later engineering a cover-up; they cited as proof the fact that there were 168 empty seats on the plane, a highly unusual pre-holiday circumstance. On February 16, 1989, British Transport Minister Paul Channon announced that the bomb had been hidden in a radio cassette player that had apparently been loaded on board in Frankfurt, West Germany, where the flight originated. The International Civil Aviation Organization adopted a resolution to tighten aviation security rules worldwide, and the U.S. Federal Aviation Administration (FAA) told American airlines to increase all inspection of electronic consumer goods taken on board aircrafts.

The public outcry against the government's failure to release a warning continued to increase. On March 15, 1989, Elizabeth Delude-Dix from Lockerbie, whose husband had been killed in the disaster, produced a document she claimed was a warning circulated by the U.S. to foreign governments two weeks prior to the explosion. Delude-Dix called for the resignation of Channon and demanded a public inquiry into the crash.

Conservative Prime Minister Margaret Thatcher was criticized for the handling of the bomb warning, as the Labor Party voiced its suspicions of a cover-up, noting that the warning letter, dated December 19, 1988, was not released to airlines until early January 1989. Though the Thatcher government did not immediately respond to these charges, a new directive to British airports required passengers to remove all electronic and electric equipment from luggage before checking in and to carry it on board in hand so that it could be inspected at boarding gates

West German detectives announced on March 20, 1989, that a Libyan terrorist known as the "Professor" was responsible for the explosion. The police reported that one of the visitors to the "Professor's" hotel room in Bonn, West Germany, included a twenty-year-old Lebanese student, Khalid Jaafar. Detectives thought Jaafar had unknowingly taken the bomb aboard the plane in a radio cassette player.

The "Professor" was also under suspicion for masterminding a wild attack on a Greek ferry on July 11, 1988, in which nine persons were killed and more than eighty injured. Jaafar's father, Nazir Jaafar, called the German investigation "anti-Arab," saying that his son had been singled out because of his Arabic name, the only one on the list of the passenger victims, and insisted that Jaafar had not been involved.

On March 24, 1989, the Bush administration admitted that the FAA had secretly warned airlines one week prior to its announcement that three Lebanese Palestinians might attempt to skyjack an American aircraft in Europe. President Bush maintained that hijacking and bombing threats should be kept secret from the public, warning that to publicly announce all terrorist threats would only serve to increase threatening calls. Said Bush: "Every nut in the world will start calling in and enjoying the silent satisfaction of fouling up the travel schedules."

Day of the Arab

As investigators continued to probe, they concentrated on Jaafar and three unnamed women who had male friends in the Middle East. Detectives pointed out that Jaafar had relatives who lived near Baalbek where the PFLP maintained several bases and where about 1,000 Iranian terrorists (Pasdaran, the Revolutionary Guards) had been stationed since 1982. Then, on April 17, a bomb expert of the West German police in Wiesbaden was blown to pieces at police headquarters while examining a device that was similar in construction and design to the one that destroyed the Pan Am flight. Police spokesman Arno Falk stated that the device had been hidden in a radio and that the bomb had been obtained "in connection with our previous investigation, but we cannot say more than that." A second device was disarmed without incident.

On April 24, 1989, the *London Times* reported that investigators believed that they had uncovered an international organized crime network that poured tens of millions of pounds into secret accounts to fund terrorist cells throughout Europe, bankrolling the PFLP and other such groups. The money was used to create schools for terrorists, to buy sophisticated equipment and explosives, and to develop means to outwit airline security systems. Seven persons were arrested in Copenhagen, Denmark, in connection with robberies five years earlier. It was thought that these funds were transferred to terrorist accounts via Paris to South Yemen.

In early May 1989, a West German press report insisted that Iran had ordered the bombing of Flight 103, paying PFLP terrorist Jibril more than $1 million to engineer the destruction and that the act was to avenge the July 1988 downing of an Iranian civilian jet in the Persian Gulf by the U.S. Officially, authorities in the U.S., Britain, and West Germany continue to maintain that they do not know who blew up Flight 103, although two terrorists, Lamen Khalifa Fhimah and Abdel Basset Ali Al-Megrahi (now hiding in Libya), are on the FBI's Ten Most Wanted list in connection with the bombing.

·TEN·
RAGE FROM THE RIGHT

1990

At the Lunatic Fringe

In the 1990s, terrorism took many forms and wore myriad faces. Lone killers with obscure motives erupted with more frequency than in any other decade, murdering their fellow citizens at random. For the innocent, instant death lurked at the most commonplace sites, a neighborhood corner or a commuter train, meted out by strangers, a new breed of terrorists without political or military cause. A birth sign or the color of skin served as the flimsy excuse to kill. In many other instances, no reason was ever discovered to explain the destruction of human life.

Typical was a faceless stranger the New York press dubbed the Zodiac Killer (not to be confused with the Zodiac Killer who had terrorized San Francisco decades earlier). The terrorist shot four persons, one fatally, in the Queens-Brooklyn border and in Central Park in 1990. The shootings occured on Thursdays, twenty-one days, or a multiple of twenty-one days, apart. The killer wrote taunting letters to the police, saying that he would

murder someone born under each of the twelve astrological signs, thus earning the sobriquet of the Zodiac Killer.

Zodiac shot a Scorpio, a Gemini, a Taurus, and a Cancer, somehow learning from the victims their astrological signs. So widespread was the 1990 panic he created in New York City that citizens were warned by the press not to divulge their birth dates to strangers. Police went on extra alert every three weeks in anticipation of Zodiac striking again. After a June 21, 1990, shooting, however, the killer vanished.

Nothing more was heard from this terrorist, and he might have slipped into a permanent police limbo had it not been for a routine domestic shooting on June 18, 1996. A family dispute erupted when twenty-six-year-old Heriberto Seda reportedly shot his teenage sister in the back for running around with a notorious street gang. When police were summoned to Seda's third-floor Brooklyn apartment, they were met by gunfire. Seda held off police in a raging gunfight for almost four hours before he surrendered.

Heriberto Seda under arrest in 1996; he proved to be New York's notorious Zodiac, a terrorist-killer who shot four persons according to their astrological signs. (Wide World)

One of the detectives inspecting Seda's apartment after the gunman was taken into custody examined the suspect's strange scrawls on paper strewn about the apartment and recognized them as those of the mysterious Zodiac killer, who had disappeared five years earlier. When Seda was confronted with evidence from his apartment, he broke down and confessed that he was, indeed, Zodiac, saying that he had been seized by "a sudden urge" to strike randomly and that he learned of his victims' astrological signs only "by chance."

It was also by chance that twenty-five unrelated strangers were shot by a black racist, Colin Ferguson, in 1993. A native of Jamaica, Ferguson had spent some time on the West Coast, a loner who was remembered for only one thing, hating whites and Asians. Obtaining an automatic pistol, Fergu-

son went to New York, where he disappeared until the evening of December 7, 1993. He suddenly resurfaced in Manhattan's Penn Station, where he boarded a 5:33 P.M. commuter train bound for Long Island.

Ferguson sat mutely staring out a window until the train rolled into Garden City. He suddenly bolted upright, producing the pistol, and began running down aisles of the train, shooting passengers at random but careful to select only whites to murder. As passengers cringed in their seats, the madman shot one helpless person after another. Three courageous commuters finally ended the terrorist's carnage by tackling and holding him until police could take him into custody. After he was wordlessly escorted from the train, grim-faced officers found six dead and nineteen wounded persons sprawled in the train cars.

The mass murderer was not brought to trial until January 26, 1996. Ferguson was dissatisified with his defense attorneys early on, including the controversial William Kunstler who planned to conduct a defense he called "black rage." Such a defense appeared to be racist at best, one that Ferguson himself apparently disliked. After his attorneys described their client as paranoid and delusional, he fired them and became his own defense lawyer. Judge Donald Belfi, presiding over the case in a Mineola, New York, courtroom, essentially invited chaos into the case when allowing the accused to defend himself, instead of insisting upon a court-appointed lawyer to handle Ferguson's trial.

The arrogant Ferguson did allow a fellow Jamaican, Alton Rose, to act as his "legal adviser." Rose described Feguson's attempt to defend himself as similar to "a patient in a doctor's office trying to perform his own spinal cord operation." Dressed in a suit, white shirt and tie, Ferguson also wore a bullet-proof vest under his shirt when in court, a protective measure he insisted upon, stating that he believed the trial was nothing more than a conspiracy to murder *him*.

Ferguson's defense of himself made a ridiculous shambles of the proceedings. He endlessly mouthed legal mumbo-jumbo. He spoke as if he understood legal terminology and knew the law, saying things like "Is it your testimony that . . ." and "Would it be fair to say that . . ." and "Was it your finding that . . ." It was all a bad imitation of a real lawyer. He picked up legal phrases and applied them where they did not fit and made no sense. He referred to himself always in the third person, as "Mr. Ferguson" and "the defendant."

After taking weeks to prepare his own case, Ferguson asked Judge Belfi for more time. He wanted to summon President Clinton and New York Governor Mario Cuomo to testify because it was reported that both had talked to witnesses in the trial. When the court ruled against these demands, the defendant angrily denounced the judicial system.

The terrorist offered several theories as to how the mass shootings took place. First, he insisted that he was asleep when a white man stole his gun out of his bag and commenced shooting everyone in sight and that he had been arrested simply because he

Colin Ferguson, the terrorist-killer who shot twenty-five persons on board a New York commuter train in 1993. (Wide World)

was black. When this argument was dismissed as ridiculous, Ferguson stated that another black man with the same name as his and looking identical to him committed the shootings.

The high point of this theater of the absurd was reached when Ferguson began raving about Wisconsin serial killer Jeffrey Dahmer and that Dahmer's recent murder by a fellow inmate was linked to a vast conspiracy against him, Colin Ferguson. Then, one after another, survivors of Ferguson's shooting spree confronted him in court. For the first time in any American trial, the victim confronted the criminal face-to-face as both the defendant and the defendant's attorney. In this bizarre dual position, Ferguson the self-appointed defense counsel asked the victims if they could identify Ferguson the accused as their attacker.

Maryanne Phillips, one of the victims, faced Ferguson cooly and said: "I saw you shoot me." This was repeated time and again, twelve out of the seventeen surviving victims saying: "It was you who shot me," and "You are the man who shot me."

He asked one witness: "Did the gunman shoot you?"

The victim replied while looking straight at Ferguson: "As soon as you had time to point the gun at me and pull the trigger."

When Robert Giugliano, a burly contractor Ferguson had shot in the chest, took the witness stand, his icy stare so unnerved Ferguson that he asked for a fifteen-minute recess. It was apparent that the strutting, posturing Ferguson was inflicting more pain upon his victims, first having shot them, then compelling them to recount in detail the horror and identify him as their assailant.

On February 15, 1996, Ferguson had run out of witnesses to identify him as a ruthless killer. He also refused to take the stand on his own behalf. It was, as the tolerant Judge Belfi stated, "the moment of truth." Ferguson rested his case, which was no case at all.

Two days later a jury deliberated ten hours and then returned six guilty verdicts in the murders of the six train passengers. Ferguson was also convicted of twenty-two counts of attempted murder. Carolyn McCarthy, whose husband had been shot to death by Ferguson and whose son Kevin had been crippled for life by a gunshot from the killer, had sat quietly behind the defendant through-

out the trial. At its conclusion she stated: "It's been a long fourteen months but justice has been done."

Judge Belfi later sentenced Ferguson to six life terms in prison, a total of 200 years with no hope for parole. He would die behind bars, the state insisted. Robert Giugliano was still enraged at the mass killer. At the sentencing, Giugliano shook his fist at the unperturbed Ferguson and shouted: "I feel this animal should suffer till the day he dies! . . . Given five minutes with Colin Ferguson, this coward would know the meaning of suffering!"

Where Colin Ferguson apparently killed out of his hatred for whites, Larry Wayne Shoemake murdered out of his loathing for blacks. On April 12, 1996, Shoemake went on a murderous rampage in a Jackson, Mississippi, shopping mall frequented mostly by blacks. Armed with four assault weapons, a shotgun, two handguns, and a great deal of ammunition, he began shooting black people in and around the PoFolks Restaurant.

Shoemake took refuge in the restaurant as it was abandoned by fleeing, screaming customers. He began shooting black passersby at random, killing D. Q. Holyfield, 49, and seriously wounding seven others, including Pamela Berry, a black reporter for the *Jackson Clarion-Ledger* who had been sent to the site to cover the ensuing gun battle between Shoemake and police.

It was several hours before the furious fusillade from the restaurant ceased, and only after the building broke into flames. Some time later, police dragged the charred body of

Shoemake from the gutted building. He had either been killed by police fire or had committed suicide when the flames closed in around him. Found in the dead killer's home were a number of messages from Shoemake, all advocating neo-Nazi and racist views. A police spokesman stated: "It appeared that he sort of expected that his house would be searched by authorities in the aftermath."

Where Heriberto Seda selected victims according to their birth signs, Colin Ferguson and Larry Shoemake according to skin color, Leon Bor killed people who happened to be German. Born in Soviet Russia as Leonid Borshevsky, Bor moved to the U.S. where he lived briefly until immigrating to Israel, becoming an Israeli citizen in 1989.

Little is known of Bor's activities in Israel except that he went to Germany in 1995, suddenly appearing on July 29 before a crowd of twenty-four people who had stepped from a sight-seeing bus in Cologne. The tourists, who were made up of Americans, Austrians, and Germans, had alighted from the bus to take snapshots of the Rhine River and a historical cathedral on the opposite bank.

Bor suddenly appeared among the tourists. He carried a bundle of black clothes, a parachute, and a sextant (used for navigation at sea). He brandished a 9mm Smith and Wesson pistol. Bor herded the tourists back onto the bus and, without a word of explanation, shot and killed the bus driver. He then unbundled the clothes, which turned out to be a black commando uniform that he put on.

Bor next ordered a terrified passenger to take his picture in the uniform and then unleased a torrent of mostly incoherent statements about the Russian Mafia, the 1994 massacre in a Hebron mosque, and a recent trip he had made to Paris. Every few minutes the terrorist shouted to the passenger holding his Polaroid camera to take his picture.

Most of the passengers realized that they were dealing with a lunatic, and three of them promptly fled the bus. One was a woman who deserted her two sons, ages eleven and twelve. She smashed the glass of the back window, jumped out and ran. Her youngest son also leaped from the bus and began running after her. Bor raced down the aisle, aiming his pistol at the fleeing boy.

Seeing that Bor was about the kill the child, Heinz Buchner, a fifty-three-year-old Austrian, heroically leaped up and jumped into Bor's line of fire, taking a bullet in the chest. Though severely wounded, Buchner himself, about two hours later, also jumped out of the rear window and escaped. (He later survived to be lauded as a hero by police commander Winrich Granitzka, who would state that Buchner had "risked his life and paid with terrible injuries.")

The bus remained stationary as Bor calmly walked down the aisle, asking passengers questions; he wanted to known their nationalities. When an elderly woman replied that she was German, Bor cooly raised his pistol and shot her. He fired three bullets into the neck and head of the sixty-four-year-old victim, killing her instantly. The terrorist then took Polaroids of the dead bus driver and the murdered German woman.

Police swat teams finally arrived and surrounded the bus. Bor cleverly kept officers at bay by displaying what the commandos thought to be dynamite, which the terrorist threatened to explode if they rushed him. The dynamite was nothing more than sticks of wood painted silver and strapped to his chest.

Using the portable phone in the bus, Bor talked softly to authorities, demanding that a Russian interpreter be brought to the bus. A short time later, officers approached the bus, holding out a cellular phone that Bor could use in talking to the interpreter. As the terrorist reached for the phone, an officer rushed forward, jumped into the bus and fired a single bullet into Bor's head, killing him.

Though Bor's motives remained unclear—some said that he was seeking vengeance against Germans for Hitler's holocaust—his murderous personality was quite clear to German prosecutor Karl Uterman who described Bor as a mad terrorist, "a killer who would stop at nothing. He was an absolute sadist who killed for the fun of it."

Three months later, another youth in France, sixteen-year-old Eric Borel, terrorized the small town of Cuers by shooting everyone in sight. His motives, too, were ambiguous. Borel lived at Soilles-Pont, a small town located six miles north of the sunny Mediterranean port of Toulon. A taciturn youth, he apparently went to pieces after his father died of cancer. An admirer of Nazi philosophy, Borel's room was plastered with photos of Adolf Hitler. On Sunday, September 24, 1995, Borel crept up on his mother, stepfather, and half-brother and crushed their skulls with a hammer and a baseball bat. He then retrieved his hunting rifle and a bag of ammunition and began strolling toward the village of Cuers.

As Borel entered the village, he began randomly shooting everyone he saw. "It was like he was hunting birds," said a cafe owner who watched the boy walk down the street, picking out his targets. He shot an old woman walking her dog. He next shot an elderly man going toward a cafe. Borel then spotted two people withdrawing money from a cash station and shot them both dead.

Turning a corner, the sharpshooting killer spotted a man playing boules, the Provencal bowling game, in the town square. He shot the man dead. Shocked villagers panicked and ran in all directions as word quickly spread that a terrorist was stalking everyone in town. They barricaded their homes and shops and watched fearfully as the youth patiently strolled the streets, looking for people to shoot, firing, and then calmly reloading his weapon as he walked along. One man emerged from a building and Borel shot him in the stomach. As the victim lay writhing on the ground, the killer walked up to him, and, at almost point-blank range, fired a lethal bullet into the man's head.

"He was very calm, very poised," reported one startled witness. "He put the gun on his shoulder, held the gun steady, adjusted his aim and fired."

One by one, unsuspecting villagers fell before Borel's unerring aim, seventeen in all, nine of whom died on the spot, another eight remaining seriously wounded.

The boy did not appear agitated as he stalked his victims. One witness reported: "I saw him go past my shop with his rifle. He was walking calmly. He wasn't in a hurry. At first, I thought he was a hunter. He was about twenty-five meters from my place when I saw him shoot a passerby, a shopkeeper who I think was hit in the head."

As heavily armed police warily tracked the terrorist through the narrow streets of the village, Borel, silent, saw that he had almost exhausted his ammunition. Leaning against a wall, he loaded his rifle once more and jammed the barrel into his mouth, pulling the trigger and killing himself. No explanation for Borel's mass murder was ever forthcoming. Shocked though the citizens of France were over this slaughter, they had, for some time, been subjected to repeated bloody attacks by terrorists.

A rash of bombings had occurred throughout France in recent months, all at the instigation of dissident Algerian separatists retaliating against the government for its continued support of the military regime ruling Algeria. The bombings had occurred chiefly in Paris. On July 25, 1995, a bomb was placed in a subway car in the Latin Quarter that exploded and killed seven persons, injuring dozens of others. Another bomb blew up in a trash can near the Arch of Triumph and another in an outdoor toilet stall near an open market. In addition to the seven killed by the sub-way blast, 130 persons had been seriously injured by six exploding bombs.

On August 16, 1995, an unexploded bomb was found on board a high-speed train traveling between Lyon and Paris. Police forensic specialists found a set of fingerprints on a piece of adhesive tape that had been wrapped around the bomb. From the prints, officials were able to identify the terrorist who had concocted the bomb, twenty-four-year-old Khaled Kelkal, one of the top-ranked Algerian separatists.

A massive manhunt ensued, with more than 750 investigators tracking Kelkal. On September 28, 1995, a mushroom hunter stumbled upon a grenade and made a police report. This led an army of police and military units to pinpoint and close in on Kelkal's forest hideout near Lyon. A shoot-out took place in which one of Kelkal's accomplices was wounded and two others were captured, but the elusive Kelkal escaped. Inside the hideout, police found Islamic literature and a map of the Lyon area that detailed safe houses that Kelkal and other terrorists were using. Kelkal's fingerprints were on the map.

The manhunt was stepped up, with hundreds of officers combing the Lyon area for the fleeing terrorist. On Friday night, September 30, 1995, military commandos spotted a man waiting at a bus stop about five miles outside of Lyon. When they approached him, the man whipped out an automatic and began firing. The return fire from dozens of machine guns was withering. It cut Khaled Kelkal in half before he dropped dead to the ground.

Blood on the Rising Sun

The history of Japan is pock-marked with terrorism. In fact, the country has been, for centuries, plagued by one form of terrorist society or another. In the late nineteenth century, the Black Dragon Society took root under the leadership of Mitsuru Toyama. The Society not only controlled all illegal activities in Japan—drugs, prostitution, gambling—but was the most potent political force in the land, its trained terrorists practicing wholesale assassination and supporting the jingoistic militarists bent on world conquest. More than any other force, the Society was responsible for launching Japan into World War II.

Ostensibly crushed after Japan's defeat, the Black Dragon Society was replaced by the Yakuza, a criminal brotherhood (its members bearing tattoo-coated bodies) that, to this day, dominates all criminal activities in Japan and has powerful chapters throughout the Pacific, in Hawaii and on the U.S. West Coast.

Yakuza, organized much like the Mafia, having a "family" or "families" presiding over towns and cities, realized like the Black Dragons before it, that its power and influence were intrinsically tied to the fortunes of the political right. Crime kingpins heading the Yakuza, such as Yoshio Kodama, Nobusuke Kishi, and Ryoichi Sasakawa, forged alliances with the political right to suppress the rising socialist movement in Japan. This led to the assassination of Socialist Party leader Asanuma Inejiro in 1960 by rightists and Yakuza members.

By that time, Tokyo police estimated that there were 70,000 Yakuza members in Japan. Ten years later, there were 250,000, making Yakuza the largest criminal organization in the world. It controlled all gambling, prostitution, drug trafficking, and extortion in Japan, and its influence became vast throughout the Pacific.

Its members were professional terrorists in that they were highly skilled in the many ways of intimidating shopkeepers and businessmen into paying large weekly tributes to Yakuza. First came polite messages to those tardy in their payments. Then came threats, then destruction to shops and businesses and, finally, severe injuries were inflicted on employees and owners and their families. Those who still refused to yield to Yakuza extortion were killed, along with their family members.

Right: Mitsuru Toyama, founder of the dreaded Black Dragon Society, which openly practiced terrorism and assassination, while controlling organized crime in Japan for sixty years.

Below right: Yoshio Kodama, left, supreme boss of Yakuza, 1960s-1980s; Yakuza evolved from the Black Dragon Society, a terrorist organization controlling all crime in Japan, as well as most of the country's finances and business.

Of all the many Yakuza gangs in Japan, the *Yamaguchi-gumi*, originally a small waterfront mob in Kobe, emerged as the most powerful under the leadership of Kazuo Taoka, who was known as Japan's Al Capone. At one time, he bossed 343 separate gangs under the Yakuza banner, controlling the entire Osaka district. More than 80 percent of all cargo loading and unloading on the Kobe docks was controlled by this gang.

By the 1970s, Yakuza gangs had established roots in Malaysia, Thailand, Hong Kong, and Taiwan, where they forged strong links with the Chinese Triads. Eventually, this criminal terrorist organization spread its influence to Hawaii where it took control of drug smuggling. Although its members donned conservative suits and became addicted to handmade sunglasses, they continued the Yakuza traditions, taking secret oaths

and enforcing Yakuza edicts with a vengeance.

Yoshio Kodama emerged in the 1980s as the supreme Yakuza leader after making an alliance with Kakuji Inagawa, Yakuza crime boss of the Yokohama-Tokyo area. Together these crime czars sided with the rightist Liberal Democratic Party to suppress

Rage from the Right

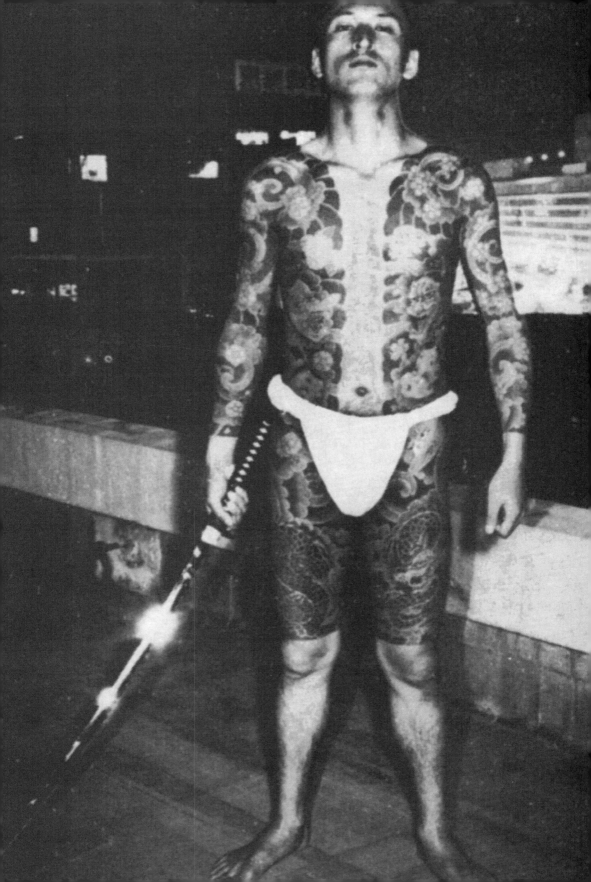

any leftist organizations in Japan that threatened the LDP's power. Leftists were sought out by Yakuza members and beaten up or even killed (one third of all murders in Japan are committed by Yakuza killers, according to Japanese police statistics).

By the early 1990s, many dissatisifed Yakuza members suddenly bolted from the Society and joined a strange political backlash movement built upon terrorism. This organization first came to international attention on March 20, 1995, when several packages left inside moving subway cars in the vast subway system of Tokyo began to spurt a powerful nerve gas that soon overwhelmed thousands of terrified passengers. Victims ran, tumbled, and staggered from the train cars and subway stations in wild panic. At the end of the day, twelve persons had died from the poison gas attacks and more than 5,500 were injured or contaminated.

The terrorists behind the horrific attack were quickly identified by police as being members of Aum Shinri Kyo (Supreme Truth), a doomsday cult that believes that the end of the world is coming soon and that only its organization will be the group to survive and rule over a mostly devastated planet.

Police by the hundreds began ferreting out cult members, following the attack, making raids on their various headquarters throughout Japan and arresting hundreds. In the village of Kamikuisiki, nestled at the foot of Mt. Fuji, sixty-three miles west of Tokyo, police assaulted a cult compound in a televised raid, taking fifty-three children belonging to cult members, fearing that these children might be somehow injured by their doomsday-obsessed parents.

The parents chased after buses carrying the children, shouting: "This is kidnapping! Return our children!" The children were taken to a welfare facility while bomb experts examined the compound. They found tons of chemicals, including trimethylphosphate and methuylphosphon acid dimethyl which are byproducts of sarin, a gas decomposition that the Nazis invented before World War II.

The use of sarin, the deadliest nerve gas ever created, caused the people of Japan to live for weeks in nerve-wracking terror, especially after cultists predicted a terrible calamity about to again engulf Japan. Cult spokesman Hirofumi Joyu, a boyish, affable lawyer, sought to calm national fear by appearing on TV news and talk-show programs, saying: "Please rest assured that Aum Shinri Kyo will not be taking any action."

More than 100 cult members were meanwhile arrested in raids against more than 130 cult facilities throughout Japan. Members were charged with possession of guns, kidnapping, and even driving without a license,

Shoko Asahara, leader of Japan's Aum Shinri Kyo, the terrorist religious sect that released a lethal nerve gas into the Tokyo subway system in 1995. (Wide World)

any offense that would allow police to take them into custody and interrogate them about cult leaders such as the forty-year-old Shoko Asahara, who was then being widely sought. (The children of cult leaders wore electrode caps that reportedly put them directly in touch with the ever-expanding brain waves of the cult leader, and thus benefited from Asahara's thoughts.)

On April 24, 1995, police were able to locate and arrest thirty-six-year-old Hideo Murai, one of the five top cult leaders and head of the cult's "Science and Technology Ministry," a department of the cult's shadow government that had been established to control Japan following doomsday. As Murai was being escorted out of the Tokyo offices of Aum Shinri Kyo, surrounded by a mob of press photographers and onlookers, an assassin named Hiroyuki

Yo, a twenty-nine-year-old South Korean, pushed his way through the crowd and fatally stabbed the cult leader in the abdomen.

As Murai clutched his abdomen and screamed in pain, police seized Yo, who later told them that he wanted to punish Murai because he believed him responsible for creating the sarin attack of March 20, and for other crimes. Murai died of his wounds a short time later. Meanwhile, more than 10,000 police officers rummaged through thousands of homes suspected of housing cult weapons and bombs. They unearthed evidence of widespread rifle production, biological warfare labs, and plans to purchase nuclear weapons from Russia.

Two days later, police learned of a secret basement beneath the Mt. Fuji headquarters of Aum Shinri Kyo. Following this tip, officers found hiding inside of the basement the much-sought Masami Tsuchiya and six other cult leaders. Considered to be one of Japan's scientific elite, Tsuchiya was the chemicals expert who was thought to have created the sarin used in the massive poison gas attack in the Tokyo subway system.

The thirty-year-old Tsuchiya was reported to be a brilliant scientist who quit a five-year chemistry doctoral program at Tsukuba University, one of the top schools in Japan, to join the doomsday cult. (Eight weeks later, Tsuchiya admitted that he and others had, indeed, made the poison gas sarin, but he would not admit that the gas had been created specifically for the purpose of the subway attack.)

Also taken into custody was thirty-four-year-old Seiichi Endo, cult leader and former genetics and virus researcher. These cult chiefs and their followers held by police universally denied having anything to do with the gas attacks in Tokyo and elsewhere. The lone exception was cultist Katsuhiko Kobayashi, who confessed that the sect produced poisoned gas at its headquarters.

More insidious were the revelations that came from two sergeants in the Japanese Army. They admitted to being cult members and that they had staged firebomb raids against some of their own cult headquarters before the March 20, 1995, attacks designed to disrupt an on-going police investigation into cult activities.

Despite the widespread police raids and arrests, cultists continued to spread terror in Japan by engineering three more gas attacks in subway stations, which sent more than 500 people to the hospital. These attacks, however, brought about no deaths. On May 5, 1995, two more attacks took place when cultists left two burning plastic bags of chemicals in a men's room. Four fast-acting train employees rushed into the men's room and extinguished the fires; they were all injured and were hailed as heroes.

One bag contained sodium cyanide, and the other, diluted sulfuric acid. Had the vapors combined properly (as was no doubt the design of the cultists), enough hydrogen cyanide would have been formed to kill more than 10,000 people. The terrorists had selected Japan's "Children's Day" for the attack.

On May 15, police stopped a car at a roadblock outside of Tokyo and took into custody twenty-five-year-old Yoshihiro Inoue, the cult's so-called "Intelligence Minister." By then, police had assembled a great deal of evidence against the cult, including the confessions of more than 200 cult members who detailed how ten of their leaders had developed the sarin gas and another ten top members had placed the gas containers in three strategic places in the Tokyo subway system on March 20. These confessions led to the discovery of Inoue's notebook, which contained a record of timetables and numbers of passengers who used the three subway lines where the sarin nerve gas was released.

The following day, an army of policemen stormed the cult compound at the base of Mt. Fuji. This time, officers were successful in unearthing and arresting the top cult leader, forty-year-old Shoko Asahara, along with fourteen of his top lieutenants, who were all charged with mass murder. Asahara was found sitting "in meditation" in a hidden room beneath the third floor of "Truth Building" Number Six. He wore long, black, flowing hair and an elegant robe.

The terrorist campaign was over, according to police. Said Metropolitan Police Chief Yukihiko Inoue of the cult attacks: "This is an unprecedented crime in our history—killing people indiscriminately by spreading gas in the subway. We devoted all our strength to investigate this case to relieve the Japanese people of their anxiety. We will continue to make efforts to prevent any recurrence of such incidents."

Hundreds of cult leaders were jailed, along with all of their top leaders, many of whom being former members of Japan's organized criminal society, Yakuza, as well as thirty members of the Japanese Army who had acted as secret agents for the cult, tipping off its members to impending police and army raids.

Asahara, whose real name is Chizuo Matsumoto, along with forty of his top followers, were charged with murder, assisting murder and a host of other charges. Many were convicted and sent to prison. Asahara, who is partially blind, had predicted that in 1997, nuclear war would destroy most of the world and his sect would be the only organized body left living. The reasons why he had ordered the gas attacks remain obscure.

Asahara was like many another false prophet. He had been educated at a school for the blind, where he was known as a terrible bully. He had experimented with acupuncture to cure his own blindness and failed. He and his wife opened a health food store where he was arrested in 1982 for selling fake medicines. He started a cult in that same year, the Heavenly Blessing Association, but he attracted few followers. After traveling to Nepal in 1987, he returned to Japan with a new credo, one made up of Hindu and Buddhist beliefs and practices, which he funneled into Aum Shinri Kyo, a cult that appealed to the insecure and the paranoid.

Asahara played upon the fears of the public and in Japan, where superstition, legends, and the prophesying of dire events has been historically popular, his ridiculous sect thrived. The cult leader ran for office in 1992, but he was soundly defeated. Bitter over this setback, Asahara ranted against the U.S., Europe, and the Japanese government for the country's recent economic recessions.

Most of Asahara's followers were youthful college students who came from middle-class or wealthy families. Through them, the cult amassed more than $1 billion in assets, which allowed Asahara to build a network of warehouses, chemical plants, computer firms, and compounds where cultists could hide weapons and themselves while they experimented with deadly chemicals and kinetic energy, seeking at the same time to purchase nuclear weapons and develop mental telepathy, which would allow them to read the minds of their enemies.

Asahara continued to deny having anything to do with the March 20, 1995, poison gas attack. At the time of his arrest, the cult leader snickered: "How can a blind person like me commit such a crime?" When police grabbed him and began leading him into custody, the fanatical cult leader shouted: "Don't touch me! I don't even allow my followers to touch me!"

The Path to Oklahoma City

Just as the cultists of Japan's Aum Shinri Kyo represented the demented, fanatical elements of that country's far right-wing, there arose in the U.S. at the same time an ever growing number of paramilitary groups advocating right-wing hatreds of old and an alarming willingness to rebel against the government. The old guardians of law and order, particularly federal agencies such as the FBI and the ATF, were suddenly branded as the enemy of the American people by these radical paramilitary organizations that chiefly infested the Midwest and far western states.

This movement had festered into existence during the 1980s, its early leaders coming from the ranks of the KKK and neo-Nazi organizations. An early-day extremist of this movement was Bruce Carroll Pierce, a rabid racist from Rossville, Georgia. He was the leader of a nationwide organization called the Order, which was loosely based upon the old Ku Klux Klan but one that adopted Nazi philosophies. Its members, as a shocked nation was later to learn, were well armed and had diligently planned to violently overthrow the government of the United States.

Pierce's revolution began with a controversial radio host, Alan Berg, who described himself as "the last angry man." A former Chicago lawyer with an abrasive personality and a reputation for bluntness, Berg once said: "You never know where the nuts are going to come from. So you live day by day." The host of a daily radio talk show on Denver station KOA, Berg's program reached nearly a quarter of a million listeners. Calling himself "the man you love to hate," Berg joked about the many death threats he received.

About midnight on June 18, 1984, one of those death threats became a humorless reality. Berg was shot to death in the driveway of his home. Police found ten .45-caliber shell casings near his bullet-riddled corpse. The performer apparently died instantly. The murder investigation produced no results until the following year. On March 25, 1985, police arrested Bruce Carroll Pierce in Rossville, Georgia, charging him with Berg's murder.

At the time of his arrest, Pierce's van contained bombs; grenades; machine guns; automatic weapons, including three pistols; dynamite; and a crossbow and arrows. Police reported that Pierce was the leader of a neo-Nazi group called the Order. An offshoot of the Church of the Aryan Nation, the group had a predominately West Coast membership. Members stood accused of engineering several armored-car robberies that had netted them about $4 million, money they used to finance violent revolutionary activities.

Police linked three other members of the Order to Berg's killing—David Lane, a Denver-based neo-Nazi leader; Robert Matthews, founder of the Order; and Richard Scutari. Matthews was never arrested in that he was dead by the time police picked up Pierce. The organization founder had burned to death after a thirty-six-hour standoff and shoot-out with FBI agents near Seattle, Washington, in December 1984. Lane, however, was arrested in a shopping center parking lot in Winston-Salem, North Carolina, on March 31, 1985, six days after Pierce had been captured in Georgia.

The Department of Justice approved federal prosecution of the Order under federal racketeering laws on April 11, 1985. Proceedings were brought against twenty-four persons, twelve being Order members, who had been arrested in September 1984, three months after Berg's murder. Of the ten Order members charged with conspiring to overthrow the U.S. government, Pierce, Lane, and Scutari were charged with Berg's killing, a charge stemming from a civil rights violation punishable with life imprisonment.

A federal district court jury found Lane and Pierce guilty of violating Berg's civil rights on December 3, 1987. Each terrorist was sentenced to 150 years in prison. Pierce was specifically convicted of shooting the talk-show host thirteen times with a submachine gun and Lane was convicted of driving the getaway car. Scutari and another defendant were found not guilty of participating in Berg's death. The Order quickly collapsed following the convictions, but by then, many other paramilitary groups, most calling themselves self-styled state militias, had come into existence.

Militia members armed themselves with assault weapons and donned battlefield fatigues. They drilled at regular meetings, going through rigorous commando exercises, wearing out ranges where they fired their automatic weapons. The basic philosophy put forth by these militant groups was one of the extreme right. It branded the federal government a dictatorial liberal power bent on destroying the individual rights of Americans, particularly the right to own and bear arms. It labeled the FBI and the ATF enemies of the people, and by the early 1990s, it openly defied federal, state, and local law enforcement agencies seeking to disarm and disband the militias.

One of their number was dissatisfied with the apparent inability of the militias to effect any real change or to move against the government in open rebellion. He thought to change all that, as well as to strike back in particular at the ATF for its 1993 attack and destruction of the Branch Davidian compound in Waco, Texas.

At 9:04 A.M. on April 19, 1995, Secretary's Day, a truck bomb went off next to the Alfred P. Murrah Federal Building in Oklahoma City, Oklahoma, vertically shearing off one third of the building, killing 168 men, women, and children and injuring hundreds more. Initially, the impact of this colossal explosion suggested at first that foreign terrorists, part of a vast anti-American conspiracy, had done the horrible deed. Then a penny-ante protestor and drifter, twenty-seven-year-old Timothy McVeigh, was identified as the chief bombing suspect.

Only an hour and fifteen minutes after the Oklahoma City explosion, McVeigh had been stopped by state trooper Charles Hangar, who had spotted a beat-up yellow Mercury Marquis without license plates outside of Perry, Oklahoma. When Hangar pulled the driver to the side of the roadway, he noticed a suspicious bulge beneath his jacket. He discovered that the driver, McVeigh, was carrying a concealed 9mm pistol, along with a six-inch knife. He placed McVeigh under arrest and took him to the Perry courthouse, where he was charged with traffic violations and carrying concealed weapons.

On April 21, Hangar saw a composite sketch of one of the suspected Oklahoma City bombers on TV and realized that it bore a strong resemblance to the man he had arrested two days earlier. Rushing to the Perry lockup, Hangar was just in time to prevent McVeigh from being released on a $500 bond. Turned over to the FBI, which had been conducting a massive, desperate search for the bombers, McVeigh was placed in federal custody and charged with the bombing.

Dressed in orange prison garb and shackled, the tall, crew-cutted, lean-faced McVeigh was implacable as he was taken from the Perry courthouse by FBI agents to a waiting army helicopter en route to Tinker Air Force Base. Dozens of heavily armed agents accompanied McVeigh through angry throngs in Perry who screamed: "Baby killer! Murdering bastard!" Once at the air force base, McVeigh was hurried to a makeshift courtroom in the supply building where he was formally charged with the bombing.

At the time, the taciturn McVeigh refused to admit anything. He did, however, express militant right-wing views and that he had visited the devastated one-time Branch Davidian compound in Waco. He stated bitter resentment against the federal government for attacking the suicidal cult members who followed David Koresh into a fiery doomsday in 1993. He told investigators that the government "should never have done what it did in Waco."

The explosion in Oklahoma City took place on the second anniversary of the destruction of the Davidian compound in Waco, where Koresh and more than eighty fanatical followers, including many innocent, helpless children, died of either self-inflicted gunshot wounds (or were executed by fellow members) or were incinerated when the complex was consumed in a towering blaze. The Waco incident had served as a rallying point for right-wing extremists and paramilitary groups in the U.S. who believed Waco

America's worst terrorist bombing on record, which claimed 168 lives: the destroyed Alfred P. Murrah Federal Building in Oklahoma City, Oklahoma, April 19, 1995. (Wide World/U.S. Department of Justice)

served as a symbol of federal government tyranny.

The same day McVeigh was identified and arrested, his cousin, forty-year-old Terry Nichols, was arrested in Herington, Kansas, and identified as the second person involved in the Oklahoma City bombing. At the same time, federal investigators swarmed onto a small farm outside of Decker, Michigan, sixty miles north of Detroit. The farm was owned by James Douglas Nichols, Terry Nichols's

brother. The federal agents searched for ingredients that might be used in the making of bombs, particularly fertilizer and fuel oil, the components used in creating the enormous bomb that destroyed the federal building in Oklahoma City.

James Nichols' neighbors thought him to be a crank, a man who bathed in peroxide (for the oxygen, he claimed) and, for the fun of it, made and exploded small bombs on his property. James' younger brother

Terry was once described by an ex-army buddy as a "spastic, nerdy kind of guy who walked with an odd waddle." Both belonged to extremist groups that were linked by fax machines and the Internet, a communications network filled with anti-government rantings. They were, like many of the oddball militants in the U.S. playing at militia, part of what was aptly called the lunatic fringe.

McVeigh stood solidly in their ranks after living with the Nichols brothers in Michigan, where he was indoctrinated at meetings of the paramilitary group called the Michigan Patriots headed by Mark Koernke, a janitor turned militia leader. Koernke preached the credo of the extreme right, urging America to arm in order to fend off an impending coup d'etat planned by bankers, politicians and media bosses.

Terry and James Nichols were later indicted for their part in the bombing conspiracy. Michael Fortier, a friend of McVeigh's and the Nichols brothers, was later indicted as having transported stolen property, chiefly guns that were sold to raise money. The cash was used to buy explosives in preparing the huge bomb used in Oklahoma City. Fortier later pleaded guilty to this charge, as well as to the charge of perjury, agreeing to testify against McVeigh and Terry Nichols.

Fortier told federal investigators that he had accompanied McVeigh to the Alfred P. Murrah Federal Building, where they closely examined the structure. McVeigh picked out the spot in the parking lot where he planned to park a rented truck filled with explosive materials some days later. The parking lot was directly in front of the building and beneath a day-care center packed with children, and, above that, the offices of the ATF, the supposed object of the bombing attack.

Taken to the federal corrections center at El Reno, Oklahoma, McVeigh was watched night and day on TV cameras monitoring his every move in his eight-foot by twelve-foot cell. Meanwhile, government officials studied the backgrounds of McVeigh and Nichols, homegrown terrorists who had reportedly committed one of the worst atrocities in American history.

McVeigh had grown up in Lockport, New York, and was an above-average student with an IQ of 128. He was known as a "pleasant, cooperative" boy. He enjoyed the comfort of a middle-class home without domestic problems and the close affection of parents and two sisters. Following his high school graduation, McVeigh entered the army, joining up the same day as Terry Nichols in 1988. They went through basic training together at Fort Benning, Georgia, and they were stationed together at Fort Riley, Kansas. Both apparently held the same political views and told one and all that they were staunchly against any federal government controls. In May 1989, Nichols was discharged for undisclosed reasons. McVeigh, however, remained in the service and achieved the rank of sergeant. He served in Operation Desert Storm, being awarded several medals, including a Bronze Star.

Exactly what McVeigh did in the

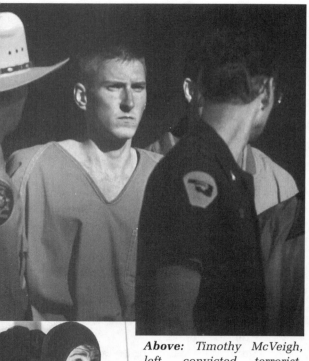

Above: Timothy McVeigh, left, convicted terrorist-bomber of the federal building in Oklahoma City, Oklahoma, in which 168 persons lost their lives on April 19, 1995. *Left:* Actor Robert DeNiro, portraying "Harry Tuttle," an engineer-turned-terrorist in the futuristic 1985 film, Brazil, *who blows up a government building packed with bureaucrats; McVeigh used the alias "Tuttle" prior to the Oklahoma City bombing, and donned the same kind of combat fatigues worn by DeNiro.*

Gulf War to earn that medal is not known. He was a gunner on a Bradley Fighting Vehicle in the First Division, the "Big Red One," as that unit was known during World War II when it stormed onto beaches in Italy and later at Normandy. He told friends that he "blew up" an Iraqi soldier, which prompted more than 500 more Iraqi soldiers to surrender to him. An

army buddy said that McVeigh shot several Iraqi soldiers who attempted to surrender. Taking prisoners was not foremost in the minds of McVeigh and others. In some instances, it was reported, hundreds of Iraqi soldiers were simply buried alive in their sand bunkers by U.S. bulldozers.

Obsessed with guns, McVeigh spent most of his service time in the barracks, reading *Guns and Ammo* magazine. Against the rules, he kept a 9mm Glock pistol with him at all times. In the trunk of his car, parked on post, McVeigh kept pistols, rifles, shotguns, and a Czech-made machine gun. Yet, he was not then thought of as a terrorist. "Something happened to Tim McVeigh between the time he left the army and the Oklahoma City bombing," said one army buddy.

Something happened before that. As early as 1989, McVeigh became obsessed with right-wing revolts in the U.S. as postured in the more absurd action fiction of the day. At one point he loaned a book he was reading, *The Turner Diaries*, to an army friend, saying: "Don't let anybody see it. I don't want to get into trouble." This hack fiction story begins with the bombing of the FBI headquarters in Washington and describes a bloody right-wing revolt and race war in America.

The actual turning point for McVeigh may have been when he applied for Special Services and was rejected, a rejection that embittered him against the army. He sought his release and was discharged a short time later. On December 31, 1991, a friend received a disturbing card from McVeigh, one that showed a skull and crossbones and a pistol aimed at the viewer. It read: "So many victims, so little time." During this period, McVeigh worked for the National Guard in New York, and he also served as a part-time security guard.

To add to his income, McVeigh, according to Terry Nichols' later statements, sold army surplus goods with Nichols throughout the country. Nichols also told authorities that McVeigh at one point called him at his home in Herington, Kansas, and asked that he pick him up in Oklahoma City. This occured a short time before the bombing. Nichols did pick up McVeigh, driving him to Junction City, 240 miles away. On this trip, McVeigh told Nichols several times: "Something big is going to happen."

It was in Junction City where McVeigh, along with "John Doe No. 2," rented the Ryder truck, which was then packed with explosives and driven to Oklahoma City, according to authorities. (Several witnesses later told federal investigators that they saw McVeigh near the federal building in Oklahoma City only minutes before the bomb went off.)

Nichols, however, could not distance himself from his close friend McVeigh as to their common interests. He, too, investigators quickly proved, was not only a gun enthusiast but a collector. His home in Herington yielded a 60mm anti-tank rocket, thirty-three assorted firearms, nonelectric detonators, four 55-gallon plastic drums, and three empty 50-pound bags that had contained ammonium nitrate fertilizer, the very material used in the Oklahoma City bombing. Also found

in Nichols' home was literature concerning the Waco incident and considerable anti-tax and anti-government literature.

McVeigh made no secret of his hatred for federal controls. He had written a letter to his hometown newspaper in Lockport, New York, in which he stated: "Is civil war imminent?" His older sister Jennifer shared his views about Waco and also wrote letters to the local paper condemning government action in that affair. She reportedly told friends in early 1995 that "something big is going to happen in March or April and Tim's involved."

For some time in 1994, McVeigh lived with the Nichols brothers on their Michigan farm. Then Terry Nichols moved to Kansas and McVeigh to Kingman, Arizona, where he roomed in a mobile home with former army chum Michael Fortier, the very man who later agreed to testify against McVeigh and Nichols. It was conjectured that McVeigh and Nichols made their moves to Kansas and Arizona in preparation for their bombing of the federal building in Oklahoma City.

In Kingman, McVeigh supported himself by selling weapons, using the alias of T. Tuttle in his mail order advertisements. This alias may be a play on the name "Harry Tuttle," a terrorist played by Robert DeNiro in the 1985 offbeat futuristic movie *Brazil*, one in which DeNiro explodes a bomb that destroys a building housing government bureaucrats. Like DeNiro in the movie, McVeigh wore combat boots and fatigues while living in

Kingman and was so attired when regularly picking up his mail. In late February and early March 1995, McVeigh uncustomarily was absent, his mail being picked up by Michael Fortier. On one occasion, another man, who was later described as "John Doe No. 2," also picked up McVeigh's mail.

In hindsight, Kingman seemed to be a logical base of operations for McVeigh. In the mid-1980s, a paramilitary group calling itself the Arizona Patriots, with an agenda similar to that of Koernke's Michigan Patriots, planned to blow up federal buildings in Phoenix and Los Angeles and execute a machine-gun attack on IRS offices in Ogden, Utah. The Arizona group expected to finance these terrorist operations by robbing an armored car en route from a Nevada casino. The conspiracy was unearthed by the FBI, and three of the plotters were sent to prison.

During his absence from Kingman, McVeigh reportedly scouted federal buildings in Phoenix, Arizona; Omaha, Nebraska; and Dallas, Texas. He apparently chose the federal building in Oklahoma City to bomb because he could more easily park the truck planted with explosives directly in front of the place, assuring himself that, when the bomb went off, the explosion would thoroughly damage the structure. Upon his return to Kingman, some time in March 1995, McVeigh went to a local video store and rented the film, *Blown Away*, a pscho-bomber movie starring Jeff Bridges and Tommy Lee Jones. He viewed this film many times.

McVeigh is thought to be the person most responsible for the ghastly Oklahoma City bombing. Reports have it that McVeigh's destruction of the day-care center in the federal building was intentional and that he purposely sought to kill as many children as possible in retaliation for the children killed in the Waco firestorm. To that end, nineteen helpless children in Oklahoma City were murdered in the towering blast.

Some authorities believe that McVeigh had more help than that given by Nichols and Fortier, that he was not able to construct the mammoth bomb himself. According to explosive experts, the bomb was made up of 4,800 pounds of ammonium nitrate fertilizer mixed with fuel oil packed in twenty blue plastic drums. This was "boosted" with metal containers of hydrogen or acetylene to make the bomb even more devastating. It would have taken several persons to load this material into the large Ryder truck McVeigh had rented.

The far-right militias and paramilitary groups throughout the U.S. ranted that the Oklahoma City bombing was actually performed by federal agents at the behest of a government that intended to use this terrible carnage to destroy the militias. Militia leaders pointed out that this was the same technique employed by Hitler when he had Goering set fire to the German government building, the Reichstag, in 1933, in order to blame political opponents for the blaze.

To many right-wing militia members, McVeigh is a hero. Phil

Markowski of the Michigan Militia said of him: "I consider Tim McVeigh to be a good guy. If I were in a war, I would want him on my side. He's the kind of a guy who forms allegiances to the death." To the surviving family members of those senselessly slaughtered in Oklahoma City, McVeigh is no hero. The mere mention of his name evokes incredible pain. Edye Smith, who lost her two small sons, Colton, 2, and Chase, 3, in the horrible blast, finds it impossible to watch little blond boys at play without thinking back on her own slain children. "There's a hole in her heart," Smith's mother stated, "that can never be replaced."

McVeigh and Nichols were granted separate trials, with McVeigh going to court first. In March 1997, a month before McVeigh went to trial, the *Dallas Morning News* reported that one of his defense attorneys had interviewed him, asking why he had not bombed the Alfred P. Murrah Federal Building at night, when fewer persons would have been killed. "That would not have gotten the point across to the government," the *News* quoted McVeigh's response. "We needed a body count to make our point."

Stephen Jones, 56, McVeigh's chief defense attorny, denied that McVeigh had made the statement to anyone working on his defense and went on to charge the paper with "jury pool contamination." When McVeigh's trial did begin, the accused terrorist and mass murderer chatted casually with paralegals in court and smiled and nodded at members of the press and the prosecutors, enjoying, it seemed,

his moment of high drama.

Jury selection began on March 31, 1997, and the case then went to court before Judge Richard Matsch, with opening statements made on April 24, 1997. A parade of witnesses came forth to state that they had seen one or two men driving the Ryder truck. Fred Skerdla, a gas station attendant in Billings, Oklahoma, reported how he had seen McVeigh driving the Ryder truck at between 1 A.M. and 3 A.M., on the morning of the bombing.

One witness, Mike Moroz, insisted that he saw McVeigh driving this truck when he stopped at Johnny's Tire Company on Tenth Street in Oklahoma City—only seven blocks from the Murrah Building about a half hour before the explosion on April 19, 1995, where McVeigh asked for directions to the building's location.

The most damaging testimony came from McVeigh's close friends, Michael Fortier and his wife Lori, who both stated that McVeigh had confided his plans to them, that he had told them he intended to blow up the Murrah Building in retaliation for the destruction of the Branch Davidians in Waco, Texas. Nothing Jones did or said in his cross-examination of these witnesses caused them to change their stories.

In June 1997, a jury of seven men and five women found the twenty-nine-year-old Timothy James McVeigh guilty and decreed the death penalty. The emotional burden endured by these jurors was deep and painful; before rendering their decision, the jurors were all reduced to tears. Vera Chubb, one of the jurors, later explained that the tears were not for the convicted McVeigh. "We were thinking about the families that were left in Oklahoma City . . . how their lives would never be the same and how mothers and fathers had to bury their loved ones."

Diane Faircloth had been moved by McVeigh's mother, Mildred "Mickey" Frazer, who had earlier appeared in court to sobbingly beg for her son's life. Faircloth nevertheless felt no sympathy for McVeigh, stating: "What he represents to me is a terrorist—someone with no regard for human life. He represents a twisted view of the intentions of the government and the principles that this country was founded upon."

Terry Nichols, McVeigh's friend and cohort in the plot to destroy the Murrah Building, was next to go to trial, even though he was not present at the time of the bombing. In fact, Nichols was seen on the morning of April 19, 1995, working on his lawn in Herrington, Kansas. He was dusting the grass with fertilizer—ammonium nitrate—the same substance used in packaging the horrendous bomb which destroyed the Murrah Building. Federal authorities insisted that Nichols was not merely fertilizing his lawn—he was destroying evidence, the remainder of the fertilizer that had not been used in the bomb packed into the Ryder Truck left outside of the Murrah Building.

The prosecution in Nichols' separate case, convinced a jury that Nichols had, indeed, aided McVeigh in building the bomb and then drove McVeigh's car to Oklahoma City and

Terry Nichols, who was convicted of conspiring with Timothy McVeight to blow up the Murrah building in Oklahoma City, Oklahoma, in 1995. (Wide World)

left it there so that McVeigh, after parking the Ryder Truck next to the Murrah Building, had the auto available for his escape. Nichols was also convicted of being an accessory to McVeigh's crime but he was given a life sentence.

To the date of this writing the impassive McVeigh has admitted nothing (despite his alleged remarks to one of his defense attorneys prior ot his trial). His death sentence (by lethal injection) is subject to appeal, one which, at this writing, is expected to take several years. Meanwhile, McVeigh sits comfortably in federal prison, having years to continue his fight for life.

The Unabomber and Beyond

FBI sketch of the Unabomber, released by the Bureau in 1995.

The ubiquitous killer and serial terrorist the press dubbed the Unabomber began murdering and maiming American citizens at will in 1978. Apparently driven by a seething hatred for modern technology, specifically computer science and the changes it brings about, he struck out at corporations, institutions and individuals.

On April 20, 1995, the terrorist sent a letter to Nobel Prize Winner Richard J. Roberts, one of four letters he mailed from Oakland, California, along with a bomb, which, on April 24, 1995, killed Gilbert Murray, the president of the California Forestry Association, an industry trade group located in Sacramento. (The package containing the bomb was addressed to Murray's associate, William Dennison.) The contents of the letters received by geneticist Roberts at New England Biolabs in Beverly, Massachusetts, were not disclosed. Roberts helped to launch the field of biotechnology and brought definition to the makeup of DNA.

Up to that time, the Unabomber had sent sixteen bombs, which killed three persons and seriously injured twenty-three people in the U.S. The first to be killed was Hugh Scrutton, owner of a computer store in Sacramento, California, who discovered a bag left behind his store on December 11, 1985. When he picked it up, it blew him to pieces. The second person murdered by the Unabomber was advertising executive Thomas Mosser of North Caldwell, New Jersey, who was killed on December 10, 1994, when he opened a package delivered to his home. The last fatality was timber lobbyist Gilbert Murray, killed when he opened a package on April 24, 1995.

In one of the letters the Unabomber sent to the *New York Times*, he stated in a typewritten note: "Clearly, we are in a position to do a great deal of damage." This was the second note the terrorist had sent to the *Times*, the first missive having been sent in 1993. In both notes, the killer described himself as an "anarchist" representing a group called "FC" (standing for "Freedom Club," according to the terrorist's later letters).

The FBI believed that the terrorist was striking back at anyone who had polluted the environment. In his 1995 note to the *Times*, the Unabomber referred to Burson-Marsteller, an agency that represented Exxon following the Exxon-Valdez oil spill in Alaska. Bureau experts pointed out that the terrorist's hatred for institutions was exemplified early on when, in his first attack, he mailed a bomb that exploded on the campus of Northwestern University in Evanston, Illinois, on May 26, 1978.

In the 1995 note, the Unabomber inexplicably claimed that he had "nothing against universities or scholars as such . . . All the university people we have attacked have been specialists in technical fields" who were involved "in certain areas of applied psychology, such as behavior modification." He added that "we would not want anyone to think that we have any desire to hurt professors who study archeology, history, literature or harmless stuff like that."

Then the Unabomber stated that he would stop killing people if a national publication would print his manuscript, one which he said he had been working on for some time and consisted of between 29,000 and 37,000 words. The terrorist added (either jocularly or as a way to gain unthinkable sympathy) that "it's no fun having to spend all your evenings and weekends preparing dangerous mixtures, filing trigger mechanisms out of scraps of metal or searching the sierras for a place isolated enough to test a bomb."

In another April 20, 1995, letter, the Unabomber taunted one of his own victims, David Gelernter, a noted computer science professor at Yale University, who received serious injuries when a bomb exploded in his hands in June 1993. Gelernter was blinded in one eye, lost part of his right hand, was deafened in one ear and was injured in the chest when the terrorist's bomb went off.

"People with advanced degrees aren't as smart as they think they are," taunted the Unabomber in his letter to Gelernter. "If you had any brains you would have realized that there are a lot of people out there who resent bitterly the way technonerds like you are changing the world and you wouldn't have been dumb enough to open an unexpected package from an unknown source."

The letter went on to criticize Gelernter's book, *Mirror Worlds*, which predicted the inevitability of widespread computerization. Remarked the Unabomber: "In the epilog of your book you tried to justify your research by claiming that the developments you describe are inevitable, and that any college person can learn enough about computers to compete in a computer-dominated world.

"Apparently people without a college degree don't count . . . In any case, being informed about computers won't enable anyone to prevent invasion of privacy (through computers), genetic engineering, environmental degradation through excessive economic growth and so forth . . . If the developments you describe are inevitable, they are not inevitable in the way old age or bad weather are inevitable. They are inevitable only because technonerds like you make them inevitable. If there were no computer scientists there would be no progress in computer science."

The Unabomber's hatred for academics like Gelernter was evident, emphasized in his letter to the *Times* in which he clearly stated that he was "out to get" computer and genetic scientists whom he felt were ruining the world and that he was dedicated to the "destruction of the worldwide industrial system." After studying the letters, the FBI stated that though the Unabomber claimed to be part of a group, agents did not "have a shred of evidence that he is connected with other people in the placing of the bombs."

It was evident, however, that the terrorist insisted upon establishing a frightening personal image. Before he sent a bomb on June 22, 1993 to geneticist Charles Epstein at the University of California in San Francisco, the Unabomber spray-painted the initials "FC" and the word "anarchy" in the campus area of Sacramento State University. Epstein lost several fingers and suffered a broken arm when he opened the package containing the bomb. Two days later, the Unabomber mailed his bomb to Gelernter.

In one of the letters the killer sent in 1995, he showed his return address as being the headquarters of the FBI in Washington, D.C., a way of sneering his contempt at those he knew were avidly pursuing him. Smugly, in his letter to the *Times*, the killer bragged about how his expertise at bomb making had improved: "Since we no longer have to confine the explosive in pipe, we are now free of limitations on the size and shape of our bombs. We are pretty sure we know how to increase the power of our explosives.

"And, we think we now have more effective fragmentation material. So we expect to be able to pack deadly bombs into ever smaller, lighter and more harmless-looking packages . . . we believe we will be able to make bombs much bigger than we've made before."

Further, the Unabomber said that he represented a movement that hoped to promote "instability in industrial society, propagate anti-industrial ideas and give encouragement to those who hate the industrial system . . ." To some academics studying the Unabomber's letters, it seemed as if he were echoing the early nineteenth century beliefs of the Luddites, an anti-industrial sect in England.

At one point in 1995, the mysterious Unabomber brought panic to air travelers and airlines when he threatened to blow up an airliner at the Los Angeles Airport. For days, FBI agents swarmed throughout southern California airports, where all passengers were stopped and ordered to identify themselves. Postal authorities announced that no mail weighing more than three quarters of an ounce would be accepted or delivered.

Then, to placate the madman, the *New York Times* and the *Washington Post* offered to publish the Unabomber's manifesto. Both publications received his 35,000-word manuscript entitled "Industrial Society and Its Future." Along with the manuscript, which the FBI certified as genuine, was a letter in which the Unabomber decried the Oklahoma City bombing, stating: "We strongly deplore the kind of indiscriminate slaughter that occurred in the Oklahoma City event."

In a precedent-setting move, the *Times* and the *Post* published a segment of the Unabomber's rambling, raving manuscript in September 1995, one in which the terrorist condemned a corrupt technocracy responsible for stamping out human freedom on behalf of the corporate and governmental elite. Said a *Times* spokesman: "We are absolutely not trying to appease the Unabomber by publishing the excerpts. It was only 3,000 words." The *Post* stated: "We thought we owed our readers the relevant excerpts. For all we know it could wind up in the Internet next week."

Hundreds of FBI agents were assigned to tracking down the elusive terrorist. As is the case with most such manhunts, FBI agents got a break when a tipster contacted them in January 1996. The unlikely informant was David Kaczynski, who had found papers with Unabomber-like rhetoric in the home of his mother, Wanda Kaczynski, in Lombard, Illinois. The papers had been written by his brother, onetime academic, social dropout and Montana hermit, Theodore "Ted" Kaczynski.

David Kaczynski, a social worker, lived quietly with his wife in Schenectady, New York. He had read the excerpts of the Unabomber's diatribes in the *Times* and realized that the writing was strikingly similar to that written by his brother over the years. Moreover, when helping his mother move from her Lombard home in January 1996, he found hundreds of letters his brother had written, all brimming with the same invective. The loyalty-torn Kaczynski agonized for some time over his decision to contact the FBI through a Washington, D.C., attorney. He offered to help the Bureau only if his name was not disclosed and that his brother, if found guilty, would not receive the death penalty. Neither promise could be kept.

Agents investigated every square inch of the Lombard home. An around-the-clock stakeout kept vigil on the house and neighborhood while other agents scoured the remote regions of Stemple Pass, Montana, where Kaczynski lived in a crude cabin. Agents kept the cabin under close surveillance while they monitored the movements of the hermit, a shaggy-haired, heavily bearded Ted Kaczynski.

Kaczynski had lived in the cabin for twenty-five years and seldom went to the town of Lincoln, which was six miles distant. When he did go to Lincoln, he peddled a battered bicycle to a dry goods store to buy meager supplies, seldom talking to storeowner Becky Garland, who described him as a "hermit kind of guy. Over the years we had a few conversations about things, but we didn't talk long. Mostly, I saw him maybe every six months or so . . ."

After observing Kaczynski for almost two months, FBI agents finally took him into custody. He offered a scuffling resistance, and then went meekly, silently behind bars. Inside his cabin, agents found ten three-ring binders full of detailed writings and diagrams of explosive devices and sketches of boxes meant to conceal the devices. They also found hand-written notes in Spanish and English describing how chemical compounds could create explosive charges. Kaczynski had also filled logs that described his experiments in determining the optimal design for pipe bombs and their effectiveness in various weather conditions. The cabin was also filled with books on chemistry and electrical circuitry.

The Kaczynski cabin had no toilet facilities or running water, but it contained a treasure trove of terrorist devices, including one unmailed finished package bomb, which bore no address; copper, plastic and galvanized metal pipes, some having plates at one end, a preliminary step in the construction of pipe bombs; containers with aluminum, zinc, lead and potassium chlorate, which can be used in constructing bombs; solid cast ingots; batteries and electrical wire that could be used to detonate explosives; and assorted drills, drill bits, wirecutters, and hacksaw blades. It also had two manual typewriters that Kaczynski used to write the Unabomber messages, according to law enforcement experts.

While Kaczynski remained in custody, his strange background was pieced together by law enforcement officials. Born on May 22, 1942, to Wanda and Theodore R. Kaczynski in Evergreen Park, Illinois, he was the first of two sons, his brother, David, born eight years later. Kaczynski's father worked in a Chicago sausage factory until managing a firm called

A heavily manacled Theodore Kaczynski is shown entering federal court in 1996; he would prove to be the notorious Unabomber, the demented killer who terrorized the nation for eighteen years. (Wide World)

Cushion Pak in Cedar Rapids, Iowa. (The elder Kaczynski committed suicide in 1990 after he was diagnosed as having cancer.)

The Kaczynski family, according to Evergreen Park neighbors, kept to themselves. Ted Kaczynski was a bright lad who spent most of his time in the family basement, tinkering. He was so brilliant that he skipped one grade in grade school and his junior year of high school, entering Harvard on a scholarship at age sixteen. During high school, Kaczynski showed a decided interest in creating homemade bombs. One school chum remembered that "he was very intelligent and had a flair for pyrotechnics." One of Kaczynski's classmates asked him how to make a bomb and Kaczynski told him; the bomb went off in a chemistry class and caused a girl to lose her hearing.

Kaczynski did not adjust well to Harvard. Though he was a brilliant math student, he was shy and retiring, wanting to be alone most of the time. He shut himself up in a single room at a fraternity house, one which was later described by a fellow student as "the messiest room I've ever seen . . . a foot or two deep in trash. And it smelled, because there was spoiled milk and sandwiches underneath all that stuff."

Never outgoing, Kaczynski did not date girls and had no close friends at Harvard. He did sit in on some "bull sessions" where the more brilliant math students met in the cafeteria and espoused the idealist philosophy of Immanuel Kant. (The Unabomber's published manifesto contains many allusions to Kantian thinking.) Following his graduation from Harvard in 1962, Kaczynski attended the University of Michigan from 1962 to 1967, receiving his doctorate in mathematics. He displayed brilliance and solved problems that stumped professors. His articles were published in academic reviews, and he was one of ten young math graduates to be hired at the University of California in Berkeley in 1967, where he was thought to be one of the few who would get tenure.

At Berkeley, Kaczynski taught without incident. Here, too, he did not mix with faculty but remained reclusive.

Though Berkeley had always been known to be a hotbed of leftist political activities, Kaczynski took no part in partisan politics. In 1969, Kaczynski shocked the staff at Berkeley by resigning, saying that he was giving up math and was uncertain as to what he might do. No amount of persuasion could compel him to reconsider.

It was later pointed out that he was feeling "inner tension" at this time as a result of his disgust with leftist activism. (The Unabomber's manifesto is highly critical of leftist political philosophies.) To family members, Kaczynski later confided that he quit Berkeley because he feared that what he taught to engineers would later be used to destroy the environment.

Kaczynski surfaced briefly in Salt Lake City, where he took menial jobs before moving to the wilds of Montana in 1970 or 1971. In 1971, Kaczynski and his brother (who apparently provided the financing) bought 1.4 acres of land outside Lincoln, Montana, next to a dirt road. Here Kaczynski built a small shack, ten feet by twelve.

From that time on, Kaczynski lived the hermit's life. He nurtured a small vegetable garden. He lived on a dollar a day, going to Lincoln only to buy supplies and visit the library. Occasionally, he traveled by bus to Helena where he bought and sold used books, staying at the $14-a-night Park Hotel. He did not remain away from his shack for long. Most of his hours he spent inside the shack, which FBI officials described as a low-tech bomb factory where Kaczynski meticulously pieced together his bombs from scraps of metal and wood that made them impossible to trace.

Not until October 1996 was Kaczynski indicted by a grand jury in Newark, New Jersey, for the 1994 murder-bombing of ad executive Thomas Mosser. By then, the FBI had put together a strong case to convict Kaczynski in the Unabomber killings. They expected to prove that the suspect's saliva matches that taken from the stamps on the packages mailed by the Unabomber, as well as matching his fingerprints to the one Unabomber print found on one of the bomb packages and that one of the two typewriters found in Kaczynski's cabin would match perfectly to the Unabomber's manifesto.

An "intellectual" match of the Unabomber's philosophy can be found in the works of novelist Joseph Conrad, who was Ted Kaczynski's favorite author. Kaczynski read and reread every novel ever written by Conrad, whose real name was Jozef Teodor Konrad Korzeniowski. More than the name similarities, Kaczynski undoubtedly took over the lifestyle of one of Conrad's fictional protagonists. In Conrad's 1907 novel, *The Secret Agent*, a brilliant but mad professor abandons academia and takes up residence in a "hermitage," where he fashions a bomb that he intends to use in destroying "that idol of science," an observatory. He eats raw carrots; Kaczynski ate raw turnips. The professor-turned-anarchist vows revenge against the advocates of modern science; so did the Unabomber.

The anarchists of *The Secret Agent* use the initials "FP" ("Future of the Proletariat") in their leaflets; the Unabomber used the initials "FC" as a signature. Like Conrad's mad professor who lived a lonely life of isolation, Kaczynski dwelled in total alienation from society. Conrad had written that the bomb-making professor saw science and technology as nefarious forces exalted by a naive public, as did the Unabomber. As Conrad wrote: "Explosives were his faith, his hope, his weapon and his shield."

For Ted Kaczynski, these weapons of destruction also powered an arrogance and vanity that led to his eventual identification, arrest and indictment as America's most wanted terrorist.

Following his arrest, Kaczynski refused to talk with his eighty-year-old mother, Wanda, and his forty-seven-year-old brother, David. He had not seen either of them in fifteen years and when first appearing in the court of Judge Garland Burrell, Jr., he walked past them without looking at them or uttering a single word. He pleaded not guilty to the charges of having killed three persons and seriously injured another twenty-nine people over his eighteen-year course of terrorism. Only four persons, all residents of tiny Lincoln, Montana, visited the terrorist in jail.

In the second week of January 1998, Kaczynski attempted to hang himself with his underwear in his jail cell, a clumsy attempt that failed. The suicide attempt, in fact, was so awkward that it was thought that Kaczynski had purposely planned to fail in taking his own life but, in so doing, try to convince authorities that he was mentally unbalanced.

Yet, Kaczynski had been fighting with his attorneys who wanted to portray him as mentally ill. He insisted that he was sane and ordered them to abandon all efforts to profile him as unbalanced. The defense lawyers agreed, but stated that they would use the insanity plea during the death penalty phase of Kaczynski's trial.

Then Kaczynski insisted that he be allowed to fire his lawyers and that he act as his own attorney.

Kaczynski, in an effort to prove that he was sane enough to represent himself, then agreed to be examined by court-appointed psychiatrists. The court was frustrated in that by allowing Kaczynski to act as his own attorney, the trial might become the same kind of farce created by the black terrorist Colin Ferguson. Many close to the case thought that Kaczynski was simply attempting to remain in control, to continue to battle the entire government arraigned against him— the federal judiciary, the FBI, the Department of Justice, all representing the social system he had vowed to destroy with his bombs.

At the end of January 1998, Kaczynski agreed to a deal: He would plead guilty in exchange for a life sentence with no right to appeal, but on the condition that Judge Burrell denied his petition to represent himself in court. This was agreed. Appearing before Judge Burrell, the defendant's bid to represent himself was denied. He was then asked if he was responsible for all of the murders and bombings of which he stood accused. "Yes, your honor," replied the terrorist. Kaczynski was formally sentenced to life behind bars in May 1998.

Three months after Kaczynski was taken into custody, the nation was shocked by the news that 230 persons had been killed when TWA Flight 800 blew up over the Atlantic shortly after takeoff on July 17, 1996. The jumbo 747 jet crashed off Long Island in full view of many observers, who later gave varying reports of what they saw in the nighttime sky. Some stated that the aircraft simply blew up. Others claimed that they saw what appeared to be "a rocket" or "a flare" shooting toward the plane before it exploded.

An army of investigators poured into the area as ships were sent to pick up possible survivors. There were none. Some bodies were found floating among the wreckage, but most of the victims were recovered only after U.S. Navy ships dredged the area for months, hauling up most of what remained of the shattered plane. Airline and FAA experts, along with the FBI, closely examined the wreckage to determine what caused the blast—a bomb, a missile, or mechanical failure.

At one point it was suggested that a U.S. warplane performing exercises in the area of Flight 800 had accidentally shot off a missile that brought down the passenger plane. A piece of flooring from the passenger compartment was retrieved, and it was field-tested by an explosive-detecting "sniffer." The flooring then underwent more sophisticated tests at the FBI lab in Washington and, in both instances, the report was the same. The floor contained microscopic traces of

PETN, a compound used in plastic explosives.

Still, government officials and FBI spokesmen refused to stipulate that the plane had been sabotaged. No terrorist organization came forward to claim responsibility, but CIA officials hinted to press members that there existed a strong possibility that the bombing had been inspired by Iranian terrorists. One report had it that transmissions tracked by the CIA out of Teheran "have raised suspicions" of an Iranian connection. The agency also reported that a terrorist summit was held in Iran a month before Flight 800 exploded and a green light to blow up an American airliner may have been flashed at that time. The CIA went no further, admitting that it had "nothing solid," to bring forth.

The FBI, meanwhile, working with Israeli intelligence, further supported the Iranian link when it recalled a recent Iranian threat in Israel involving a Hizbollah terrorist named Hussein Mikdad. On April 4, 1996, Mikdad, reportedly Iranian-backed, flew from Zurich to Tel Aviv with bomb parts hidden in a carry-on bag.

On April 12, while assembling the bomb in an east Jerusalem hotel room, Mikdad accidentally detonated the device, which contained a powerful plastic explosive called RDX. The explosion blew off Mikdad's legs and an arm. This was the first time that Hizballah had managed to slip a terrorist into Israel by way of an international airline, and it was thought that he was only one of many terrorists assigned to Western targets and that Flight 800 was on that target list.

Moreover, U.S. Defense Secretary William Perry gave an interview in which he pointed to an ongoing Saudi investigation into the June 23, 1996, bombing of a U.S. military complex in Dhahran, which "possibly" pointed to Iran's involvement in that terrorist explosion. The Iranian link, however, was never officially affixed to the destruction of Flight 800.

The existence of a missile of any kind was ruled out as that theory "just didn't stand up to scrutiny," but some investigators unofficially came to believe that the plane was destroyed by a bomb planted somewhere in the midsection of the 747 jumbo jet.

Following months of expensive dredging, most of what was left of TWA's Flight 800 was recovered from the sea. The 747 was reconstructed piece by piece in an enormous hangar in Calverton, on Long Island, N.Y. The ninety-four-foot long, twenty-seven-foot high plane was reassembled and, after a period of extensive investigation, the FBI announced that Flight 800 was not the victim of a terrorist bomb but had most probably blown up because of a mechanical failure, possibly when the center fuel tank blew up from the inside as a result of a fuel-vapor explosion.

Officially, in July 1997, the National Transportation Safety Board announced that sloshing or leaking fuel had most likely built up a static charge which caused a deadly spark that created the explosion in the center fuel tank. Yet, others continue at this writing to believe that small explosives could have been planted on the center fuel tank and set off the blast. Since the

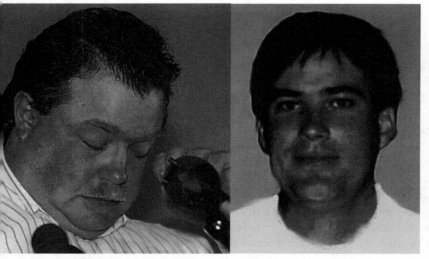

Far left: *Richard Jewell, who was wrongly accused of planting the bomb at Atlanta's Centennial Park in 1996. (Wide World)* **Left:** *Eric Robert Rudolph, still hunted at this writing for several terrorist bombings, including the 1996 bombing at Atlanta's Centennial Park. (Wide World)*

NTSB's conclusion contained speculation, doubts remain and suspicions linger that the hand of a terrorist had somehow touched this horrible tragedy.

Ten days after Flight 800 collapsed, flaming into the sea, a pipe bomb rocked Atlanta's Centennial Park. At 1:25 A.M., on July 27, 1996, while hundreds were dancing to rock music in the park, the bomb went off with a deafening roar, wounding 112 people, who fell to the ground, their bodies riddled with shrapnel or flying debris from the blast. Of these, Alice Hawthorne, a forty-three-year-old black businesswoman, was mortally wounded.

Despite immediate first aid administered by osteopath John Vogel, Hawthorne was pronounced dead upon arrival at Grady Memorial Hospital a short time later. Melih Uzunyol, a cameraman for Turkish TV, died of a heart attack while rushing forth to videotape the aftermath of the bombing. The other 111 wounded persons received medical attention and recovered.

Atlanta police later came under severe criticism for failing to act promptly on a 911 call from a male informant who stated with no dis-

cernable accent that "there is a bomb in Centennial Park. You have thirty minutes." During that time, Richard Jewell, a temporary guard for a private security firm, reported a suspicious knapsack and helped other guards clear people from the site before the bomb exploded.

At first, Jewell was hailed as a hero who may have saved dozens of lives. He appeared a short time later on the *Today Show* with Katie Couric, telling the interviewer: "I just happened to be at the right place at the right time and doing the job I was trained to do." But Jewell himself became a suspect after Atlanta authorities received a call from Ray Cleere, president of Piedmont College in Demorest, Georgia. Cleere stated that Jewell had been a security guard at the college but had been fired after "erratic" behavior, including one instance where he arbitrarily flagged down motorists to administer sobriety tests.

A gung-ho law enforcement advocate, Jewell had previously worked as a deputy for the Habersham County, Georgia, sheriff's department but was reprimanded and demoted to jail guard after crashing his police car while racing with another officer. He resigned from the department, picking up security guard jobs. This was the position he held when the Olympic Park bomb exploded.

It was thought that Jewell had planted the bomb so that he could discover it himself, appear to save countless lives through his warning, and emerge a hero. The FBI conducted a twelve-hour search of Jewell's two-bedroom apartment, which he shared with his mother. Agents removed scores of boxes from the apartment, including dozens of videotapes. Still, Jewell was not charged, especially since the Bureau could not find a shred of evidence linking Jewell to the crime. By September, Jewell's mother, Barbara Jewell, appealed to President Clinton, asking that her son be cleared of any wrongdoing, saying: "He is a prisoner in my home."

Jewell's attorneys went on the attack, demanding that either their client be charged with the bombing or that the FBI and other federal authorities apologize for ruining his reputation. C. Watson Bryant, Jr., one of Jewell's attorneys, fumed: "These jerks [federal authorities] need to get up off their butts and tell the truth." Jewell was not officially dropped as a suspect, however, for another two months. By then, investigators were no closer to solving the Olympic Park bombing than other investigators were to finding the cause of the explosion of Flight 800.

Not until October 26, 1996, however, was Jewell officially notified by the Department of Justice that he was no longer a suspect in the Atlanta bomb-

ing. The federal investigation of Jewell was, at best, flimsy, based upon allegations and accusations that could have been examined without a warrant. One of the reports to the federal investigators was that Jewell "trolled the Internet" in search of bomb-making data. He was analyzed by so-called "experts" in the press on national television.

Following the exoneration of Jewell, Atlanta continued to suffer from bombings. In January 1997, a suburban abortion clinic was bombed and, on February 28, 1997, a gay and lesbian bar was also bombed, an explosion that injured at least five persons. These two bombings were thought to be the work of the same terrorist and, perhaps, the same terrorist who had planted the bomb at Atlanta's Centennial Park.

The Atlanta bombing paled by comparison with the twin terrorist bombings of U. S. embassies in Nairobi, Kenya, and Dar es Salaam, Tanzania, on August 7, 1998, both gigantic explosions taking place within seconds of each other at 10:40 a.m. The bomb in Tanzania exploded some distance from the U. S. Embassy, which, thanks to the building having been constructed far from the street, created less damage. Ten Tanzanians were nevertheless killed and many injured. In Nairobi, however, the explosion was devastating, claiming the lives of twelve Americans and more than 250 Kenyans, collapsing an entire building next to the embassy and blowing out the windows of scores of buildings nearby, causing more than 5,000 to be injured.

American intelligence and other foreign agencies scurried to identify those behind the horrific bombings. The first "break" was the apprehension of Mohammed Saddig Odeh, also known as Abdul Bast Awadh and Mohammad Sadig Howaida. He had been arrested by Pakistani officials on August 7, 1998, the very day of the explosion, after arriving in Karachi, Pakistan, from Nairobi. Returned to Nairobi, Odeh underwent relentless interrogation by Kenyan investigators, as well as FBI agents who had flown to Nairobi.

Odeh would admit nothing, even though he had earlier confessed to Pakistani officials that the bombings had been ordered by errant 42-year-old Saudi Arabian millionaire and terrorist leader, Osama bin Laden. Bin Laden, whose father became a construction billionaire in Saudi Arabia, had studied engineering in England. Using his father's riches, he amassed his own fortune--between $200 and $300 million. He volunteered his services to the CIA in the Afghan war against the U.S.S.R., his mountain guerrillas defeating the Russians at almost every turn.

Following the war, bin Laden organized his own terrorist organization, the Islamic Front for Jihad Against Jews and Crusaders. He was suspected of being behind the bombing of the World Trade Center in 1993, the prime suspect in that case, Ramzi Ahmed Yousef, convicted of the bombing in 1996. Yousef had been reportedly captured in a bin Laden family guest house in Pakistan.

Bin Laden had become as fanatical a terrorist as the mystical figure he sought to emulate--the Old Man of the Mountain (Hasan ibn-al-Sabah), creator of the Order of the Assassins, an eleventh century killer cult seeking to murder the Christian leaders of the Third Crusade which invaded the kingdoms of Islam. (This undoubtedly explains why bin Laden's organization was against "Crusaders.")

In the last decade, bin Laden, posing as an "agriculturalist," began expanding his terrorist organization. Saudi officials became so unnerved by his activities that he was "denaturalized" in 1991, many of his bank accounts frozen three years later. He moved to the Sudan where, through a front, he invested in, among many enterprises, the Military Complex, an industrial compound in Khartoum where the plant for Shifa Pharmaceutical Industries was located. It was in this plant, U. S. officials later claimed, that the deadly nerve gas, VX, was to be produced and then later used in terrorist attacks against the U. S. and its allies.

Bin Laden's terrorist activities throughout the 1990s were intensified. He was pinpointed as the person behind several bombings of U.S. facilities in Saudi Arabia in 1995 and 1996, although these attacks still remain unsolved. After the U. S. pressured Sudan to expel him (and his three wives) in 1996, he established a terrorist training compound at Zhawar Kili, Afghanistan, near the Pakistan border. Bin Laden had long endeared himself to the fundamentalist Islamic Taliban regime controlling Afghanistan and its leader, Mullah Mohammad Omar.

In his mountain retreat, bin Laden granted interviews and publicly condemned Western "non-believers," telling one ABC reporter that U.S.

forces should "leave Saudi Arabia or die." His terrorist compound boasted anti-aircraft missile systems, radar, and a sophisticated communications systems allowing bin Laden to uplink faxes and video by satellite and to tap into the Internet. It was from this remote staging area that bin Laden allegedly ordered the bombings of the U. S. embassies in Africa.

In retaliation, on August 20, 1998, President Clinton ordered American warships in the Red Sea to launch cruise missiles into Khartoum, utterly destroying the Shifa Pharmaceutical plant. At the same time, U. S. warships in the Arabian Sea unleashed long-range Tomahawk missiles which targeted bin Laden's camp at Zwahar Kili. The damage inflicted was reported to be considerable but bin Laden, according to several accounts, survived the attack. One of the reasons why the camp was targeted was to disrupt a conference of many top level Islamic terrorists who were to meet on that day, including members of the Islamic Jihad.

It was not learned if, indeed, the conference took place, but it was believed that among those scheduled to attend were representatives of the PFLP, a terrorist arm of the Al Fatah Council (as is Islamic Jihad) which is directly linked to the PLO and Yasir Arafat. Although he was profiled as the director of the August 1998 bombings, it was obvious to trained observers that bin Laden's posturing and threats, his willingness to give interviews and be photographed and filmed in his Afghanistan hideout, made him too much of a public figure to be the actual mastermind of the bombings; he was simply another high-profile PFLP front man. None of the real Islamic terorist leaders in the past two decades would ever think to seek the limelight.

The Islamic terrorist leaders always opted for the shadows, as has been the case with Abu Abbas (Mohammed Zaidan Abbas; AKA: Abu Khalid), the insidious PFLP leader, and one of Arafat's foremost aides and advisers, who engineered the Black September killings of the Israeli Olympic team in 1972, the seizing of the cruise ship *Achille Lauro* in 1985 and the destruction of Pan Am Flight 103 over Lockerbie, Scotland in 1988, the bomb that destroyed that plane placed by two Abbas' hand-picked terrorists who are presently hiding in Libya to his day, guests of Muammar Qaddafi. It was Abbas who directed countless terrorist attacks against Israel, usually from Lebanon bases, as well as numerous skyjackings through the 1970s and 1980s.

By the 1990s, the PFLP/Al Fatah had a strutting, arrogant Saudi millionaire, bin Laden, to do their bidding, one whose gnawing vanity, these shrewd manipulators knew, would insist that he assume the successor mantle of the legendary Old Man of the Mountain (which undoubtedly explains bin Laden's proclivity for residing in mountaintop caves). Bin Laden would not only help fund PFLP operations but would happily take credit for its heinous crimes in the name of "holy Jihad."

Bin Laden certainly represented the terrorist arm that launched the August 1998 embassy bombings but he was not the catalyst--that was the PFLP, which has historically directed and approved of almost all major Islamic terrorist attacks against the U. S. and Israel in the last three decades. Through this attack, a PFLP message was sent to both the U.S. and one of his most ardent allies, Israel: Give up the territories along the West Bank demanded by the Palestinians and Arafat and give them up quickly.

The historical precedent, modus operandi and motive for the attack were all deeply rooted to the PFLP, not to the publicity-seeking bin Laden. Two months before the attacks in Nairobi and Dar es Salaam, on June 19 and June 21, 1998, two bomb attacks in Beirut were made by PFLP terrorists, a car bomb killing two persons and, two days later, rocket-propelled grenades which were exploded near the U.S. Embassy, which brought about no injuries. The attacks were symbolic demonstrations against the U.S. to compel America to further pressure Israel into giving up West Bank territory. Prime Minister Benjamin Netanyahu's government, despite U.S. pressure, resolved not to give up territory until the Palestinians (Arafat) cracked down on terrorism.

The PFLP's answer was to order bin Laden's attacks in Africa, returning to the very city, Nairobi, where the PFLP had exploded a tremendous bomb on December 31, 1980, destroying the Zionist-owned Norfolk Hotel, killing between sixteen and twenty persons and injuring another eighty-five. In that explosion, as well as those of August 7, 1998, the PFLP left its calling card, traces of Semtex, an explosive manufactured in Czechoslovakia and used consistently by the PFLP in its terrorists bombings.

The 1980 and 1998 bombings followed an identical attack plan, a vehicle packed with explosives driven close to a parking area before the explosives were detonated. The 1980 Nairobi bombing was conducted by the PFLP in retaliation for the successful raid by Israeli commandos at Entebbe four years earlier when Israeli hostages were rescued by the daring commandos who had used Nairobi (and Tanzania) as a staging area for the raid. (More than irony can be found in the fact that only one fatality among the commandos was inflicted by the PFLP terrorists--that of its heroic leader, Col. Netanyahu, the brother of Israel's present-day prime minister.)

Moreover, the August 1998 attacks against U. S. embassies occurred in the year marking the fiftieth anniversary of Israel as a sovereign state, the U.S. being one of the first nations to acknowledge it as such. To Yasir Arafat, the PFLP and its allied terrorist groups, Israel and the U.S. are one-in-the-same, a common enemy; they are the "Jews and Crusaders" Osama bin Laden has vowed to destroy. Bin Laden, despite his menacing threats, is not the present-day Old Man of the Mountain--that dubious distinction belongs to only one man (who uttered not a word of condemnation for those who set off the deadly African explosions): Yasir Arafat.

As the twentieth century closes, the shadows of faceless terrorists lengthen throughout all countries. Until governments and law enforcement agencies develop better warning systems, improved technologies, and make the conscious and universal decision to wage total war upon terrorists and their powerful organizations and sponsors, victims will continue to fall in record numbers.

A CHRONOLOGY OF 20th CENTURY TERRORISM, 1900—1998

The following chronology includes major worldwide terrorist acts (assassinations, bombings, kidnappings, lootings, lynchings, riots, serial terrorist killers, and skyjackings). Specific dates are given for those entries where such dates are verifiable. Also see cross-references in the Glossary of Terrorist Organizations and the Index.

1900

Klemens von Ketteler, German minister to Peking, China, is hacked to death by a Boxer terrorist while being carried in a litter next to the German Embassy. This scene is depicted, along with the terrorism practiced by the Boxers against the foreign enclave at Peking, in the 1963 film, *55 Days at Peking*, starring Charlton Heston and Ava Gardner, with Flora Robson giving an accurate performance of the insidious Tzu Hsi, the dowager empress of China, who secretly backed the Boxer terrorists.

March 23: Lewis Rice, a Negro who has testified on behalf of another black man accused of murder, is lynched in Ripley, Tennessee.

June 10: A white mob in Sneads, Florida, tracks down and shoots to pieces John Sanders and another Negro who are suspected of being accessories to the murder of Ernest Hardwick, a white farmer earlier beaten to death by a group of black men.

July 29: Humbert I (Umberto I), king of Italy, is fatally shot at Monza by Gaetano Bresci, an anarchist and terrorist who has

traveled from Patterson, New Jersey, to carry out the assassination.

August 23: More than 150 white cotton-mill workers storm the Huntsville, Alabama, jail and shoot to death Elijah Clark, a twenty-year-old black, who is charged with sexually assaulting thirteen-year-old Susan Priest, a white girl.

September 8: Following a devastating hurricane that destroys most of Galveston, Texas, widespread terrorism ensues, created mostly by unemployed blacks who swarm into destroyed business districts, raping and looting. Troops are called out and are ordered to shoot on sight all looters and others committing criminal acts. More than 500 persons are shot to death, most of these being blacks.

October 24: Two black men, James Caleaway and James Guer, are lynched by a mob at Liberty Hill, Georgia. Both victims have been murdered because of "racial prejudice"—they publicly cursed whites.

1901

Wilhelm II, emperor of Germany and king of Prussia, is attacked by a Bremen shipyard worker and terrorist, but he survives the assassination attempt.

January 3: In Rome, Georgia, George Reed, a Negro, is released to a mob of more than 150 men. Reed is shot and hanged, despite the fact that the woman he is accused of sexually assaulting, Mrs. J. M. Locklear, has been unable to identify her assailant.

February 26: George Ward, a black man, is dragged by a large white mob from his Terre Haute, Indiana, prison cell and hanged from a tree at the banks of the Wabash River. Ward has been awaiting trial on a charge of murdering Ida Finkelstein, a school teacher.

March 13: More than 5,000 persons in Corsicana, Texas, watch as John Henderson, a black man, is burned at the stake after being charged with raping a white woman.

March 14: When immigrant Frank Latito is shot in broad daylight, crowds in the Italian quarter of Denver, Colorado, riot and almost lynch Frank Sposato, the suspected shooter, but he is saved by Denver police, who will rush Sposato out of the community. (Sposato will be acquitted for the shooting on November 19, 1901.)

March 16: Ballie Crutchfield, a black woman in Rome, Tennessee, is dragged from her cabin by a white mob, shot in the head, and her body tossed into a nearby creek. Crutchfield has been murdered after her brother has earlier escaped from the same mob intending to lynch him for a reported theft.

May 31: Five white men, Calvin Hale, Frank Hale, James Hale, Martin Hale, and B. D. Tantis, who have been accused of theft, are lynched by a mob at Lookout, California.

July 27: Accused horse thief Ignacio Rivera is lynched by a mob at Hent's Ranch, Arizona.

August 7: John Pennington, a black man accused of sexually attacking Mrs. J. C. Davis, a white woman, is chased through a swamp near Enterprise, Alabama, by a mob using bloodhounds, and, when caught, chained to a tree and burned to death.

August 15: Race riots erupt in New York City, and white mobs attempt to kill several black entertainers, including Ernest Hogan, Williams & Walker, and Coke & Johnson.

August 20: In Pierce City, Missouri, a mob of white men terrorizes the black community for fifteen hours, burning the homes of five black families and causing the death of seventy-one-year-old Peter Hampton. The violence has occurred in the aftermath of the murder of Casselle Wilds, for which two black men have been lynched the previous day.

September 6: William McKinley, president of the U.S., is fatally shot in Buffalo, New York, by anarchist and terrorist Leon Czolgosz. McKinley died of his wound on September 14. Czolgosz will be executed for the assassination on October 29, 1901.

September 28: Antonio Maggio, a notorious terrorist and anarchist, is apprehended on charges of conspiring to kill state officials in Santa Fe, New Mexico.

October 31: Silas Esters, a white man who has forced a boy to commit a crime, is lynched by a mob in Hodgenville, Kentucky.

1902

M. Kanchev, a minister of the Bulgarian cabinet, is slain by a terrorist in Sofia.

January 18: Accused horse thief John Yellowwolf is lynched by a mob in Rosebud, South Dakota.

March 30: A black man is burned at the stake near Savannah, Georgia, by a posse that has mistaken his identity for Negro Richard Young, who is sought for the murder of Dower Fountain.

April 1: A mob of more than 4,000 persons batters down the doors of the Rome, Georgia, jail and seizes prisoner Walter Allen, a Negro charged with sexually assaulting fifteen-year-old Blossom Adamson. After hanging Allen from a light pole, the terrorists fire more than 1,000 rounds from pistols and rifles into his swaying body.

April 15: Dimitri S. Sipiagin, Russia's minister of the interior, is assassinated by terrorist S. V. Balmashov.

May 8: Following the horrific explosion of Mt. Pelée on the island of Martinique, which utterly destroys the city of St. Pierre, killing almost all 36,000 residents, looters swarm into the area. Police arrive to arrest twenty-seven looters and shoot two others who resist arrest.

May 22: Dudley Morgan, a black man accused of sexually assaulting a married white woman, is taken into the custody of the sheriff in Lansing, Texas, and is tortured for hours before being burned to death at the stake.

September 28: A white mob in Corinth, Mississippi, seizes black man Tom Clark, who has confessed on August 10 to the murder of Mrs. Carey Whitfield. The mob comes to near riot while members violently argue as to whether Clark should be hanged or burned. He is finally hanged *and* burned.

November 1: A burgermeister in Stujely, Hungary, is lynched by townspeople after he has set fire to his own house, killing his wife, parents, and three children.

1903

April 19–20: Russian anti-Jewish riots erupt in the town of Kishinef, where authorities show marked sympathy for the rioters.

April 26: A mob of whites breaks into the home of Rebecca and Ida Stephens in Bloomington, Indiana, and whips the women and their black boarder, Joe Shively, accusing the white women of "race contamination."

April 29: Revolutionaries explode dozens of bombs throughout Bulgaria during the Salonica Coup, which is designed to overthrow Turkish rule.

June 11: Alexander I (Obrenovic), king of Serbia, and his wife, Queen Draga, are assassinated—hacked to pieces by swords wielded by officers of the secret military cabal known as the "Black Hand Society," a Serbian terrorist organization created and led by Dragutin Dimitrijevic (AKA: "Colonel Apis").

July 14: A man falsely believed to be Ed Claus, a Negro who has been accused of raping white school teacher Susie Johnson, is tied to a tree near Eastman, Georgia, and shot to death. The real Ed Claus will later be located in Darien, Georgia.

July 26: A white mob seizes Jennis Sturs, a black woman accused of giving sixteen-year-old Elizabeth Dolan a tainted glass of lemonade. Sturs is lynched, hanged from a tree on a plantation outside of Shreveport, Louisiana.

September 17: An unidentified Chinese man accused of speaking disrespectfully toward whites is lynched by a mob in Tonopah, Nevada.

October 9: Samuel Williams, a white man who refuses to supply information about a black resident, is lynched by a white mob in Lawby, Florida.

November 21: At the instructions of IWW leader William "Big Bill" Hayward, bomber and terrorist Harry Orchard blows up the main shaft of the Vindicator Mine in Cripple Creek, Colorado. (Orchard will later blow up a train in Independence, Colorado, carrying strikebreakers to their homes; twenty-six men will be killed and fifty others injured, many crippled for life. Orchard, also in the same year, will attempt to murder Mine Owner's Association member Fred Bradley by planting a bomb at Bradley's home; the explosion will blow Bradley across the street and demolish his home, but he will miraculously survive.)

1904

After several times ruling against the IWW, Judge Luther M. Goddard of the

Colorado Supreme Court becomes the target of a bomb planted by Wobbly terrorists; Goddard survives the explosion but bystander Merritt W. Walley is killed.

Nicholas I. Bobrikov, Russian general and brutal governor of Finland, is assassinated by a student terrorist who commits suicide.

February 7: Following the murders of white plantation owner James Eastland and a black employee, John Carr, a white mob of more than 200 men, accompanied by packs of bloodhounds, tracks and catches Luther Holbert and his wife near Doddsville, Mississippi. The Holberts, thought to be the killers of Eastland and Carr, are hanged, and then their bodies are burned at the stake. Other posse members pursuing the Holberts near Doddsville catch three other unidentified black men and lynch them, even though they have nothing to do with the Eastland and Carr murders.

March 26: A mob of white residents in St. Charles, Arkansas, makes up a list of local black men, thirteen in all, who are thought to be talking disrespectfully to whites. All thirteen black men are rounded up and lynched. On their swaying bodies, signs are hung that read: "Killed for racial prejudice."

July 28: Vyacheslav K. Plehve (Wenzel von Plehwe), Russian minister of interior during an oppressive administration, is assassinated by a terrorist bomb in St. Petersburg.

1905

Wu Yueh, a Chinese terrorist, attempts to murder five Chinese ministers in Peking but is instead killed when his bomb explodes prematurely.

Professor Mikhail I. Gertsenstein, a Jewish member of the Russian Duma, is killed by an anti-Semitic terrorist.

Pavel A. Shuralov, prefect of police in Moscow, is slain by terrorists.

Theódoros Dhiliyiánnis, prime minister of Greece, after ceding valued land to Turkey, is slain by national terrorists.

A plot by two members of the Polish Socialist Party to murder the Police Chief of Warsaw fails; both terrorists are killed.

E. Soisalon Soininen, procurator (attorney general) of Finland, is murdered by a terrorist.

Peter Arkadevich Stolypin, premier of Russia, is the target of several assassination attempts by terrorists, including the bombing of his villa, the explosion killing thirty-two of his guests.

February 17: Grand Duke Sergei Alexandrovich, uncle of Czar Nicholas II and governor of Moscow, is killed by a bomb thrown by terrorist and revolutionary Ivan Kalayev.

December 30: IWW terrorist Harry Orchard kills former Idaho governor Frank Steuenberg with a dynamite blast at Steuenberg's house in Caldwell.

1906

January 6: Within a twenty-four-hour period, ten persons in Chicago are killed from bombs exploded by Black Hand terrorists.

March 17: William Carr, a black man accused of stealing a white man's cow, is lynched from a railroad trestle in Planquemines, Louisiana, by a mob of thirty masked men.

April 18: Following a massive earthquake and fire that destroy San Francisco, California, thousands of criminals displaced from the devastated Barbary Coast, swarm throughout the ruins, raping and looting. Mayor Eugene E. Schmitz endorses General Frederick Funston's order to his troops to execute on sight all looters and others found committing criminal acts. More than 100 persons are shot or hanged. Dozens of bodies will sway from lampposts for days following the quake, signs adorning their bodies that read: "Shot and hanged for looting."

May 8: George Whitney, a black man accused of insulting a white woman, is lynched by a white mob in Ethel, Louisiana.

May 31: Alfonso XIII, king of Spain, and his bride, Victoria, are returning from their wedding when a terrorist bomb explodes, missing the carriage in which the royal couple are riding, but killing and wounding several members of the procession, along with spectators.

August 15: Several police officers in Warsaw, Poland, are attacked by terrorists in what comes to be known as Bloody Wednesday.

September 22: Twelve purported assaults by black men on white women reported in "extras" in the Atlanta, Georgia, press result in widespread violence against blacks in which twelve are killed and more than seventy are wounded.

October 26: "Slab" Pitts, a Negro, is lynched by a white mob for marrying a white woman in Toyah, Texas.

1907

Amin-es Sultan, premier of Persia, is stabbed to death by a banker turned terrorist.

En-ling, Manchu governor of Chekiang, is assassinated by terrorist Hsu-Hsi-lin, who is promptly executed.

Dimiter Petkov, a minister of the Bulgarian cabinet, is murdered by a terrorist in Sofia.

May–October: More than thirty bombs hurled by mobster terrorists of rival gambling syndicates destroy each other's pool rooms and off-track betting parlors in Chicago, producing considerable damage but no serious injuries.

September 30: A bomb linked to IWW terrorists kills Sheriff Harvey K. Brown of Baker City, Idaho; the bomber is never apprehended.

October 23: Henry Sykes, a black man accused of insulting a white woman, is lynched in Van Fleet, Mississippi.

1908

John F. Fort, governor of New Jersey, is the target of an unknown dynamite terrorist who is believed to be an opponent of the state's rigid liquor laws.

Michael Silverstein throws a homemade bomb into a squad of New York City police in Union Square to protest the harrassment of prostitutes by corrupt law enforcement officers. A pedestrian is killed.

Andreas Potacki, Polish nobleman and Hapsburg governor of Polish Galicia, is slain by terrorists.

January 12: An unidentified black man attempting to entertain a crowd of Negro spectators, is lynched by a black mob in Pine Level, North Carolina, for "being a poor performer."

February 1: Carlos I (Charles I), king of Portugal, and his son, Crown Prince Luis, are shot to death by political terrorists while riding in a carriage in Lisbon.

June 20: Ernest Williams, a black man accused of using "offensive language," is lynched in Parkdale, Arkansas.

June 22: Nine black men accused of murder are dragged from a local jail and all are lynched by a large white mob in Hemphill, Texas. The bodies are left to rot; a sign posted by the mob reads: "Anyone cutting down these niggers will be shot!"

August 4: Four black men are lynched in Russellville, Kentucky, after they publicly express sympathy with the murder of a white man.

December 13: A terrorist bomb is detonated in the Chicago Coliseum, causing considerable damage but no serious injuries.

December 28: Following an underwater earthquake and a massive seismic sea wave that destroys Messina, Reggio di Calabria, and the surrounding area, thousands of criminals rape and loot at will.

Armed sailors from Russian warships, the only peace-keeping force available to local authorities, are sent ashore to deal with the criminal terrorists. They shoot and kill more than 500 persons.

1909

January 18: A black man named Hilliard is accused of insulting a white girl in Hope, Arkansas, and is lynched.

February 22: Three white men accused of rape are lynched in Mineral Bluff, Georgia.

March 12: NYPD Lt. Joseph Petrosino, while investigating the backgrounds of Black Hand terrorists who have immigrated from Sicily to America, is shot to death at Palermo, at the foot of the Garibaldi statue in the Piazza Marina, by Black Hand terrorists under the direction of Mafia don, Vito Cascioferro, who later proudly claims that he has fired the fatal shot into Petrosino's head as the heroic police detective lies wounded. This terrorist murder touches off an international incident resulting in strained relations between the U.S. and Italy.

April 19: Western gunman Jim "the Killer" Miller and three other white men accused of murder are lynched in a horse barn in Ada, Oklahoma.

July 1: Sir William Hutt Curzon Wylie, former British administrator in India, and a bystander, are shot dead by Madar Lai Dhingra, an Indian terrorist who opposes British rule in India. The terrorist will be hanged on August 17, 1909.

July 31: Simon Anderson, a black man accused of window peeping, is lynched in Wellston, Georgia.

October 24: Ito Hirobumi, prince and prime minister of Japan, is assassinated in Harbin, China, by a Korean terrorist.

1910

Butros Ghali Pasha, prime minister of Egypt, is slain by Egyptian terrorists fearing that Ghali might give over control of the Suez Canal to foreign powers.

January 10–March 26, 1911: Thirty-eight persons in Chicago are murdered on one street corner—Oak and Milton streets in Little Italy—by Black Hand terrorists.

March 25: "Judge" Jones, a Negro accused of improper conduct with a white woman, is removed from the Pine Bluff, Arkansas, jail and hanged by a mob of forty white men.

June 14: William Hunter, a black man accused of insulting a white woman, is lynched in Star City, Arkansas.

July 31: Between fifteen and twenty black men are killed in race riots by a mob of white men in Palestine, Texas.

October 1: The *Los Angeles Times* building is bombed; twenty-one employees are killed. Labor terrorists James and John McNamara are arrested, tried, and convicted, despite the efforts of Clarence Darrow, their defense attorney, to have them acquitted.

October 12: Mrs. Crow, a white woman, accuses Grant Richardson, a Negro, of assaulting her and fathering her child. As

Richardson is being escorted to the Centreville, Alabama, jail, a group of white men seize him and shoot him to pieces.

December 10: Six or more European anarchists, a terrorist group led by Peter Piatkow (AKA "Peter the Painter"), attempt to rob a jewelry store in the Exchange Buildings in Houndsditch, a section of London's East End, and are interrupted by police. The terrorists shoot five officers, killing three of them, before fleeing.

1911

January 3: Two Russian anarchists, Fritz Svaars and Jacob Vogel (Joseph Marx), part of a terrorist ring led by Peter Piatkow, barricade themselves in second-floor rooms at 100 Sidney Street, battling more than 200 armed policemen personally directed by Home Secretary Winston Churchill. After a fierce fight, the building catches fire; both terrorists are found dead, their bodies charred. Both have died of gunshot wounds; Svaars' fatal wound has been self-inflicted.

January 11: Gene Marshall, a Negro accused of murder, is seized by a white lynch mob, which also decides to hang two other blacks, Wade Patterson and James West, who have been accused of insulting white women. All three are lynched.

August 4: Unable to locate Richard Verge, a black man accused of murdering white planter Vernon Tutt, a white mob seizes Sam Verge, the brother of the accused, and lynches him in Demopolis, Alabama.

August 14: While recuperating in a Coatsville, Pennsylvania, hospital from self-inflicted wounds, Zachariah Walker, suspected of murdering policeman Edgar Rice, is seized by a mob of masked men, carried away on the hospital mattress, and then burned to death.

September 1: Peter A. Stolypin, stern Russian prime minister, is slain at the Kiev Opera House, fatally shot in full view of Emperor Nicholas II and two of his daughters, by Mordka Bogrov, a police spy who is also a secret Bolshevik terrorist. Bogrov is quickly tried, convicted and hanged. Stolypin lingers for five days before dying from his mortal wound.

December 21: The terrorist robbery gang led by Jules Bonnot shoots and robs a bank messenger for the Societé Générale in the Rue Ordener in Paris, stealing a half million francs ($200,000).

1912

January 26: Liang-pi, leader of the Manchu court in Peking, is shot to death by P'eng Chia-chen, a terrorist in the employ of Chinese leaders opposed to Liang-pi's move to force Henry Pu-Yi, the child emperor, to abdicate.

April 9: Acquitted of writing "insulting letters" to a white girl, twenty-nine-year-old Tom Miles, a Negro, is seized by a white mob and hanged, his body riddled with bullets, in Shreveport, Louisiana.

April 26: Henry Etheridge, a Negro attempting to secure recruits for a proposed African colony, is lynched near Jackson, Georgia.

September 7: Negro Walter Johnston is lynched by a white mob for the murder of fourteen-year-old Nite White in Bluefield, West Virginia, even though authorities have issued a statement saying that Johnston did not commit the murder.

October 14: Theodore Roosevelt, former president of the U.S., is shot and wounded in Milwaukee, Wisconsin, at a political rally (Roosevelt is running for the presidency on the Bull Moose ticket) by terrorist John Schrank, who is later judged insane. The sturdy Roosevelt not only survives the attack but gives a brief speech before being taken to a hospital.

November 12: Jose Canalejas y Mendez, a leading Spanish politician supporting the monarchy, is assassinated by anarchists in Madrid, Spain.

December 21: Negro Henry Fitts of Norway, South Carolina, refuses to repay a loan and is lynched by a white mob.

1913

Nazim Pasha, Turkey's minister of war, is slain by terrorists directed by Enver Pasha.

February 9: In Houston, Mississippi, a mob of more than 1,000 seizes David Rucker, a Negro, and, in a mock trial, convicts him of the murder of Mrs. J. C. Williams. Rucker is then chained to a steel pump, soaked in oil, and burned alive.

February 19: Gustavo Madero, Mexican political leader and brother of the overthrown president of Mexico, is shot at night by terrorist agents directed by Mexican strongman General Victoriano Huerta.

February 23: Francisco Indalecio Madero, president of Mexico—illegally usurped and ousted on February 13, 1913, by General Victoriano Huerta—and Vice President Jose Pino Suarez, are slain in Mexico City by terrorist Francisco Cardenas and others at the direction of Huerta.

March 7: Abraham Gonzalez, pro-Madero governor of Chihuahua, Mexico, is murdered by Huerta terrorists.

March 18: George I, king of Greece, is murdered by terrorists in Salonika.

April 21: Three of Jules Bonnot's terror gang are beheaded by the guillotine in Paris after having been found guilty of robbery and murder.

April 26: Mary Phagan, a thirteen-year-old girl working in an Atlanta pencil factory, is raped and murdered in the factory, her body found the next day. Factory manager Leo Frank is railroaded for the killing, even though authorities know that Jim Conley, a brutal black janitor, is the real killer. The case is used by William Joseph Simmons, a traveling salesman and preacher, to form a secret cabal called the "Knights of Mary Phagan," that later becomes the resurgent Ku Klux Klan.

May 25: Peter Kürten, a lone terrorist killer who will be labeled the "Monster of Düsseldorf," or the "Düsseldorf Vampire," commits his first murder in Kuln-Mülheim, Germany, by slitting the throat of thirteen-year-old Christine Klein, an innkeeper's daughter. He returns to the inn the following day to share in the local gossip following the discovery of the body, later stating: "All of this amount of indignation and horror did me good." Kürten, who will be executed in 1930, will be charged with nine murders and seven other assaults with intent to murder. In his lengthy confession to the police, the terrorist will admit to sixty-eight serious crimes. Kürten will announce that, in many instances, he drank the blood of his dying victims, often attaining sexual climax afterward. Peter Lorre will enact the role of Kürten in Fritz Lang's 1933 classic horror movie, *M*.

June 11: Mahmud Sevket Pasha, grand vizier of the Ottoman Empire, is slain by terrorists.

June 21: William Redding, a black man, incurs the wrath of residents in Americus, Georgia, by firing a shot at police chief William Barrow. A white mob of more than 500 strings Redding up to an overhead cable and then fires at him from all angles until his dead body is riddled with bullets.

August 12: Negro Richard Puckett, who is accused of sexually attacking a white woman on a rural road, is dragged from his jail cell in Laurens, South Carolina, by a mob of more than 2,000 and hanged from a railroad trestle, his lifeless body then shot with several hundred bullets.

August 24: Wilson Gardner, a young, retarded Negro who has threatened to hang with a rope he carries anyone who attacks him, is beaten to death by a mob and his body strung up with his own belt from a railroad trestle near Kilgore, Alabama.

August 25: Negro Virgil Swanson is lynched in Greenville, Georgia, for the murder of planter L. C. Marchman. A short time later, Walter Brewster, also black, confesses to killing Marchman.

1914

January 10: John and Arling Morrison, staunch opponents of the IWW, are shot to death in their Salt Lake City store by two Wobbly terrorists. The killers manage to escape, but one is wounded; he is later identified as union terrorist Joe Hill.

March 31: A group of heavily armed men storm the jail at Muskogee, Oklahoma, easily overpowering a one-armed jailer (all of the other guards are inexplicably missing), and abduct Marie Scott, a black woman accused of stabbing a young white man. Scott is dragged to a nearby telephone pole and hanged.

April 29: A white mob in Marshalltown, Texas, castrates and kills Charles Fisher, a black youth, who has kissed the daughter of a local white farmer.

June 28: A group of Serbian nationalist terrorists, led by Gavrilo Princip (as part of a plot by the secret Serbian Black Hand Society), assassinate Francis Ferdinand (Franz Ferdinand), archduke of Austria, and his morganatic wife, Countess Sophie Chotek, in Sarajevo, Bosnia. Princip and others are sent to prison. The assassination touches off World War I.

July 31: Jean-Joseph-Marie-Auguste Jaurès, French socialist leader, is killed in Paris by terrorist Raoul Villain.

November 25: A black man, Fred Sullivan, and his wife, who are accused of burning a plantation barn, are lynched by a white mob in Byhalia, Mississippi. A deputy sheriff and his posse arrive to prevent the hangings, but they are disarmed by the mob and forced to watch the lynching.

December 4: William Grier, a Negro who is accused of frightening a white woman, is lynched in aptly named Coward, South Carolina.

1915

February 17: John Richards, a Negro accused of insulting a white woman, is lynched by a large mob near Sparr, Florida.

April 17: Caesar Sheffield, a black man accused of stealing meat from a smokehouse, is taken from a jail by a white mob and is later found shot to death in a field near Valdosta, Georgia.

July 28: Terrorists oust and murder Vilbrun Guillaume Sam, president of Haiti.

August 16: Leo Frank, who, in 1913, had been wrongly convicted of murdering Mary Phagan, a fourteen-year-old employee in his Atlanta pencil factory, is dragged from the prison farm at Milledgeville, Georgia, by the so-called Knights of Mary Phagan and lynched near Marietta. The terrorist group will become the core of the reborn Ku Klux Klan. The powerful 1937 film *They Won't Forget*, directed by Mervyn LeRoy, has Edward Norris essaying a role based on Frank.

November 19: Union terrorist Joe Hill is executed by a firing squad for his murders of two anti-IWW men in Salt Lake City a year earlier.

1916

Beverly Wyly Dunn engineers the Black Tom explosion in Jersey City, New Jersey.

March 31: Jeff Brown, a black man who accidentally brushes against a white woman while attempting to board a freight train, is seized by a gang of whites that witnessed the incident and is lynched in Cedar Bluff, Mississippi.

April 3: A mob of more than 500 men overpowers officers at the Idabel, Oklahoma, Court House, and seizes Oscar Martin, a black man on trial for sexually attacking a thirteen-year-old white girl. Martin is hanged from a second-floor balcony of the courthouse.

May 15: Following his conviction for the murder of Lucy Fryer, eighteen-year-old Jesse Washington, a Negro, is dragged from the Waco, Texas, courtroom and burned to death before a crowd of more than 15,000 cheering people.

July 22: A bomb explodes in downtown San Francisco during the Preparedness Day Parade, killing nine people and injuring forty-one others. Labor leaders Tom Mooney and Warren Billings are wrongly convicted for the terrorist bombing and will spend more than two decades in prison before being released.

October 21: Count Karl von Stürgkh, prime minister of Austria-Hungary, while having dinner in his favorite Vienna restaurant, is fatally shot by terrorist Freidrich Adler.

1917

May 22: Ell Person, a black man suspected of rape and murder, is burned to death by a mob and his head severed, in Memphis, Tennessee. A photograph of Person's mutilated head is widely published in the Northern black press as a grim reminder of Southern racial attitudes.

May 28: Racial tensions fueled by rumors that blacks have been perpetrating crimes against whites, particularly white women, bring more than 3,000 whites into the downtown area of East St. Louis, Illinois, where a race riot ensues in which scores of blacks are beaten, but no fatalities occur.

July 2: Bloody race riots erupt in East St. Louis, Illinois, after a Negro shoots his white attacker. When whites drive through the Negro district shooting randomly into homes, blacks return fire and kill two policemen. White rioters are particularly brutal, killing women and children and tossing bodies onto large bonfires. More than 300 buildings in the black ghetto are burned, eight whites and thirty-nine blacks are killed, and hundreds of blacks are wounded.

August 1: Frank Little, a white union organizer, is lynched in Butte, Montana, by a mob backed by mine owners.

September 21: Bert Smith, a black cook on an oil reservation in Goose Creek, Texas, is accused of assaulting a white woman. More than 800 fellow workers seize Smith and hang him, then his body is riddled with bullets and mutilated with sledgehammers and knives.

November 16: Terrorist Reinhold Faust plants a bomb in Chicago's Auditorium Theatre, but it is defused by fireman Michael Corrigan before it can explode.

November 17: Two black men, Collins Johnson and D. C. Johnson, are lynched for calling a white man a liar.

1918

Count Stephan Tisza, premier of Hungary, is assassinated by terrorists for not backing the Centralists in World War I.

January 26: Jim Hudson, who is accused of living with a white woman, is lynched in Benton, Louisiana.

February 12: Twelve masked men abduct Negro Jim McIlherron from a train near Estill Springs, Tennessee, accusing him of killing two white men and wounding another. McIlherron is tortured with a red-hot crowbar, then nailed to boards and burned to death.

May 17: Eleven blacks accused of murdering a white man are lynched by KKK terrorists in Brooks and Lowndes counties, Georgia.

May 23: A slaughterhouse terrorist called "the Ax Man of New Orleans" by the press, and who has chopped three persons to death in 1911, strikes again, invading the New Orleans grocery store of Joseph Maggio, and slitting the throats of Maggio and his wife while they sleep, then chopping them with an ax. The bloody ax is found on the back porch after the fiend flees as Maggio's brothers, Andrew and Jake, responded to the sounds of their brother's struggle.

June 28: "The Ax Man of New Orleans" attacks grocer Louis Besumer and his common-law wife, Mrs. Harriet Lowe, as they sleep, inflicting terrible wounds with an ax before fleeing. The victims survive, but Mrs. Lowe dies in August from her terrible wounds, after suggesting that Besumer himself has been the attacker. He is jailed but later released.

July 6: Terrorist gunmen shoot and kill Count Wilhelm von Mirbach, German ambassador to Russia, in Moscow.

August 5: Mrs. Edward Scheider, whose husband is a grocer, is attacked by "the Ax Man of New Orleans," the pregnant woman's head struck repeatedly with an ax. She miraculously survives.

August 10: "The Ax Man of New Orleans" breaks into the home of barber Joseph Romano, crushing his skull and almost decapitating him with an ax. Romano's nieces rush into the room as the terrorist flees. They will describe their uncle's berserk murderer as a "tall, heavyset white man." As with all of the previous killings performed by this terrorist, he has gained entry by chiseling out a panel of a back door.

August 28: Frederick Wagner, who is of German extraction, is accused of making disloyal remarks about America and is lynched near Hot Springs, Arkansas.

September 23: The first of six bombs is thrown at the Chicago home of a Negro citizen who has moved into a previously all-white neighborhood.

December 21: Four blacks accused of murdering a white man are lynched by KKK terrorists in Shubuta, Mississippi.

December 26: Akron, Ohio, patrolman Robert Norris, is shot while walking his beat at night, this being the first of several murders of police officers in the city at the hands of a terror gang intending to kill the entire police force. Gang leader Rosario Borgio has offered to pay $250 for each police officer killed.

1919

January 15: Rightist Free Corpsmen, a military terrorist organization, abduct Rosa "Red Rosa" Luxemburg and Karl Liebknecht, leaders of the left-wing Spartacus Party, holding them incommunicado for some hours in Berlin's Eden Hotel. Two cars are brought to the rear entrance of the hotel that evening. Liebknecht and Luxemburg are knocked senseless by a gun butt wielded by a terrorist named Runge, and each is thrown into the rear of a car. As Luxemburg lies unconscious in the rear seat of a car, a German Navy officer empties his revolver into the back of her head, killing her. Her body is later thrown into the Landwehr canal. Liebknecht is driven to a deserted area, shoved from a car, and ordered to begin walking. He is then shot to death by several officers who later report that he has been killed while attempting to escape.

January 21: Racial tensions in Chicago result in more than thirty bombs being thrown at the homes of Negro residents.

February 20: Habibollah Khan, amir of Afghanistan, is killed by terrorists who are backed by Nasr Ullah Khan and who are jailed for complicity in the assassination.

March 10: "The Ax Man of New Orleans" invades the home of Charles Cortimiglia, attacking the grocer and his wife, wounding them. Despite pleas from Rose Cortimiglia, the terrorist strikes her baby square on the head with his ax, killing the child instantly before fleeing.

March 13: The *New Orleans Times-Picayune* prints a letter dated "from Hell" and signed "The AXMAN," a missive ostensibly written by the terrorist who has killed several persons since 1911, stating that he will visit the city on March 19, 1919, but that he will not enter any home or establishment where jazz music—his favorite—is being played.

March 19: In response to the threat of "the Ax Man of New Orleans" visiting the city to again murder helpless victims, residents everywhere play jazz music around the clock—the deranged killer having said he would spare any household that played such music. The terrorist fails to appear.

April 4: William Little, a black soldier who has returned from World War I, is found beaten to death outside Blakely, Georgia, while still wearing his army uniform. Local residents had objected to Little wearing the uniform, and his murder is attributed to KKK terrorists.

April 29: George Holden, a black man who is accused of writing insulting notes to Onlie Elliot, a white woman, and who has miraculously survived two lynching attempts on his life, is taken from a train near Monroe, Louisiana, by an armed mob and shot to death.

May 1: May Day riots occur throughout the U.S. when citizens attack Socialist May Day celebrations. Socialist offices are wrecked in Cleveland where one person is killed and forty injured when army veterans attack a May Day parade.

May 21: Frank Jordano is arrested, identified by victim Rose Cortimiglia as being the dreaded terrorist known as "the Ax Man of New Orleans." Without any evidence other than Mrs. Cortimiglia's testimony (her husband, also a victim of the serial killer, refutes her statements as being hysterical), Jordano is convicted and sentenced to death.

May: Chicago whites bomb a building rented to Negroes by attorney William Austin.

June: After renting a West Side building to Negroes, the home of Chicago attorney William Austin is bombed.

June 2: The Washington, D.C., home of U.S. Attorney General A. Mitchell Palmer is bombed by an anarchist who becomes the only casualty of the explosion. The group to which the terrorist belongs also sets off eight other bombs in Washington, which destroy the facades of several government buildings. Thirty-eight other bombs are sent to government officials throughout the country but none claim any lives. The anarchist terrorism will bring about the notorious "Red Raids" of 1919–1921.

July 30: Race riots erupt in Chicago, Illinois, after a black youth goes swimming on a South Side beach reserved for whites and is stoned and drowned. The ensuing race riots leave twenty-two blacks and fourteen whites dead and 500 wounded.

August 10: New Orleans resident Steve Boca is attacked by the city's persistent "Ax Man," but he survives his wounds. Frank Jordano, who has earlier been convicted for the "Ax Man's" crimes, is released.

August 12: Jim O'Leary's saloon at 4183 Halsted, Chicago, is bombed by gambling syndicate terrorists.

August 19: A bomb explodes in the front yard of the Chicago home of powerful gambler Mont Tennes.

September 2: "The Ax Man of New Orleans" attempts to chisel out a a backdoor panel to gain entrance to a pharmacy, but pharmacist William Carlson fires several bullets through the door, driving off the terrorist.

September 3: Sarah Laumann is attacked while she sleeps by "the Ax Man of New Orleans." Despite terrible head wounds from the killer's ax, she survives, but she cannot identify her assailant.

September 9–12: When police in Boston, Massachussetts, go on strike, the city is overrun with criminals committing blatant crimes, causing Governor Calvin Coolidge to call out the national guard, which shoots thieves and looters on sight. Nine rioters are killed and fifty-eight are wounded.

September 22–October 5: More than 250,000 U.S. Steel workers in Pennsylvania go on strike and clash with state militia and special police, resulting in several deaths and many injuries.

September 29: Joe Coe, a black man wrongly accused of assaulting a five-year-old girl, is dragged from his jail cell in Omaha, Nebraska, by a crowd of more than 1,000 persons, taken to a telephone pole, and hanged. When Omaha Mayor Edward P. Smith attempts to stop the lynching, he is almost hanged next to Coe. Smith is so roughly handled by the lynch mob that he dies from injuries hours later.

October 8: Hugo Haase, German socialist leader, is assassinated in Berlin by terrorists.

October 27: Michele Pepitone is murdered in New Orleans in reprisal for the killing of Black Hand terrorist chief Paul di Cristina (Paulo Marchese); Pepitone's father, Pietro Pepitone, a New Orleans grocer, had shot and killed di Cristina a decade earlier when the terrorist attempted to extort money from him. Pepitone's murder is attributed to "the Ax Man of New Orleans," who is later identified by Mrs. Pepitone as Joseph "Doc" Mumfre, a mysterious figure and much-feared extortionist and terrorist. Two years later, in October 1921, after remarrying (to Angelo Albano) and moving to Los Angeles, Mrs. Pepitone-Albano shoots and kills Mumfre. She is sent to prison for ten years but is released in three years and insists that Mumfre was the notorious "Ax Man." No other support for this claim is forthcoming, and the infamous terrorist remains unknown to this day.

December 21: Emma Goldman, Alexander Berkman and 245 other radicals, all thought to be part of the anarchist terror campaign begun earlier this year, are deported to Russia on the ship *Buford*.

1920

May 8: Henry Scott, a black railway porter, is accused of insulting a white female passenger and is dragged from a train near Tampa, Florida, by a lynch mob that has filled three railroad cars. Scott is lynched in full view of white passengers on the train, many of whom cheer at the sight of the dangling body.

June 16: Three black circus workers, who are accused of raping a seventeen-year-old white girl in Duluth, Minnesota, are lynched from telephone poles.

August 23: Droubi Pashda is killed in Syria by a terrorist.

September 16: Thirty-eight persons are killed when a horse-drawn wagon loaded with dynamite and scrap iron explodes outside the Assay Building at the corner of Broad and Wall Streets in New York City. The bomb also destroys the offices of many businesses nearby, including that of J. P. Morgan. The terrorist responsible for the bomb is never identified.

September 28: A series of bombings occur on Chicago's near South Side between the rival gangs of Alderman Johnny Powers and the D'Andrea family, both fighting for control of the Nineteenth Ward; no one is killed but a restaurant is destroyed.

December 24: Dejelal Munif Bey is murdered in Hungary by terrorists.

1921

February 7: The Powers-D'Andrea political feud in Chicago escalates after a bomb explodes at a Blue Island dance hall when a number of D'Andrea supporters are present.

March 8: Eduardo Data Iradier, premier of Spain, is fatally shot by an anarchist.

July 22: Milorad Drakovic, minister of interior of Yugoslavia, is murdered by a Bosnian terrorist.

October 26: Two former army officers belonging to a right-wing terrorist organization shoot and kill Matthias Erzberger, chief of the German leftist Center Party at a Black Forest retreat.

November 4: Takashi Hara (Kei Hara), prime minister of Japan, is stabbed to death in the Tokyo Railroad Station by a right-wing terrorist, Nakaoka Konichi, who will be sent to prison.

December 11: Fred Rouse, a black packing-house worker, in the hospital with a fractured skull from a fight with two other workers, is dragged from his bed and hanged on a nearby tree in Fort Worth, Texas.

1922

February 15: Heikki Ritavouri, minister of the interior for Finland, is assassinated by a terrorist who disagrees with the way the minister has handled Red prisoners following the 1918 war.

March 22: Alex Smith, a black man who runs a bordello in Gulfport, Mississippi, is lynched by an angry white mob after two white girls are found in his establishment.

May 6: Three black men, who are accused of murdering seventeen-year-old Eula Ausley, are tied together and burned alive in the city square of Kirvin, Texas, by an angry white mob. Two white men later confess to the murder.

June 22: Sir Henry Wilson, British military advisor to Protestant troops during the Irish Civil War in Belfast, Ireland, is shot to death by two IRA members, Reginald Dunne and Joseph O'Sullivan.

June 22: Union members in Herrin, Illinois, attack strikebreakers. Men are ordered to run and are then shot. Some are tied together and shot, others have their throats slit, and some are hanged. Nineteen strikebreakers are killed.

June 24: Walter Rathenau, Germany's foreign minister, is shot to death by two right-wing terrorists, in Berlin, Germany.

July 28: Black laborer John West uses a cup reserved for white workers when taking a drink of water and is lynched by his irate fellow white workers near Guernsey, Arkansas.

August 10: Reginald Dunne and Joseph O'Sullivan, the IRA murderers of Sir Henry Wilson, are executed.

August 14: Terrorists assassinate Baron Udekem D'Acoz in Belgium.

August 22: Michael Collins, the great revolutionary leader of Ireland, is assassinated by IRA members in an ambush at Beal-n-Blath, Cork, Ireland.

October 30: Benito Mussolini, through intimidation and threats of death from his Black Shirts, a widespread and powerful terrorist organization, comes to power in Italy.

December 14: George Gay, a Negro accused of attacking a white woman, is abducted from the state penitentiary at Huntsville, Texas, and is lynched by a white mob of more than 1,500 men.

December 14–15: Charles Wright, a twenty-five-year-old black man, confesses to the murder of Ruby Hendry, a white school teacher, and is burned alive in Perry, Florida, by a lynch mob. The following day, Arthur Young, a Negro, is lynched in Perry, Florida, by the same mob for the same crime, even though he is innocent and Charles Wright has confessed to committing the murder.

December 16: Only a few days after taking office, Gabriel Narutowicz, president of Poland, is assassinated by anarchist Eligius Niewiadomski.

1923

January 9: Leslie Legget, a swarthy-skinned white man, is mistaken by a lynch mob for a Negro when accused of consorting with a white woman and is shot to death in Shreveport, Louisiana.

April 29: James T. Scott, a Negro janitor at the University of Missouri at Columbia, is accused of attempting to assault the fourteen-year-old daughter of a faculty member and is abducted by a mob of more than 500 and hanged from a bridge.

June 14: Alexander Stamboliski, the overthrown dictator of Bulgaria, is assassinated by terrorists.

August 25: Len Hart, a thirty-four-year-old Negro, is lynched after being accused of peeping into the window of a white girl in Jacksonville, Florida.

September 1–3: In the wake of the great Kwanto Earthquake that devastated Tokyo-Yokohama, killing 143,000, injuring 200,000, and making another half million persons homeless, Regent Hirohito, to absolve the throne of unworthy rule as deigned by the superstitious Japanese and the ancient dogmas of Shinto, announces that Koreans have "offended the spirits before the earthquake" and were taking advantage of the disaster by setting fires (which will cause the most loss of life) and pillaging shops. Thousands of sabre-wielding members of the secret Black Dragon Society, Hirohito's private terrorist organization, round up more than 4,000 hapless Koreans from the Tokyo slums and, after holding brief mock trials in the streets, behead them all. Hirohito also uses the earthquake to get rid of political opposition (as would the Nazis in 1934 by burning down the Reichstag Building and blaming the arson on Communists). Osugi Sake, a socialist orator, his wife, and his seven-year-old nephew are accused of urging earthquake survivors to avoid the fire by breaking through police lines and wading into the pools of the imperial palace, thus violating the sanctity of the throne. For this "offense," Sake, his wife, and his nephew are thrown into a dungeon and shortly thereafter strangled to death by a sadistic police captain, Masahiko Amakasu, who acts at Hirohito's behest. Amakasu, a Black Dragon terrorist, is later convicted of these killings and sent to prison for ten years, released within three years through Hirohito's influence, and then given considerable sums from a "friend of the throne" to relocate in Europe.

November 7: Dallas Sewell, a Negro accused of "passing for white and associating with white women," is lynched in Eufala, Oklahoma, by a large mob dressed in the robes and hoods of the Ku Klux Klan.

December 27: Crown prince (later emperor) Hirohito of Japan, is the unsuccessful assassination target of terrorist Daisaku Namba, who will be beheaded.

1924

May 30: Baron Saito, a liberal peace-seeker, is attacked but survives an assassination attempt by a terrorist in Korea.

June 2: Ignatz Seipel, chancellor of Austria, survives an assassination attempt by terrorists.

June 10: Giacomo Matteotti, the Socialist leader of the Italian parliament and an outspoken opponent of dictator Benito Mussolini, is kidnapped and murdered by Black Shirt terrorists in Rome.

July 13: Said Zaghloul Pasha ibn Ibrahim, premier of Egypt, survives an assassination attempt by terrorists.

September 13: Amando Casalini, Fascist deputy, is shot dead in Rome, allegedly by Giovanni Corvi, who claims when arrested that he wants revenge for the death of Giacomo Matteotti, slain in June. It is later claimed that Corvi is a secret Black Shirt member and murder specialist who has been ordered to kill Casalini to make it appear that dictator Benito Mussolini's government faces an actual threat from the Socialists.

September 16: Greek terrorists murder Todor Aleksandrov, leader of the Internal Macedonian Revolutionary Organization.

October 8: William Bell, a Negro, is beaten over the head with a baseball bat and dies at the hands of a mob of more than 100 in Chicago

November 19: Sir Lee Oliver Fitzmaurice Stack, British commander of the Egyptian Army, is riding in his car in Cairo, Egypt, when he is shot dead by Egyptian nationalists, these terrorists directed by Shafik Mansur.

December 4: The trial of Fritz Haarmann, called the "Ogre of Hanover," begins. Haarmann is a terrorist killer who may have killed and cannibalized as many as one hundred young boys following World War I in Hanover, Germany, then awash with thousands of homeless youths. Haarmann, who is tried with his accomplice, Hans Grans, his homosexual lover, for years has served as a police informant and has used his police badge to compel youths he has picked up at Hanover's train stations to accompany him to his apartment in Hanover's Jewish ghetto from 1920 to 1924. He admits to twenty-four of the twenty-seven murders with which he is charged, calmly describing how he has murdered the youths, ages twelve to twenty, by biting their throats, then butchering the bodies in an attic room, selling off the clothes, dumping the bones in a nearby river and carrying the "edible" portions of the butchered flesh in buckets to the open market in Hanover where he sells it as "horse meat" to Hanover's starving citizens. Haarmann is found guilty and sentenced to death. Hans Grans is given a life sentence that is later reduced to twelve years.

1925

January 11: Takakira Kato, prime minister of Japan, survives an assassination attempt by military terrorists reportedly on secret orders from Emperor Hirohito.

January 23: Italian dictator Benito Mussolini appears before his puppet parliament and takes responsibility for the actions of his Black Shirts, including the kidnapping and murder of his chief political opponent, Giacomo Matteotti, daring anyone to challenge his terrorist governmental rule. No one voices opposition.

March 15: David Curtis Stephenson, Grand Dragon of the Ku Klux Klan in Indiana, a state he virtually controls, abducts Madge Oberholtzer, and, with the aid of two Klansmen, drags her aboard a train, drugging and raping her. She later takes poison and dies. Stephenson will be charged with her murder and be sent to prison for life.

April 14: Boris III, czar of Bulgaria, survives an assassination attempt by terrorists in Sofia.

April 15: Communist terrorists kill General Kosta Georgiev in Sofia, Bulgaria. The victim is a close associate of Boris III, czar of Bulgaria, who has a day earlier survived an assassination attempt.

April 15: Terrorist killer Fritz Haarmann, the "Ogre of Hanover," who has murdered and cannibalized at least forty youths by his own admission, is beheaded at Hanover Prison.

April 16: Boris III, czar of Bulgaria, attends the funeral of General Georgiev and is nearly killed by a bomb explosion, set off by Communist terrorists, which demolishes St. Nedelja Cathedral in Sofia, Bulgaria, and leaves 125 dead.

May 2: Boris III, czar of Bulgaria, survives a third attempt on his life by terrorists in Sofia.

September 11: Italy's dictator, Benito Mussolini, survives an assassination attempt, allegedly made by Socialist terrorists, but some claim that the attempt is bogus, a Black Shirt ruse to make it appear that Mussolini is facing a Socialist menace and giving him an excuse to persecute Socialists and Communists.

December 19: Lindsay Coleman, a Negro, is lynched in Clarksdale, Mississippi, after being acquitted of the murder of a local plantation owner, Grover C. Nichols.

1926

February 20: Earle Leonard Nelson, a psychopathic killer, strangles Mrs. Clara Newman, his landlady, in San Francisco, his first of many victims. Nelson, a necrophiliac who violates Mrs. Newman's body after murdering her, a pattern consistent with his many subsequent murders, displays amazing agility in escaping police dragnets and will be dubbed the "Gorilla Murderer." His gruesome murders will terrorize whole communities, particularly those on the West Coast, and across the U.S. and in Canada. Most of Nelson's victims will be his landladies. (Alfred Hitchcock's 1942 motion picture, *Shadow of a Doubt*, the director's favorite, will be based, in part, on Nelson.)

March 2: Earle Leonard Nelson strangles and rapes Mrs. Laura Beale in California.

April 21: Father Gregorio Esparragoza is murdered in Mexico by military officers under orders from dictator Alvaro Obregón, who has initiated a terrorist campaign against Catholic clergy in the country.

April 25: Chicago crime boss Al Capone personally executes William H. McSwiggin, an Illinois state's attorney, who has been investigating his widespread illegal operations, firing a submachine gun from a moving car, a terrorist killing Capone designs to silence political opposition to his gang rule and one witnessed by a dozen witnesses. The witnesses cannot later recall the identity of the killer, causing the refrain: "Who Killed McSwiggin?" to be repeatedly uttered in Chicago whenever Capone's name is mentioned.

May 25: Simon Petlura, Ukrainian nationalist leader, is slain in Paris, France, by Communist terrorist Simon Schwarzbart, reportedly on orders from Soviet dictator Joseph Stalin.

June 2: Albert Blazes, a twenty-two-year-old Negro accused of assaulting a white girl (who appears to have been only frightened), is hanged by a lynch mob in Osceola, Arkansas, and his body burned.

June 10: Strangler and necrophile Earle Leonard Nelson murders Mrs. Lillian St. Mary in California.

June 26: Earle Leonard Nelson strangles and rapes Mrs. George Russell in Santa Barbara, California.

August 16: Earle Leonard Nelson strangles and rapes Mrs. Mary Nesbit in Oakland, California.

August 24: More than 80,000 movie fans, mostly women, riot outside Campbell's Funeral Home in New York City, wherein rests the body of silent film star Rudolf Valentino. The riot ensues when the fans are informed that, after 30,000 mostly female fans have already trampled the funeral home to a shambles, no more visitors will be allowed to view Valentino's fast-decomposing body. More than 200 mounted policemen wielding clubs disperse the crowds; dozens of persons are injured.

October 19: Earle Leonard Nelson strangles and rapes Mrs. Beta Withers in Portland, Oregon.

October 20: Earle Leonard Nelson strangles and rapes Mrs. Mabel Fluke in Portland, Oregon.

October 26: Earle Leonard Nelson strangles and rapes Mrs. Virginia Grant in Portland, Oregon.

November 10: Earle Leonard Nelson strangles and rapes Mrs. William Edmonds in San Francisco, California.

November 15: Earle Leonard Nelson strangles and rapes Mrs. Blanche Meyers in Portland, Oregon.

December 12: Joe Adams, mayor of West City, Illinois, is shot and killed by two terrorists under orders from southern Illinois crime boss and bootlegger Charles Birger, who is later hanged for the killing.

December 23: Earle Leonard Nelson strangles and rapes Mrs. John Bernard in Council Bluffs, Iowa.

December 24: Adolfo Diaz, president of Nicaragua, survives an assassination attempt by terrorists.

December 28: Earle Leonard Nelson strangles and rapes Mrs. Germania Harpin and also murders her eight-month-old child in Kansas City, Missouri.

1927

April 16: Father David Uribe is slain in Mexico by military officers under orders from dictator Alvaro Obregón, who continues his anti-Catholic terrorist campaign.

April 27: Earle Leonard Nelson strangles and rapes Mrs. Mary McConnell in Philadelphia.

May 1: Earle Leonard Nelson strangles and rapes Jennie Randolph in Philadelphia, Pennsylvania.

June 1: Earle Leonard Nelson strangles and rapes two sisters, Minnie May Atorthy and Mrs. M. C. Atorthy, in Detroit, Michigan.

June 3: Earle Leonard Nelson strangles and rapes Mary Sietsome in Chicago, Illinois.

June 8: Earle Leonard Nelson strangles and rapes Lola Cowan in Winnepeg, Manitoba, Canada.

June 9: Earle Leonard Nelson strangles and rapes Mrs. Emily Patterson in Winnepeg, Manitoba, Canada.

June 13: Two black brothers, Jim and Mark Fox, are accused of killing a sawmill foreman. They are seized by a lynch mob, soaked in gasoline and burned to death.

July 10: Kevin C. O'Higgins, vice president of Ireland, is slain by IRA gunmen who are never apprehended.

November 13: Mexican dictator Alvaro Obregón survives an assassination attempt on his life.

November 14: Serial strangler, necrophile and terrorist Earle Leonard Nelson is convicted in Winnepeg, Manitoba, Canada, of the murder of Mrs. Emily Patterson and is sentenced to death.

1928

January 12: Serial killer and terrorist Earle Leonard Nelson, who has murdered at least twenty persons over a two-year period, is hanged in Winnepeg, Manitoba, Canada.

June 4: Chang Tso-lin, a powerful Chinese warlord, is assassinated when Japanese military officers, all members of the Black

Dragon Society, a secret terrorist organization promoting foreign aggression on behalf of Emperor Hirohito, blow up the train on which he is riding as it arrives in Mukden, Manchuria.

June: Two black brothers, Lee and David Blackman, are seized by a lynch mob and hanged in Rapides Parish, Louisiana, after their brother, William Blackman, has been shot to death by police officers in a shootout where William Blackman has shot and killed a white deputy.

July 17: Plutarco Elias Calles, president of Mexico, survives an assassination attempt.

July 17: Alvaro Obregón, Mexican general and former president who has persecuted and terrorized the Catholic clergy in Mexico, is shot to death by José de Leon Toral, an artist who pretends to draw Obregón's portrait as he sits in La Bombita (Little Bomb) Restaurant in San Angel, Mexico. Toral will be executed.

1929

January 12: A group of suspects is arrested in Miami, Florida, on charges of conspiring to assassinate President Herbert Hoover, but is freed for lack of evidence.

February 2: Terrorist killer Peter Kürten stabs Appollonia Kuhn with a pair of scissors in Düssseldorf, Germany, but her screams scare off the murderer and the victim survives. In this year alone, Kürten will attack twenty-three persons.

February 8: Peter Kürten stabs nine-year-old Rosa Ohliger to death near the Vinzenz Church in Düsseldorf, Germany. Kürten, who thrills to his reputation as the terror-ist known as the "Monster of Düsseldorf," soaks Ohliger's body with kerosene and burns it.

February 12: Terrorist killer Peter Kürten repeatedly stabs Rudolf Sheer, a drunk, in Düsseldorf, Germany. As Sheer lays dying, Kürten, by his own later admission, drinks the blood from his victim's open wounds.

July 28: Overcrowding causes more than 1,700 prisoners at Auburn Prison, New York, to riot. Many inmates seize the arsenal and try to escape. During the five-hour riot, two prisoners are killed and eleven escape. Damage to the prison is estimated at about $450,000. Six convicts are later given additional prison terms for leading the riot.

August 11: Maria Hahn, a housemaid enamored with terrorist killer Peter Kürten, is stabbed to death by Kürten who dumps her body in a ditch in Düsseldorf, Germany.

August: Terrorist killer Peter Kürten kills five-year-old Louise Lenzen in the suburb of Flehe, Düsseldorf, Germany. He then attacks a twenty-six-year-old servant woman, Gertrude Schulte, near the fairgrounds in Neuss, repeatedly stabbing her and drinking her blood before her screams scare him off. These and previous attacks cause the citizens of Düsseldorf to panic. Children are locked in their homes or escorted everywhere by armed parents. Newspapers print lurid stories about the madman terrorist in their community, describing him as a Satanist and vampire.

September 29: Terrorist killer Peter Kürten employs a hammer to kill servant girl Ida Reuter in woods outside of Düsseldorf, Germany.

October 11: Peter Kürten uses a hammer to crush the skull of Elizabeth Dorrier in the woods outside of Düsseldorf, Germany. A few days later, he will kill Gertrude Albermann, a five-year-old, stabbing her thirty-six times with a pair of scissors.

December 11: Fifty men who have been confined to solitary in Auburn Prison, New York, break out of confinement, holding the warden hostage. Police and guards fire on the prisoners and, after a six-hour siege, the riot is quelled; nine guards and prisoners are dead and many are wounded. Three of the ringleaders of the mass breakout will be executed on August 28, 1930.

1930

January 11: Will W. Alexander, director of the Commission on Inter-Racial Cooperation, declares that lynching in the U.S. will vanish by 1940, wiped out by radio, good roads, and newspapers.

January 14: Horst Wessel, one of Hitler's Brown Shirt (SA, Stormtroopers) terrorists, is fatally shot by Ali Hoehler, another Brown Shirt thug, over the control of Erna Jaenecke, a prostitute (both Wessel and Hoehler are pimps). Wessel will be promoted as a Brown Shirt hero by Nazi propaganda chief Paul Josef Goebbels, who creates a false background for the terrorist, who dies of his wound on February 23.

February 5: Pascual Ortiz-Rubio, president of Mexico, survives an assassination attempt by terrorists.

April 26: Terrorists fail to assassinate Augusto Bernardino Leguia y Salcedo, president of Peru.

May 9: George Hughes, a Negro who has pleaded guilty to assaulting a white woman, is incinerated in Sherman, Texas, when a lynch mob burns down the courthouse and jail in which Hughes is being held.

May 10: Race riots erupt in Sherman, Texas, where white mobs burn down several homes occupied by black residents.

May 24: With police detectives closing in, Peter Kürten confesses his terrorist murders of many years to his startled wife, urging her to turn him in to the authorities. She does, collecting one third of the reward money offered for the apprehension of the "Monster of Düsseldorf." Says Kürten: "It was not easy convincing her that this was not betraying me."

June 8: Dr. Henry Albert von Baligand, German minister to Portugal, is assassinated by a terrorist.

June 11: Joseph Moyzynsky is shot to death while spooning with his girlfriend at Whitestone, Queens, New York, the first of many victims claimed by a terrorist who will be known only as "3-X."

June 17: The "3-X" terrorist shoots to death Noel Sowley, who is sitting with his girlfriend at Creedmore, Queens, New York.

June 25: Rebecca Hirsch is attacked in her Brooklyn, New York, room by the "3-X" slayer, who ties her to her bed and then sets fire to her clothes. She survives.

July 4: Six persons—two white men, three black men, and a black woman—are all accused of murder and are lynched by a large mob in Emelle, Alabama.

July 5: Reginald Arthur Lee, British acting consul-general in Marseilles, France, vanishes completely, his disappearance attributed to a kidnapping by political terrorists.

August 15: George Robinson, a Negro accused of resisting arrest, is lynched in Raymond, Mississippi.

September 9: Police Captain Grover C. Fain, an articulate and compassionate official, faces an irate lynch mob in Atlanta, Georgia, that is bent on storming the jail and hanging Negro Robert Glaze, who is being held in connection with the murder of a streetcar conductor. Fain persuades the mob to disperse.

September 10: Pig Lockett and Holly White, both black, are accused of robbing tourists and are stopped en route to Scooba, Mississippi, by a lynch mob and hanged.

September 25: Willie Kirkland, a young black man accused of attacking a young white girl, is dragged from his jail cell by a mob of seventy-five men and lynched in Magnolia Gardens, Georgia.

October 2: Gordon Stewart Northcott, who has in the late 1920s terrorized Mexican-American communities by murdering and beheadeding almost two dozen young boys, burying the dismembered corpses on his run-down ranch in Riverside County, California, is hanged at San Quentin.

October 14: Josef Pilsudski, general and premier of Poland, survives an assassination attempt by terrorists.

November 14: Yoko Hamaguchi, prime minister of Japan, is shot by Black Dragon terrorist Toomeo Sagoya. Hamaguchi will die of his wounds six months later. Sagoya is imprisoned for three years before he is pardoned by his secret sponsor, Emperor Hirohito.

1931

January 1: Terrorist Sylvestre Matuschka blows the Vienna-Passau Express train off its tracks in a wild insurance scheme.

January 8: Emperor Hirohito of Japan survives an assassination attempt by I Pong-chang, who is later executed.

February 21: Zog I, premier and king of Albania, survives an assassination attempt by terrorists.

February 25: Gerado Machado, Cuban strongman and president of Cuba, survives an assassination attempt by terrorists while on a visit to New York City.

February: The first known skyjacking on record occurs when revolutionaries attempt to take over a Peruvian domestic flight, ordering the pilot, Captain B. D. Richards, to drop propaganda leaflets over Peruvian cities. Richards refuses and the revolutionaries back down.

April 13: The trial of Peter Kürten, the "Monster of Düsseldorf," begins in Düsseldorf, Germany. Thousands pack into the courthouse, lining the hallways to catch a glimpse of the terrorist killer who has claimed dozens of lives over the last two decades and to view the gruesome exhibits of his crimes—skulls, bones, and his murder weapons: scissors, hammers, and knives. Kürten is matter-of-fact in the dock, saying in a monotone: "I did not kill either people I hated or people I loved. I killed whomever crossed my path at the moment my urge for murder took hold of me." He is convicted within nine days and sentenced to death.

July 2: Terrorist killer Peter Kürten is taken from his cell in Klingelputz Prison in Cologne, Germany, and into a courtyard where prison officials witness the serial murderer walk calmly to a waiting headsman. He asks the executioner who is about to decapitate him: "After my head has been chopped off, will I be able to hear at least for a moment the sound of my own blood gushing from the stump of my neck? That would be the pleasure to end all pleasures." Kürten is beheaded without further ceremony. As Kürten's eyes seem to blink in his decapitated head, the executioner reportedly remarks to it: "Can you hear the voice of God directing you to hell, Mr. Kürten?"

July 23: T. V. Soong, minister of finance for China, survives an assassination attempt.

July 30: Chiang Kai-shek, president of China, survives an assassination attempt by Black Dragon terrorists.

August 8: Near Juelerboy, Hungary, terrorist Sylvestre Matuschka ignites a dynamite bomb that derails a passenger train, injuring twenty-five persons.

August 28: Richard and Charles Smoke, a black father and son accused of assault, are lynched in Blountstown, Florida.

October 2: Ismet Innü, prime minister of Greece, survives an assassination attempt by terrorists.

November 9: Henry Pu-Yi (Hsan T'ung), last emperor of China, survives an assassination attempt, but the attack is staged by Japanese terrorists pretending to be Chinese terrorists representing China's president, Chiang Kai-shek, in order to move Pu-Yi into accepting Japanese "protection" and thus becoming a puppet of Japan and Emperor Hirohito.

1932

January 17: Antonio Oscar de Fragosa Carmona, president of Portugal, survives an assassination attempt by terrorists.

February 9: Junnosuke Inouye, minister of finance in Japan, is murdered by Black Dragon terrorists.

March 7: Thousands of unemployed auto workers march on the Ford Motor Company plant in Dearborn, Michigan, and they are repulsed by firehoses, pistols, and a machine gun. Four marchers are killed and twenty more are injured.

May 7: Paul Doumer, president of France, is assassinated by a Russian anarchist.

May 15: Ki Tsuyoshi Inukai, prime minister of Japan, is assassinated by army and navy officers in Tokyo; many of the killers are members of the secret Black Dragon Society of terrorists who support Emperor Hirohito's secret plans of aggression.

June 14: A white mob in Winnsboro, South Carolina, is so intent on abducting a black prisoner from the local jail, that Sheriff Hood is killed by mob members, who also wound six deputies before extracting the Negro prisoner, who is shot to death.

July 28: Thousands of unemployed veterans who have marched on Washington, D.C., to obtain a promised "bonus" for their World War I service, are dispersed by U.S. Army troops commanded by General Douglas MacArthur (and his aides Dwight David Eisenhower and George Patton). Soldiers burn the hobo camps occupied by the Bonus Army veterans at Anacosta Flats, accidentally kill an infant, and wound dozens of resisting veterans.

September 12: Terrorist Sylvestre Matuschka explodes a bomb beneath the Hungarian RR Express, sending the passenger train crashing off a viaduct near Bio-Torbagy, killing twenty-two people and injuring scores more.

1933

February 15: Terrorist Joseph Zangara attempts to assassinate President Franklin Delano Roosevelt when the president visits Miami, Florida, but Zangara's bullets accidentally strike Chicago mayor Anton Joseph Cermak, who will die on March 6, 1933.

March 20: Terrorist Joseph Zangara is executed for killing Chicago mayor Anton Cermak.

April 30: Luis M. Sanchez Cerro, president of Peru, is assassinated by terrorists.

July 5: Norris Bendy, a Negro truck driver, is arrested after fighting with white truck driver Marvin Tollis, in Clinton, South Carolina. A mob drags Bendy from his cell, beating and shooting him before hanging him from a tree.

October 4: Engelbert Dollfuss, chancellor and dictator of Austria, is the target of a failed assassination attempt on the part of Nazi Brown Shirts in Vienna.

October 9: Bennie Thompson, a young black man, is taken from the jail at Ninety Six, North Carolina, by a mob and is beaten to death. Four white men are later charged with the killing, one of whom implicates local police officers as accomplices.

October 11: Freddy Moore and Norman Thibodeaux, two young black men

accused of murdering a white girl, are grabbed by a lynch mob. Moore is hanged but Thibodeaux manages to escape. The slain girl's stepfather will confess to the killing a short time later.

October 12: Carol II, king of Rumania, is the target of a failed attempt on his life.

October 18: A mob of more than 3,000 overwhelms fifty state troopers at the Princess Anne, Maryland, jail, abducting and lynching George Armwood, a twenty-four-year-old Negro who is accused of murdering eighty-two-year-old Mary Denston.

October 23: Oscar Raimundo Benavides, president of Peru, is the target of an unsuccessful attempt on his life.

November 13: J. A. Primo de Rivera, dictator of Spain, is the target of an unsuccessful attempt on his life.

November 26: A fierce mob of more than 15,000 persons overwhelms jailers at San Jose, California, dragging away Thomas Harold Thurmond and John Maurice Holmes, who have kidnapped and murdered twenty-two-year-old Brooke Hart, the son of a local department store owner. Both men are lynched while thousands of residents cheer and pose for photos beneath the swaying bodies. California governor James "Sunny Jim" Rolfe, who has failed to send additional guards to the jail to prevent the lynchings, later praises the mob for meting out lynch-law justice, saying that the mob has given "the best lesson ever given the country. I would pardon those fellows if they were charged. I would like to parole all kidnappers in San Quentin to the fine, patriotic citizens of San Jose." Though there are newsreels taken of the lynch-mob members storming the jail, as well as photos taken by newspaper photographers, none of the well-known leaders are ever charged. Film director Fritz Lang will make a memorable film based on this terrorist incident in 1936, *Fury*, starring Spencer Tracy.

December 15: After a grand jury refuses to indict Cord Cheek, a twenty-year-old Negro who has been accused of molesting an eleven-year-old white girl, a lynch mob breaks into a Columbia, Tennessee, jail and hangs the black man.

December 30: Ion Duca, prime minister of Rumania, is assassinated by terrorist members of the fascist Iron Guard.

1934

February 27: Nazi reichsmarshal Hermann Goering orders Brown Shirt terrorists led by Karl Ernst to set fire to the Reichstag Building in Berlin, an act of sabotage that Adolf Hitler will blame Communist opponents for and use as an excuse to purge leftist radicals in Germany. (A half-witted Communist, Marinus van der Lubbe, is convicted of committing the arson and is later beheaded.)

April 8: During a pro-Nazi rally, American Nazis and Communists clash in eighteen separate riots throughout the U.S., which leave scores injured and twelve persons arrested.

April 15: Major Emil Fey, minister of the interior for Austria, is the target of an unsuccessful attempt on his life by Nazi Brown Shirts.

June 16: Colonel Bronislaw Pieracki, Polish minister of the interior, is assassinated in Poland by terrorists.

June 21: A mob of 200 armed men seize John Criggs, a Negro accused of associating with white women, and lynch him in Newton, Texas.

June 30: Adolf Hitler, accompanied by heavily armed members of his SS bodyguard, travels to Munich and then to a Lake Wiesee resort where he confronts Ernst Roehm, head of the Brown Shirts (SA), his long-established terrorist organization, catching Roehm and other top storm-trooper leaders in homosexual liaisons and accusing them of treason. He orders all the SA leaders shot; these executions carried out by Heinrich Himmler's SS troops, a massive blood purge of hundreds, later called the Night of the Long Knives. Included in the mass murders are many of Hitler's old enemies, including Gustav von Kahr, Kurt von Schleicher, and Gregor Strasser.

July 9: Andrew McCloud, a twenty-six-year-old Negro accused of attempting to assault a white girl, is dragged from the Moorehouse Parish jail by a mob of more than 3,000 and hanged in the public square of Bastrop, Louisiana.

July 16: A mob in Bolton, Mississippi, shoots to death James Sanders, a twenty-five-year-old black man accused of writing indecent and insulting letters to a white girl.

July 25: Englebert Dollfuss, chancellor and dictator of Austria, is fatally shot by Austrian Nazis and Brown Shirts headed by Otto Planetta, in an unsuccessful coup. Planetta and others are later executed.

September: The dissected remains of an unknown woman are found in the Kingsbury Run section of Cleveland, the first known victim of a mad terrorist who will be called the "Mad Butcher of Cleveland."

October 9: Alexander I, king of Yugoslavia (and grandson of Alexander Karageorgevic), and Jean Louis Barthou, foreign minister for France, are both assassinated in Marseilles by Vlada Chermozamsky, a killer working for the Croatian terrorist organization led by Ante Pavelic. Chermozamsky is fatally shot at the same time.

November 5: During a political parade in Kelayres, Pennsylvania, five participants are shot and killed by political rival John J. Bruno and his relatives, who have been conducting a campaign of terrorism. Bruno and others responsible are sent to prison.

December 1: As part of his terrorist purge to eliminate all suspected political enemies, Joseph Stalin sends an assassin to murder Sergei Mironovich Kirov, Russian revolutionary leader. The assassin and 116 others are executed as part of an assassination plot invented by Stalin himself. Stalin has and will be conducting for several years a nation-wide purge of kulaks, nomads, gypsies, and others he considers "undesirables," a terrorist murder campaign that will claim between six and twelve million lives.

1935

For several months, the interracial Southern Tenant Farmers' Union, consisting of more than 10,000 black and white sharecroppers, goes on strike, refusing to plant or harvest crops, until given better wages or increased portions of profits. Union members in Arkansas and other neighboring states are terrorized by absentee corporations owning their lands; corrupt officials; and police, special police, or goon squads, privately paid armies of thugs who harrass, attack, jail, and murder scores of Union members.

January 28: Wilhelm II, king of the Netherlands, is the target of an unsuccessful assassination attempt by Nazi terrorists.

March 19: After sixteen-year-old Lino Rivera, a black youth, is arrested in Harlem for shoplifting, a widespread race riot ensues. One Negro is shot and more than 100 are injured. More than 200 stores in Harlem are gutted by fires, and damage soars beyond $2 million.

March 25: Thomas J. Courtney, an Illinois state's attorney, is shot to death by Capone gang terrorists.

March 25: R. J. Tyrone, a black farmer in Hattisburg, Mississippi, who is having financial problems with a neighboring white farmer, is visited by a white mob and is shot dead in his home. A coroner rules his death a suicide.

June 3: Gabriel Terra, president of Uruguay, is the target of an unsuccessful assassination attempt in Uruguay.

1936

January 26: The decapitated, dissected remains of Florence Polillo are found in Kingsbury Run, Cleveland, another victim of the killer terrorist called the "Mad Butcher of Cleveland."

February 13: Leon Blum, president of France, is the target of an unsuccessful assassination attempt on his life.

February 26: Keisuke Okada, prime minister of Japan; Makoto Saito, former prime minister of Japan; Korekiyo Takahashi, former premier of Japan; and General Watanabe are all assassinated by Black

Dragon members supported by Emperor Hirohito.

April 7: Spanish intellectual and Republican Eduardo Ortega Gasset is the target of a failed assassination attempt on his life by right-wing terrorists working with insurgent leader Colonel Francisco Franco.

May: The bullet-ridden body of Charles Poole is found behind the wheel of his car on Gulley Road on the far West Side of Detroit, Michigan. It is later determined that Poole is one of many murder victims of the dreaded secret terrorist society, the Black Legion.

June 1: Arrested on disorderly charges in Elizabethtown, N.Y., Frank Engel confesses to being the infamous "3-X" terrorist, who had plagued Queens and Brooklyn in the 1930s, but he is judged insane and sent to an asylum for life.

June 18: A mob of 300 persons attempts to lynch five men and four women, all black, for a murder that has occurred in an El Campo, Texas, cafe, but the Texas Rangers succeed in driving off the would-be lynchers, who next vent their wrath by burning down the cafe.

June 29: Robert Nixon, a youthful Negro who will invade many U.S. residences, killing his victims with a brick (the press will label him the "Brick Moron"), climbs the fire escape of Chicago's Devonshire Hotel and enters the room of Florence Thompson Castle, a cocktail waitress, killing her with a brick. Her son, hiding in a closet, tells police the killer is a white man painted black.

June: The headless, dissected corpse of a young man is found at Kingsbury Run, Cleveland, another victim of the much-sought "Mad Butcher."

July 16: Michael Stelescu, a Rumanian political leader, is recovering in a Bucharest hospital when eight members of the Iron Guard, a right-wing terrorist organization, enter his room and shoot him to death.

August 18: Frederico Garcia Lorca is assassinated in Spain.

1937

January 23: Suleiman Bey Salah is slain by terrorists in Palestine.

February 2: Wesley Johnson, a Negro accused of attacking a white woman, is lynched in Henry County, Alabama. Four months later, Sheriff J. L. Corbett is charged with failing to protect Johnson from the lynch mob, and in the charges is a report that the mob has lynched the wrong man.

March 2: Robert Nixon, a Negro terrorist called the "Brick Moron," invades the Los Angeles home of Rose G. Valdez, crushing her head with a brick.

March 4: Robert Nixon, the "Brick Moron," attacks and injures Mrs. Zoe Damrell in her Los Angeles home.

April 4: Robert Nixon, the "Brick Moron," bludgeons Edna Worden and her twelve-year-old daughter, Marguerite, to death in their Los Angeles home.

May 27: Robert Nixon, the "Brick Moron," crushes the skull of Florence Johnson in her Chicago, Illinois, home.

May 30: Police and special company deputies fire upon a crowd of more than 3,000 striking employees of the Republic

Steel Company in South Chicago, Illinois, killing ten strikers, six of whom are shot in the back. Fifty-eight strikers and sixteen police officers are injured in the struggle.

August 11: Bakir Sidky Pasha, Iraqi strongman, is assassinated by terrorists in a successful coup.

November 28: Mustafa an-Nahhas Pasha, prime minister of Egypt, is the target of an unsuccessful assassination attempt in Cairo.

1938

May 11: Getúlio Dornelles Vargas, dictator of Brazil, is the target of an unsuccessful assassination attempt.

November 7: Ernst von Rath, a Nazi official at the German Embassy in Geneva, Switzerland, is shot and killed by Hershel Grynszpan, a Jewish student. German dictator Adolf Hitler uses this assassination to launch a campaign of terror throughout Germany against Jews, called "Kristallnacht" (Night of the Broken Glass), occurring on the night of November 9, 1938, when thousands of homes and businesses owned by Jews are ransacked and vandalized by Nazi thugs.

November 21: Wilder McGowan, a twenty-four-year-old black man accused of assaulting a seventy-four-year-old white woman is hunted down by bloodhounds and hanged by a lynch mob of more than 200 white men near Wiggins, Mississippi.

November 29: Cornelius Zelea-Codreanu, a leader of the Rumanian terrorist organization, the right-wing Iron Guard, and seventeen others are shot to death by agents of the Rumanian government.

1939

June 15: Robert Nixon, a Negro who has used a brick to kill at least a half dozen persons in Chicago and Los Angeles, is executed in Illinois's electric chair for the murder of Florence Johnson.

August 25: IRA members Peter Barnes and James Richards explode a bomb in Coventry, England, which kills five and wounds fifty others.

September 21: Armand Calinescu, premier of Rumania, is assassinated by Rumanian Nazis known as Iron Guardists.

1940

January 29: General R. Valazquez Rivera is murdered in the Dominican Republic by terrorists.

March 13: Sir Michael Francis O'Dwyer, former governor of Punjab, is shot to death in London by Sikh terrorist Udham Singh.

March 15: Les Wilson, a candidate for sheriff in Okaloosa County, Florida, is fatally shot at his home by Jessie and Doyle Cayson, who have conducted a terrorist campaign against Wilson in order to protect profitable contracts won through political ties jeopardized by Wilson. The Caysons will be sent to prison for life.

May: Three bodies, all decapitated, are found in an abandoned freight car in Pittsburgh; police believe these are victims of the "Mad Butcher of Cleveland," a berserk killer who is never apprehended.

June 25: Sikh terrorist Udham Singh, killer of Sir Michael O'Dwyer, is hanged.

August 20: Leon Trotsky, who has helped Lenin achieve a Communist revolution in Russia, and who has been exiled from Russia for his anti-Stalin posture, is assassinated in his villa outside of Mexico City, Mexico, by Stalinist terrorist and assassin Jacques Mornard, who will be sent to prison. The political murder is retold in the 1972 film, *The Assassination of Trotsky*, in which Richard Burton essays Trotsky and Alain Delon portrays Mornard.

October 24: Andino Carias, president of Honduras, is the target of an unsuccessful assassination attempt.

November 16: Terrorist George Peter Metesky, who will come to be known as New York's "Mad Bomber," plants a pipe bomb at the Edison Building (he was a former, disgruntled employee) at West Sixty-Fourth Street in Manhattan, the first of thirty-seven bombs he will plant all over the city in the next sixteen years.

November 29: Nicola Iorga, former prime minister of Rumania, is assassinated by members of the Iron Guard.

1941

Boris III, czar of Bulgaria, is the target of three unsuccessful assassination attempts.

April 1: José Manuel Cortina y Garcia, president of the Cuban delegation to the League of Nations, is the target of an unsuccessful assassination attempt in Havana, Cuba.

May 13: A. C. Williams, a twenty-two-year-old Negro accused of assaulting a twelve-year-old white girl in Quincy, Florida, is abducted from his jail cell by a mob of white men and is shot in the head and left for dead. While being taken to a hospital, the ambulance is stopped by the same mob, and Williams is seized again and shot to death.

August 14: Baron Kichiro Hiranuma, former jurist and premier of Japan and imperial adviser who apparently has fallen out of favor with Emperor Hirohito, is assassinated by terrorists thought to be members of the Black Dragon Society.

December 6: Aturo Alessandro Palma, former president of Chile, is the target of an unsuccessful assassination attempt.

1942

February 25: Franz von Papen, German politician, intriguer, and ambassador to Turkey, is the target of an unsuccessful assassination attempt in Ankara; it is later claimed that the assassination attempt has been staged by Nazi terrorists in order to blame Allied agents and to win favor with Turkish officials.

June 4: Reinhard Heydrich, the dreaded SS leader and "Protector" of Czechoslovakia, dies of wounds received from an attack in Prague on May 27; Heinrich Himmler, head of the SS, uses Heydrich's death to unleash a terrorist campaign throughout the country, beginning with the destruction of the town of Lidice, where all the men and boys are murdered.

July 10: Helen Brown, pregnant, is attacked in her Tulsa, Oklahoma, home shortly after her husband goes off to work; she is strangled and later dies in a hospital, the first of several murders committed by an unknown terrorist.

October: Two unidentified fourteen-year-old black boys accused of attempting to rape a white girl are hanged by a lynch mob in Shubuta, Mississippi.

1943

January 11: Carlo Tresca, a staunch anti-Communist newspaper publisher and editor, is shot and killed in New York City, reportedly by Carmen "the Cigar" Galante, a Mafia terrorist and killer who has been hired by Communists to kill Tresca.

January 14: Georgia Green and her mother, Mrs. Clara Luzila Stewart, are found hacked to pieces in their Tulsa, Oklahoma, home, their deaths attributed to the "Tulsa Bludgeon Killer," an unknown terrorist who has been plaguing the town since mid-1942.

June 3–8: Rioting in Los Angeles, California, breaks out when soldiers begin fighting with Mexican-Americans wearing zoot suits. Hundreds are injured. The Los Angeles City Council will later ban the wearing of zoot suits. The offbeat 1981 film *Zoot Suit* is loosely based on this event.

June 20: Following a fight between blacks and whites in an amusement park, widespread race riots erupt in Detroit, Michigan. Blacks sack and loot white stores while whites randomly shoot blacks. Nine whites and twenty-nine blacks are killed.

August 24: Boris III, czar of Bulgaria, is assassinated by terrorists.

October 18: Captain Felix Tropschuh, one of the hundreds of thousands of captured German prisoners-of-war kept in American internment camps, is murdered by fellow prisoners, diehard Nazis, at Camp Concordia, Kansas, after Nazis read his diary, in which he has criticized Hitler's philosophy. Tropschuh is only one of at least 100 other German prisoners-of-war to be executed for deserting Hitler's cause.

November 4: Corporal Johann Kunze, a prisoner-of-war at the American internment camp at Camp Tonkawa, Oklahoma, is beaten to death by Nazi prisoners for giving information to G-2 interrogators upon his capture. Five of the assailants were later identified, tried, convicted and executed.

December 17: Nazi terrorists at an American internment camp, Camp Hearne, Texas, beat to death Corporal Hugo Krauss, a fellow prisoner, for acting as an interpreter for the American camp commander.

1944

March 13: Werner Dreschler, a German POW at Papago Park Camp, Arizona, is murdered by Nazi terrorists who labeled him a traitor. His seven killers will later be tried, convicted, and executed.

March 25: German POW Hans Geller is murdered by Nazi terrorists at Camp Chaffee, Arkansas, for appearing to be too cooperative with American officers in charge of the internment camp.

March 26: Rev. Isaac Simmons, a sixty-six-year-old black minister and farmer, suspects that there is oil on his property, and he hires a lawyer to safeguard the title to his land; he is lynched in Amite County, Mississippi.

April 6: Corporal Horst Gunther, a POW at the internment camp at Camp Gordon, Georgia, is hanged by Nazi terrorists. Two of his murderers will later be tried, convicted, and executed.

April 10: Manuel Avila Camacho, president of Mexico, is the target of an unsuccessful assassination attempt in Mexico City.

August 13: Sir Harold McMichael is the target of a failed assassination attempt in Palestine.

November 6: Walter Edward Guinness (Lord Moyne), former chief of the Irish House of Lords and British minister of state for the Middle East, is assassinated by terrorists in Cairo, Egypt.

1945

February 24: Ahmed Maher Pasha, Egyptian premier, is murdered in Cairo by a terrorist.

April 28: Deposed Italian dictator Benito Mussolini, Clara Petacci, his mistress, and several Fascist followers, are shot to death by Italian Communists as they attempt to flee to Switzerland.

April 29: The bodies of dictator Benito Mussolini, his mistress, Clara Petacci, and some of Mussolini's Black Shirt followers—all having been executed by parti-

sans—are strung up by the heels from the girders of a gas station in Milan, a gruesome end to Fascist terrorism in Italy.

May 15: Mrs. Panta Lou Liles is found raped and murdered in her Tulsa, Oklahoma, home, her body reduced to pulp after the so-called Tulsa Bludgeon Killer struck her repeatedly with a blunt instrument.

June 7: Leroy Benton, a black cafe porter, is arrested by Tulsa Police and charged with the "bludgeon murders" of recent years; Benton, after being grilled, confesses to murdering Mrs. Panta Lou Liles two months earlier, but he later recants his confession. He is convicted and sent to prison for life.

October 3: Alcide De Gaspari, prime minister of Italy, is the target of an unsuccessful assassination attempt.

December 7: Mustafa an-Nahhas Pasha, prime minister of Egypt, is the target of several attempts on his life in Cairo by terrorists.

1946

February: Lou Denton and his girlfriend, Irma Black, parked on Morris Lane, a mile west of Texarkana, Texas, are attacked and the girl raped before the assailant flees.

March 24: Richard Griffin and his girlfriend, Polly Ann Moore, parked on North Park Road, outside of Texarkana, Texas, are attacked. Griffin is shot to death, and Moore is raped and then also shot to death. The bodies are discovered the following day, the murders attributed to the same person who assaulted Lou Denton and Irma Black a month earlier. The unknown terrorist is called the "Lover's Lane Murderer."

March: The Mink Slide area of Columbia, Tennessee, erupts into riots after blacks shoot four policemen whom they mistake for a rampaging white mob. Police, later accused of causing considerable damage in the Negro section, round up 104 blacks, killing 2 who reportedly try to escape. Two blacks are convicted of attempted murder and sent to prison.

April 14: Paul Martin and his girlfriend, Betty Jo Booker, after parking a car on the North Park Road, outside of Texarkana, Texas, close to where two others have been murdered three weeks earlier, are attacked by the "Lover's Lane Murderer." Martin is shot and killed, three bullets fired into his back. Booker is raped before being savagely slashed to death.

May 3: A bullet smashes through a window of Virgil Starks' home, ten miles outside of Texarkana, Texas, mortally wounding him. His wife is struck by two more bullets but manages to flee to the home of a neighbor. The shooting is attributed to the "Lover's Lane Murderer."

May 7: With more than 1,000 armed deputies searching for the Texarkana, Texas, terrorist, a drifter wearing good clothes and carrying cash steps in front of a fast-moving train and is killed. He bears no identification and will never be given a name. Nearby, a car, stripped of its tires, is found burning. Police surmise that the suicidal stranger is the "Lover's Lane Murderer," who has ended his life before being trapped by lawmen closing in on his trail.

June 9: Rama VIII (Ananda Mahidol), king of Siam (Thailand), is shot and killed in his palace in Bangkok by unknown terrorists.

July 26: Roger Malcolm and George Dorsey, two twenty-seven-year-old black men accused of attacking a former employer, are, along with their wives, shot to death by a white mob of about twenty unmasked men near Monroe, Georgia.

December 27: Emir Mohammed Zeinati is slain by terrorists in Palestine.

1947

May 5: Ernest Bevin, British secretary of state for foreign affairs, is the target of an unsuccessful attempt on his life in England. Anthony Eden, who has earlier held Bevin's post, also escapes an assassination attempt in England.

July 19: Aung San, head of the anti-Fascist People's Freedom League and virtual prime minister of the interim Burmese government, is slain by terrorists led by U. Saw, former prime minister.

July 25: Three men skyjack a Rumanian plane to Canakkale Province, Turkey. One crew member is killed.

September 12: Political leader Jan Masaryk is the target of an unsuccessful assassination attempt in Czechoslovakia.

September 23: Paul I, king of Greece, is the target of an unsuccessful assassination attempt in Greece.

October 7: Paul Ramadier, former French prime minister, is the target of an unsuccessful assassination attempt in France.

1948

January 6: A middle-aged man wearing a white smock and an armband labeled "SANITATION," enters the manager's office of a branch of the Teikoku Bank in Tokyo, introducing himself as Dr. Jiro Yamaguchi, and saying he has come from General Douglas MacArthur's headquarters (MacArthur is then the Allied Governor of post–World War II Japan), and that he has instructions from the Americans to administer medicine to the bank's employees to prevent them from contracting dysentery, then attacking Tokyo in epidemic proportions. The visitor pours a mixture containing potassium cyanide into teacups, ordering the employees to drink the "medicine." Of the fifteen bank employees immediately stricken by the poison, twelve die. The terrorist, who has used the same ruse twice earlier in other Tokyo banks, then collects 180,000 yen (roughly $600) and flees. Hirasawa Sadamichi, fifty-seven, an artist living in Otaru, is later arrested and charged with the mass murders and robbery. He is convicted and sentenced to death, but he remains on death row for thirty-two years because there is some doubt as to his being the actual criminal. Hirasawa will die on May 10, 1987, in a medical detention center in Hachioji.

January 30: India's great leader Mohandas Karamchand (Mahatma) Gandhi, is slain in New Delhi, India, by political terrorist Nathuram Vnayak Godse, and others.

February 17: Yahya Mahmud al-Mutawakkil (Mohammed ton Yahya), imam (ruler) of Yemen, is killed in Yemen by terrorists.

March 3: Leroy Benton's murder conviction as the "Tulsa Bludgeon Killer," is overturned by the Oklahoma Criminal Court of Appeals on grounds that he had been coerced by "third degree" methods. Benton goes to Hammond, Indiana.

April 6: A Czechoslovakian plane is skyjacked by seventeen people (with the pilot and two crew members participating) fleeing Communist domination, the plane later landing in the U.S. zone of Germany.

April 9: Terrorists slay Jorge Elicer Gaitán, Columbian presidential candidate, in Columbia.

April 20: Union leader Walter Reuther is the target of an unsuccessful assassination attempt by labor terrorists in Detroit, Michigan.

May 3: A bomb is sent to Captain Roy Alexander Farran, one-time British officer in Palestine; his brother, Rex Farran, opens the package containing the bomb and is killed. The bomb is traced to the Israeli terrorist organization known as the Stern Gang.

May 4: Two men fleeing Communist domination skyjack a Czechoslovakian plane and force it to land in the U.S. zone in Germany.

June 4: Two men skyjack a Yugoslavian plane flying from Belgrade to Sarajevo and force it to land in Bari, Italy.

June 17: A Soviet-Rumanian Airways C-47 is skyjacked to Salzburg, Austria.

June 30: A Bulgarian Junkers 52 flying from Varna to Sofia, Bulgaria, is skyjacked by several men and forced to land in Istanbul, Turkey. The pilot is killed and two members of the crew are wounded.

July 2: Four women are attacked in their beds in Tulsa, Oklahoma, three of them beaten to death. Their killer, thought to be the "Tulsa Bludgeon Killer," is never found.

July 16: Chinese skyjackers take over a Cathay Pacific Catalina flying boat, but the crew resists; the pilot and copilot are killed. The plane crashes, killing twenty-five people. Only one of the skyjackers survives.

September 4: A Communist-sponsored concert in Peekskill, New York, erupts into riot when American Legionnaires, Westchester police, and anti-Communists attack the Communists and their supporters. Dozens of cars are damaged and scores of persons are injured.

September 12: Eight people take control of a Greek Dakota plane flying from Athens to Salonika, Greece. They force the plane to land in Tetovo, Yugoslavia.

September 17: Count Folkke Bernadotte of Wisborg, a mediator for the United Nations who has arranged for a truce between Israelis and Arabs in Palestine, is slain by Israeli terrorists in Jerusalem. (The Stern Gang is suspected of committing the assassination.)

December 28: Mahmoud Nurkrashy Pasha, premier of Egypt, is killed in Egypt by members of the Muslim Brotherhood, a secret terrorist organization attempting to overthrow the government.

1949

January 4: Twenty-two persons, including pilot Milos Kuhn, skyjack a Hungarian plane flying from Peos to Budapest, Hungary, forcing it to land in the U.S. zone in Germany.

January 30: Six skyjackers take a China National Aviation Corp. airplane flying from Shanghai to Taingtao, China, forcing it to land in Tainan, China. Passengers are held for over a month before being released. The plane is retained by the skyjackers.

February: Hasan al-Banna, Egyptian politician who has established the Muslim Brotherhood, is killed in a plot involving the Egyptian administration.

April 26: Elihu H. Bailey, mayor of Evarts, Kentucky, is the target of an unsuccessful assassination plot by bootleggers, who try to murder Bailey with dynamite.

April 29: Skyjackers take a Soviet-Rumanian Dakota jet flying from Timisoara to Bucharest, Rumania, to Salonika, Greece, where three persons are given political asylum.

May 7: The first bomb placed within a commercial airline explodes over the Philippines, killing thirteen persons. Terrorist Crispin Vergo will be sent to prison for planting the bomb on board the Philippines Airlines jet, which was en route from Daet to Manila.

August 14: Terrorist Fadallah Abu Mansur kills Colonel Husni Zaim in Syria.

September 5: Howard Unruh, a decorated World War II veteran, goes berserk and terrorizes a section of Camden, New Jersey, by shooting victims on the streets at random, killing thirteen persons within twelve minutes before barricading himself in his house. He later surrenders to police and is confined for life in an insane asylum.

September 16: Five men skyjack a LOT Polish plane flying from Gdansk to Lodz. It lands at Nykoeping Military airfield, sixty-five miles south of Stockholm, Sweden.

November 15: Nathuram Vinayak Godse, the terrorist who assassinated Mohandas (Mahatma) Gandhi on January 30, 1948, is executed. The assassination of Gandhi will be portrayed in the 1963 film, *Nine Hours to Rama*, with Horst Buchholz essaying Godse and J. S. Casshyap in the role of Gandhi.

December 9: Four skyjackers take over a Soviet-Rumanian DC-3, scheduled to fly from Sibiv to Bucharest, Rumania. They kill a security guard before landing in Belgrade, Yugoslavia.

December 16: Sixteen skyjackers take a Polish plane flying from Lodz to Gdansk. It lands in Roenna, Bornholm Island, Denmark.

1950

March 24: Three Czechoslovakian DC-3 planes are skyjacked and all land in the U.S. zone in Germany.

March 29: George Peter Metesky, New York's "Mad Bomber," plants a bomb at Grand Central Station, but police manage to defuse the device before it can explode.

April 13: A bomb placed in a towel holder in the lavatory of a British European airliner bound from London to Paris explodes and injures one passenger.

August 11: Two skyjackers compel the pilot of a Czechoslovakian transport plane to land in Pottmes, in the U.S. zone in Germany.

October 31: Terrorist Ahmad al-Barazi assassinates Colonel Same Al-Hinnawi in Lebanon.

November 1: Puerto Rican terrorists Griselio Torresola and Oscar Collazo attempt to assassinate President Harry Truman in Washington, D.C., but the president's guards kill Torresola and wound Collazo, who is sentenced to death. Leslie Coffelt, one of Truman's guards, is killed in the shootout, which takes place in front of Blair House in Washington, D.C. Truman will commute Collazo's death penalty to life imprisonment. Collazo will be freed in September 1979 by President Jimmy Carter.

November 13: Colonel Carlos Delgado Chalbaud, president of Venezuela, is slain by terrorists in Caracas.

1951

March 8: General Ali Razmara, prime minister of Iran, is assassinated by terrorists in Iran.

July 16: Riad Al-Sulh (Riad Solh Bey), prime minister of Lebanon, is assassinated.

July 20: Abdullah (Abdul ibn Hussein, Abd Allah ibn al-Husayn), king of Jordan, is assassinated by Palestinian terrorists.

October 16: Liaquat Ali Khan, prime minister of Pakistan, is murdered in Pakistan by terrorists.

1952

February 16: Hussein Fatemi, Iran's minister of foreign affairs, is assassinated in Iran.

September 25: Gangs of Mau Mau terrorists attack fellow blacks in the Kenya village of Timau, setting fire to the place and slaughtering 120 cattle in an effort to intimidate villagers into joining their secret criminal society.

November 26: Tom Mbotela, a black councillor in Nairobi City, is murdered by Mau Mau terrorists after having publicly denounced the secret society.

December 30: An Tie Cho skyjacks a Philippines DC-3 traveling from Laong to Aparii, killing the pilot and purser, and demanding to go to Red China. The co-pilot lands the plane at Quemoy and Tie Cho is arrested.

1953

January 11: George Peter Metesky, New York's "Mad Bomber," explodes a bomb in New York's Pennsylvania Station, injuring several people.

March 26: Mau Mau terrorists attack and capture the police station at Naivashi, Kenya, slaughtering all the officers and their families.

April 15: Juan Domingo Perón, president of Argentina, is the target of a failed assassination attempt in Argentina.

April: Mau Mau leader Jomo Kenyatta and other leaders of the secret criminal society are identified and tried. Kenyatta is given a seven-year prison sentence.

September 11: Sidi Muhammad ben Moulay Arafa, sultan of Morocco, is the target of a failed assassination attempt in Morocco by Allal ben Abdallah, a Moroccan terrorist who is shot during the attack.

1954

March 1: Puerto Rican nationalists terrorize the U.S. House of Representatives in Washington, D.C., by spraying gunfire into the assembly, injuring Congressmen Alvin Morell Bentley, Clifford Davis, George Hyde Fallon, Benton Franklin Jensen, and Kenneth Allison Roberts. The attackers, including Lolita Lebron, are sent to prison.

March 22: Sir Winston Churchill, prime minister of England, is the target of a failed assassination attempt when a bomb arrives in the mail at 10 Downing Street, London. It is disarmed.

August 5: Carlos Lacerda, an outspoken journalist who has openly criticized the Brazilian government, is injured during a failed assassination attempt in Brazil by terrorists thought to be backed by the regime in power. An air force major accompanying Lacerda is killed.

October 27: Gamal Abdel Nasser, president of Egypt, is the target of a failed assassination attempt in Egypt.

1955

January 2: Jose Antonio Remon, president of Panama, is visiting a Panama race track when he is shot dead by machine gun fire sprayed by terrorists.

March 12: Motilal Nehru, prime minister of India, is the target of an unsuccessful assassination attempt in India.

April 2: Sir Robert Armitage, governor of Cyprus, is the target of a failed assassination attempt in Cyprus.

April 11: A bomb placed in the wheel well of an Air India Constellation jet explodes over Great Naturna Island in the South China Sea, killing sixteen. Three passengers survive.

April 22: Lieutenant Colonel Adan Al-Malki, ruler of Syria, is assassinated in Syria by terrorist members of the Syrian army.

May 7: Reverend George W. Lee, a fifty-one-year-old Negro preacher who refuses to withdraw his name from a voting list, is shot to death by Ku Klux Klan members in Bezoni, Mississippi.

May 14: Konrad Adenauer, chancellor of Germany, is the target of an unsuccessful assassination attempt in Germany.

June 16: Juan Perón, president of Argentina, is the target of an unsuccessful assassination attempt in Argentina.

June 25: William Vacanarat Shadrach Tubman, president of Liberia, is the target of an unsuccessful assassination attempt in Liberia.

July 14–17: Following a terrorist bomb explosion on Bastille Day that destroys a cafe in Casablanca, Morocco, killing six Europeans, widespread rioting ensues for three days.

August 6: Lamar D. Smith, a sixty-three-year-old Negro who has been encouraging blacks to register to vote, is shot to death by white supremacists on the courthouse lawn of Brookhaven, Mississippi.

August 31: Emmett Louis Till, a fifteen-year-old black youth who has reportedly whistled at an attractive white woman, is shot to death by white supremacists and his body thrown into the Tallahatchie River near Greenwood, Mississippi.

November 1: Jack Gilbert Graham, in order to collect insurance on his mother's life, plants a bomb on a passenger plane that explodes over a Colorado beet farm, killing all forty-four persons on board, including Graham's mother. Graham will be convicted and executed.

November 17: Hussein Ala, premier of Iran, is the target of an unsuccessful assassination attempt in Iran.

1956

February 28: Mao Tse-tung, Communist dictator of China, is the target of an unsuccessful assassination attempt in China.

June 26: Fulgencio Batista, dictator and president of Cuba, is the target of an unsuccessful assassination attempt in Havana, Cuba.

September 21: Anastasio Somoza, president and dictator of Nicaragua, is fatally shot by terrorists in León, Nicaragua. He will die on September 29, 1956.

October 10: Chinese triads in Hong Kong create riots that last for several days, committing many murders and causing more than $25 million in damages.

October 26: Dedan Kimathi, the last of the important Mau Mau leaders still at large, and who has been one of the most ruthless mass murderers of the secret criminal society in Kenya, is captured. He is later executed for his countless murders and the Mau Mau movement is broken (10,527 Mau Maus have been killed, and an equal number of blacks killed by Mau Maus, as well as thirty-two white settlers in the five-year reign of terror in Kenya).

1957

February 23: Ngo Dinh Diem, president of South Vietnam, is the target of an unsuccessful assassination attempt by Communist terrorists.

March 13: Fulgencio Batista, dictator and president of Cuba, is the target of an unsuccessful assassination attempt in Cuba.

April 17: Nnamdi Azikiwe, premier of the Eastern Region of Nigeria, is the target of a failed assassination attempt by terrorists.

May 25: Kliment Yefremovich Voroshilov, chairman of the Russian presidium, is the target of an unsuccessful assassination attempt in Indonesia.

July 12: Mohammed Zahir Shah, king of Afghanistan, along with Sadar Mohammed Daud Khan, the country's prime minister, are the targets of unsuccessful assassination attempts in Afghanistan.

July 26: Carlos Castillo Armas, president of Guatamala, is slain by one of his own guards in Guatamala City.

August 4: Three men—Clyde Bates, Manuel Chavez, and Manuel Hernandez—firebomb a neighborhood bar in Los Angeles, California, killing six people. All

three men will be convicted of murder on August 16, 1958.

December 1: Terrorists attack A. Sukarno (Kusnasosro), president of Indonesia, in Jakarta, Indonesia, spraying the president's entourage with gunfire and hurling grenades into the group. Sukarno escapes injury, but ten other persons are killed, including the terrorists.

1958

January 23: More than 100 persons are killed in widespread street rioting in Caracas, Venezuela, as militants oppose the dictatorship of General Marcos Perez Jimenez, whose regime will be toppled.

February 8: Jacques Soustelle, minister of information for France, is the target of a failed assassination attempt. Another attempt by terrorists will be made on Soustelle's life on September 15, 1958.

July 14: Faisal III, king of Iraq, is assassinated at the Baghdad palace, along with most of his top aides and advisers in a coup led by General Abdul Karim Kassem (Qassim).

August 12: Twenty-one segregationists are arrested outside Central High School in Little Rock, Arkansas, for refusing an order to disperse when protesting integration by black students.

September 20: Rev. Martin Luther King, Jr., civil rights leader, is the target of an unsuccessful assassination attempt in New York City.

1959

April 10: Six skyjackers force a Haitian DC-3 traveling from Auxcayes to Port-au-Prince to fly to Cuba. The pilot is killed and the copilot takes the plane to Havana.

April 12: James Lindsay Almond, Jr., governor of Virginia, is the target of an unsuccessful assassination attempt, possibly by segregationists.

April 16: Three Cubans skyjack a Cuban Aerovias DC-3 flying from Havana to the Isle of Pines, landing the plane in Miami, where the skyjackers are taken into custody.

April 25: Antonio Rodrigues Diaz, a general under the deposed Cuban dictator Fulgencio Batista, and several others, skyjack a Cuban Vicker Viscount flying from Varadero Beach to Havana, ordering the pilot to fly to Miami, Florida. The plane, lacking fuel, lands at Key West, Florida.

September 25: Solomon West Ridgeway Dias Bandaranaike, prime minister of Ceylon, is assassinated in Colombo.

September 26: Hurricane Vera ravishes Nagoya, Japan, killing more than 5,000 persons, prompting scores of criminals to rape and loot at will. Police arrive to shoot and kill at least 100 looters and rapists.

1960

January 6: A National Airlines jet, flying from New York to Miami, explodes over Bolivia, North Carolina, and crashes after a passenger sets off a dynamite bomb in the forward fuselage. Thirty-four persons are killed.

February 18: Norodom Sihanouk, king of Cambodia, is the target of a failed assassination attempt in Cambodia.

March 8: Felton Turner, a twenty-seven-year-old Negro accused of improprieties with white women, is abducted outside of Houston, Texas, by four members of the Ku Klux Klan and hanged by his heels from a tree, while a series of KKK's is carved into his chest and stomach.

March 9: A. Sukarno, president of Indonesia, is the target of a failed assassination attempt in Indonesia.

March 28: Arturo Frondizi, president of Argentina, is the target of a failed assassination attempt in Argentina.

April 9: Hendrik Frensch Verwoerd, prime minister of South Africa, is critically wounded by gunshots fired by a white farmer opposed to apartheid, in Johannesburg. He will survive.

April 28: A bomb explodes in the cockpit of a Linea Aeropostal jet bound from Caracas to Puerto Ayacucho, Venezuela. Thirteen people are killed.

June 17: Japanese socialist leader Jotaro Kawakami is stabbed to death in Japan.

June 24: Romulo Betancourt, president of Venezuela, is wounded by a bomb set off by terrorists in Caracas. One of Betancourt's aides is killed; many others are wounded.

July 8: Patrice Lumumba, prime minister of the Congo, is the target of an unsuccessful assassination attempt in the Congo. It is later claimed that the CIA has been behind this murder plot.

July 14: Nobusake Kishi, premier of Japan, is stabbed in a failed attempt to assassinate him in Japan.

July 19: Alex Hildebrant skyjacks a Trans-Australia Electra L-188 headed for Brisbane, Australia. He is overpowered by the copilot and taken into custody in Singapore, and imprisoned.

August 29: Hazza Majali, premier of Jordan, and ten others are killed when terrorists bomb government offices in Amman, Jordan.

September 15: Patrice Lumumba, prime minister of the Congo, is the target of an unsuccessful assassination attempt in the Congo. It is later claimed that the CIA has been behind this second attempt on Lumumba's life.

October 12: Inejiro Asanuma, secretary-general of the Socialist Party in Japan, is stabbed to death by a terrorist.

October 29: A Cubana DC-3 is skyjacked by nine men who shoot and kill a security guard. The plane lands in Key West, Florida. The pilot, copilot, and one passenger are injured.

December 8: Five skyjackers take over a domestic Cuban flight, but the pilot crash-lands. One is killed and four are injured.

1961

January 1: Two skyjackers wave pistols at the pilot of a Cubana domestic flight in the Havana terminal, forcing the plane to fly to New York. The skyjackers are Batista supporters fleeing Communist Cuba and dictator Fidel Castro.

January 17: Patrice Lumumba, prime minister of the Congo (now Zaire), is kidnapped by agents of President Joseph Kasavubu and is assassinated in the back of a truck in Katanga Province.

May 27: Imam Ahmed Ibn Yahya of Yemen is shot and critically wounded at Hodeida, but he will survive. Five terrorists making the attack receive the death penalty.

May 30: Rafael Leónidas Trujillo Molina, dictator of the Dominican Republic, is traveling in his car when he is shot to death from ambush by Pedro Cedeno and Amado Garcia in an unsuccessful coup.

May: Freedom Riders arrive in Alabama to aid blacks in securing their civil rights. One of their buses is burned in Anniston by KKK members. Another bus is boarded by KKK thugs who club and beat occupants, who suffer concussions and broken ribs and arms.

July 31: Bruce Britt skyjacks a DC-3 Chico, California, to San Francisco flight, shooting and injuring the pilot and a ticket agent. Britt will be arrested and imprisoned.

August 3: Leon Bearden, an unemployed used-car salesman, and his teenage son Cody skyjack a Continental Airlines jet in Phoenix, Arizona. The Beardens hold the passengers and crew hostage, demanding that they be flown to Cuba. Lawmen recapture the plane from the Beardens when it lands in El Paso, Texas. Leon Bearden is sent to prison for life.

August 9: Albert Cadon skyjacks a Pan American DC-8 with seventy-nine aboard, flying from Mexico City to Guatemala, ordering the pilot to land in Cuba. He is deported from Cuba back to Mexico, where he is imprisoned.

August 9: Five skyjackers take over a Cuban C-46 on its way to the Isle of Pines. The pilot and two others are killed, and six are wounded. The copilot makes a crash landing.

September 9: Charles de Gaulle, president of France, is the target of an unsuccessful assassination attempt in Paris, France. Six more attempts on de Gaulle's life will be made in 1962, three attempts in 1963, five attempts in 1964, and three attempts in 1965.

September 10: Three skyjackers skyjack a U.S.S.R. Yak-12 plane that crashes in Armenia, killing one of the skyjackers. The other two skyjackers are captured and put to death.

November 27: Five men skyjack a Venezuelan DC-6B on its way to Maracaibo. It lands in Curacao. The skyjackers will be extradited and imprisoned.

1962

April 13: David Healy and Leonard Oeth skyjack a chartered plane over Miami to Cuba. They will be deported back to the U.S. and imprisoned.

April 16: Edgar Da Silva skyjacks a Royal Dutch Airlines plane heading for Lisbon, demanding to go to East Berlin. The plane lands in Holland, where Da Silva is taken into custody.

May 22: A bomb placed inside the towel holder in the rear lavatory of a Continental Airlines jet bound from Chicago, Illinois, to Kansas City, Missouri, explodes and kills all forty-five persons on board.

September 30: Two persons are killed and more than seventy others are injured when a mob attacks U.S. marshals escorting Negro student James Meredith to the University of Mississippi during federally mandated intergration. A fifteen-hour attack by white supremacists is finally halted when 3,000 U.S. troops and the Mississippi National Guard are called to the scene.

December 6: An unsuccessful assassination attempt is made on the life of Teamster's president James Hoffa in Tennessee.

1963

January 13: Sylvanus Olympio, president of Togo, is assassinated at Lomé, Togo, by terrorists who have been former soldiers serving Olympio.

February 8: General Abdul Karim Kassem, prime minister of Iraq, is ousted and assassinated in a military coup in Baghdad, Iraq.

March 8: Members of the Front du Libération du Québec (FLQ) throw Molotov cocktails at military establishments in Canada, marking the start of a wave of FLQ bombings throughout the country.

April 1: Quinim Pholsena, foreign minister of Laos, is assassinated in Vietiane by Chy Kong, who leads a terrorist group and who later confesses to the murder.

April 11: Mohammed Khemisti, foreign minister of Algeria, is shot to death in Algiers, Algeria, by a Muslim terrorist.

April 20: An FLQ bomb explodes at an army recruiting center in Montreal, Canada, killing a guard.

June 12: Medgar W. Evers, Mississippi field secretary for the National Association for the Advancement of Colored People, is shot to death in front of his Jackson, Mississippi home. Though the assailant is never apprehended, the Ku Klux Klan is thought to be behind the murder. (Not until 1994 will Evers' killer, Byron de la Beckwith, be convicted of the terrorist murder.)

September 15: White supremacists thought to be members of the Ku Klux Klan bomb the 16th Street Baptist Church in Birmingham, Alabama, killing four black school girls.

November 2: Ngo Dinh Diem, president and dictator of South Vietnam, and his brother, Ngo Dinh Nhu, are murdered in the back of an armored personnel carrier by an unidentified South Vietnamese army officer, a secret agent and terrorist for the North Vietnamese Communists, according to one report.

November 22: U.S. President John Fitzgerald Kennedy is fatally shot by Lee Harvey Oswald in Dallas, Texas. Also wounded in the gunfire directed to the open-top presidential car is Texas Governor John B. Connally. Oswald will be shot and killed two days later by underworld character Jack Ruby, who is given the death penalty but dies of cancer in prison. Though the exhaustive Warren Commission Report later issued contends Oswald has acted alone, many believe that others have been involved in the conspiracy to kill Kennedy and that other shootists have been present in Dallas, who actually fired the fatal bullets into Kennedy. This was the contention of Oliver Stone's movie, *JFK*, which was widely criticized for being ambiguous and offering no new evidence to support the claim. (The assassination of Kennedy will receive more coverage than

any other act of terrorism in the twentieth century, so much so that a more detailed examination of this extraordinary case within these pages is precluded for reasons of space and the unnecessary exercise of repeating endless, oft-told theories.)

November 28: Six skyjackers take over a Venezuelan Convair twin engine plane, landing it in Trinidad, where the skyjackers are taken into custody. They will be extradicted and imprisoned.

1964

January 10: Provoked by inflammatory radio broadcasts, anti-American riots break out throughout Panama, in which dozens are killed.

February 4: Hassan II, king of Morocco, is the target of an unsuccessful assassination attempt in Morocco.

June 21: Three northern civil rights workers, Michael Schwerner, Andrew Goodman, and James Chaney, while traveling at night between Philadelphia and Meridian, Mississippi, are stopped by Neshoba County Deputy Sheriff Cecil R. Price, a Klan member, who turns the trio over to KKK leader Sam H. Bowers, Jr., and other Klan members. All three are shot and killed, their bodies dumped into shallow graves that have been prepared in advance of the premeditated murders.

July 1: Race riots take place in Philadelphia, Pennsylvania, in which 150 persons are injured and 165 (mostly blacks) are arrested for attacking police.

July 16: After a Negro youth is shot and killed for attacking a policeman in

Harlem, New York, widespread rioting and looting by blacks ensues. One looter will be killed, dozens arrested, and 140 others will be injured.

October 9: U.S. Air Force Lieutenant Colonel Michael Smolen is abducted in Caracas, Venezuela, by Castroite terrorists demanding the release of a terrorist held in Saigon, Vietnam. The prisoner's execution will be delayed and Smolen released.

October 20: In a startling verdict from an all-white Alabama jury, KKK members Sam. H. Bowers, Cecil R. Price, and five others are found guilty of conspiracy to murder the three civil rights workers (of CORE) on June 21, 1964. All seven will be sent to prison.

December 8: A dynamite charge apparently planted by a passenger who has insured himself for a large amount of money kills fifteen passengers aboard an ALAS Airline jet bound from Tipuani to LaPaz, Bolivia.

December 20: Simon Wiesenthal, the celebrated Nazi hunter, is the target of an unsuccessful assassination attempt in Vienna, Austria.

December 26: Ian Brady and his lover Myra Hindley, both sadistic killers, kidnap their third victim (two boys, John Kilbride and Keith Bennett, both twelve, having been earlier abducted and killed by the couple), ten-year-old Lesley Ann Downey, forcing her to pose nude before strangling her to death and burying her body on the Saddleworth Moors—the hatchet killings of the couple will be known as the "Moors Murders." The couple will go on to murder seventeen-year-old Edward Evans, before David Smith, Hindley's brother-in-law, turns the kidnapping killers over to police. Both Brady and Hindley will be sent to prison for life.

1965

January 21: Terrorists assassinate Hassan Ali Mansour (Ali Mansour), premier of Iran, in Teheran, Iran. All four assassins will be executed.

February 9: Colonel Harold Hauser, head of the U.S. military mission to Guatemala, is the target of an unsuccessful assassination attempt by terrorists of the Movimiento Revolucionario.

February 21: Malcolm X, a black nationalist leader, is shot to death during a meeting in New York, New York, by three Black Muslims, who are later sent to prison.

July 8: A Canadian Pacific airline flying over British Columbia crashes en route to Whitehouse in the Yukon. A bomb planted in the fuselage is blamed for the terrorist act that kills all fifty-two passengers on board.

July 20: General Maxwell D. Taylor is the target of an unsuccessful assassination attempt in Vietnam.

July 27: Fidel Castro, Communist dictator and premier of Cuba, is the target of an unsuccessful assassination attempt in Havana, Cuba, one which is later attributed to the CIA.

August 8: Widespread rioting in the Los Angeles suburb of Watts takes place. Blacks run amuck, starting hundreds of fires (even their own homes), then severing the hoses of firemen who arrive to fight the fires, stoning the firemen. Half the entire area will be gutted, 34 persons will die, and 1,032 will be injured. More than 4,000 blacks will be arrested and damages will exceed $34 million.

August 11: A widespread race riot in Cape Town, South Africa, results in seventeen blacks being killed and another fifty injured.

August 31: Harry S. Fergerstrom, armed with a knife and glass from a broken bottle, skyjacks a Hawaiian DC-3 scheduled to fly from Honolulu to Kauai, Hawaii. He orders the pilot to return to Honolulu, where he is taken into custody and sent to a correctional school.

October 11: Lawrence D. Heisler and Richard K. Boyd, both U.S. Navy seaman, skyjack an Aloha F-27 en route from Molokai, Hawaii, to Honolulu. They will be dishonorably discharged and imprisoned.

October 20: John Kilpatrick, president of the United Industrial Workers' Union, is fatally shot by Dana H. Nash, who will be sent to prison.

October 26: Luis Medina Perez attempts to skyjack a National L-188 with thirty-three aboard, heading from Miami to Key West, Florida. He uses a BB pistol to order the pilot to land in Cuba. He will later be found mentally incompetent.

October 29: Diosdado Macapagal, president of the Philippines, is the target of an unsuccessful assassination attempt in the Philippines.

November 17: Thomas H. Robinson, brandishing two revolvers, skyjacks a National DC-8 flight carrying ninety-one people from Houston to New Orleans. He orders the pilot to fly to Cuba. Robinson will later be sent to a correctional school.

1966

January 10: Negro activist Vernon Dahmer is killed by a Ku Klux Klan bomb in Hattiesburg, Mississippi.

January 15: Sir Abubakar Tafawa Balewa, prime minister of Nigeria, is assassinated in Nigeria.

January 29: Five Yugoslavian consulates in the U.S. are bombed by political dissidents.

March 27: Angel Betancourt Gueto, a flight engineer, attempts to flee Communist Cuba by skyjacking a Cubana IL-18 heading for Havana. After the plane lands in Cuba, the pilot and a guard are killed, and the copilot wounded. Gueto, who thinks he has landed in Miami, is captured.

May 6: An FLQ bomb explodes in a Quebec arms manufacturing plant, killing one employee, Therese Marin.

May 18: General Maximiliano Hernandez Martinez is assassinated in Honduras.

June 6: James Meredith, civil rights worker, is the target of a failed assassination attempt.

June 19: Arthur Calwell, head of the Labor Party, is the target of an unsuccessful assassination attempt in Australia by Peter R. Kocan, who will be sent to prison for life.

June 30: Thomas Albert Tarrant and Kathy Ainsworth, two anti-Semitic terrorists, attempt to plant a bomb at the home of a Jewish businessman in Meridian, Mississippi, but are interrupted by police. Ainsworth flees and is shot and killed.

July: Race riots in Chicago, Cleveland, and New York leave dozens injured.

September 6: Hendrik Frensch Verwoerd, prime minister of South Africa, is stabbed to death in parliament at Capetown, South Africa, by terrorist Dimitri Stifanos, who will be judged insane.

September 28: Maria Varrier and nineteen others skyjack an Argentine DC-4, which lands in the Falkland Islands. The three leaders of the skyjacking group are sentenced to death, the others imprisoned.

September 29: National Guardsmen are called into San Francisco to quell widespread race rioting, where dozens are injured.

November 13: A bomb blows up on the *Grand Integrity* five days after the ship sails from Portland, Oregon. Captain Ho Lien-Siu and a motorman are killed as they inspect the device just before it explodes, but the ship is not seriously damaged.

November 22: An Aden Airways jetliner crashes in Southern Yemen after an explosive device hidden in a piece of carry-on luggage is detonated. Twenty-eight persons are killed.

December 17: Homosexual serial killers Myron Lance and Walter Kelbach abduct, rape, and murder Stephen Shea, a Salt Lake City, Utah, service station attendant. They will go on to murder another service station attendant, a cab driver, and three persons in a bar before being apprehended and sent to prison for life.

1967

January 7: Army deserter Richard James Paris detonates a dynamite bomb with a .38-caliber pistol in the honeymoon suite of the Orbit Inn in Las Vegas, Nevada, killing himself, his wife, and five other newlyweds.

February 7: Terrorist Riyad Kamal Hajjaj skyjacks an Egyptian AN-24 domestic flight, forcing the plane to land in Jordan. Hajjaj will escape to Sweden, but will later be arrested and imprisoned for other crimes.

April 5: Hubert Humphrey, vice president of the U.S., is the victim of an apparent assassination plot during a visit to West Berlin by eleven terrorists, who are arrested.

April 19: Sheik Salem Al-Amoodi is assassinated in Aden.

June 2: Massive riots by students protesting the visit of the Shah of Iran result in widespread injuries and damage in Berlin. The riots are used by Ulrike Meinhof, a Marxist, and playboy student Berndt Andreas Baader to form the dreaded terrorist group known as the Baader-Meinhof Gang.

June 9: Charles Eustis Bohlen, U.S. Ambassador to France, is the target of a failed assassination attempt in Paris.

June 22: Roy Wilkins, civil rights leader, is the target of an unsuccessful assassination attempt in New York City.

June 25: Francois Duvalier, dictator and president of Haiti, is the target of a failed assassination attempt in Port-au-Prince.

June 30: Francois Bodenan skyjacks a private United Kingdom jet carrying Moise Tshombe, former prime minister of the Congo. The plane lands in Algeria where Tshombe is held captive until his death on June 29, 1969.

July 12–18: Over a six-day period, 127 separate race riots break out across the U.S. They will leave dozens injured and millions of dollars in property damage.

July 23: Angered over police raids on black nightclubs breaking mandatory closing times, Negro rioters take to the streets of Detroit, Michigan, and begin looting stores. Police and National Guardsmen battle the enormous black crowds, and thirty-three blacks and ten whites are killed, with more than 600 injured and 3,800, mostly blacks, arrested. Property damage attributed to black rioters is estimated at $46 million.

August 26: George Lincoln Rockwell, head of the Nazi Party in the U.S., is slain in Virginia.

September 28: Levi Eshkol, prime minister of Israel, is the target of an unsuccessful assassination attempt in Israel.

October 12: A British European Airways jet flying over the Mediterranean Sea explodes in midair when a bomb planted in the passenger cabin goes off. Sixty-six lives are lost.

November 20: Louis G. Babler takes control of a chartered Piper Apache, taking three persons from Hollywood, Florida, to Bimini, Bahama Islands. He demands that the plane be flown to Cuba, where he will escape.

1968

January 16: Colonel John D. Webber, Jr., commander of a U.S. special service squad in Guatemala, and Lieutenant Commander Ernest A. Munro, are shot to death by terrorists in Guatemala.

February 9: William Clark, a Marine, skyjacks a Pan American military chartered DC-6, flying from South Vietnam to Hong Kong. Clark will be court-martialed and sentenced, but charges will be dropped when he is diagnosed as schizophrenic.

February 18: James Boynton skyjacks a private plane to Cuba, but he is returned by the Castro government and is sent to prison.

February 18: One person is killed and fourteen others are injured when a terrorist bomb explodes in the basement of the Yugoslav ambassador's home in Paris, France.

February 21: Lawrence M. Rhodes skyjacks a Delta DC-8 flying from Tampa to West Palm Beach, Florida, demanding that he be taken to Cuba. He will be committed to a mental institution.

April 3: Four members of the Baader-Meinhof gang—Berndt Andreas Baader, Gudrun Ensslin, Thorwald Proll and Horst Sohnlein, all heavily drugged, plant firebombs in Berlin's largest department stores. One bomb, planted in the toy department, causes a small fire that will be extinguished; another firebomb fails to ignite. All four terrorists will be captured and sent to prison for three years. All will be released on bond on June 13, 1969, to await an appeal hearing. They flee to France while Ulrike Meinhof, who emerges as the leader of the terrorist gang, begins organizing.

April 4: Civil rights leader Martin Luther King, Jr., is shot to death in Memphis, Tennessee, by James Earl Ray, who is sent to prison for life. Though many claim that Ray has not acted alone, no other conspirators are ever identified.

April 5–9: In response to the assassination of black leader Martin Luther King, Jr., Negro rioters swarm through the streets of Chicago, Baltimore, Washington, and Cincinnati, looting stores and attacking police and National Guardsmen. Thirty-one will die in the various city riots, and millions of dollars in damage will be done.

April 23–28: Students belonging to the radical Students for a Democratic Society, seize five buildings on the Columbia University campus in New York. After six days of occupation, the students are dispersed by police. More than 130 persons are injured and 600 are arrested.

May 6: A drunken patron ejected from a Fort Worth, Texas, nightclub returns to firebomb the place, killing seven customers and horribly burning six others.

May 21–22: After four students are suspended for their roles in the April Columbia University riot in New York, SDS members seize the main classroom building on May 21, holding it for forty-eight hours before they are dislodged. Sixty-eight persons are injured, 177 more are arrested, and damage is put at $300,000.

June 5: Robert Francis Kennedy, U.S. senator from New York, is shot to death in Los Angeles by Sirhan Bishara Sirhan, a Palestinian terrorist. Sirhan will be sent to prison for life.

June 29: E. H. Carter, armed with a revolver, skyjacks a Southeast Airlines DC-3 carrying seventeen people from Miami to Key West, Florida, to Cuba, where he remains.

July 1: Mario Velasquez Fonseca skyjacks a Northwest Airlines B-727, carrying eighty-five passengers and crew, from Chicago to Cuba.

July 4: John H. Morris boards a TWA B-727 in Kansas City, telling the crew that he is carrying dynamite and will ignite the explosives unless he is taken to Cuba. When it is learned that he has no weapons, Morris is overpowered and later sent to prison.

July 12: A private Cessna-210 with two persons on board is skyjacked in Miami by Leonard S. Bendicks and taken to Cuba on his orders. The Castro government will return Bendicks to the U.S., where he will be imprisoned.

July 12: Boarding a Delta CV-880 in Baltimore, Oran D. Richards orders the pilot to fly to Cuba instead of Houston. Richards is later returned to the U.S., where he is judged insane and confined in an asylum.

July 22: Three Habash Front terrorists skyjack an El Al plane traveling from Rome to Tel Aviv, Israel, forcing the pilot to land in Algeria. They will be imprisoned.

July 27: Armed with a pistol, Rogelio Hernandez Leyva skyjacks a National Airlines DC-8, ordering the pilot to fly to Cuba with his fifty-seven passengers. Leyva, identified as a Communist terrorist, disappears after the plane arrives in Havana.

August 4: Willis Jesse and his three-year-old daughter board a chartered private plane in Naples, Florida. Jesse skyjacks the plane to Cuba. He is later returned, charged, convicted of kidnapping, and sent to prison.

Chronology

August 13: George Papadopoulis, premier of Greece, is the target of a failed assassination attempt in Greece.

August 21: Antonio LoBianco, twenty-nine, and Barbara Locci, who sit in a parked car in a cemetery fifteen miles outside of Florence, Italy, are shot and killed by a terrorist who will be dubbed the "Monster of Florence" and whose killings will be almost identical to New York's "3-X" and the Son of Sam (David Berkowitz), San Francisco's Zodiac, and the Texarkana, Texas, slayer of the 1940s. The "Monster of Florence" follows an identifiable pattern: After shooting his victims through car windows, he will use a scalpel to remove the sex organs of his female victims.

August 22: Bill McBride forces the pilot of a chartered Cessna-182, flying from Naples, Florida, to fly to Cuba, where he vanishes.

August 26: Thousands of anti-establishment youths, led by radical leftists Abbie Hoffman, Jerry Rubin, and others, begin three days of violent opposition to the Democratic National Convention then convening in Chicago, labeling the Democrats as being members of a "war party." The protestors hurl rocks, bricks, and other objects against police and National Guardsmen, as well as use razors affixed to their shoes to bloody the shins of officers. Police retaliate with mass clubbings. Hundreds on both sides are injured.

September 11: Charles Beasley skyjacks an Air Canada plane flying to Toronto, demanding to be flown to Cuba. He will be imprisoned.

September 20: Jose A. Suarez Garcia skyjacks an Eastern B-720, flying from San Juan, Puerto Rico, to Miami, Florida, with forty-six passengers on board, diverting it to Cuba, where he will vanish.

October 12: Captain Charles R. Chandler of the U.S. Army, is slain outside his home in Sao Paulo, Brazil, by Vanguarda Popular Revolucionaria (VPR) terrorists.

October 23: Anti-Castro El Poder Cubano terrorists are arrested in New York for attempting to assassinate the Cuban ambassador to the United Nations.

October 26: Three Croatian leaders opposed to communism are killed by Communist terrorists in Munich, Germany.

November 2: Roger A. Pastorcich takes control of an Eastern DC-9 with fifty-four persons on board, flying to Chicago from Birmingham, Alabama. His demand to be flown to South Vietnam is rejected. He will later be captured and placed in a juvenile detention center.

November 4: Raymond Johnson, Jr., skyjacks a National B-727 carrying sixty-five people from New Orleans to Miami, ordering the plane to fly to Cuba, where he will disappear.

November 22: Twelve people are killed and 52 more injured when a bomb explodes in Jerusalem's busiest open-air market.

November 23: Six Latin-Americans armed with four pistols skyjack an Eastern B-727 Chicago-to-Miami flight with ninety persons on board, taking the plane to Cuba, where they escape.

December 11: James and Gwendolyn Patterson, armed with a revolver, skyjack a St. Louis-to-Miami TWA B-727 flight carrying thirty-nine persons to Cuba, where they disappear.

December 14: Charles Senecal, director of Chanbly Transport, is the target of a terrorist bombing in Canada.

December 19: Thomas G. Washington, carrying a fake pistol and phony nitro, takes 142 passengers and nine crew members hostage when he skyjacks a Miami-bound Eastern DC-8 to Cuba. He will be returned to the U.S. and imprisoned.

December 20: The terrorist who would be called the Zodiac Killer, and whose body count would range between nine to more than forty (depending upon lawmen who credited killings to him), struck for the first time on a deserted road outside Vallejo, California, shooting and killing David Faraday, seventeen, and Bettilou Jenson, sixteen, as they sit in a parked car.

December 26: Two Habash Front terrorists, armed with hand grenades and small arms, attack an El Al jetliner in Athens, Greece, killing one Israeli passenger before being captured by police.

1969

January 2: Tyrone and Linda Austin, armed with a pistol, skyjack a 138-passenger Eastern DC-8 heading for Miami from New York. They order the pilot to fly to Cuba, where they escape. Tyrone Austin will later be killed in a bank robbery.

January 2: George Flamourides (AKA: G. Paravolidakis) skyjacks a Greek DC-6B flying to Athens, Greece. The plane lands in Cairo, where Flamourides is captured and imprisoned.

January 9: Ronald T. Bohle, wielding a knife, skyjacks a seventy-three–passenger Nassau-bound Eastern B-727 to Cuba. He will later be imprisoned.

January 11: Robert M. Helmey, brandishing a revolver, skyjacks a B-727 Jacksonville-to-Miami flight, taking twenty persons to Cuba. He will later be found insane and acquitted.

January 17: Kenneth E. McPeek takes over a Delta CV-880 en route from Detroit to Miami, carrying seventy-seven people. Wielding a shotgun, McPeek unsuccessfully attempts to force the pilot to fly to Cuba. He will be captured and imprisoned.

January 28: Clinton R. Smith and Byron V. Booth, armed with a revolver and dynamite, skyjack a National DC-8 Miami-bound flight with thirty-two persons aboard to Cuba. They will escape.

January 28: Larry F. Brooks, Noble B. Mason, and Everett L. White, wielding three pistols, skyjack an Eastern DC-8 Atlanta-to-Miami flight and its 105 passengers. They force the pilot to fly to Cuba, but they will later be imprisoned.

January 31: Allan C. Sheffield skyjacks fifty-five passengers on board a National DC-8 en route from San Francisco to Tampa, Florida, forcing it to land in Cuba. He will be arrested and imprisoned.

February 3: Dr. Eduardo Mondran, president of the Mozambique Liberation Front, is killed when he receives a bomb in the mail at Dar es Salaam, Tanzania.

February 3: Michael Anthony Peparo and Tasmin Rebecca Fitzgerald, armed with a knife and an aerosol insecticide cylinder, attempt to skyjack a National B-727 New York-to-Miami flight carrying seventy passengers and crew to Cuba. They will be arrested and sent to prison.

February 14: A number of people are injured and substantial damage is done when an FLQ bomb demolishes part of the Montreal Stock Exchange building.

February 18: Four Habash Front terrorists armed with guns and hand grenades attack an El Al jet in Zurich, Switzerland, killing the copilot and injuring five passengers. One skyjacker will be killed and the other three arrested and later imprisoned.

February 21: Two persons are killed and eight more are injured when a bomb explodes in a Jerusalem food store.

February 25: Lorenzo Ervin, Jr., uses a revolver to take over an Eastern DC-8 Atlanta-to-Miami flight carrying sixty-seven people and forces the pilot to land in Cuba. He will later be imprisoned.

March 1: Clay Shaw, a wealthy entrepreneur in New Orleans, is acquitted on charges of conspiring to assassinate President John F. Kennedy.

March 5: Anthony G. Bryant skyjacks a National B-727 New York-to-Miami flight carrying twenty-six people, threatening the pilot with a revolver and forcing him to fly to Cuba. Bryant will later be imprisoned.

March 17: Robert L. Sandlin, who will later be sent to an insane asylum, skyjacks a Delta DC-9 carrying sixty-three persons from Atlanta to Augusta, Georgia, diverting the plane to Cuba. Sandlin threatens the crew with a bomb that turns out to be a fake.

March 19: Dallas A. Dickey skyjacks a Delta CV-880, with ninety-seven people on board, scheduled to fly from New Orleans to Dallas, Texas. He orders the pilot to fly to Cuba. Dickey will later be sent to an insane asylum.

March 25: Luis A. Frese skyjacks a Delta DC-8 scheduled to fly 114 people to San Diego from Dallas, Texas. At gunpoint, Frese orders the pilot to fly to Cuba, where he will be imprisoned and die in his cell.

March 30: The New African Organization, a militant group in Detroit, Michigan, erupts in a gun battle after a meeting. One policeman is killed and four blacks are injured, while 135 others (mostly blacks) are arrested for rioting.

April 15: Terrorist Cameron David Bishop is placed on the FBI's Ten Most Wanted List for bombing a defense plant in Colorado in January 1969.

May 5: Jean P. Charrette and Alain Allard use two revolvers and a knife to skyjack a National B-727 flying from New York to Miami with seventy-five people on board, ordering the pilot to fly to Cuba. They will later be imprisoned in Canada.

May 13: Race rioting in Kuala Lampur, Malaysia, results in more than 100 deaths.

May 30: Terrance Niemeyer attempts to skyjack a Texas International CV-600 New Orleans–Alexandria, Louisiana, flight carrying forty-four people, to Cuba. Niemeyer, who falsely claims to have a hand grenade, will later be sent to an insane asylum.

June 17: William L. Brent uses a revolver to skyjack a TWA B-707 Oakland, California–New York flight carrying ninety people, to Cuba. He will escape.

June 26: Thoroughly drunk and wearing only shorts, a T-shirt, and sandals, Anthony Raymond boards an Eastern Airlines 727 in Miami. He suddenly flashes a penknife and is able to terrify the entire crew and passengers, although it was later admitted that he could easily have been overpowered. Once in the cockpit, Raymond orders the pilot to fly to Cuba, which he does.

Raymond is welcomed in Havana, but when he sobers up, he demands that he be returned to the U.S. When he does return, Raymond is sent to prison for fifteen years.

June 26: The Fuerzas Armadas Rebeldes (FAR) bombs fourteen minimax supermarkets in Argentina, causing $3 million in damage.

June 26: Joseph C. Crawford skyjacks a Continental DC-9 destined for Midland from El Paso, Texas. Brandishing a knife, he forces the pilot to land in Cuba. He will be returned to the U.S. and imprisoned.

July 4: The Zodiac Killer shoots and kills a nineteen-year-old girl and wounds her companion as they sit in a car near San Francisco. The terrorist will later stab Cecelia Shephard twenty-four times in the back when killing her, and carve an outline of a cross on her skin. Zodiac still later tries to kill a cabdriver who survives and gives the only description of this maniac—a man approximately five feet eight inches tall, with short reddish brown hair and thick glasses. Zodiac will send dozens of taunting letters to police and leave cryptograms at the scenes of his many murders, one reading: "I like killing people because it is so much fun." By 1975, Zodiac will cease to communicate with police and authorities will believe him dead or committed to an insane asylum. San Francisco police estimate his murders at six, but Don Striepeke, sheriff of Sonoma County, believes the Zodiac is responsible for more than forty slayings.

July 5: Tom Mboya, minister of economic planning and development in Kenya, is assassinated in Nairobi by members of the Kikuyu Tribe. Some fear that the killing signals a rebirth of the terrorist organization, Mau Mau.

July 30: A. H. Meyer, U.S. ambassador to Japan, is the target of a failed assassination attempt when he is accosted by a Japanese citizen armed with a knife in Tokyo.

July 31: Lester E. Perry, wielding a razor blade, skyjacks a TWA B-727 flying 123 passengers from Pittsburgh to Los Angeles, forcing the pilot to fly to Cuba, where he will escape.

August 5: A Philippines Airlines jet explodes over Zamboanaga, Philippines. The bomb is detonated in one of the restrooms, killing the person setting it off and injuring four others.

August 5: John S. McCreery attempts to skyjack an Eastern DC-9 flying from Philadelphia to Tampa, Florida. McCreery, who wields a knife and a razor blade, will later be sent to an insane asylum.

August 29: Leila A. Khaled and Salim K. Essawai of the PFLP skyjack a TWA B-707 flying from Rome to Athens with 127 persons on board. Armed with pistols and hand grenades, the terrorists order the pilot to fly to Syria. In Damascus, two passengers are exchanged for two Syrian pilots. Everyone aboard deplanes and the skyjackers demolish the cockpit before escaping.

September 3: Three terrorists of ELF skyjack an Ethiopian DC-6 flying from Addis Ababa to Dijibouti. When the plane lands at Aden, South Yemen, one skyjacker is shot and the other two captured.

September 4: Charles Burke Elbrick, U.S. ambassador to Brazil, is abducted in Rio de Janiero by MR-8 (Revolutionary Movement of the Eighth) and ALN terrorists who demand that several political prisoners be freed and the group's manisfesto be printed. Some of the demands will be met and Elbrick set free.

September 21: Muslims and Hindus in western India riot over alleged mistreatment of sacred Hindu cows and Hindu spiritual leaders by Muslims. More than 1,000 persons are killed.

September 26: The trial of the so-called "Chicago Eight" (Jerry Rubin, Abbie Hoffman, Rennie Davis, David Dellinger, Thomas Hayden, John Froines, Lee Weiner, and Bobby Seale of the Black Panther Party) commences in Chicago before Judge Julius Hoffman. The defendants are charged with intent to commit a conspiracy and inciting to riot prior to and during the Democratic National Convention. The five-month trial is a farce, with the defendants and their attorneys creating mayhem and confusion in the court.

September 29: Two Habash Front terrorists skyjack a TWA plane flying from Rome to Lodi, Italy, forcing it to land in Damascus, where two Israeli passengers are freed in exchange for the release of two Syrian pilots being held in Israel.

October 6: José Strassle, son of the Swiss consul in Cali, Colombia, and Hermann Bluff, consul secretary, are kidnapped by a terrorist group called the Invisible Ones but are later set free. Officials deny media reports that a ransom of several thousand dollars has been paid.

October 17: Abdi Rashid Ali Shermarke, president of Somalia, is assassinated at Las Anos, Somalia.

October 21: Henry Shorr skyjacks a Pan American B-720 scheduled to carry its twenty-eight passengers from Mexico City to Merida, Mexico. Shorr wields a revolver to divert the plane to Cuba. He will commit suicide a year later.

November 10: Fourteen-year-old David Booth, wielding a knife, attempts to skyjack a Delta DC-9 en route from Cincinnati to Chicago, with 75 persons on board. Booth demands to be flown to either Sweden or Mexico but he is unsuccessful and is later sent to a juvenile detention center.

November 27: Two Jordanian terrorists launch a grenade attack on the El Al Airlines office in Athens, Greece, killing a Greek child and wounding thirteen others.

December 2: Benny R. Hamilton, armed with a knife, skyjacks a TWA B-707, flying from San Francisco to Philadelphia, forcing the pilot to fly to Cuba. He will later be imprisoned in the U.S.

December 12: Red Brigadists explode a bomb in the Piazza Fontana, in Milan, Italy, that kills sixteen people. Seven persons are later put on trial, five acquitted, and on March 20, 1981, two others sentenced to prison on lesser charges.

December 21: Three Habash Front terrorists plan to skyjack a TWA plane arriving at Athens, Greece, from Tel Aviv, but they are apprehended by police and will be imprisoned until July 1970.

December 22: A bomb explodes in a lavatory on an Air Vietnam jet, killing thirty-two people near Nha Trang, South Vietnam. The landing brakes are damaged by the bomb and the plane careens into a school when landing.

1970

January 6: Anton Funjek skyjacks a Delta DC-9 taking sixty passengers from Orlando to Jacksonville, Florida. Brandishing a knife, Funjek attempts to force the pilot to land in Switzerland. He will later be imprisoned.

January 8: Christian Belon "to spite Americans and Israelis for their aggression in the Middle East," skyjacks a TWA 707 carrying twenty persons from Paris to Rome. Belon orders the pilot at gunpoint to fly to Beirut, where he will be arrested and imprisoned.

January 30: A state of siege is declared in Guatemala following the attempted assassination of a presidential candidate and the murder of a newspaper editor opposed to communism by Communist terrorists.

February 10: A bus at the airport in Munich, Germany, is attacked with grenades by three Arab terrorists. An Israeli citizen is killed and eleven other passengers are injured.

February 15: Some of the members of the original "Chicago Eight" trial in Chicago are acquitted of the charge to commit a conspiracy before and during the 1968 Democratic National Convention, but Jerry Rubin, Abbie Hoffman, Rennie Davis, David Dellinger, and Thomas Hayden are convicted of crossing a state line to incite a riot. Further, Judge Hoffman has sentenced several of the defendants, along with their attorneys, William Kunstler and Leonard Weinglass, to long terms for contempt of court. None of the terms are served. A federal district judge will overturn the convictions on a technicality—that Hoffman waited too long to impose sentencing.

February 21: A Swissair jet flying from Zurich, Switzerland, to Tel Aviv, Israel, is blown up in midair, claiming forty-seven lives. It is believed that the bomb has been planted by Abu Ibrahim of the Popular Front for Liberation of Palestine (PFLP).

February 27: Fuentes Mohr, Guatemalan foreign minister, is abducted by leftist FAR terrorists. He will be released after a terrorist is set free from prison.

March 3: Takeshi Okamoto, a fanatical member of the terrorist Japanese Red Army, boards a Japanese jet and, brandishing a sword, forces the pilot to fly to North Korea.

March 6: Sean M. Holly, U.S. labor attaché in Guatemala, is abducted by FAR terrorists and is later released when three terrorists are set free from prison.

March 11: Nobuo Okuchi, Japanese consul general in Sao Paulo, Brazil, is kidnapped in Brazil by VPR terrorists, who demand the release of prisoners. The diplomat is released after the prisoners are set free.

March 11: Clemmie Stubbs skyjacks a United B-727, scheduled to fly from Cleveland to Atlanta. Stubbs threatens the 106 passengers and crew members with a revolver and compels the pilot to fly to Cuba, where he is imprisoned. He will later be killed while attempting to escape his Cuban jail cell.

March 17: John Divivo unsuccessfully tries to skyjack an Eastern DC-9 flight taking seventy-three persons and crew from Newark, N.J., to Boston. Divivo shoots and kills the pilot and wounds the copilot, who resist his orders. He is overpowered and later imprisoned, committing suicide in his cell.

March 21: Joaquin Waldemar Sanchez, Paraguayan consul in Ituzaingó, Argentina, is kidnapped by FAL terrorists. When their demand for the release of two other terrorists in prison is refused, Sanchez is released.

March 24: Lieutenant Colonel Donald J. Crowley, U.S. air attaché to the Dominican

Republic, is kidnapped. Crowley will be freed after twenty political prisoners are allowed to leave the country.

March 29: MANO terrorists kidnap Yuri Pivovarov, U.S.S.R. assistant commercial attaché in Argentina, but police rescue Pivovarov after a harrowing car chase.

March 31: Count Karl von Spreti, West German ambassador to Guatemala, is abducted, his terrorist kidnappers demanding the release of twenty-two political prisoners, along with $700,000. When the Guatemalan government refuses, Spreti will be slain.

March 31: Nine URA terrorists skyjack a Japan Airlines plane, ordering it to fly to Pyongyang, North Korea. The plane instead flies to Seoul, where the airport has been quickly disguised to look like the Pyongyang airport. The terrorists are not deceived but allow the passengers to deplane, then order the pilot to fly them to Pyongyang, where they vanish.

April 5: Curtis S. Cutter, U.S. consul general in Brazil, is nearly kidnapped in Pôrto Alegre, but he escapes and three VPR terrorists are arrested.

April 21: Seventy-five miles north of Manila, Philippines, a bomb hidden in the lavatory of a Philippines Airlines jet explodes in midair, killing all thirty-six passengers.

April 22: Ira D. Meeks and Diane V. McKinney, wielding a revolver, skyjack a chartered Cessna-172 from Gastonia, North Carolina, to Cuba. Both will later be captured; Meeks will be found mentally incompetent and charges against both skyjackers will be dropped.

April 23: Using a toy pistol and an alleged bomb, Joseph A. Wagstaff unsuccessfully

attempts to skyjack a DC-9 en route from Pellston to Sault St. Marie, Michigan, to Detroit. He will be seized and sent to an insane asylum.

May 4: Students at Kent State University protesting the Vietnam War are fired upon by nervous National Guardsmen and four students are killed.

May 4: Al Fatah terrorists invade the Israeli Embassy in Asunción, Paraguay, and shoot to death the wife of the first secretary, and another person.

May 11: Rioting blacks in Augusta, Florida, are dispersed by police who shoot and kill six black demonstrators.

May 14: Ulrike Meinhof and other terrorists free Andreas Baader from prison guards in Berlin's Tegel Library, where Baader has been allowed to do research. The terrorists fire submachine guns, injuring the guards and several employees and patrons.

May 22: Members of the Feyedeen cross into Israel into Lebanon and fire three bazooka rockets into a school bus, killing eight Israeli children and injuring twenty-two others.

May 25: Nelson Molina skyjacks an American Airlines B-727 en route from Chicago to New York. Molina brandishes a pistol when ordering the pilot to fly the seventy-four passengers and crew to Cuba, where he will escape.

May 25: Graciella C. Quesada Zamora skyjacks a ninety-six–passenger Delta CV-880 en route from Chicago to Miami. Flashing a revolver, she forces the pilot to fly to Cuba. She will be returned to the U.S. in 1980 and imprisoned.

May 29: Pedro Eugenio Arambaru, former president of Argentina, is abducted and murdered by terrorists whose demands for freeing political prisoners are denied.

June 2: One person is killed and twelve others are injured when a hand grenade explodes beneath a seat on a Philippines Airlines jet en route to Bacolod Negros Island. The plane lands safely at Roxas, Philippines.

June 4: Arthur Barkley attempts to hold hostage the fifty-six people aboard a TWA B-727 en route from Phoenix, Arizona, to St. Louis, Missouri. Brandishing a revolver, razor blade, and a bottle of gasoline, Barkley demands a $100 million ransom. He is seized, then found temporarily insane and acquitted.

June 7: Morris Draper, U.S. political secretary, is abducted in Amman, Jordan, by PFLP terrorists. He will later be released.

June 10: Major Robert Perry, U.S. military attaché in Amman, Jordan, is at home when he is fatally shot by terrorists.

June 11: Ehrenfried von Holleben, West German ambassador to Brazil, is kidnapped by terrorists who demand that forty prisoners be released. The demands are met and Holleben is set free.

June 18: The Parke-Davis plant in Buenos Aires, Argentina, is bombed, killing three employees.

June 22: Terrorist Haxhi H. Xhaferi skyjacks a Pan American plane carrying 133 passengers from Beirut to Rome. Flashing a pistol, Xhaferi orders the plane flown to Cairo. He will be tried and sent to prison three years later.

July 3: Five persons are killed in Belfast, Ireland, in a clash between IRA forces and British troops.

July 9: Fernando Londone y Londone, ex-foreign minister of Colombia, is kidnapped by Colombian terrorists who demand and receive $200,000.

July 21: Two West Germans are kidnapped in Teoponte, Bolivia, by ELN terrorists whose demands for the release of prisoners will be met and the Germans will be set free.

July 24: Quick-acting police arrest several terrorists who are about to abduct Donner Lyon, U.S. consul in Recife, Brazil.

July 31: Aloisio Mares Dias Gomide, Brazilian vice consul in Uruguay, is kidnapped by Tupamaro terrorists who allegedly receive a $250,000 ransom. Gomide is then released.

July 31: U.S. diplomat Daniel A. Mitrione is kidnapped by Uruguayan terrorists, Tupamaro, who demand the release of all Tupamaros held in prison. The demand will be refused, and Mitrione will be slain by his captors.

July 31: Michael Gordon Jones, second consul to the U.S. embassy in Montevideo, Uruguay, along with cultural attaché Nathan Rosenfeld are kidnapped by Tupamaro terrorists, but they manage to escape.

August 2: Rudolfo Rivera Rios skyjacks a Pan American B-747 scheduled to fly from New York to San Juan, Puerto Rico. Rios threatens 360 passengers and 17 crew members with a pistol and alleged nitroglycerin, ordering the pilot to fly to Cuba. He will later be imprisoned.

August 7: Claude L. Fly, U.S. agronomist, is abducted in Montevideo, Uruguay, by

Tupamaro terrorists who demand that 150 political prisoners be freed. Fly will suffer a heart attack and be set free.

August 15: Alfredo Stroessner, president of Paraguay, is the target of a failed assassination attempt.

August 20: Gregory A. Graves skyjacks a Delta DC-9 scheduled to fly from Atlanta to Savannah, Georgia, to Cuba. Graves threatens the eighty-two passengers and crew with an alleged bomb. He will be returned to the U.S. in 1975 and be imprisoned.

August 24: Karleton Armstrong, David S. Fine, and other members of the Students for a Democratic Society (SDS) detonate a bomb at the University of Wisconsin in Madison, Wisconsin, killing Robert Fassnacht and injuring several other persons. Armstrong will later be sent to prison for this terrorist act.

August 24: Robert J. Labadie skyjacks a TWA B-727 scheduled to fly from Chicago to Philadelphia, to Cuba. Labadie claims to have a bomb while threatening the eighty-six passengers and crew. He will later be sent to an insane asylum.

August 30: Johan Huber unsuccessfully attempts to skyjack a Pan American B-727 en route from Munich to West Berlin with 125 persons on board. Using a starter pistol, Huber tries to force the pilot to fly to Budapest, Hungary. He will be sent to an insane asylum.

September 6: Terrorists of the Habash Front skyjack a Pan American 747 to Beirut, and then to Cairo, where its 171 passengers and crew are disembarked. The terrorists then blow up the plane. The same terrorist organization will skyjack three other planes this same day, one of these being an El Al plane on which ter-

rorist Patrick Arguello will be killed and Leila Khaled will be injured. An Israeli flight attendant is injured, along with four passengers.

September 12: Members of the Jewish Defense League take three hostages at the Egyptian embassy in London, England. The captors demand the release of airplane passengers held hostage in Jordan by Arab terrorists.

September 15: Donald B. Irwin attempts to skyjack a TWA B-707 scheduled to fly from Los Angeles to San Francisco. Irwin flashes an unloaded pistol to control fifty-nine passengers and crew members, ordering the pilot to fly to North Korea. He will be thwarted and imprisoned.

September 19: Richard D. Witt skyjacks a 727 jet flying from Pittsburgh to Philadelphia. Using a pistol and an alleged bomb, Witt commandeers the aircraft and its ninety-eight passengers and crew, having the pilot fly to Egypt and then to Cuba. He will later be imprisoned in the U.S.

September 22: David W. Donovan fails to skyjack an Eastern DC-8 en route from Boston to San Juan, Puerto Rico. Donovan threatens to set the plane on fire if his demands are not met but he will not state his demands. He is seized and skyjacking charges dropped, but he will be imprisoned for an unrelated robbery and murder.

October 5: Four FLQ terrorists kidnap James Richard Cross, the British trade commissioner for Canada, in Quebec in the country's first political kidnapping. The kidnappers demand $500,000 in gold, the reinstatement of recently fired postal workers, and safe passage to Cuba or Algeria. When the government fails to comply, the terrorists kidnap Pierre

Laporte, Quebec's Minister of Labor, threatening to kill Laporte unless their demands are met.

October 18: When their demands are refused by the Canadian government, FLQ terrorists murder hostage Pierre Laporte; his bullet-riddled body is found in the trunk of a car parked at St. Hubert's Airport near Montreal. Three of Laporte's kidnappers and killers will be sent to prison for life.

November 6: The central bus station in Tel Aviv, Israel, is devastated by two explosions that kill two persons and injure twenty-four others.

November 27: Pope Paul VI is threatened but not harmed by Benjamin Mendoza, a Bolivian terrorist, who confronts the Catholic leader at the airport in Manila, Philippines.

December 1: Eugen Beihl, a West German consul, is abducted in San Sebastián, Spain, by ETA Basque terrorists. Biehl will be set free on December 25.

December 2: The FLQ terrorists still holding James Richard Cross are located in a Montreal house and are surrounded by police, who agree to allow them safe passage to Cuba if they release Cross. The terrorists release their hostage and are flown safely out of the country.

December 7: Giovanni Enrico Bucher, Swiss ambassador to Brazil, is abducted in Rio de Janeiro by members of the National Liberation Alliance (ALN). After seventy political prisoners are released, Bucher will be set free.

1971

January 3: Arthur J. Wilson, Lolita K. Graves, Carl White, and Norma Jean White skyjack a National DC-8 scheduled to fly eighty-nine passengers from Los Angeles to Tampa, Florida, to Cuba. All four will later be apprehended. Charges against Norma White will be dropped, but the other three terrorists will be sent to prison.

January 8: Tupamaro terrorists kidnap Geoffrey M. S. Jackson, British ambassador to Uruguay, in Montevideo. Jackson will be released after 106 political prisoners are set free.

January 15: The Baader-Meinhof gang robs two banks in Kassel, Germany, using the money to buy guns from Al Fatah, an Arab terrorist organization.

January 22: Garland J. Grant skyjacks a Northwest B-727, scheduled to fly sixty people from Milwaukee, Wisconsin, to Detroit, Michigan, to Cuba. Grant has boarded the plane with a hatchet and an alleged bomb. He will be returned to the U.S. and imprisoned.

February 1: Jibril Front terrorists attempt to blow up an El Al plane en route from London to Lod. A bomb is planted in the luggage of an unwitting woman and is located. The woman is released.

February 4: Walter C. Hines, allegedly armed with nitroglycerin, skyjacks a Delta DC-9 set to fly twenty-seven people from Chicago to Nashville, Tennessee, to Cuba. He will be imprisoned.

February 10: Two Croatian terrorists take over the Yugoslavian consulate in Gothenburg, Sweden, demanding that prisoners in Yugoslavia be freed. When their demands are not met, the terrorists surrender.

February 15: James Finlay, U.S. Air Force security officer in Ankara, Turkey, is abducted by TPLA terrorists who make no demands. Finlay will be released a short time later.

February 25: Chapin S. Paterson, allegedly carrying a bomb, skyjacks a B-737 scheduled to fly ninety-eight people from San Francisco to Seattle, to Cuba and then Canada. He will be deported from Canada to the U.S. and imprisoned.

March 4: Four U.S. Air Force members are kidnapped in Ankara, Turkey, by TPLA terrorists who demand but do not receive $400,000 ransom. The airmen will be set free and the terrorists captured and convicted.

March 6: Colonel Delgado Villegas, former prominent Guatemalan police official, is fatally shot following three previous attempts on his life by terrorists.

March 8: Thomas K. Marston, seventeen, attempts to skyjack a B-727 flying forty-six persons from Mobile, Alabama, to New Orleans. Marston, armed with a pistol, orders the pilot to fly to Canada, but he is overpowered. He will later be sent to prison.

March 10: Berro Oribe, attorney general of Uruguay, is kidnapped by Tupamaro terrorists, who grill him about legal cases against terrorists and then, surprisingly, set him free.

March 31: John M. Matthews, Jr., fourteen, armed with a pistol, attempts to skyjack a Delta DC-9 Birmingham, Alabama–Chicago flight, to Cuba. He is seized and

later put on a three year probation for carrying a weapon aboard an airplane.

April 7: The Yugoslavian ambassador to Sweden is killed and other Yugoslavian statesmen are injured in Stockholm, Sweden, by Croatian terrorists.

May 17: Ephraim Elrom, Israeli consul general in Istanbul, Turkey, is kidnapped by terrorists who demand the release of imprisoned terrorists. When the demand is refused, Elrom is shot and killed.

May 21: Three members of the Black Liberation Army (BLA), a Negro terrorist organization, shoot and kill two police officers in Harlem who have answered a bogus call for help placed by the terrorists. Members of the same group will, five months later, shoot and kill a police desk sergeant at Ingleside, California, and two more NYPD officers in January 1972. The killers will be apprehended and the BLA will soon go out of existence.

May 23: Stanley Sylvester, honorary British consul and administrator of Swift & Co., in Rosario, Argentina, is kidnapped by ERP terrorists whose demands for the distribution of $62,500 in goods and foodstuffs to the poor are met. Sylvester will be released.

May 29: Henri Wolimer, French consul in San Sebastian, Spain, evades a kidnapping attempt by Basque terrorists.

June 11: Gregory L. White skyjacks a TWA B-727 en route from Chicago to New York. Holding twenty-six persons hostage with a pistol, White demands $75,000 ransom and to be flown to North Vietnam. He is seized and sent to an insane asylum, where he will later kill himself.

June 23: Alfredo Cambron, legal adviser to U.S.-financed companies in Uruguay, is kidnapped by OPR-33 terrorists, but he will later be set free.

July 2: Robert L. Jackson and Ligia Sanchez Archila skyjack a B-707 en route from Mexico City to San Antonio, Texas. Wielding pistols and alleged nitroglycerin, they terrorized the 110 passengers and crew, demanding a $100,000 ransom and to be flown to Brazil, Argentina, and Algeria. They will later be imprisoned.

July 15: Petra Schelm and Werner Hoppe, two members of the Baader-Meinhof gang who have just stolen a BMW, are halted by a police roadblock outside of Hamburg. The terrorists fire upon the officers. Schelm is killed by return fire, and Hoppe is captured and later sent to prison.

July 23: Richard A. Obergfell is killed while attempting to skyjack a TWA B-727 New York–Chicago flight to Italy with sixty-one people on board. Although Obergfell has claimed to have a pistol and a bomb, no weapons are found on his dead body.

August 9: Twelve persons are killed and 300 arrested and 150 houses burned in widespread rioting in Belfast, Ireland.

September 3: Armed only with an icepick, Juan M. Borges Guerra attempts to skyjack an Eastern DC-9 Chicago-to-Miami flight, to Cuba. He is overpowered and later sent to prison.

September 9: Inmates at Attica Prison near Buffalo, New York, seize the facility, taking fifty hostages and demanding better conditions. Twenty-nine inmates and ten hostages are killed when state police and military units storm the prison. Eighty-five inmates, three hostages, and a state trooper are wounded. None of the surviving prisoners will be punished.

September 24: Barbara H. Pliskow attempts to skyjack an American Airlines B-727 Detroit–New York flight, to Algeria, wielding a pistol and dynamite, and demanding that some prisoners be released. She will be captured and put on probation for two years.

September 25: Holger Meins and Magrit Schiller, two members of the Baader-Meinhof gang, are stopped by two police officers on the Freiburg-Basel motorway. The terrorists shoot and kill the officers and speed off.

October 4: George Giffe, Jr., and Bobby Wayne Wallace, armed with pistols, try to skyjack a Big Brother, Inc. Aero Commander Hawk 681 to the Bahamas. Giffe kills his wife and the pilot of the Nashville, Tennessee–Atlanta flight before committing suicide.

October 9: Richard F. Dixon skyjacks an Eastern B-727 Detroit-to-Miami flight, to Cuba, terrorizing the forty-six passengers and crew members with a revolver. He will be imprisoned five years later.

October 18: Del L. Thomas skyjacks a B-737 Anchorage, Alaska–Bethel, Arkansas, flight to Cuba. He overpowers thirty-five passengers and crew with a pistol. Thomas will later be imprisoned.

October 25: Angel Lugo Casado skyjacks an American Airlines B-747 New York–San Juan, Puerto Rico, flight, to Cuba. He terrorizes the 236 passengers and crew members with a pistol that turns out to be fake. He will be returned to the U.S. in 1978 and imprisoned.

November 4: A middle-aged man giving his name as Dan B. Cooper (or D. B. Cooper) purchases a ticket for Northwest Airlines Flight 305, flying from Portland,

Oregon, to Seattle, Washington. When airborne, Cooper shows a stewardess a dynamite bomb and demands that $200,000 and parachutes be delivered to him upon landing at Seattle. The cash and parachutes are delivered and Cooper allows the thirty-two passengers to go free. Once again airborne, the skyjacker instructs the four crew members of the 727 Trijet to maintain a 200 m.p.h. speed and fly at 10,000 feet, the destination being Reno, Nevada. Cooper then goes to the back of the plane and lowers the stairs beneath the tail and parachutes with the money. He is never seen again, although several thousand dollars of the ransom money will be found in February 1980 near Vancouver, Washington. At one point, it is claimed that Cooper is really Jack Coffelt, a burglar and con man from Missouri, but Coffelt, who will die in 1976, is never confirmed as being the legendary skyjacker.

November 19: Jaime Castrejon Diez, rector of the State University of Guerrero, Mexico, is abducted by terrorists. After nine political prisoners are set free and the kidnappers paid $500,000 in ransom, Diez will be released.

November 20: An explosion rips apart a China Airlines Caravelle over the South China Sea, killing twenty-five persons. There are no survivors.

November 27: Michael R. Finney, Charles R. Hill, and Ralph L. Goodwin commandeer a TWA B-727 en route from Albuquerque, New Mexico, to Chicago. Brandishing two pistols and a knife, the terrorists divert the flight to Cuba. Goodwin will later drown and Finney and Hill become fugitives.

November 28: Wasif Tell, prime minister of Jordan, is shot and killed by four members of Black September (BSO), a

Palestinian terrorist organization, as he arrives at the Sheraton Hotel in Cairo.

November 30: French reporter Michele Ray claims to have been kidnapped by OPR-33 terrorists in Uruguay, but officials believe she has arranged the abduction in order to interview the terrorists and sell a sensational, though faked, story.

December 15: Zaid Rifai, Jordan's ambassador to England, is injured by gunshots in a failed attempt on his life in London by Black September terrorists.

December 22: Klaus Junschke and three other members of the Baader-Meinhof terrorist gang rob the Bavarian Mortgage and Exchange Bank in Kaiserslautern, Germany, killing a policeman before fleeing.

December 24: Everett L. Holt skyjacks a B-707 taking thirty-five persons from Minneapolis, Minnesota, to Chicago. He wields a revolver and alleged bomb, demanding a $500,000 ransom. He will be captured and sent to an insane asylum.

December 26: Donald L. Coleman attempts to skyjack an American Airlines B-707 en route from Chicago to San Francisco, carrying eighty-five persons. Using a knife, toy pistol, and a fake bomb, Coleman also demands $200,000 ransom. He will be captured and imprisoned.

1972

January 7: Brandishing a pistol and a shotgun, Allen G. Sims and Ida P. Robinson skyjack a B-727 San Francisco–Los Angeles flight, with 151 persons on board, to Africa and then to Cuba. Sims will later be imprisoned, but Robinson will escape.

January 12: Billy E. Hurst, Jr., skyjacks a B-727 en route from Houston to Dallas, Texas, with 100 persons on board. Waving a pistol and an alleged bomb, Hurst demands $1 million ransom and ten parachutes. He will later be imprisoned.

January 20: Richard C. LaPoint skyjacks a DC-10 Las Vegas–Reno, Nevada, flight with seventy-three persons on board. Claiming to have a bomb, LaPoint demands $500,000 and two parachutes. He will parachute from the in-flight plane, be captured, and be imprisoned.

January 26: A bomb explodes in the luggage compartment of a Yugoslavian jet en route from Copenhagen, Denmark, to Zagreb, Yugoslavia, killing twenty-seven persons. One person survives.

January 26: Croatian terrorists explode a bomb aboard a Stockholm-to-Belgrade jetliner, killing twenty-six passengers.

January 26: Members of the Jewish Defense League (JDL) firebomb the New York City offices of entertainment empressario Sol Hurok, who has managed the performances of Soviet entertainers in the U.S. Considerable damage is done but no injuries are reported.

January 26: Merlyn L. St. George, armed with a starter pistol and an alleged bomb and demanding $200,000 ransom and four parachutes, is killed while attempting to skyjack an FH-227 plane flying forty-six people from Albany to New York City.

January 26: Patrick H. McAlroy, brandishing a pistol, attempts to skyjack an SFO helicopter about to leave Berkeley, California, for San Francisco, to Cuba. He is seized and sent to a mental institution.

January 27: Croatian terrorists explode a bomb aboard a train en route from Vienna, Austria, to Zagreb, Yugoslavia, injuring six passengers.

January 29: Garrett B. Trapnell, armed with a pistol and a phony bomb, fails to skyjack a B-707 en route from Los Angeles to New York with 101 people aboard. Trapnell demands $306,800 ransom, the release of a prisoner in Dallas, Texas, and flight to Europe. He is shot, captured, and imprisoned.

February 22: The IRA sets off a bomb at the Parachute Regiment headquarters at Aldershot, England, killing nine soldiers and civilians and injuring three others.

February 22: Habash Front terrorists skyjack a Lufthansa Airlines plane en route from New Delhi to Athens, and order it to fly to Aden, South Yemen, where the passengers and crew are released after the West German government has paid the terrorists $5 million and allowed them to go free.

March 2: Wolfgang Grundmann and Manfred Grashof, two members of the Baader-Meinhof gang, are captured after a wild shootout in their Hamburg apartment.

March 3: Members of Italy's Red Brigades, a terrorist group, kidnap businessman Idalgo Macchiarini but release him a short time later.

March 3: Black September Palestinian terrorists try to assault the London headquarters of Hussein I, King of Jordan, or so it is reported. (Some terrorist authorities believe that Hussein is a secret backer of Palestinian terrorists and that the feeble attack is only a ruse to convince the West that Hussein is opposed to Arab terrorism.)

March 7: James W. Brewton and Joseph T. Bennett, armed with guns, skyjack to Cuba a Chalk's Flying Service Grumman 73 scheduled to fly to the Bahamas from Miami. Bennett will escape to Cuba. Brewton will be fatally shot in Jamaica three years later.

March 21: Oberdan Sallustro, president of Fiat in Argentina, is kidnapped by ERP terrorists in Argentina, who demand $1 million in ransom and the release of political prisoners. Fiat agrees to pay the ransom, but the government refuses to release the prisoners. Sallustro is killed.

March 27: One Canadian and two British NATO radar technicians are kidnapped in Turkey by TPLA terrorists whose demands for the release of prisoners are refused. All three captives will be slain, along with the terrorists, who are gunned down as police raid their hideout.

April 4: The Cuban Trade Office in Montreal is bombed, killing one person and injuring seven others.

April 7: Richard F. McCoy skyjacks a United 727 taking ninety-one persons from Denver to Los Angeles. McCoy brandishes a pistol, a hand grenade, and a phony bomb when demanding $500,000 ransom and six parachutes. He escapes but will later be killed when resisting arrest.

April 9: Stanley H. Speck, claiming to have a hand grenade, attempts to skyjack a B-727 with ninety-two aboard en route from Oakland to San Diego, California. He demands four parachutes and $500,000 ransom. Speck will be captured in San Diego and sent to an insane asylum.

April 17: Kenneth L. Smith forces his way on board a B-727 scheduled to fly from Seattle to Annette Island, Arkansas.

Claiming to have a pistol, Smith orders the pilot to fly to Cairo, Egypt, but his plans are foiled. He will be sent to an insane asylum.

April 17: William H. Greene III attempts to skyjack a Delta CV-880 en route from West Palm Beach, Florida, to Chicago. Threatening the seventy-six persons on board with a phony gun, Greene demands $500,000 ransom and a flight to Nassau, Bahamas. He will surrender and be imprisoned.

May 3: Four TPLA members demanding the release of three prisoners in Turkey skyjack a Turkish plane to Sofia, Bulgaria, where they surrender.

May 5: Frederick W. Haneman, armed with a pistol and a fake bomb, skyjacks an Eastern B-727 carrying forty-nine passengers from Allentown, Pennsylvania, to Washington, D.C. Haneman demands $303,000 ransom, six parachutes, and a flight to Central America. He will later surrender and be imprisoned.

May 5: Michael L. Hansen, armed with a pistol, skyjacks a B-737 en route from Salt Lake City, Utah, to Los Angeles, diverting the seventy-five–passenger craft to Hanoi, North Vietnam, and then Cuba. He will later be imprisoned.

May 7: Ulrich Schmucker, a member of the Baader-Meinhof gang, is captured by German police but released. He is later thought to have turned police informant and is murdered by gang members.

May 11: Four members of the Baader-Meinhof terrorist gang—Ulrike Meinhof, Gudrun Ensslin, Andreas Baader, and Jan-Carl Raspe—plant bombs at the U.S. Army headquarters in Frankfurt. Lt. Col. Paul Abel Bloomquist is killed by one of the exploding bombs and twelve other U.S.

servicemen are injured. The blasts cause more than $1 million in damage.

May 15: George Wallace, the segregationist governor of Alabama, while giving an open-air speech in Laurel, Maryland, is shot and severely crippled for life by Arthur Bremer, who will be sent to prison.

May 24: The Baader-Meinhof gang explodes two car bombs outside the U.S. Army's European headquarters in Heidelberg, Germany, killing one soldier and wounding two others.

May 30: Three members of the Japanese terrorist organization known as the Red Army (who have been recruited by Black Septemberists) machine-gun and blow up with grenades innocent travelers at Lod Airport terminal. They kill twenty-four persons and wound another twenty-six, four of whom later die. Police kill two of the suicidal terrorists and capture the third, Kozo Okomoto, who will be sent to prison for life.

June 1: An informant gives police in Frankfurt, Germany, the address of the "bomb factory" used by the Baader-Meinhof terrorist gang. Officers capture Jan-Carl Raspe and surround the garage containing the bombs and two of the terrorists—Andreas Baader and Holger Meins. After a shootout, both terrorists are wounded and captured. A short time later, gang leader Ulrike Meinhof is captured in Hanover.

June 2: William Holder and Katherine Kerkow, armed with a fake bomb, skyjack a B-727 en route from Los Angeles to Seattle carrying ninety-seven people. They demand to be flown to Algeria, a $500,000 ransom, and five parachutes. The ransom will be returned. Holder will be given a suspended sentence and Kerkow will escape.

June 2: Robb D. Heady skyjacks a United Airlines B-727.

June 15: A bomb placed beneath a passenger seat of a CV-880 jet of Cathay Pacific Airways (Hong Kong), reportedly by a police officer whose fianceé and daughter are on board, explodes over the central highlands of South Vietnam, killing eighty-one people.

June 23: Martin J. McNally and Walter J. Petlikowsky, wielding a submachine gun, a hand grenade, and a phony bomb, skyjack an American B-727 en route with 101 people from St. Louis to Tulsa, Oklahoma. They demand $502,000 and five parachutes. Both will later be captured and imprisoned.

June 30: Daniel B. Carre, claiming to have a knife, skyjacks a DC-9 en route to Portland, Oregon, from Seattle. He demands $50,000 and a parachute. Carre will later be sent to an insane asylum.

July 2: Thai Binh Nguyen, wielding a knife and showing alleged hand grenades, skyjacks a Pan American B-747 en route from Honolulu, Hawaii, to Saigon, South Vietnam, with 135 passengers on board. The terrorist demands to be flown to Hanoi, North Vietnam, but he is killed by another passenger when the plan first lands in Saigon.

July 5: Dimitz K. Alexiev and Michael D. Azmanoff, armed with pistols, skyjack a B-737 en route with eighty-six people aboard from Sacramento to San Francisco, California. The terrorists demand $800,000 and two parachutes. Both terrorists and one passenger will be killed. Lubomir Peichev, a conspirator, will be imprisoned.

July 8: Members of Israel's Mossad detonate a car bomb that kills PFLP terrorist leader Ghassan Kanafani in Beirut.

July 21: IRA terrorists explode twenty-two bombs in downtown Belfast, Ireland, killing eleven people and injuring 130 more; the day is thereafter known as Bloody Friday.

July 28: Hector Menoni, director of United Press International in Uruguay, is abducted by OPR-33 terrorists. He will later be set free.

July 31: Wielding handguns, Melvin and Jean McNair, George Wright, George Brown, and Joyce Burgess, all members of the terrorist Black Panther Party, skyjack a Delta DC-8 en route from Detroit to Miami with 101 people aboard. They demand $1 million ransom and a flight to Algeria. All but Wright will later be imprisoned.

August 4: A murderous Negro gang styling itself after the terrorist Mau Maus of Kenya of the 1950s, calling itself the De Mau Mau Gang, invades the western suburbs of Chicago. The gang kills four members of the Corbett family in Barrington Hills and then, in Monee, slaughters the Stephen Hawtree family. In Highland Park, gang members murder William Richter. In Frankfort, they kill Michael Gerschenson. After claiming nine victims, the six bloodthirsty gang members are captured. Tried and convicted, the gang members escape the death penalty and are given long prison terms.

September 5: Eight Black September terrorists, all Syrian-trained commandos, invade the Olympic compound housing athletes participating in the XX Olympiad in Munich, Germany. (Black September is the official enforcement arm of Al Fatah, which is directed by Yasir Arafat.) The terrorists kill two members of the Israeli team and hold the rest hostage, demanding the release of the imprisoned Ulrike Meinhoff and other members of the Baader-Meinhof

gang, along with 234 other Arab terrorists then in jail. When the terrorists are provided a jet to fly them out of the country, they are attacked by German police. The terrorists immediately kill nine more members of the Israeli team. Five of the Arab terrorists are killed and three taken prisoner. The organizer of the massacre, Ali Hassan Salemeh, will be killed in reprisal by Mossad agents in 1979.

September 5: Jan J. Van de Panne, Dutch chief of Philips Electronics Co. in Argentina, is kidnapped by Montoneros terrorists. When the firm pays $500,000 ransom, Panne is set free.

September 9: Dr. Ami Shachori, agricultural adviser to the Israeli Embassy in London, is slain by a mail bomb sent by Black September terrorists. Forty-nine other letter bombs mailed by Black September are intercepted and disarmed.

September 11: Salvador Allende Gossens, president of Chile, is ousted in a military coup led by General Augusto Pinochet Ugarte. Allende either commits suicide or is assassinated in this supposedly CIA-backed coup.

October 16: Wael Zuaiter, Al Fatah official in Rome, is fatally shot near his apartment, reportedly by Mossad agents.

October 16: Two Americans are injured and a Canadian is killed by a bomb blast at the Sheraton Hotel in Buenos Aires, Argentina. The bombing is attributed to Maximo Mena Command.

October 29: Black Septemberists skyjack a Lufthansa Boeing jet bound from Beirut, Lebanon, to Ankara, Turkey, demanding that three terrorists imprisoned for the 1972 massacre of the Israeli athletes during the XX Olympiad in Munich, Germany, be released. The plane lands in Libya and, following negotiations, the three terrorists are first arrested and then set free.

November 2: Three terrorists bomb the French consulate in Zaragoza, Spain, killing one person.

November 3: A French woman is killed while attempting to plant a bomb at the U.S. Embassy in Amman, Jordan.

November 7: Enrico Barrella, Italian industrialist, is abducted in Buenos Aires by terrorists who later release him after collecting $500,000 in ransom money.

December 7: Imelda Marcos, wife of Philippines president Ferdinand Edralin Marcos, is stabbed and critically injured, but survives the terrorist attack in Pasay City, Philippines.

December 8: Mahmoud Hamshari, the primary official of Al Fatah and the Palestinian Liberation Organization (PLO) in France, dies when a bomb explodes in his Paris apartment. Mossad agents are allegedly responsible.

December 8: Seven terrorists attempt to skyjack an Ethiopian Airlines craft over Addis Ababa, Ethiopia; a grenade blast injures eleven persons before the plane safely lands.

December 28: Black September terrorists hold six hostages at the Israeli embassy in Bankok, Thailand. They demand the release of terrorists imprisoned in Israel. When the demands are not met, the terrorists later back down and are allowed to leave the country.

1973

January 23: Three armed terrorists abduct U.S. ambassador Clinton Knox and U.S. consul general Ward Christensen, demanding the release of prisoners and ransom. The demands are met and the prisoners set free.

February 3: Norman Lee, administrator of a Coca-Cola plant in Buenos Aires, Argentina, is abducted by terrorists who later release him after collecting a ransom.

February 20: Three Pakistani terrorists take hostages at the Indian High Commission offices in London, England, demanding that Pakistanis imprisoned in India be released. Their demands will not be met and two of the three terrorists will be killed by police, the third captured.

February 23: Believing that a Libyan Boeing 727 jet is "a flying bomb," Israelis shoot the plane down over the Sinai, killing 106 passengers and crew.

March 1: Black September terrorists take ten hostages at the Saudi Arabian embassy in Khartoum, Sudan, demanding the release of several imprisoned terrorists in several countries. When their demands are not met, the terrorists will kill three diplomats and then surrender to authorities.

March 2: Cleo A. Noel, Jr., U.S. ambassador; George C. Moore, U.S. charge d'affaires; and Guy Eid, Belgian charge d'affaires, are assassinated in Khartoum, Sudan, by Palestinian terrorists.

March 8: Two IRA bombs explode in London, England, killing one person and injuring more than 200 others.

March 19: An Air Vietnam passenger jet is blown apart over Ban Me Thuot when a bomb explodes in the cargo area, killing all fifty-nine persons aboard.

March 28: Gerardo Scalmazzi, manager of the First National Bank of Boston's Rosario branch, is kidnapped by terrorists in Rosario, Argentina, and will later be released after the terrorists receive between a reported $500,000 to $1 million in ransom money.

April 2: Anthony R. DaCruz, a technical operations manager for Eastman Kodak, is abducted by terrorists in Argentina. He will later be released after a $1.5 million ransom is paid.

April 8: Francis Victor Brimicombe, president of Nobleza Tobacos, a subsidiary of the British-American Tobacco Co., is kidnapped by terrorists in Argentina. He will be set free after the firm pays between $1.5 and $1.8 million.

April 9: Al Fatah chief Kamal Adwan is assassinated in Beirut, Lebanon, by Israeli terrorists.

April 12: An Arab terrorist carrying a Jordanian passport is killed when a bomb in his luggage accidentally explodes in his hotel room in Athens, Greece.

May 4: Terrance G. Leonhardy, U.S. consul general in Guadalajara, Mexico, is abducted by terrorists of the People's Revolutionary Armed Forces, who demand that political prisoners be released and an $80,000 ransom be paid. The demands are met and Leonhardy is later released.

May 21: Oscar Castel, president of a Coca-Cola bottling plant in Córdoba, Argentina, is kidnapped by terrorists, who later set him free after collecting $100,000 ransom.

May 21: ERP terrorists kidnap and fatally shoot Luis Giovanelli, the administrator of a Ford Motor plant, in Buenos Aires, Argentina. ERP states that they will continue kidnapping Ford employees until a $1 million ransom is paid. The company later complies.

June 2: Lieutenant Colonel Lewis Hawkins, U.S. military adviser in Iran, is shot to death by Iranian terrorists.

June 6: Charles Lockwood, a British executive of an Acrow Steel division in Argentina, is kidnapped by terrorists. He will later be set free after a $2 million ransom is paid.

June 18: Roberto Galvez, manager of a U.S. company in Guatemala, is kidnapped by FAR terrorists. He will be released later, after a ransom of $50,000 is paid.

June 18: West German businessman Hans Kurt Gebhardt is kidnapped in Argentina by terrorists. He will be set free after a $100,000 ransom has been paid.

June 18: ERP terrorists abduct John R. Thompson, president of a Firestone subsidiary in Buenos Aires, Argentina. After a $3 million ransom is paid, Thompson will be released.

June 25: Mario Baratella, vice president of the Italian-owned Bank of Rio de la Plata in Buenos Aires, Argentina, is abducted and released after the terrorist kidnappers receive an undisclosed ransom (reported to be $2 million).

June 28: Mohammed Boudia, the most prominent Arab terrorist in Europe, is slain by a car bomb in Paris, one planted by Mossad agents.

July 1: Colonel Josef Alon, Israeli military attaché in Washington, D.C., is fatally shot by Arab terrorists in his Chevy Chase, Maryland home.

July 2: Terrorists kidnap Raul Bornancini, assistant manager of the Córdoba, Argentina, branch of the First National City Bank of New York. He will later be set free after the kidnappers receive a reported $1 million ransom.

July 21: A Japan Airlines plane traveling from Paris via Amsterdam to Tokyo with 137 passengers is skyjacked by four terrorists who force the pilot to land in Dubai. The plane is then flown to Libya, the passengers deplaned and the plane blown up.

August 2: Juan Felipe de la Cruz Serafin, a leading member of the anti-Castro Cuban Revolutionary Directorate, is killed by a bomb explosion in his hotel room in Avrainville, France.

August 4: A train station in Belgrade, Yugoslavia is bombed by terrorists, killing one person and injuring seven others.

August 5: The Libyan-based National Arab Youth for the Liberation of Palestine (NAYLP) carries out a machine gun and hand grenade attack against a TWA jet at the airport in Athens, Greece, killing five passengers and injuring fifty-five others.

August 27: Ian Martin, British manager of a meat firm, is abducted by terrorists in Asunción, Paraguay. Police raid the terrorist hideout and rescue Martin, killing two terrorists and arresting others.

September 5: Palestinian terrorists take thirteen hostages at the Saudi Arabian embassy in Paris, France, demanding that Jordan free the imprisoned Abu Daoud, a terrorist leader. Daoud is not released and the terrorists free their hostages, then surrender.

September 8: Three persons are injured when IRA terrorists explode bombs at the King's Cross and Euston railway stations in London, England.

October 10: Anthony Williams, British consul in Mexico, is kidnapped by terrorists, who demand the release of political prisoners. The prisoners are not released, but a ransom of $200,000 is reportedly paid and Williams is set free.

October 22: Kurt Schmid, an executive for Swissair, is abducted by ERP terrorists in Argentina, who demand a $10 million ransom. An unspecified ransom is later paid and Schmid is released.

October 23: David Wilkie, Jr., president of an Amoco International Oil Co. subsidiary, is abducted by terrorists in Buenos Aires, Argentina. He will be set free after a reported $3.5 million ransom is paid.

November 6: Marcus Foster, the black superintendent of schools in Oakland, California, who has proposed that all students be photographed for identification purposes, is shot to death with cyanide-tipped bullets by members of the Symbionese Liberation Army (SLA).

November 22: John A. Swint, general manager of a Ford subsidiary, is shot to death with his three bodyguards in Córdoba, Argentina, by terrorist members of the Fuerzas Armadas Peronistas (FAP).

December 6: Victor E. Samuelson, U.S. administrator of Exxon Co., is kidnapped by ERP terrorists in Buenos Aires, Argentina. He will later be released after a staggering $14.2 million ransom is paid.

December 13: George Peter Metesky, the infamous "Mad Bomber" of New York, is released from a mental facility.

December 17: Five NAYLP terrorists carry out an unauthorized operation in Rome, Italy, by hurling thermite bombs into a Pan Am jetliner, burning thirty-two passengers to death, and injuring eighteen others.

December 18: Sixty persons are injured when two car bombs and a parcel bomb explode in London, England.

December 29: FAR terrorists abduct Yves Boisset, director of Peugeot in Argentina, demanding a $4 million ransom. An unspecified ransom is paid and Boisset is set free.

December 30: Teddy Seiff, prominent British Zionist, is slain in London by a PFLP terrorist.

1974

January 10: Two members of the SLA are stopped by police near Concord, California, and shoot it out; Russell Little is wounded and Joseph Remiro escapes, only to be captured a short time later. The SLA's bomb-making factory catches fire in Concord a few days later, and police find revolutionary pamphlets and a note (later determined to be the handwriting of SLA leader Donald DeFreeze), reading: "Patricia Campbell Hearst on the night of the full moon of January 7." Little and Remiro will later be convicted of murdering Marcus Foster in 1973 and will be sent to prison for life.

January 24: The international terrorist Carlos (Ilyich Ramirez Sanchez) throws a bomb into the Israeli Bank Hapoalim in London, England. A woman is injured.

February 4: Publishing heiress Patricia Campbell Hearst is reportedly kidnapped from a San Francisco, California, apartment she shares with her fiancé Stephen Weed, by members of the Symbionese Liberation Army (SLA), in liaison with the Black Muslims, and headed by Negro terrorist Donald DeFreeze. She is held for $70 million in foodstuffs that are to be distributed to the poor. The distribution of food will be begun in Oakland, California, but a near riot ensues when 13,000 persons arrive to obtain the food parcels. It will later be concluded that Hearst has faked her own kidnapping and has been part of the SLA conspiracy all along.

February 22: Samuel J. Byck, armed with a gun and a bomb, kills a policeman in the Baltimore, Maryland, terminal before forcing his way aboard a Delta DC-9 scheduled to fly to Atlanta with fourteen people aboard. Byck kills the copilot, wounds the pilot, then kills himself.

February 23: Two demolition experts are killed in an explosion while trying to defuse a bomb placed in the Dow Chemical plant in Lavrion, Greece.

March 20: Ian Ball attempts to kidnap Princess Anne of England in London, planning to demand a £3 million ransom. Ball shoots three persons before he is captured. He will be sent to an institution for the criminally insane.

March 23: A disgruntled bar patron ejected from an Allentown, Pennsylvania, bar returns to hurl a Molotov cocktail inside, killing eight persons and injuring a dozen more. The mass murderer is never found.

April 12: Alfred Albert Laun III, chief of the U.S. Information Service section in Córdoba, Argentina, is severely injured when he is abducted by ERP terrorists. He will be set free the next day, apparently due to his injuries.

April 18: Members of the Red Brigades kidnap deputy prosecutor Mario Sossi, demanding the release of eight imprisoned terrorists. The demand is agreed to by Genoa prosecutor Francesco Coco and Sossi is released. Coco reneges on his promise and is murdered by the terrorists two years later.

May 17: Acting on a tip, more than 400 heavily armed L.A. police surround a small house at 1466 E. 54th Street, a hideout for SLA terrorists. A fierce fight ensues with more than 6,000 shots exchanged by the terrorists and police. The building catches fire and police later find in the smoldering ruins the bodies of SLA leader Donald DeFreeze, William Wolfe (reported to be Patricia Hearst's lover), Nancy Ling Perry, Camilla Hall, and Patricia Soltysik.

July 17: An IRA bomb explodes in the Tower of London, killing one person and injuring forty-one others.

July 26: Small-time thief Paul John Knowles breaks out of a Jacksonville, Florida, jail and immediately kills Alice Curtis. He will go on to murder another seventeen persons in four states until he is captured. He will be killed by a police detective on November 18, 1974, while attempting to escape.

August 4: The neo-fascist Ordine (Black Order) of Italy explodes a bomb on a Rome-to-Munich train near Bologna, Italy, killing twelve persons and injuring forty-eight others.

August 15: Park Chung Hee, president of South Korea, is the target of a failed assassination attempt by terrorists who fatally shoot his wife instead.

August 19: Rodger P. Davies, U.S. ambassador to Cyprus, is shot to death in Nicosta by a terrorist.

September 4: Marshall Collins III skyjacks an Eastern DC-9 en route from New York to Boston with 100 people. Collins uses a razor blade and a nail to intimidate the crew, demanding a $10,000 ransom. He will be sent to an insane asylum.

September 7: Barbara Hutchinson, chief of the U.S. Information Service in the Dominican Republic, and six others are abducted by terrorists, who demand that prisoners be freed and a $1 million ransom be paid. The demands will not be met, and the terrorists release their hostages before being allowed to leave the country.

September 8: The NAYLP plants a bomb on board a TWA jet bound from Athens to Rome. The explosion damages the plane's engines and the jet crashes into the Ionian Sea, killing all eighty-five persons on board.

September 13: Terrorists of the Japanese Red Army, the German RAF, and the PFLP take eleven hostages at the French embassy in The Hague, Netherlands, demanding that a hostage held in France be set free. Following negotiations, the hostages will be set free and the terrorists allowed to leave the country.

September 14: Pasquale Gentilcore, nineteen, and his girlfriend, Stefania Pettini, eighteen, are shot to death as they sit in their car fifteen miles outside of Florence, Italy, by the "Monster of Florence," who has used the same weapon, a .22-caliber pistol, that he used on two victims in 1968.

September 15: An Air Vietnam jet is hijacked over Phan Rang, a terrorist suicidally exploding two hand grenades and causing the plane to crash, killing all seventy persons on board.

September 16: Jorge and Juan Born, sons of the chairman of Argentina's largest firm, Bunge Born, are kidnapped by Montoneros terrorists who receive a $60 million ransom. The brothers are set free.

October 5: Three British soldiers and two women are killed when IRA bombs explode in several pubs in Guildford, Ireland, that cater to military personnel. Fifty-four patrons are injured.

November 14: Gunter von Drenckmann, president of the West German Supreme Court, is shot to death at his Berlin home by members of the Baader-Meinhof gang on orders from the imprisoned Ulrike Meinhof, who has marked the jurist for death as an example of the power she still wields even behind bars.

November 21: The IRA explodes a series of bombs in Birmingham, England, which kills 21 people and wounds another 168.

December 1: Charles Jackson, forty-six, is the first of eight persons who fall victim to the lone terrorist known as the "Los Angeles Slasher" or the "Skid Row Slasher." Jackson is found sprawled on the lawn of the Los Angeles Public Library with his throat slashed.

December 8: Moses August Yakanak, forty-seven, is found slashed to death in a Los Angeles alley, another victim of the "Los Angeles Slasher."

December 11: Drifter Arthur Dahlstedt, fifty-four, is found dead in the doorway of an abandoned Skid Row building, the third known victim of the "Los Angeles Slasher."

December 22: The "Los Angeles Slasher" kills David Perez, whose sliced-up body is found in some bushes on Flower Street.

1975

January 8: Casimir Strawinski, fifty-eight, is found slashed to death in his third-floor room at the Pickwick Hotel, the fifth victim of the "Los Angeles Slasher." Strawinski has earlier remarked to a friend: "I won't be around too long," and police believe he was predicting his own murder. It is later learned that the murder victim was referring to his advanced cancer and not to the murdering Skid Row terrorist.

January 15: Robert "Tex" Shannahan, forty, is found slashed to death in a Skid Row room, another "Los Angeles Slasher" victim.

January 25: Samuel Suarez is found cut to pieces in his fifth-floor room at the Barclay Hotel, the seventh victim of the "Los Angeles Slasher."

January 31: Clyde C. Hay, thirty-four, is found slashed to death in his cheap Hollywood apartment, another "Los Angeles Slasher" victim. The slasher, originally described as a wiry man with long, blond hair, is portrayed by LAPD Lieutenant Dan Cooke as a "human jackal. . . . We're dealing with a real monster." In each murder, the terrorist has performed a strange ritual, sprinkling salt about the bodies, removing the victim's shoes and pointing them at the feet, facts kept secret by the police to prevent copycat killings.

February 3: Vaughn Greenwood, a thirty-one-year-old Negro, is arrested and charged with the deaths committed by the "Los Angeles Slasher." He is indicted for the eight known slasher murders and three more homicides, two of these dating back to 1964.

February 11: Richard Ratsimandrava, president of Madagascar, is shot dead in Tananarive by terrorists.

February 27: German politician Peter Lorenz is kidnapped in Berlin by terrorists. The West German government releases five members of the Baader-Meinhof gang and pays a ransom for Lorenz's release.

March 25: Faisal, king of Saudi Arabia, is killed in the royal palace at Riyadh by Prince Faisal Bin Musaed Bin Abdulaziz in retaliation for the murder of his brother nine years earlier.

March 27: Susan Edith Saxe, a leader of a student terrorist organization that has looted a federal arsenal and robbed a Boston bank in 1970, is arrested in Philadelphia. She later pleads guilty and receives a long prison sentence.

April 24: Members of the Baader-Meinhof gang invade the West German Embassy in Stockholm, holding hostages and demanding that their leader Ulrike Meinhof and others be released from prison. The terrorists kill Lt. Col. Andreas Baron von Mirbach, a military attaché, and an official before Swedish police storm the building, killing two terrorists, including Ulrich Wessel, the leader, and capturing four other terrorists.

April 25: Francis P. Covey skyjacks a United B-727 en route with sixty-seven people from Raleigh, North Carolina, to Newark, New Jersey. Covey demands to be flown to Cuba. He will later be imprisoned.

May 15: Deborah L. Crawford attempts to skyjack a United B-737 en route from Eugene, Oregon, to San Francisco with eighty people aboard. Claiming she has a knife, she forbids the pilot to land in San Francisco. She will be institutionalized.

May 21: The trial of German terrorists Ulrike Meinhof, Andreas Baader, Gudrun Ensslin, and Jan-Carl Raspe begins, with more than 600 capital offenses charged against them. The trial will go on for almost two years.

June 3: A Philippines Airlines passenger jet makes an emergency landing 200 miles south of Manila, after a bomb planted in the lavatory explodes, killing one person and injuring forty-five others.

June 6: Morris E. Colosky, wielding a knife, skyjacks a chartered helicopter en route from Plymouth to Lansing, Michigan. Colosky forces the pilot, Richard Jackson, to fly to the Southern State Prison at Jackson, Michigan, and land inside the walls on the athletic field, where a red handkerchief has been placed by prisoner Dale Otto Remling. Seconds after the helicopter lands, Remling dashes forth and leaps inside. Jackson is then ordered by Colosky to land the helicopter on a roadway where two cars are waiting. After landing, Colosky and Remling disable Jackson by spraying him with mace, and then make their escape in the cars. Both Remling and Colosky will later be captured, along with six accomplices, and imprisoned. Remling has schemed up the helicopter escape, modeling it after a prison escape by helicopter as shown in the trailers for the movie, *Breakout*, which Remling has seen on the prison TV only weeks earlier.

August 3: Fifty-three hostages are taken at the U.S. embassy in Kuala Lampur, Malaysia, by Japanese Red Army terrorists, who demand that Japan release imprisoned terrorists. The demand is met and the hostages are released before the terrorists are allowed to fly to Libya.

August 15: Seven patients at the Veterans Administration Hospital in Ann Arbor,

Michigan, suffer lung and heart failure within the same hour, and, despite the frantic efforts of physicians, four patients die. FBI agents will determine that between July 1 and August 15, eleven suspicious deaths have occurred (out of fifty-six patients stricken with breathing failures in the six-week period). The victims have been given Pavulon, a powerful muscle relaxant, which has been added to the dextrose and water solutions administered to these patients. (Pavulon is a derivative of curare, a vegetable poison South American Indians ritualistically use on blow-gun darts to paralyze enemies and animals.) Though two Filipino nurses are later charged with the killings, they are exonerated and the culprit is not found.

August 15: Sheik Mujibur Rahma, president of Bangladesh, is assassinated in a coup.

September 5: U.S. President Gerald Rudolph Ford survives an assassination attempt on his life in Sacramento, California, by Charles Manson devotee Lynette Alice "Squeaky" Fromme, who is sent to prison.

September 15: Arab terrorists take the Egyptian ambassador and others hostage in the Egyptian embassy in Madrid, Spain, insisting that Egypt repudiate the Sinai Agreement with Israel. After several Egyptian diplomats sign such a statement, the hostages are released. Egypt then refuses to recognize the statement as valid.

September 15: Frederick Saloman attempts to skyjack an out-of-service B-727 in San Jose, California. Saloman takes four hostages, two of whom escape. He releases another hostage and wounds the fourth before he is fatally shot by police officers.

September 22: U.S. President Gerald Ford is assaulted by an armed political activist, Sarah Jane Moore, but the attack is thwarted. Moore is sent to prison.

September 27: A bombing in a Lowell, Massachusetts, cafe injures twenty-three people and causes considerable damage to Jake's Cafe and sixty-eight neighboring businesses. The bomb has been set off by two persons who open a gas main in the cafe under the directions of a terrorist who is later sent to prison.

September 30: A bomb explodes inside a Hungarian passenger jet en route from Budapest to Beirut, causing it to crash into the Mediterranean Sea, killing all sixty-four persons on board.

October 3: IRA terrorists abduct and hold hostage the manager of a steel plant in Limerick, Ireland, demanding that prisoners be released. After the hostage is released, the IRA terrorists are captured.

November 8: A suicidally bent Jack R. Johnson skyjacks a chartered Tri State Aero Cessna flying over Evansville, Idaho. Wielding a pistol, Johnson orders the pilot to dive straight into the ground below. The pilot struggles with Johnson, finally pushing him out of the in-flight plane. Johnson is killed by the fall.

December 2: Six South Moluccan terrorists take about fifty persons hostage on a train near Beilen, Netherlands, demanding independence for their homeland. Three hostages will be killed before the terrorists surrender on December 14, 1975.

December 4: Forty-seven hostages are taken at the Indonesian consulate in Amsterdam, Netherlands, by South Moluccan terrorists who demand autonomy for their homeland. The demand is refused and, on December 19, 1976, the hostages are set free and the terrorists surrender.

December 21: Ilyich Ramirez Sanchez, an infamous terrorist better known as Carlos or "the Jackal," leads seven other PFLP terrorists in a raid on an OPEC conference in Vienna, Austria, holding eighty-one representatives hostage. Sanchez, his men, and hostages are given a $50 million ransom and flown safely to Algiers.

December 23: Richard S. Welsh, chief of the CIA in Athens, Greece, is fatally shot by unknown terrorists as he arrives at his home.

December 29: Eleven persons are killed and seventy more are injured when a bomb explodes in one of the terminals at New York's LaGuardia Airport. The terrorist is not found.

1976

January 1: A bomb explodes in the luggage compartment of a Lebanese jetliner flying between Saudi Arabia and Kuwait, killing all eighty-two persons on board.

January 15: Sixteen-year-old Cynthia Cadieux vanishes from her Roseville, Michigan, home. She will be found the next morning on Franklyn Road, her head crushed by a blunt instrument, her body naked on a snow drift, and her clothes piled neatly nearby. She is the first of seven victims killed by what police believe is a lone killer-terrorist who murders young boys and girls in the Detroit suburbs through 1977. Despite the efforts of a massive police task force, the murderer will not be caught.

February 13: General Murtala Ramat Mohammed, president of Nigeria, is assassinated by terrorists during a coup attempt.

February 27: Business executive William Niehous is kidnapped by terrorists from his home in Caracas, Venezuela. The abductors demand a $3.5 million ransom and concessions for Niehous' employees. After negotiations, Niehous is released.

March: Five Negro terrorists, who make up San Francisco's "Death Angels," are tried for the random murders of fifteen whites, slain in the city as part of the group's "initiation" rites. After 371 days, the terrorists are convicted and sent to prison for life.

May 4: Gudrun Ensslin of the Baader-Meinhof Gang confesses to three bombings for which her group has been charged.

May 21: Moslem terrorists skyjack a Philippines Airlines jetliner at Zamboanga, Philippines, exploding hand grenades on board and killing thirteen persons and injuring fourteen others.

May 23: Armed Vanguard of the Proletariat terrorists abduct Gayle Moony, daughter of a U.S. businessman, in Acapulco, Mexico, and hold her for ransom. She will later be set free unharmed.

June 2: Don Bolles, a reporter investigating organized crime in Phoenix, Arizona, is blown up and killed when a car bomb in his auto explodes. John Harvey Adamson will later be convicted of this bombing and sent to prison for twenty years.

June 16: Anti-apartheid riots take place in Soweto, South Africa, in which 176 persons, mostly blacks, are killed. Rioting will spread to Transvaal, Natal, and Pretoria.

June 24: Seven terrorists, two West Germans, and five PFLP members skyjack an Air France Airbus en route from Tel Aviv to Paris with 245 passengers on board. They order the pilot to fly to Entebbe, Uganda, where, through the collusion of military dictator Idi Amin, the mostly Israeli passengers will be held hostage at the airport until rescued by Israeli commandos. Two captives will die while being held hostage and all of the terrorists will be killed in the commando raid, after which the passengers are flown to safety.

July 15: Richard and James Schoenfeld kidnap a school bus carrying twenty-six children near Chowchilla, California, demanding $5 million ransom. The abductors bury the bus and collect the ransom. The children are later found unharmed.

July 21: An IRA bomb kills British Ambassador Christopher Ewart-Biggs as he drives from his residence outside of Dublin, Ireland, to the embassy in Merrion Square.

July 29: David Berkowitz, the New York City terrorist who will call himself "Son of Sam" (after a dog named Sam), kills his first random victim, Donna Lauria, and wounds Jody Valenti, after firing several shots into the car in which both girls are sitting, parked in the Bronx.

September 21: Orlando Letelier, former foreign minister of Chile, dies when his car blows up in Washington, D.C., the victim of unknown terrorists.

September 28: An Army bomb expert is killed and a state arson expert wounded while attempting to defuse one of five dynamite bombs blown up at the Quincy Compressor Company in Quincy, Illinois, shortly after a visit from vice presidential

candidate Robert Dole. Three men are later sent to prison, convicted of murder and arson.

October 6: Nine minutes after taking off from Barbados, West Indies, a Cuban jet bound for Kingston, Jamaica, explodes, killing all seventy-three passengers on board.

October 11: Three Palestinian terrorists attempt to seize the Syrian embassy in Islamabad, Pakistan, but are foiled by police, who kill two terrorists and capture the third.

October 11: Palestinian terrorists belonging to the Black June group hold five hostages at the Syrian embassy in Rome, Italy, to state that Syria has not treated their terrorist group fairly. After injuring one hostage, the terrorists surrender to police.

October 17: A movie theater in Buenos Aires, Argentina, is destroyed and fifty persons are injured when a bomb explodes during a Peronist "Loyalty Day" celebration.

October 20: Members of the People's Revolutionary Front kidnap financier Tulio Oneto in Buenos Aires, Argentina. Oneto will be murdered after his family refuses to pay the $2 million ransom.

October 23: Terrorist David Berkowitz ("Son of Sam") shoots and wounds Carl Denaro, who has been sitting in his car with girlfriend Rosemary Keenan, in front of a Flushing bar.

November 26: David Berkowitz ("Son of Sam") approaches two girls, Donna DeMasi and Joanne Lomino, who are sitting on a stoop chatting in the Floral Park section of Queens. He asks for directions, then draws a gun from a paper bag and fires blindly at the girls, wounding both of them. Lomino will be paralyzed. Police match the bullets from this shooting to that of the Lauria-Valenti shooting and realize they are dealing with a berserk terrorist.

December 15: Fifteen persons are killed and thirty more are injured when a dynamite bomb planted by leftist Montoneros terrorists explodes in the Defense Ministry Building in Buenos Aires, Argentina.

1977

January 11: William Saupe attempts to skyjack a TWA B-747 en route from New York to London, with 333 persons on board. Saupe claims to have hand grenades and demands to be flown to Uganda. He will be seized and later put on probation.

January 19: Vaughn Greenwood, who has been tried and convicted for eleven murders, including those 1974–1975 murders committed by the "Los Angeles Slasher," is sentenced to life imprisonment.

January 30: David Berkowitz ("Son of Sam") finds a couple necking in a car in Ridgewood, Queens, and fires a bullet into the head of Christine Freund, who falls into the arms of her boyfriend, John Diehl. She is pronounced dead on arrival when reaching a hospital.

January 31: Following a heavy snowfall in Buffalo, New York, dozens of homes, businesses, and vehicles are looted by thieves. Police attempt to track them down on snowmobiles but are largely unsuccessful.

February 3: General Teferi Bante, Ethiopian head of state, and six others on the military council of power, are assassinated during a coup led by Lieutenant Colonel Mengistu Haile-Mariam.

March 8: David Berkowitz ("Son of Sam") walks up to Virginia Voskerichian, an Armenian student, on a Forest Hills street and fires a bullet point-blank into her face, killing her instantly.

March 9: Haamas Abdul Khaalis, a Negro whose real name is Ernest Timothy McGhee, leads a group of black terrorists calling themselves the Hanafi Muslims (a splinter group of the Black Muslims), in a terror campaign in Washington, D.C., invading three buildings, killing one person and wounding eleven others. Khaalis and his terrorists hold 100 hostages and demand that the movie *Mohammad, Messenger of God*, which he deems sacrilegious, be banned, and that five Black Muslims responsible for the 1973 slayings of seven Khaalis family members be turned over to him for execution. Some of the demands are met and Khaalis releases the hostages.

March 15: Luciano Pocari skyjacks an Iberia Airlines B-727 scheduled to take thirty-seven people from Barcelona to Palma de Mallorca, forcing the pilot to fly to the Ivory Coast. Pocari demands $120,000 to recover his daughter from her mother. He will be arrested and imprisoned.

March 16: Kamal Jumbat, Lebanese Druse leader, is shot to death by terrorists outside of Beirut.

March 18: Marien Ngouabi, president of the Congo, is shot to death by terrorists in Brazzaville.

March 27: Nine persons are injured when six bombs are exploded in the Sheraton Hilton Hotel in Buenos Aires, Argentina.

April 10: Abdullah al-Henjiri, ex-prime minister of Yemen, his wife, and the Yemen Embassy minister, are all fatally shot in London by Zohair Akache, a Palestinian terrorist.

April 15: Luchino Rewvelli-Beaumont, head of a French Fiat subsidiary is kidnapped near his apartment in Paris by nine South American terrorists calling themselves the Committee for Socialist Revolutionary Unity. A $2 million ransom is reportedly paid for the executive's release.

April 17: David Berkowitz ("Son of Sam") shoots Alexander Esau and Valentina Suriani, who sit in a parked car in the Bronx. Suriani dies instantly, and Esau dies three hours later.

April 28: Ulrike Meinhof (tried *in absentia*; she has committed suicide in 1976 inside her cell), Andreas Baader, Gudrun Ensslin, and Jan-Carl Raspe, the leadership core of the dreaded Baader-Meinhof terrorist gang, are all convicted of murder, robbery, and terrorism and sent to prison for life. The three remaining terrorists will commit suicide in their cells.

May 8: Bruce J. Trayer, armed with a razor blade, tries to skyjack a Northwest B-747 en route from Tokyo to Honolulu with 262 persons on board. He demands to be taken to Moscow, but Trayer is overpowered and the plane returns to Tokyo. Trayer will be sent to an insane asylum.

May 23: South Moluccan terrorists take 55 persons hostage on board a train close to Glimmen, Netherlands, and demand the release of imprisoned terrorists and an escape bus. Police storm the train and the resulting shootout leaves two hostages and six terrorists dead. On the same day, South Moluccan terrorists seize an ele-

mentary school in Bovensmilde, Netherlands, holding 125 children and 5 teachers hostage. The children will be freed by the terrorists and the police will rescue the teachers while capturing the terrorists.

June 6: Nasser Mohammed Ali Abu Khaled skyjacks a Lebanon Middle East Airways B-707 bound for Baghdad, Iraq, with 115 passengers aboard. The terrorist demands $5 million ransom. He will be subdued by commandos and later released for health reasons.

June 26: David Berkowitz ("Son of Sam") shoots and wounds Salvatore Lupo and Judy Placido as they sit in a car parked in Queens.

July 23: Hanafi Muslim terrorist Haamas Abdul Khaalis and seven of his followers are convicted of kidnapping and murder during their March 9, 1977, terrorist spree in Washington, D.C. They are all given long prison terms.

July 30: Jürgen Ponto, a prominent German banker, is slain in Frankfurt, Germany, by Red Army Faction (RAF) terrorists.

July 31: David Berkowitz ("Son of Sam"), while prowling through Brooklyn streets, finds Robert Violante and Stacy Moskowitz sitting in a parked car with the windows rolled up. He fires four times through the window, killing Moskowitz and blinding Violante.

August 2: David Berkowitz ("Son of Sam"), who has been identified when running from the scene of the Violante-Moskowitz shooting in Brooklyn to his car, which bore a traffic ticket, is tracked down by police, who have identified his auto. The terrorist will plead guilty at his arraignment and never be tried; he is given 365 years in prison with no hope of parole.

August 6: A bomb explodes in a Woolworth store in Salisbury, Rhodesia, killing eleven people and injuring another seventy-six.

October 6: Kenneth Bianchi and Angelo Buono begin their long series of serial killings in the Los Angeles area, which will be attributed to a terrorist labeled the "Hillside Strangler," by abducting, raping, and strangling twenty-one-year-old Elissa Teresa Kastin, dumping her naked body on Chevy Chase Drive.

October 13: Four PFLP terrorists skyjack a Lufthansa 737 jet from Palma de Mallorca, to Frankfurt, Germany. The plane lands in Rome for refueling and then flies to several Middle Eastern countries, where it is refused the right to land. During the flight, the Arab terrorists demand that eleven political prisoners be released and $15 million paid to them. After fatally shooting the pilot, the terrorists order the co-pilot to fly to Mogadishu, where German commandos storm the plane, killing three of the terrorists. Other than the pilot, the passengers and crew members miraculously remain unharmed.

October 18: Yolanda Washington is slain by Kenneth Bianchi (the "Hillside Strangler") and Angelo Buono, her naked body scrubbed clean to eliminate clues, dumped on the slopes of Forest Lawn Cemetery.

October 19: German industrialist Hans Martin Schleyer, who has been kidnapped in Cologne, Germany, is murdered by members of the Baader-Meinhof gang after authorities refuse to exchange Schleyer for imprisoned B-M gang members.

October 20: Thomas M. Hannan skyjacks a B-737 en route from Grand Island to Lincoln, Nebraska, with thirty-four per-

sons on board. He wields a shotgun and demands to be flown to Atlanta, Georgia, to pick up a convict. Hannan also demands a $3 million ransom, parachutes, and weapons. The hostages will be released and Hannan will fatally shoot himself.

October 31: Judith Lynn Miller, fifteen, is abducted, raped, and strangled by Kenneth Bianchi (the "Hillside Strangler") and Angelo Buono, her naked body scrubbed clean and dumped close to a road on a hillside in Glendale, California.

October: Sayf bin Sa'id al-Ghubash, the foreign minister of the United Arab Emirates, dies in an assault at the Abu Dhabi airport, apparently assassinated by Abu Nidal terrorists in an unsuccessful attempt to kill Abd al-Halim Khaddam, the Syrian foreign minister.

November 15: Muhammed Salah, director of the Arab Library in Paris, France, is slain by Abu Nidal terrorists.

November 20: Kenneth Bianchi (the "Hillside Strangler") and Angelo Buono abduct, rape, and strangle three females—Dolores Cepeda, twelve; Sonja Johnson, fourteen; and Kristina Weckler, twenty. Weckler's naked body is dumped on a hillside in Highland Park, California, the nude bodies of Cepeda and Johnson are placed on slopes in Elysian Park, California.

November 23: Kenneth Bianchi (the "Hillside Strangler") and Angelo Buono abduct, rape, and strangle Jane Evelyn King, twenty-eight, dumping her naked body onto an offramp of the southbound Golden State Freeway.

November 29: Lauren Rae Wagner, eighteen, and Kimberly Diane Martin, eighteen, are abducted, raped, and strangled by Kenneth Bianchi (the "Hillside

Strangler") and Angelo Buono. The killers dump Wagner's body on a slope of Cliff Drive in Glassell Park, California, and Martin's body some miles away.

December 14: Achilleas Kypianou, son of the Cyprus president, is abducted by terrorists. He will be released after political concessions are made to the terrorists.

December 25: Nikolai Wischnewski skyjacks an Eastern DC-9 en route from Jacksonville, Florida, to Atlanta, with thirty-six people aboard. He wields a toy pistol and phony bomb, and demands to be flown to Cuba. He will later be imprisoned.

1978

January 1: Said Hammami (Hamami), Palestinian Liberation Organization agent in London, is slain in London by Abu Nidal terrorists.

January 10: Pedro Chamorro, an editor and publisher who publishes an anti-government newspaper, is murdered by terrorists in Managua, Nicaragua.

February 2: Seven hostages are taken at the United Nations office in San Salvador by Popular Revolutionary Bloc terrorists whose demands for the release of political prisoners are not met. The hostages are released after the U.N. promises to make an official inquiry into human rights violations in El Salvador.

February 3: Ten persons are killed in widespread rioting in Nicaragua by those opposing the Somoza regime.

February 17: The naked body of Cindy Lee Hudspeth is found by Los Angeles

officers in the trunk of a car; she has been abducted, raped, and strangled by Kenneth Bianchi (the "Hillside Strangler") and Angelo Buono.

February 18: Yusuf Siba'i (Yousseff el-Sebai), leader of the Committee for Afro-Asian Solidarity and editor of *Al Ahram*, an Egyptian newspaper, is murdered in Nicosia, by Abu Nidal Palestinian terrorists.

March 12: PLO terrorists from South Lebanon blow up a public bus in Tel Aviv, Israel, killing thirty-seven people.

March 13: Seventy-two hostages are taken at government offices in Assen, Netherlands, by South Moluccan terrorists who demand the release of fellow imprisoned terrorists, a $12 million ransom, and an escape bus. The demands are refused and police storm the offices. One hostage is slain and three terrorists are apprehended.

March 16: Aldo Moro, who has served as Italy's prime minister, is kidnapped as five of his bodyguards are shot and killed by Red Brigades terrorists. The terrorists demanded the release of all Communist prisoners to guarantee Moro's safe return.

March 27: Chief Kapuuo, who has been appointed president of Nambia by South African officials, is slain by terrorists.

April 1: Richard Bland, sixteen, attempts to skyjack a B-737 en route from Richmond to Norfolk, Virginia, with sixty-six persons aboard. Brandishing a rifle, Bland demands $1 million ransom and a flight to New York, and then France. He will be captured and later put under psychiatric care.

May 8: After the Italian government refused to yield to the Red Brigades kidnappers of Aldo Moro, the body of the former prime minister is found in Rome, stuffed into the trunk of car. Moro, his hands and feet bound with chains, had been shot eleven times in the heart.

May 11: Mario Astarita, Italian manager of the Chemical Bank of New York, is shot in the legs in Milan, Italy, apparently by a terrorist group calling itself the Front Line and Fighting Communist Formations, a faction of the Red Brigades. The shooting is apparently a reprisal against the Italian Government's refusal to exchange Aldo Moro (the former prime minister who has been killed days earlier by Red Brigadists) for imprisoned terrorists.

May 24: Four persons flying in a small Piper Aztec plane are killed by an explosion over Nairobi, Kenya.

May 24: Barbara A. Oswald, armed with three pistols, skyjacks a chartered helicopter out of St. Louis. She demands the release of G. Trapnell, a federal prisoner. The pilot struggles with her, grabs her pistol, and fatally shoots her.

June 15: Ali Yasin, an agent of the Palestinian Liberation Organization, is slain in Kuwait by Abu Nidal terrorists.

June 24: President Ghashmi of North Yemen is assassinated by terrorists at a conference in Beirut, Lebanon.

July 9: Abdul Razak Al-Naif, ex-premier of Iraq, is shot dead in London by members of Al Mukharabat, Iraq's secret intelligence service, which functions as a terrorist organization.

July 21: General Juan Sanchez and Lieutenant Colonel Juan Perez Rodriguez are assassinated in Spain by a terrorist who will be sent to prison.

August 3: Ezzedine Kalak, director of the Palestinian Liberation Organization in Paris, and Adnan Hamid, a journalist for the Palestine news organization, are both slain in Paris by Abu Nidal terrorists.

August 17: Two Croatian terrorists take eight persons hostage at the West German consulate in Chicago, Illinois, demanding that a Croatian in Cologne, West Germany, be set free. The terrorists later give themselves up and free the hostages.

August 18: A terrorist accidentally sets off a bomb he is planting in the lavatory of a Philippines Airlines jetliner en route from Cebu to Manila, killing himself and wounding three others.

August 27: Diana L. Benson skyjacks a United DC-8 en route from Denver to Seattle with 159 people aboard. Claiming to possess a bomb, Benson demands to be flown to Vancouver, Canada. She will be captured and found to be mentally incompetent before being released.

November 23: John R. Prindle attempts to skyjack a DC-9 en route from Madison to Milwaukee, Wisconsin, with twenty-three persons on board. Prindle brandishes a knife and claims to have a bomb, but when asked for his demands, Prindle only grins and babbles incoherently—"Take me to Paris . . . no, no, maybe New York is better . . . What do you think about Dallas?" He will be seized and found to be mentally incompetent.

November 27: Mayor George Mascone of San Francisco, and supervisor Harvey Milk, a professed homosexual, are both slain by former supervisor Daniel James White. White will be sent to prison for manslaughter, instead of the more serious crime of murder, a verdict that will spark massive riots by the homosexual community on July 15, 1979.

December 7: Abdul Wahhab Kayali, former leader of the pro-Iraqi Liberation Front, is shot by terrorists in his office in Beirut, Lebanon.

December 11: Ayatollah Abdol Hossein Dastgheib, an aide to militant Iranian religious leader Ayatollah Ruhollah Khomeini, is killed by a bomb blast set off by terrorists near his home in Shiraz, Iran.

December 11: Fifteen-year-old Robert Piest is abducted, sodomized, and murdered by serial killer John Wayne Gacy. The search for Piest will lead to Gacy's arrest, conviction, and life sentence for killing the boy and twenty-six others over many years.

December 17: U.S. President Ronald Reagan is the target of an assassination attempt when he receives a letter bomb, which is disarmed.

December 21: Robyn S. Oswald, claiming to carry a bomb, skyjacks a TWA DC-9 en route from St. Louis to Kansas City, Missouri, to help G. Trapnell escape from prison—her mother has attempted the same thing in skyjacking a St. Louis helicopter seven months earlier—but she is seized, and will be put into a juvenile home and then placed on probation.

December 23: Paul Grimm, manager of the Oil Service Company of Iran, is shot to death by terrorists as he drives to work in Ahwaz, Iran.

1979

January 12: Ali Hassan Salemeh, organizer of the Black September (the enforcement arm of Al Fatah) massacre of Israeli athletes at the XX Olympiad in Munich,

Germany, on July 18, 1972, is slain by a car bomb planted by members of the Mossad, Israeli intelligence, which has sought Salemeh for seven years. Six passersby are also killed in the blast.

January 16: More than 100 hostages are taken from the Mexican Embassy, Red Cross and the Organization of American States, in El Salvador by United Popular Action Front terrorists who demand the release of prisoners and other political concessions. The hostages will be released and the terrorists will leave the country.

January 27: Irene McKinney, claiming to have nitroglycerin, skyjacks a United B-747 carrying 131 persons from Los Angeles to New York. She demands that a number of celebrities read a message on television. She will be seized and placed on probation.

January: Kenneth Bianchi, California's "Hillside Strangler," after moving to Bellingham, Washington (where he has applied for a position with the police department), abducts, rapes, and strangles college girls Diane Wilder and Karen Mandic, stuffing the bodies into the trunk of Mandic's car.

February 14: About 100 hostages at the U.S. Embassy in Teheran are seized for about two hours by Iranian terrorists. An Iranian embassy worker is slain before the terrorists leave the embassy grounds.

February 14: Adolph Dubs, U.S. ambassador to Afghanistan, is shot dead in Kabul by Afghan Muslim terrorists.

March 16: John C. Kivlen, claiming to have a knife, skyjacks a B-727 en route from Los Angeles to Tuscon, Arizona, carrying ninety-four people. He demands $200,000 ransom and a flight to Cuba. He will be seized and sent to an insane asylum.

March 22: Sir Richard Sykes, British ambassador to the Netherlands, is fatally shot at his home at The Hague by terrorists.

March 30: Airey Neave, Tory member of the British parliament, is slain when a bomb explodes in his car, one reportedly planted by IRA terrorists.

April 4: Zulfikar Ali Bhutto, former president and prime minister of Pakistan, overthrown in 1977, is put to death in Rawalpindi, Pakistan.

April 4: Domenico Speranza attempts to skyjack a Pan American B-747 in Sydney, Australia, which is scheduled to fly to Auckland, New Zealand. Wielding a knife and showing two cans of gunpowder, Speranza demands to be flown to Rome and then on to Moscow. He will be killed before the plane leaves Sydney.

May 4: The Metropolitan Cathedral in San Salvador is seized by Popular Revolutionary Bloc terrorists, who demand the release of five political prisoners and an investigation into human rights violations in El Salvador. Seventeen persons will die and another thirty-five are injured when police storm the building.

May 15: Farabundo Marti Popular Liberation Forces terrorists fail to take over the South African Embassy in San Salvador. Two police officers die in a shootout and the terrorists escape.

May 29: U.S. District Judge John H. Wood, Jr., is shot to death by Charles B. Harrelson in San Antonio, Texas. Harrelson, a professional killer, who previously served time for a 1968 murder, is convicted of killing Wood and given two consecutive life sentences. His employer, drug king James Chagra, who was to appear before Wood on a drug conviction, is also sent to prison for life.

June 11: Eduardo Guerra Jimenez skyjacks a Delta L-1011 en route from New York to Fort Lauderdale with 204 people on board. Jimenez carries a pocketknife and claims to have a bomb and a gun. He demands to go to Cuba, where he will escape.

June 20: Nikola Kavaja skyjacks an American Airlines B-727 en route from New York to Chicago with 136 people aboard. Claiming to have dynamite, he demands the release of a prisoner and a flight to Ireland. He will be seized and imprisoned.

June 29: U.S. General Alexander Haig, NATO commander, is the target of a failed attempt on his life with a car bomb in Belgium.

June 30: Rigoberto Gonzalez Sanchez attempts to skyjack an Eastern Airlines L-1011 en route from San Juan, Puerto Rico, to Miami carrying 306 people. Threatening to ignite a bottle of gasoline (it is rum), he orders the pilot to fly to Cuba. Gonzalez Sanchez is overpowered and will later be institutionalized.

July 15: Thousands of homosexuals enraged at the lenient sentence given to former Supervisor Daniel James White for his killing of gay Supervisor Harvey Milk (and straight Mayor George Mascone), create widespread rioting, which results in millions of dollars in damage to businesses.

July 20: Ronald A. Rimerman skyjacks a United B-727 en route from Denver to Omaha, Nebraska, carrying 126 people. He claims to have plastic explosives and orders the pilot to fly to Cuba. He will be seized and sent to an insane asylum.

July 25: Zuhair Moshin, head of the Syrian-dominated Sa'ika, is fatally shot near his apartment in Cannes, France, by

Abu Nidal terrorists acting for Al Mukharabat, the Iraqi secret service.

August 16: Alfred R. Kagan skyjacks an Eastern B-727 en route from Guatemala City, Guatemala, to Miami with ninety-one people on board. Brandishing a penknife and claiming to have a bomb, Kagan demands he be flown to Cuba. He will be seized and institutionalized.

August 22: James R. Albee will become a convicted skyjacker, sentenced to sixty years in prison in Oregon for threatening with a bomb the pilot of a Los Angeles-bound United B-727 en route from Portland, Oregon, to Los Angeles with 120 people on board.

August 27: World War II hero First Earl Louis Mountbatten is blown up and killed on his boat as he fishes in Donegal Bay, off the coast of County Sligo, Ireland; the cause of the explosion is an IRA bomb.

August 27: Eighteen British soldiers are killed by two IRA bombs exploding in Warrenpoint, Ireland.

September 12: Rafael Keppel, employing a toy pistol, skyjacks a Lufthansa B-727, flying from Frankfurt, Germany with 119 persons and eight crew members. Keppel forces the pilot to land at the Bonn-Cologne airport, holding all on board hostage for seven hours while reading a rambling manifesto demanding a "more humane world." Keppel will later surrender and be imprisoned.

October 26: Park Chung Hee, president of South Korea, and several aides and body-guards, are shot to death in Seoul, South Korea, by Kim Jae Kyu, South Korean intelligence chief, and others during a military coup. Kyu will be sentenced to death on December 20, 1979.

October 30: John E. Gray skyjacks a B-727 en route from Los Angeles to San Diego, California, with 108 people on board, ordering the pilot to fly to Mexico. He will be seized and imprisoned.

October 30: About 300 leftwing terrorists attempt to storm the U.S. Embassy in San Salvador but are repulsed by U.S. Marines and local police and troops. Two Marines are injured and the terrorists driven off.

November 4: Sixty-three hostages are taken at the U.S. Embassy in Teheran by Iranian terrorists, who demand the return of the Shah of Iran to Iran for trial. Though the demands of the terrorists will not be met, and a poorly organized rescue attempt of the hostages will fail, the American hostages, after enduring prolonged captivity, will eventually be released, their freedom negotiated by officials of President Ronald Reagan's administration. (The failure of President Jimmy Carter to effect the release of the hostages greatly contributes to Reagan's election as president.)

November 13: Efraim Eldar, Israel's ambassador to Portugal, is the target of an unsuccessful assassination in Lisbon, by Abu Nidal terrorists.

November 21: A bomb thrown from a passing car into Junior's Lunch Cafe in Lynchburg, Virginia, injures three people and causes $28,000 worth of damage.

November 21: Thousands of Muslim terrorists attack and burn the U.S. Embassy in Islamabad, Pakistan. Local troops manage to rescue more than 100 U.S. citizens. One U.S. Marine is killed while defending the embassy.

November 24: Gerald J. Hill, claiming to carry a knife and dynamite, skyjacks an American Airlines B-727 en route from San

Antonio to El Paso, Texas with seventy-four persons aboard. Hill demands to be flown to Iran, but he is seized and imprisoned.

November 29: A seventeen-year-old boy is killed while attempting to place a bomb inside a soda-pop machine in St. Stephens, South Carolina.

November: Five Communist Workers Party members are killed by terrorists in Greensboro, North Carolina. Six members of the Ku Klux Klan are indicated for the slayings, but they will be acquitted a year later.

December 3: Eleven persons are trampled to death in a riot created by fans trying to enter a crowded Cincinnati, Ohio, rock concert given by the rock-and-roll group, The Who.

1980

January 25: Samuel A. Ingram, claiming to have a bomb and a pistol, skyjacks a Delta L-1011, compelling the pilot to fly sixty-three people to Cuba, where the crew and most of the passengers escape. Ingram insists that he then be flown to Iran, but he surrenders and will be imprisoned.

January 31: Left-wing terrorists seize the Spanish Embassy in Guatemala City, Guatemala, holding eight hostages. The police do not negotiate but storm the building, which catches fire. Only one of the terrorists and the Spanish ambassador will survive the blaze.

February 3: Thirty-two persons are killed and scores more injured when inmates of the New Mexico State Prison riot over conditions.

February 27: Fifty-seven hostages are taken at the Dominican Republic Embassy in Bogotá, Colombia, by M-19 terrorists, who demand $50 million ransom and political concessions. They will accept $2 million and be given permission to leave the country.

March 10: Four persons are killed in a Paris synagogue bombed by the PFLP, the explosive device placed on the back of a motorcycle parked in front of the temple.

March 24: Oscar Arnulfo Romero, archbishop of San Salvador, an outspoken critic of the country's oppressive military leaders, is killed by terrorists

April 12: William Richard Tolbert, Jr., president of the Republic of Liberia, is assassinated after being overthrown in a coup led by Sergeant Samuel K. Doe.

April 14: Indira Gandhi, prime minister of India, is the target of an unsuccessful assassination when a terrorist hurls a knife at her in New Delhi.

April 14: Thomas C. Wiltgen, carrying a knife and claiming to be an IRA member, skyjacks a Continental B-727 in Denver, demanding to be flown to Libya. He allows the seventy-five passengers to deplane before surrendering. He will be imprisoned.

April 30: Five Arab terrorists from Iran take twenty-six hostages at the Iranian embassy, demanding the release of political prisoners in Iran. Two hostages will be slain, five set free, and the others rescued when British forces storm the embassy, killing two of the terrorists and taking the other three prisoner.

May 1: Stephen W. Bilson sneaks onto a Pacific Southwest B-727 in Stockton,

California, taking the flight engineer hostage. He reads a rambling statement about Iran and hostages in Iran before he is overpowered by the flight engineer and arrested. He will be imprisoned.

May 10: Omran el-Mehdawi, second secretary of the Libyan Embassy in Bonn, Germany, is killed by terrorists.

May 19: Race riots in Miami see eighteen persons killed, scores injured, more than 1,300 people, mostly blacks, arrested, and more than $100 million in damage. Only when 3,500 National Guardsmen are called to the scene will the riots be quelled.

May 29: Vernon E. Jordan, Jr., civil rights leader and president of the National Urban League, is shot and injured in Fort Wayne, Indiana, but survies the attack.

June 12: FAR terrorists kidnap the president of a subsidary of Nestle Company in Guatemala, receiving a reported $4.7 million for the executive's release.

June 27: A bomb, or a ground-to-air missile, explodes a DC-9 jetliner, causing it to crash ninety miles southwest of Naples, Italy, killing eighty-one persons.

July 11: Glen K. Tripp, threatening to blow up a Northwest B-727 about to depart for Portland, Oregon with sixty-four people, demands $100,000 and two parachutes. He later changes his mind, and demands a car. While walking to the auto he is arrested. He will be imprisoned.

July 22: Silvio Mesa Cabrera skyjacks a 144-passenger Delta L-1011 en route from Miami to San Juan, Puerto Rico. He demands that the plane be flown to Havana but poor weather conditions force the craft to land at Camaguey, Cuba, where he vanishes.

July 22: Thousands of blacks riot in Chattanooga, Tennessee, after two Ku Klux Klan members are acquitted by an all-white jury of shooting four black women. Eight policemen are injured and widespread damage done.

August 2: The Armed Revolutionary Nuclei (NAR), a neo-fascist Italian terrorist group, causes the bombing of the Bologna railway station, killing seventy-five persons and injuring another 186 people.

August 10: Manuel Soto, threatening to blow up a Key West–bound Air Florida plane carrying thirty passenges and five crew members, orders the pilot to fly to Cuba. Upon landing in Havana, Soto surrenders to local police. His "bomb" turns out to be a box of soap.

August 20: More than 150 are killed and a dozen towns in Northern India are left in smoldering ruins following riots between Hindus and Muslims.

August 27: A well-constructed homemade bomb explodes in Harvey's Casino in Stateline, Nevada, causing $18 million in damages. There are no injuries.

August 27: Thousands of blacks riot in Philadelphia, Pennsylvania, after a police officer shoots and kills a black youth.

September 17: Anastasio Somoza, former president of Nicaragua, who has been ousted in 1979 by the Sandinistas, is shot to death by terrorists in Paraguay.

September 26: A member of the neo-Nazi Wehrsportsgruppe (Military Sports Group) explodes a bomb during the bierfest in Munich, Germany, killing himself and twelve bystanders. More than 300 people are injured.

November 14: Sixteen children, a school bus driver, and a teacher are taken hostage in Vielsalm, Belgium, by Mark Frank, Michael Stree, and another terrorist, who demand social reforms. The terrorists will drive the bus to Brussels, where police capture them and free the hostages.

November: Countess Giovanna di Porta Puglia is rescued from the castle of Castell Arguanto, south of Milan, Italy, after she has been held captive for more than forty years by her brothers Luigi and Alfredo Puglia, and Luigi's wife, who are all arrested and imprisoned.

December 7: Clifford Bevens, U.S. manager of a Goodyear subsidiary, Ginsa Tire, is kidnapped from his Guatamala City apartment by terrorists who demand $10 million ransom. Soldiers will locate the terrorist hideout and, when they storm this place, Bevens and his five kidnappers are killed.

December 28: Members of the Red Brigades, a terrorist organization responsible for countless kidnappings, robberies, and assassinations, imprisoned at Trani, Italy, lead a mass breakout attempt, holding hostages. Two days later, Italian commandos in helicopters land inside the prison yard and free the hostages.

December 31: General Enrico Galvaligi, chief of security for prisons confining terrorists, is shot to death by Red Brigadists in Italy, in reprisal for suppressing the revolt of terrorist prisoners in Trani, Italy, three days earlier.

December 31: The PFLP avenges itself for the Entebbe raid by blowing up the Zionist-owned Norfolk Hotel in Nairobi, Kenya, killing between sixteen and twenty people. Eighty-five others are injured in the resulting fire.

1981

January 3: Jose Rodolfo Viera, president of the Salvadoran Institute for Agrarian Transformation; Michael Peter Hammer, U.S. agrarian reform authority; and Mark David Pearlman, U.S. attorney, are all shot to death by terrorists in San Salvador, El Salvador.

January 12: Sheik Hammad Abu Rabia, chief of one of the largest Negev tribes, is shot to death by terrorists in Jerusalem.

January 12: Muslim rioting in Kano, Nigeria, leaves between 7,000 and 10,000 dead.

January 13: Bernadine Dohrn, the most fanatical of the Weathermen terrorist organization of the 1960s and 1970s, goes to trial for organizing the infamous "Days of Rage" riots in Chicago in 1969 and other crimes. She pleads guilty and is given a three-year suspended sentence and is fined $1,500.

January 16: Bernadette Devlin McAliskey, Irish political activist, and her husband, Michael, survive an attack after they are shot and wounded in County Tyrone, Ireland, by three members of a Protestant paramilitary organization.

January 18: Facundo Guardado, Salvadoran terrorist, is apprehended by Honduras' National Intelligence Division. After he is later set free, the terrorist will claim that he has been kidnapped and tortured.

January 19: Chester A. Bitterman III, a U.S. linguist, is abducted from the Summer Institute of Linguistics in Bogotá, Colombia, by terrorists who claim he is a CIA agent. Bitterman will be slain.

January 21: Sir Norman Stronge, Protestant speaker of the Northern Ireland Parliament, and his son, James, former speaker of the Stormont Parliament, are shot to death in their Armagh home, presumably by IRA terrorists in reprisal for the attack on Bernadette Devlin McAliskey.

January 27: More than 400 imprisoned IRA terrorists riot at Maze Prison, smashing furniture and windows and creating widespread damage.

February 6: Mahmut Dikler, deputy director of police for Istanbul, Turkey, and a bodyguard, are shot to death in Instanbul by left-wing terrorists.

February 6: Jose Maria Ryan, head engineer of a nuclear plant being built at Lemoniz, is killed by members of the Basque Fatherland and Liberty Group (ETA), a terrorist organization.

February 9: Eighteen peasants are killed when a bomb strikes the truck in which they are riding in Suchitoto, El Salvador. Thirty others are injured.

February 16: Pope John Paul II is the target of a failed assassination attempt when a bomb explodes just before his appearance in Pakistan. Muslim terrorists are suspected.

February 17: Muslim terrorists are suspected of exploding a bomb in Davao, Mindanao, Philippines, two days before Pope John Paul II is to arrive. One person is killed and eleven are wounded.

February 17: Luigi Maragoni, head of the state-run Polyclinic Hospital in Milan, is fatally shot by four attackers.

February 19: A bomb explosion at KGB headquarters in Moscow, U.S.S.R., kills an officer and his driver, an event the Soviet government officially denies.

February 20–21: Three separate bomb explosions in Teheran, Iran, kill two persons and injure thirty-one others.

February 23: The Munich, Germany, offices of Radio Free Europe and Radio Liberty are bombed and eight persons are injured.

March 7: PFLP terrorist leader Mohammed Zaidan Abbas, and top adviser to Yasir Arafat, sends two suicidal terrorists over Israeli territory in hang gliders to drop explosives on a refinery in Haifa. Both terrorists missed their objectives and fell into the hands of Israeli soldiers.

March 17: A bazooka shot is fired at a U.S. Embassy van in San Jose, Costa Rica, injuring three Marines and their Costa Rican driver.

March 28: Jihad Command terrorists skyjack an Indonesian Airways jet flying within Sumatra, taking the fifty-seven persons on board hostage and demanding the release of eighty political prisoners. When the plane lands, a shootout with police ensues and four of the terrorists are killed before the hostages are set free.

March 30: U.S. President Ronald Reagan, press secretary James Brady, police officer Thomas Delahanty, and Secret Service agent Timothy J. McCarthy, are shot and wounded (all survive) in Washington, D.C., by John W. Hinckley, Jr., who will be sent to an institution for the mentally ill.

April 2: A bomb demolishes a garage in Newport, Kentucky, killing two persons, injuring twenty-one others, and causing $1 million in property damage.

April 3: Scattered bombings and rioting in West Bengal, India, kill 8 persons and injure another 200 people.

April 6: Under orders from PFLP director Mohammed Zaidan Abbas, two terrorists attempt to infiltrate Israel in a hot-air balloon, but they are shot down by Israeli troops and killed.

April 14: Guiseppe Salvia, deputy director of Poggioreale Prison, is shot to death in his car in Naples, Italy, by Red Brigadists.

April 16: Joseph Munhangi, member of the Ugandan parliament, is assassinated by terrorists in Kampala, Uganda.

April 19: Thirteen people are killed and 177 injured when terrorists of the New People's Army of the outlawed Communist Party throw hand grenades into a Roman Catholic Church in Davao, Philippines, during an Easter Mass.

April 19: Two eighteen-year-old youths are killed in Londonderry, Ireland, when a British army vehicle rams into a crowd throwing gas bombs.

April 23: Naser Almaneih, a former Iranian police chief, is sentenced to fifty years in prison in California for the August 20, 1980, bombing of a high school in Berkeley, California, and for conspiring to bomb an Iranian meeting at San Jose State University.

April 25: A car bomb kills seven people and injures another thirty-five in the Iranian city of Kermanshah.

May 1: Heinz Nittel, Vienna councilman and president of the Austrian-Israel Friendship League, is shot to death near his apartment in Vienna, Austria, by terrorists who later identify themselves as members of Al-Asifa.

May 2: Laurence James Downey, an Australian, skyjacks an Aer Lingus B-737 flying from Dublin, Ireland, demanding publication of "The Third Secret of Fatima," a prophecy of global war held secret by the Vatican. Police will capture Downey upon the plane's landing.

May 4: General Andreas Gonzalez de Suso is shot to death by leftist terrorists near his home in Madrid, Spain.

May 7: Three Spanish military officers are killed and eleven passersby injured when Basque separatists lob a bomb into a staff car waiting for a red light in Madrid, Spain.

May 11: Heinz Herbert Karry, minister of econcomics of Hesse, West Germany, is shot to death in the bedroom of his apartment by terrorists in Frankfurt, Germany.

May 12: Otto Walter Garcia, one of the leaders of the Leftist United Revolutionary Front, is killed in Guatemala.

May 13: Pope John Paul II and two others are shot and wounded in St. Peter's Square, Rome, Italy, by Mehmet Ali Agca, a Turkish terrorist, acting on orders from Communist leaders in the Balkans. Agca will be sent to prison.

May 14: Carlos Humberto Mendez Lopez, deputy commander of the private army of the National Liberation Movement, is fatally shot by two terrorists in Guatamala City, Guatamala.

May 15: Following the death of hunger striker Francis Hughes, the IRA fires a rocket through the roof of a police car in West Belfast, Ireland, killing one officer and wounding three others.

May 16: The Puerto Rican Armed Resistance Group claims responsibility for a pipe-bomb explosion that kills Alex McMilan, an employee at Kennedy Airport in New York. Two other bombs are found in the airport within the next twenty-four hours.

May 20: New York Police receive 487 bomb threats in the wake of the May 16 bombing by Puerto Rican terrorists at Kennedy Airport.

May 20: Guiseppe Tagliercio, an administrator of a Montedison petrochemical firm, is kidnapped from his apartment in Mestre, Italy, by Red Brigades terrorists. Tagliercio will be murdered by his captors.

May 24: A Turkish Airlines DC-9 with 112 persons on board flying from Ankara to Istanbul, Turkey, is skyjacked by two Dev Sol terrorists who demand $500,000 ransom and the release of prisoners held in Turkey. The plane will land in Burgas, Bulgaria, where no demands will be met and the siege ended.

May 30: Ziaur Rahman, president of Bangladesh, is assassinated in Chittagong, Bangladesh, along with six bodyguards and two aides in a short-lived coup under General Abul Manzur, who will be killed by guards on June 1, 1981.

May 31: Warrant Officer Michael O'Neill, a member of a British bomb disposal unit, is killed near Newry, Ireland, while he is examining an auto.

June 1: Na'im Khadir, agent for the Palestinian Liberation Organization in Brussels, Belgium, is killed by Abu Nidal terrorists.

June 3: Though no injuries occur, damage in the millions of dollars is done when time bombs destroy two huge department stores and six adjacent buildings in Athens, Greece. The Revolutionary Anti-Capitalist Action and the New Organization claim responsibility.

June 6: The "Monster of Florence" kills again by shooting Giovanni Foggi, twenty-one, and his fiancée, Carmela Di Nuccio, nineteen, as they sit in a car in the southwest Florence suburb of Scandicci. The killer removes Di Nuccio's genitalia with a scalpel or razor-sharp knife.

June 11: A bomb explosion at the Arab Socialist Union Building in Tyre, Lebanon, kills twenty-five people.

June 23: An explosion at the Qom Railroad Station in Iran kills four persons and wounds fifty-eight.

June 28: The headquarters of the Islamic Republican Party in Teheran, Iran, is bombed, killing seventy-two persons, including Ayatollah Behesti, chief justice of the Supreme Court, and four cabinet ministers.

June 28: Muhammed Kacu'i, governor of Evin Prison, is murdered in Teheran by terrorists.

July 5: More than 200 persons are injured in Liverpool, England, when thousands riot in protest over the policies of Prime Minister Margaret Thatcher.

July 10: Kenneth Rex McElroy, a towering, beefy man, has, since dropping out of school thirty years earlier, terrorized the town of Skidmore, Missouri, by picking fights, shoving people off the sidewalks, barreling his pickup truck down roads to force others into ditches, and firing shotgun pellets into the ceiling of the local grocery store. He has shot two residents and escaped punishment. He has even bullied the local police into shunning him and ignoring his constant abuses. On this day more than eighty residents hold a town hall meeting to discuss McElroy and his incessant terror tactics. A short time later, as McElroy parks his pickup truck outside a local bar, dozens of residents surround his truck, while a man fires four rifle bullets into McElroy, killing him. All in the town refuse to identify McElroy's killer.

July 14: Three persons are killed by a bomb explosion in a movie theater in Banqui, in the Central African Republic.

August 1: Abu Da'ud (Abu Daoud), a leader of Black September and the Palestinian Liberation Organization (PLO), is slain in Warsaw, Poland, by Abu Nidal terrorists.

August 2: A bomb explodes during a wedding ceremony at the Christian Coptic Church in Cairo, Egypt, killing three people and injuring fifty-six others. The Arab Steadfastness Front, a terrorist organization, is held responsible.

August 18: Rosa Judith Cisneros, civil rights leader and legal adviser to the Salvadoran Communal Union, is killed as she leaves her home in San Salvador, El Salvador.

August 22: Forty-eight persons are injured by two IRA bombs set off in Belfast, Ireland, following the death of hunger striker Michael Devine.

August 30: Mohammed Ali Rejai, president of Iran, and Mohammed Javar Bahonar, prime minister, are assassinated and other officials are injured in a bomb blast in Teheran.

August 30: Eighteen people are injured when a bomb explodes at the Intercontinental Hotel in Paris, France.

August 31: A car bomb planted by the German Red Army at the U.S. Air Force Base in Ramstein wounds twenty persons.

September 3: A car bomb explodes in front of Syrian Air Force Headquarters in Damascus, killing twenty persons and wounding fifty others.

September 4: Louis Delamare, French ambassador to Lebanon, is shot to death by terrorists while driving his car in Beirut.

September 17: A car bomb explodes in Sidon, Lebanon, killing twenty-three persons. The Front for the Liberation of Lebanon from Foreigners, a right-wing terrorist group, takes credit.

September 18: A car rigged with bombs explodes in West Beirut on a street infested with drug dealers. Three persons are killed and many more injured. A group calling itself the Front for the Liberation of Lebanon from Foreigners takes credit for the explosion. The Palestinian Liberation Organization (PLO) claims the group is an Israeli front.

September 20: A bomb explodes in the Muslim section of Beirut, killing four persons and injuring thirty-five others. The Front for the Liberation of Lebanon from Foreigners takes credit.

September 28: A car bomb explodes at the Palestinian checkpoint in Zrariyeh, Lebanon, killing fifteen patrons in a nearby restaurant. The pro-Amal Shiites are believed to be responsible.

September 29: Hojatoleslam Abdulkarim Hashemi-Nejad, secretary general of the Islamic Republic Party, is killed and others are wounded in Mashad, Iran, by a hand grenade held by Hadi Alavai Fitilechi, a Mujahedeen terrorist.

Chronology

September 29: An India Airlines B-737 is skyjacked by five Sikhs after takeoff from New Delhi and forced to land in Lahore, Pakistan. The skyjackers demand $500,000 ransom and the release of Sant Jarnail Singh Bhindranwale and others. The terrorists will be overpowered and arrested.

October 1: A car bomb explodes next to the PLO offices in Beirut, Lebanon, killing 50 persons and wounding another 250 people. The attackers are believed to be members of the Front for the Liberation of Lebanon from Foreigners.

October 6: Khaled Islambouli, an Egyptian army officer and leader of the terrorist sect, Takfir Wal-Hajira, and four others, attack the reviewing stand in which Anwar Sadat, President of Egypt, and other Eygptian notables are sitting, watching a Cairo military parade. The terrorists hurl grenades and spray the reviewing stand with bullets from automatic weapons. Sadat is fatally struck by four bullets, and eleven other dignitaries are killed, along with many guards. Scores are wounded. The terrorists are quickly captured and it is later learned that they have been backed by Libyan strongman Muammar Qaddafi, who considers Sadat a traitor to the Arab cause because of Sadat's friendly relations with Israel.

October 10: A nail bomb attack is launched by the IRA on a bus in London, England, killing two persons and injuring thirty-five others.

October 17: Sir Stuart Pringle, general and ex-commandant of the British Marines and Northern Ireland commando leader, loses part of a leg when a bomb planted by IRA terrorists explodes in his car.

October 22: The "Monster of Florence" again murders a couple spooning in their car, twelve miles northwest of Florence, shooting twenty-four-year-old Stefano Baldi and Susanna Cambri. The woman is sexually mutilated as has been the case with previous victims. Police conclude from footprints that the killer is a large, heavyset man. Several suspects will be taken into custody but none will prove to be the serial killer.

November 4: Roland Smith receives a three-year prison sentence for threatening the life of U.S. President Ronald Reagan.

November 6: Israel Borquez, president of the Supreme Court of Chile, is slightly wounded in Santiago by terrorist gunmen.

November 14: Reverend Robert Bradford, member of the British parliament and Ulster unionist, is fatally shot in Belfast, Ireland, reportedly by IRA gunmen.

November 21: Terrorist Khaled Islambouli, killer of Egyptian President Anwar Sadat and many others, is tried in Cairo, along with twenty-two others of his terrorist organization, Takfir Wal-Hajira. All are found guilty of assassination. Islambouli and four others are condemned to death; seventeen others are given prison sentences.

December 15: A suicide car loaded with explosives is driven into the Iraqi Embassy in Beirut, Lebanon, killing thirty-seven people and injuring another fifty. The Kurdistan Liberation Army takes credit.

December 17: U.S. Brigadier General James Lee Dozier is kidnapped from his Verona apartment on orders of Antonio Savasta, fanatical leader of the Red Brigades terrorists in Italy. Savasta demands that hundreds of Red Brigadists be released from prison in exchange for Dozier.

December 18: The headquarters of the Zimbabwean African National Union in Salisbury is destroyed by a bomb, killing 6 persons and injuring another 150.

December 19: Libyan dictator Muammar Qaddafi is injured and his driver slain by Khalifa Khadir, a Libyan Army colonel.

December 19: A time bomb placed inside a pickup truck explodes in Beirut, Lebanon, killing five policemen and injuring six persons.

1982

January 1: Terrorists kidnap fifty residents of San Francisco El Tablon, Guatemala. Most will be tortured and shot to death.

January 5: Jose Lipperheide, a Basque businessman, is abducted near Bilbao, Spain, by ETA terrorists. He will be released after the kidnappers receive a $1.2 million ransom.

January 13: Rabeh Jerwa, minister plenipotentiary of the Algerian Embassy in Beirut, Lebanon, is kidnapped from his apartment by terrorists and assassinated, three bullets being fired into his head.

January 15: Twenty-five persons are injured by an explosion at the Migash-Israel Restaurant in Berlin, Germany. The 15th of May Arab Movement for the Liberation of Palestine explodes the bomb.

January 18: Lieutenant Colonel Charles Robert Ray, U.S. military attaché, is shot to death near his apartment by FARL terrorists in Paris, France.

January 26: Jacoobo Ramon Larach, general manager of the Pepsi-Cola bottling company in San Pedro Sula, Honduras, is fatally shot when terrorists attempt to kidnap him.

January 28: Members of Italy's Nucleo Operativo Centrale, a crack antiterrorist organization, locate the apartment in Padua where American General James Dozier is being held by Antonio Savasta and other members of the Red Brigades. They break down the door just in time to prevent Savasta from killing Dozier, rescuing the hostage and taking the Red Brigadists prisoner.

January 28: Kemal Arikan, consul general of Turkey, is shot to death in his car in Los Angeles, California, by Armenian terrorists who claim responsibility for the assassination.

January 29: John McKeague, Loyalist leader and possibly chief of clandestine Red Hand Commandos, is shot to death in Belfast, Ireland.

February 5: Roberto Giron Lemus, editor of *La Nacion*, is going to work when he is assassinated by terrorists in Guatemala City, Guatemala.

February 22: Fifteen people are killed and sixty-one injured when a bomb explodes in a garbage truck in Teheran's Seapah Square during rush hour.

February 24: Several badly informed Shiite Muslim terrorists skyjack a Kuwaiti Boeing 707 in Beirut as a protest against Libya's arrest of Shiite Muslim leader Imam Moussa Sadr. The plane will be flown to Iran, where the terrorists will surrender after learning that the plane they have skyjacked is not Libyan.

February 27: Eight are killed and thirty-five are injured when a car bomb planted by the Front for the Liberation of Lebanon from Foreigners explodes at the Syrian Army checkpoint in West Beirut.

March 14: The trial of Red Brigades leader Antonio Savasta and sixteen others begins and will end in conviction and imprisonment of the defendants. The power of Italy's worst terrorist organization is finally broken.

March 15: An eleven-year-old boy is killed and two women injured by an IRA bomb exploding in Banbridge, Ireland.

March 18: Several terrorists hurl gasoline bombs at a political rally for the Functional Groups Party in Jakarta, Indonesia, killing seven persons and injuring more than 100 others.

March 29: The international terrorist Carlos (Ilyich Ramirez Sanchez) bombs a Paris-Toulouse express train near Limoges, killing six persons and injuring another fifteen.

April 3: Yacov Barsimantov, second secretary of the Israeli Embassy in Paris, is shot to death in his Paris apartment.

April 3: Wandee Throngprapa, managing editor of *Tawan Siam*, a Bangkok newspaper, is shot to death by terrorists in his office.

April 9: Kani Gungor, a commerical officer of the Turkish Embassy in Ottawa, is injured by gunshots fired by terrorists. The Secret Army for the Liberation of Armenia takes credit for the shooting.

April 15: Khaled Islambouli and four other conspirators of the Egyptian terrorist organization Takfir Wal-Hajira are hanged

for their part in the 1981 assassination of President Anwar Sadat.

April 27: Raffaele de Cogliano, Christian Democrat and commissioner of the Campania administration, and his driver are fatally shot by terrorists in Naples, Italy.

April 28: Pio La Torre, member of parliament and leader of the Communist Party in Sicily, and his driver are shot to death in Palermo.

May 4: Orhan R. Gunduz, honorary Turkish consul to New England, is shot to death in Sommerville, a Boston suburb. The Justice Commandos of the Armenian Genocide claim credit.

May 5: Angel Pascual Mugica, general manager of the Lemoniz nuclear plant, is driving outside of Bilbao, Spain, when he is shot to death by terrorists.

May 21: Juan Cleano skyjacks a Philippines Airlines BAC-111 before it lands at Cebu, demanding a ransom of 60,000 pesos ($7,270, the amount of his mortgage) and political reforms (added to make his crime appear politically motivated). He will be overpowered and imprisoned.

May 24: A bomb hidden in a car belonging to the secretary of the French Embassy in Beirut is detonated as the vehicle enters the embassy gates, killing fourteen persons and injuring twenty-one.

May 27: Hamid Alaou skyjacks a Royal Air Morocco B-727 after it departs Athens, Greece, demanding a flight to Tunis and improvements in the morality of observance of Islam in Morocco. He will surrender to Tunisian officials.

June 4: Mustafa Marzook, first secretary of the Kuwaiti Embassy in New Delhi, India, is shot to death in his home. The Arab Brigades Movement takes credit.

June 4: Petrus Nyaose, secretary general of the African National Congress, and his wife, Jabu, are murdered by a car bomb in Swaziland.

June 17: Kamal Hussein, deputy director of the Palestinian Liberation Organization, is slain by terrorists in Rome, Italy.

June 18: The terrorist known as the "Monster of Florence" strikes again fifteen miles southwest of Florence, where he shoots and kills Paolo Mainardi, twenty-two, and Antonella Migliorini, nineteen. Police will later conclude from the tire tracks of Mainardi's car that Mainardi apparently saw the killer approaching and attempted to drive away; the killer leaped in front of the car and fired several shots through the front window of the car with his .22-caliber Beretta pistol, killing the victims, but left before performing his usual mutilations.

June: General Yekotiel Adam, former deputy chief of staff and leader of Israel's intelligence agency, Mossad, is murdered by members of the Palestinian Liberation Organization.

July 17: Fifteen terrorists kill Peruvian governor Zenon Palomino Flores in Callera and then loot stores and rape women at will in the mountain village.

July 20: IRA bombs exploding in Hyde Park and Regent's Park, London, kill eight persons and injure forty-seven.

July 25: Five workers from Xian take control of a Chinese passenger plane heading from Xian to Shanghai and demand to go to Hong Kong. The passengers and crew members will overpower the skyjackers, causing a bomb that one of the skyjackers is carrying to go off, damaging the plane and forcing it to make an emergency landing. The terrorists will be arrested and imprisoned.

August 7: A bomb thrown by two members of the Armenian Secret Army for the Liberation of Armenia into a crowded waiting room at the Esenboga Airport in Ankara, kills three Turkish policeman and one American, as well as injuring seventy-two others.

August 9: A terrorist flings a bomb into the Jo Goldenberg kosher restaurant in Paris, France. As patrons flee, the gunmen opens fire with a machine gun, killing six persons and injuring another twenty-two people.

August 10: Members of the Mozambique National Resistance fire a bazooka shell at a passing train near Beira, in Mozambique, killing fourteen persons and wounding another fifty people.

August 13: Dr. Hector Zevalloses, abortion clinic operator, and his wife are abducted in Edwardsville, Illinois, but later freed by anti-abortionist Army of God terrorists led by Don Benny Anderson. Several of the terrorists will be sent to prison.

August 27: Colonel Atilla Atikat, the Turkish military attaché in Ottawa, Canada, is fatally shot in his car. The Justice Commandos of the Armenian Genocide takes credit.

September 3: General Carlo Alberto Dalla Chiesa, chief of an anti-Mafia task force, is slain, along with his wife and bodyguard, in Sicily, by Mafia killers.

September 6: A truck bomb explodes on the Avenue Khayyam, opposite the ministries of justice and interior, in Teheran, Iran, killing 20 people and injuring 100 more.

September 11: A bomb blast outside an employment agency in Manila, Philippines, kills two employees and injures twenty-five people.

September 14: Bashir (Bishin) Gemayel, president-elect of Lebanon, is assassinated in East Beirut by a bomb planted by Syrian terrorists. The 440-pound bomb, planted by Habib Shartouni, also kills eight other persons and injures more than fifty.

September 14: Hamad Jutaili, acting consul general of the Kuwaiti Embassy, is shot by terrorists when he stops his car in a service station in Karachi, Pakistan.

September 16: Najeeb Sayeb Refai, first secretary of the Kuwaiti Embassy in Madrid, is fatally shot by gunmen, including Abu Nidal terrorist Ibrahim Nasser Hamdan.

September 27: Abu Walid (Kafr Kalil), general and Palestinian Liberation Organization chief of operations, is slain in Lebanon.

October 1: A TNT-bomb blast at the Iman Square in Teheran, Iran, kills sixty or more persons riding on a double-decker bus, and a nearby five-story hotel is completely leveled.

October 15: Ashrafi Isfahani, ayatollah, is hugged by an assassin carrying a grenade and both are blown up in Bahtaran, Iran. The assassin may have been a member of the Mujahedeen Khalq.

October 22: The FBI announces that five Armenian terrorists have been arrested for assaults on Turkish statesmen in southern California.

November 4: General Victor Lago Roman, commander of the Brunete First Armored Division of Spain, is assassinated in Madrid, Spain, by terrorists.

November 7: Three Russian terrorists skyjack a Soviet plane flying from Novorossisk to Odessa. They stab the pilot, wound two passengers, and force the plane to land in Sinop, Turkey, where they are arrested.

November 14: Four restaurants in Kabul, Afghanistan, that are frequented by Soviet officials are hit by terrorist bombs, killing twenty-four persons.

November 17: Edwin Wilson, former CIA agent and arms dealer, is found guilty of sending explosives to Libya and sent to prison for thirty years.

November 23: A bomb wrecks a building in the suburb of Shiyah, outside Beirut, killing six persons and injuring another twenty.

November 25: Two terrorist bombs explode in a shopping center in Kabul, Afghanistan, killing five persons and injuring thirty-two others.

December 1: Walid Jumblatt, Druse Muslim leader, is injured with thirty-eight others and four are killed when a bomb explodes near Jumblatt's car in Lebanon.

December 5: Salvadoran terrorists kidnap 136 persons on a bus bound for a soccer game in an attempt to recruit members to their ranks. One captive tries to escape and is killed, and the other hostages will be released when no one volunteers to become a terrorist.

December 8: Norman Mayer, an antinuclear protestor, drives his truck to the base of the Washington Monument in Washington, D.C., threatening to blow it up unless a ban on nuclear weapons is discussed in Congress. Mayer tries to drive away in the afternoon, but police open fire and he is fatally wounded. There are no explosives in his truck.

December 9: Zola Ngini, Adolph Mpongosohe, and Jackson Tayo, leaders of the African National Congress, are slain with thirty-nine others when South African raiders attack an ANC camp in Lesotho.

December 14: Dr. Judith Xionara Suazo Estrada, daughter of the president of Honduras, while going to the hospital in Guatemala City, Guatemala, is kidnapped by terrorists. She will be released after the government publishes a left-wing manifesto.

December 15: A pressure-sensitive bomb placed under the driver's seat of a car seriously injures U.S. Army captain Howard Bromberg in Darmstadt, Germany. This is the sixtieth terrorist attack against Americans on German soil in 1982.

1983

January 10: More than 550 prisoners at Sing Sing Prison in New York riot, holding seventeen guards hostage for twenty-four hours, until prison officials promise reforms.

January 13: Robert S. Hester, a Memphis, Tennessee, police officer, is taken hostage by six religious cult members led by Lindberg Sanders. Hester will be murdered by the terrorists, and a Memphis SWAT team will later kill all of the kidnappers.

February 14: Riots between Hindus and Muslims during the elections throughout India cause more than 1,500 deaths.

February 20: A Libyan Arab Airways B-727 en route from Sebha, Libya, to Tripoli is skyjacked by two Libyan Army officers, who hold the 158 passengers hostage at the airport in Valletta, Malta, for three days. They will surrender on the promise of political asylum.

March 9: Galip Balkar, Turkish ambassador to Yugoslavia, is fatally shot and his driver critically wounded in Belgrade, Yugoslavia. Balkar will die on March 11, and two terrorist groups take credit.

April 10: Dr. Issam Sartawi, prominent Palestinian Liberation Organization moderate, is shot to death in Albufeira, Portugal, by Abu Nidal terrorists.

April 18: Sixty-three persons are killed in a bomb explosion at the U.S. Embassy in Beirut. The bomb has been planted by the Islamic Jihad.

May 5: Tjou Chang-Jen skyjacks a jet en route from Manchuria to Shanghai, China, demanding that he be flown to Taiwan. Instead, the pilot hoodwinks the skyjacker and flies to South Korea, where the terrorist is seized and imprisoned.

May 14: Serial killer Randolph Kraft (the "Freeway Killer") is stopped by police in California and the body of Terry Lee Bambrei, a Marine, is found in his trunk. Kraft will be convicted of murdering sixteen men in California between 1982 and 1983 (and he has committed perhaps as many murders in five other states). He will be sentenced to death.

May 22: A bomb explodes in downtown Pretoria, South Africa. The outlawed

African National Congress (ANC) takes credit for the blast, which kills 19 people and injures another 200.

July 15: Orly Airport in Paris, France, is bombed by a terrorist group known as the Secret Army for the Liberation of Armenia. Seven persons are killed and sixty more are injured.

August 21: Benigno S. Aquino, Jr., a Filipino politician opposed to the Marcos regime, returns to the Philippines and is fatally shot at the Manila International Airport. A leftist terrorist is responsible, reports the Marcos administration, but the assassination is attributed by others to military personnel acting on behalf of Marcos.

September 9: The "Monster of Florence" enters a van parked alongside a road outside of Florence and murders two homosexual lovers in their sleep, killing Horst Meyer and Uwe Rusch Sens. He does not perform his usual mutilations but tears up the couple's homosexual magazines before fleeing.

September 29: A Gulf Air jetliner of the United Arab Emirates is blow up in midair by Abu Nidal terrorists, killing all 122 persons on board.

October 9: Four cabinet ministers of South Korea and fifteen others die in a bomb explosion in Rangoon, Burma. One of the assassins is killed by Burmese guards. Two North Korean military officers will be sentenced to death on December 8, 1983, by a Burmese court for the attack.

October 19: Maurice Bishop, premier of Grenada, who has been placed under house arrest on October 13, is slain by insurgent military members.

October 21: Judge Henry A. Gentile is murdered and divorce attorney James A.

Piszcor is wounded by ex–police officer Hutchie T. Moore in a Chicago, Illinois, courtroom.

October 23: A suicidal terrorist drives a TNT-packed truck into Marine headquarters at Beirut International Airport, the horrific explosion killing 241 U.S. Marines and sailors who are part of the multinational peace-keeping force. Another suicidal terrorist drives a second truck with explosives into a barracks two miles away, killing fifty-eight French paratroopers. The attack has been made by terrorists belonging to the Islamic Jihad in an effort to rid Lebanon of the multinational peace-keeping force in Lebanon.

November 4: Sixty Israelis are killed when a suicide truck bomb explodes in Tyre. Islamic Jihad terrorists are blamed.

November 15: George Tsantes, a U.S. Navy captain, is shot to death by left-wing terrorists in Athens, Greece.

December 12: A suicide truck driven by members of the Al-Dawa movement attacks the U.S. Embassy in Kuwait. The French Embassy is also attacked, leaving four persons dead and at least fifty injured.

December 17: A car bomb explodes outside of Harrods, the famous department store in London, England, killing six persons and wounding ninety-four others. The IRA disclaims responsibility after universal condemnation for the terrorist outrage is expressed by world leaders.

1984

January 9: Kenneth Bianchi (the "Hillside Strangler"), after being apprehended in

Washington and turning state's evidence to avoid the death penalty in that state for murdering two college girls, and being returned to California, where he implicates his cousin, Angelo Buono, in their 1977–1978 murders, is convicted and sent to prison for life. Buono is also convicted of the terrorist murders and sent to prison for life.

January 29: Guillermo Lacaci, Spanish general, is fatally shot in Madrid by terrorists.

February 2: Judge Braxton Kittrell, Jr., after an Alabama jury of eleven whites and one black have found racial terrorists Henry Francis Hays and James Llewellyn Knowles guilty of the 1981 murder of Michael Donald, a black, sentences Hays to death and Knowles to life imprisonment.

March 8: Kiichi Miyazawa, prominent political figure in Japan, is attacked and wounded by knife-wielding terrorist Hirosato Higashivama.

March 10: Several bombings attributed to the Libyan Secret Service are set off at Arba businesses in London, England, the most serious incident occurring in Berkeley Square, where twenty-seven persons are injured.

March 24: Elizbeth II, queen of England, receives death threats on her trip to Jordan, reportedly from Abu Nidal terrorists.

March 28: Kenneth Whitty, first secretary of the British Embassy in Athens, is fatally shot in Athens, Greece. The Revolutionary Organization of Socialist Muslims take credit for the assassination.

April 3: A car bomb thought to be planted by the outlawed African National Congress (ANC) explodes in Durban, South Africa,

killing three people and wounding sixteen others.

May 10: Prompted by terrorists, Hindu-Muslim riots break out in Bombay, India, causing more than 230 deaths in 11 days.

May 29: Two Negro serial killers, Alton Coleman and Debra Brown, kidnap and strangle Vernita Wheat of Kenosha, Wisconsin, one of many murders committed in several states by these terrorists, who will later be convicted of several killings and sentenced to death.

June 5: PFLP terrorist leader Mohammed Zaidan Abbas sends four of his most ruthless terrorists to attack the Israeli kibbutz of Ein-Gev, but all are captured and imprisoned.

June 16: Hardayal Singh, chief of the Jullundur district committee of the Congress Party, is shot to death in Goraya, India, by Sikh terrorists.

June 18: Alan Berg, controversial talk-show host in Denver, Colorado, is shot and killed by members of the Order, a terrorist organization loosely structured after the Ku Klux Klan.

July 6–August 5, 1987: Serial killer and terrorist Robert Berdella abducts and kills his first of six victims in the Kansas City, Missouri, area. Berdella will be apprehended when his seventh victim manages to escape. He will be sent to prison for life.

July 29: The "Monster of Florence" shoots and kills Claudio Stefanacci, twenty, and Pia Rontini, eighteen, as they sit in their car near Vicchio.

July 31: Islamic Jihad terrorists skyjack an Air France B-737 en route from Frankfurt to Paris, to Teheran, Iran. The terrorists demand the release of terrorists jailed in France. Two persons are killed, but the demands are not met.

September 20: The Islamic Jihad attempts another suicide bombing of the U.S. Embassy in Beirut, the driver aiming his bomb-packed truck at the embassy annex, but alert guards open up on the speeding vehicle, killing the driver. The truck swerves off course and explodes, killing at least fourteen people.

October 12: Margaret Thatcher, prime minister of England, and members of the British cabinet are the target of IRA terrorists who plant a bomb at the Grand Hotel in Brighton, England, where Thatcher and her cabinet are holding high-level conferences. Five persons are killed, including John Wakeham, chief whip of the Tory Party, and others injured when the bomb explodes, but Thatcher survives.

October 19: Jerzy Popieluszko, one of the leaders of the Polish trade union Solidarity, is kidnapped by Polish secret police. He will be killed and his body later found.

October 31: Indira Gandhi, prime minister of India, is shot to death in New Delhi, by two of her Sikh bodyguards.

November 4: More than 2,000 Sikhs are killed in rioting throughout India, sparked by the assassination of Prime Minister Indira Gandhi by her two Sikh bodyguards.

November 27: Percy Morris, British deputy high commissioner, is fatally shot in Bombay, India, by Abu Nidal terrorists.

December 3: Five Arab terrorists skyjack a Kuwaiti jet flying from Dubai to Karachi and order it flown to Teheran, demanding freedom for Shiites held in Kuwait for bombing the U.S. embassy. The terrorists

will murder two U.S. officials before Iranian troops take them into custody.

December 22: Bernard Goetz, who has suffered earlier beatings by terrorists in New York, and who is armed with an unlicensed .38-caliber pistol, shoots four Negro youths who have attempted to rob him at knifepoint on a New York subway train.

1985

January 25: General René Audran, chief of the French international arms sales group, is fatally shot in Paris, France, by members of Action Directe.

February 1: Ernst Zimmermann, president of the West German Aerospace and Armaments Association, is fatally shot in Munich by terrorists of the Red Army Faction (RAF).

February 3: A terrorist bomb explodes near the U.S. air base near Athens, Greece, injuring seventy-nine persons.

February 7: Enrique Camarena Salazar, U.S. drug enforcement agent, and Alfredo Azaval Avelar, his pilot, are kidnapped in Mexico, tortured, and then slain by Raul López Alvarez and two other terrorists acting on the orders of drug trafficking king Rafael Cèro Quintero.

March 16: Journalist Terry Anderson is kidnapped in Lebanon by Islamic Jihad terrorists. He will be held many years before being released.

March 24: Arthur Nicholson, U.S. Army major whom the U.S.S.R. claims to be a spy, is slain in Ludwigslust, Germany, by a Soviet guard.

March 25: Bruce Carroll Pierce, leader of the neo-Nazi group calling itself the Order, is arrested in Rossville, Georgia, and charged with the murder of radio talk-show host Alan Berg.

March 26: A Turkish terrorist group sets off a bomb on a train bound from Burgos, Bulgaria, to Sofia, killing seven persons.

March 31: In Winston-Salem, North Carolina, FBI agents arrest David Lane, the Denver-based leader of the neo-Nazi group called the Order, charging him, along with Bruce Carroll Pierce, with the murder of Denver talk-show host Alan Berg. Lane, Pierce, and ten other Order members are also charged with conspiring to overthrow the U.S. government.

May 10–12: Two days of terrorist bombings in New Delhi and other cities in northern India cause eighty-five deaths and hundreds of injuries.

June 14: TWA flight 847 is skyjacked by two radical Shiites, members of Hizbollah (or Hezbollah)—the Party of God—just after the plane takes off from Athens. The Arab terrorists, who have smuggled guns on board, beat passengers, then order the plane to land at Beirut. Refused the right to land, the TWA plane is flown to Algiers, refueled, then flown back to Beirut. Before landing, the terrorists kill passenger Robert Stethem, a U.S. Navy diver, throwing his body onto the tarmac upon landing. The flight then flies back and forth between Algiers and Beirut for seventeen agonizing days, while the skyjackers unsuccessfully attempt to have 700 Shiite and Palestinian prisoners released from Israeli prisons. On June 30, 1985, the terrorists finally release their hostages, including thirty-nine Americans in Beirut. Mohammed Ali Hamadi, leader of the two-man terrorist team, will later be imprisoned.

June 23: Sikh terrorists are held responsible for the in-flight explosion of an Air India 747 bound from Toronto to London. All 329 persons on board are killed.

July 11: Fifteen persons are killed and ninety more are wounded by bombs set off in Kuwait cafes by Abu Nidal terrorists.

August 14: A car bomb in the Christian section of East Beirut kills 15 persons and injures about 120 others.

August 17: A second car bomb in the Christian section of East Beirut kills fifty-five persons and injures seventeen others.

August 19: Christian Lebanese retaliate against Arab terrorists by exploding a bomb in the Muslim suburbs of Beirut, killing twenty-nine persons and injuring nineteen.

August 20: Albert Atrakchi, first secretary of the Israeli Embassy in Cairo, Egypt, is shot to death. The Egyptian Revolution, a terrorist group, will take credit.

August 20: Forty-four persons are killed when a car bomb explodes in Tripoli.

September 8: The "Monster of Florence" shoots and kills French tourists Jean-Michel Kraveichvili, twenty-five, and Nadine Mauriot, thirty-six. As with the previous 1984 killing, the killer not only removes the genitalia of the female victim but her left breast. The terrorist later mails two strips of skin from Mauriot's breast to an attorney. Although the terrorist has not struck since this last killing, the authorities of Florence, Italy, take precautions by posting signs on all roads outside the city, warning children and lovers not to stop in isolated areas.

September 18: Michel Namri, publisher of the anti-Syrian *Arab News Letter* in Athens, Greece, is slain by Abu Nidal terrorists.

September 30: Four Soviet diplomats are kidnapped in Beirut, Lebanon, by Sunni terrorists, who demand that the U.S.S.R. force Syria to halt attacks on Tripoli. One diplomat, Arkady Kathov, is slain. The other three hostages will be set free.

October 7: Four PFLP terrorists, on orders from Mohammed Zaidan Abbas, seize the Italian cruise ship, *Achille Lauro*, but their intentions are unclear. The terrorists randomly select an American passenger, Leon Klinghoffer, shooting and killing the sixty-nine-year old invalid—he is confined to a wheelchair—and ordering other passengers at gunpoint to dump his body into the sea. The vessel sailed to Port Said, where the terrorists surrendered to Egyptian authorities. Accompanied by Abbas, they then flew to Sicily. Abbas was allowed by Italian authorities to escape to Belgrade, where he disappeared. The four terrorists who had taken over the ship were tried, convicted, and given prison sentences, the longest being thirty years, given to Yussef Magid Molqi, the killer of Leon Klinghoffer. A 1990 made-for-television miniseries, *Voyage of Terror: The Achille Lauro Affair*, starring Burt Lancaster in the role of Klinghoffer, and using the actual ship and its route, painfully recaptures this tragedy.

November 23: Libyan Abu Nidal terrorists skyjack an Egyptair 737 bound from Athens to Cairo. The plane is forced to land at Luga, Malta, where it is stormed by an Egyptian antiterrorist task force. The skyjackers blow open the cargo doors, killing all fifty-nine persons, including the skyjackers, except for one terrorist.

December 11: The Unabomber, a lone terrorist, strikes for the first time, planting a bomb outside a Sacramento, California, computer store, where owner Hugh Scutton picks it up and is blown to bits.

December 15: African National Congress (ANC) terrorists plant a land mine in

Transvaal, South Africa, which kills six whites, prompting an angry warning from President P. W. Botha to officials of Zimbabwe.

December 23: African National Congress (ANC) terrorists cause a bomb explosion at a shopping center in Durban, South Africa, that kills six whites and injures forty-eight others.

1986

February 6: Vice Admiral Cristobal Colon, a descendant of Christopher Columbus, is murdered by ETA terrorists, who throw grenades at his car in Madrid, Spain.

February 6: A terrorist bomb injures twenty-one persons in Paris, France.

February 14: Jean-Claude "Baby Doc" Duvalier, dictator of Haiti, flees the country after looting government coffers of more than $400 million. Duvalier's reign, and that of his father, Francois "Papa Doc" Duvalier, begun in 1957, has been a horrific dictatorship supported by the Duvaliers' terrorist organization, the Ton Ton Macoutes. The terrorist regime is profiled in the 1967 film, *The Comedians*, a far-fetched drama with Richard Burton and Elizabeth Taylor, who gather their tourist friends on Haiti to plot the overthrow of the Duvaliers.

February 28: Olaf Palme, prime minister of Sweden, is shot dead in Stockholm, Sweden.

March 2: Zafr al-Masri, mayor of Nablus, is fatally shot by Palestinian terrorists.

March 26: A Dutch court in Amsterdam refuses to extradite IRA terrorist Gerard Kelly on the grounds that his crimes are political. The Netherlands is accused, as have been Germany, Italy and other European countries, of being intimidated by terrorists into equivocational postures, in order to avoid retaliation.

April 3: PFLP terrorists plant a bomb on board TWA Flight 840, flying from Athens to Cairo. The explosion blows a hole in the side of the 727 jet and kills four Americans, including an infant, and injures nine others. May Mansur, the widow of a Syrian militant leader, is held responsible. Mansur was a passenger on the flight and present at the time of the explosion. She denies any responsibility.

April 5: A bomb blast at the La Belle disco in West Berlin, Germany, kills a U.S. soldier and a Turkish woman, injuring 204 others. Intercepted messages from the Libyan Embassy in East Berlin indicate that Libya is responsible for the explosion.

April 17: Two British citizens and a U.S. citizen are kidnapped and slain in Beirut, Lebanon, by Libyan terrorists after the U.S. and England bomb Libya in response to the Libyan bombing of the La Belle disco in West Berlin on April 5, 1986.

May 3: The Liberation Tigers of Tamil Eelam (LTTE) explode a bomb on board an Air Lanka Tristar in Colombo, killing 17. The attack is aimed at pressuring Margaret Thatcher, Prime Minister of England, into aiding the Sri Lankan government.

May 3: Seamus McElwaine and Kevin Lynch, two IRA terrorists, are shot in an ambush in Dublin, Ireland, as they are about to set off an 800-pound boobytrap bomb.

May 7: The Central Telegraph office in Colombo, Sri Lanka, is bombed by LTTE terrorists. Fourteen persons are killed and 100 more are injured.

June 9: Rival black groups riot at the Crossroads, South Africa, leaving 20 dead,

hundreds wounded and 20,000 homeless.

June 14: A car bomb explosion in Durban, South Africa, kills three people and injures another sixty-nine.

June 23: IRA terrorist Patrick Magee is sentenced to thirty-five years in a British prison for bombing a hotel in Brighton, England, on October 12, 1984, in an attempt to assassinate Prime Minister Margaret Thatcher and her entire cabinet.

June 26: Seven tourists are killed in a terrorist attack by the Sendero Liminoso aboard a train en route to the Inca ruins of Machu Pichu in Cuzco, Peru.

August 18: Blacks protesting evictions of rent boycotters clash with police in Soweto, South Africa, which leads to rioting, causing twenty-one deaths and more than 100 injuries.

September 5: Four Abu Nidal terrorists skyjack a Karachi Pan American B-747 carrying 389 passengers. The crew escapes, the plane is immobilized, and the terrorists murder twenty of the passengers before they are seized and imprisoned.

September 7: General Augusto Pinochet Ugarte, president of Chile, is riding in a car when he is assaulted by insurgents armed with grenades, guns, and rockets. Ugarte survives but six bodyguards die.

September 17: A bomb blast in a crowded department store in Paris kills five persons and injures another sixty-one. The Lebanese Armed Revolutionary Faction (FARL) has carried out the attack in order to force the French to release their imprisoned leader, Georges Abdallah.

October 15: Palestinian terrorists throw hand grenades in front of the Wailing Wall in Jerusalem, killing one person and injuring sixty-nine others.

October 27: Two children, Samuel Johnson, Jr., and Emmanuel Dalieh, are abducted at a parade in Harper City, Liberia, Africa, for sacrificial use by a murder cult led by Joshua Bedell and Samuel Cummings. The terrorists will be tracked down, convicted and sentenced to death.

December 25: An Iraqi plane is skyjacked while en route from Baghdad to Amman. It crashes and sixty-two persons are killed.

1987

January 16: Ecuadorian President Cordero Febres is abducted by terrorists, who demand the release of insurgent General Vargas Pasos. Cordero will be set free when the general is released.

January 20: Terry Waite, a special envoy of the Archbishop of Canterbury, meets in Beirut, Lebanon, with terrorists who have kidnapped Terry Anderson in 1985, in an effort to negotiate his release and that of others. Instead, Waite himself is taken hostage by the treacherous Islamic Jihad terrorists.

January 24: Four professors at the University College in Beirut, Lebanon (Alan Steen, Mithileshwar Singh, Jesse Turner, and Robert Polhill), are kidnapped by Islamic Jihad, working hand-in-glove with Yasir Arafat and his PLO, demanding that the U.S. acknowledge Palestinian rights.

February 12: Buelah May Donald, the mother of Michael Donald, along with the NAACP, is awarded $7 million damages against the Ku Klux Klan in a wrongful death suit by an all-white jury. The financial burden breaks the back of the Klan, which is almost universally condemned by whites in the South, where the once-feared terrorist organization is no longer a viable force.

March 20: Licio Giorgieri, chief air force general in charge of space research for Italy, is slain by Italian terrorists.

June 1: Rashid Karami, premier of Lebanon, is traveling in a helicopter when a bomb is detonated, killing him.

July 24: Hussein Ali Hariri, a Lebanese Shiite terrorist, skyjacks a plane to Geneva, Switzerland, where he demands the release of a Lebanese terrorist held in West Germany. One French passenger is killed and the rest escape when Swiss police storm the plane, taking Hariri prisoner.

July 30: Sixty-eight persons are injured in the terrorist bombing of a military barracks in Johannesburg, South Africa.

July 31: Iranian pilgrims to Mecca, some of these being terrorists, clash with Saudi Arabian security forces, resulting in riots that leave 400 dead.

August 18: A bomb explodes in the Sri Lankan parliament building, killing one person and injuring fifteen others.

October 15: President Thomas Sankara of Burkina Faso is overthrown and assassinated by Captain Blaise Compaoré, his deputy.

November 8: Remembrance Day ceremonies in Northern Ireland are disrupted by a bomb blast, which kills eleven persons and wounds sixty-one others.

December 3: David Lane and Bruce Carroll Pierce, leaders of the neo-Nazi terrorist group the Order, are convicted of murdering Denver talk-show host Alan Berg, and each receives a 150-year prison sentence.

December 9: Palestinian terrorists instigate anti-Israeli rioting on the East Bank and in the Gaza Strip in which 12 Palestinians will be killed by January 9, 1988. Nine of the terrorists will be identified and deported.

December 23: Zino Scioni, falsely claiming to carry a bomb, skyjacks a Rome KLM B-737 en route to Milan from Amsterdam. Holding the ninety-seven people aboard hostage, Scioni demands $1 million ransom. He will be arrested four hours later.

1988

January 25: Carlos Hoyos, attorney general of Colombia, is abducted and murdered near Medellin by drug traffickers, who also slay two of Hoyos' bodyguards.

February 10: More than 200 persons are killed and thousands injured during riots between rival factions, fueled by terrorists on either side, in Bangladesh during the nationwide elections in 4,376 villages.

March 6: The British Special Air Service (SAS) kills three suspected IRA terrorists in Gibraltar as they are about to detonate a car bomb with a remote control device.

March 29: Dulcie September, European agent of the outlawed African National Congress, is fatally shot near her office in Paris, France, by terrorists.

April 5: Eight Arab terrorists skyjack a B-747 flying from Thailand to Kuwait, demanding the release of terrorists imprisoned in Kuwait. Two passengers will be released and others freed as the plane lands in Iran, Cyprus, and Algeria, where the skyjackers will be allowed to leave the country.

April 7: Albie Sachs, a well-known South African lawyer opposed to apartheid, is the target of an assassination attempt when he is critically wounded by a car bomb in Maputo, Mozambique.

April 12: Yu Kikumura, a Japanese citizen who is thought to be a leader of the terrorist Red Army, is arrested in New Jersey with three pipe bombs in his possession.

April 14: Five persons are killed in a Naples, Italy, nightclub that caters to U.S. servicemen, when a car packed with explosives is driven into the club by Junzo Okudaira, a suicidal member of the Red Army terrorist group.

April 16: Khalil al-Wazir, military leader of the Palestinian Liberation Organization, a gardener, and two bodyguards are shot to death at his home near Tunis.

April 23: A truck carrying 300 pounds of TNT explodes in a crowded marketplace in Tripoli, Lebanon, killing scores of people.

August 22: At least 5,000 persons are killed during a week of ethnic violence between the majority Hutu tribe and the smaller Tutsi tribe of Burundi, many of the clashes prompted by terrorists on both sides.

September 24: Raimundo Alves da Conceicao skyjacks a Brazilian B-737 en route from Porto Velho to Rio de Janeiro. He shoots the copilot, and, when landing and attempting to flee to another, smaller plane, is himself shot and wounded by police.

December 21: Pan Am Flight 103, a 747 jumbo jet en route to New York with 259 passengers, blows up over Lockerbie, Scotland, after PFLP terrorists plant a bomb aboard, apparently at Frankfurt, Germany. All on board, as well as eleven persons on the ground, are killed in one of the worst terrorist attacks on record.

1989

January 24: Theodore Bundy, who has been convicted of the 1978 murders of Lisa Levy, twenty, and Kimberly Leach, twelve (and, according to best reports a terrorist killer who abducted and murdered as many as ten to twenty more young girls and women from 1974 to 1978 and has fought off his execution through eleven years of appeals) is executed in Florida's electric chair.

January 31: Alvin Antonio Siu, a Nicaraguan Indian exiled in Colombia, skyjacks a Costa Rican Ace Airline B-727 carrying 122 people to Medellin, Colombia, by threatening to set a passenger on fire. An antiterrorist squad storms the plane in Costa Rica and captures Siu.

February 7: Sources in the international terrorist movement report that Ahmed Jibril, a former Syrian military intelligence officer and head of the PFLP, at the urging of Libyan strongman Muammar Qaddafi (who seeks revenge for the U.S. air raids in his country in 1986), is responsible for ordering Pan Am's Flight 103 blown up. The PFLP denies the allegation, although best information confirms the PFLP as responsible. A subsequent report has it that Iran paid $1 million to Jibril to destroy Flight 103.

July 5: Sikh terrorists skyjack an Indian Airlines A-300 Airbus carrying 225 passengers from Srinager, Kashmir, to New Delhi, to Pakistan. The terrorists have threatened to blow up the plane unless their demands for ransom money and release of prisoners are met. They are later taken into custody.

November 16: Terrorists of the Farabundo Marti National Liberation Front (FMLN) shoot to death six Jesuit priests, as well as a cook and her daughter in José Simeón Caias University of Central America in San Salvador, El Salvador.

November 21: Twelve members of a U.S. Special Forces group (Green Berets) are trapped in a San Salvador hotel and are forced, under threat of death, to surrender to FMLN terrorists.

November 22: René Moawad, president of Lebanon, is assassinated when a bomb explodes along the route of his motorcade in Beirut, killing another twenty-three persons, this being the work of Arab terrorists.

November 27: FMLN terrorists seize several homes of U.S. diplomats in San Salvador, causing the U.S. to order all U.S. citizens to leave El Salvador.

November 27: An Avianca Airlines jetliner explodes over Colombia, killing 110, including some persons on the ground. Government officials state that the explosion has been the result of a bomb planted by drug-trafficking terrorists.

November 30: Terrorists plant a bomb beneath the presidential palace in Manila, as well as seizing several radio stations in an unsuccessful coup attempt.

December 6: In the worst mass killing in Canadian history, lone terrorist Marc Lepine, armed with a hunting rifle, shoots and kills fourteen women (six in one classroom) on the campus of the University of Montreal, before killing himself. Police state the following day that Lepine has left a note in which he states that women have ruined his life.

December 6: Drug-trafficking terrorists defying government efforts to eradicate their operations explode a half ton of dynamite in front of the Administrative Security Building in Bogotá, Colombia, killing sixty persons and seriously injuring another 1,000.

December 16: Judge Robert Vance of the U.S. Court of Appeals for the 11th District is killed in his surburban Birmingham, Alabama, home when he opens a package that explodes a pipe bomb, one reportedly sent by white supremacists angered at Vance's recent rulings against them.

December 18: White supremacists (reportedly Ku Klux Klan members), kill Robert Robinson, a black alderman and lawyer who has represented the NAACP, in Savannah, Georgia, by sending him a pipe bomb.

December 18: Two unexploded bombs are defused in the federal court building in Atlanta, Georgia, reportedly planted by KKK terrorists.

December 19: Bomb experts defuse a bomb planted in the NAACP headquarters in Jacksonville, Florida, reportedly sent by white supremacists. The FBI claims that the bombs that killed Judge Robert Vance in Birmingham, Alabama, and black lawyer Robert Robinson in Savannah, Georgia, along with those found in a federal court building in Atlanta, Georgia, and the Jacksonville bomb, are all linked through "hard forensic evidence."

1990

January 19: Nine soldiers (three officers and six enlisted soldiers), one of whom is still being sought, are indicted in El Salvador for the murders of six Jesuit priests and two others on November 16, 1989, in San Salvador. All are reported members of the terrorist group FMLN.

February 4: Palestinian terrorists attack a bus carrying Israeli academics and their wives en route to Cairo on the main highway east of the city, killing eight persons and wounding another seventeen.

February 11: Nelson Mandela, imprisoned in South Africa for more than 27 years for plotting to overthrow the govern-

ment and for terrorist activities, is released. He urges that pressure be applied against the white minority government.

March 25: Police arrest Julio Gonzalez in New York City, charging him with deliberately setting fire to a Bronx social club, where 87 persons perish from burning or asphyxiation in a blazing inferno.

March 27: William Robinson, a U.S. missionary, is slain in the Israeli-designated "security zone" in Lebanon by Palestinian terrorists to deter the establishment of Israeli settlements.

April 9: IRA terrorists explode a bomb that wrecks two vehicles of a British Army patrol on a country road near Downpatrick, County Down, killing four British soldiers.

April 10: Arab terrorists release three hostages—a French woman, her Belgian companion, and daughter, who have been kidnapped on a Mediterranean cruise two years earlier.

April 22: Robert Polhill, a fifty-five-year-old American taken hostage by pro-Iranian terrorists three years earlier, is released in Beirut, Lebanon.

April 30: Frank Herbert Reed, a fifty-seven-year-old American abducted by Arab terrorists almost four years earlier, is released in Beirut, Lebanon.

May 13: Communist terrorists shoot and kill two U.S. airmen near Clark Air Force Base in the Philippines.

May 20: A mentally unbalanced Israeli in the occupied Gaza Strip, opens fire on Arab construction workers, killing seven before being subdued.

May 21: Islamic leader Maulvi Mohammed Farooq, forty-five, is assassinated in Srinagar, Kashmir.

May 30: PLO terrorists attempt raids along the coast of Israel, but Israeli troops wreck the attacking speedboats, killing four and capturing twelve of the raiders. Yasir Arafat denies PLO involvement.

July 20: The London Stock Exchange is bombed by IRA terrorists, who give warning, allowing the safe evacuation of more than 300 persons; no one is injured.

July 24: IRA terrorists are blamed for the explosion of a bomb that kills three policemen in a car and a Catholic nun near Armagh in Northern Ireland.

July 30: An IRA bomb claims the life of Ian Gow, fifty-three, a Conservative member of the British parliament who has repeatedly condemned the IRA terrorists.

August 1: Muslim terrorists in Trinidad, after seizing Prime Minister Arthur N. R. Robinson and others, surrender to local authorities, releasing their hostages.

August 25: Brian Keenan, fifty-two, a Belfast-born teacher who has been held for four years as a hostage in Lebanon, is released by Arab terrorists.

September 9: President of the Republic of Liberia, Samuel K. Doe, thirty-eight, who has murdered his predecessor in 1980, is himself assassinated. His mutilated body will later be put on display.

September 28: A Filipino general and fifteen soldiers are convicted of killing Benigno S. Aquino, Jr., in 1983, and all are sent to prison for life.

October 22: The White Aryan Resistance, a group of supremacist terrorists, is found liable by a Portland, Oregon, jury of inciting the 1988 beating death of an Ethiopian man; and $12.5 million damages are assessed against the leaders, along with the two skinheads responsible for the beating.

1991

January 14: Two PLO leaders are shot dead in Tunis, along with a bodyguard, by rival Arab terrorists.

February 7: IRA terrorists fire three rounds at 10 Downing Street, residence of the British prime minister, but no one is injured.

February 16: Drug-trafficking terrorists explode a car bomb in Medellín, Colombia, killing 22 persons and injuring another 140 near a bullfighting ring.

February 18: IRA terrorists bomb two railway stations, Victoria and Paddington terminals in London, England, killing one person and injuring another forty.

May 13: A South African judge in Johannesburg brands as a terrorist Winnie Mandela, wife of Nelson Mandela, leader of outlawed African National Congress, finding her guilty of kidnapping four youths, who were to her home and beaten for not supporting her political cause. She is sentenced to six years in prison the following day.

May 21: Mengistu Haile Mariam, president and dictator of Ethiopia, who has led a hard-line Marxist government employing terrorism, flees the country as rebels approach the capital of Addis Ababa.

May 26: An Austrian Boeing 767-300 jetliner explodes over the jungle in Thailand, killing all 223 persons on board; a terrorist bomb is suspected but remains unproven.

July 31: Six Lithuanian border guards are slain by terrorists, who challenge Lithuania's claim of independence from the Soviet Union.

August 8: Pro-Iranian terrorists release hostage John McCarthy, a British journalist.

August 11: Edward Austin Tracy, an American who has been held hostage for five years by Lebanese terrorists, is released in Beirut. Hours earlier, French hostage Jérome Leyraud, abducted a week before, has been released by the same terrorist group.

August 30: Federal agents storm the Federal Correctional Institution at Talladega, Alabama, freeing 9 hostages from prison-inmate terrorists and capturing 121 rebelling prisoners.

September 13: Police in Phoenix, Arizona, arrest six persons, charging them with the terrorist slayings of nine persons at a Buddhist temple outside of Phoenix.

September 24: Pro-Iranian terrorists release British hostage Jack Mann, seventy-seven and in poor health, to Syrian officials. Mann has been held captive for more than two years.

September 30: Colonel Guillermo Benevides Moreno, a Salvadoran officer, is found guilty of ordering the terrorist slayings of six Jesuit priests, their cook, and her daughter in 1989.

November 4: The trial of Arab terrorist El Sayyid Nosair opens in New York City. Nosair has shot and killed rabbi and former head of the Jewish Defense League, Meir Kahane, outside a New York hotel in November 1990. Nosair will be found guilty only of assault with a deadly weapon and be sentenced to a term of seven to twenty-two years in prison.

1992

January 4: Members of a black teenage gang who terrorized a tourist family on a New York subway platform, killing one, are sentenced to twenty-five years in prison.

January 5–6: IRA terrorists attack civilians working at a British Army base in Ulster, with a bomb that kills eight persons and wounds another six as they are riding home.

January 10: IRA terrorists explode a bomb less than 300 yards from 10 Downing Street, the prime minister's residence in London, England. No one is injured.

January 15: Joseph Doherty, IRA terrorist and convicted killer of a British soldier, who has taken refuge in the U.S., is ordered deported back to Great Britain after court rules that he is not entitled to political asylum.

February 17: Serial killer, cannibal, and terrorist, Jeffrey Dahmer, who has claimed insanity in the torture and sex murders of fifteen victims, mostly homosexual youths in Milwaukee, Wisconsin, is sentenced to fifteen consecutive life terms.

February 19: IRA terrorist Joseph Doherty, convicted in 1980 of killing a British soldier and jailed in the U.S. in 1983 after fleeing to that country, is deported to Great Britain, his claim for political asylum earlier denied.

March 17: A powerful car bomb explodes at the Israeli embassy in Buenos Aires, Argentina, killing at least fourteen persons and injuring another 252 people. The bomb has been planted by Islamic terrorists.

April 10: IRA terrorists explode a bomb inside of a van parked in London's financial district, killing three and wounding ninety-one others. A second IRA bomb exploding in northwest London causes no injuries.

April 29–May 1: Three days of widespread violence in minority sections of Los Angeles that claim fifty lives, injure thousands, and cause millions of dollars in damages, erupt after a jury acquits four white LAPD officers charged in the terror beating of black motorist Rodney G. King.

June 8: Atef Bseiso, considered to be a PLO terrorist leader by the Mossad (Israeli intelligence), is shot dead outside of his hotel in Paris, France.

June 29: Mohammed Boudiaf, the seventy-three-year-old president of Algeria (installed in January 1992, following a coup), is assassinated, shot in the back and head by terrorists as he delivers a speech.

July 19: Mafia terrorists kill Paolo Borsellino, fifty-four, an Italian prosecutor responsible for convicting Mafia members, by blowing him up with a bomb when he visits his mother in Palermo, Sicily.

July 28: Giovanni Lizzio, forty-seven, who heads investigations into Mafia extortions, is slain by Mafia terrorists in Catania, Sicily.

August 12: An Amtrak train is derailed near Newport News, Virginia, with seventy-four passengers injured. Federal investigators state that criminal vandalism to a switch has caused the wreck.

August 13: ABC-TV new producer David Kaplan, forty-five, is shot in the back and killed in Sarajevo, by terrorist snipers firing on a caravan carrying Milan Panic, prime minister of Yugoslavia, into Sarajevo.

August 25: Neo-Nazi terrorists bomb a hotel housing refugees seeking asylum from communism in the Baltic seaport of Rostock, Germany, in an effort to drive out all foreigners. No serious injuries occur.

August 31: Randall "Randy" Weaver, forty-four-year-old member of a white supremacist group, and a fugitive on gun charges, surrenders after a long siege to federal agents at Ruby Ridge in northern Idaho,

where William Degan, who is a deputy marshal, Weaver's wife Vicki, and son, Samuel, have been killed. Weaver is a hero of terrorist hate groups in the far American West because of his defiance of gun laws.

September 7: Twenty-four protestors are machine-gunned to death as they flee Ciskei troops in South Africa, where terrorist tactics are enacted to support oppressive military rule.

September 13: Abimael Gutzman Reynoso, leader of the Shining Path terrorist organization of Peru, is captured after a twelve-year search, along with about a dozen of his top aides. Gutzman Reynoso's decade-long terror campaign has cost 25,000 lives and $22 billion in damages.

October 3: To mark the second anniversary of Germany's reunification, more than 1,000 neo-Nazis march through the streets of Arnstadt, Germany, and another 500 neo-Nazis march through downtown Dresden, Germany, shouting "Foreigners Out!" and "Germany for Germans!"

October 9: An engineer in a Russian nuclear plant is caught just before leaving for Moscow to sell to terrorists 1,538 kilos of highly enriched uranium (HEU).

October 14: Ex-hostages Joseph Cicippio and David Jacobsen file suit against the government of Iran, claiming that their abductions and others were directed and financed by Iran in order to force the U.S. into freeing frozen Iranian assets.

1993

January 8: A European inquiry board reports that more than 20,000 Muslim women in Bosnia and Hercegovina have been raped by mostly Serbian terrorists in an effort to drive them from their homes.

January 8: Hakija Turajlic, one of three Bosnian deputy prime ministers, is assassinated after a U.N. vehicle is halted. Serbian military leaders later apologize, saying that an overanxious Serbian draftee responsible for the killing has been detained.

February 24: Mobs in Mogadishu spread terror for hours, creating widespread destruction and looting, and firing guns for more than six hours in challenge to the presence of U.N. peacekeeping forces, which eventually return fire.

February 26: A powerful bomb explodes in the parking garage beneath the World Trade Center in New York City. Six persons are killed and more than 1,000 are injured in the worst terrorist attack on U.S. soil to date. Four Islamic terrorists, and their leader, Ramzi Ahmed Yousef, will later be sent to prison for life.

February 28: The Branch Davidians, a so-called religious cult led by hustler David Koresh, which has holed up in a compound outside of Waco, Texas, resists federal officers attempting to confiscate a cache of illegal weapons, killing six persons, including four federal agents, and wounding fourteen others in a siege of the fortified compound. Koresh has kept his followers inside the compound by terrorist tactics, many of his closest supporters carrying automatic weapons and threatening to murder anyone attempting to desert.

March 1: More than 400 federal agents participate in the siege of the Branch Davidian cult compound outside of Waco, Texas. Cult leader David Koresh arrogantly defies agents to attack and seize the enormous cache of illegal weapons held by him and his followers. Koresh says that he is Jesus Christ.

March 12: Terrorists kill 232 persons and injure hundreds more with several bomb explosions in Bombay's financial district. Fifty persons, mostly brokers, are killed at the stock exchange.

March 17: Terrorists set off a bomb in a central residential area of Calcutta, India, killing forty-five persons and injuring dozens more when two apartment buildings are leveled by the blast.

March 30: Two Serbian terrorists are sentenced to death by firing squad on orders of a military tribunal that has found them guilty of mass rape and genocide against Muslims.

April 1: U.S. indicts four Palestinian terrorists on charges of plotting to blow up the Israeli Embassy in Washington, D.C., as part of a terror campaign against Jews in the U.S. and abroad by the Abu Nidal network.

April 12: Neo-Nazi racist Larry Wayne Shoemake terrorizes a Jackson, Mississippi, mall by invading a restaurant with an arsenal and randomly shooting black passersby, killing one and wounding seven others before police arrive and a gun battle ensues. Shoemake is killed (or commits suicide) as the restaurant catches fire.

April 17: After the four LAPD officers in the Rodney King beating have been acquitted by a California jury, a federal trial has ensued against the four men, and two of these, Sgt. Stacey C. Koon and Officer Laurence M. Powell are found guilty by a federal jury, the other two officers being acquitted.

April 19: The Branch Davidian cult compound outside of Waco, Texas, is stormed by federal officers, who batter holes in buildings and inject tear gas. Cult members set fire to the buildings, while cult leader David Koresh, who has held many of his followers captive through terrorist tactics (his heavily armed aides reportedly threatening to kill any deserters), dies along with seventy-two followers in the inferno, ending the fifty-one-day federal siege. Koresh and some of his top aides are found dead with bullets in their heads, apparent suicides. U.S. Attorney General Janet Reno, along with FBI agents in charge, are severely criticized for mishandling the Waco siege and attack.

April 24: An IRA bomb explodes in London's financial district, killing one person and wounding forty-four others.

May 1: A terrorist with explosives strapped to his body blows himself and eleven others to pieces, including Ranasinghe Premadasa, president of Sri Lanka, at a May Day political rally in Colombo, the capital. The assassination is in retaliation for the killing of a politician opposed to the Premadasa regime a week earlier.

May 15: A terrorist takes six children hostage in a Paris nursery, but he is killed by French police, who catch him asleep. The children are rescued without injury.

May 22: An Egyptian court sentences six Muslim terrorists to death and two others to life sentences for attacks on tourists and plotting to assassinate Egyptian officials.

May 27: A terrorist bomb explodes outside the Uffizi art gallery in Florence, Italy, killing six persons and injuring dozens more, as well as causing damage to priceless art works.

May: Lithuanian police raid a bank vault and discover a rod of beryllium with about 150 grams of highly enriched uranium (HEU), which is apparently intended for sale to terrorists planning on the construction of a nuclear bomb.

June 22: The Unabomber sends a bomb to geneticist Charles Epstein at the University

of California. The scientist loses several fingers when the bomb blows up.

June 24: Federal agents seize eight Muslim terrorists in New York City before they can execute their planned campaign of political bombings and assassinations.

June 29: Two Russian seaman are apprehended after stealing 1.8 kilos of highly enriched uranium and before they can sell the HEU to terrorists planning on constructing a nuclear bomb.

July 2: FBI agents arrest Omar Abdel Rahman, Islamic fundamentalist leader and suspected organizer of terrorist operations, outside of a mosque in Brooklyn, New York. His followers have been linked to bombing plots.

July 17: Egypt hangs five more Islamic terrorists who have been found guilty of bombings and mass killings, a government campaign that has shut down terrorist operations of militant fundamentalists.

July 27: Terrorists (reportedly Red Brigadists) explode a car bomb in downtown Milan, Italy, killing at least five persons. Another bomb exploding in the center of Rome, Italy, injures twenty-four persons, and damages the basilica of St. John Lateran, the Pope's See.

August 4: A U.S. federal judge sentences Sgt. Stacey C. Koon and Officer Laurence M. Powell, who have been found guilty by a federal jury of the terrorist beating of black motorist Rodney G. King, to two and a half years in prison. The judge explains the lenient sentence by stating that King had provoked the police violence.

August 15: Gold miners invading Brazil's Yanomamo Indian reservation kill seventy-three Indians and terrorize whole communities in the nation's largest massacre of the century.

August 18: Four are killed and fifteen others are injured when Islamic terrorists attack new Egyptian security chief (he is wounded and survives) in downtown Cairo.

November 7: Three Russian naval officers steal 4.5 kilos of highly enriched uranium (HEU), apparently intent on selling this to terrorists who plan to construct a nuclear bomb. The thieves and fuel are located by authorities six months later.

December 7: Black racist Colin Ferguson, carrying an automatic pistol, boards a commuter train at Penn Station and, as the train arrives at Garden City, leaps from his seat and goes swiftly down the aisles of the train, from car to car, picking out victims at random and shooting twenty-five persons, killing six of these helpless victims.

1994

March 4: Four Islamic terrorists responsible for the bombing of the World Trade Center in New York City on February 26, 1993, are sent to prison for life. Charges will be brought against their leader, a religious fanatic, Ramzi Ahmed Yousef, mastermind behind the attack, which has killed six persons and injured more than 1,000 others.

May 10: Police in Bavaria discover 5.6 gm of pure plutonium-239 in the garage of a professional criminal who has links to the KGB and Bulgarian terrorists. It is believed that this fuel was to be used by terrorists for the construction of a nuclear bomb.

June 13: German police seize 800 mg of highly enriched uranium (HEU) that has been smuggled from Prague to Bavaria.

August 10: Police in Munich, Germany, intercept at the airport a suitcase shipped from Moscow, containing lithium-6 and nuclear fuel that are apparently intended for terrorists planning on building a nuclear bomb.

December 10: Advertising executive Thomas Mosser opens a package delivered to his North Caldwell, New Jersey, home and is killed when it contents, a bomb, goes off. This terrorist act is attributed to the Unabomber.

December 14: Investigators in Prague, in the Czech Republic, discover 2.72 kilos of highly enrich uranium (HEU) in the back seat of a parked car. They will find another kilo of the same shipment in January 1995, all of this fuel apparently intended for delivery to terrorists planning on constructing a nuclear bomb.

1995

January 22: Two Palestinian terrorists kill eighteen Israeli soldiers, a civilian, and themselves by exploding a bomb outside a military camp in central Israel. The bomb also injures sixty-five other persons. The Islamic Jihad terrorist group claims responsibility for the bombing.

January 30: A terrorist car bomb explodes on a crowded Algiers street, killing forty-two persons and injuring another 300 people.

February 6: Twelve Islamic terrorists are tried in U.S. federal court in New York for the 1993 bombing of the World Trade Center. Siddig Ibrahim Siddig Ali, one of the accused, changes his plea from not guilty to guilty, saying that Sheik Omar Abdel Rahman, one of his fellow defendants and for whom he has served as bodyguard and translator, has played a significant role in the bombing conspiracy.

In addition to the U.N. building in New York, Siddig Ali tells the court, the terrorists have planned the destruction of an FBI office, a bridge, and two tunnels.

February 7: Ramzi Ahmed Yousef, the Islamic terrorist leader who has masterminded the 1993 bombing of the World Trade Center in New York, is arrested in Islamabad, Pakistan, and will be flown to New York the following day to face trial. He will, on February 9, 1995, plead not guilty to eleven counts.

March 20: Members of the Aum Shinri Kyo, a fanatical terrorist organization and offshoot of the Japanese criminal society, Yakuza, plant several packages inside the Tokyo subway system that emit a powerful nerve gas (sarin, which can paralyze the central nervous system and cause death), which kills 12 persons and injures another 5,500 people. A massive hunt ensues as police search for the cult leaders.

April 2: The Islamic Resistance Movement of Hamas explodes a bomb in Gaza that kills eight persons and wounds another thirty. Police report that the terrorists were assembling a bomb that went off by accident.

April 4: Francisco Duran, 26, of Colorado Springs, Colorado, is convicted of attempting to assassinate President Bill Clinton by firing an assault rifle at the White House in Washington, D.C., in October 1994. Duran will be convicted and, on June 29, 1995, sentenced to forty years in prison.

April 9: Two suicide terrorists kill themselves, seven Israeli soldiers, and an American student, and wound another forty-five persons, mostly Israeli soldiers, when they detonate bombs in the Gaza Strip. Both Hamas and Islamic Jihad take credit for the terrorist explosions.

April 19: A powerful truck bomb explodes outside the Alfred P. Murrah Federal Building in Oklahoma City, Oklahoma, at 9:02 A.M., shearing away half the nine-story building and killing 168 men, women, and children, the worst terrorist attack in U.S. history. About an hour later, Timothy McVeigh, who will become the prime suspect in the bombing, is arrested near Perry, Oklahoma, for carrying concealed weapons.

April 21: FBI agents charge Timothy McVeigh, in custody in Perry, Oklahoma, for carrying concealed weapons, with blowing up the Murrah Building in Oklahoma City. McVeigh's cousin, Terry Nichols, is arrested the same day in Herington, Kansas, charged with aiding McVeigh in blowing up the Murrah Building.

April 24: Police locate the hideout of Hideo Murai, one of the five top leaders of the terrorist cult, Aum Shinri Kyo, which is responsible for planting the nerve-gas bombs that have killed twelve persons and injured thousands more on the Tokyo subway system a month earlier. Murai is the cult's chemist, who packaged the deadly sarin nerve gas. As he is being escorted from the hideout, the thirty-six-year-old Murai is fatally stabbed by Hiroyuki Yo, a South Korean.

April 24: Gilbert Murray, president of the California Forestry Association, is killed in Sacramento, California, by a package bomb sent by the Unabomber. Murray will be the third and final fatality claimed by the terrorist. Two dozen others will be injured and maimed by bombs sent by the Unabomber.

May 15: At a roadblock outside of Tokyo, police apprehend Yoshihiro Inoue, head of "intelligence" for the murderous Aum Shinri Kyo cult. Officers obtain Inoue's notebook, which details timetables and numbers of passengers using Tokyo's three subway lines where the sarin gas attacks were unleashed on March 20.

May 16: Police and paramilitary units storm the secret compound of Aum Shinri Kyo, the terrorist cult responsible for the poison-gas attacks in the Tokyo subway system on March 20, at the base of Mt. Fuji, capturing, among others, the cult leader, Shoko Asahara, who is later sent to prison. With Asahara's capture, Am Shinru Kyo is no longer an effective terrorist organization.

June 26: Islamic terrorists attack the limousine carrying Egyptian President Hosni Mubarak during his visit to Addis Ababa, Ethiopia. The attackers fire from rooftops, on the street, and in a passing Jeep, but they fail to injure the Egyptian leader, killing two Ethiopian policemen instead. Two of the terrorists are killed and many passersby are wounded in the gunfight.

July 25: Algerian separatists, as part of a terrorist campaign, plant a bomb in a subway car of the Paris metro system; it explodes in the Latin Quarter stop, killing seven persons and wounding dozens more.

July 29: Leon Bor, an Israeli citizen, boards a tourist bus in Cologne, Germany, shooting the driver and holding twenty-six sightseers hostage. He randomly shoots and kills an elderly woman who identifies herself as a German. After terrorizing the passengers for several hours, Bor is shot and killed by police.

August 11: FBI director Louis Freeh suspends four Bureau officials, including agent Larry Potts, after it is disclosed that the Bureau either withheld or destroyed documents relating to the 1992 Ruby Ridge siege in Idaho in which three persons have been killed.

August 15: The Department of Justice agrees to pay $3.1 million to Randall Weaver and his daughters, who have filed a $200 million wrongful death suit against the Department for the shooting deaths of Weaver's wife, Vicki, and son, Samuel, during the FBI's 1992 siege of Randall's cabin in Idaho.

August 16: An unexploded bomb is discovered on board the high-speed train racing between Lyon and Paris, France. Forensic specialists lift a fingerprint that identifies Khaled Kelkal, an Algerian separatist leader and terrorist.

August 29: Eduard Shevardnadze, the head of Georgia, escapes an assassination attempt in Tbilisi, the capital, when a terrorist bomb explodes close to his motorcade. Shevardnadze is slightly wounded.

September 19: On the recommendations of U.S. Attorney General Janet Reno and FBI director Louis Freeh, the *Washington Post* publishes the thirty-five-thousand-word manifesto that has been sent by the Unabomber, in the hopes that someone will recognize the writing style of the terrorist and identify him. The manifesto is a rambling tirade of intellectual gobbldygook that essentially attacks the Industrial Revolution.

September 24: Eric Borel, a sixteen-year-old French youth, enters the village of Cuers with a hunting rifle and terrorizes the town for several hours as he hunts down residents, randomly killing nine persons and wounding another eight before killing himself when he runs out of ammunition.

September 28: Outside Lyon, French police and paramilitary units locate a hideout of Algerian separatists led by Khaled Kelkal, shooting it out with the terrorists, wounding one of three who are captured; Kelkal escapes.

September 30: French commandos hunting for terrorist Khaled Kelkal find him waiting for a bus five miles outside of Lyon, France. Following a shootout, Kelkal is killed.

October 1: Ten Islamic fundamentalist terrorists, tried before a federal court in

New York, are convicted of conspiracy to destroy U.S. public buildings and structures. One of their leaders, Sheik Omar Abdel Rahman, a blind Eygptian cleric and Islamic fanatic, is convicted of directing the conspiracy and attempting to assassinate Egyptian president Hosni Mubarak. El Sayyid Nosair is convicted of the 1990 murder of Rabbi Meir Kahane (he was acquitted of murder charges in a state court in 1991 and convicted at that time only of assault). The case has been won for the prosecution largely on tapes secretly recorded by undercover FBI informant, Emad Salem. One of these tapes showed four of the Islamic terrorists making a bomb by mixing diesel oil and fertilizer in a Queens, New York, garage.

October 3: Terrorists attempt to assassinate Macedonian President Kiro Gilgorov, in Skopje, the capital, as Gilgorov is being driven to the National Parliament Building. Gilgorov is seriously wounded in the head; his driver and three bystanders are killed.

October 9: According to federal investigators, a terrorist group calling itself Sons of the Gestapo derails an Amtrak train southwest of Phoenix, Arizona, which kills one of the twenty crew members and injures 100 of the 248 passengers.

1996

January 15: Ramzi Ahmed Yousef, Islamic terrorist and mastermind behind the bombing of the World Trade Center in New York City on February 26, 1993, a terrorist attack in which six persons have been killed and more than 1,000 others injured, is sentenced in Manhattan to life imprisonment plus 240 years. Before his sentence, Yousef screamed out a diatribe, saying: "I am a terrorist, and I am proud of it!" To federal judge Kevin Duffy, he ranted: "Your God is

not Allah. You worship death and destruction." Yousef has been sentenced for two crimes—the attack on the World Trade Center and an unsuccessful plot to blow up a dozen U.S. airliners in Asia.

January: David Kaczynski, who has read the Unabomber's rambling manifesto published, in part, by the *New York Times*, finds similar writings in his mother's Lombard, Illinois home, those written by his brother, Theodore "Ted" Kaczynski. He will later inform authorities. Six months later, Kaczynski will be arrested by FBI agents at his remote cabin in Montana, identified as the Unabomber and charged with the terrorist's many crimes.

February 17: Mass murderer and terrorist Colin Ferguson, who has acted as his own lawyer in defense of his shooting spree aboard a New York commuter train in 1993, is convicted of murdering six persons and attempting to murder twenty-two others. He is given a life sentence with no hope for parole.

March 7: A bomb explodes on a bus in Beijing, China, killing two people and injuring many others. Communist authorities blame "hooligans," but others report the explosion being created by anti-Communist terrorists.

June 18: After a four-hour gunfight with police in Brooklyn, Heriberto Seda surrenders to police; evidence found in Seda's apartment pinpoints him as the lone terrorist known as "Zodiac," who has, in 1990, shot four persons. Before going to prison, Seda confesses, saying he has been moved to murder by a "sudden urge."

July 17: TWA Flight 800, a jumbo 747 jetliner, just after taking off, blows up over the ocean off Long Island, with all 230 persons on board killed. It will later be claimed that the airplane was downed by a missile, fired accidentally by a U.S. military training plane or by terrorists from shore or a ship at sea.

July 27: At 1:25 A.M., Atlanta's Centennial Park is rocked by a pipe-bomb explosion, which kills one and injures another 112 persons. Richard Jewell, a guard, earlier reported a suspicious knapsack placed in the area where hundreds of persons were dancing to rock music, and helped other guards clear the area just before the explosion. Jewell is, at first, hailed as a hero, but he later becomes the chief suspect of the FBI.

October 26: The Department of Justice officially announces that Richard Jewell is no longer a suspect in the bombing of Atlanta's Centennial Park. Jewell's life has been thoroughly disrupted and he has been all but charged as being the terrorist bomber by the nation's press.

November 5: Haitian police shoot and kill five men, one in handcuffs, in Port-au-Prince, another example of terrorist tactics by what has been described as a "constabulary of thugs." The Haitian police force, poorly trained in a crash four-month course by U.S. advisers, following the free election of President Jean Bertrand Aristide (with the help of a strong U.S. military presence in Haiti in 1994), has sadistically beaten prisoners, some to death, and indiscriminately used deadly force, firing after autos (killing a small girl riding in one).

December 2: Martin Bryant, twenty-nine, the gunman who has terrorized a Tasmanian resort, killing thirty-five and wounding nineteen in a wild shooting spree in April 1996, is sentenced to thirty-five life terms in Hobart, Australia.

December 11: The U.S. Air Force clears General Terry J. Schwalier of responsibility for the terrorist bombing of the U.S. military camp in Dhahran, Saudi Arabia in June 1996, in which nineteen Americans were killed and another 500 wounded,

saying that Schwalier had taken reasonable steps to protect the base. Terrorist Hani al-Sayegh, a Saudi citizen, is later arrested and held in Canada as the mastermind behind the attack.

December 17: In the worst terrorist attack in the 133-year history of the Red Cross, five women, four being nurses, and a construction worker are shot to death while they sleep in a hospital compound in Chechnya. Veselin Sljivancanin, a Serbian terrorist, is thought to have led the raid against the hospital.

December 18: Fourteen Túpac Amaru Revolutionary Movement (MRTA) terrorists, led by Néstor Cerpa Cartolini, swarm into the Japanese Embassy in Lima, Peru, during a party, taking 490 hostages, many of these being top-ranking international diplomats, threatening to kill the hostages unless imprisoned terrorists are released by the Peruvian government.

December 23: MRTA terrorists occupying the Japanese Embassy in Lima, Peru, release 225 of their 490 hostages as a Christmas gesture, but keep the remainder under threat of death while they continue negotiating with Peruvian officials for the release of fellow imprisoned terrorists.

December 28: MRTA terrorists occupying the Japanese Embassy in Lima, Peru, release more hostages but the Peruvian government will not agree to release imprisoned terrorists, offering only a safe passage to Cuba for the terrorists inside the embassy.

December 30: Separatist Bodo terrorists explode two bombs beneath the tracks of a packed train as it leaves Kokrajhar, India, killing eighteen persons and injuring sixty more.

1997

January 16: Two bombs explode at an abortion clinic in Atlanta, Georgia. The first explosion creates only damage, the second injures 6 persons, including investigators and reporters covering the first explosion. Eric Robert Rudolph will become a suspect in this and the Olympic Park bombing and will be widely sought by FBI and police, with a $1 million price tag on his head.

January 20: Islamic terrorists raid a village south of Algiers, murdering thirty-six residents, decapitating some of these victims. Hours later, these same terrorists explode a car bomb outside of a cafe in Algiers, killing more than thirty persons and wounding scores more.

February 23: A Palestinian gunman terrorizes tourists and sightseers on the 86th-floor observation deck of New York's Empire State Building, murdering one tourist and wounding 7 others before killing himself.

February 28: A gay and lesbian bar in Atlanta is bombed and five persons are injured; it is believed that this terrorist act is the work of the same person or persons who have bombed Atlanta's Centennial Park.

March 13: A Jordanian soldier, an Islamic fanatic and terrorist, fires at Israeli school girls in the area of the Jordan Valley shared by Jordan and Israel, killing seven before his gun jams and he is seized. The soldier is allegedly imprisoned.

March 21: A suicide bomber kills himself and four others, and wounds dozens more when exploding a bomb in a cafe in Tel Aviv, Israel, setting back the Israeli-Palestinian peace negotiations.

April 22: In a dramatic rescue, 170 Peruvian shock troops blow down doors and walls and dash into the terrorist-held Japanese Embassy in Lima, Peru, liberating all the diplomats held hostage, while killing all fourteen MRTA terrorists. Two soldiers are slain by the terrorists, along with one of the hostages.

April 24: Opening statements are made in the trial of Timothy McVeigh for the 1995 terrorist bombing of the Murrah Building in Oklahoma City, Oklahoma. Within two months, McVeigh will be convicted and receive a death sentence for committing the worst terrorist act in U.S. history.

May 7: In the first war-crimes trial dealing with the civil strife in Bosnia, Dusan Tadic, a Bosnian Serb, forty-one, is found guilty by a U.N. panel of killing two policemen and torturing and terrorizing scores of Muslim civilians in Bosnia.

June 13: A federal jury in Denver, Colorado, votes unanimously to sentence twenty-nine-year-old Timothy McVeigh to death for the 1995 terrorist bombing of the federal building in Oklahoma City, Oklahoma.

June 16: IRA terrorists kill two policemen in Northern Ireland, which prompts the British government to call off peace talks.

June 17: Pakistani officials and Afghan tribal leaders are instrumental in capturing Min Aimal Kansi, suspected of the terrorist killings of two CIA officials outside of the agency's headquarters in Virginia, in 1993.

July 14: A U.N. tribunal sentences Bosnia-Serb terrorist Dusan Tadic to twenty years in prison for terrorist murders and "crimes against humanity" in "ethnic cleansing" terrorist campaigns in Bosnia.

July 15: Celebrated fashion designer Gianni Versace, fifty, is shot dead outside his mansion by serial killer Andrew P. Cunanan, in Miami Beach, Florida.

July 24: Andrew P. Cunanan, twenty-seven, a pronounced homosexual who has killed five persons, including gay fashion designer Gianni Versace, and terrorized the gay community nationwide (by reportedly stalking wealthy gays on an exclusive "sugar daddy" list throughout the country), is killed (either by his own hand or by police gunfire) in a deserted Miami Beach, Florida, houseboat.

July 30: Two terrorists carrying bombs in a crowded Jerusalem market explode (on purpose or accidentally) the devices, killing themselves and thirteen innocent passersby and seriously injuring another 150 persons. Hamas, an Islamic terrorist organization, takes credit for the mass murder.

July: The National Transportation Safety Board announces that TWA Flight 800, which blew up over the ocean on July 7, 1996, killing all 230 persons on board, has been destroyed, most probably, by an explosion in the center fuel tank, one resulting in an accident. Others still persist in believing that the plane was purposely exploded by a terrorist missile.

July: The FBI states that there were at least five potential members of the bombing conspiracy involved in planting the bomb that killed four Negro schoolgirls in Birmingham, Alabama, in 1963. Agents name three living members: Robert "Dynamite Bob" Chambliss, Thomas E. Blanton, Jr., and Bobby Frank Cherry.

August 14: Timothy McVeigh, convicted terrorist bomber of the federal building in Oklahoma City, Oklahoma, in which 168 persons have perished and scores have been injured, is sentenced to death by a federal judge in Denver, Colorado, expediting a jury decree. After hearing his death sentence, McVeigh, cryptically quotes a dissenting opinion of the late U.S. Supreme Court justice, Louis Brandeis: "'Our government is the potent, the omnipotent teacher. For good or for ill, it teaches the whole people by its example,' That's all I have to say." Terry Nichols, who has aided McVeigh, will receive a life sentence.

August: Koichiro Tarutani, an executive of Yamaichi Securities, is murdered in Tokyo while walking home, slashed to death as if his killer(s) have employed a Samurai sword, which is the traditional weapon of the secret Japanese criminal society, Yakuza. Tarutani has been killed by Yakuza thugs, according to one report, because he has attempted to collect on bad loans to crime boss Ryuchi Koike (who runs the Yakuza's enforcement and extortionist arm, Sokaiya). Koike has been loaned 79 million yen by Yamaichi Securities, and as much as 30 billion yen by the huge Dai-Ichi Kangyo Bank, its chairman, Kunjii Miyazaki, when confronted with this loan, committing suicide by hanging. It is believed that many top government leaders, business and banking executives, are all members of Yakuza's hierarchy (members of high standing being covered from neck to ankles by tattoos that signify their rank). Yakuza, which may have as many as a million members, is the offshoot of the old Black Dragon Society, which secretly aided Emperor Hirohito in his plans to begin World War II in the Pacific. One intelligence source privately states: "Japan from top to bottom is thoroughly polluted by Yakuza, which has corrupted its government and financial institutions, not unlike the Mafia in Sicily." The close to one trillion (in U.S. dollars) in Japan's bad loans have reportedly been made to the country's criminal elements and therefore cannot be recovered or sold off.

August: Carl Drega, sixty-seven, shoots and kills four residents in Colebrook, New Hampshire, before police shoot him to death. Drega has been amassing pipe bombs, apparently as part of an intended but unfulfilled terrorist campaign.

September 4: Three terrorists suicidally explode a bomb in a Jerusalem marketplace, killing themselves and one other, while seriously wounding another 200 Israelis and tourists. Hamas, an Islamic terrorist organization, is thought to be responsible.

September 23: Terrorists of the Islamic Salvation Front are held responsible for widespread attacks on civilians, killing 85 and injuring another 67 persons.

September 25: Two Israeli agents try to kill Hamas leader Khalid Mashaal, in Amman, Jordan, but are foiled in their attempt.

September 30: Israel, in a concessionary gesture, releases twenty terrorists from prison, including Hamas founder, Sheik Ahmed Yassin.

October 8: The U.S. government labels 30 international groups as terrorist groups and bans contributions to these foreign organizations, making it illegal for any member of such terrorist groups to enter the U.S.

December 22: Terrorists of the Institutional Revolutionary Party are blamed for killing forty-five Zapatista members in San Cristobal de Las Casas, Mexico.

December 24: After having been captured in Sudan in 1994 and extradited to France, Ilyich Ramirez Sanchez, the notorious Carlos (or "Jackal"), is convicted of kidnapping and murder in Paris and is sent to prison for life.

1998

January 29: An abortion clinic in Birmingham, Alabama, is bombed by an unknown terrorist, killing Robert Sanderson, an off-duty policeman, and injuring a nurse.

January: Theodore "Ted" Kaczynski, the notorious Unabomber, attempts to hang himself in his jail cell. He surives to cut a deal with prosecutors, confessing to his many bombings in exchange for receiving a life sentence behind bars.

February 9: Eduard Shevardnadze, seventy, the head of Georgia, escapes another assassination attempt in Tbilisi, the capital, when terrorists fire a rocket-propelled grenade at his passing car. Seven suspected terrorists will be arrested and charged with the attack, these being supporters of Shevardnadze's predecessor, Zviad Gamsakhurdia, a former Soviet foreign minister, overthrown in a 1992 coup and who has died in mysterious circumstances in 1993.

February 14: A bomb explodes aboard a bus in the central Chinese city of Wuhan, killing at least sixteen persons (one report has thirty fatalities) and injuring scores more. Two taxis and three other buses are badly damaged by the explosion, which is attributed to anti-Communist terrorists.

February 14: The FBI announces that Eric Robert Rudolph is sought as a fugitive suspect in the January 29, 1998, bombing of a Birmingham, Alabama, abortion clinic. Media reports have it that traces of explosives have been found in Rudolph's truck and storage locker.

February 14: Milan Simic and Miroslav Tadic, two Bosnian Serb leaders accused of conducting a "campaign of terror," turn themselves in to a United Nations war crimes tribunal at Bosanski Samac, Bosnia.

February 14: Thirteen bombs are exploded by Muslim terrorists in several crowded sections of Coimbatore, India, prior to a speech by Hindu leader Lal Krishna Advani. Hindu-Muslim clashes have increased since a Hindu policeman was killed by two Muslims in November 1997.

February 15: The bodies of seven men, Zapatista sympathizers, are found in a pit near San Cristobal de Las Casas, Mexico, victims, it is reported, of terrorists from the Institutional Revolutionary Party.

February 17: Milan Simic and Miroslav Tadic, accused of conducting a "campaign of terror" in Bosnia, plead innocent before a court in The Hague, Netherlands. Another accused terrorist mastermind, Simo Zaric, agrees to surrender to the court.

March 9: A time-activated bomb explodes inside of a compartment on the Chiltan Express train as it is crossing a bridge over a canal forty-five miles southwest of Lahore en route to Quetta, Punjab, India. Seven persons are killed and thirty-five are wounded by the terrorist explosion. Another terrorist bomb explodes the same day outside a court building in the province of Sind, injuring thirteen, six of whom are policemen.

March 9: Serbian terrorist Dragoljub Kunarac, thirty-seven, admits before a court in The Hague, Netherlands, that he has raped several Muslim women in 1992 during the Bosnian war. Human-rights groups state that more than 30,000 Muslim women have been raped during 1992–1995 Bosnian conflict by Serbian terrorists, many of whom tell their victims that it is their purpose to impregnate them with Serbian babies and thus increase the Serbian population (and its voting power) in the area.

March 25: Salvador Valdez and Jose Santos Vasquez, two men who have been jailed for attempting to abduct small girls in Huejutla, Mexico, and are about to be released on bond, are seized by a crowd of more than 1,000 persons and lynched. It has been reported that the two victims have been kidnapping small girls in order to kill them and sell their organs on the black market.

March 29: Mohiyedine Sharif, chief bomb maker for the Hamas terrorist organization, is killed in a premature car bombing in the West Bank town of Ramallah. Officials for the Palestinian Authority claim that Sharif was murdered by gunfire before the bomb exploded, shot to death by Adel Awadallah, a rival member of his own terrorist group involved in an Islamic power struggle with Sharif. Awadallah and Ghassan Addasi, a teenage bomb maker, drove Sharif to a remote spot, shot and killed him, then packed his body into the car, driving to Ramallah. The terrorists then placed their leader's body near the bomb-laden car and detonated the explosives with a timer to make it appear that he was killed by Israelis. Hamas will deny this report.

March 31: Gocha Esebua, leader of a twenty-man terrorist group opposed to Eduard Shevardnadze, leader of Georgia, is shot and killed by police. Esebua and others had captured United Nations observers and held them hostage for more than a week in February 1998, before releasing them and escaping. Esebua has been a fugitive for several weeks.

April 5: Terrorists open fire and throw a grenade at a funeral procession for rebel militant Gocha Esebua, killing five persons and wounding another eight in Zugdidi, Georgia, a former province of Soviet Russia. Esebua, killed in a shootout with police a week earlier, has been an ardent foe of Eduard Shevardnadze, whom he apparently tried to assassinate on Febuary 9, 1998.

April 5: Terrorists explode two bombs— one on the terrace of the Speke Hotel, the other at the Nile Grill restaurant in Kampala, Uganda. Five persons are killed and five others are injured in the blasts.

April 6: A terrorist bomb explodes outside the Russian Embassy in Riga, Latvia. An antipersonnel mine has been detonated, officials claim, by right-wing terrorists, who have recently bombed a synagogue in Riga, an act reportedly inspired by SS veterans of World War II. Fascism is reportedly on the rise again in Latvia.

April 23: James Earl Ray, convicted and imprisoned for life for assassinating civil rights leader Martin Luther King, Jr., dies in prison of liver failure.

April 26: Bishop Juan Gerardi Conedera, seventy-five, is beaten to death with a concrete block by terrorists in Guatemala City only two days after the Catholic prelate has released a shocking report on human-rights violations in Guatemala during that country's thirty-six-year civil war.

May 4: Theodore "Ted" Kaczynski, the notorious Unabomber, who has confessed to mailing many bombs over two decades, is officially sentenced by a California judge to four consecutive life terms in prison. Susan Mosser, whose husband, Thomas Mosser, an advertising executive of North Caldwell, New Jersey, has been killed by one of Kaczynski's mail bombs in 1994, tells the court sentencing the Unabomber to "lock him so far down he'll be closer to hell." David Kaczynski, the Unabomber's brother and the man responsible for identifying the terrrorist, says to the families of his brother's bomb victims: "The Kaczynski family offers its deepest apologies. We are very, very sorry."

May 12: Akin Birdal, fifty, Turkey's most outspoken human-rights activist, who has publicly supported the much-oppressed Kurdish communities, is shot and seriously wounded by two terrorists in his office after the would-be assassins pretend to seek legal advice. The shootists escape and later state that they are members of the ultranationalist Turkish Revenge Brigade, a terrorist organization.

May 12: General Gernando Landazabal Reyes, seventy-six, a conservative political activist, is shot dead in front of his Bogotá, Colombia, residence by terrorists.

May 12: U.S. President William Clinton announces that he will ask Congress to pass legislation providing for $280 million more in combating terrorism and drug trafficking.

May 12–15: Thousands riot in Jakarta, Indonesia, against the thirty-two-year authoritarian regime of President Suharto. On May 12, more than 5,000 students formed on the campus of the Trisatki University in West Jakarta, encouraged, one report has it, by radical instructors and student terrorists. Taking to the streets, the students throw rocks and other items at police who first fire rubber bullets (that can be fatal at less than 150 feet), and then change to real bullets after a police spy is publicly beaten by students. By Friday, May 15, tens of thousands invade the Chinese district, destroying whole blocks of Chinese businesses, which represent the richest minority in Indonesia. This section catches fire and several hundred looters are trapped in the flames and killed. Suharto, away on a state visit, returns to call out more than 10,000 troops and police to quell the worst rioting in Indonesian history.

May 15: A federal judge in New York sentences Abdul Hakim Murad, thirty, a commercial pilot who was born in Kuwait and has lived in Pakistan, to life in prison for bombing a Philippines Airlines jet in 1994, in which a Japanese passenger died, and for plotting to bomb eleven U.S. airliners over the Far East in January 1995.

May 17: At least ten persons were killed and twenty more injured by right-wing terrorists who swept through Barrancabermeja, in northeastern Santander province of Colombia. The country's main oil town has been plagued by "death squads" intent upon sowing terror throughout the province prior to the May 31, 1998, presidential elections.

June 9: FBI agents seize more than $1.4 million in assets belonging to the Quranic Literacy Institute in Oak Lawn, Illinois, and its chief officer, Mohammad Salah, whom federal officials describe as "a poster boy for Hamas." Salah has spent five years in an Israeli prison for funneling funds to Hamas, the outlawed terrorist organization in the Middle East.

June 19: A PFLP car bomb explodes in Beirut, killing two persons. This terrorist bombing is thought to be a signal to U.S. officials to pressure Israel into relinquishing West Bank territory to the Palestinians.

June 20: FBI Director Louis Freeh pulls out his agents in Saudi Arabia who have been investigating the 1996 truck bombing which took the lives of nineteen Americans and wounded 500 more persons. Freeh leaves behind only one agent to continue the investigation, which has been stymied by uncooperative Saudi officials reluctant to attach blame for the 1996 bombing to Iran. Saudi dissident Hani al-Sayegh, who is being held by U.S. authorities at an undisclosed location, and is thought to have been part of the 1996 bombing, awaits deportation to Saudi Arabia where he is expected to be beheaded. His testimony concerning the bombing is so contradictory as to be useless.

June 21: The PFLP orchestrates an attack of rocket-propelled grenades, which are fired close to the U.S. Embassy in Beirut, an attack that causes no injuries.

July 25: Russell E. "Rusty" Weston, Jr., 41, who believes that President Clinton has ordered the Navy Seals to hunt him down, either at his rural Montana cabin, a crude dwelling without plumbing located near Rimini (not unlike the hermit-like dwelling of Unabomber Ted Kaczynski) or his parents' Valmeyer home in rural southern Illinois. He is also convinced that government agents are watching him through

his TV set. When he and some fellow gold-hunters are ordered off federal land in Montana, Weston jumps into his red Chevy pickup and drives to the home of his parents. There Weston broods, then begins shooting cats in the backyard of his parents' home, which brings about an argument with his father. Stealing his father's handgun, Weston, who had been committed to a Montana mental hospital for fifty-three days in 1996, drives to Washington, D.C., arriving in the afternoon of July 24, 1998, a Friday. He joins hundreds of tourists flocking into the Capitol Building. As Weston approaches the security desk in a corridor near the Documents Room, he suddenly bolts past security officer Jacob J. Chestnut, producing a gun. Chestnut gropes for his weapon, but before he can draw his gun from the holster, Weston shoots him point blank in the head, killing him. Weston then races down the corridor, firing wildly and wounding twenty-four-year-old tourist Angela Dickinson. Opening the door to a suite of offices occupied by Texas Congressman Tom DeLay, he rushes inside. Security officer John Gibson, who shouts for all inside the suite to get under their desks, draws his weapon. Both he and Weston advance toward each other firing. Gibson falls first, but the heroic officer continues to fire, several of his shots finding their mark. Weston himself then collapses. Gibson, rushed to a hospital, will die a short time later, but Weston will survive to face murder charges.

August 7: The U.S. embassies in Nairobi, Kenya, and Dar es Salaam, Tanzania, are bombed. In Dar es Salaam, ten Tanzanians are killed and dozens injured in the blast, but little damage is done to the embassy building which sits some distance from the street. The explosion in Nairobi is tremendous, totally collapsing a building next to the U.S. Embassy. The bombers have attempted to drive a Mitsubishi pickup truck into the embassy ramp area but have been turned back by an alert guard who trades gunshots with them. Going up an alleyway, the vehicle suddenly explodes, demolishing the building next to the embassy. Twelve Americans are killed, along with more than 250 Kenyans. The blast blows out countless office windows, sending debris through the streets and wounding more than 5,000 persons. Osama bin Laden, a multimillionaire Saudi Arabian, who heads the terrorist group Islamic Front for Jihad Against Jews and Crusaders, is later identified as having ordered the bombings.

August 15: A car bomb explodes in a crowded street in Omagh, Northern Ireland, seventy miles west of Belfast, and takes the lives of 28 persons, wounding another 220, one of the deadliest attacks in the long history of this terrorist-plagued land. The fatalities have been increased, according to Omagh officials, after a warning call from the perpetrators informs authorities that the bomb is located near a building. Passersby are moved from the site and actually closer to the location of the bomb. Many women and children are slain (thirteen women, nine children), others crippled. The Real IRA, a splinter group of the IRA, claims responsibility and states that it has exploded the bomb in protest over the ongoing peace settlement between the IRA and Protestant authorities. The Real IRA is universally condemned by IRA, Sinn Fein, and Protestant leaders, as well as governments around the globe. Leaders of the Real IRA (consisting of fewer than 100 members) later apologize for the attack and say that they will abide by the peace settlement. The terrorists, however, are religiously hunted by anti-terrorist forces. (Nine hardcore members of the IRA were released from

prison on April 14, 1998, before the end of their terms, in an effort to strengthen the peace accords. At that time, Irish political leaders feared that some of these diehard IRA members would form splinter groups and contest the peace with terrorist acts.)

August 20: President Clinton orders simultaneous attacks against a bin Laden–backed pharmaceutical plant in Khartoum, Sudan, which has reportedly been developing VX, a deadly nerve gas for future terrorist attacks (and which has recently been found in Iraqi warheads), and bin Laden's mountain terrorist training camp at Zhawar Kili, Afghanistan. More than 75 Mohawk cruise missiles (at a cost of more than $1 million per missile) are fired by U.S. warships in the Red and Arabian seas. The retaliatory strike against Khartoum is extremely effective, utterly destroying the pharmaceutical plant. The bombing against bin Laden's stronghold in Afghanistan has caused considerable damage and some casualties, but, according to several accounts, bin Laden and the many leaders of Middle Eastern terrorist organizations with whom he was reportedly meeting on this day are not injured. (Bin Laden was to meet with leaders of Islamic Jihad, the PFLP and other long-established terrorist organizations, which are his true mentors and directors.)

August 20: Terrorists slip into the Hebron mobile home of Rabbi Schlomo Raanan, stabbing the sixty-three-year-old Zionist leader to death. The attackers are believed to be PLO killers resentful of the Israeli settlers living among them. As a result of this attack, riots will ensue and Israel will further delay the relinquishing of West Bank territories.

GLOSSARY OF TERRORIST ORGANIZATIONS

The following compendium represents all major worldwide terrorist organizations from 1900 through the 1990s. Acronyms for many entries are cross-referenced to full proper names.

AAA, See: Argentine Anticommunist Alliance

AALA, See: Afro-American Liberation Army

AAPRA, See: All-African People's Revolutionary Army

Abdalla: An anti-Castro terrorist organization active chiefly in New York City during the 1970s.

Abu Abbas: A Syian terrorist organization, named after Abu Abbas, chief terrorist organizer of the PFLP and top aide to Yasir Arafat, aligned with the Al-Fatah faction of the PFLP. This group was condemned by President Clinton in his 1995 executive order.

Abu Musa: A Syrian terrorist group, a faction of the Al-Fatah faction.

Abu Nidal Faction: (Al Fatah Revolutionary Council), a Middle Eastern terrorist organization chiefly based in Syria and Libya, named after Abu Nidal (Sabri al-Banna), one of the world's most dangerous terrorists, who, for decades, has conducted terrorist attacks on both Israelis and Palestinians and who remains a man of mystery, his appearance allegedly altered through plastic surgery; he has been in hiding in Libya and was reported to have been detained in Egypt where he had gone in August 1998 to be treated for terminal leukemia (Egyptian officials denied the report.) President Clinton proscribed the Abu Nidal Organization in his executive order of 1995, prohibiting any U.S. organization or citizen from contributing to this terrrorist group.

Acao Libertadora Nacional (ALN): A Brazilian terrorist organization.

Action Directe (Direct Action, AD): An anti-NATO terrorist organization headquartered in France. AD was responsible for the murder of Georges Besse in 1986.

Action Organization for the Liberation of Palestine: A terrorist organization credited with the February 1970, attack on Israeli passengers at the Munich airport.

Action pour la Renaissance de la Corse (Corsican Resistance Action, ARC): Founded in 1967, ARC was created to protect the regional identity of Corsica. It has been responsible for various bombings throughout Corsica.

AD, See: Action Directe.

African National Congress (ANC): An organization working for the anti-apartheid movement in South Africa, accused of terrorist activities and bombings, many of these being confirmed.

Afro-American Liberation Army (AALA): A terrorist organization in Los Angeles, Calif., active in the 1970s.

AIM, See: American Indian Movement.

Al-Asifa: A European terrorist organization active during the 1980s.

Al-Dawa (The Call): An Islamic Shiite organization consisting of Ayatollah Khomeini supporters and Iraqi dissidents; Al Dawa took credit for the bombing of a British embassy.

Al Fatah: A Middle East terrorist organization active for the past four decades, often working in cooperation with the PFLP and sometimes Abu Nidal. President Clinton proscribed this group in his 1995 executive order in which all U.S. organizations and citizens are prohibited from contributing to this organization.

Al Fatah Revolutionary Council: A hierarchy of terrorist leaders from Abu Nidal, Al Fatah and PFLP, working with PLO and Yasir Arafat, which has planned and ordered innumerable world-wide terrorist attacks over the last four decades, and, most probably, was involved in the U.S. embassy bombings in Kenya and Tanzania in August 1998. President Clinton proscribed this group in his 1995 executive order in which all U.S. organizations and citizens are prohibited from contributing to this organization. The Council reportedly broke with Yasir Arafat and the PLO but many believe that this report is nothing more than a smokescreen.

Al Jihad Al Mudaddas Front: A Lebanese terrorist organization active since the 1980s. Condemned by President Clinton in his 1995 executive order.

al Qaeda: a Middle Eastern terrorist organiztion, reportedly led by Osama (Usama) bin Laden, as reported by Mohammed Saddiq Odeh, one of the two terrorists caught following the August 7, 1998 bombings of the U.S. embassies in Nairobi, Kenya and Dar es Salaam (the other being Khald Salim, AKA: Mohammed Rashid Daoud Al-'Owhali.).

Al Zulifikar: A Pakistani terrorist organization active during the 1980s.

ALF, See: Arab Liberation Front.

Algerian Separatists: A terrorist organization in Algeria seeking indedependence.

Aliens of America: A U.S. terrorist organization, based in Los Angeles during the 1970s.

All African People's Revolutionary Army (AAPRA): An African terrorist organization.

All India Communist Party: A terrorist organization active during the 1980s.

Alliance of the Lao Reactionary Group Fronts: A terrorist organization formed in China during 1982.

ALN, See: Acao Libertadora Nacional.

Alpha 66: An anti-Castro terrorist organization active in the Miami, Fla., area.

ALQ, See: Armee de Liberation Quebecois.

Amal (Islamic Hope): A Shiite organization of more than 5,000 members, headed by Nabih Berri; founded as the Movement of the Disinherited.

American Indian Movement (AIM): Founded to preserve Indian reservations in the upper plains; best known for the 1973 occupation of Wounded Knee, which resulted in several shootouts with federal marshals and FBI agents.

American Nazi Party: A U.S. terrorist organization begun by George Lincoln Rockwell, who was killed on August 25, 1967, John Patler charged with the shooting; Matt Koehl succeeded Rockwell but the organization broke into disorganized splinter groups throughout the U.S.

Americans for Justice: A U.S. terrorist organization active on the West Coast during the 1970s.

ANC, See: African National Congress.

Angry Merchants: A terrorist organization responsible for bombings in France in 1982.

Animal Rights Militia: A group responsible for numerous letter bombing incidents in Britain during the 1980s.

ANM, See: Arab National Movement.

Anti-Capitalist Action: A terrorist organization in Greece.

Anti-Communist Commandos: A terrorist organi-

zation active in Puerto Rico during the 1970s.

AOLP, See: Action Organization for the Liberation of Palestine.

April 19 Movement, See: Movimiento 19 Abril (M 19).

April 6 Liberation Movement: A Philippine terrorist organization movement.

ARC, See: Action pour la Renaissance de la Corse.

Arab Brigades Movement: A terrorist organization active in India during the 1980s.

Arab Communist Organization: A Middle Eastern terrorist organization during the 1970s.

Arab Liberation Front (ALF): A terrorist organization founded in Iraq in 1968 for the purpose of attacking Israeli interests.

Arab National Youth for the Liberation of Palestine: A Middle Eastern terrorist organization during the 1970s.

Arab Nationalist Movement: A Middle Eastern terrorist organization.

Arab Revolution Vanguards: A Middle Eastern terrorist organization during the 1980s.

Arab Steadfastness Front: A terrorist organization active in Egypt during the 1980s.

ARENA, See: Nationalist Republican Alliance.

Argentine Anti-Communist Alliance (AAA): An Argentine terrorist organization.

Argentinian Revolutionary Workers Party: A Latin American terrorist organization active during the 1980s.

Armed Commandos of Liberation: A Puerto Rican terrorist organization responsible for bombings during the 1970s.

Armed Communist Formations: An Italian terrorist organization active during the 1970s.

Armed Communist League: A terrorist organization active in Mexico during the 1970s.

Armed Forces of National Liberation of Puerto Rico: A terrorist organization working for total independence.

Armed Forces of National Resistance (FARN): A terrorist organization based in El Salvador.

Armed Guard of the Proletariet: A terrorist organization in Mexico.

Armed Nationalist Reactionary Group: A terrorist organization in the Dominican Republic during the 1980s.

Armed Nuclei for Popular Autonomy (NAPAP): A terrorist organization based in France.

Armed Proletarian Nucleus, See: Nuclei Armati Proletari.

Armed Resistance Group: A U.S.-based Puerto Rican terrorist organization.

Armed Revolution Squads: A right-wing terrorist organization in Italy during the 1980s.

Armed Revolutionary Nuclei (NAR): An Italian

terrorist organization during the 1980s.

Armed Revolutionary Vanguard-Palmares, See: Vanguarda Armada Revolucionaria-Palmares.

Armed Struggle: A Middle Eastern terrorist organization most active during the 1980s.

Armed Vanguard of the Proletariet: A terrorist organization based in Mexico during the 1970s.

Armee de Liberation Quebecois (ALQ): A separatist terrorist organization in Quebec, responsible for the 1964 invasion of a Montreal armament factory.

Armenian Orly Group: A terrorist organization active during the 1980s in Paris, France.

Armenian Secret Army for the Liberation of Armenia (ASALA): An Armenian nationalist terrorist organization.

Army of God: U.S.-based anti-abortion terrorist organization.

ASALA, See: Armenian Secret Army for the Liberation of Armenia.

As-Sa'iqa (Thunderbolt): A Palestinian group which is headquartered in Damascus, the Sa'iqa aligns itself with the Syrian Baath Party.

Aum Shinri Kyo (Supreme Truth): A religious cult and terrorist organization in Japan, which was responsible for the nerve gas attacks in the Tokyo subway system in 1995.

AUTOP, See: Workers Autonomy.

Azedegan: An Iranian pro-monarchist terrorist organization active in the 1980s.

Baader-Meinhof Gang (BM): A terrorist organization founded in West Germany by Berndt Andreas Baader and Ulrike Meinhof in the 1967, supported by East Germany, Moscow and the PFLP; the worst terror gang in German history which threatened the government itself and was not eradicated until the mid-1980s.

Bakunin-Gdansk: A terrorist ogranization active in Paris, France, during the 1980s.

BAMM, See: Black Afro Militant Movement.

Basque Fatherland and Liberty Group: A terrorist organization seeking independence for the Basque territories of Northern Spain, allied with the ETA.

Basque Nationalists, See: Euzkadi Ta Azkatazuna-Basque Homeland and Liberation.

Bay Bombers: A terrorist organization located in San Francisco, California, during the 1970s.

BFO: A Middle Eastern terrorist organization active in the 1970s.

BLA, See: Black Liberation Army.

Black Afro Militant Movement: A U.S. terrorist organization.

Black Dragon Society: Begun in the 1890s by Mitsuru Toyama, this criminal-terrorist organization was all pervasive in Japan until the end of World War II, at which time it was succeeded by the Yakusa.

Black Hand, The (La Mano Negra): Italian/Sicilian extortionist-terrorists operating in Italy and throughout Europe from the sixteenth century and in the U.S. from the 1890s, particularly in New York, Chicago, New Orleans and other metropolitan areas having large Italian/Sicilian populations who were their prey. The Black Hand all but disappeared during the early 1920s, the members of its many disassociated gangs turning to the more lucrative racket of bootlegging.

Black Hand Society: Serbian nationalist-terrorist organization seeking independence for Serbia, first from the Austro-Hungarian Empire, later from the federation of Slavic states known as Yugoslavia. Responsible for many assassinations, particularly that of Archduke Francis Ferdinand in Sarajevo in 1914, considered to be the catalyst of World War I.

Black June: A Middle Eastern terrorist organization active in the 1970s.

Black Legion, The: An American terrorist organization operating in and around Detroit, Mich., in the 1930s. The Legion was modeled after the Ku Klux Klan, its members terrorizing and killing minorities and immigrants in an effort to keep them out of the auto industry workforce.

Black Liberation Army (BLA): A U.S. terrorist organization of Negroes which was an offshoot of the Black Panthers, founded in 1971. BLA members murdered several police officers (white and black) in New York and California. Within two years, most of the group's members had been imprisoned or shot to death.

Black Muslims: Originally a black separatist organization based on the teachings of Elijah Muhammad, the Muslims often resorted to violence to perpetuate their religious and commercial empire. They have been involved in numerous shoot-outs with police and were responsible for fourteen murders in San Francisco, California, these slayings known as the Zebra killings.

Black Nation of Islam (BNI): A U.S. terrorist organization.

Black Panther Party (BPP): A militant Negro organization founded in Oakland, California, in 1966 by Huey Newton and Bobby Seale, the BPP was active in campus and ghetto protests. Its members were involved with numerous shootings and bombings until the late 1970s when surviving leaders turned to the formation of all-black private enterprises.

Black Revolutionary: A terrorist organization

active in New York City during the late 1970s.

Black September (BSO): A terrorist organization based in the Middle East which worked closely with Al Fatah, the PFLP and Yasir Arafat's PLO. Founded in 1970, BSO was responsible for the massacre of Israeli atheletes at the Munich Olympics. President Clinton condemned this organization in his 1995 executive order.

Black Shirts: Terrorist paramilitary and terrorist organization founded by Italian dictator Benito Mussolini which enforced Mussolini's edicts throughout Italy from his rise to power in 1922 to his fall from power during World War II.

BM, See: Baader-Meinhof Gang.

BNI, See: Black Nation of Islam.

Boxers: Chinese paramilitary and terrorist organization aimed at driving all foreigners out of China; the Boxers were secretly directed by Tzu Hsi, the dowager empress of China at the turn of the century, but their power was crushed by multi-national forces in 1900.

BOZKURTLAR, See: Grey Wolves.

BPP, See: Black Panther Party.

BPR, See: Popular Revolutionary Bloc.

Breakthrough: A reactionary terrorist group in Detroit, Mich., headed by Donald Lobsinger, which attacked left-wing groups at rallies during the 1970s.

Brigate Rosse, See: Red Brigades.

Brotherhood of Aleppo: A Middle Eastern terrorist organization during the 1980s.

Brown Shirts (Sturmabteilung, SA, Stormtroopers): German paramilitary and terrorist organization created by Adolf Hitler and his National Socialist Party in the early 1920s, one which grew to have millions of members--malcontents, misfits, criminals of all stripes--who persecuted and terrorized all enemies designated by Hitler throughout the 1920s and 1930s in Germany, until Hitler purged the organization and its leaders in 1934, replacing it with the state-sponsored SS and Gestapo.

BSO, See: Black Semptember.

CAL, See: Commandos Armados de Liberacion.

Carlos Aguero Echevarria: A terrorist organization in Costa Rica during the 1980s.

CCC, See: Cellules Communistes Combattantes.

Camorra: Italian criminal society, begun in the eighteenth century and later dominated Italy, practicing widespread extortion and terrorism.

Cellules Communistes Combattantes (CCC): A terrorist organization headquartered in Belgium.

Chicano Liberation Front (CLF): Founded in Los Angeles in the early 1970s to protest the deaths of Chicanos at anti-war rallies; involved with numerous attacks in public buildings and at

least one death in a bombing incident.

Chinese Triads: Terrorist organizations in China, Taiwan, Hong Kong, Singapore and throughout the Pacific, begun in the late seventeenth century in China to overthrow the oppressive Ch'ing dynasty, evolving into a criminal organization with millions of members, terrorizing fellow Chinese into paying extortion and ramsom money.

Chukaku-Ha: A terrorist organization in Japan.

CLF, See: Chicano Liberation Front.

COLINA, See: Commando da Libertacao Nacional.

Commando da Libertacao Nacional (COLINA, National Liberation Commando): A South American terrorist organization.

Comite Argentino de Lucha Anti-Imperialista: An Argentine terrorist organization active in the 1970s.

Commando Boudia: The opeational name for the terrorist Carlos (Ilyich Ramirez Sanchez) in London and Paris; named for the Algerian terrorist Mohammed Boudia.

Commandos Armados de Liberacion (CAL): A terrorist organization operating in Puerto Rico.

Communist Armed Nuclei: A terrorist organization in Italy during the 1980s.

Communist Front for Counter Power: A terrorist organization active in Italy during the 1980s.

Communist Groups for Proletarian Internationalism: A terrorist organization active in Italy during the 1980s.

Continental Revolutionary Army: A U.S. terrorist organization active in the Denver, Colorado, area during the 1970s.

Coordination of United Revolutionary Organizations (CORU): A consortium of terrorists organizations in Spain.

Corsican National Liberation Front (FLNC): A terrorist organization in Corsica.

CORU, See: Coordination of United Revolutionary Organizations.

Croatian Revolutionary Brotherhood (Hvratsko Revolucionarno Bratsvo, HRB): A nationalist-terrorist organization based in Yugoslavia.

Crypto: A Malaysian terrorist organization active in the 1980s.

Cuban Action Commandos: Founded in Los Angeles, California, in the late 1960s, this right-wing terrorist organization was responsible for bombing embassies of countries friendly to Fidel Castro's government. In 1975, this group bombed a number of left-wing bookstores.

Cuban Anti-Communist League, See: FLNC-Cuban Anti-Communist League.

Cuban Power, See: El Poder Cubano.

Cuban Revolutionary Directorate: An anti-Castro

terrorist organization active in Europe during the 1970s.

Dagger Society: A Chinese Triad and terrorist organization in China.

Death Angels: A terrorist-murder cult of Negroes in San Francisco who, in 1973-1974, killed fifteen persons as part of its initiation rites, initiates obligated to murder white persons to gain membership. Five members were tracked down and sent to prison for life.

De Mau Mau Gang: A Negro terrorist-murder gang in Illinois, which killed several white persons in 1972; its members, styling themselves after Mau Mau terrorists of Kenya, were sent to prison for life.

Democratic Front Against Repression: A Latin American terrorist organization active during the 1980s.

Democratic Front for the Liberation of Palestine (DFLP): A Middle Eastern terrorist organization formed in 1969 by extremists breaking away from the PFLP (or so the PFLP let it be known). The actual founder was Nayef Hawatmeh. This group, now based in Syria, was responsible for countless terrorist massacres, skyjackings and bombings, including a 1974 attack which killed twenty-two Israeli children. President Clinton proscribed this group in his executive order of 1995, prohibiting any U.S. organization or citizen from contributing to this terrrorist organization. This group is also known as the Popular Democratic Front for the Liberation of Palestine (PDFLP)

DEV SOL: A terrorist organization operating in Turkey.

DFLP, See: Democratic Front for the Liberation of Palestine.

DGI, See: Directoria General de Inteligencia.

Direct Action, See: Action Directe.

Directoria General de Inteligencia (DGI): A Cuban intelligence organization, directed by Fidel Castro and supported by the KGB during the Cold War, aligned with Western European terrorist activities.

Eagles of National Unity: A Middle Eastern terrorist organization active during the 1970s.

Eagles of the Revolution: A Middle Eastern terrorist organization active during the 1980s.

Eagle Warrior Society: A U.S. terrorist organization active on Indian reservations during the 1970s.

EAN: An anti-dictator terrorist organization made up of youths in Greece.

Easter Commandos: A terrorist faction of Black September.

Eelam Revolutionary Organization of Students (EROS): A terrorist organization based in Sri Lanka.

EGP: A terrorist organization based in Guatemala during the 1980s.

Ejercito de Liberacion National (ELN): A terrorist organization in Peru.

Ejercito Popular de Liberacion (EPL): A terrorist organization operating in Colombia.

Ejercito Revolucionario del Pueblo (ERP): A terrorist organization operating in Argentina and El Salvador, most active in the 1970s.

El Poder Cubano (Cuban Power): An anti-Castro terrorist organization active in the U.S.

El Salvador Democratic Revolutionary Front: An anti-government terrorist organization in El Salvador.

ELF, See: Eritrean Liberation Front.

ELN, See: Ejercito de Liberacion National.

ELS, See: Southern Liberation Army.

Emiliano Zapata Unit (EZP): Based in San Francisco, the EZP was responsible for four bombings in 1975 and 1976. This terrorist organization later merged with the New Dawn Collective.

English Republican Army: A terrorist organization in England during the 1980s.

Enlightened Path: A terrorist organization in Peru during the 1980s.

EOKA, See: Ethniki Oganosis Kyprion Agoniston.

EPL, See: Ejercito Popular de Liberacion.

EPLF, See: Eritrean People's Liberation Front.

Eritrean Liberation Front: A terrorist organization in Ethiopia.

Eritean People's Liberation Front (EPLF): A secessionist-terrorist group in Ethiopia which sabotaged food shipments to the starving nation in the 1980s.

EROS, See: Eelam Revolutionary Organization of Students.

ERP, See: Ejercito Revolucionario del Pueblo.

ETA, See: Euzkadi Ta Azkatazuna-Basque Homeland and Liberation.

Ethniki Organosis Kyprion Agoniston (EOKA): A terrorist organization based in Cyprus.

Euzkadi Ta Azkatazuna-Basque Homeland and Liberation (ETA): A terrorist organization active in Spain since the 1940s (following the fall of the Spanish Republic to Franco's Falangist/fascist forces in 1939) seeking independence from Spain for the Basque provinces.

EZP, See: Emiliano Zapata Unit.

FAL, See: Frente Argentino de Liberacion.

Falangists: A Bolivian right-wing terrorist organization during the 1980s.

FALN, See: Fuerzas Armadas de Liberacion Nacional.

Family of Jihad: A terrorist faction of Al Fatah.

FANE, See: Federation National Europe.

FAP, See: Fuerzas Armadas Peronistas.

FAR, See: Fuerzas Armadas Rebeldes.

Farabundo Marti National Liberation Front (FMLN): A terrorist organization active in El Savaldor during the 1980s.

FARC, See: Fuerzas Armadas Revolucionarias de Colombia.

FARL, See: Lebanese Armed Revolutionary Faction.

FARN, See: Armed Forces of National Resistance.

Fatah Revolutionary Council, See: Abu Nidal Faction, Al Fatah, Al Fatah Revolutionary Council.

Fedaj Khalq: A terrorist organization headquartered in Iran.

Fedayeen: A Middle Eastern terrorist organization active since the 1970s.

Federation National Europe: A neo-fascist terrorist organization active during the 1980s.

FFI, See: Fighters for the Freedom of Israel.

Fighters for the Freedom of Israel (FFI): A terrorist organization in Israel.

15th of May Arab Movement for the Liberation of Palestine: A Middle Eastern terrorist organization active in the 1980s.

Fighting Communist Formation: A terrorist organization in Italy during the 1970s.

FIN Cuban National Front: A terrorist organization active in New York City during the 1970s, which worked against the Cuban regime of Fidel Castro.

FINC–Youth of the Stars: A terrorist organization active in Miami, Florida during the 1970s.

First Line Armed Cell: A terrorist organization in Italy during the 1980s.

First of October Autonomous Revolutionary Group (GRAPO): A left-wing terrorist organization active in Spain during the 1970s.

FLB-ARB, See: Front de Liberation de la Bretagne-Armee Revolutionnaire Bretonne.

FLN, See: Front de Liberation National.

FLN, See: Front de Liberation of Algeria.

FLNC, See: Corsican National Liberation Front.

FLNC–Cuban Anti-Communist League: A Cuban terrorist organization active in the Miami, Florida area during the 1970s.

FLOSY, See: Front for the Liberation of Occupied South Yemen.

FLQ, See: Front du Liberation du Quebec.

FMLN, See: Farabundo Marti National Liberation Front.

FMPR, See: Manuel Rodriguez Patriotic Front.

Forcas Populares do 25 Abril (FP 25): A terrorist organization based in Portugal.

14K Association: A Chinese Triad criminal-terrorist organization, imported from China to Hong Kong after the fall of Chiang Kai-shek's regime.

FP 25, See: Forcas Populares do 25 Abril.

FRAP, See: Frente Revolucionario AntiFascista y Patriotica.

FRAP, See: Fuerzas Revolucionarias Armadas del Pueblo.

Free Corps: A right-wing terrorist organization in Germany during the early 1920s, which assassinated moderate and left-wing politicians and was backed by the German military.

Freedom Front/Revolutionary Fighting Group: A U.S. terrorist organization active in New York City during the 1980s.

French Revolutionary Brigades: A terrorist organization active in the 1980s in France and throughout Europe.

Frente Argentino de Liberacion (FAL): A terrorist organization in Argentina.

Frente Revolucionario AntiFascista y Patriotica (FRAP): A terrorist organization in Spain, founded in 1971.

Frente Sandinista de Liberacion Nacional (FSLN): A terrorist organization based in Nicaragua.

Frente Urbana Zapatista (ZAPATISTA): A terrorist organization based in Mexico.

Front de Liberation de la Bretagne-Armee Revolutionnaire Bretonne (FLB-ARB): An Algeria-based terrorist organization active in the 1980s.

Front de Liberation of Algeria (FLN): A terrorist organization in Algeria active during the 1980s.

Front de Liberation National: A separatist-terrorist organization in Quebec active during the 1960s.

Front du Liberation du Quebec (FLQ): Founded in 1963, this terrorist organization, its activities centered in Quebec, conducted many kidnappings, killings and bombings and proved to be one of the worst terrorist groups in Canadian history.

Front for the Liberation of Lebanon (from Foreigners): A right-wing terrorist organization active during the 1980s.

Front for the Liberation of Occupied South Yemen (FLOSY): A Middle Eastern terrorist organization.

Front Line and Fighting Communist Formations: A terrorist organization in Italy which served as a companion group to the Red Brigades.

FSLN, See: Frente Sandinista de Liberacion Nacional.

Fuerzas Armadas de Liberacion Nacional Puertoriquena (Armed Forces of Puerto Rican National Liberation, FALN): Originally created as a lobby for Puerto Rican independence, the FALN resorted to terrorism with the bombings of five banks in New York City in 1974. Other

FALN bombings of public places in New York and Chicago caused four deaths and dozens of injuries.

Fuerzas Armadas Peronistas (FAP): A terrorist organization in Argentina consisting of Juan Peron followers.

Fuerzas Armadas Rebeldes (FAR): A terrorist organization in Guatemala aligned with the Communist Party.

Fuerzas Armadas Revolucionarias de Colombia (FARC): A terrorist organization operating in Colombia.

Fuerzas Revolucionarias Armadas del Pueblo (FRAP): A terrorist organization based in Mexico.

George Jackson Brigade: A U.S. terrorist organization active in the Pacific Northwest during the 1970s.

German-American Bund: A Nazi organization in the U.S. during the 1930s that was often involved in terrorist activities, including riots and extortion of German-born Americans who were forced by the Bund to spy for Hitler's Third Reich.

German People's Socialist Movement (USBD): A West German terrorist organization active during the 1980s.

Gestapo: Secret police and terrorist organization in Germany during Hitler's Third Reich.

Ghassan Kanafi: A terrorist organization in Italy during the 1970s.

GRAPO, See: First of October Autonomous Revolutionary Group.

Greek Armed Group for the Support of the Northern Irish Struggle: A terrorist organization in Greece during the 1980s.

Greek People: An anti-government terrorist organization in Greece during the 1970s.

Green Pang: A Chinese Triad terrorist organization, first in China, then, after the fall of mainland China to the Communists, in Hong Kong.

Grey Wolves (BOZKURTLAR): A terrorist organization in Turkey.

Groupe de Liberation Armee de La Guadaloupe: A terrorist organization in Paris, France, during the 1980s.

Groupe de Liberation de la Martinique: A terrorist organization in Martinique which was responsible for the bombing of the Palace of Justice in 1981.

Guatemalan Committee of Patriotic Unity: A terrorist organization created by combining four terrorist factions in 1982 in Guatemala.

Guatemalan Labor Party's National Directorate Nucleus: A terrorist organization in Guatemala.

Guatemalan National Revolutionary Unity: A terrorist consortium in Guatemala formed in 1982 by combining EGP, FAR, OPRA and the National Directorate Nucleus terrorist groups.

Guatemalan Work Party: A Latin American terrorist organization active during the 1980s.

Guerrilla Army of the Poor: A terrorist organization in Guatemala active in the 1980s.

Guerrilla Party: A terrorist organization in Sicily during the 1980s.

Guerrilleros Del Cristo Rey (Warriors of Christ the King): A terrorist organization in Spain active in the 1970s.

Habash Front: A terrorist organization active in Europe since the 1970s. Its founder and leader, George Habash, condemned by President Clinton in his 1995 executive order, is also the leader of the much larger and more lethal Popular Front for the Liberation of Palestine (PFLP).

Hamas, See: Islamic Resistance Movement.

Hanafi Muslims: A terrorist organization in the U.S., active in Philadelphia and Washington, D.C. in the 1970s.

Harakat Tahrir Filastin, See: Al Fatah.

Hawatmah Front: A terrorist organization in Turkey operating during the 1970s.

Heaven and Earth Society: A Triad terrorist organization in China from the seventeenth century.

Hizbollah (Herzbollah, Hizballah, Party of God): A pro-Iranian Shiite terrorist organization based in Lebanon, founded in 1982, and responsible for the 1985 hijacking of a TWA flight in Beirut. Hizbollah is affiliated with Amal and the Soldiers of God, another Iranian terrorist group. President Clinton proscribed this group in his executive order of 1995, prohibiting any U.S. organization or citizen from contributing to this terrrorist group, while also condemning its leader, Mohammed Hussein Fadlallah.

HRB, See: Croatian Revolutionary Brotherhood.

Hung Society: A Triad terrorist organization in China since the seventeenth century.

Hvratsko Revolucionarno Bratsvo, See: Croatian Revolutionary Brotherhood.

IMRO, See: Inner Macedonian Revolutionary Organization.

Independence Liberation Resistance Organization: A terrorist organization active in Greece during the 1970s.

Industrial Workers of the World (IWW): A union of miners in the Western U.S. during the 1900s, its leaders resorting to terrorism to achieve benefits from mine owners, ordering killings and bombings in Colorado, Idaho, Montana and elsewhere.

INLA, See: Irish National Liberation Army.

Inner (Internal) Macedonian Revolutionary Organization (IMRO): A terrorist organization, created in 1893, thought to be extinct by 1934 but re-emerged in the 1950s, remaining active in the Balkan regions of Greece and Yugoslavia.

Invisible Ones: A terrorist organization in Colombia, since the 1960s, responsible for several political kidnappings.

Iparretarrak: A terrorist organization in Europe during the 1980s.

IRA, See: Irish Republican Army.

Iraqi Islamic Revolution: A dissident terrorist organization exiled in Iran which supports such splinter groups as the Iraqi Al-Dawa and the Iraqi Mujaheddin.

Irgun Zvai Leumi (Irgun, IZL): A Palestinian terrorist organization.

Irish National Liberation Army (INLA): A terrorist organization in Northern Ireland.

Irish Republican Army (IRA): A terrorist organization since 1922 active against the British occupation of Northern Ireland; responsible for countless bombings and killings in Ireland and England.

Iron Guard: Terrorist organization in Rumania from late 1920s to the end of World War II.

Islamic Amal: A Shiite terrorist organization headquartered in Baalbek, Lebanon, which broke away from the larger Amal group.

Islamic Front for Jihad Against Jews and Crusaders: A Middle Eastern terrorist organization reportedly headed by Arab millionaire Osama bin Laden during the 1990s and responsible for the bombings of the U.S. embassies in Nairobi, Kenya and Dar es Salaam, Tanzania, in cooperation with another bin Laden terrorist group, Al-Qaeda. This may be a front for the PFLP which oversees its operations.

Islamic Gama'at: A Middle Eastern terrorist organization which was condemned in President Clinton's 1995 executive order.

Islamic Jihad: A Middle Eastern terrorist organization best known for its suicide bombings of the U.S. Marine barracks in Beirut, and the U.S. embassies in Lebanon and Kuwait. This large and widespread organization has affiliations with various Lebanese, Iraqi and Iranian Shiite terrorist groups dedicated to the Islamic revolution in the Middle East. This group was condemned by President Clinton in his 1995 executive order.

Islamic Resistance Movement (Hamas): A title used by various Middle Eastern terrorist groups with Shiite affiliations, active chiefly against Israel and its allies. This group was condemned by President Clinton in his 1995 executive

order.

Islamic Revolutionary Guards: A Middle Eastern terrorist organization active in the 1980s.

Islamic Salvation Front: A Middle Eastern terrorist organization.

Islamic Unification Movement (Tawhid): A terrorist organization based in Tripoli, Lebanon, and made up of Sunni Moslems.

IWW, See: Industrial Workers of the World.

IZL, See: Irgun Zvai Leumi.

January 31 Popular Front: A terrorist organization based in Guatemala during the 1980s.

Japanese Red Army, See: Red Army of Japan.

JCAG, See: Justice Commando of the Armenian Genocide.

JDL, See: Jewish Defense League.

Jewish Armed Resistance: A terrorist organization based in the U.S. during the 1970s.

Jewish Defense League (JDL): Formed by rabbi Meir Kahane and lawyer Bert Zweibon in 1968 to protest the treatment of Soviet Jews, the JDL evolved into a counteractive terrorist organization, credited with several bombings in the Middle East, as well as in New York City.

Jewish Underground Army: A U.S. terrorist organization in New York City during the 1970s.

Jibril Front: A Palestinian terrorist organization responsible for many bombings and commanded by Ahmed Jabril who was condemned by President Clinton in his 1995 exeuctive order.

Jihad Command, See: Al Jihad Al Muddas Front.

JIN: An anti-Castro terrorist organization active in the 1970s in Miami, Florida.

JRA, See, Red Army of Japan.

June 9 Organization: An Armenian terrorist organization active in the 1980s.

Justice Commando of Armenian Genocide (JCAG): An Armenian terrorist organization.

JVP–People's Liberation Front: A terrorist organization active in the 1980s in Sri Lanka.

Kabataang Makabayan: A student terrorist organization in the Philippines active in the 1970s.

Kach: A right-wing Israeli terrorist organization, outlawed in Israel and condemned by President Clinton in his 1995 executive order.

Kahane Chai: An Israeli terrorist organization, outlawed in Israel and condemned by President Clinton in his 1995 executive order.

KGB: Soviet intelligence service which often functioned as a terrorist organization.

KKK, See: Ku Klux Klan.

Knights of Mary Phagan: A terrorist organization begun in 1915 in Georgia and modeled after the Ku Klux Klan, its members seeking vengeance for the murder of its 13-year-old namesake. This group became the precursor to the reorganized

Ku Klux Klan.

Knights of the Ku Klux Klan, See: Ku Klux Klan.

Ku Klux Klan (KKK, Knights of the Ku Klux Klan): America's most visible symbol of racism and hatred, the KKK has been practicing terroristic bombings, lynchings, murders and beatings since its inception following the Civil War. Blatant and open during the 1920s, the Klan, during the Civil Rights movement of the 1960s became more furtive. Its heinous crimes have diminished along with its membership in the last few decades, chiefly due to lack of local support and heavy damages awarded to victims or relatives of victims for the Klan's brutal offenses.

Kurdistan Liberation Army: A Middle Eastern terrorist organization.

La Mano Negra, See: Black Hand, The.

Lebanese Armed Revolution Brigades: A terrorist organization headquartered in Lebanon.

Lebanese Armed Revolutionary Faction (Fractions armee es revolutionaires libanaises, FARL): A Christian Lebanese terrorist organization.

Lebanese National Resistance Front: A blanket named used by several Middle Eastern terrorist organizations.

Lebanese Socialist Revolutionary Organization: A Middle Eastern terrorist organization most active in the 1970s.

Leftist Patriotic Honduran Front: A terrorist organization based in Honduras during the 1980s.

Legion of Justice: A terrorist organization based in Chicago, Illinois, active between 1969 and 1971. This group attacked anti-war protestors and Communist sympathizers.

LEHI, See: Lohame Herut Israel.

Lesotho Liberation Army: A terrorist organization active in the 1980s.

Liberation Tigers of Tamil Eelam (LTTE): A secessionist terrorist organization headquartered in Sri Lanka.

Libyan Secret Service: Libya's intelligence service which functions as Muammar Qaddafi's personal terrorist organization; this state-sponsored organization works hand-in-glove with all major Middle Eastern terrorist organizations against Israel, the U.S. and its allies.

Lohame Herut Israel (LEHI), See: Stern Gang.

Lorenzo Zelaya Popular Revolutionary Command: A terrorist organization located in Honduras, most active during the 1980s.

LTTE, See: Liberation Tigers of Tamil Eelam.

M-19, See: Movimiento 19 Abril.

Macheteros: A terrorist organization in Puerto Rico active in the 1980s.

Mafia: An international criminal organization of Italian/Sicilian members that often practices

terrorist activities.

Manipur: A terrorist organization in India active in the 1980s.

MANO, See: Movimiento Argentino Nacional Organisacion.

Mano Blanco: A terrorist organization in Guatemala.

Manuel Rodriguez Patriotic Front (FMPR): A terrorist organization in Chile.

MAR, See: Movimiento de Accion Revolucionaria.

Masada Action and Defense Movement: A terrorist organization active in Europe in the 1970s.

Mau Mau: A terrorist organization headed by Jomo Kenyatta in Kenya during the early 1950s which committed hundreds of bloody murders and massacres, its aim being to drive out all foreigners from the country.

Maximo Mena Command: A terrorist organization in Argentina which broke away from MANO.

Menominee Warrior Society: A U.S. Indian terrorist organization active in the 1970s and located in Wisconsin, Minnesota and Michigan.

Mexican People's Revolutionary Army: A terrorist organization in Mexico and in the U.S.

Militant Jewish Defense League, See: Jewish Defense League.

Military Sports Group Hoffmann (Wehrsportsgruppe): A neo-Nazi terrorist organization based in West Germany, responsible for many bombings and killings.

Minutemen: A U.S. terrorist organization created by Robert DuPugh in the late 1950s. DuPugh, who had been given a Section 8 (psychologically impaired) discharge from the U.S. Army in World War II, formed this right-wing organization in the wake of the Red Scare of the 1950s and the election of liberal Democrat John F. Kennedy to the presidency. Hundreds, if not thousands, joined the Minutemen and huge arsenals were amassed, the paramilitary members marching boldly down American streets to display their weapons. The organization suffered a serious setback in October 1966 when nineteen of its members were arrested while preparing to attack the offices of three liberal organizations in New York City. The organization declined drastically after DuPugh was arrested and imprisoned for a Federal firearms violation.

MIR, See: Movimiento de la Izquerda Revolucionaria.

MIRA, See: Movimiento Independista Revolucionario Armada.

MLN, See: Tupamaros-Movimiento de Liberacion Nacional.

Montoneros: A terrorist organization in Argentina

named after Juan Jose Valle Montoneros.

MoPoCo: A terrorist organization based in Paraguay.

MOVE: A terrorist organization based in Philadelphia, Pennsylvania, during the 1980s.

Movement for the Restoration of Democracy: A terrorist organization in Pakistan during the 1980s.

Movement of Southward Brothers: A pro-Palestinian terrorist organization in Europe which was chiefly active during the 1970s.

Movimiento Argentino Nacional Organisacion (MANO): A terrorist organization based in Argentina.

Movimiento de Accion Revolucionaria (MAR): A terrorist organization based in Mexico in the 1970s.

Movimiento de la Izquerda Revolucionaria (MIR): A terrorist organization operating in Chile, Peru and Venezuela.

Movimiento Independista Revolucionario Armada (MIRA): A Puerto Rican terrorist organization during the 1970s which was responsible for many bombings.

Movimiento 19 Abril (April 19 Movement, M-19): A terrorist organization in Colombia.

Movimiento Revolucionario do Octobre 8 (MR-8): A terrorist organization in Brazil which is affiliated with the Brazilian Communist Party and responsible for (among countless terrorist activities) kidnapping the U.S. ambassador in 1969.

Movimiento Revolucionario Alejandro de Leon 13 Noviembre (MR-13): A Trotskyite terrorist organization in Guatemala, named after an unsuccessful military coup on November 13, 1960.

Mozambican National Resistance: A terrorist organization operating in Mozambique during the 1980s.

Mozambique Liberation Front: A terrorist organization active in Tanzania.

MPLA: An Angolan terrorist organization active in the 1970s.

MR-8, See: Movimiento Revolucionario do Octobre 8.

MR-13, See: Movimiento Revolucionario Alejandro de Leon 13 Noviembre.

MRTA, See: Tupac Amaru Revolutionary Movement.

Mujaheddin (Mujahedeen Kalq): A terrorist organization based in Iran.

Mushala Gang: A terrorist group located in Zambia during the 1980s.

Muslim Brotherhood: A Middle Eastern terrorist organization chiefly active during the 1980s.

Muslims Against Global Oppression: A terrorist group in South Africa which claimed responsiblity for the bombing of a Planet Hollywood restaurant in Cape Town, on August 25, 1998, in which a woman was killed and twenty-four others injured.

NAP, See: Nuclei Armati Proletari-Armed Proletarian Nuclei.

NAPAP, See: Armed Nuclei for Popular Autonomy.

NAR, See: Armed Revolutionary Nuclei.

Nat Turner–John Brown Faction: A terrorist splinter group of the New World Liberation Front.

National Arab Youth for the Liberation of Palestine (NAYLP): A Middle Eastern terrorist organization.

National Committee to Combat Fascism: A terrorist organization based in Detroit, Michigan, during the 1970s.

National Directorate Nucleus: A terrorist faction of the Labor Party in Guatemala which was chiefly active during the 1980s.

National Fatherland Front: A terrorist organization located in Kabul, Afghanistan during the 1980s.

National Liberation Armed Forces: A terrorist organization operating chiefly in the 1970s in Venezuela.

National Liberation Army: A terrorist organization in Colombia responsible for many kidnappings and bombings.

National Liberation Commando, See: Commando da Libertacao Nacional.

National Liberation Front (NLF): A terrorist organization based in South Yemen and aligned with the PFLP and PDFLP.

National Liberation Movement: A terrorist organization in Guatemala which was chiefly active during the 1980s.

National Peasant Movement: A terrorist organization in Honduras during the 1980s.

National Resistance Army: A terrorist organization in Uganda.

National Socialist Liberation Front (NSLF): A reactionary terrorist group led by Joseph Tommasi, the NSLF bombed the offices of four left-wing organizations in Los Angeles in 1975, before Tommasi was shot and killed by Nazis, his death causing the group to disband.

National Youth Resistance Organization: A terrorist organization based in Greece and most active in the 1970s.

Nationalist Group for the Liberation of Palestine: A Middle Eastern terrorist organization.

Nationalist Republican Alliance (ARENA): A Salvadoran conservative terrorist organization which conducted "death squad" activities.

NAYLP, See: National Arab Youth for the Liberation of Palestine.

Nazi-American Bund, See: German-American Bund.

Neo-Nazi groups: Many present-day terrorist organizations advocating Hitler's Nazi beliefs are active in Europe and, to a lesser degree, the U.S. The leading neo-Nazi group in America is the American Nazi Party which has a limited membership. Many neo-Nazi terrrorist organizations are based in Europe, particularly the Military Sports Group Hoffman in West Germany and others in the Baltic states.

New African Organization: A terrorist organization of blacks that operated in Detroit, Michigan, in the late 1960s and early 1970s.

New Dawn Collective: A U.S. terrorist organization in Northern California, chiefly active in the 1970s.

New Organization: A terrorist organization in Greece which was active during the 1980s.

New People's Army (NPA): A leftist terrorist organization which attacks police officers and U.S. military personnel in the Philippines.

New World Liberation Front (NWLF): A West Coast terrorist organization in the 1970s, the NWLF advocated the beliefs of Carlos Marighella, a Brazilian revolutionary. It was responsible for eight bombings in 1974 and twenty-two bombings the following year. The NWLF acted as a shelter organization for the splintered factions of other leftist groups such as the Chicano Liberation Front, Red Guerrilla Family and the Symbionese Liberation Army (SLA).

19th of May: A terrorist organization active during the 1980s in Latin America.

NLF, See: National Liberation Front.

NOA, See: Nueva Organizacion Anticommunista.

November 17 Terrorist Group: A terrorist organization founded in the 1970s and based in Greece.

NPA, See: New People's Army.

NSLF, See: National Socialist Liberation Front.

Nuclei Armati Proletari-Armed Proletarian Nuclei (NAP): A terrorist organization most active in the 1970s and based in Italy.

Nueva Organizacion Anticommunista (NOA): A terrorist organiation in Guatemala.

NWLF, See: New World Liberation Front.

October 1 Anti-Fascist Revolutionary Group: A terrorist organization in Spain which was active in the 1980s.

Okhrana: the secret police of czarist Russia which operated as a nation-wide terrorist and counter-terrrorist organization.

OPRA: A terrorist group active in Guatemala in the 1980s.

OPR-33, See: Organization of the Popular Revolution-33.

Order, The: A neo-Nazi terrorist organization in the American South and Pacific Northwest during the 1980s.

Order of Assassins, The: An eleventh century terrorist organization which attempted to murder both Christian and Islamic leaders opposed to its fanatical beliefs, its credos and modus operandi embraced by today's millionaire terrorist Osama bin Laden.

Ordine: A neo-fascist terrorist organization in Italy.

Organization for Victims of Zionist Occupation: A Palestinian terrorist organization responsible for several skyjackings.

Organization of Struggle Against World Imperialism: A front for the PFLP terrorist organization.

Organization of the National Confrontation Front: A Middle Eastern terrorist organization chiefly active during the 1980s.

Organization of the Oppressed on Earth: A terrorist group in Lebanon which is made up of pro-Iranian Shiite Moslems and which was responsible for the kidnapping of U.S. Marine officer William Higgins in 1988.

Organization of the Popular Revolution-33 (OPR-33): A terrorist organization operating in Uraguay during the 1970s.

Orly Group, See: Armenian Orly Group.

Palestine Liberation Army: A terrorist organization which serves as the military component of the PLO.

Palestine Liberation Front (PLF): A terrorist organization based in Syria and condemned by President Clinton in his 1995 executive order.

Palestine Liberation Organization (PLO): A Middle Eastern political organization headed by Yasir Arafat which has, over the last four decades been directly or indirectly (through the PFLP and other groups) involved with terrorists activities.

Palestinian Communist Party: A Middle Eastern terrorist organization.

Palestinian Islamic Jihad-Shiqaqi Faction (PIJ): A Middle Eastern terrorist organization condemned by President Clinton in his 1995 executive order.

Palestinian Popular Struggle Front: A Middle Eastern terrorist organization.

Partido Revolucionario Dominican (PRD): A terrorist organization operating in the Dominican Republic.

Party of God, See: Hizbollah.

Pattani Liberation Front: A Muslim separatist terrorist organization based in Thailand during the 1970s.

PDFLP, See: Democratic Front for the Liberation of Palestine.

Peace and Freedom Fighters: A reactionary group

made up of Hungarian exiles in Los Angeles; this terrorist group was reportedly responsible for many attacks against left-wing organizations during the 1970s.

People's Army, See: New People's Army.

People's Forces Unit IX: A terrorist faction of the New World Liberation Front.

People's Front 31st January: A terrorist organization operating during the 1980s in Latin America.

People's Liberation Army: A terrorist organization operating in Burma in the 1980s.

People's Liberation Forces: A terrorist organization operating in El Salvador during the 1980s.

People's Redemption Council: A terrorist organization in Liberia most active during the 1980s.

People's Revolutionary Armed Forces: A terrorist organization in Mexico which was chiefly active in the 1970s.

People's Revolutionary Army: A terrorist group active during the 1970s in Latin America.

People's Revolutionary Army: A terrorist organization in Uganda which was active during the 1980s.

People's Revolutionary Front: A terrorist group in the Philippines which was active during the 1970s.

People's Revolutionary Party (PRP): A terrorist group active in the 1970s in Northern California.

Peykar Group: A left-wing terrorist organization in Iran which operated chiefly during the 1980s.

PFLP, See: Popular Front for the Liberation of Palestine.

PFLP-CG, See: Popular Front for the Liberation of Palestine–General Command.

PIJ, See: Palestinian Islamic Jihad-Shiqaqi.

PIRA, See: Provisional Irish Republican Army.

PLA, See: Palestine Liberation Army.

PLO, See: Palestine Liberation Organization.

Popular Democratic Front for the Liberation of Palestine (PDFLP), See: Democratic Front for the Liberation of Palestine (DFLP).

Popular Forces of April 25: A terrorist organization based in Portugal and active during the 1980s.

Popular Front for the Liberation of Palestine (PFLP): A Middle Eastern terrorist organization founded in 1967 and one which is considered to be the most dangerous terrorist groups in the world. The PFLP is responsible for countless bombings, skyjackings, kidnappings and murders and is closely allied with Black September, the PLO, and, through his top advisers, Yasir Arafat. The PFLP, branded a top terrorist organization in President Clinton's 1995 executive

order, is most probably the organization behind Osama bin Laden, and gave the order for bin Laden's terrorist group to bomb the two U.S. embassies in Kenya and Tanzania in August 1998. This organization was condemned by President Clinton in his 1995 executive order, which specified that the group was last based in Syria.

Popular Front for the Liberation of Palestine–General Command (PFLP-GC): A branch of the Popular Front for the Liberation of Palestine which is strongly supported by Syria. This group was condemned in President Clinton's 1995 executive order.

Popular League: A left-wing terrorist organization in El Salvador during the 1980s.

Popular Liberation Forces (PLF): A component of the PLO terrorist organization, PLA, serving as the PLA's commando wing.

Popular Resistance Group: A terrorist organization in Greece which was most active in the 1970s.

Popular Revolutionary Bloc (BPR): A terrorist group in El Salvador during the 1970s.

Popular Revolutionary Struggle: A terrorist organization in Greece most active in the 1980s.

Popular Struggle Front: A terrorist organization in Turkey which operated in the 1970s.

Posse Commitatus: A vigilante group founded by Mike Beach in Portland, Oregon, in 1968; this group was menacing and made many threats but was not particularly violent.

P.P.S. Okrezeva: A socialist terrorist organization in Poland which was involved in several assassinations in the 1900s.

PRD, See: Partido Revolucionario Dominican.

Prima Linea: A terrorist group in Italy which was active in the 1980s.

Progressive Labor Party: A reactionary terrorist organization based in Southern California during the 1970s.

Proletarian Action Group: A terrorist organization in Italy which was active in the 1970s.

Proletariat Organized Group: A terrorist organization active in Sicily during the 1980s.

Proud Eagle Tribe: A U.S. terrorist group and a faction of the Weather Underground; Proud Eagle was responsible for several bombings in the Boston area during the 1970s.

Provisional Irish Republican Army (PIRA): Begun in 1969 as a splinter group of the IRA, it has practiced countless terrorist activities in Northern Ireland.

PRP, See: People's Revolutionary Party.

Puerto Rican Armed Resistance Group: A terrorist organization in New York during the 1980s.

Puerto Rican Liberation Front: A U.S. terrorist

organization which was most active in the 1970s along the East Coast.

Puerto Rican Resistance Movement: A terrorist group active in the 1970s.

Puerto Rican Revolutionary Workers: A terrorist group in Puerto Rico.

Purple Sunshine: A U.S. terrorist organization operating in Northern California in the 1970s.

Quarter Moon Society: A U.S. terrorist group responsible for several bombings in the 1970s in Seattle, Washington.

Quebec Separatist Movement: A terrorist organization in Canada which was founded in the 1960s.

RAF, See: Rote Armee Fraktion.

RAJ, See: Red Army of Japan.

RAM, See: Revolutionary Action Movement.

Real IRA, The: A splinter group of the Provisional IRA which emerged in 1998 to set off a bomb in Omagh, Ireland in August 1998, one which killed twenty-eight persons and injured hundreds more, including many women and children. The Real IRA took credit and was universally condemned for the terrorist attack, causing its members to apologize and call a halt to their terrorist attacks.

Red Army Faction, See: Rote Armee Fraktion.

Red Army of Japan (Rengo Sekigun, Japanese Red Army, United Red Army, JRA, RAJ): A left-wing Japanese terrorist organization founded in 1969; the RAJ operated in Japan, across the Pacific, in the Middle East, Europe and even the U.S., aligning itself with the PFLP when some of its members attacked passengers in Tel Aviv's Lod Airport in 1972.

Red Brigades: A terrorist organization headed by Renato Curcio during the 1970s and was responsible for many assassinations, kidnappings and bombings.

Red Cloud Group: A U.S. Indian terrorist organization which was active during the 1970s.

Red Flag: A terrorist organization active in the 1970s in Venezuela.

Red Guards: A terrorist organization operating in Italy.

Red Guerrilla Family (RGF): A U.S. terrorist organization headquartered in San Francisco where it exploded numerous bombs during the 1970s.

Red Hand Commandos: A Northern Ireland terrorist organization active in the 1980s.

Red Panthers: A French terrorist organization based in Paris during the 1980s.

Red Placard: A French terrorist organization most active in the 1980s in Paris.

Red Society: A Chinese Triad terrorist organization.

Rengo Sekigun, See: Red Army of Japan.

Republic of New Africa (RNA): A U.S. terrorist group made up of militant blacks which was founded in 1968, mostly from former members of RAM. Eleven members were charged with assault and murder in Mississippi in 1970.

Revolutionare Zellen (RZ): A West German terrorist organization.

Revolutionary Action Force East: A U.S. terrorist group made up of dissident American students which commited several robberies during the early 1970s.

Revolutionary Action Movement (RAM): A U.S. terrorist organization which was active on the East Coast between 1963 and 1968, RAM advocated a militant black independence. In June 1967, sixteen members were arrested after large caches of weapons were seized in New York and Philadelphia. Four more members were arrested later in Philadelphia for attempting to poison the city's water supply.

Revolutionary Anti-Capitalist Action: A terrorist group in Greece during the 1980s.

Revolutionary Armed Action: A terrorist organization active during the 1970s in Portugal.

Revolutionary Armed Forces: A terrorist group in Guatemala during the 1970s which conducted several political kidnappings and bombings.

Revolutionary Cells: A West German terrorist group active in the 1980s.

Revolutionary Commandos for Solidarity: A terrorist organization in Costa Rica most active in the 1970s.

Revolutionary Council: A terrorist group active in North Africa in the 1970s.

Revolutionary Force 9: A terrorist organization operating in the U.S. in the early 1970s, one responsible for the 1970 bombings of several corporate headquarters in New York City.

Revolutionary Force 7: A terrorist organization which was responsible for the bombings of several embassies in Washington, D.C. in 1970.

Revolutionary Justice Organization: A pro-Iranian terrorist organization responsible for many kidnappings in the 1980s.

Revolutionary Movement: A terrorist group in Honduras in the 1980s.

Revolutionary Organization of Socialist Muslims: A Middle Eastern terrorist group which operated in Europe and the Middle East, mostly in the 1980s.

Revolutionary Organization of the People in Arms: A terrorist organization in Guatemala which was most active in the 1980s.

Revolutionary Party of Central American Workers: A Latin American terrorist group most active in the 1970s.

Revolutionary Popular Struggle: A terrorist group responsible for numerous bombings in Greece during the 1980s.

Revolutionary Student Brigade: A terrorist group active in the 1970s on the U.S. East Coast.

Revolutionary Sympathizers Union: A terrorist organization in Turkey which was most active during the 1980s.

RGF, See: Red Guerrilla Family.

RNA, See: Republic of New Africa.

Rote Armee Fraktion (RAF): A terrorist organization in West Germany which was dominated by the Baader-Meinhof Gang during the 1970s and 1980s.

Russian Mafia: A criminal-terrorist organization which has taken considerable control of Russian banks and businesses during the 1990s.

RZ, See: Revolutionare Zellen.

SA, See: Brown Shirts.

S.A.O. Terrorists: A terrorist organization in France founded in 1962.

Scottish National Liberation Army: A terrorist group active during the 1980s.

SDS, See: Students for a Democratic Society.

SDS, See: Sozialisticher Deutscher Studenbund.

Second of June Movement: A terrorist group in West Germany.

Secret Anti-Communist Army: A pro-government terrorist group made up of paramilitary "death squads" in El Salvador which tortures and mutilates non-combative civilians and members of the clergy.

Secret Army for the Liberation of Armenia: An Armenian terrorist organization chiefly active during the 1980s.

Secret Army Organization (SAO): A reactionary terrorist group in the U.S. which harassed student protestors in Arizona and Southern California during the late 1960s and 1970s. It was claimed that the SAO was secretly funded by J. Edgar Hoover's FBI, but this rumor was never confirmed.

Secret Cuban Government: An anti-Castro terrorist group which was based in New York City in the 1970s.

SEEK: A U.S. student terrorist organization which perpetrated considerable violence on several New York City campuses during the 1970s.

Self Defense Against All Authority: A terrorist group based in France during the 1980s.

Sendero Luminoso (Shining Path): A terrorist organization in Peru.

September 23 Communist League: A terrorist group in Mexico responsible for many murders and kidnappings during the 1970s.

Seventh Suicide Squad: A Greek terrorist organization that claimed responsibility for the 1973 attack on the Athens Airport.

Shield Society: A terrorist group of extreme nationalists in Japan led by writer Yukio Mishima in the 1960s.

Shining Path, See: Sendero Luminoso.

Sidamo Liberation Movement: A terrorist organization based in Ethiopia in the 1980s.

Skinheads: A U.S. terrorist organization founded in 1988, one having a large membership in a loosely-based national network of mostly social and educational dropouts; Skinheads are often aligned with the American Nazi Party and other extreme right-wing terrorist groups.

SLA, See: Symbionese Liberation Army.

SMERSH: The terrorist and assassination arm of the KGB, Russian intelligence, an organization created in the 1930s, which has been revamped and is known today as CUKR, hidden within the Fourth Bureau of the Russian army.

SNCC: See: Student Nonviolent Coordinating Committee.

Socialist People's Movement: A right-wing terrorist group in West Germany active in the 1980s.

Socialist White People's Party: A reactionary terrorist group in Southern California most active in the 1970s.

Society for International Involvement: A terrorist organization in California most active in the 1970s.

Sokaiya: The terrorist enforcement arm of the Yakusa, the criminal society which dominates Japan's econmy.

Sons of Liberty: A U.S. terrorist group based in Boston in the 1970s.

Sons of the Gestapo: A U.S. terrorist group based in Arizona which was credited with derailing an Amtrak train near Phoenix, on October 9, 1995.

South Moluccas: A terrorist organization based in the Netherlands.

Southern Liberation Army (ELS): A terrorist organization based in Mexico.

Sozialisticher Deutscher Studenbund (SDS): A left-wing militant terrorist group in West Germany which supported the Baader-Meinhof Gang from the 1960s to the 1980s.

Spanish Basque Battalion: A terrorist organization in Spain during the 1980s.

Spartacus Party: A sometimes terrorist political party of the extreme left in Germany following World War I; the group was led by Rosa Luxemburg and Karl Liebknecht, who were both assassinated by terrorist members of the Free Corps.

SPK (Socialist Patients' Collection): A terrorist

group of certified lunatics who escaped from a West German asylum to join forces with the Baader-Meinhof Gang in the 1970s.

SS: German secret police and Hitler's personal guard led by Heinrich Himmler during the 1930s until the end of World War II which committed countless atrocities and operating concentration camps in which millions were slaughtered.

Stern Gang (Lohame Herut Israel): A Zionist terrorist gang formed by Abraham Stern in the late 1930s which attacked British installations and officials for two decades, as well as sending bombs to England's allies, including President Harry Truman.

Stormtroopers, See: Brown Shirts.

Student Nonviolent Coordinating Committee (SNCC): Originally formed in the 1960s to aid black voter registration in the South, SNCC was taken over by militants Stokely Carmichael and H. Rap Brown who advocated terrorism to secure rights for blacks. The group was involved in violence on U.S. campuses.

Students for a Democratic Society (SDS): A U.S. terrorist organization which caused widespread violence on college campuses and in major urban centers. In 1968, following the riots in Chicago at the Democratic Convention, a splinter terrorist group, the Weathermen, broke away from SDS.

Sturmabteilung, See: Brown Shirts.

SWAPO: A terrorist organization in South Africa which was chiefly active during the 1980s.

Symbionese Liberation Army (SLA): A California-based terrorist organization created in 1973 and led by Donald DeFreeze, which was responsible for the murder of Oakland school superintendent, Marcus Foster, prior to the so-called kidnapping of newspaper heiress, Patricia Campbell Hearst in 1974. DeFreeze and six members of the SLA died in a terrific gun battle with Los Angeles police in May 1974. The group dissipated after Bill and Emily Harris, and Patricia Hearst were apprehended in 1975.

Takfir Wal-Hajira (Repentence of the Holy Flight): The Egyptian terrorist organization that engineered the assassination of President Anwar Sadat in 1981.

Tamil Eelam Liberation Organization (TELO): A terrorist group based in Sri Lanka.

TELO, See: Tamil Eelam Liberation Organization.

Terror Brigade: A Russian terrorist ogranziaton active in the 1900s.

Third Force: A Protestant terrorist organization active in Northern Ireland in the 1980s.

Third Position: A terrorist group active in Padua

during the 1980s.

Thunderbolt, See: As-Sa'iqa.

Ton Ton Macoutes: A terrorist secret police maintained by Francois "Papa Doc" Duvalier, dictator of Haiti.

TPLA, See: Turkish People's Liberation Army.

TPLF, See: Turkish People's Liberation Front.

Triad Society: A blanket name for the many Chinese terrorist groups belonging to the Triads.

Tupac Amara Revolutionary Movement (MRTA): A terrorist organiztion active in Peru for the last several decades.

Tupamaros-Movimiento de Liberacion Nacional (MLN): An ultra-left Marxist terrorist organization based in Chile, Guatemala and Uruguay which was chiefly active during the 1970s.

Turkish People's Liberation Army (TPLA): A militant terrorist organization founded in the 1970s and operating throughout Turkey.

Turkish People's Liberation Front (TPLF): A terrorist group based in Turkey.

Turkish Revenge Brigade: A terrorist group in Turkey.

Turkish Revolutionary Left Group: A terrorist organization operating in Turkey during the 1980s.

28 February Popular League: A terrorist group operating in the 1980s in El Salvador.

23rd of September Communist League: A terrorist organization active in Mexico during the 1970s.

UDA, See: Ulster Defense Association.

UFF, See: Ulster Freedom Fighters.

Ugandan Freedom Movement: An African terrorist organization which chiefly operated during the 1980s.

Ugandan Patriotic Movement: An African terrorist group operating in the 1980s.

Ulster Defense Association (UDA): A terrorist organization based in Northern Ireland.

Ulster Freedom Fighters (UFF): A terrorist group making its headquarters in Northern Ireland.

Ulster Volunteer Forces (UVF): A terrorist organization based in Northern Ireland.

Umkonto Wesizwe: A terrorist faction of the African National Congress (ANC) which was most active during the 1980s.

Union de Travailleurs Agricoles: A terrorist group active in the 1980s in Guadalupe.

UNITA: A terrorist organization based in Angola.

United Anti-Reelection Command: A left-wing terrorist group based in the Dominican Republic which has conducted several kidnappings.

United Front for Guerrilla Action: A terrorist organization based in Colombia and active in the 1970s.

United Front for the Revolution: A terrorist group

in Guatemala which was chiefly active during the 1970s.

United Popular Action Front: A terrorist group in El Salvador.

United Popular Liberation Army: A terrorist organization based in Mexico and active in the 1970s.

United Red Army, See: Red Army of Japan.

United Revolutionary Front: A terrorist group in Guatemala which was most active during the 1980s.

USBD, See: German People's Socialist Movement.

U.S. Cultural Organization (US): A Negro terrorist group best known for its clashes with other black organizations during the 1960s. Members of this group stood accused of murdering at least three membgers of the Black Panther Party.

UVF, See: Ulster Volunteer Forces.

Vanguard Group: A U.S. terrorist organization active during the 1970s.

Vanguarda Armada Revolucionaria-Palmares: A terrorist organization formed by the merger of COLINA and VPR, two Brazilian-based terrorist groups.

Vanguarda Popular Revolucionaria (VPR): A terrorist organization located in Brazil which conducted numerous political kidnappings in the 1970s.

VAR–Palmares, See: Vanguarda Armada Revolucionaria-Palmares.

Vieques Group: A terrorist organization in Puerto Rico.

VPR, See: Vanguarda Popular Revolucionaria.

Warriors of Christ the King, See: Guerrilleros Del Cristo Rey

Way of Eternal Bliss: A European terrorist group which conducted several skyjackings in the late 1970s.

Weathermen: A U.S. terrorist organization founded in the 1960s.

Weather Underground Organization (Weathermen, WU): A U.S. terrorist organization made up of dissident students and responsible for many terrorist bombings between 1969 and 1974. Formed by former SDS members, it staged its "Days of Rage" in October 1969 in Chicago which coincided with the trial of the Chicago Eight (later the Chicago Seven), and it conducted a second wave of massive destruction and violence in Chicago following the deaths of two Black Panther members in a police shootout. In 1970, three Weather Underground members blew themselves to pieces in their Greenwich Village bomb factory. The WU was directly responsible for nineteen bombings, including one at the U.S. Capitol in 1971 and another at the Pentagon in 1974.

Wehrsportsgruppe, See: Military Sports Group Hoffman.

White Aryan Resistance: A racist-terrorist organization in Oregon.

White Panthers: A terrorist organization based in the U.S. in the 1970s.

Wobblies, See: Industrial Workers of the World.

WOG, See: Wrath of God.

Workers Army of the Welsh Republic: A terrorist organization based in Wales and active during the 1980s.

Workers Autonomy: A terrorist organization based in Italy.

Wrath of God (WOG): A group of Zionists operating in Europe, its purpose to avenge the Israeli massacre at the 1972 Olympics in Munich, Germany.

Yakusa: The criminal-terrorist society which controls most of the financial and economic destiny of Japan, and, in recent years, is responsible for defaulting on billions in loans from Japanese banks and bringing about Japan's current financial crisis.

Young Croation Republican Army: A terrorist group based in Croatia and operating during the 1970s.

Youth Action Group: A terrorist organization operating in the 1970s and based in Paris, France.

Youth Council: A militant Negro group which conducted terrorist acts in Milwaukee, Wisconsin, during the 1960s.

Youth League to Crush the Y and P System: A terrorist organization made up of nationalists in Japan, who, in 1977, seized the headquarters of Keidanren, a business and industries federation.

Young Lords: A terrorist group of youthful Puerto Ricans who were based in New York City during the late 1960s.

Zapata Urban Front (ZUF): A terrorist organization operating in Mexico and the West Coast of the U.S.

Zapatista, See: Frente Urbana Zapatista.

ZAPU Patriotic Front: A terrorist organization active in the 1980s in Zimbabwe.

Zengakuren: A terrorist group in Japan made up of left-wing students.

Zero: A pro-Castro terrorist organization based in Miami, Florida and active during the 1970s.

ZUF, See: Zapata Urban Front.

BIBLIOGRAPHY

Thousands of sources have been employed by the author in researching this work, including books, pamphlets, periodicals, reports and newspapers, as well as personal interviews and correspondence with law enforcement agencies. What follows are the basic published reference sources used in the preparation of this work.

Acerbo, Giacomo. *Fascism in the First Year of Government.* Rome: Giorgio Berlutti, 1923.

Adams, Graham, Jr. *Age of Industrial Violence, 1910–1915: The Activities and Findings of the U.S. Commission on Industrial Relations.* New York: Columbia University Press, 1966.

Adams, James. *The Funding of Terror.* New York: Simon and Schuster, 1986.

Albrecht-Carré, René. *Italy from Napoleon to Mussolini.* New York: Columbia University Press, 1960.

Alexander, Charles C. *The Ku Klux Klan in the Southwest.* Lexington: University of Kentucky Press, 1965.

Alexander, Henry A. *Some Facts About the Murder Notes in the Phagan Case.* Atlanta, Ga.: Published by the author, n.d.

Alfieri, Dino. *Dictators Face to Face.* (trans., David Moore) London: Elek Books, 1954.

Alix, Ernest Kahlar. *Ransom Kidnappings in America, 1874–1974.* Carbondale, Ill.: Southern Illinois University Press, 1974.

Allen, Frederick Lewis. *Only Yesterday: An Informal History of the Nineteen Twenties.* New York: Harper & Bros., 1931.

Alnwick, Kenneth J., and Thomas A. Fabyanic, (eds.). *Warfare in Lebanon.* Washington, D.C.: National Defense University, 1988.

Andrew, Roland G. *Through Fascist Italy.* London: Harrap, 1935.

Arnett, Alex Mathews. *The Populist Movement in Georgia.* New York: Columbia University Press, 1922.

Asbury, Herbert. *The Gangs of New York.* New York: Alfred A. Knopf, 1927.

———. *The French Quarter: An Informal History of the New Orleans Underworld.* New York: Alfred A. Knopf, 1936.

———. *Gem of the Prairie: An Informal History of the Chicago Underworld.* New York: Alfred A. Knopf, 1940.

Ashton-Wolfe, H. *The Underworld.* New York: George H. Doran, 1936.

Askwith, T. G. *Kenya's Progress.* Nairobi, Kenya: Eagle Press, 1958.

Attwood, William. *The Reds and the Blacks: A Personal Adventure.* New York: Harper & Row, 1967.

Avrich, Paul. *The Russian Anarchists.* Princeton, N.J.: Princeton University Press, 1967.

Bailey, Thomas A. *America Faces Russia.* Ithaca, N.Y.: Cornell University Press, 1950.

Baldwin, W. W. *Mau Mau Manhunt: The Adventures of the Only American Who Fought the Terrorists in Kenya.* New York: Dutton, 1957.

Barnett, D. L., and Karari Najama. *Mau Mau from Within: Autobiography and Analysis on Kenya's Peasant Revolt.* New York: Monthly Review Press, 1966.

Barzini, Luigi. *The Italians.* New York: Atheneum, 1964.

———. *From Caesar to the Mafia.* New York: The Library Press, 1961.

Bar-Zohar, Michael, and Eitan Haber. *The Quest for the Red Prince.* New York: William Morrow, 1983.

Baskerville, Beatrice. *What Next, O Duce?* London: Longmans, 1937.

Beals, Carleton. *Rome or Death!* New York: Century, 1923.

Beard, James Melville. *K.K.K. Sketches.* Philadelphia: Claxton, 1877.

Becker, Jillian. *Hitler's Children: The Story of the Baader-Meinhof Terrorist Gang.* New York: Lippincott, 1977.

———. *The PLO: The Rise and Fall of the Palestine Liberation Organization.* New York: St. Martin's, 1984.

Bell, J. Bower. *Transnational Terror.* Washington,

D.C.: American Enterprise Institute for Public Policy Research, 1975.

———. *Terror Out of Zion.* New York: St. Martin's Press, 1977.

———. *Assassin!: The Theory and Practice of Political Violence.* New York: St. Martin's Press, 1979

———. *The Secret Army: The IRA, 1916–1979.* Cambridge, Mass.: MIT Press, 1980.

Bellini, Delle Stelle. *Dongo: The Last Act.* London: MacDonald, 1964.

Bennecke, Heinrich. *Hitler und die S.A.* Munich: Gunter Olzob Verlag, 1962.

Bentley, George R. *A History of the Freedman's Bureau.* Philadelphia: University of Pennsylvania, 1955.

Benvenisti, Meron. *The Sling and the Club.* Jerusalem: Keter Publishing, 1988.

Beraud, Henri. *Men of the Aftermath.* London: Grant Richars & Humphrey Toulmin, 1929.

Berkman, Alexander. Prison *Memoirs of an Anarchist.* New York: Mother Earth, 1912.

Bianchi, Giuseppe. *The Work of the Fascist Government and the Economic Reconstruction of Italy.* Milan: Unione Economica Italiana, 1925.

Binchy, D. A. *Church and State in Fascist Italy.* Oxford, Eng.: Oxford University Press, 1941.

Blake, Aldrich. *The Ku Klux Kraze.* Oklahoma City: n.p., 1924.

Blaxland, G. *The Regiments Depart: A History of the British Army, 1945–1970.* London: Kimber, 1973.

Blum, John Norton. *V Was for Victory: Politics and American Culture During World War II.* New York: Harcourt, Brace & Jovanovich, 1976.

Blundell, Sir M. *So Rough a Wind: Kenya Memoirs.* London: Weidenfeld & Nicholson, 1964.

Bojano, Filippo. *In the Wake of the Goose-Step.* London: Cassell, 1944.

Bolitho, William. *Italy Under Mussolini.* New York: Macmillan, 1926.

Bond, John. *Mussolini: The Wild Man of Europe.* Washington, D.C.: Independent Publishers, 1929.

Borah, William Edgar. *Haywood Trial: Closing Arguments of W. E Borah.* Boise, Id.: Statesman Shop, 1907.

Bordeux, V. J. *Benito Mussolini—The Man.* London: Hutchinson, 1927.

Borgese, G. A. *Goliath: The March of Fascism.* New York: Viking, 1938.

Borghi, Armando. *Mussolini Red and Black.* London: Wisehart, 1935.

Bornstein, Joseph. *The Politics of Murder.* New York: William Sloan, 1950.

Bosworth, Allan R. *America's Concentration Camps.* New York: W. W. Norton, 1967.

Brantley, C. *The Giriama and Colonial Resistance in Kenya, 1800–1920.* Berkeley: University of California Press, 1981.

Brett, E. A. *Colonialism and Underdevelopment in East Africa: The Politics of Economic Change, 1919–1939.* London: Heinemann, 1973.

Briggs, I. Vernon. *The Manner of Man That Kills: Spencer, Czolgosz, Richeson.* Boston: Richard G. Badger, The Gorman Press, 1921.

Brissenden, Paul F. *The IWW: A Study in American Syndicalism.* New York: Columbia University Press, 1919.

Brock, Alan. *A Casebook of Crime.* London: Watmoughs, 1948.

Brockway, F. *African Journeys.* London: Gollancz, 1955.

Brown, John Mason. *Many a Watchful Night.* New York: McGraw-Hill, 1944.

Browne, Douglas G., and E. V. Tullett. *The Rise of Scotland Yard.* New York: G. P. Putnam's Sons, 1956.

Bullock, Alan. *Hitler: A Study in Tyranny.* New York: Harper & Row, 1962.

Burgess, John W. *Reconstruction and the Constitution.* New York: Charles Scribner's Sons, 1902.

Burns, William J. *The Masked War: The Story of a Peril That Threatened the U.S., by the Man Who Uncovered the Dynamite Conspirators and Sent Them to Jail.* New York: George H. Doran, 1913.

Burt, Olive Woolley. *American Murder Ballads.* New York: Oxford University Press, 1958.

Busch, Francis X. *Prisoners at the Bar.* Indianapolis, Ind.: Bobbs-Merrill, 1952.

———. *Guilty or Not Guilty.* Indianapolis, Ind.: Bobbs-Merrill, 1952.

Butterfield, Roger. *The American Past.* New York: Simon and Schuster, 1947.

Caesar, Gene. *Incredible Detective: The Biography of William J. Burns.* Englewood Cliffs, N.J.: Prentice-Hall, 1968.

Cameron, J. *The African Revolution.* London: Thames & Hudson, 1961.

Carey-Jones, N. S. *The Anatomy of Uhuru: An Essay on Kenya's Independence.* Manchester, Eng.: Manchester University Press, 1966.

Carothers, J. C. *The Psychology of Mau Mau.* Nairobi, Kenya: Government Printer, 1955.

Carter, Hodding. *The Angry Scar.* Garden City, N.Y.: Doubleday, 1959.

Cash, W. J. *The Mind of the South.* London: Thames & Hudson, 1971.

Chabod, Federico. *A History of Italian Fascism.* (trans., Muriel Grindrod) London: Weidenfeld & Nicolson, 1963.

Chaffee, Zachariah. *Free Speech in the United States.* Cambridge, Mass.: Harvard University Press, 1946.

Chalmers, David Mark. *Hooded Americanism.* Garden City, N.Y.: Doubleday, 1965.

Chaplin, J. P. *Rumor, Fear and the Madness of Crowds.* New York: Ballantine Books, 1959.

Chaplin, Ralph. *Wobbly: The Rough-and-Tumble Story of an American Radical.* Chicago: University of Chicago Press, 1948.

Ciano, Count Galeazzo. *Ciano's Diaries, 1939–1943.* Garden City, N.Y.: Doubleday, 1946.

Clark, R. T. *The Fall of the German Republic.* London: Allen & Unwin, 1935.

Clayton, A. *Counter-Insurgency in Kenya, 1952–1960.* Nairobi, Kenya: Transafrica, 1975.

Cline, Ray S. *Terrorism: The Soviet Connection.* New York: Crane Russak, 1984.

Clough, M. S. *Chiefs and Politicians: Local Politics and Social Change in Kiambu, Kenya, 1918–1936.* Palo Alto, Calif.: Stanford University Press, 1977.

Clutterbuck, Richard. *Living with Terrorism.* New Rochelle, N. Y.: Arlington House, 1975.

———. *Guerrillas and Terrorists.* London: Faber & Faber, 1977.

Cobb, Belton. *Murdered on Duty: A Chronicle of the Killing of Policemen.* London: W. H. Allen, 1961.

Coben, Stanley. *A. Mitchell Palmer, Politician.* New York: Columbia University Press, 1963.

Cohen, B. M., and M. Z. Cooper. *A Follow-up Study of World War II Prisoners of War.* Washington, D.C.: Government Printing Office, 1954.

Collier, Richard. *Duce!: A Biography of Benito Mussolini.* New York: Viking, 1971.

Collins, Frederick Lewis. *The FBI in Peace and War.* New York: G. P. Putnam's Sons, 1943.

Collins, Larry, and Dominique Lampierre. *O Jerusalem.* New York: Simon and Schuster, 1988.

Commons, John R. (ed.). *History of Labor in the United States.* (6 vols.) New York: Macmillan, 1918.

Connolly, C. P. *The Truth About the Frank Case.* New York: Vail-Ballou, 1915.

Cook, Ezra A. *Ku Klux Klan Secrets Exposed.* Chicago: Published by the author, 1922.

Cooley, John K. *Libyan Sandstorm.* New York: Holt, Rinehart and Winston, 1982.

Cooper, Herston. *Crossville: How Did We Treat POW's?* Chicago: Adams Press, 1965.

Corfield, I. D. *Historical Survey of the Origins and Growth of Mau Mau.* London: H. M. Stationary Office, 1960.

Cornish, M. *An Introduction to Violence.* London: Cassell, 1960.

Cox, J. R. *Kenyatta's Country.* London: Hutchinson, 1965.

Crandall, Allen. *The Man from Kinsman.* Sterling, Colo.: Published by the author, 1933.

Crankshaw, Edward. *Gestapo: Instrument of Tyranny.* New York: Viking, 1956.

Cranworth, L. A. *Colony in the Making, or Sport and Profit in British East Africa.* London: Macmillan, 1912.

Cressey, Donald R. *Theft of the Nation.* New York: Harper & Row, 1969.

Crouse, Russell. *Murder Won't Out.* Garden City, N.Y.: Doubleday, Doran, 1932.

Curry, Leroy A. *The Ku Klux Klan under the Searchlight.* Kansas City, Mo.: Western Baptist, 1924.

Darrow, Clarence. *The Story of My Life.* New York: Charles Scribner's Sons, 1932.

Davidson, B. *The People's Cause: A History of Guerrillas in Africa.* London: Longmans, 1981.

Davidson, Eugene. *The Making of Adolf Hitler.* New York: Macmillan, 1977.

Davis, Susan Lawrence. *Authentic History: Ku Klux Klan, 1865–1877.* New York: American Library Service, 1924.

Deakin, F. W. *The Brutal Friendship.* New York: Anchor Books, 1966.

Dean, Vera Michele. *Fascist Rule in Italy.* London: Nelson, 1934.

Demaris, Ovid. *Captive City: Chicago in Chains.* New York: Lyle Stuart, 1969.

———. *Brothers in Blood: The International Terrorist Network.* New York: Charles Scribner's Sons, 1977.

Dilnot, George. *Rogues' March.* London: Geoffrey Bles, 1934.

Dineson, I. *Out of Africa.* New York: Random House, 1938.

Dinnerstein, Leonard. *The Leo Frank Case.* New York: Columbia University Press, 1958.

Dobson, Christopher. *Black September: Its Short, Violent History.* New York: Macmillan, 1974.

———. *Counterattack: The West's Battle Against the Terrorists.* New York: Facts on File, 1982.

———. *The Terrorists: Their Weapons, Leaders and Tactics.* New York: Facts on File, 1982.

Dobson, Christopher, and Ronald Payne. *The Carlos Complex: A Study in Terror.* New York:

Putnam, 1977.

Dombrowski, Roman. *Mussolini: Twilight and Fall.* London: Heinemann, 1956.

Dorman, Michael. *The Secret Service Story.* New York: Delacorte Press, 1967.

Downes, Donald. *The Scarlet Thread.* London: Derek Verschoyle, 1953.

Draper, Theodore. *The Roots of American Communism.* New York: Viking, 1957.

Drinnon, Richard. *Rebel in Paradise: A Biography of Emma Goldman.* Chicago: University of Chicago Press, 1961.

Duke, Thomas S. *Celebrated Criminal Cases of America.* San Francisco: James H. Barry, 1910.

Ebenstein, William. *Fascist Italy.* New York: American Books, 1939.

Eddy, J. P. *Mystery of Peter the Painter.* London: Stevens & Sons, 1946.

Eden, Anthony. *Facing the Dictators.* London: Cassell, 1962.

Edgerton, Robert B. *Mau Mau: An African Chronicle.* New York: The Free Press, 1989.

Evans, P. *Law and Disorder, or Scenes of Life in Kenya.* London: Secker & Warburg, 1986.

Everett, Marshall. *Complete Life of William McKinley and the Story of His Assassination.* Chicago: Donohue, 1901.

Fadiman, J. A. *An Oral History of Tribal Warfare: The Meru of Mt. Kenya.* Athens: Ohio University Press, 1982.

Falk, Candace. *Love, Anarchy and Emma Goldman.* New York: Holt, Rinehart & Winston, 1984.

Falzone, Gaetano. *Histoirie de la Mafia.* Paris: Fayard, 1973.

Farson, N. *Last Chance in Africa.* London: Gollancz, 1953.

Fermi, Laura. *Mussolini.* Chicago: University of Chicago Press, 1963.

Fest, Joachim. *Hitler.* London: Wiedenfeld & Nicolson, 1974.

Fiaschetti, Michael. *You Gotta Be Rough.* Garden City, N.Y.: Doubleday, Doran, 1930.

Finer, Herman. *Mussolini's Italy.* New York: Holt, 1935.

Flanagan, Mike. *Out West.* New York: Harry N. Abrams, 1987.

Fleming, John S. *What is Ku Kluxism?* Goodwater, Ala.: Masonic Weekly Recorder, 1923.

Flory, William S. *Prisoners of War: A Study in the Development of International Law.* Washington, D.C.: American Council on Public Affairs, 1942.

Foner, Philip S. *History of the Labor Movement in the United States: From Colonial Times to the Founding of the Federation of Labor.* New York: International, 1947.

Fontaine, Roger. *Terrorism: The Cuban Connection.* New York: Crane Russak, 1988.

Foran, W. R. *The Kenya Police, 1887–1960.* London: Hale, 1962.

Ford, Franklin L. *Political Murder.* London: Harvard University Press, 1985.

Ford, Patrick H. (ed.). *The Darrow Bribery Trial with Background Facts of McNamara Case and Including Darrow's Address to the Jury.* Whittier, Calif.: Western Printing, 1956.

Fox, Frank. *Italy Today.* London: Herbert Jenkins, 1927.

Franzero, C. M. *Inside Italy.* London: Hodder & Stoughton, 1941.

Frost, Richard H. *The Mooney Case.* Stanford, Calif.: Stanford University Press, 1968.

Fuller, Edgar I. *The Visible of the Invisible Empire.* Denver: Maelstrom, 1925.

Gage, Nicholas. *Mafia, USA.* Chicago: Playboy Press, 1972.

Gallo, Max. *Mussolini's Italy: Twenty Years of the Fascist Era.* (trans., Charles Lam Markman) New York: Macmillan, 1973.

Gansberg, Judith M. *Stalag, U.S.A.* New York: Crowell, 1977.

Garrat, G. T. *Mussolini's Roman Empire.* London: Penguin Books, 1938.

Gatheru, Reuel Mugo. *Child of Two Worlds.* London: Routledge & Kegan Paul, 1964.

Gentry, Curt. *Frame-Up: The Incredible Case of Tom Mooney and Warren Billings.* New York: W. W. Norton, 1967.

Germino, Dante L. *The Italian Fascist Party in Power.* Minneapolis: University of Minnesota Press, 1959.

Gibbs, Sir Philip. *Since Then.* London: Heinemann, 1930.

Godden, Gertrude M. *Mussolini.* London: Burns & Oates, 1923.

Golan, Galia. *The Soviet Union and the Palestine Liberation Organization: An Uneasy Alliance.* New York: Praeger, 1980.

Goldberg, Robert Alan. *Hooded Empire.* Chicago: University of Illinois Press, 1981.

Golden, Harry. *A Little Girl Is Dead.* New York: World, 1965.

Goldman, Emma. *Anarchism and Other Essays.* New York: Mother Earth, 1911.

———. *Living My Life.* New York: Alfred A. Knopf, 1931.

Gompers, Samuel. *The McNamara Case.* Washington, D.C.: American Federation of Labor, 1911.

Gordon, John J. *Unmasked.* New York: Published

by the author, 1924.

Gossett, Thomas F. *Race: The History of an Idea in America.* New York: Schocken Books, 1965.

Grover, David H. *Debaters and Dynamiters: The Story of the Haywood Trial.* Corvallis, Ore.: Oregon State University Press, 1965.

Gunn, John W. *Wisdom of Clarence Darrow.* Girard, Kan.: Haldeman-Julius, 1947.

Gunther, John. *Taken at the Flood.* New York: Harper, 1960.

Gurko, Miriam. *Clarence Darrow.* New York: Thomas Y. Crowell, 1965.

Haas, Ben. *KKK.* Evanston, Ill.: Regency, 1963.

Hacker, Frederick J. *Crusaders, Criminals, Crazies: Terror and Terrorism in Our Time.* New York: W. W. Norton, 1976.

Halstead, Murat. *The Illustrious Life of William McKinley.* Chicago: n.p., 1901

———. *Life and Distinguished Services of William McKinley, Our Martyr President.* Chicago: Vosbrink Mercantile, 1901.

Hanser, Richard. *Putsch: How Hitler Made a Revolution.* New York: Peter H. Wyden, 1970.

Harkabi, Yehoshafat. *Fatah in the Arab Strategy.* Tel Aviv: Marachot Publishers, 1969.

Harrison, Charles Yale. *Clarence Darrow.* New York: Jonathan Cape & Harrison Smith, 1931.

Hart, Alan. *Arafat: Terrorist or Peacemaker?* London: Sidgwick & Jackson, 1984.

Haywood, William D. *Bill Haywood's Book.* New York: International, 1929.

Heaps, Willard A. *Riots U.S.A., 1765–1965.* New York: Seabury Press, 1966.

———. *Assassination: A Special Kind of Murder.* New York: Meredith, 1969.

Heiden, Konrad. *A History of National Socialism.* Berlin: Rowohlt, 1932.

———. *The Birth of the Third Reich.* Zurich, Switz.: Europa, 1934.

———. *Der Fuehrer.* Boston: Houghton Mifflin, 1944.

Heinz, H. A. *Germany's Hitler.* London: Hurst & Blackett, 1934.

Henderson, Ian, and P. Goodhart. *Manhunt in Kenya.* Garden City, N.Y.: Doubleday, 1958.

Henson, Allen L. *Confessions of a Criminal Lawyer.* New York: Vantage, 1959.

Hibbert, Christopher. *Benito Mussolini.* London: Longmans Green, 1962.

Hicks, John D. *The Populist Revolt.* Minneapolis: University of Minnesota Press, 1931.

Higham, John. *Strangers in the Land: Patterns of American Nativism, 1860–1925.* New York: Atheneum, 1973.

Hindlip, L. *British East Africa: Past, Present and Future.* London: Unwin, 1905.

Hinshaw, David. *The Home Front.* New York: G. P. Putnam's Sons, 1943.

Hobley, C. W. *Kenya: From Chartered Company to Crown Colony.* London: Witherby, 1929.

Hohne, Heinz. *The Order of the Death's Head.* New York: Coward-McCann, 1970.

Holman, D. *Bwana Drum.* London: Allen, 1964.

Holroyd, James Edward. *The Gaslight Murders.* London: George Allen & Unwin, 1960.

Hoover, J. Edgar. *Masters of Deceit.* New York: Henry Holt, 1958.

———. *A Study of Communism.* New York: Holt, Rinehart and Winston, 1962.

———. *J. Edgar Hoover on Communism.* New York: Random House, 1969.

Hopkins, Ernest Jerome. *What Happened in the Mooney Case?* New York: Brower, Warren & Putnam, 1932.

Horn, Stanley F. *Invisible Empire: The Story of the Ku Klux Klan, 1866–1871.* Boston: Houghton-Mifflin, 1939.

Hornung, Manfred. *PW.* Vienna: Eduard Wancura Verlag, 1959.

Howard, Milford W. *Fascism: A Challenge to Democracy.* New York: Fleming H. Revell, 1928.

Howe, Irving, and Lewis Coser. *The American Communist Party: A Critical History.* New York: Frederick A. Praeger, 1962.

Huie, William Bradford. *Three Lives for Mississippi.* New York: Signet, 1968.

Hullinger, Edwin Ware. *The New Fascist State.* New York: Rae D. Henkle, 1928.

Hunt, Henry T. *The Case of Thomas J. Mooney and Warren K. Billings.* New York: G. G. Burgoyne, 1929.

Hurwood, Bernhardt J. *Society and the Assassin.* New York: Parent's Magazine Press, 1970.

Hyams, Edward. *Killing No Murder: A Study of Assassination as a Political Means.* London: Thomas Nelson & Sons, 1969.

Ingham, K. *A History of East Africa.* London: Longmans, 1962.

Ivianski, Zeev. *Individual Terror: Theory and Deed.* Tel Aviv: Hakibbutz Hameuchad, 1977.

Jackson, Kenneth T. *The Ku Klux Klan in the City.* New York: Oxford University Press, 1970.

Jaffe, Philip J. *The Rise and Fall of American Communism.* New York: Horizon, 1975.

Jarman, T. L. *The Rise and Fall of Nazi Germany.* New York: New American Library, 1961.

Jetzinger, Franz. *Hitler's Jugend.* Vienna, Aust.: Europa Verlag, 1956.

Johns, A. Wesley. *The Man Who Shot McKinley.* South Brunswick, N.J.: A. S. Barnes, 1970.

Johnson, Francis. *Famous Assassinations of*

History. Chicago: A. C. McClurg, 1903.

Jones, Winfield. *Story of the Ku Klux Klan.* Washington, D.C.: American Newspaper Syndicate, 1921.

————. *Knights of the Ku Klux Klan.* New York: Tocsin, 1941.

Kaggia, B. M. *Roots of Freedom.* Nairobi, Kenya: East African, 1975.

Kanogo, T. *Squatters and the Roots of Mau Mau, 1905–1963.* London: James Curry, 1987.

Kaplan, Justin. *Lincoln Steffens: A Biography.* New York: Simon & Schuster, 1974.

Kariuki, J., and P. Ochieng. *Mau Mau Detainee.* London: Oxford University Press, 1963.

Kazziha, Walid. *Revolutionary Transformation in the Arab World.* New York: St. Martin's, 1975.

Kennedy, D. *Islands of White: Settler Society and Culture in Kenya and Southern Rhodesia, 1890–1939.* Durham, N.C.: Duke University Press, 1987.

Kennedy, William Sloane. *Italy in Chains.* West Yarmouth, Mass.: Stonecroft Press, 1927.

Kenyatta, Jomo. *Suffering Without Bitterness.* Nairobi, Kenya: East African, 1968.

Kiernan, Thomas. *Arafat: The Man and the Myth.* New York: Norton, 1976.

King, Bolton. *Fascism in Italy.* London: William & Norgate, 1931.

King-Hall, Sir Stephen. *Three Dictators.* London: Faber & Faber, 1964.

Kirkpatrick, Sir Ivone. *Mussolini: Study in Power.* New York: Hawthorn, 1964.

Kitson, Frank. *Gangs and Counter-Gangs.* London: Barrie & Rockliffe, 1960.

Kobler, John. *Capone: The Life and World of Al Capone.* New York: G. P. Putnam's Sons, 1971.

Kogon, Eugen. *The Theory and Practice of Hell.* (trans., Heinz Norden) London: Secker & Warburg, 1950.

Kohlsaat, H. H. *From McKinley to Harding: Personal Recollections of Our Presidents.* New York: Charles Scribner's Sons, 1923.

Krammer, Arnold. *Nazi Prisoners of War in America.* New York: Stein and Day, 1979.

Kurland, Gerland. *Clarence Darrow: Attorney for the Damned.* New York: SamHar Press, 1972.

Kurz, Anat, and Ariel Merari. *ASALA: International Terrorism or Political Tool?* Jerusalem: Westview Press, 1985.

Lander, C. *My Kenya Acres: A Woman Farms in Mau Mau Country.* London: Harrap, 1957.

Lapping, B. *End of Empire.* New York: St. Martin's, 1985.

Laqueur, Walter. *Terrorism.* Boston: Little, Brown, 1977.

Lawson, John D. (ed.). *American State Trials.* (17 vols.) St. Louis: Thomas, 1914–1937.

Leakey, L. S. B. *Mau Mau and the Kikuyu.* London: Methuen, 1953.

————. *Defeating Mau Mau.* London: Methuen, 1954.

Leech, Margaret. *In the Days of McKinley.* New York: Harper & Brothers, 1959.

Leigh, I. *In the Shadow of Mau Mau.* London: Allen, 1955.

Leighton, Isabel (ed.). *The Aspirin Age, 1919–1941.* New York: Simon and Schuster, 1949.

Leo, C. *Land and Class in Kenya.* Toronto, Ont.: University of Toronto Press, 1984.

Lester, David, and Gene Lester. *Crime of Passion.* Chicago: Nelson-Hall, 1975.

Lester, John C., and D. C. Wilson. *Ku Klux Klan: Its Origin, Growth and Disbandment.* New York: Neale, 1905.

Lindemann, Albert S. *The Red Years: European Socialism versus Bolshevism, 1919–1921.* Berkeley: University of California Press, 1974.

Livingston, Neil C. *The War Against Terrorism.* Lexington, Mass.: Lexington Books, 1982.

————. *Fighting Back: Winning the War Against Terrorism.* Lexington, Mass.: Lexington Books, 1986.

————. *Beyond the Iran-Contra Crisis.* Lexington, Mass.: Lexington Books, 1988.

Livingston, Neil C., and David Halevy. *Inside the PLO.* New York: Morrow, 1990.

Loucks, Emerson Hunsberger. *The Ku Klux Klan in Pennsylvania.* Harrisburg, Pa.: The Telegraph Press, 1936.

Lusso, Emilio. *Enter Mussolini.* (trans., Marion Rawson) London: Methuen, 1936.

Lynch, Denis Tilden. *Criminals and Politicians.* New York: Macmillan, 1932.

Lytle, Andrew Nelson. *Bedford Forrest and His Critter Company.* New York: Minton, Balch, 1931.

McCarver, Norman L., and Norman L. McCarver, Jr. *Hearne on the Brazos.* San Antonio: San Antonio Century Press, 1958.

MacGregor-Hastie, Roy. *The Day of the Lion: The Rise and Fall of Fascist Italy, 1922–1945.* New York: Coward-McCann, 1963.

McKenna, Marion C. *Borah.* Ann Arbor, Mich.: University of Michigan Press, 1961.

Mackenzie, Norman. *Secret Societies.* New York: Holt, Rinehart & Winston, 1967.

McLellan, Vin, and Paul Avery. *The Voices of Guns.* New York: G. P. Putnam's Sons, 1977.

MacNaughten, Sir Melville. *Days of My Years.* London: Edward Arnold, 1914.

McPhaul, John J. *Johnny Torrio.* New Rochelle, N.Y.: Arlington House, 1970.

Maina, P. *Six Mau Mau Generals.* Nairobi, Kenya: Gazelle Books, 1977.

Majdalany, Fred. *State of Emergency: The Full Story of Mau Mau.* Boston: Houghton Mifflin, 1963.

Manvell, Roger. *Hermann Goring.* London: Heinemann, 1962.

———. *Heinrich Himmler.* New York: G. P. Putnam's Sons, 1965.

———. *SS and Gestapo: Rule by Terror.* London: MacDonald, 1970.

Martelli, George. *Italy Against the World.* London: Chatto & Windus, 1937.

Martin, David C. *Best Laid Plans.* New York: Harper, 1988.

Maser, Werner. *Hitler: Legend, Myth and Reality.* New York: Harper & Row, 1974.

Massock, R. G. *Italy from Within.* London: Macmillan, 1943.

Mast, Blaine. *K.K.K., Friend or Foe: Which?* Pittsburgh, Pa.: Herbrick & Held Printing, 1924.

Matteotti, Giacomo. *The Fascisti Exposed.* (trans., E. W. Dickes) London: ILP, 1924.

Matthews, Herbert L. *The Fruits of Fascism.* New York: Harcourt, Brace, 1943.

Mecklin, John M. *The Ku Klux Klan: A Study of the American Mind.* New York: Russell & Russell, 1963.

Megaro, Gaudens. *Mussolini in the Making.* Boston: Houghton Mifflin, 1938.

Melman, Yossi. *The Master Terrorist: The True Story Behind Abu Nidal.* New York: Adami Books, 1986.

Merami, Ariel, and Schomi Elad. *The International Dimension and Palestinian Terrorism.* Boulder, Colo.: Westview Press, 1986.

Messick, Hank. *The Mobs and the Mafia.* New York: Ballantine Books, 1971.

Mickolus, Edward P. *Transitional Terrorism.* Westport, Conn.: Greenwood Press, 1980.

Miller, C. *The Lunatic Express: An Entertainment in Imperialism.* New York: Macmillan, 1971.

Mitchell, David. *1919: Red Mirage.* New York: Macmillan, 1970.

Monelli, Paolo. *Mussolini: An Intimate Life.* (trans., Brigid Maxwell) London: Thames & Hudson, 1953.

Monroe, James L. (ed.). *Prisoners of War and Political Hostages.* Springfield, Va.: Monroe Corp., 1973.

Monteval, Marion. *The Klan Inside Out.* Claremore, Okla.: Monarch, 1924.

Mooney-Billings Report Suppressed by the Wickersham Commission. New York: Gotham House, 1932.

Moorehead, Caroline. *Hostages to Fortune.* New York: Atheneum, 1980.

Morain, Alfred. *The Underworld of Paris.* London: Jarrolds, 1929.

Mordell, Albert. *Clarence Darrow, Eugene V. Debs and Haldeman-Julius.* Gerard, Kan.: Haldeman-Julius, 1950.

Morgan, H. Wayne. *William McKinley and His America.* Syracuse, N. Y.: Syracuse University Press, 1963.

Mori, Cesare. *The Last Stuggle with the Mafia.* (trans., Orlo Williams) New York: G. P. Putnam's Sons, 1933.

Mosley, Leonard. *On Borrowed Time.* New York: Random House, 1969.

Munro, Ion S. *Through Fascism to World Power.* London: Alexander Maclehose, 1933.

Murithi, J. K., and P. N. Ndoria. *War in the Forest: An Autobiography of a Mau Mau Leader.* Nairobi, Kenya: East African, 1971.

Murphy, John T. *A Manual on the Rise and Fall of Italy's Fascist Empire.* London: Crowther, 1943.

Murray, Robert K. *Red Scare: A Study in National Hysteria, 1919–1920.* New York: McGraw-Hill, 1964.

Murray-Brown, J. *Kenyatta.* London: Allen, 1972.

Myers, Gustavus. *History of Bigotry in the United States.* New York: Random House, 1943.

Nash, Jay Robert. *Citizen Hoover: A Critical Study of J. Edgar Hoover and His FBI.* Chicago: Nelson-Hall, 1972.

———. *Bloodletters and Badmen: A Narrative Encyclopedia of American Criminals from the Pilgrims to the Present.* New York: M. Evans and Company, 1973.

———. *Among the Missing: An Anecdotal History of Missing Persons from 1800 to the Present.* New York: Simon and Schuster, 1978.

———. *Murder, America: Homicide in the United States from the Revolution to the Present.* New York: Simon and Schuster, 1980.

———. *Almanac of World Crime.* New York: Doubleday, 1981.

———. *Look for the Woman.* New York: M. Evans and Company, 1981.

———. *Open Files.* New York: McGraw-Hill, 1983.

———. *Crime Chronology.* New York: Facts on File, 1984.

———. *Encyclopedia of World Crime.* (6 vols.) Wilmette, Ill.: CrimeBooks, Inc., 1990.

Nenni, Pietro. *Ten Years of Tyranny in Italy.* (trans., Anne Steele) London: Allen & Unwin, 1932.

Nolte, Ernst. *Three Faces of Fascism.* New York:

Holt, Rinehart and Winston, 1966.

Nott-Bower, Sir William. *Fifty-two Years a Policeman.* London: Edward Arnold, 1926.

O'Ballance, Edgar. *Language of Violence: The Blood Politics of Terrorism.* San Rafael, Calif.: Presidio Press, 1979.

Olcott, C. *The Life of William McKinley.* (2 vols.) Boston: Houghton Mifflin, 1916.

Olden, Rudolf. *Hitler.* New York: Covici-Friede, 1936.

Orchard, Harry (Albert E. Horsley). *The Confessions and Autobiography of Harry Orchard.* New York: Doubleday, Page, 1907.

Orlow, Dietrich. *The History of the Nazi Party.* (2 vols.) Pittsburgh, Pa.: University of Pittsburgh Press, 1969.

Overstreet, Harry, and Bonaro Overstreet. *The FBI in an Open Society.* New York: W. W. Norton, 1969.

Owen, Frank. *The Three Dictators.* London: Allen & Unwin, 1941.

Pabel, Reinhold. *Enemies Are Human.* Philadelphia: Winston Press, 1955.

Pacepa, Ion Mihai. *Red Horizons.* Washington, D.C.: Regnery Gateway, 1987.

Packard, Reynolds, and Eleanor Packard. *Balcony Empire.* London: Chatto & Windus, 1943.

Paine, Lauren. *The Assassin's World.* New York: Taplinger, 1975.

Parry, Albert. *Terrorism: From Robespierre to Arafat.* New York: Vanguard, 1976.

Patti, Ercole. *Roman Chronicle.* London: Chatto & Windus, 1965.

Payne, Robert. *The Life and Death of Adolf Hitler.* New York: Praeger, 1973.

Pearl, Jack. *The Dangerous Assassins.* Derby, Conn.: Monarch Books, 1964.

Pellizzi, C. *Italy.* London: Longmans, 1933.

Perry, Louis B., and Richard S. Perry. *A History of the Los Angeles Labor Movement, 1911–1941.* Berkeley: University of California Press, 1963.

Petrie, Sir Charles. *Mussolini.* London: Holme Press, 1931.

Pfeffer, Leo. *This Honorable Court.* Boston: Beacon Press, 1965.

Phillips, Sir Percival. *The Red Dragon and the Black Shirts.* London: Daily Mail, 1923.

Pini, Giorgio. *Mussolini.* (trans., Luigi Villari) London: Hutchinson, 1939.

Post, Louis F. *The Deportations Delirium of Nineteen-Twenty.* Chicago: C. H. Kerr, 1923.

Powers, Richard. *Secrecy and Power.* New York: Free Press, 1987.

Price, G. Ward. *I Know These Dictators.* London: Harrap, 1937.

Raffolovich, George. *Benito Mussolini.* Florence, Italy: Owl, 1923.

Randal, Jonathan. *Going All the Way.* New York: Viking, 1983.

Randel, William Pierce. *The Ku Klux Klan: A Century of Infamy.* New York: Chilton Books, 1965.

Raushenbush, Stephen. *The March of Fascism.* New Haven, Conn.: Yale University Press, 1940.

Raven, S. S. *The Feathers of Death.* London: Anthony Blond, 1959.

Rawcliffe, D. H. *The Struggle for Kenya.* London: Gollancz, 1954.

Reid, Ed. *Mafia.* New York: Random House, 1952.

Remak, Joachim. *The Nazi Years.* Englewood Cliffs, N.J.: Prentice-Hall, 1969.

Reppetto, Thomas A. *The Blue Parade.* New York: Free Press, 1978.

Richter, Hans Werner. *The Conquered.* Munich: K. Desch, 1949.

Roberts, Kenneth. *Black Magic.* Indianapolis, Ind.: Bobbs-Merrill, 1924.

Roberts, Stephen H. *The House That Hitler Built.* New York: Harper, 1938.

Robertson, Angus. *Mussolini and the New Italy.* London: Allenson, 1929.

Robinson, W. W. *Bombs and Bribery.* Los Angeles: Dawson's Book Shop, 1969.

Roche, John P. The Quest for the Dream: The Development of Civil Rights and Human Relations in Modern America. New York: Macmillan, 1963.

Rochester, Anna. *The Populist Movement in the United States.* New York: International, 1943.

Rossi, Angelo T. *The Rise of Italian Fascism.* (trans., Peter and Dorothy Wait) London: Methuen, 1938.

Rowe, Gary Thomas, Jr. *My Undercover Years with the Ku Klux Klan.* New York: Bantam Books, 1979.

Rubenberg, Cheryl. *The Palestine Liberation Organization.* Belmont, Mass.: Institute of Arab Studies, 1983.

Sahliyeh, Emil. *The PLO After the Lebanon War.* Boulder, Colo.: Westview Press, 1985.

Salvamini, Gaetano. *The Fascist Dictatorship in Italy.* New York: Holt, Rinehart and Winston, 1927.

———. *Under the Axe of Fascism.* New York: Viking, 1936.

Samuels, Charles, and Louise Samuels. *Night Fell on Georgia.* New York: Dell, 1956.

Santoro, Cesare. *Hitler Germany as Seen by a Foreigner.* Berlin: Internationaler, 1938.

Saporiti, Piero. *Empty Balcony.* London:

Gollancz, 1947.

Sarfatti, Margherita. *Dux: The Life of Benito Mussolini.* (trans., Fredric Whyte) London: Thornton Butterworth, 1925.

Sayer, James Edward. *Clarence Darrow: Public Advocate.* Dayton, Ohio: Wright State University, 1978.

Schneider, H. W. *Making of the Fascist State.* New York: Oxford University Press, 1928.

Schoenbaum, David. *Hitler's Social Revolution: Class and Status in Nazi Germany, 1933–1939.* Garden City, N.Y.: Doubleday, 1966.

Schramm, Percy Ernst. *Hitler: The Man and the Military Leader.* Chicago: Quadrangle Books, 1971.

Schrieber, Jan. *The Ultimate Weapon: Terrorists and World Order.* New York: William Morrow, 1978.

Schriftgeisser, Karl. *This Was Normalcy.* Boston: Atlantic, Little, Brown, 1948.

Schuman, Frederick L. *The Nazi Dictatorship.* New York: Alfred A. Knopf, 1936.

Seldes, George. *Sawdust Caesar.* New York: Harper, 1938.

Servadio, Gaia. *Mafioso: A History of the Mafia from Its Origins to the Present Day.* New York: Dell, 1976.

Shawcross, William. *The Shah's Last Ride.* New York: Simon and Schuster, 1988.

Shew, E. Spencer. *A Companion to Murder.* New York: Alfred A. Knopf, 1960.

Shirer, William L. *Berlin Diary.* New York: Alfred A. Knopf, 1941.

———. *The Rise and Fall of the Third Reich.* New York: Simon and Schuster, 1960.

Silvestri, Carlo. *Matteotti, Mussolini e il dramma italiano.* Rome: Ruffolo, 1947.

Sims, Patsy. *The Klan.* New York: Stein & Day, 1978.

Sivan, Emmanuel. *Radical Islam.* Tel Aviv: Am Oved Publishers, 1985.

Slater, M. *Trial of Jomo Kenyatta.* London: Secker & Warburg, 1955.

Slosson, Preston William. *The Great Crusade and After, 1914–1928.* New York: Macmillan, 1930.

Smith, Colin. *Carlos: Portrait of a Terrorist.* New York: Holt, Rinehart & Winston, 1977.

Smith, Dennis Mack. *A History of Sicily.* London: Chatto & Windus, 1968.

Smith, Dwight C., Jr. *The Mafia Mystique.* New York: Basic Books, 1975.

Smith, Gibbs M. *Joe Hill.* Salt Lake City: University of Utah Press, 1969.

Spivak, J. L. *Europe Under the Terror.* London:

Gollancz, 1936.

Spolansky, Jacob. *The Communist Trail in America.* New York: Macmillan, 1951.

Starhemberg, E. R. von. *Between Hitler and Mussolini.* London: Hodder & Stoughton, 1941.

Steiner, H. A. *Government in Fascist Italy.* New York: McGraw-Hill, 1938.

Sterling, Claire. *The Terror Network.* New York: Holt, Rinehart and Winston, 1981.

Stimson, Grace Heilman. *Rise of the Labor Movement in Los Angeles.* Berkeley: University of California, 1955.

Stone, Irving. *Clarence Darrow for the Defense.* Garden City, N.Y.: Doubleday, 1941.

Stoneham, C. T. *Mau Mau.* London: Museum Press, 1953.

———. *Out of Barbarism.* London: Museum Press, 1955.

Stripling, Robert E. *The Red Plot Against America.* New York: Bell, 1949.

Sutherland, Sidney. *Ten Real Murder Mysteries.* New York: G. P. Putnam's Sons, 1929.

Swarthout, Glendon. *The Eagle and the Iron Cross.* New York: New American Library, 1966.

Swisher, Carl Brent. *American Constitutional Development.* Boston: Houghton-Mifflin, 1943.

Taheri, Amir. *Holy Terror.* Bethesda, Md.: Adler & Adler, 1987.

Taylor, Telford. *Sword and Swastika: Generals and Nazis in the Third Reich.* Chicago: Quadrangle, 1969.

Thompson, Sir Basil. *The Story of Scotland Yard.* London: Grayson & Grayson, 1925.

Throup, D. W. *Economic and Social Origins of Mau Mau, 1945–1953.* London: James Currey, 1988.

Tierney, Kevin. *Clarence Darrow: A Biography.* New York: Thomas Y. Crowell, 1979.

Tiltman, Hessell. *The Terror in Europe.* London: Jarrolds, 1931.

Tobias, Fritz. *The Reichstag Fire.* New York: G. P. Putnam's Sons, 1964.

Toledano, Ralph de. *J. Edgar Hoover: The Man and His Times.* New Rochelle, N.Y.: Arlington House, 1973.

Tolstoy, Nicolai. *The Night of the Long Knives.* New York: Ballantine Books, 1972.

Tompkins, Peter. *Italy Betrayed.* New York: Simon and Schuster, 1966.

Trelease, Allen W. *White Terror: The KKK Conspiracy and Southern Reconstruction.* New York: Harper & Row, 1971.

Treves, Paolo. *What Mussolini Did to Us.* (trans.,

Bibliography

Casimiro Isolani) London: Gollancz, 1940.

Truman, Harry S. *Memoirs.* (2 vols.) Garden City, N.Y.: Doubleday, 1955.

Truman, Margaret. *Harry S. Truman.* New York: William Morrow, 1973.

Ungar, Sanford J. *FBI.* Boston: Little, Brown, 1975.

Valera, Paolo. *Mussolini.* Milan, Italy: La Folla, 1924.

Van Passen, Pierre. *To Number Our Days.* New York: Charles Scribner's Sons, 1964.

Venys, L. *A History of the Mau Mau Movement.* Prague, Czech.: Charles University, 1970.

Viereck, Peter. *Metapolitics: The Roots of the Nazi Mind.* New York: G. P. Putnam's Sons, 1961.

Villari, Luigi. *The Fascist Experiment.* London: Faber & Gwyer, 1926.

Vizetelly, Ernest Alfred. *The Anarchists.* New York: John Lane, 1911.

Vogt, Hannah. *The Burden of Guilt: A Short History of Germany, 1914–1945.* New York: Oxford University Press, 1964.

Walther, Herbert (ed.). *Der Fuhrer: The Life and Times of Adolf Hitler.* Secaucus, N.J.: Bison Books, 1978.

Weinberg, Arthur (ed.). *Attorney for the Damned.* New York: Simon & Schuster, 1957.

Weinberg, Arthur, and Lila Weinberg. *Clarence Darrow: A Sentimental Rebel.* New York: G. P. Putnam's Sons, 1980.

Wensley, Frederick Porter. *Forty Years of Scotland Yard.* New York: Garden City Publishers, 1930.

———. *Detective Days.* London: Cassell, 1931.

Wepman, D. *Jomo Kenyatta.* New York: Chelsea House, 1985.

Wheaton, Eliot B. *The Nazi Revolution, 1933–35:*

Prelude to Calamity. Garden City, N. Y.: Doubleday, 1969.

Wheeler-Bennett, Sir John. *The Nemesis of Power: The German Army in Politics, 1918–1945.* New York: St. Martin's, 1953.

Whitehead, Don. *The F.B.I. Story.* New York: Random House, 1956.

———. *Attack on Terror: The F.B.I. Against the Ku Klux Klan in Mississippi.* New York: Funk & Wagnalls, 1970.

Whitehead, George G. *Clarence Darrow—The Big Minority Man.* Gerard, Kan.: Haldeman-Julius, 1931.

———. *Clarence Darrow: "Evangelist" of Sane Thinking.* Gerard, Kan.: Haldeman-Julius, 1931.

Whitney, Richard. *Reds in America.* New York: Beckwith, 1924.

Whittingham, Richard. *Martial Justice: The Last Mass Execution in the United States.* Chicago: Regnery, 1971.

Wicker, Tom. *Investigating the FBI.* Garden City, N.Y.: Doubleday, 1973.

Wilson, Colin, and Patricia Pittman. *Encyclopedia of Murder.* New York: G. P. Putnam's Sons, 1961.

Witcher, W. C. *The Unveiling of the Ku Klux Klan.* Fort Worth, Tex.: American Constitutional League, 1922.

———. *The Reign of Terror in Oklahoma.* Fort Worth, Tex.: Published by the author, 1923.

Wolf, Marvin J., and Katherine Mader. *Fallen Angels.* Facts on File, 1986.

Woodward, C. Vann. *Tom Watson: Agrarian Rebel.* New York: Macmillan, 1938.

Wykes, Alan. *Hitler.* New York: Ballantine Books, 1971.

Yari, Ehud. *Fatah.* Tel Aviv: A. Levin-Epstein, 1970

INDEX

Categories for Arson, Assassinations, Bombings, Kidnappings, Looting, Lynchings, Riots, Serial Killer-Terrorists and Skyjackings listed below reference only those entries appearing in the Chronology. Also see information on terrorist groups and organizations in the Glossary of Terrorist Organizations.

Abbas, Abu (Mohammed Zaidan Abbas; AKA: Abu Khalid), 241, 243, 244, 245, 287, 376, 377, 387, 390
ABC-TV (Network), 286, 398
Abdallah, Allal ben, 326
Abdallah, Georges, 392
Abdullah (Abdul ibn Hussein, Abd Allah ibn al-Husayn, king of Jordan), 325
Abdullah, Mohammed, 215
Abraham, 156
Ab Dhabi Airport, 367
Abu Nidal Faction (part of the Al-Fatah Revolutionary Council, a Middle Eastern terrorist group named after its leader Abu Nidal), 247, 367, 368, 369, 371-72, 372, 378, 379, 384, 385, 386, 387, 388, 389, 390, 391, 400
Acao Libertadora Nacional, See: ALN
Ace Airline (Costa Rica), 394
Achille Lauro (cruise ship), xi, 240, 241-45, 287, 390
Acrow Steel Co., 356
Action Directe (AD, Direct Action, anti-NATO terrorist group in France), 388
Adam, Gen. Yekotiel, 383
Adams, Joe, 309
Adams, Steve, 13, 14-15
Adamson, Blossom, 291
Adamson, John Harvey, 363
Addasi, Ghassan, 410-11
Aden Airways, 335
Adenauer, Konrad, 327
Adler, Freidrich, 299
Administrative Security Building (Bogotá, Col.), 395
Adwan, Kamal, 356

Aer Lingus Airlines, 377
AFL (American Federation of Labor), 40
African National Congress (ANC, an oft-times terrorist organization in South Africa), 383, 385-86, 387, 390, 393, 397
Afrika Korps, 131, 134, 135
Agca, Mehmet Ali, 377
Ahmed Maher Pasher, 321
Ainsworth, Kathy, 174, 334
Air Florida, 374
Air France, 364, 387
Air India, 327, 380, 389, 394
Air Lanka, 391
Airplane hijackings, See: Skyjackings
Air Vietnam, 342, 356, 359
Akache, Zohair, 366
Ala, Hussein, 327
Al Ahram, 368
Al-Amoodi, Salem, 335
ALAS Airlines, 333
al-Ashker, Bassam, 245
Al-Asifa (European terrorist group), 377
al-Assad, Hefez, 242
Albano, Angelo, 303
Albee, James R., 372
Alberman, Gertrude, 311
Albrecht, Susanne, 207
Al-Dawa (Middle Eastern terrorist organization), 386
Alexander I (Karageorgevic, king of Yugo.), 316
Alexander I (Obrenovic, king of Serbia), 291
Alexander, Will W., 311
Alexandrov, Todor, 306
Alexandrovich, Grand Duke Sergei, 293
Alexiev, Dimitz K., 353

Al Fatah (Arab terrorist group largely connected with the PFLP and the PLO), 193, 214, 215, 231, 241, 247, 344, 347, 354, 355, 356, 370
Alfano, Enrico, 22
Alfanso VIII (king of Spain), 293
Alfred P. Murrah Federal Building (Oklahoma City, Okla.), 267, 269, 273, 274, 403, 407
Algerian Embassy, Beirut, Leb., 381
Algerian Separatists (terrorist group), 257
al-Ghubash, Sayf bin Sa'id, 367
al-Halim Khaddam, Abd, 367
al-Hamid Labib, Abdullah abed (AKA: Col. Hawari), 247
al-Henjiri, Abdullah, 366
Al-Hinnawi, Col. Same, 325
Ali, Prophet Drew, 220
Allam, Gen. Hassam, 235
Allard, Alain, 340
Allen, Walter, 291
Allende Gossens, Salvador, 354
Al-Malki, Adan, 327
Almaneih, Naser, 377
al-Masri, Zafr, 390
Al-Megrahi, Abdel Basset Ali, 250
Almond, James Lindsay, Jr., 329
Al-Mukharabat (Iraq Secret Police and terrorist organization), 369, 371-72
ALN (Acao Libertadora Nacional; National Liberation Alliance; Brazilian terrorist group), 341, 347
Al-Naif, Abdul Razak, 369
Alon, Col. Josef, 356-57
al-Sayegh, Hani, 406, 411

Al-Sulh, Riad (Riad Solh, Bey), 325
Alves da Conceicao, Raimundo, 394
al-Wazir, Khalil, 393
Amakasu, Masahiko, 306
Amal Shi'ites, 379
AMAN (Israeli military intelligence), 244
American Airlines, 344, 349, 350, 353, 371, 372-73
American Federation of Labor, *See:* AFL
American Muslim Mission, 228
Amerio, Ettore, 209
Amin, Idi, 364
Amin-es (Sultan of Persia), 294
Amoco International Oil Co., 357
Amtrak, 398, 405
ANC, *See:* African National Congress
Anderson, Don Benny, 383
Anderson, Simon, 295
Anderson, Terry, 388, 392
Andrassy, Edward, 118
Ann Arbor (Mich.) Murderer, 361-62
Anne (Princess of England), 358
Anti-Capitalist Action (terrorist group in Greece), 378
An Tie Cho, 326
Appeal to Reason, 50
Applequist, Otto, 46, 47
April 19 Movement, *See:* M-19
Aquino, Benigno S., Jr., 386, 396
Arab Brigades Movement (terrorist group in India), 382-83
Arab League, 245
Arab Library (Paris, Fr.), 367
Arab News Letter, 389
Arab Socialist Union Building (Tyre, Leb.), 378
Arab Steadfastness Front (terrorst group based in Egypt), 379
Arafa, Sidi Muhammad ben Moulay, 326
Arafat, Yasir (PLO leader often linked with the terrorist groups Al Fatah, PFLP and Black September), ix, 213, 215, 231, 232, 241, 243, 244, 245, 287, 354, 376, 392, 396
Arambaru, Pedro Eugenio, 345
Arch of Triumph (Paris, Fr.), 257
Arguello, Patrick, 346
Arizona Patriots, 272
Arikan, Kemal, 381
Aristide, Jean Bertrand, 406
Arledge, Jimmy, 173
Arlington Cemetary, 144
Armed Guard of the Proletariat

(Mexican terrorist group), 363
Armed Proletarian Nucleus (NAP, Italian terrorist group), 210
Armed Resistance Group (U.S. Puerto Rican terrorist group), 377-78
Armed Revolutionary Nuclei (NAR, Italian terrorist group), 374
Army of God (U.S. anti-abortion terrorist group), 383
Armitage, Sir Robert, 327
Armour, Edward, 122
Armstrong, Karleton, 346
Armwood, George, 314
Arsenic and Old Lace (film), 148
Arson
    Berlin, Ger. (Reichstag Bldg.), 315 (1934)
    New York, N. Y., 395 (1990)
    Pierce City, Mo., 290 (1901)
    Tokyo-Yokohama, Jap., 305-06 (1923)
Artichoke King, The, *See:* Terranova, Ciro
Asahara, Shoko (Chizuo Matsumoto), 262-64, 403
Asanuma, Inejiro, 330
Ashby-Jones, Rev. M., 84
Ashton-Wolfe, H., 36
Assadi, Marouf, 245
Assassination of Trotsky, The (film), 319
Assassinations and assassination attempts (victims—heads of state, corporation executives, and representatives of government, law enforcement, military and political organizations)
    Abdullah, 325 (1951)
    Adam, Gen. Yekotiel, 383 (1982)
    Adams, Joe, 309 (1926)
    Adenauer, Konrad, 327 (1955)
    Adwan, Kamal, 356 (1973)
    Ahmed Maher Pasha, 321 (1945)
    Al-Amoodi, Salem, 335 (1967)
    Ala, Hussein, 327 (1955)
    Alexander I (Karageorgevic), 316 (1934)
    Alexander I (Obrenovic), 291 (1903)
    Alexandrov, Todor, 306 (1924)
    Alexandrovich, Grand Duke Sergei, 293 (1905)
    Alfonso VIII, 293 (1906)
    al-Ghubash, Sayf bin Sa'id, 367 (1977)

    al-Henjiri, Abdullah, 366 (1977)
    Al-Hinnawi, Same, 325 (1950)
    Allende Gossens, Salvador, 354 (1972)
    Al-Malki, Adan, 327 (1955)
    al-Masri, Zafr, 390 (1986)
    Al-Naif, Abdul Razak, 369 (1978)
    Almond, James Lindsay, Jr., 329 (1959)
    Alon, Col. Josef, 356-57 (1973)
    Al-Sulh, Riad, 325 (1951)
    al-Wazir, Khalil, 393
    Amin-es, 294 (1907)
    Aquino, Benigno S., Jr., 386 (1983)
    Arafa, Sidi Muhammad ben Moulay, 326 (1953)
    Arambaru, Pedro Eugenio, 345 (1970)
    Arikan, Kemal, 381 (1982)
    Armitage, Sir Robert, 327 (1955)
    Asanuma, Inejiro, 330 (1960)
    Astarita, Mario, 369 (1978)
    Atikat, Col. Atilla, 383 (1982)
    Atrakchi, Albert, 389 (1985)
    Audran, Gen. René, 388 (1985)
    Avila Camacho, Manuel, 321 (1944)
    Azaval Avelar, Alfredo, 388 (1985)
    Azikiwe, Nnamdi, 328 (1957)
    Bahonar, Mohammed Javar, 379 (1981)
    Bailey, Elihu H., 324 (1949)
    Bakir Sidky Pasha, 318 (1937)
    Balewa, Sir Abubakar Tafawa, 334 (1966)
    Baligand, Dr. Henry Albert von, 311 (1930)
    Balkar, Galip, 385 (1983)
    Banna, Hasan, 324 (1949)
    Bante, Gen. Teferi, 365 (1977)
    Barsimantov, Yacov, 382 (1982)
    Barthou, Jean Louis, 316 (1934)
    Batista, Fulgencio, 327 (1956), 328 (1957)
    Behesti, Ayatollah, 378 (1981)
    Bentley, Alvin Morell, 326 (1954)
    Berg, Alan, 387 (1984)
    Betancourt, Romulo, 329 (1960)
    Bevens, Clifford, 375 (1980)
    Bevin, Ernest, 322 (1947)
    Bernadotte, Count Folkke, 324 (1948)
    Bhutto, Zulfikar Ali, 371 (1979)
    Bishop, Maurice, 386 (1983)

(1931)
Hoffa, James, 331 (1962)
Hoover, Herbert, 310 (1929)
Hoyos, Carlos, 393 (1988)
Humbert I, 289 (1900)
Humphrey, Hubert, 335 (1967)
Hussan II, 332 (1964)
Hussein, Kamal, 383 (1982)
Ibrahim, Said Zaghloul, 306 (1924)
Innü, Ismet, 313 (1931)
Inouye, Junnosuke, 313 (1932)
Inukai, Ki Tsuyoshi, 313 (1932)
Iradier, Eduardo Data, 304 (1921)
Iorga, Nicola, 319 (1940)
Isfahani, Ashrafi, 384 (1982)
Jaurès, Jean-Joseph-Marie-Auguste, 298 (1914)
Jenson, Benton Franklin, 326 (1954)
John Paul II (Pope), 376 (1981), 377 (1981)
Jordan, Vernon E., Jr., 374 (1980)
Jumbat, Kamal, 365 (1977)
Jutaili, Hamad, 384 (1982)
Kacu'i, Muhammed, 378 (1981)
Kahane, Meir, 397 (1990)
Kahr, Gustav von, 315 (1934)
Kalak, Ezzedine, 369 (1978)
Kanchev, M., 291 (1902)
Kaplan, David, 398 (1992)
Kapuuo, Chief, 368 (1978)
Karami, Rashid, 392 (1987)
Karry, Heinz Herbert, 377 (1981)
Kassem, Abdul Karim, 331 (1963)
Kathov, Arkady, 390 (1985)
Kato, Takakira, 307 (1925)
Kawakami, Jotaro, 329 (1960)
Kayali, Abdul Wahhab, 370 (1978)
Kennedy, John Fitzgerald, 332 (1963)
Kennedy, Robert Francis, 337 (1968)
Ketteler, Klemens von, 289 (1900)
Khadir, Na'im, 378 (1981)
Khan, Liaquat Ali, 325 (1951)
Khan, Sadar Mohammed Daud, 328 (1957)
Khemisti, Mohammed, 331 (1963)
Kilpatrick, John, 334 (1965)
King, Martin Luther, 328 (1958), 337 (1968)
Kirov, Sergei Mironovich, 316 (1934)

Kishi, Nobusake, 330 (1960)
Lacaci, Gen. Guillermo, 387 (1984)
Lacerda, Carlos, 326 (1954)
Lago Roman, Gen. Victor, 384 (1982)
Landazabal Reyes, Gen. Gernando, 411 (1998)
Larach, Jacoobo Ramon, 381 (1982)
La Torre, Pio, 382 (1982)
Leguia y Salcedo, Augusto Bernardino, 311 (1930)
Letelier, Orlando, 364 (1976)
Liang-pi, 296 (1912)
Liebknecht, Karl, 301 (1919)
Lizzio, Giovanni, 398 (1992)
Lumumba, Patrice, 329 (1960), 330 (1960), 330 (1961)
Luxemburg, Rosa, 301 (1919)
Macapagal, Diosdado, 334 (1965)
Machado, Gerado, 312 (1931)
Madero, Francisco Indalecio, 297 (1913)
Madero, Gustavo, 297 (1913)
Mahmud Sevket Pasha, 298 (1913)
Majali, Hazza, 330 (1960)
Malcolm X (Malcolm Little), 333 (1965)
Mansour, Hassan Ali, 333 (1965)
Manzur, Gen. Abul, 378 (1981)
Mao Tse-tung, 327 (1956)
Maragoni, Luigi, 376 (1981)
Marcos, Imelda, 355 (1972)
Marzook, Mustafa, 382-83 (1982)
Mascone, Mayor George, 369 (1978)
Massaryk, Jan, 322 (1947)
Matawakkil, Yahya Mahmud al, 323 (1948)
Matteotti, Giacomo, 306 (1924)
Mbotela, Tom, 326 (1952)
Mboya, Tom, 341 (1969)
McAliskey, Bernadette Devlin, 375 (1981)
McKeague, John, 381 (1982)
McKinley, William, 290 (1901)
McMichael, Sir Harold, 321 (1944)
Mendez Lopez, Carlos Humberto, 377 (1981)
Meredith, James, 334 (1966)
Meyer, A. H., 341
Milk, Harvey, 369 (1978)
Mirbach, Count Wilhelm von, 301 (1918)
Mirbach, Lt.-Col. Andreas

Baron von, 361 (1975)
Miyazawa, Kiichi, 387 (1984)
Moawad, René, 394 (1989)
Mohammed, Gen. Murtala Ramat, 363 (1976)
Mondran, Dr. Eduardo, 339 (1969)
Moore, George C., 355 (1973)
Moro, Aldo, 368 (1978)
Morris, Percy, 388 (1984)
Moshin, Zuhair, 371-72 (1979)
Mpongosohe, Adolph, 385 (1982)
Mubarak, Hosni, 403-04 (1995)
Mugica, Angel Pascual, 382 (1982)
Munhangi, Joseph, 377 (1981)
Munro, Lt.-Comm. Ernest A., 336 (1968)
Mussolini, Benito, 321 (1945)
Nahhas, Mustafa, 318 (1937)
Narutowicz, Gabriel, 305 (1922)
Nasser, Gamal Abdel, 326 (1954)
Nazim Pasha, 297 (1913)
Neave, Airey, 371 (1979)
Nehru, (Pandit) Motilal, 326 (1955)
Ngini, Zola, 385 (1982)
Ngouabi, Marien, 365 (1977)
Nicholson, Arthur, 388 (1985)
Nittel, Heinz, 377 (1981)
Noel, Cleo A., 355 (1973)
Nurkrashy, Mahmoud, 324 (1948)
Nyaose, Petrus, 383 (1982)
Obregón, Alvaro, 309 (1927), 310 (1928)
O'Dwyer, Sir Michael Francis, 318 (1940)
O'Higgins, Kevin, 309 (1927)
Okada, Keisuke, 316-17 (1936)
Olympio, Sylvanus, 331 (1963)
Oneto, Tulio, 364 (1976)
Ortega y Gasset, Eduardo, 317 (1936)
Ortiz-Rubio, Pascual, 311 (1930)
Palma, Aturo Alessandro, 319 (1941)
Palme, Olaf, 390
Palomino Flores, Zenon, 383 (1982)
Papadoupolis, George, 338 (1968)
Papen, Franz von, 319 (1942)
Park Chung Hee, 372 (1979)
Paul I, 322 (1947)
Paul VI (Pope), 347 (1970)
Pearlman, Mark David, 375

Index

Yahya, Imam Ahmed Ibn, 330 (1961)

Zaim, Husni, 324 (1949)

Zahir Shah, Mohammed, 328 (1957)

Zeinati, Emir Mohammed, 322 (1946)

Zelea-Codreanu, Cornelius, 318 (1938)

Zimmermann, Ernst, 388 (1985)

Zog I, 312 (1931)

Zuaiter, Wael, 354 (1972)

Assay Building (New York, N. Y.), 304

Astarita, Mario, 369

ATF, 265, 266, 269

Atikat, Col. Atilla, 383

Atlanta Constitution, 69, 87

Atorthy, Mrs. M. C., 309

Atorthy, Minnie May, 309

Atrakchi, Albert, 389

Attica Prison (New York), 349

Atwood, Angela, 225

Auburn Prison (New York), 8, 310, 311

Audran, Gen. René, 388

Augsberg (Ger.) Police Station, 199-200

Aum Shinri Kyo (Supreme Truth, Japanese relious sect and terrorist group), 261-64, 402-03

Austin, Linda, 339

Austin, Tyrone, 339

Austin, William, 302

Austrian-Israel Friendship League, 377

Avianca Airlines (Col.), 394

Avila Camacho, Manuel, 321

Avolone, Hector, 117

Awadallah, Adel, 410-11

Ax Man of New Orleans, The, vii, 300, 301, 302, 303

Ayers, William, 182, 183

Azaval Avelar, Alfredo, 388

Azmanoff, Michael D., 353

Azikiwe, Nnamdi, 328

Baader, Berndt Andreas, 187, 188, 189, 190, 191, 192, 197, 198, 200, 201, 202, 205, 206, 207, 208, 215, 246, 335, 336, 344, 352, 353, 361, 366

Baader-Meinhof Commission, 201

Baader-Meinhof Gang (German terrorist group), viii, xi, 186, 187-208, 213, 217, 234, 240, 335, 336, 347, 349, 350, 351, 352, 353, 354, 360, 361, 363, 366, 367

Babler, Louis G., 336

Baby Doc, *See:* Duvalier, Jean-Claude

Baecher, Sgt. Werner, 132

Bakir Sidky Pasha, 318

Balbo, Italo, 95

Baldi, Stefano, 380

Baligand, Dr. Henry Albert von, 311

Balkar, Galip, 385

Ball, Ian, 358

Balmashov, S. V., 291

Bambrei, Terry Lee, 385

Bank of Rio de la Plata (Buenos Aires, Argen.), 356

Banna, Hasan al, 324

Bannerman, John, 123

Bante, Gen. Teferi, 365

Baratella, Mario, 356

Barazi, Ahmed al, 325

Barclay Hotel (Los Angeles, Calif.), 361

Baring, Sir Evelyn, 153

Barkley, Arthur, 345

Barnes, Peter, 318

Barnette, Horace D., 173

"Baron Semedi," 162

Barrella, Enrico, 355

Barrett, John J., 50-51

Barrow, William, 298

Barry, Marion, 227

Barsimantov, Yacov, 382

Barthou, Jean Louis, 316

Bartlett, "Soup," 28

Barz, Ingeborg, 195-96, 197-98

Bates, Clyde, 328

Batista, Fulgencio, 327, 328, 329, 330

Batuni Oath (Mau Mau secret oath), 151-52

Bavarian Mortgage and Exchange Bank (Kaiserslautern, Ger.), 196, 350

Beale, Mrs. Laura, 308

Bearden, Cody, 165-66, 330

Bearden, Leon, 165-66, 330

Beavers, Police Chief John, 70, 73

Bedell, Joshua, 392

Begin, Menachem, 231

Behesti, Ayatollah, 378

Beihl, Eugene, 347

Beirut International Airport, 1986

Belcastro, James (AKA: King of the Bombers), 90-92

Belfi, Judge Donald, 252, 253

Bell, Herman, 186

Bell, William, 306

Bell Federal Savings and Loan (Philadelphia, Pa.), 184, 185

Belon, Christian, 343

Bendicks, Leonard S., 167, 337

Bendy, Norris, 314

Benevides Moreno, Col. Guillermo, 397

Bennett, Joseph T., 352

Bennett, Keith, 333

Benson, Diana L., 369

Bentley, Alvin Morell, 326

Bentley, Sgt., 30

Benton, Leroy, 127, 321, 323

Berdella, Robert, 387

Berg, Alan, 265, 266, 387, 389, 393

Berkman, Alexander, 3, 50, 60, 61, 62, 181, 303

Berkowitz, David (AKA: Son of Sam), vii, 115, 338, 364, 365, 366

Berlin (Ger.) Telephone Co., 195

Bernadotte, Count Folkke, 324

Bernard, Mrs. John, 309

Berry, Pamela, 254

Besumer, Louis, 301

Betancourt, Romulo, 329

Betancourt Gueto, Angel, 334

Bevens, Clifford, 375

Bevin, Ernest, 140, 322

Bhindranwale, Sant Jarnail Singh, 380

Bhutto, Zulfikar Ali, 371

Bianchi, Kenneth (AKA: Hillside Strangler), 367-68, 370, 386-87

Bielak, John, 122

Big Brother, Inc. Airlines, 349

Billings, Warren Knox, 49, 50, 51, 52, 53, 54, 299

Billington, Dr. J. Jeff, 126

Bilson, Stephen W., 373-74

bin Laden, Osama, 286-288, 412

Bingham, Police Commissioner Theodore (New York), 22

Binh Nguyen, Thai, 353

Biondo, Lorenzo, 56, 58

Biondo, Pasquale, 56, 57, 58

Birdal, Akin, 411

Birdzell, Donald T., 143, 144

Birger, Charles, 309

Birth of a Nation, The (film), 75, 80

Bir ad Dawim (Libyan terrorist camp), 240

Bishop, Cameron David, 340

Bishop, Maurice, 386

Bitterman, Chester A., III, 375

BLA (Black Liberation Army, U. S. terrorst group), 186, 348

Black, Irma, 128, 129, 321-22

"Black Codes," 67

Black Dragon Society (Japanese criminal organization and terrorist group), 258, 259, 305-06,

Linea Aeropostal, 329 (1960)
London, Eng., 354 (1972), 355 (1973), 357 (1973), 358 (1974), 380 (1981), 383 (1982), 386 (1983), 387 (1984), 396 (1990), 397 (1991), 398 (two entries, 1992)
Londonderry, Ire., 377 (1981)
Los Angeles, Calif., 295 (1910), 328 (1957)
Lowell, Mass., 362 (1975)
Lynchburg, Va., 372 (1979)
Madison, Wis., 346 (1970)
Madrid, Spain, 377 (1981)
Manila, Philippines, 384 (1982), 395 (1989)
Medellín, Col., 397 (1991)
Meridian, Miss., 334 (1966)
Milan, Italy, 342 (1969), 401 (1993)
Montreal, Can., 331 (1963), 339-40 (1969), 352 (1972)
Moscow, U. S. S. R., 376 (1981)
Munich, Ger., 343 (1970), 374 (1980), 376 (1981)
Nairobi, Kenya (plane explosion), 369 (1978), 375 (1980)
Naples, Italy (plane explosion), 374 (1980), 393 (1988)
National Airlines, 329 (1960)
New Delhi, Ind., 389 (1985)
Newport, Ky., 376 (1981)
New York, N. Y., 294 (1908), 304, (1920), 319 (1940), 325 (1950), 326 (1953), 351 (1972), 363 (1975), 377-78 (1981), 399 (World Trade Center bombing, 1993)
Newry, Ire., 378 (1981)
North Caldwell, N. J., 402 (1994)
Oklahoma City, Okla., 403 (1995)
Pan Am (Flight 103), 394 (1988)
Paris, Fr., 336 (1968), 373 (1980), 379 (1981), 383 (1982), 386 (1983), 390 (1986), 391-92 (1986), 404 (1995)
Philippines Airlines, 324 (first bombing of a commercial plane, 1949), 344 (1970), 345 (1970), 361 (1975), 369 (1978)
Phoenix, Ariz., 363 (1976)
Pretoria, S. Afr., 385-86 (1983)
Quebec, Can., 334 (1966)
Quincy, Ill., 364 (1976)
Ramallah, West Bank, 410 (1998)
Ramstein, Ger., 379 (1981)
Rangoon, Burma, 386 (1983)
Riga, Latvia, 411 (1998)
Rome, Italy, 358 (1973), 401 (1993)
Rostock, Ger., 398 (1992)
Sacramento, Calif., 390 (1985), 403 (1995)
St. Stephen's, S. C., 373 (1979)
Salisbury, Rhodesia, 367 (1977), 381 (1981)
San Francisco, Calif., 299 (1916)
Savannah, Ga., 395 (1989)
Shiraz, Iran, 370 (1978)
Sidon, Lebanon, 379 (1981)
Sri Lanka, 392 (1987)
Stateline, Nev., 374 (1980)
Suchitoto, El Salvador, 376 (1981)
Swedish Airlines, 351 (1972)
Swissair, 343 (1970)
Teheran, Iran, 376 (1981), 378 (1981), 379 (1981), 381 (1982), 383 (1982), 384 (two entries, 1982)
Tel Aviv, Israel, 347 (1970), 353 (Lod Airport, 1972), 368 (1978), 407 (1997)
Thailand (airplane explosion), 397 (1991)
Transvaal, S. Afr., 390 (1985)
Tripoli, Leb., 389 (1985), 393 (1988)
Tyre, Lebanon, 378 (1981)
TWA, 359 (1974), 391 (1986), 405-06 (1996?), 408 (1996?)
United States, 334 (five Yugoslavian consulates, 1966)
University of California, 401 (1993)
Vienna-Passau Express train, Hung., 312 (1931)
Washington, D. C., 302 (1919), 364 (1976)
Wuhan, China, 409-10 (1998)
Yugoslavian Airlines, 351 (1972)
Zaragoza, Spain, 355 (1972)
Zrariyeh, Leb., 379 (1981)
Zugdidi, Georgia (Russia), 411 (1998)
Bonaccorsi, Arconovaldo, 98, 100
Bond, Stanley, 184
Bonner, Capt. Clyde, 199
Bonnet, Jules Joseph, 34-39, 296
Bonus Army, 313
Booker, Betty Jo, 129, 322
Booth, Byron V., 339
Booth, David, 342
Booth, John Wilkes, 5
Bor, Leon (Leonid Borshevsky), 255-56, 404
Borah, William E., 15
Borel, Eric, 256-57, 404
Borges Guerra, Juan M., 349
Borgio, Rosario, 55-56, 58, 301
Borgnine, Ernest, 23
Boring, Floyd, 144
Boris III (czar of Bulgaria), 307, 319, 320
Born, Jorge, 359-60
Born, Juan, 359-60
Bornancini, Raul, 357
Borquez, Israel, 380
Borsellino, Paolo, 398
Boston Globe, 133
Botha, P. W., 390
Bottom, Anthony, 186
Boudia, Mohammed, 240, 356
Boudiaf, Mohammed, 398
Boudine, Kathy, 182
Bourassa, Robert, 218
Bovone, Domenico, 98
Bowers, Sam H., Jr., 171, 172, 173, 332, 333
Bowyer, Eric, 153
Boxers (Chinese terrorist organization), 159
Boyd, Inspector Frank R., 117
Boyd, Richard K., 334
Boynton, James, 167, 336
BPR, *See:* Popular Revolutionary Bloc
Bradley, Fred, 12, 15, 292
Brady, Ian, *See:* Moors Murderers
Brady, James, 376
Branch Davidians (U.S. religious sect), 266, 267, 273, 399, 400
Brandeis, Supreme Court Justice Louis, 408
Brandeis University, 184
Brando, Marlon, 192
Brandt, Willy, 197
Brazil (film), 270, 271
Breakout (film), 361
Bremer, Arthur, 353
Brent, William L., 340
Bresci, Gaetano, 3, 289
Brewster, Walter, 298
Brewton, James W., 352
Brick Moron, *See:* Nixon, Robert
Bridge and Structural Iron Workers Union, 41
Bridges, Jeff, 272
Brimicombe, Francis Victor, 356
British-American Tobacco Co., 356
British European Airlines, 325
Britt, Bruce, 330

Esau, Alexander, 366
Esebua, Gocha, 411
Eshkol, Levi, 336
Eselius brothers, 46, 47
Esparragoza, Father Gregorio, 308
Esposito, Joseph (AKA: Diamond Joe), 90, 91
Essawai, Salim K., 341
Esenboga Airport (Ankara, Turkey), 383
Esters, Silas, 290
ETA (Euzkadi Ta Azkatazuna-Basque Homeland and Liberation/Basque Fatherland and Liberty Group), 347, 376, 381, 390
Etheridge, Henry, 296
Ethiopian Airlines, 355
Euzkadi Ta Azkatazuna-Basque Homeland and Liberation, *See:* ETA
Evans, Edward, 333
Evans, Hiram Wesley, 79, 87
Evers, Lt.-Col. C. P., 134
Evers, Medgar W., 332
Evin Prison (Teheran, Iran), 378
Ewart-Biggs, Christopher, 240, 364
Exchange Building (Houndsditch, London, Eng.), 29, 296
Exodus (film), 142
Exxon Oil Co., 276, 357
Exxon-Valdez Oil Spill, 276
FAA, 247, 249, 282
Fain, Capt. Grover C., 312
Faircloth, Diane, 274
Faisal III (king of Iraq), 328
Faisal (king of Saudi Arabia), 361
Faisal (prince of Saudi Arabia; Faisal Bin Musaed Bin Abdulaziz), 361
FAL (Frente Argentino de Liberacion, Argentine terrorist group), 343-44
Falk, Arno, 250
Fallon, George Hyde, 326
FAP, *See:* Fuerzas Armadas Peronistas
FAR, *See:* Fuerzas Armadas Rebeldes
Farabundo Marti National Liberation Front (FMLN, El Salvadoran terrorist group), 371, 394
Faraday, David, 339
Fard, Wallace D., 220
FARL (Lebanese Armed Revolutionary Faction, Lebanese terrorist group), 381, 391

Farooq, Maulvi Mohammed, 396
Farouk (King of Egypt), 230, 233
Farrakhan, Louis, 228
Farran, Rex Francis, 140, 323
Farran, Capt. Roy Alexander, 140, 323
Fasci di Combattimento, 93
Fassnacht, Robert, 346
Fatah, See: Al Fatah
Fataier, Ibrahim Abdelatif, 244-45
Fatemi, Hussein, 325
Faust, Reinhold, 300
FBI (U.S. Federal Bureau of Investigation), vii, 61, 127, 166, 172, 173, 182, 227, 248, 250, 265, 266, 267, 270, 275-76, 277, 278-79, 282, 283, 284, 340, 384, 389, 395, 400, 402, 403, 404, 405, 406, 407, 408, 411
FBI Headquarters (Washington, D.C.), 277
Fedayeen (Middle Eastern terrorist group), 344
Federal Aviation Administration, See: FAA
Federal Bureau of Investigation, *See:* FBI
Federation of the Russian Workers, 60
Federzoni, Luigi, 97
Fergerstrom, Harry S., 334
Ferguson, Colin, 252-54, 255, 282, 401, 405
Fhimah, Lamen Khalifa, 250
Fiaschetti, Lt. Michael, 57-58
Fiat Co., 352
Fickert, Charles, 52, 53
15th of May Arab Movement for the Liberation of Palestine (Middle Eastern terrorist group), 381
55 Days at Peking (film), 289
Filippelli, Filippo, 96, 97, 98
Fine, David S., 346
Finkelstein, Ida, 290
Finlay, James, 348
Finney, Michael R., 350
Finzi, Aldo, 96
Firestone Co., 356
First National Bank of Boston (Rosario, Argen.), 356
First National City Bank of New York (Córdorba, Argen.), 357
Fisher, Charles, 298
Fitilechi, Hadi Alavai, 379
Fitts, Henry, 297
Fitzgerald, Judge Richard J., 157-58
Fitzgerald, Tasmin, 339
Fitzmorris, Charles C., 91

Five Points Gang, 19, 27
Flamourides, George (AKA: G. Paravolidakis), 339
Flight 103 (Pan-Am), 245, 247-50, 287, 394
Flight 800 (TWA), 282-84, 405-06
Flight 840 (TWA), 247, 391
Flight 847 (TWA), 247, 389
FLQ (Front du Liberation du Quebec, Canadian terrorist group), 217-19, 331, 334, 339-40, 346-47
Fluke, Mrs. Mabel, 308
Fly, Claude L., 345-46
Flynn, William J., 61, 62
FMLN, See: Farabundo Marti National Liberation Front
Foggi, Giovanni, 378
Folsom Prison (Calif.), 50, 53
Fonseca, Mario Velasquez, 167, 337
Foran, Thomas, 179
Ford, Gerald Rudolph, 362
Ford Motor Co., 313 (Dearborn, Mich.), 356 (Buenos Aires, Argen.), 357 (Córdoba, Argen.)
Formby, Nina, 71
Forrest, Gen. Nathan Bedford, 65, 66, 68
Forsyth, Frederick, 216
Fort, John F., 294
Fortier, Lori, 273
Fortier, Michael, xii, 269, 270, 272, 273
Fort Benning (Ga.), 269
Fort Bragg (N. C.), 243
Fort Devens (Mass.), 137-38
Fort DuPont (Del.), 133
Fort Leavenworth (Kan.), 136
Fort McPherson (Ga.), 137
Fort Riley (Kan.), 269
Foster, George, 4, 5
Foster, Gregory, 186
Foster, Marcus, 221-22, 224, 225, 357
Fountain, Dower, 291
14K Association (Triad society), 160
Fox, Jim, 309
Fox, Mark, 309
Fragosa Carmona, Antonio Oscar de, 313
France Embassy, Beirut, Leb., 382
Francis Ferdinand (Franz Ferdinand, archduke of Aust.), 298
Franco, Francisco, 317
Frank, Leo Max, 69-78, 171, 297, 299
Frank, Lucille, 70, 72, 77

Gunduz, Orhan R., 382
Gungor, Kani, 382
Guns and Ammo Magazine, 270
Gunther, Cpl. Horst, 136-37, 321
Gutzman Reynoso, Abimael, 399
Haarmann, Fritz (AKA: Ogre of Hanover), vii, 306-07
Haase, Hugo, 303
Habash, George, 240, 342
Habash Front (Arab terrorist group), 337, 338, 340, 342, 346, 351
Habibollah Khan, 301
Hafex, Abd Rabb Enabi, 236
Haganah, 139, 140
Hägglund, Joel Emmanuel, *See:* Hill, Joe
Hägglund, Olaf, 45
Hahn, Maria, 310
Haig, Gen. Alexander, 371
Haile-Mariam, Lt.-Col. Mengistu, 397
Hajjaj, Riyad Kamal, 335
Hale, Calvin, 290
Hale, Frank, 290
Hale, James, 290
Hale, Martin, 290
Hall, Camilla, 224, 225, 359
Hall-Mills Murder Case, 117
Hamadi, Mohammed Ali, 389
Hamaguchi, Yoko, 312
Hamas (Middle Eastern terrorist group), 403, 408, 409, 410-11
Hamdan, Ibrahim Nasser, 384
Hamid, Adnan, 369
Hamilton, Benny R., 342
Hamilton, Wade, 53
Hammami (Hamami), Said, 368
Hammer, Michael Peter, 375
Hampton, Fred, 185-86
Hampton, Peter, 290
Hanafi Moslems (U. S. terrorist group), xi, 226-28, 365, 366
Haneman, Frederick W., 352
Hangar, Off. Charles, 267
Hannan, Thomas M., 367
Hanselbauer Inn (Lake Wiesee, Ger.), 110
Hansen, Michael L., 352
Hanrahan, Edward V., 185-86
Hapsburg Empire, 112
Hara, Takashi (Hei Hara), 304
Harding, Warren G., 175
Hardwick, Ernest, 289
Hariri, Hussein Ali, 392
Harpin, Mrs. Germania, 309
Harrelson, Charles B., 371
Harriman, Joseph, 40, 43
Harris, Anthony, 225
Harris, Emily, 224
Harris, William, 224

Harrison, Carter (Mayor of Chicago), 8
Harrods Department Store (London, Eng.), 386
Hart, Brooke, 314
Hart, Len, 305
Harvard University, 279, 280
Harvey, Judge Alexander H. II, 169
Harvey, George U., 116
Harvey's Casino (Stateline, Nev.), 374
Hashemi-Nejad, Hojatoleslam Abdulkarim, 379
Hauser, Col. Harold, 333
Hauser, Siegfried, 206
Havrill, Jim, 123
Hawaiian Airlines, 334
Hawkins, Lt.-Col. Lewis, 356
Hawley, James H., 15
Hawthorne, Alice, 284
Hawtree, Stephen, 157, 354
Hay, Clyde C., 361
Hayden, Tom, 178, 179, 180, 342, 343
Haymarket Riot (Chicago, Illinois), 5
Hayn, Hans, 111
Hays, Bennie Jack, 174
Hays, Henry Francis, 174, 387
Hayward, William Dudley (AKA: Big Bill), 9-16, 42, 43, 46, 47, 48, 50, 61, 292
Heady, Rob D., 353
Healy, David, 167
Hearst, Patricia Campbell, 220-24, 358, 359
Hearst, William Randolph, Jr., 221
Heathrow Airport (London, Eng.), 247
Heaven and Earth Society (Triad society and terrorist group), 159
Heavenly Blessing Association (Jap. cult), 264
Hebrew University, 139
Hefez, Fawzi Abdul, 235
Heines, Edmund, 108, 110, 111
Heisler, Lawrence D., 334
Hell Gate Plant (Consolidated Edison, N.Y.), 146
Helmey, Robert M., 339
Henderson, Ian, 155-56
Henderson, John, 290
Hendry, Ruby, 85, 305
Hennessey, Police Chief David, 25
Hensley, Dep. Zeke, 128
Hernandez, Manuel, 328
Hernandez Leyva, Rogelio, 337

Hernandez Martinez, Gen. Maximiliano, 334
Hester, Robert S., 385
Heston, Charlton, 289
Heydebreck, Hans Peter von, 111
Heydrich, Reinhard, 319
Hezbollah, See: Hizbollah
Hibernia Bank (San Francisco, Calif.), 224
Higashivama, Hirosato, 387
Hildebrant, Alex, 330
Hill, Charles R., 350
Hill, Gerald J., 372-73
Hill, Joe (Joel Emmanuel Hägglund; AKA: Joe Hillstrom), 45-48, 50, 298, 299
Hillside Strangler, See: Bianchi, Kenneth
Hillstrom, Joe, See: Hill, Joe
Himmler, Heinrich, 102, 108, 110, 133, 245, 315, 319
Hinckley, John W., Jr., 376
Hindley, Myra, See: Moors Murderers
Hines, Walter C., 347
Hiranuma, Baron Kichiro, 319
Hirobumi, Ito, 295
Hirohito (Emperor of Jap.), 305-06, 307, 310, 312, 313, 317, 319, 409
Hirsch, Phoebe, 182
Hirsch, Rebecca, 116, 311
Hitchcock, Alfred, 34, 308
Hitler, Adolf, x, 100, 101-104, 106, 107, 108, 110, 111, 131, 134, 138, 187, 256, 272, 311, 315, 318
Hizbollah (Hezbollah, Hizballah, Party of God, Iranian terrorist group), 247, 283
Hoehler, Ali, 104, 105, 311
Hoff, Dierk Ferdinand, 198
Hoffa, James, 331
Hoffman, Abbie, 176, 178, 179, 180, 338, 342, 343
Hoffman, Judge Julius, 179, 180, 342, 343
Hogan, Ernest, 290
Hogan, Tom, See: Orchard, Harry
Holbert, Luther, 292
Holden, George, 302
Holder, William, 353
Ho Lien-Siu, 335
Holleben, Ehrenfried von, 345
Holmes, John Maurice, 314-15
Holmes, Justice Oliver Wendell, 72
Holt, Everett L., 350
Holyfield, D. Q., 254
Homann, Peter, 192-93
Hood, Sheriff, 313

group), 347
Jihad Command (Al-Jihad Al Mudaddas Front, Lebanese terrorist group), 376
Jihaz el-Rasd, 214
Jo Goldenberg Restaurant (Paris, Fr.), 383
John Paul II (Pope), 376, 377
Johnny's Tire Co. (Oklahoma City, Okla.), 273
Johns, Cloudsley, 50
Johnson, Collins, 300
Johnson, D. C., 300
Johnson, Florence, 317, 318
Johnson, Jack R., 362
Johnson, Lyndon Baines, 175
Johnson, Raymond, Jr., 338
Johnson, Samuel, Jr., 392
Johnson, Sonja, 367
Johnson, Susie, 292
Johnson, Wesley, 317
Johnston, Walter, 297
Jones, Jeff, 182
Jones, "Judge," 295
Jones, Michael Gordon, 345
Jones, Stephen, 273
Jones, Tommy Lee, 272
Jones Act (U.S.), 142
Jordan, James E., 173
Jordan, Vernon E., Jr., 374
Jordano, Frank, 302
José Simeón Caias University, 394
Joyce, Thomas, 63
Joyu, Hirofumi, 261
J. P. Morgan Company, 63, 304
Jumbat, Kamal, 365
Jumblatt, Walid, 384
Junior's Lunch Cafe (Lynchburg, Va.), 372
Junschke, Klaus, 196-97, 350
Justice Commandos of the Armenian Genocide (JCAG, Armenian terrorist group), 382, 383
Jutaili, Hamad, 384 (1982)
Kacu'i, Muhammed, 378
Kaczynski, David, 278, 279, 281, 411
Kaczynski, Theodore (Unabomber), vii, viii, xii, 275-82, 390, 401, 404, 405, 409, 411
Kaczynski, Theodore R., 279
Kaczynski, Wanda, 278, 279, 281
Kagan, Alfred R., 372
Kahane, Meir, 397, 405
Kahr, Gustav von, 111, 315
Kalak, Ezzedine, 369
Kalil, Kafr, See: Walid, Abu
Kamau, Johnstone, See: Kenyatta, Jomo

Kanafani, Ghassan, 353
Kanchev, M., 291
Kansas City, Mo., Police Department, 127
Kansi, Mir Aimal, 407
Kant, Immanuel, 280
Kaplan, David, 398
Kapuuo, Chief, 368
Karami, Rashid, 392
Karim, Surgeon-General, 236
Karry, Heinz Herbert, 377
Kasavubu, Joseph, 330
Kassem (Qassim), Gen. Abdul Karim, 328, 331
Kastin, Elissa, 367
Kathov, Arkady, 390
Kato, Takakira, 307
KAU, See: Kenyan African Union
Kaufholf Department Store, 190
Kavaja, Nikola, 371
Kawakami, Jotaro, 329
Kayali, Abdul Wahhab, 370
KCA, See: Kikuyu Central Association
Keenan, Brian, 396
Keenan, Rosemary, 364
Kelbach, Walter, 335
Kelkal, Khaled, 257, 404
Keller, Helen, 47
Kelly, Alice, 148
Kelly, Gerard, 391
Kennedy, Carolyn, 164
Kennedy, Jackie, 164
Kennedy, John Fitzgerald, 164, 166, 170, 332, 340
Kennedy, John, Jr., 164, 171
Kennedy, Michael, 183
Kennedy, Robert Francis, 171, 337
Kennedy Airport, 377, 378
Kent State University, 184, 344
Kenya Civil Service Agency, 150
Kenya Teacher's College, 150
Kenya-Uganda Railroad, 150
Kenyan African Union (KAU), 150-51, 152, 155, 156
Kenyatta, Jomo (Johnstone Kamau), 150-51, 153, 155, 156, 326
Keppel, Rafael, 372
Kerkow, Katherine, 353
Kerr, Andrew, 28
Ketteler, Kelmens von, 289
Kettner, Franz, 135-36
Key, Mayor James, 83
KGB (secret police and intelligence service of U.S.S.R.), 376, 402
Khaalis, Haamas Abdul (Ernest Timothy McGhee), 226-28, 365, 366

Khadir, Khalifa, 381
Khadir, Na'im, 378
Khalaf, Salah, See: Iyad, Abu
Khaled, Abdel Rahim, 244
Khaled, Leila, 341, 346
Khaled, Nasser Mohammed Ali Abu, 366
Khalid (King of Saudi Arabia), 216
Khalifa, Monzer, 214
Khan, Liaquat Ali, 325
Khan, Sadar Mohammed Daud, 328
Khemisti, Mohammed, 331
Khomeini, Ayatollah Ruhollah, ix, 233, 236, 370
Kidnappings (victims of political terrorists)
Anderson, Terry, 388 (1985)
Arambaru, Pedro Eugenio, 345 (1970)
Azaval Avelar, Alfredo, 388 (1985)
Baratella, Mario, 356 (1973)
Barrella, Enrico, 355 (1972)
Beihl, Eugene, 347 (1970)
Bevens, Clifford, 375 (1980)
Bluff, Hermann, 342 (1969)
Boisset, Yves, 358 (1973)
Bornancini, Raul, 357 (1973)
Brimicombe, Francis Victor, 356 (1973)
Bucher, Giovanni Enrico, 347 (1970)
Cambron, Alfredo, 348-49 (1971)
Camarena Salazar, Enrique, 388 (1985)
Castel, Oscar, 356 (1973)
Castrejon Diez, Jaime, 350 (1971)
Christensen, Ward, 355 (1973)
Cordero Febres, Leon, 392 (1987)
Cross, James Richard, 346 (1970)
Crowley, Lt.-Col. Donald J., 343-44 (1970)
DaCruz, Anthony R., 356 (1973)
Dias Gomide, Aloisio Mares, 345 (1970)
Dozier, Gen. James Lee, 380 (1981)
Draper, Morris, 345 (1970)
Elbrick, Charles Burke, 341 (1969)
Fly, Claude L., 345-46 (1970)
Galvez, Roberto, 356 (1973)
Gebhardt, Hans Kurt, 356 (1973)

Gernando, 411
Lance, Myron, 335
Lane, David, 266, 389, 393
Lanford, Chief of Det. Newport, 70
Lang, Fritz, 298, 315
LaPoint, Richard C., 351
Laporte, Pierre, 217-18, 346-47
Larach, Jacoobo Ramon, 381
Latin Quarter (Paris, Fr.), 257
Latito, Frank, 290
Laumann, Sarah, 303
Laun, Alfred Albert III, 358
Lauria, Donna, 364, 365
Laurie, Rocco, 186
Lavin, Belle, 52
Leach, Kimberly, 394
League of Nations, 319
Leatherheads, *See:* NOCS
Lebanese Armed Revolutionary Faction, *See:* FARL
Lebowitz, Judge Samuel, 148
Lebron, Lolita, 326
Lee, Rev. George W., 327
Lee, Irwin, 123
Lee, Newt, 69-70
Lee, Reginald Arthur, 311-12
Leeson, Sgt., 32
Legget, Leslie, 305
Leguia y Salcedo, Augusto Bernardino, 311
Lemiuex, 217, 218
Lenin, 16, 191, 319
Lenzen, Louise, 310
Leonhardy, Terrance G., 356
Leopold, Nathan, 44
Lepine, Marc, 395
Lerch, Gen. Archer L., 133
LeRoy, Mervyn, 299
Letelier, Orlando, 364
Levi, Joseph, 29
Levy, Lisa, 394
Lewis, Austin, 50
Leyraud, Jérome, 397
Leyva, Rogelio Hernandez, 168
Liang-pi, 296
Liberation Tigers of Tamil Eelam (LTTE, terrorist group in Sri Lanka), 391
Libyan Embassy, East Berlin, Ger., 391
Libyan Airlines, 355, 385
Libyan Secret Service (Libyan terrorist organization), 387
Liebknecht, Karl, 301
Liles, Panta Lou, 126-27, 321
Lincoln, Abraham, 4
Lipperheide, Jose, 381
Lippert, Michael, 111
Little, Frank, 300
Little, Russell, 222, 224, 358

Little, William, 302
Lizzio, Giovanni, 398
Lo Bianco, Antonio, 338
Locci, Barbara, 338
Lockett, Pig, 312
Locklear, Mrs. J. M., 290
Lod Airport (Tel Aviv, Israel), 213-14, 353
Loeb, Richard, 44
Lombardo, Albert, 115
Lomino, Joanne, 364-65
London Daily Mail, 34
London (Eng.) Stock Exchange, 396
London Times, 250
Londone y Londone, Fernando, 345 (1970)
López Alverez, Raul, 388
Looting
    Baltimore, Md., 337 (1968)
    Boston, Mass., 303 (1919)
    Buffalo, N. Y., 365 (1977)
    Callera, Peru, 383 (1982)
    Chicago, Ill., 337 (1968)
    Cincinnati, Ohio, 337 (1968)
    Galveston, Tex., 289 (1900)
    Messina, Sicily, 294-95 (1908)
    Mogadishu, 399 (1993)
    Nagoya, Jap., 329 (1959)
    San Francisco, Calif., 293 (1906)
    Washington, D. C., 337 (1968)
Lorenz, Peter, 205, 361
Lorre, Peter, 34, 298
Lortie, Bernard, 219
Lover's Lane Murderer of Texarkana (Tex.), 128-30, 321-22
Los Angeles Airport, 277
Los Angeles Library, 360
Los Angeles Slasher (Skid Row Slasher), See: Greenwood, Vaughn
Los Angeles Times, 40
Los Angeles Times Building, 40, 41, 45, 50, 295
Loust, LAPD Sgt. Charles, 226
Lowe, Mrs. Harriet, 301
Luciano, Charles (AKA: Lucky), 24
Luddites (U. K. religious sect), 277
Ludendorff, Gen. Erich, 101
Lufthansa Airlines, 207, 246, 351, 354-55, 367, 372
Lugo Casado, Angel, 349
Luis, Crown Prince (Portugal), 294
Luka, Chief, 155
Lumumba, Patrice, 329, 330
Luongo, Judge Alfred, 185

Lupo, Salvatore, 366
Lupo the Wolf, *See:* Saietta, Ignazio
Luther, Angela, 200, 205
Luxemburg, Rosa (AKA: Red Rosa), 301
Lynch, Kevin, 391
Lynchings (victims burned, hanged, shot)
    Allen, Walter, 291 (1902)
    Anderson, Simon, 295 (1909)
    Armwood, George, 314 (1933)
    Barrow, William, 298 (1913)
    Bell, William, 306 (1924)
    Bendy, Norris, 314 (1933)
    Blackman, David, 310 (1928)
    Blackman, Lee, 310 (1928)
    Blazes, Albert, 308 (1926)
    Brooks and Lowndes counties, Ga., 300 (eleven blacks, 1918)
    Brown, Jeff, 299 (1916)
    Caleaway, James, 289 (1900)
    Carr, William, 293 (1906)
    Chaney, James, 332 (1964)
    Cheek, Cord, 315 (1933)
    Clark, Elijah, 289 (1900)
    Clark, Tom. 291 (1902)
    Coe, Joe, 303 (1919)
    Coleman, Lindsay, 307 (1925)
    Criggs, John, 315 (1934)
    Crutchfield, William, 290 (1901)
    Dahmer, Vernon, 334 (1966)
    Dorsey, George, 322 (1946)
    Duluth, Minn., 303, (three blacks, 1920)
    Emelle, Ala., 311 (two whites, four blacks, 1930)
    Esters, Silas, 290 (1901)
    Etheridge, Henry, 296 (1912)
    Fisher, Charles, 298 (1914)
    Fitts, Henry, 297 (1912)
    Fox, Jim, 309 (1927)
    Fox, Mark, 309 (1927)
    Frank, Leo Max, 299 (1915)
    Gardner, Wilson, 298 (1913)
    Gay, George, 305 (1922)
    Goodman, Andrew, 332 (1964)
    Grier, William, 299 (1914)
    Guer, James, 289 (1900)
    Hale, Calvin, 290 (1901)
    Hale, Frank, 290 (1901)
    Hale, James, 290 (1901)
    Hale, Martin, 290 (1901)
    Hart, Len, 305 (1923)
    Hemphill, Tex., 294 (nine blacks, 1908)
    Henderson, John, 290 (1901)
    Hilliard, 295 (1909)
    Holbert, Luther, 292 (1904)

Marston, Thomas K., 348
Martin, Ian, 357
Martin, Kimberly, 367-68
Martin, Oscar, 299
Martin, Paul, 129, 322
Marx, Joseph (AKA: Jacob Vogel), 32, 33, 296
Marzook, Mustafa, 382-83
Masaryk, Jan, 322
Mascone, Mayor George, 369, 371
Mashaal, Khalid, 409
Mason, Noble B., 339
Massie Murder Case, 44
Mathu, Eliud, 150
Matrisciano, George (AKA: Martini), 28
Matsch, Judge Richard, 273
Matteotti, Giacomo, 94-98, 306, 307
Matthews, John M., 348
Matthews, Robert, 266
Matuschka, Sylvestre, viii, 112-14, 312, 313, 314
Mau Mau, x, 149-57, 325-26, 327-28, 341, 354
Mauriot, Nadine, 389
Maximo Mena Command (splinter Argentine terrorist group of MANO), 354
May, Catherine, 115, 117
Mayer, Norman, 384-85
Maze Prison, 376
Mazzano, Guiseppe, 56
Mbotela, Tom, 153, 326
Mboya, Tom, 341
McAdoo, Police Commissioner William (New York), 22
McAliskey, Bernadette Devlin, 375, 376
McAliskey, Michael, 375
McAlroy, Patrick H., 351
McArthur, Gen. Douglas, 313, 323
McBride, Bill, 168, 338
McCarthy, Carolyn, 254
McCarthy, John, 397
McCarthy, Kevin, 254
McCarthy, Timothy J., 376
McCloud, Andrew, 315
McConnell, Mrs. Mary, 309
McCoy, Richard F., 352
McCreery, John S., 341
McCutcheon, Sam, 128
McDonald, John, 52, 53, 54
McElroy, Kenneth Rex, 378-79
McElwaine, Seamus, 391
McGhee, Ernest Timothy, *See:* Khaalis, Haamas Abdul
McGowan, Wilder, 318
McHugh, Dr. Frank E., 46-47
McIlherron, Jim, 300

McKeague, John, 381
McKinley, William, ix, 1-8, 60, 290
McKinney, Diane V., 344
McKinney, Irene, 370
McKnight, Minola, 71
McLaughlin, Judge Walter, 185
MacLeod, Ian, 203-04
McManigal, Ortie, 41-42
McMichael, Sir Harold, 321
McMilan, Alex, 377-78
McNair, Jean, 354
McNair, Melvin, 354
McNally, Martin J., 353
McNamara, James, 41, 42, 43, 44, 50, 295
McNamara, John J., 41, 42, 43, 44, 50, 295
McNamara brothers, ix, 43, 45, 61
McNutt, Maxwell, 50-51
McParland, James, 13
McPeek, Kenneth E., 339
McSwiggin, William H., 308
McVeigh, Jennifer, 271
McVeigh, Timothy James (AKA: T. Tuttle), viii, xii, 267-74, 403, 407, 408
Means, Col. A. H., 136
Medellín (Col.) Drug Cartel, 393, 397
Medina Perez, Luis, 334
Meeks, Ira D., 344
Meese, Edwin, 243
Meiklejohn, Commander, 153
Meinhof, Ulrike, 187-88, 189, 191-92, 193, 194, 195, 197, 198, 199, 203, 204, 205, 206-07, 215, 234, 335, 336-37, 344, 352, 353, 354, 360, 361, 366
Meins, Holger, 194, 198, 200, 201-202, 204, 349, 353
Mein Kampf (My Struggle, book), 101
Mellon, Jim, 182
Mendez Lopez, Carlos Humberto, 377
Mendoza, Benjamin, 347
Menoni, Hector, 354
Menschner, Sgt. Edgar, 136
Merchants and Manufacturers Association, 40
Meredith, James, 331, 334
Merrion Square (Dublin, Ire.), 240
Mesa Cabrera, Silvio, 374
Metesky, George Peter (AKA: Mad Bomber), viii, 146-48, 319, 325, 326, 357
Metropolitan Cathedral (San Salvador), 371
Metropolitan Opera House (New

York), 21
Mexican Embassy, El Salvador, 370
Meyer, A. H., 341
Meyer, Horst, 386
Meyers, Mrs. Blanche, 309
Mezzano, Vito, 58
Michigan Militia, 273
Michigan Patriots, 269, 272
Middle East Airways, 366
Migash-Israel Restaurant (Berlin, Ger.), 381
Migliorini, Antonella, 383
Mikdad, Hussein, 283
Milburn, John G., 6
Miles, Tom, 296
Military Sports Group Hoffman (Wehrsportsgruppe), 374
Milk, Harvey, 369, 371
Milledgeville Prison Farm (Ga.), 74, 75, 76, 299
Miller, Fred, 14
Miller, Jim (AKA: The Killer), 295
Miller, Judith M., 367
Milstein, Luba, 31
Mine Owners Association, 12, 292
Mineo, Sal, 142
Mirbach, Lt.-Col. Andreas Baron von, 205, 361
Mirbach, Count Wilhelm von, 301
Mirror Worlds (book), 276
Mitchell, Gov. Sir Philip, 150
Mitrione, Daniel A., 345
Miyazaki, Kunjii, 408-09
Miyazawa, Kiichi, 387
M-19 (Moviemiento Abril 19/April 19 Movement, Colombian terrorist group), 373
Moawad, René, 394
MOBE (National Mobilization to End the War), 175, 178
Mohammed, Gen. Murtala Ramat, 363
Mohammad, Messenger of God (film), 227, 365
Mohr, Fuentes, 343
Molina, Nelson, 344
Moller, Irmgard, 200
Molly McGuires, 13
Molqi, Yussef Magid, 244-45, 390
Mondran, Dr. Eduardo, 339
Monster of Dusseldorf, *See:* Kürten, Peter
Monster of Florence, vii, 338, 359, 378, 380, 383, 386, 387, 389
Montoneros (Argentine terrorist group), 354, 359-60, 365
Montreal (Can.) Stock Exchange,

Niemeyer, Terrance, 340
Niewiadomski, Eligius, 305
Night of the Long Knives, 315
Nile Grill (Kampala, Uganda), 411
Nine Hours to Rama (film), 325
Nittel, Heinz, 377
Nixon, Robert (AKA: The Brick Moron), 317, 318
Nobel Peace Prize, 231
Nobleza Tobacos (Argen.), 356
NOCS (*Nucleo Operativo Centrale di Sicurezza*; AKA: Leatherheads, Italian anti-terrorist oganization), 212-13, 381
Noel, Cleo A., 215, 355
Nolan, Dr. Edward D., 52, 53
Norfolk Hotel (Nairobi, Kenya), 288, 375
Norris, Edward, 299
Norris, Off. Robert, 56, 301
North, Lt.-Col. Oliver, 244
North Atlantic Treaty Organization, See: NATO
Northcott, Gordon Stewart, 312
Northwest Airlines, 167, 337, 347, 349-50, 366, 374
Northwestern University, 276
Norton, Ruth, 127
Nosair, El Sayyid, 397, 405
Nuclear fuel thefts by terrorists
  Czechoslovakia, 402 (two entries, 1994)
  Germany, 402 (1994)
  Lithuania, 400 (1993), 402 (1994)
  Russia, 399 (1992), 401 (1993)
Nucleo Operativo Centrale di Sicurezza, See: NOCS
Nugent, John, 14
Nurkrashy, Mahmoud, 324
Nyaose, Jabu, 383
Nyaose, Petrus, 383
Oath of Unity (*Ndemwa Ithatu*, Mau Mau secret oath), 151-52
Obergfell, Richard A., 349
Oberholtzer, Madge, 87-88, 307
Obregón, Alvaro, 308, 309
O'Brien, Inspector John, 117
O'Brien-Moore, Erin, 123
Odeh, Mohammed Saddig, 286
O'Dwyer, Sir Michael Francis, 318, 319
Oeth, Leonard, 167
Ogre of Hanover, *See:* Haarmann, Fritz
O'Higgins, Kevin, 309
Ohliger, Rosa, 310
Ohnesorg, Benno, 187, 189, 190
Oil Service Company, 370
Okada, Keisuke, 316-17

Okhrana (Czarist secret police), 29
Oklahoma City (Okla.) Bombing, 267-74
Okomoto, Kozo, 214, 353
Okomoto, Takeshi, 343
Okuchi, Nobuo, 343
Okudaira, Junzo, 393
Okudeira, Rakeshi, 214
Old Man of the Mountain (Islamic terrorist chieftan), ix, 232, 286
Olson, Culbert Levy, 54
Olympic Park (Atlanta, Ga.), *See:* Centennial Park (Atlanta, Ga.)
Olympics, *See:* XX Olympiad
Olympio, Sylvanus, 331
O'Neill, Michael, 378
Oneto, Tulio, 364
OPEC Conference (1975, Vienna, Aust.), 216, 363
Operation Desert Storm, 269, 270
Operation Zebra, 225
OPR-33 (Organization of the Popular Revolution 33, Uruguayan terrorist group), 348-49, 350, 354
Orbit Inn (Las Vegas, Nev.), 335
Orchard, Harry (Albert E. Horsley; AKA: Tom Hogan), ix, 10, 11, 12, 13, 14, 15, 45, 292, 293
Order, The (U.S. terrorist group), 265, 266, 387, 389, 393
Order of the Assassins (Islamic terrorist organization), ix, 232, 234, 286
Ordine (Black Order, Italian neo-fascist terrorist group), 359
Organization of American States, 370
Organization of Struggle Against World Imperialism (front for PFLP), 246
Oribe, Berro, 348
Orly Airport (Paris, Fr.), 386
Ortega y Gasset, Eduardo, 317
Ortiz-Rubio, Pascual, 311
Oswald, Barbara, 369, 370
Oswald, Lee Harvey, 332
Oswald, Robyn S., 370
O'Sullivan, Joseph, 304, 305
Otis, Harrison Gray, 40, 43, 44, 50
Ottaway, Det. Supt. John, 31, 32
Oxman, Frank C., 53, 54
Pacific Gas and Electric Company of California, 50
Pacific Southwest Airlines, 373-74
Paddington Station (London, Eng.), 397

Palestinian Authority, 410-11
Palestinian Liberation Organization, See: PLO
Palestinian National Council (Algiers), 245
Palma, Aturo Alessandro, 319
Palme, Olaf, 390
Palmer, A. Mitchell, 59, 60, 62, 64, 302
Palomino Flores, Zenon, 383
Pan American Airlines, 245, 247, 248, 330, 336, 342, 345, 346, 353, 358, 371, 391
Pan-American Exposition (Buffalo, New York), 3-4
Papa Doc, See; Duvalier, Francois
Papadopoulis, George, 338
Papen, Franz von, 319
Paramount Theatre (Brooklyn, N. Y.), 147
Parchman State Penitentiary (Miss.), 171
Paris, Richard James, 335
Park Chung Hee, 372
Park Hotel (Helena, Mt.), 280
Partito Nazionale Fascista, 93-94
Pasdaran (Iranian Revolutionary Guards), 250
Pastorcich, Roger A., 338
Paterson, Chapin S., 348
Patterson, Mrs. Emily, 309
Patterson, Gwendolyn, 338
Patterson, James, 338
Patterson, Gov. John, 171
Patterson, Wade, 296
Patton, George, 313
Paul I (king of Greece), 322
Paul VI (Pope), 347
Pavelic, Ante, 316
Pay or Die (film), 23
Pearlman, Mark David, 375
P'eng Chia-chen, 296
Peichev, Lubomir, 353
Pennington, John, 290
Pennsylvania Station (New York City), 252, 326, 401
Pentagon (Washington, D. C.), 182
People's Arditi, 94
People's Revolutionary Armed Forces (Mexican terrorist group), 356
People's Revolutionary Front (Philippine terrorist group), 364
Peparo, Michael Anthony, 339
Pepitone, Pietro, 26, 303
Pepitone, Michele, 27, 303
Pepitone, Mrs. Michele, 303
Pepsi-Cola Co., 381
Perez, David, 360

(1975)

Ax Man of New Orleans, 300, 301 (1918), 301 (1919), 302 (1919) 303, (1919)

Bedell, Joshua (and Samuel Cummings), 392 (1986)

Berdella, Robert, 387 (1984)

Berkowitz, David (AKA: Son of Sam), 364-65 (three entries, 1976), 365 (two entries, 1977), 366 (four entries, 1977)

Bianchi, Kenneth (AKA: Hillside Strangler; with Buono, Angelo), 367-68 (five entries, 1977), 368 (1978), 370 (1979), 386-87 (1984)

Bundy, Theodore, 394 (1989)

Coleman, Alton (and Debra Brown), 387 (1984)

Cunanan, Andrew P., 408 (1997)

Dahmer, Jeffrey, 398 (1992)

Gacy, John Wayne, 370

Greenwood, Vaughn (AKA: Los Angeles Slasher, Skid Row Slasher), 360 (four entries, 1974), 360 (four entries, 1975)

Haarmann, Fritz, 306-07 (1924)

Knowles, Paul John, 359 (1974)

Kraft, Randolph (AKA: Freeway Killer), 385

Kürten, Peter, 297-98 (1913), 310 (1929), 311 (1929), 311 (1930), 312-13 (1931)

Lance, Myron (and Kelbach, Walter), 335 (1966)

Lepine, Marc, 395 (1989)

Lover's Lane Murderer (Texarkana, Tex.), 321-22 (1946)

Mad Butcher of Cleveland, 315 (1934), 316 (1935), 317 (1936), 318 (1940)

Michigan Child Killer, 363 (1976)

Monster of Florence, 338 (1968), 359 (1974), 378 (1981), 380 (1981), 383 (1982), 386 (1983), 387 (1984), 389 (1985)

Moors Murderers (Ian Brady and Myra Hindley), 333 (1964)

Nelson, Earle Leonard, 308 (1926), 309 (1926), 309 (1927), 309 (1928)

Northcott, Gordon Stewart, 312 (1930)

Nixon, Robert (AKA: Brick Moron), 317 (1936), 317 (1937), 318 (1938)

3-X (anonymous terrorist killer in NYC), 311 (1930), 317 (1936)

Sadamichi, Hiresawa, 323 (1948)

Tulsa (Okla.) Bludgeon Killer, 319-20 (1942), 320 (1943), 321 (1945), 323 (1948)

Unruh, Howard, 324 (1949)

Zodiac Killer (San Francisco), 339 (1968), 341 (1969)

Zodiac Killer (New York, N. Y.), 405

Sewell, Dallas, 86, 306

Shachori, Dr. Ami, 354

Shadow of a Doubt (film), 308

Shah of Iran, ix, 187, 188, 189, 216, 231, 335, 372

Shannahan, Robert, 361

Sharif, Mohiyedine, 410-11

Shartouni, Habib, 384

Shaw, Clay, 340

Shea, Con, 28

Shea, Stephen, 335

Sheer, Rudolf, 310

Sheffield, Allan C., 339

Sheffield, Caesar, 299

Shehabi, Omar, 248

Shephard, Cecelia, 340

Sheraton Hotel (Buenos Aires, Argen.), 354, 365

Sheraton Hotel (Cairo, Egypt), 214, 350

Sheridan, Ann, 123

Shermarke, Abdi Rashid Ali, 342

Shevardnadze, Eduard, 404, 409, 411

Shirru, Michele, 98

Shively, Joe, 291

Shoemake, Larry Wayne, 254-55, 400

Shorr, Henry, 342

Shotgun Man (Chicago Black Hand enforcer), 27

Shuralov, Pavel A., 293

Siba'i, Yusuf (Yousseff el-Sebai), 368

Siddig Ali, Siddig Ibrahim, 402

Sieff, J. Edward, 238

Siege of Sidney Street (London, Eng.), 32-34

Sietsome, Mary, 309

Sigonella Air Base (Sicily), 244

Sihanouk, Norodom, 329

Silverstein, Michael, 16, 294

Simard, Francis, 219

Simard, Jacques, 219

Simic, Milan, 410

Simmons, Rev. Isaac, 321

Simmons, "Col." William Joseph, 72, 75, 77, 79-81, 82, 83, 84, 87, 297

Simon, J. C., 225

Simpkins, Jack, 13

Sims, Allen G., 350

Singh, Hardayal, 387

Singh, Mithileshwar, 392

Singh, Udham, 318, 319

Sing Sing Prison (New York), 385

Sinn Fein, 412

Sipiagin, Dimitri S., 291

Sirhan, Sirhan Bishara, 337

Siu, Alvin Antonio, 394

Skerdla, Fred, 273

Skid Row Slasher (Los Angeles Slasher), *See:* Greenwood, Vaughn

Skyjackings (countries of plane origin are listed)

Argentina, 335 (1966)

Australia, 330 (1960)

Brazil, 394 (1988)

Bulgaria, 323 (1948)

Canada, 338 (1968)

China, 324 (1948), 324 (1949), 383 (1982), 385 (1983)

Costa Rica, 394 (1989)

Cuba, 329 (two entries, 1959), 330 (two entries, 1960; one entry, 1961), 331 (1961), 334 (1966)

Czechoslovakia, 323 (two entries, 1948), 325 (two entries, 1950)

Egypt, 335 (1967), 390 (1985)

Ethiopia, 341 (1969), 355 (1972)

France, 387 (1984)

Germany, 351 (1972), 354-55 (1972), 367 (1977)

Great Britain, 336 (1967)

Greece, 324 (1948), 339 (1969)

Haiti, 329 (1959)

Hungary, 324 (1949)

India, 380 (1981) 389 (1985), 394 (1989)

Iraq, 392 (1986)

Ireland, 377 (1981)

Israel, 337 (1968), 339 (1968), 340 (1969), 346 (1970)

Italy, 393 (1987)

Japan, 343 (1970), 344 (1970), 357 (1973)

Kuwait, 388 (1984), 393 (1988)

Lebanon, 366 (1977), 392 (1987)

Libya, 385 (1983)

Mexico, 330 (1961)

Morocco, 382 (1982)

Netherlands, 331 (1962)

464 •

Sturmabtelung, See: Brown Shirts

Sturs, Jennis, 292

Stürgkh, Count Karl von, 299

Suarez, Jose A., 338

Suarez, Samuel, 361

Suazo Estrada, Dr. Judith Xionara, 385

Suez Canal, 231

Suharto, President, 412

Sullivan, Charles, 117

Sullivan, Fred, 298

Sullivan, Frederick, 84

Sullivan Mine, 10

Sukarno (Kusnasosro), A., 328, 329

Sun Yat-sen, 159

Sûreté Nationale, 36, 37

Suria, Judge Fred E., Jr., 183

Suriani, Valentina, 366

Svaars, Fritz, 31, 33, 296

Swanson, Judge John A., 91, 92

Swanson, Martin, 52

Swanson, Virgil, 298

Sweeney, Jim, 28

Swift & Co., 348

Swint, John A., 357

Swissair, 343, 357

Sykes, Henry, 294

Sykes, Sir Richard, 371

Symbionese Liberation Army, See: SLA

Sylvester, Stanley, 348

Syria
Air Force headquarters (Damacus), 379
Embassy, Islamabad, Pak., 364
Embassy, Rome, Italy, 364

Tadic, Dusan, 407, 408

Tadic, Miroslav, 410

Tagliercio, Guiseppe, 378

Taliercio, Guiseppe, 212

Takahashi, Korekiyo, 316-17

Takfir Wal-Hajira (Repentence of the Holy Flight), 229, 232, 234, 380, 382

Tammany Ring, 68

Tantis, B. D., 290

Taoka, Kazuo, 259

Tarrant, Thomas Albert, 174, 334

Tarutani, Koichiro, 408-09

Taufer, Lutz, 206

Tawan Siam, 382

Taylor, Donald, 157-58

Taylor, Elizabeth, 390

Taylor, Gen. Maxwell D., 333

Taylor, Reuben, 157-58

Tayo, Jackson, 385

Tegel Library (Berlin, Ger.), 344

Tegel Prison (Berlin, Ger.), 192

Teikoku Bank (Tokyo, Jap.), 323

Tell, Wasif, 214, 350

Temple of Music (Pan-American Exposition, Buffalo, New York), 4

Ten Days That Shook the World, 16

Tennes, Mont, 44, 303

Terra, Gabriel, 316

Terranova, Ciro (AKA: Artichoke King), 19

Terruzi, Attilio, 95

Teufel, Fritz, 205

Texarkana (Tex.) Lover's Lane Murderer, See: Lover's Lane Murderer

Texas International Airlines, 340

Texas Rangers, 129, 317

Teymour, Prince Shabeb bin, 235

Thatcher, Margaret, 240, 249, 378, 388, 391

They Won't Forget (film), 299

Thibodeaux, Norman, 314

Third Crusade, 232

Thomas, Del L., 349

Thompson, Bennie, 314

Thompson, John R., 356

Thompson, William Hale (AKA: Big Bill), 89, 91, 92

3-X (anonymous terrorist killer), vii, 114-18, 311, 317, 338

Throngprapa, Wandee, 382

Thurmond, Thomas Harold, 314-15

Tilgener, Gotz, 204

Till, Emmett Louis, 327

Tinker Air Force Base, 267

Tisza, Count Stephen, 300

Tjou Chang-Jen, 385

Today Show, 284

Tolbert, William Richard, Jr., 373

Tollis, Marvin, 313

Ton Ton Macoutes (Haitian terrorist organization), 162-64, 390

Toral, José de Leon, 310

Torresola, Griselio, 142-45, 325

Torrio, John (Johnny), 19, 27, 90

Tower of London, 32

Toyama, Mitsuru, 258, 259

TPLA (Turkish People's Liberation Army, Turkish terrorist group), 240, 348, 352

Tracy, Edward Austin, 397

Tracy, Spencer, 315

Trani Prison (Italy), 212, 375

Trans-Australia Airlines, 330

Trans-World Airlines, See: TWA

Trapnell, Garrett B., 351, 369, 370

Trayer, Bruce J., 366

Tresca, Carlo, 320

Triad Society (Chinese extortion-

ist-terrorist group), 159-62

Tripp, Glen K., 374

Trisatki University (Jakarta, Indo.), 412

Tropschuh, Capt. Felix, 134, 320

Trotsky, Leon, 319

Trudeau, Pierre, 217

Trujillo Molina, Rafael Leónidas, 330

Truman, Bess, 144

Truman, Harry, x, 136, 139-45, 146, 325

Truman, Margaret, 144

Tsantes, Capt. George, 386

Tshombe, Moise, 336

Tsuchiya, Masami, 262

Tsukuba University (Jap.), 262

Tubman, William Vacanarat Shadrach, 327

Tucker, Constable, 30

Tully, Jim, 236

Tulsa (Okla.) Bludgeon Killer, vii, 125-28, 319-20, 321, 323-24

Túpac Amaru Revolutionary Movement (MRTA, terrorist group in Peru), 406, 407

Tupamaro (Tupamaros-Movimiento de Liberacion Nacional, terrorst group in Guatamala, Uruguay and Chile), 345, 345, 347, 348

Turajlic, Hakija, 399

Turkish Embassy, Ottawa, Can., 382

Turkish Airlines, 378

Turkish People's Liberation Army, See: TPLA

Turkish Revenge Brigade (Turkish terrorist group), 411

Turner, Felton, 329

Turner, J. W., 75

Turner, Jesse, 392

Turner Diaries, The (book), 270

Tutt, Vernon, 296

Tyler, Mrs. Elizabeth, 86, 87

TWA (Trans-World Airlines), 167, 247, 282-84, 285, 337, 338, 340, 341, 342, 343, 345, 346, 348, 349, 350, 357, 359, 365, 370, 389, 405-06, 408

XX Olympiad, 214-15, 354, 354-55, 370

Tyrone, R. J., 316

Tzu Hsi (Empress of China), 289

Uale, Frank, See: Yale, Frank

Uffizi Art Gallery (Florence, Italy), 400-01

Uhlig, Gunter, See: Mahler, Horst

U. K. Embassy, Athens, Greece, 387

Ulster Defense Association

Bibliography

Weaver, Samuel, 399, 404
Weaver, Vicki, 399, 404
Webber, Col. John D., Jr., 336
Weckler, Kristina, 367
Weed, Stephen, 220, 358
Wegener, Lt.-Col. Ulrich, 246
Weinberg, Israel, 52, 53
Weiner, Lee, 179, 180, 342
Weinglass, Leonard, 179, 180, 343
Welch, Chief of Det. Harry, 57
Welsh, Richard S., 363
Wensley, Inspect. Frederick, 31, 32
Wessel, Horst, 104-05, 106, 187, 311
Wessel, Ulrich, 206, 361
West, James, 296
West, John, 86, 305
West German Aerospace and Armaments Association, 388
West German Embassy, Stockholm, Swed., 205
West German Intelligence, 189
West German Ministry of Defense, 200
West Germany
  Consulate, Chicago, Ill., 369
  Embassy, Stockholm, Swed., 361
Western Federation of Miners (arm of IWW), 9, 13
Weston, Russell E., Jr., 411
Wheat, Vernita, 387
White, Carl, 347
White, Daniel James, 369, 371
White, Police Chief David Augustus, 52
White, Everett L., 339
White, Gregory L., 348
White, Holly, 312
White, Nite, 297
White, Norma Jean, 347
White Aryan Resistance (U.S. terrorist group in Oregon), 396
White Hand Society, 27
White House (Washington, D.C.), 140-41, 142
Whitfield, Mrs. Carey, 291
Whitney, George, 293

Whitty, Kenneth, 387
Who, The, 373
Wiesenthal, Simon, 333
Wilder, Diane, 370
Wilds, Casselle, 290
Wilhelm II (German Kaiser), 31, 39, 290
Wilhelm II (king of Neth.), 316
Wilkerson, Kathy, 182
Wilkie, David, Jr., 357
Williams, A. C., 319
Williams, Anthony, 357
Williams, Ernest, 294
Williams, Mrs. J. C., 297
Williams, Maurice, 227
Williams, Samuel, 292
Williams & Walker, 290
Wilson, Arthur J., 347
Wilson, Edgar, 14
Wilson, Edwin, 384
Wilson, Sir Henry, 304
Wilson, Les, 318
Wilson, Methodist Bishop, 79
Wilson, Robert, 157-58
Wilson, Woodrow, 47, 51, 53
Wiltgen, Thomas C., 373
Winn, Alexander, 85
Wischnewski, Nikolai, 368
Withers, Mrs. Beta, 308
Witt, Richard D., 346
Wobblies, See: IWW
Wolfe, William, 224, 225, 359
Wolimer, Henri, 348
Wolverine Republican Club, 121
Wood, Judge John H., Jr., 371
Woodhams, Constable, 30
Woods, John, 236
Woodward, Ronald, 199
Woolworth Co., 367
Worden, Edna, 317
Worden, Marguerite, 317
World Trade Center (New York, N. Y.), viii, 286, 399, 401-02
Wright, Charles, 85, 305
Wright, George, 354
Wu Yueh, 292-93
Wylie, Sir William Hutt Curzon, 295
Wynter, Dana, 151
Xhaferi, Haxhi H., 345

Yahya, Imam Ahmed Ibn, 330
Yakanak, Moses August, 360
Yale, Frank (Frank Uale), 19
Yale University, 276
Yakuza (Japanese extortionist-terrorist organization), 258-61, 402-03, 408-09
Yamaguchi, Dr. Jiro, See: Sadamichi, Hiresawa
Yamaguchi-gumi, 259
Yamaichi Securities (Tokyo, Jap.), 408-09
Yasin, Ali, 369
Yassin, Ahmed, 409
Yasuda, Yoshuyiki, 214
Yellowwolf, John, 291
Yippies (Youth International Party), 175, 176, 178
Yo, Hiroyuki, 262, 403
Yoshimura, Wendy, 224
Young, Arthur, 85, 305
Young, Richard, 291
Yousef, Ramzi Ahmed, 286, 399, 401-02, 405
Youth International Party, See: Yippies
Yugoslav Airlines, 244
Yugoslavian Consulate in Gothenburg, Sweden
Zaim, Col. Husni, 324
Zahir Shah, Mohammed, 328
Zangara, Joseph, 314
Zaric, Simo, 410
Zebra Killings, 225-26
Zeinati, Emir Mohammed, 322
Zelea-Codreanu, Cornelius, 318
Zevalloses, Dr. Hector, 383
Zevalloses, Mrs. Hector, 383
Zimbabwean African National Union, 381
Zimmermann, Ernst, 388
Zodiac Killer (New York), See: Seda, Heriberto
Zodiac Killer (San Francisco), 338, 339
Zog I (king of Albania), 312
Zoot Suit (film), 320
Zuaiter, Wael, 354